PERFECTING PARLIAMENT

This book explains why contemporary liberal democracies are based on historical templates rather than revolutionary reforms; why the transition in Europe occurred during a relatively short period in the nineteenth century; why politically and economically powerful men and women voluntarily supported such reforms; how interests, ideas, and preexisting institutions affected the reforms adopted; and why the countries that liberalized their political systems also produced the Industrial Revolution.

The analysis is organized in three parts. The first part develops new rational-choice models of (a) governance, (b) the balance of authority between parliaments and kings, (c) constitutional exchange, and (d) suffrage reform. The second part provides historical overviews and detailed constitutional histories of six important countries: the United Kingdom, Sweden, the Netherlands, Japan, Germany, and United States. In all the countries discussed, liberal democracy emerged from a long series of constitutional reforms, rather than as a quantum leap from authoritarian to democratic governance. The third part provides additional quantitative evidence in support of the theory and summarizes the results. It also contrasts the approach taken in this book with that of other scholars and discusses methodological issues.

Roger D. Congleton is Professor of Economics and Senior Research Associate, in the Center for Study of Public Choice at George Mason University, Fairfax, Virginia, where he has taught since 1988. His research focuses on the political economy of constitutions and public policy. Professor Congleton's most recent books include *40 Years of Research on Rent Seeking* (two edited volumes, 2008), which surveys the theoretical and applied literatures on rent seeking; *Democratic Constitutional Design and Public Policy* (2006), which surveys the empirical literature on the effects of democratic constitutional design on public policies and economic growth; *Improving Democracy through Constitutional Reform* (2003), which analyzes the effects of constitutional reform on policies and economic developments within Sweden during the past two centuries; and *Politics by Principle, Not Interest* (Cambridge University Press, 1998, written with Nobel Prize winner James Buchanan), which analyzes how a generality rule can improve the performance of democratic governments.

In addition to his books, Professor Congleton has published more than one hundred papers in academic journals and edited volumes. That body of research analyzes the politics of constitutional reform, the importance of information in democratic decision making, the emergence and significance of norms, and contemporary policy making within national governments and international organizations.

Perfecting Parliament

Constitutional Reform, Liberalism, and the Rise of Western Democracy

ROGER D. CONGLETON
George Mason University, Virginia

CAMBRIDGE UNIVERSITY PRESS
Cambridge, New York, Melbourne, Madrid, Cape Town, Singapore,
São Paulo, Delhi, Dubai, Tokyo, Mexico City

Cambridge University Press
32 Avenue of the Americas, New York, NY 10013-2473, USA

www.cambridge.org
Information on this title: www.cambridge.org/9780521151696

First published 2011

Printed in the United States of America

A catalog record for this publication is available from the British Library.

Library of Congress Cataloging in Publication data
Congleton, Roger D.
Perfecting parliament : constitutional reform, liberalism, and the rise of Western democracy / Roger D. Congleton.
p. cm.
Includes bibliographical references and index.
ISBN 978-0-521-76460-5 – ISBN 978-0-521-15169-6 (pbk.)
1. Democratization–Western countries–History–19th century. 2. Democracy–Western countries–History–19th century. 3. Constitutional history–Western countries. 4. Liberalism–Western countries–History–19th century. 5. Western countries–Politics and government–19th century. 6. Rational choice theory–Political aspects. I. Title.
JC423.C685 2010
328.309182′1–dc22 2010031756

ISBN 978-0-521-76460-5 Hardback
ISBN 978-0-521-15169-6 Paperback

*****

This book is dedicated to my teachers, colleagues, family, and friends, without whose support and thoughtful criticism over many years, it could never have been written.

*****

* * *

[The] members of parliament had been recalled, so far as the government was concerned, for one reason and one reason alone: money …

In the end the members of parliament accepted the king's assurances and decided to "proceed notwithstanding." They now wanted confirmation of the adequacy of their offer, and also a more concrete set of proposals outlining what the king might surrender in return …

Rabb (1998, 140, 149) on Sir Edwin Sandys
and the great contract of 1610

* * *

The **best aristocracy** is that in which **those who have no share in the legislature are so few** and inconsiderable that the governing party has no interest in oppressing them.

Thus, when Antepater made a law at Athens, that whosoever was not worth two thousand drachmas should have not power to vote, **he formed by this method the best aristocracy possible**; because this was so small a sum as to **exclude very few**, and not one of any rank or consideration in the city.

Montesquieu (1748, 15)

* * *

Contents

Preface

Two political revolutions occurred gradually in northern Europe during the nineteenth and early twentieth centuries. First, political authority shifted from kings to parliaments. Second, parliaments became more broadly grounded in popular suffrage. This century-long shift in political authority was a major event, although the individual shifts of power and expansions of suffrage were often relatively small events. Nor were these two shifts of policy-making power entirely connected. European parliaments had occasionally gained power in previous periods without broadening their electoral bases, which before 1800 were generally limited to well-organized and well-born elites. In some cases, suffrage expanded more rapidly than power shifted to the parliament, as in Germany, whereas in other cases, such as England, parliament became the dominant institution for public policy making well before universal suffrage was obtained. Yet by the 1920s, the new democratic parliamentary governments were broadly similar throughout Europe and were radically different from previous governments that Europe and the world had experienced during recorded history. These new parliamentary governments were revolutionary, although not products of war or sudden breaks with the past. Something evidently had happened during the nineteenth-century in Europe that gave rise to gradual but extraordinary changes in governance in the course of only a century or so.

It has often been suggested that industrialization played a role in these constitutional reforms. To the best of my knowledge, however, no one has provided a peaceful mechanism through which industrialization – itself largely an economic activity – may induce major political reforms. Whether economic development induces constitutional reform or constitutional reform induces industrialization is not obvious. After all, it is political decisions that determine contract, property, and tax laws, and it is political decisions that largely determine how those rights and obligations will be enforced. Economics suggests that such political decisions can have large effects on a nation's path of economic development by affecting transaction costs, technological innovation, and market size. One could argue that national governance largely determines market activity, even in a fairly complete model of political economy.

It seems likely, however, that causality is not unidirectional from the political to the economic sphere. An interdependence clearly exists between economic and political activities in the small, as when individual pieces of legislation or administrative rulings are influenced by the testimony and lobbying efforts of organized economic interests. The present analysis suggests that this is also true in the large, because major constitutional reforms can be induced by politically active groups whose economic interests are advanced by such reforms. Technological and ideological innovations may create new opportunities and new pressures for peaceful constitutional reform that favor particular political and economic interests. The effectiveness of such groups tends to be enhanced by industrialization, but the groups are not products of industrialization.

The analysis developed in this book suggests that the road to democracy requires institutions in which constitutional bargaining and reforms can take place and support of politically active persons with an interest in more liberal forms of political decision making.

ONE

On the Origins of Western Democracy

INTRODUCTION: ON THE EVOLUTIONARY CHARACTER OF WESTERN DEMOCRACY

Most of us in the West take our contemporary form of governance and political theories for granted. The practices of selecting representatives through elections based on broad suffrage, the concentration of legislative authority in elected parliaments (legislatures), and the holding of annual meetings of parliaments have become the normal routines of political life in the West. That governance should be grounded in the consent of the governed, that various civil liberties should be essentially absolute, and that all citizens should be equal before the law are nearly universally supported and largely unquestioned. That representative governments should adopt laws in a manner consistent with constitutional procedures and constraints is so broadly accepted that it is hard for most of us to imagine any other legitimate form of government.

Most of us also acknowledge that much of the general architecture and many of the principles of contemporary governance are far older than our governments. The idea of the rule of law, if not equality before the law, can be traced back at least as far as the code of Hammurabi, which was chiseled into stone tablets in about 1775 BCE. The foundation of many of our political theories about representative government can be found in classical Greek philosophy, as in Aristotle's *Politics* written in about 330 BCE. Parliaments themselves date back at least to the late Middle Ages, as do elections for seats in parliament. Yet we also understand that constitutional governance based on equality before the law and broad suffrage is a relatively new phenomenon.

Although parliaments, diets, and assemblies have long played a role in Western governance, membership in medieval parliaments was grounded not in broad suffrage, but rather in heredity and occupation. Medieval parliaments were, for the most part, populated from relatively wealthy families and were subordinate to their kings or queens. Medieval parliaments were not self-calling. Kings and queens called "their" parliaments into session whenever convenient and dismissed them on a whim. Their relatively short meetings were largely a method for kings to communicate their ideas and policies to regional elites and to request new taxes from them. Apart from veto power over new taxes, medieval parliaments had very limited authority. As a consequence of the success and defense of those institutions, analysis of alternative institutions for governance largely disappeared from European philosophical and political discourse during the thousand years prior to the sixteenth century.

To simultaneously accept the "newness" and "oldness" of contemporary political theory and institutions is not evidence of poor training or confusion, but rather acknowledgment of elements of continuity in both the theories and institutions of governance. The ideas of popular suffrage and representative governance are quite old, but broad support for popular sovereignty, equality before the law, and universal suffrage is much newer. Many European parliaments are centuries old, but much about the institutions of contemporary parliamentary democracy is quite new.

The emergence of contemporary Western democracy from the medieval template required two major reforms of the routines of governance, and these reforms were widely adopted in northern Europe, North America, Australia, and Japan during the nineteenth and early twentieth centuries. First, policy-making authority had to shift from kings to parliaments. Second, representation in parliament had to become more broadly grounded in popular suffrage. Perhaps surprising, these reforms were not products of war or sudden breaks with the past. Indeed, even in the United States and France where "revolutionary" wars were fought, the wars themselves did not produce democratic parliamentary governance. Nor was there an obvious trend in medieval governance that somehow culminated in the nineteenth century. Something extraordinary happened during the eighteenth and nineteenth centuries that gradually produced parliamentary democracy through a long series of reforms.

This book explains (a) why contemporary liberal democracies are based on historical templates rather than revolutionary reforms; (b) why the transition in Europe occurred during a relatively short period in the nineteenth century; (c) why politically and economically powerful men and women voluntarily supported such reforms; (d) how interests, ideas, and preexisting institutions affected the reforms adopted; and (e) why the countries that liberalized their political systems also produced the Industrial Revolution. The analysis is organized in three parts. The first part of the book develops a bargaining-and-exchange theory of constitutional governance and reform. The second part uses historical case studies to determine the relevance of the theory. These historical narratives provide evidence that Western democracy emerged from a long series of liberal constitutional reforms, rather than from a single great leap from authoritarian to democratic governance. The last part provides additional quantitative evidence in support of the theory, summarizes the results, contrasts the approach taken in this book with that used by other scholars, and discusses methodological issues.

WEAKNESSES OF REVOLUTIONARY EXPLANATIONS OF THE EMERGENCE OF PARLIAMENTARY DEMOCRACY

The leading alternatives to the explanation provided in this volume are based on theories of revolutionary constitutional development. The militant version of the revolutionary hypothesis argues that major economic and political reforms occur in great leaps associated with broad public uprisings that threaten political elites. The fear that their regimes will be overthrown through civil war induces the elite to flee or to accept the demands made by their revolutionary opponents. In this manner, it is argued, credible threats of violence can produce radical democratic reforms, sometimes without much actual warfare (Acemoglu and Robinson 2000, Palmer 1959).

There are several major problems with such "popular revolt" theories of the emergence of liberal democracy. Neither major revolutionary threats nor wholesale reform of institutions are evident in the histories of countries that adopted liberal reforms in the nineteenth century, except occasionally in France. Moreover, serious revolutionary threats require well-organized, hierarchical organizations with guns, which tend to promote post-revolution dictatorships, rather than democracies. Here, one can recall that civil wars in England, France, Russia, and China produced Cromwell, Napoleon, Lenin, and Mao, rather than durable liberal reforms and democratic rule by the people through elected representatives. Outside of France, there are no cases in which armed conflicts produced even temporary democratic reforms during the nineteenth or early twentieth centuries. And, neither of the two French revolutions created durable democratic systems of government. The first Republic quickly succumbed to the Committee of Public Safety, followed closely by the rule of Napoleon I. About a half century later, King Louis-Philippe abdicated in the face of a popular uprising. The latter was a rare instance of regime change generated by widespread revolt, which seems to be largely responsible for the militant explanation of the emergence of democracy. The second Republic, however, lasted just four years before yielding to the rule of Napoleon III. The subsequent emergence of liberal democracy after Napoleon III was largely evolutionary in nature. The French Parliament had already acquired considerable authority over public policy, and suffrage had been expanding before the second revolution.

In cases in which the force of arms played a role in assembling new, more centralized nation-states, as in Germany and Italy, the new national governments were only slightly more liberal than the typical regional governments they included. In cases in which wars of secession were successful, as in Belgium and the United States, relatively democratic representative systems of government were already in place prior to secession. These systems were often liberalized after the war was won, but over many years. Military organizations are rarely themselves liberal forms of government.

The other revolutionary explanation for liberal reforms in the nineteenth century focuses on intellectual and ideological changes, rather than military threats or peasant uprisings. Such theories argue that radically new ideas swept through Europe that persuaded everyone of the merits of new forms of government. There is more historical and constitutional support for the intellectual-innovation thesis than for the military-threat models and for intermediate models that combine ideological shifts with revolutionary threats.

It is certainly true that the intellectual base for governance changed in the nineteenth century. It is also clear that enlightenment theories of the state, society, and economy affected nineteenth-century constitutional developments. For example, by the early twentieth century, many European constitutions explicitly mentioned popular sovereignty and equality before the law. These foundations for governance clearly contrasted with claims made in older documents that stressed noble family trees, divine providence, and history. However, the timing was wrong for the enlightenment theory of liberal constitutional reform.

Theories supporting popular sovereignty, contract-based governance, and civic equality were penned many decades, indeed centuries, before the political reforms of the nineteenth century began in Europe. Locke, Montesquieu, Rousseau, Paine, Smith, and Madison wrote in the seventeenth and eighteenth centuries, rather than the nineteenth century. Moreover, the writings of these influential political and economic theorists were preceded by earlier arguments and documents associated with the Dutch revolt of the late sixteenth century and by the English Levelers and North American colonists of the early seventeenth century. Although enlightenment scholarship – as well as nineteenth-century restatements and extensions of them – affected debates on institutional reform within literate society and relatively open parliaments in the eighteenth century, it seems clear that simply writing down and circulating such "revolutionary" ideas was not sufficient to cause significant democratic reform.[1]

Given this timing problem, those stressing the role of revolutionary ideas might argue that it was nineteenth-century – rather than seventeenth- and eighteenth-century – ideas that motivated constitutional demonstrations and reforms. Perhaps the ideas of Mill, Marx, and other late-nineteenth-century social reformers generated the democratic impulse for democratic reforms, rather than enlightenment scholars. Again, some evidence supports this idea. Large-scale demonstrations were organized by radical liberals, labor unions, and social democratic political movements in the late nineteenth century, and these often supported suffrage expansion even in cases in which the main goals were economic, rather than political, reforms. However, again the timing is wrong. Shifts of authority from kings to parliaments and a gradual increase in suffrage often began in the first half of the nineteenth century, well before blue-collar labor movements emerged. Moreover, such shifts were often completed before radical liberals or labor and social-democratic parties became significant participants in government.

Another significant weakness in these theories is their "quantum leap" hypothesis. Shifts to democratic governance in the nineteenth century were rarely sudden and did not require radical breaks with older institutions. Rather, new systems of governance emerged gradually, as long-standing political institutions were revised a little at a time. In some countries, the steps were larger than others, but in no case did parliamentary democracy emerge in a single great constitutional leap. The gradual emergence of modern parliamentary democracy is evident in the core architecture of contemporary constitutional democracies. The most obvious cases are those in which a monarch still occupies the national throne, as in the United Kingdom, Koninkrijk der Nederlanden (the kingdom of the Netherlands),

[1] It can be argued that the intellectual basis for governance began to shift much earlier. Some scholars argue that this shift began with the renewal of interest in Greek political philosophy, with its emphasis on reason, observation, deduction, dialogue, and education in the mid to late Middle Ages. This renaissance accelerated in southern Europe in the fifteenth and sixteenth centuries after the fall of Byzantium in 1453 (Wilson 1992). In the seventeenth and eighteenth centuries, however, scholars and practitioners went beyond the Greek theories of the state and developed new theories of legitimate governance, including new contractarian arguments for states grounded on popular sovereignty.

Konungariket Sverige (the kingdom of Sweden), and Royaume de Belgique (the kingdom of Belgium). It also bears noting that modern democratic republics have an executive branch headed by a single person and a parliament or legislature organized more or less as a large committee that makes decisions by casting votes.

There was nothing particularly unusual about the adoption of modest constitutional reforms in the nineteenth and early twentieth centuries. Individual constitutional and regulatory reforms of similar magnitude had occurred in previous centuries in most of the West. What was unusual about the nineteenth century was a strong trend in the policy, legal, and constitutional reforms in a handful of countries, which was a departure from the usual random series of reforms and counter-reforms commonplace in history. At the end of a century or two of more or less peaceful and lawful reform, there was a completely new method of choosing parliament and completely new division of policy-making authority between the king and parliament. Parliamentary democracy had emerged.

THE "KING-AND-COUNCIL" TEMPLATE FOR GOVERNANCE

In practice, most governments include a "king" and a "council," that is, a branch of government headed by a single chief executive and another composed of a committee of more or less equals who make important decisions by counting votes.[2] Such divided forms of government extend back to the dawn of recorded history (Bailkey 1967). This template for governance might have been called a "chief and council of wise men" in early societies, a "king and royal council" in early medieval times, a "king and parliament" in the late medieval and early modern periods, and a parliament and prime minister (or congress and president) in contemporary governance. By sharing this essential architecture, modern parliamentary governments reveal their deep historical roots, and also suggest that contemporary divided forms of governance reflect a good deal of past institutional experience.

A wide variety of governments can be formed from the king-and-council template, because policy-making authority can be distributed in a number of ways between the king and council and because both the king and the council can be chosen in a number of ways. Such divisions of authority and selection procedures allow the king-and-council template to be used

[2] This general architecture also tends to be commonplace among most contemporary dictatorships.

to make policy decisions in dictatorships, mixed governments, and parliamentary democracies. In authoritarian states, the executive has most of the policy-making and appointment authority, and the council serves a largely advisory role. In such cases, the council makes suggestions to the ruler – rather than rules – and kings and authoritarian presidents accept or reject this advice insofar as it advances their interests. In mixed or intermediate forms of the king-and-council architecture, authority to direct governmental resources to particular courses of action is divided between the king and council. For example, the king may decide on international relations and the parliament may decide on domestic budgets. The authority to select new policies may also be shared. In contemporary presidential systems, the parliament and the president jointly determine public policy, insofar as veto and agenda control are distributed between the legislature and president. In contemporary parliamentary democracies, the council (parliament) is dominant. The parliament makes the rules and appoints the chief executive (prime minister), who serves at the pleasure of parliament.

Procedures for selecting officeholders may also be varied. For example, officeholders may inherit their positions, be appointed by one or more preexisting bodies, or be elected. When elected by committees or larger groups, the voting rules may be adjusted in numerous ways. The qualifications for suffrage may be varied to include more or fewer voters. Votes may be weighted in various ways; supermajorities may be required or not, and constructed in various ways. Together, the variations in the division of authority and in the rules for selecting officeholders create a continuum of governmental institutions, as is necessary for democratic governance to emerge gradually, without radical changes in the core procedures of governance.

Together, the "political property rights" established by a given implementation of the king-and-council template and the many possible divisions of policy-making authority within that template allow the possibility of constitutional exchange. Authority to revise public policy within divided governments may peacefully (and lawfully) shift from one branch of government to another through formal and informal amendments, without changing the essential architecture of government. Both reform and continuity are evident in the nineteenth-century constitutional bargains that gradually produced Western democracy.

Aristotle called these intermediate cases mixed governments, but devoted most of his analytical work to the extremes (pure forms), an emphasis that continues to the present day in most theoretical work on political decision making. Nonetheless, the classical Greek scholars who produced the discrete classification schemes of political institutions so widely used today (autocracy, aristocracy, and democracy) acknowledged that "mixed" governments were more common than the pure forms they named and analyzed. The medieval governments from which Western democracies emerged were all based on the king-and-council template, and all modern democratic governments continue to be based on that template.

In national governments, there are normally a variety of councils (committees) with somewhat different responsibilities. For example, most medieval kings had executive councils (a council of state or a cabinet) in addition to "their" parliaments. Today's parliamentary democracies also include an executive cabinet or ministry. It is, however, the relationship between parliament and executive (king, prime minister, or president) that is most relevant for this book, although shifts in the authority to appoint executive cabinets play an important role in transitions to parliamentary rule.

The shifts of policy-making authority that occurred in the nineteenth century were not inevitable. They had not happened before, and they did not happen in many places. They did not happen suddenly, but through the cumulative effects of a long series of reforms to a single, relatively stable architecture of governance. In most cases, these reforms were adopted without obvious threats of civil war, although there were often large peaceful demonstrations favoring relatively narrow economic and political reforms. The theory developed in this book provides an explanation for both the timing and direction of these constitutional reforms.

A THEORY OF PEACEFUL AND LAWFUL CONSTITUTIONAL REFORM

The analysis and historical narratives focus on two neglected features of constitutional (rule-based) governance. First, they focus on the divided nature of essentially all medieval national and duchy governments. Second, they note that the written (and unwritten) constitutions of these governments defined political property rights, which could be and were traded, just as property rights for ordinary commodities can. The multidimensional nature of authority over policy making within divided governments, perhaps surprisingly, implies that reassignments of political power are not always zero-sum games.

The term "compromise" is often used to describe bargaining within parliaments and between parliaments and their sovereigns, but compromise is in most cases simply another word for negotiation and exchange. The parties to a compromise gain advantages from the terms negotiated at the same time they sacrifice other aims to bring negotiations to a successful conclusion. It is clear that the same terms could also be used to describe haggling over prices in markets without posted prices. Mutual gains from constitutional exchange occasionally emerge, which can be realized by amending the preexisting constitution. Such shifts of political power within divided governments may advance some aims more than others, but they are rarely forced, any more than sales in commercial markets are.

In the nineteenth century, trends in constitutional and economic reforms emerged from technological and ideological innovations that jointly produced new economic and ideological interests. The consequent trends in political and economic reforms were termed "liberal" in the nineteenth century, as they are throughout this book. Liberal reformers pressed for policy and constitutional changes that increased civil equality, which opened both commerce and politics to value-increasing forms of competition, and increased rates of technological innovation throughout the West. Both parliamentary democracy and industrialization were consequences of the political successes of liberal reformers.

The exchange-based theory of constitutional reform proposed in this volume can account for the historical roots of parliamentary governance, for the timing of the liberal transitions, and for the path of reform through which parliamentary democracy emerged. It bears noting, however, that the constitutional-exchange path to democracy is not a one-way street. In opposite circumstances, policy-making authority of parliament can be shifted to a king, and suffrage may be restricted, rather than expanded. The former is a relatively common event in history, and the latter also occurs from time to time, as noted in the case studies.

ORGANIZATION OF THE BOOK

Part I develops a theory of governance grounded on a theory of organizations. The theory is for the most part developed using nontechnical prose, although some mathematics is used to illustrate problems that can be solved through organization and also to demonstrate that opportunities for constitutional reform can emerge as a consequence of changes in the distribution of wealth and ideology among those with the power to adopt such reforms. For the most part, the mathematics can be neglected by readers who are more interested in the essential logic of the analysis than in demonstrations of logical consistency.

The models imply that constitutional bargaining is likely to be nearly constant, although constitutional bargains will be less commonplace. The models also suggest that the reforms adopted will be relatively small and reflect both the preexisting amendment procedures and the ideological and economic interests of those sitting at the table at the time that reforms are adopted. This is not to say that every constitutional exchange leaves those at the table with smiles on their faces any more than every market transaction equally pleases buyers and sellers. It is to say, however, that the bargains reflect the interests of those at the table, given the circumstances at the time the terms of trade were negotiated. Civil war or threats of such wars can create opportunities for constitutional exchange, as argued by Acemoglu and Robinson (2000), but they are not prerequisites for constitutional reform, nor are they likely to induce liberalization.

Part II of the book develops a series of case studies in order to determine the extent to which the models of governance and reform developed in Part I can account for the emergence of Western democracy in the late nineteenth and early twentieth centuries. The case studies suggest Western constitutional history is largely consistent with the models. Western democracy emerged from a long series of fine-grained formal and informal bargains over constitutional details, rather than bold, ingenious, revolutionary innovations adopted under the threat of violence.

A variety of exogenous shocks can produce new alignments of constitutional interests. For example, many European constitutional reforms were indirectly triggered by innovations in political theory and in technologies of production. Liberal ideas penetrated into elite circles, and the liberal direction for reform was supported by various coalitions of liberals and pragmatists that stood to profit from political and economic liberalization. Late-nineteenth-century liberalization in Japan was triggered by military concerns and increased access to European ideas and technologies. Early liberal reforms in the United States were triggered by labor scarcity during its colonial period and reinforced by subsequent technological and ideological shifts. In all cases, a large number of new, relatively liberal economic and political interest groups pressed for a broad range of reforms.

Part III concludes the analysis by providing some additional statistical support for the models of Part I, summarizing the main argument, and discussing its relevance for contemporary democratic transitions. A methodological appendix provides a rationale for the approach taken and addresses anticipated criticisms of the book's grand ambition and scope.

Readers are likely to find some parts of the book to be of greater interest than others. This is a natural result of an interdisciplinary and multimethodological enterprise such as this one. Indeed, some readers have suggested that the history should come before, rather than after, the models.

That suggestion was resisted for methodological reasons. Economists will probably find Parts I and III to be of greater interest than Part II. Political scientists, constitutional scholars, and historians will probably find Parts II and III to be of greater interest than Part I. All three parts, however, seem necessary to develop and test the theory of constitutional governance and reform proposed by this volume.

Part I: Sharing Sovereignty

Analytical histories have long been used to focus attention on key factors in political and economic development, and that approach is used in Part I. Classic works from political science, such as Aristotle's *Politics* (330 BCE) and Hobbes's *Leviathan* (1651), use analytical histories to discuss the evolution of institutions and the normative case for particular forms of governance. Contemporary scholars such as Rawls (1971) and Nozick (1974) have used this technique to develop theories of distributive justice. Olson (1993, 2000) has used the analytic approach to develop an explanation for the emergence of regional governments from bands of roving and stationary bandits. Analytical histories allow a few essential features of a choice setting to be analyzed in an environment that abstracts from the idiosyncrasies of real people and places.

The analytical foundation for the present analysis is a theory of organizational governance. Part I provides an analytical history of governance that begins with a general theory of organizational governance and ends with models of constitutional bargaining and suffrage reform. Chapters Two to Four analyze the formation and evolution of formal organizations, their internal incentive structures, and their standing decision-making procedures. That analysis, perhaps surprisingly, provides an explanation for some of the main features of medieval and modern territorial governance and for the constitutional dynamics of such governments.

Chapter Two characterizes some general features of organizations. Organizations are artificial choice settings in which a variety of conditional economic and social rewards and punishments are used to align the interests of the organization's team members with the organization's survival and success. The reward systems used are partly products of design and partly products of evolution. The persons that create new organizations (formeteurs) normally choose from preexisting organizational templates and modify those templates for the purposes at hand. Both the internal incentive structures and decision-making procedures of formal organizations are chosen by formeteurs and thus tend to advance their interests.

Large organizations normally have a standing decision-making process to devise and modify internal incentive systems and to determine which goals an organization's resources should be used to advance. Even profit-maximizing firms tend to have such governmental systems.

The king-and-council template is widely used for choosing policies because it reduces information problems and also tends to reduce unproductive intra-organizational conflict. In cases in which a single person creates an organization, the king tends to be the dominant policy maker. In cases in which a small group creates an organization, the council tends to be the dominant policy maker. In cases in which a large group creates an organization, a council may be elected or appointed by the larger group to represent their interests in the organization.

Chapter Three analyzes long-term survival advantages of organizational rule of law. Organizations that have stable reward systems, standing procedures for policy making, and standing procedures for replacing organizational leaders tend to have lower decision-making and recruiting costs, which make such organizations more robust in the short and medium run. In the long run, however, some degree of flexibility is necessary. The founders and their successors will need to be replaced, and decision-making procedures that worked well for the founding generation may need to be adjusted to reflect the talents of new officeholders and new circumstances if the organization is to remain viable. The king-and-council template for governance allows several possible solutions to an organization's transition problems, and it also allows responsibilities to shift among top officeholders to take advantage of changes in talent and to facilitate adjusting to external circumstances.

Chapter Four provides an explanation for the emergence of regional governments as one of many kinds of organizations in a setting in which migration is possible. Any durable organization with a bit of monopoly power can impose and enforce rules on persons outside their organization. For example, fine restaurants often impose dress codes on their customers. The more important the service monopolized, the greater is an organization's ability to impose such rules without inducing substitution or out-migration. In contemporary circumstances, access to air transport requires a number of rather inconvenient and somewhat embarrassing behaviors by passengers. From this perspective, territorial governments are simply durable organizations that have extraordinary monopoly power.

Territorial governments are not necessarily the first formal organization, nor are they necessarily central to the emergence of civil society, as often argued (Hobbes 1651; North, Wallis, and Weingast 2009). Moreover, the ability of an organization to impose rules on nonmembers does not necessarily require substantial military power.

The ability to organize violence, however, can make such organizations more durable. For example, regional governments may have to respond to threats from rival organizations outside their territories to protect their monopolies and organizational surplus. Olson (2000) calls such external rivals "roving bandits." Note, however, that Olson's roving bandits cannot emerge first, because there would be too little for them to steal without preexisting productive organizations and communities.

Chapters Five to Eight analyze the extent to which a territorial government's decision-making procedures can be reformed through internal bargaining and exchange. An important question for the purposes of the book is whether shifts of policy-making authority from the king to the council can ever simultaneously advance the interests of king and council. If such cases exist, it implies that constitutional terms of trade can be negotiated and freely adopted. Chapters Five and Six demonstrate that constitutional gains to trade can arise and that voluntary transfers of authority are possible within the king-and-council template for governance. Particular assignments of authority (distributions of veto power and agenda control) and procedures for selecting members of government are "political resources" that can be traded much as ordinary goods and services are in ordinary markets.

Chapters Seven and Eight explore the extent to which economic and political shocks can induce parliament to change the manner in which its members are selected. Chapter Seven demonstrates that peaceful changes in suffrage law cannot be explained by economic changes, such as increased income. Suffrage is not simply a superior good that people purchase more of as they become wealthier. Chapter Seven also argues that suffrage reform is unlikely to emerge from a civil war or threat of civil war, because democratic revolutions are difficult to organize, and the hierarchical organizations necessary are not usually inclined to transform themselves into representative democracies after such improbable wars are won. Chapter Eight suggests that peaceful suffrage reform is most likely to occur when ideas about the proper bounds of suffrage change. Ideology and ideological change appear to be more critical for suffrage expansion than for shifts of policy-making authority from kings to parliament. This partly accounts for differences in the timing of increased parliamentary authority and expansion of suffrage during the various Western transitions to democracy.

Together, the prose and mathematics of Part I provide several explanations for the widespread use of the king-and-council template for governance. It provides an explanation for the distribution of authority within that template, for changes in that distribution through time, and for the stability of selection procedures for high office. The models also suggest that the standing procedures of governance tend to be fairly stable through time, unless there are trends in external shocks. Without such trends, the distribution of authority between king and parliament (and between the central and regional governments) will resemble a random walk as reforms are adopted and reversed.

With favorable trends, the models imply that liberal trends in constitutional reform are possible. In such cases, constitutional bargaining and exchange can gradually produce parliamentary democracy through a series of reforms that gradually shift policy-making authority from kings to parliament and extend the electoral base for selecting members of parliament to include most adults.

Part II: Historical Evidence on Western Democratic Transitions

If the choice settings analyzed in the first part of the book are representative of those confronting real persons in real governments, the predicted institutions, interest groups, constitutional bargaining, and reforms should be commonplace in history. For example, one should observe widespread use of the king-and-council template. There should be ongoing constitutional negotiations and occasional reforms within such governments, but few long-run trends in the reforms adopted. The individual reforms adopted should be relatively small but discrete changes. In periods in which external shocks exhibit strong trends, as in the nineteenth century, there should be similar broad trends in both policy and constitutional reforms. These predictions are largely borne out in the case histories and historical overviews developed in Part II.

Part II begins with a general account of the emergence of Western democracy and then explores the transitions of six countries in greater detail. The case studies include three cases in which the theory applies very naturally (England, Sweden, and the Netherlands) and three more difficult cases (Germany, Japan, and the United States). In four of the cases, transitions to parliamentary democracy occurred without dethroning the royal families. In one of those cases, the transition reversed and the king regained his authority. All but one of the narratives focus on developments in the nineteenth and early twentieth centuries. The exception is the American case, where the transition began nearly two centuries earlier than in Europe and Japan, although the American transition can be said to have ended at about the same time (with the adoption of women's suffrage in the early twentieth century). Other case studies could easily be developed, but that is left for future research.

Both the overviews and the case histories are somewhat novel in that they focus narrowly on constitutional developments, rather than personalities, international entanglements, or sociological trends, except as these bear directly on constitutional bargaining and reform. Needless to say, more could be written about every case developed. Indeed, in a few cases, historians have written books on material covered here in just paragraphs. However, sufficient detail is provided to give readers a sense of the interest groups at work, the ongoing constitutional bargaining, and the long series of reforms that produced parliamentary democracy in the countries of interest. Most general national or period histories include a wide range of details that had little effect on constitutional developments and tend to neglect minor constitutional reforms that play important roles in the emergence of parliamentary democracy. Most narrow historical studies focus on a single reform and country at a single point in history and fail to note parallels in other national histories.

Chapters Nine to Eleven provide an overview of political, economic, and constitutional developments in the West during the eighteenth and nineteenth centuries. The overview focuses for the most part on European developments because most Western democracies are either physically in Europe or initially had governments whose structures were determined by European politics. (In many cases, European templates for government were simply exported to their colonies with minor adaptations for local conditions. Those of Meiji Japan were also influenced by European ideas and templates.)

The process through which the constitutional reforms were adopted is consistent with the analysis of Part I. In all cases, parliamentary democracy emerged from a series of reforms, rather than in one or two great quantum leaps, although some reforms could be said to be more important or larger than others. Constitutional bargaining is evident in most countries prior to 1830, and significant institutional innovations were adopted, but the balance of authority between king and parliament lacked a clear long-run trend. In contrast, constitutional reforms in the century between 1830 and 1930 exhibited clear liberal trends. In essentially all cases, liberal reforms were adopted using preexisting constitutional rules for amendment. In no case is every liberal reform preceded by a large-scale revolt, and in most cases, there are examples of large-scale demonstrations that failed to produce obvious reform.

The main trigger for the constitutional reforms of nineteenth-century Europe is argued to be changes in economic and ideological interests associated with new economies of scale in production, which favored economic and political liberalization. Liberal trends in reform are evident in many areas of policy, including education, civil liberties, and more open trade. Liberal trends are also evident in political reforms that affected the division of authority between the king and parliament and the basis for holding seats in parliament. Both industrialization and democracy were consequences of a long series of liberal successes in policy and constitutional debates within preexisting governments. In countries where liberals were unsuccessful, neither industrialization nor democratization took place in the nineteenth century.

The historical overview is followed by six more detailed constitutional histories. The first three country studies are cases in which all the elements of the model are evident: the United Kingdom (Chapters Twelve to Thirteen), Sweden (Chapter Fourteen), and the Netherlands (Chapter Fifteen). The timing of their transitions differ somewhat, but in all three cases, parliaments gradually gained authority, suffrage was gradually broadened, and kings and queens gradually lost most of their authority over public policy. Their respective royal families, nonetheless, retained their titles, palaces, and modest formal authority, which would not have been the case if true revolutions had occurred. Similar chapters could have been written about Belgium, Denmark, and Norway.

The second three cases are more difficult ones, in which some elements from the theory are missing. The purpose of exploring such cases is partly to show that similar negotiations were taking place elsewhere and partly to demonstrate that technological and ideological shocks do not always produce parliamentary democracy, even when substantial internal pressure for liberalization exists. Such economic and political changes simply make liberal transitions more likely. The three difficult cases are Germany (Chapter Sixteen), Japan (Chapter Seventeen), and the United States (Chapter Eighteen). Germany failed to find a bargain that would allow the last steps to parliamentary democracy to take place prior to World War I, although negotiations were undertaken and helped produce parliamentary democracy after the war was over. In roughly the same period, Japanese political leaders engaged in nonstop constitutional bargaining that gradually produced universal male suffrage and party governance in 1925, but political and economic policy shifted in an authoritarian direction in the next decade. The United States succeeded in its transition to liberal democracy, but it took a longer time, was initially catalyzed by somewhat different factors, and produced a somewhat different political system. Similar difficult-case chapters could have been written about France, Italy, Spain, and several South American countries.

Overall, the six country studies demonstrate that new economic and ideological interests and preexisting institutions played important roles in the constitutional bargains that gradually produced Western democracy. The cases also cast doubt on several alternative nonrevolutionary explanations for the emergence of the West. For example, they demonstrate that religion and other preexisting aspects of culture and institutions are less important factors than one might have expected. Belgium and Japan were not Protestant. Neither Sweden nor Japan was ever ruled by Rome. The transitions in the United States and the Netherlands were not preceded by long periods of stable more or less constitutional rule by a monarch.

Part III: Analytical History as Social Science

Part III addresses significant methodological issues not addressed in the analytical history of Part I or case studies of Part II. Chapter Nineteen provides statistical evidence in support of the hypothesized links among technology, liberal interest groups, and constitutional reforms. The statistical evidence affirms the hypothesis that Western democracy and industrialization were interdependent phenomena. There is evidence of boot strapping and joint causality. Chapter Twenty summarizes the main results, contrasts the approach used here with that used by other scholars, and suggests possible extensions. Additional methodological issues are addressed in a short appendix.

Although the book includes a good deal of history and reflects many years spent reading early constitutional documents and books written by careful historians, *Perfecting Parliament* is not intended to be primarily an historical work, but rather a contribution to social science. It attempts to develop and test a particular theory of constitutional reform.

The lasting effects of the reforms adopted in the nineteenth century are still evident in the West today. Trade is substantially free, public education is widespread, equality before the law is taken nearly for granted, and governance "of the people for the people" has proven to be a remarkably good form of government relative to the others that remain. The West dominates lists of countries ranked by average income, civil liberties, political liberties, lack of corruption, literacy, and longevity, and it continues to be a magnet for emigration from other parts of the world. Essentially all of today's mainstream Western political parties would be considered liberal on the great constitutional issues of the nineteenth century.

Yet there is nothing really unique about the West beyond its fortunate century or two of liberal reform. It is not uniquely populated with wise leaders, clever entrepreneurs, or political philosophers. Thus it is quite possible that similar, essentially peaceful reforms can occur elsewhere, as seems to have been the case in several other parts of the world in the past half century.

ACKNOWLEDGMENTS: SUPPORT AND INFLUENTIAL PRECURSORS

It can be said that this book began as a short paper on Swedish constitutional reform, which through the support and encouragement of the constitutional project at the Studieförbundet Näringsliv och Samhälle (SNS) became a short book on Swedish constitutional reform. That project raised questions that required a much longer book to answer.

At first, I believed that Swedish constitutional history was unique, because most general histories of other countries emphasize revolutions of one kind or another. The words "revolution" and "crisis" appear over and over in historical work. However, as I read more detailed accounts of constitutional developments, they seemed to be more similar to the Swedish constitutional history than one might have expected, given their revolutionary narratives. There was little evidence that violence or major threats of violence played a direct role in those reforms, although there were often peaceful demonstrations in support of reform. It seemed clear that liberalization took place through a variety of legal and procedural reforms, rather than through a single democratic leap forward. Bargaining and lawful constitutional reforms appeared to be much more common than the violent, illegal uprisings and constitutional conventions that revolutionary narratives required.

How peaceful and lawful transitions could occur, however, remained a great puzzle, and to piece together an answer took seven more years of reading, puzzle solving, and writing.

The Rational-Choice Approach to Constitutional Analysis

Contemporary analysis of constitutional designs using rational-choice models began in 1962 with the publication of *The Calculus of Consent* by James Buchanan and Gordon Tullock. They used models of individual interests and elementary game theory to assess the properties of a fairly broad range of constitutional alternatives. Their work and much that followed provided new rational-choice foundations for an older political science literature on the role of institutions in governance that extends back to Aristotle's *Politics* and beyond. Buchanan's subsequent work stressed the distinction between two levels of analysis: the constitutional level, which determines the rules of the game, and the ordinary play of the game under those rules. This volume essentially adds a third level of analysis – that of constitutional reform – to the Buchanan schema of "rules of the game" and "play under the rules."

The analytical literature on constitutional design now includes hundreds of academic papers that attempt to determine the interdependence between the standing routines of governance and public policy. See, for example, Riker (1962), Buchanan (1975), Baron and Ferejohn (1989), and Mueller (1996). Surveys of the theoretical and empirical literature are provided by Mueller (2003), Cooter (2002), Persson and Tabellini (2003), and Congleton and Swedenborg (2006). The evolution of economic and political institutions has been discussed by Hayek (1973, 1979), North (1990), Ostrom (1991), Vanberg (1994), Spruyt (1994), Finer (1997), Mesquita, Smith, Siverson, and Morrow (2003), and North, Wallis, and Weingast (2009), among many others. In most cases, however, the research provides more insight about the effects of particular institutions than about how those institutions came into existence at particular times and places.

The process through which durable procedures for policy making are adopted and refined through time has attracted surprisingly little attention from rational-choice-based research. This lacuna is important because the existing literature implies that small changes in political architecture can have significant effects on the course of public policy, which in turn can have significant effects on economic and social life. This book shows that a particular model of divided government can shed very useful light on the development and evolution of contemporary institutions for democratic governance.

Support of Colleagues

The research and writing of this manuscript took place over many years at several institutions of higher learning throughout the West, and thanks are due to a broad group of colleagues scattered around the world: at the Center for Study of Public Choice at George Mason University, Studieförbundet Näringsliv och Samhälle (SNS), University of Leiden, Nuffield College at Oxford University, University of Rome, University of Bayreuth, University of Southern Denmark, and University of Amsterdam. Many helpful conversations also took place at academic conferences and seminars in Europe,

Japan, China, Korea, and the United States. Students at the University of Leiden, University of Bayreuth, and University of Southern Denmark directly and indirectly helped bring the book to final form through their feedback in courses based on the early-draft chapters of the book.

George Tridimas and Dennis Mueller carefully read through preliminary drafts of the book and made very helpful comments and suggestions that greatly improved the final version. Toke Aidt, James Buchanan, Mario Ferrero, Klas Fregert, Hans Bernd Schäfer, Gordon Tullock, and Akira Yokoyama also read several preliminary chapters of the manuscript and provided helpful comments and suggestions. Other colleagues made short comments in conversations about the book that helped clarify my thinking. These include conversations with Cheryl Schonhardt-Bailey, Geoffrey Brennan, Charles Breeden, Bryan Caplan, Mark Crain, Lars Feld, Paal Foss, Georgio Galeotti, Robin Hanson, Rainer Hegselmann, Douglas Hibbs, Arye Hillman, Larry Iannaccone, Sarah Jennings, Gebhard Kirschgässner, David Levy, Arthur Lupia, Iain McClean, Bruce Bueno De Mesquita, Mike Munger, Rob Nelson, Douglas North, John Nye, Elinor Ostrom, Scott Paris, Torsten Persson, Olof Petersson, Roald Ramer, Illia Rainer, Christilla Roederer-Rynning, Pierre Salmon, Bernard Steunenberg, Birgitta Swedenborg, Thomas Stratmann, Yoshifumi Ueda, Stefan Voigt, Viktor Vanberg, Karl Warneryd, Barry Weingast, Stanley Winer, and Ronald Wintrobe.

Thanks are due to these and many other colleagues for their interest, criticism, and support, although they bear no responsibility for the use to which I put their comments and suggestions. Pamela Cubberly helped transform a series of drafts into forms suitable for circulation and also provided a number of helpful comments. Additional editorial suggestions were made by Jane Perry and the references were carefully checked by Marta Podemska. Scott Paris's encouragement helped carry the project through to completion, although it took many years longer than I expected. Very helpful suggestions were also provided by three anonymous readers for Cambridge University Press.

Overlap with Previously Published Work

Material from several of the chapters has been published in academic journals, partly because of the usual pressures of American academia and partly to have the analysis carefully examined by reviewers and editors in Europe, Japan, and the United States:

"From Royal to Parliamentary Rule without Revolution, the Economics of Constitutional Exchange within Divided Governments," *European Journal of Political Economy* 23 (2007): 261–84.

"Constitutional Exchange in Japan: From Shogunate to Parliamentary Democracy," *Public Choice Studies* 47 (2006): 5–29.

"Amendment Procedures and Constitutional Stability" (with B. E. Rasch) in *Democratic Constitutional Design and Public Policy: Analysis and Evidence*. R. D. Congleton and B. Swedenborg, eds., Cambridge, MA: MIT Press (2006): 319–42.

"Science and History: How Predictable is Political Behavior?" in *Understanding Change: Models, Methodologies, and Metaphors*. A. Wimmer and R. Kossler, eds., New York: Palgrave Macmillan (2005): 260–69.

"Economic Development and Democracy, Does Industrialization Lead to Universal Suffrage?" *Homo Oeconomicus* 21 (2004): 283–311.

"Mutual Advantages of Coercion and Exit within Private Clubs and Treaty Organizations: Toward a Logic of Voluntary Association," *Revista de Political Economy* 94 (2004): 47–75.

"A Theory of Menu Federalism, Decentralization by Political Agreement" (with Andreas Kyriacou and Jordi Bacaria), *Constitutional Political Economy* 14 (2003): 167–90.

"Economic and Cultural Prerequisites for Democracy," in *Rational Foundations of Democratic Politics*. A. Breton, G. Galeotti, P. Salmon, and R. Wintrobe, eds., New York: Cambridge University Press (2003): 44–67.

"On the Durability of King and Council: the Continuum between Dictatorship and Democracy," *Constitutional Political Economy* 12 (2001): 193–215.

Although most of the material taken from the book was substantially rewritten for journal publication, permission to reproduce previously published figures, tables, and some text from the published pieces is gratefully acknowledged.

What is Entirely New?

As to how much is truly new in the pages that follow is for readers to judge. Much seems both very new and very old to this author. The theory of governmental reform developed in Part I is in many respects a natural extension of the Virginia school of political economy, although the theory departs from and extends that tradition in a number of ways. As a past student and colleague of James Buchanan and Gordon Tullock, I have enjoyed many constitutional and methodological discussions with them over the course of four decades and read many of their books and articles. However, the perspective on the origins of government developed in this book owes more to Montesquieu than to Hobbes, the enlightenment scholar most stressed in their work. Moreover, none of their research focuses on the king-and-council template, nor has it been used as a lens through which to understand long-run constitutional reform and evolution.

Bargaining theories of constitutional design are evident in a good deal of work in political science, law, and economics; however, they have not previously been used to provide a unified theory of the evolution of organizational and territorial governance, to explain core features of medieval and modern governance, or to provide a continuum that can account for the gradual transitions from late-medieval governance to parliamentary democracy. Indeed, relatively few late-twentieth-century political scientists or historians have focused much attention on constitutional reform. Constitutional settings are taken for granted in most mainstream research, so that the effects of different leaders or circumstances can be examined. In other research, institutions are regarded to be cultural phenomena that have little direct effect on policy making or constitutional reform.

Of those political historians who focus on constitutional developments, most focus on single periods within single countries. This book takes the opposite approach. It neglects the idiosyncrasies of particular leaders and circumstances to focus on general features of organizations, constitutional governance, and reform. The narratives also depart from previous work in that they are grounded in models of constitutional exchange, and account for more of the core procedures of contemporary Western constitutions.

Nonetheless, many of the insights and much about the general approach that seemed novel when first conceived and written now seem like natural extensions of older theories and contemporary work by others in related fields. That the present analysis seems to echo the ideas and words of long-dead scholars is, of course, a mark in favor of the theory and evidence developed in this volume. The most general and robust conclusions of past scholars have, in a manner analogous to institutions, survived the test of time.

Aristotle's analyses are remarkable in this regard. Although he focused for the most part on pure forms of government – monarchy, aristocracy, and democracy – he did so in order to better understand the more commonplace mixed forms of government present in classical Greece.

> The reason why there are many forms of government is that *every state contains many elements* ... For a constitution is an organization of offices [among] which all the citizens distribute among themselves, according to the power which different classes possess ... There *must therefore be as many forms of government as there are modes of arranging the offices*, according to the superiorities and differences of the parts of the state. (*Politics*, Book IV, Part III)

And although the most famous Greek philosophers disagreed about the nature of an ideal constitution, they agreed that polities based on better constitutions tend to produce more robust governments and better societies than those grounded on less perfect and less robust procedures for devising and enforcing laws. Aristotle, for example, concludes that

> The more perfect the admixture of the political elements, the more lasting will be the constitution. (*Politics*, Book IV, Part XII)

Similar conclusions are reached in this book, although from a much different methodological and historical perspective.

PART I

SHARING SOVEREIGNTY

TWO

Team Production, Organization, and Governance

In the days before histories were recorded, there were few distinctions between governments and other organizations. Most were evidently familial and clan based. As agriculture emerged and people settled in particular places, the variety and size of organizations and governments tended to increase, and distinctions began to emerge between organizations that could impose rules only on their own members and those that could impose rules on persons outside their organizations. That more activities took place within formal organizations and within territories ruled by governments does not imply that all activities were organized from the top down, as in totalitarian states, nor do the distinctions between governments and other organizations imply that the procedures used by territorial governments had become completely different from those used in other organizations. More people were simply being organized to engage in more tasks because the advantages of formal organizations with artificial incentive systems had increased for both the leaders and members of organizations.

With such distant beginnings in mind, the analytical history of this book begins with an analysis of the emergence and evolution of formal organizations. All organizations share the property that they are formed to advance goals that can best be achieved by coordinating the efforts of more than one person. All organizations make decisions that focus the organization's resources on particular activities and induce their members to function as more or less productive teams, rather than as unproductive assemblies of individual shirkers and rent seekers. It is these effects that make them organizations, rather than simply groups of unrelated persons, all doing their own thing. Hunting clubs, farm cooperatives, churches, commercial enterprises, pirate ships, and governments all select projects to undertake and provide internal incentives for undertaking them.

The first half of Chapter Two discusses several natural solutions to internal incentive problems drawing on the economics literature and extending it to take account of culture. The remainder of the chapter and the rest of Part I of this book focus on the emergence and evolution of standing procedures for making organizational decisions, that is, on organizational governance. This contrasts with most work in economics and managerial science, which focuses on solutions to organizational incentive problems, and tends to neglect organizational institutions for making day-to-day and long-run decisions.

To organize a team, decisions have to be made about a number of practical details: What is the purpose of the team, how can team production be used to advance that purpose, and what kind of team members make team production cost-effective? After the team is assembled, decision making continues, as purpose, team members, and use of team members are adjusted to correct initial mistakes and adjust to changing circumstances. There are many ways that an organization can choose its objectives and strategies, although some procedures work better than others, and consequently, only a few templates for governance tend to be widely used at a given time and place.

Elinor Ostrom (2005, chapter 8) argues that a very large number of contemporary institutions can be classified using a relatively small number of general characteristics, although great variety may exist among organizations. This allows the theory of organizational design to be far simpler than the organizations themselves, the specific problems addressed by them, or the environments in which they function.

The present chapter and the next two may be regarded as an effort to provide a somewhat simpler, less fine-grained schema for analyzing institutions (organizations) than the one proposed by Ostrom, although it is very much in the spirit of her work. Of particular importance for the purposes of this book are solutions to the problem of organizational governance based on the king-and-council template. Chapters Two to Four provide a series of explanations for the widespread use of this form of divided government by both governmental and nongovernmental organizations. Chapters Five to Eight demonstrate that the king-and-council organizational template provides a number of ways for parliamentary democracy to emerge gradually from authoritarian territorial governments without revolutions.

FORMETEURS, TEAM PRODUCTION, AND THE FOUNDING OF ORGANIZATIONS

To begin with, all formal organizations have a beginning; formal organizations are initiated by an individual or group of individuals with particular purposes or goals in mind. A hunting party is to meet at a particular place and time, a barn or house is to be raised, a new product is to be made and sold, trade is to be expanded or contracted, an idea is to be promoted or dismissed, a swamp is to be drained or protected, a village is to be defended or attacked, rights and privileges are to be created, extended, or reduced. In this, formal organizations differ from "spontaneous" systems that may be said to emerge without much conscious thought, as with galaxies, ecological systems, or trading networks – although these too may be said to have a beginning, and the latter may also be said to be piecewise the result of intent.

Many formal organizations also have an end. Small organizations often end when their goals have been achieved, as with informal pickup sports games and academic conferences. Some organizations function well only because they include particular constellations of personalities and talents and end when critical members depart. Others end because important incentive or decision problems are not solved, and the organization is unable to produce sufficient surplus to sustain itself. Hunting clubs must produce food to be self-sustaining. Churches must attract sufficient donations to maintain their clergy and buildings. Economic enterprises must produce sufficient revenues to pay employees and assure reasonable profits for entrepreneurs. Governments must have sufficient tax resources and/or loyalty to retain control of their territories.

New organizations are created every day because new (potential) advantages from joint enterprises are constantly being imagined. They may be created by single individuals with very narrow purposes in mind, as often assumed by economists about the origins of organizations with profits as their principal goal. Or new organizations may be formed by groups of individuals or organizations that wish to advance common purposes, as is often assumed in rational-choice-based analyses of private clubs and treaty organizations and in contract-based theories of the state. Intermediate cases also exist in which a small group organizes a larger one, as when tribal leaders organize a work gang, a group of investors creates a new production team, or a group of political activists organizes a mass demonstration of support for or in opposition to existing policies. And cases also exist in which a large group organizes a small one to advance common interests, as when members of a club or cooperative organize small groups to produce services for the cooperative or create an oversight committee to manage such activities.

The individuals or groups that found an organization will be called "formeteurs" and the persons recruited by formeteurs will be called "team members." Except in the very unusual cases in which an entire society is the formeteur, organizations are not designed to maximize their membership's or society's welfare, but rather to maximize that of their formeteurs. This does not imply that member interests are ignored, only that team members are not the persons to focus on if one wants to understand organizational incentive and governance systems.

Why Organizations Are Founded

Many scholars have remarked that humans are social animals and that some instinct drives people to form groups of one kind or another. This book suggests, in contrast, that groups come together because people are often more effective in groups than as unaffiliated individuals. There are often good practical advantages for hunting, farming, building, worshipping, and governing in groups. If an instinct exists, it is because group activities generally advance individual interests.

Team production, however, is not entirely natural for human beings, although it often advances shared interests. A variety of incentive and governance problems have to be overcome for a group of individuals to become an effective team. As a consequence, most productive groups are *organized* in some way.

The left-hand side of Table 2.1 illustrates a common incentive problem faced by informal groups that simply share the output jointly produced. The output might be fish caught from a pond or fruit harvested from a natural orchard. The "natural cooperative" is assumed to be viable in that its members produce more jointly than they would have by working alone. The group may be better at finding the best fishing spot or trees to exploit, or the sharing of output may simply reduce the risk associated with a bad day of fishing or poor choice of fruit tree. Consequently, the exit option is not exercised (2 > 1) and group production is undertaken, rather than solitary production.

However, the natural cooperative produces less output than it could have because its members shirk too much, rather than working in equilibrium. "Shirking" may involve a number of behaviors, including low effort at productive activities, high effort at unproductive activities, or various combinations of both. Group members may simply fish from convenient spots and/or take only the low-hanging fruit. They may harvest fish or fruit too early or too late. They may take fish or fruit home that should have been turned over to the shared harvest. The assumed equal distribution of the natural co-op's production also tends to limit opportunities for taking advantage of specialization. Fish and fruit may go uncaught and unpicked in difficult locations. Fishing nets and ladders may be underproduced

Table 2.1. *On the Origins of Organizations*

The shirking dilemma for team production in natural cooperatives				An artificial incentive system as a solution to the shirking dilemma			
	Team Member B				Team Member B		
	Work	Shirk	Exit		Work	Shirk	Exit
Work (A)	3, 3	1, 4	1, 1	Work (A)	R, R	R, R-P	R, 2
Shirk (A)	4, 1	2, 2	1, 1	Shirk (A)	R-P, R	R-P, R-P	R-P, 2
Exit (A)	1, 1	1, 1	1, 1	Exit (A)	2, R	2, R-P	2, 2

The cell entries are output shares, which provide the rank order of subjective payoffs for the team members (A, B). (Utility is assumed to vary directly with rewards or output shares.) The dilemma in the "natural cooperative" case is that both team members shirk, rather than work.

because the group's output is shared equally among all members of the co-op, regardless of effort levels, risks taken, or investments made.

Most formal organizations differ from natural cooperatives in that they use artificial incentive and recruiting systems. In the case illustrated, team production can be increased by replacing the natural system of rewards on the left with the artificial system of rewards on the right. Under the artificial reward system, the formeteur promises to pay R dollars (or units of output) to people who join his organization and work, but threatens to impose a penalty of amount P on those who join and shirk. Those harvesting fish or fruit too early, for example, may be paid less than those who wait until the appropriate time.

A new formal organization is viable as long as the anticipated net reward (*R*) from being a member of the formal organization is larger than that available from the natural co-op (2). The formeteur(s), for example, can promise to pay 2.2 units of output to team members and threaten to impose a punishment of 1.1 units of output on shirkers. Solving the shirking dilemma makes team members better off than they would have been in the natural cooperative and in this case generates an organizational surplus (of 1.6 units of output) for the formeteur(s), which provides an incentive to form the organization. In such cases, natural cooperatives tend to disappear as individuals exit to join formal organizations offering greater rewards.

In equilibrium, relatively few punishments are imposed by formal organizations because relatively few team members shirk and because team members often have reasonably attractive exit options. Nonetheless, the threat of punishment remains an important part of artificial incentive systems because it reduces the private advantage of shirking associated with natural cooperatives. In modern economic organizations, the most obvious conditional reward structures are those associated with wages, salaries, and promotion. The most obvious threats are wage reductions, demotions, and being expelled (fired) from the organization.

Choosing Reward Systems

A broad range of team-production and recruiting techniques can be represented as solutions to prisoner's dilemma with exit problems (PDEs) similar to that represented in Table 2.1. Coordination problems also exist, as stressed by Hardin (1999), but these are easier to solve than PDE problems because solutions to coordination games are stable once established. Organizational PDE problems are also more challenging to solve than simple prisoner's-dilemma problems because the solutions are constrained by exit options, and exit options tend to change through time, partly because formeteurs may compete with one another to attract team members.

An important feature of artificial incentive solutions to PDE problems is that the conditional payoffs of the intra-organization game can be manipulated by formeteurs to achieve the desired team behavior, but only within the limits determined by the exit options of team members. Self-interested formeteurs naturally favor reward systems that minimize the overall cost of solving the incentive problems at hand because this maximizes the organizational surplus available for solving other problems and for advancing other formeteur goals.

The exit options of potential team members, however, create a lower bound for expected rewards and an upper bound for expected penalties (if any are imposed). Team members must receive at least as much compensation (adjusted for risk) as is available from other formal organizations and natural cooperatives. At the hypothetical extreme of what economists call perfect competition, exit options are so great and easy to realize that each team member has to be paid his or her full contribution to team production. As exit options become less attractive or more costly to realize, smaller rewards can be used to retain team members. In the extreme case of teams composed of persons without exit options (slaves), rewards can be set at subsistence levels and punishments used to encourage work in every case in which penalties are more cost-effective than rewards.

From the perspective of formeteurs, the ideal reward system aligns the interests of team members with those of the formeteurs at the lowest possible cost in the circumstances at hand.

FORMETEURS, CULTURE, AND ORGANIZATIONAL OPPORTUNITIES

In Schumpeter's (1934) and Kirzner's (1978) terms, a formeteur creates, or recognizes organizational opportunities that others do not have or cannot see. Consequently, innovation, foresight, and boldness are often associated with organizational leadership along with an exceptional ability to recruit and motivate team members. Formeteurs may also be said to be less risk averse than others (Knight 1921) insofar as they are more willing to accept the risks associated with launching new enterprises. Formeteurs, however, differ from the entrepreneurs of classic economic models because they form organizations, rather than engage in price arbitrage or product innovation. Consequently, formeteurs cannot be loners, and they tend to have unusual motivational skills and organizational insight.[1]

Organizational founders are often charismatic leaders who can easily persuade team members to accept their direction. Such persons can solve many of the incentive problems of team production by encouraging personal and organizational loyalty. They may, for example, induce team members to internalize various duties, such as working hard to advance the formeteur's and their organization's interest, simply as a method of obtaining the formeteur's approval. Here, one can imagine the charismatic founders of fishing clubs, pear-harvesting co-ops, and cherry-picking firms encouraging team members to "pull hard on the net," "climb to the highest branch," and "not miss anything." Less skilled or less naturally charismatic formeteurs will require more generous and sophisticated pecuniary reward systems to accomplish similar results, which is, of course, part of the reason that successful formeteurs tend to be relatively talented at assembling and motivating people.

If team members can be induced to work hard at advancing their organization's goals simply because they are persuaded that it is the right thing to do, reward systems can be simpler and, in many cases, less generous. If team members can be induced to feel loyal to the organization, subjective exit costs increase, and smaller rewards and larger penalties can be used to solve the organization's internal incentive problems. If an organization's internal culture causes individual members to feel worse off when they act in a manner that conflicts with organizational goals, even when his or her performance cannot be observed by others, monitoring efforts can be reduced.

[1] It should be acknowledged that many new organizations fail, which implies that formeteur insight tends to be quite imperfect.

It is therefore not surprising that farming cooperatives, private firms, religious groups, and roving bandits all attempt to build team loyalty within their organizations and to promote other internal norms that reduce shirking and increase team spirit.

Efforts to develop and support an internal organizational culture may also indirectly support or produce complementary communitywide norms, particularly if several organizations in the same community promote similar intra-organizational norms. If team members prosper and take their internalized organizational norms home at the end of the workday, their corporate norms may be taught to children and friends. Such norms may also indirectly help solve other coordination, public goods, and prisoner's-dilemma problems among families and friends and within the community at large. Moreover, if some potential team members (employees) are easier to motivate with nonpecuniary rewards than others or are intrinsically more motivated to advance organizational goals, team-production costs can be reduced by recruiting such "honest, hardworking team players," which further encourages the spread of corporate norms in the communities from which team members are recruited.

Culture and Organizational Opportunities

It bears noting, however, that not all norms or propensities to cooperate provide opportunities for formeteurs. Some norms may reduce the effectiveness of artificial reward systems. For example, team members may cooperate to escape from prisoner's-dilemma games designed by formeteurs, such as competitive piece-rate schedules, with coordinated work slowdowns and sick-outs. Other internal norms that predispose team members to work, rather than shirk, may simultaneously reduce organizational costs and the need for formal organizations. Simulation studies by Axelrod (1986), Boyd and Richerson (1992), and Vanberg and Congleton (1992, 2001) demonstrate that strategies of conditional cooperation can be privately advantageous for individual team members in settings in which exit is possible and organizations last more than a few periods. A community that supports a work ethic requires fewer formal organizations and less sophisticated artificial incentive systems within its organizations because its informal reward and punishment systems will solve many team production, coordination, and rent-seeking problems. Members of natural cooperatives in such cultures are encouraged to "show up" and "do good work" by their peers within the organization and also by their friends and families (Congleton 1991b).

Both norms that reduce the need for artificial incentive systems and norms that make artificial incentive systems more difficult to design make formal cooperatives less viable, which reduces formeteur opportunities for creating formal organizations.[2]

A niche for formal organizations, nonetheless, remains unless the norms of conditional cooperation solve all coordination and team-production problems or completely undermine all systems of artificial incentives (Ostrom, Walker, and Gardner 1992). For example, Congleton and Vanberg (2001) show that the ability to target punishments at shirkers can be sufficiently important to the success of joint enterprises that norms may emerge so that a subset of team and community members will punish shirkers, even if personally costly. Team members will often have better information about who is shirking and thus be better able to target penalties at those "not carrying their load." Such norms, however, are not always sufficient to solve the externality and coordination problems that must be addressed. Active management and active rule enforcement are often necessary to solve team-production problems.

This niche can be enlarged by other culturally transmitted values that allow formeteurs to economize on rewards by solving team-production and coordination problems with praise, status, and informal perks for outstanding work, rather than with (or in addition to) money or physical output rewards. Community norms may encourage persons to keep their promises, be punctual, and follow instructions. Indeed, formeteurs may also be informally rewarded for founding organizations with additional status or opportunities within some communities. Here one might note the number of plaques, ribbons, medals, and certificates handed out to successful formeteurs for "outstanding achievement" by territorial governments, military or civic organizations, and schools. Similar rewards are also conferred by profit-maximizing firms to their most productive employees.

Culture Reduces the Convergence of Reward Systems

Whenever a variety of methods can be used to achieve the same end, formeteurs will use the combination that is least costly to implement, other things being equal. This common economic interest of formeteurs causes considerable convergence among organizational reward systems. Complete convergence in reward systems does not occur, however, because not all motivational devices are equally available to or subject to manipulation by all formeteurs.

[2] See Congleton (1982) for a relatively simple rational-choice model of organizational inertia and bias.

Some organizational goals are better aligned with preexisting local norms than others, which implies that some organizations have larger pools of potential team members that are naturally predisposed to promote their goals than others. For example, during the medieval period in Europe, it is clear that religious orders were able to attract very talented members with relatively small pecuniary rewards because so many persons in their communities were already interested in advancing the same religious goals. Similarly, in the nineteenth and twentieth centuries, formeteurs that created new politically active groups to advance nationalistic, economic, or ecological goals could often draw from relatively large pools of patriots, economic liberals, and greens to write books and give speeches, staff their interest groups, and support their political parties.

Culturally favored organizations can assemble more effective teams at a lower cost than organizations with other goals. Conversely, the willingness of customers to pay more for some services than others allows some organizations to provide stronger pecuniary rewards than others. As a consequence, the feasible mix of pecuniary and nonpecuniary rewards varies among organizations. Investment bankers are generally paid more than fishermen, pear pickers, and priests.

The best feasible combination of conditional rewards tends to be more similar among organizations that produce similar services than among those producing different ones. For example, contemporary religious organizations and governments rely extensively on selection, internal values, culture, and financial rewards – roughly in that order – to motivate their team members. Commercial organizations also attempt to recruit team members who are easy to motivate, but the organizations use a somewhat different mix of rewards. They rely more extensively on conditional pecuniary rewards (hourly wages, bonuses, sales commissions, stock options, and promotions), than on internal culture to solve their team-production problems.[3]

CULTURAL AND ECONOMIC RATIONALES FOR ORGANIZATIONAL CONSERVATISM

Overall, the interplay among pecuniary, cultural, and team-member norms implies that the best reward systems are complex, which provides

[3] See Iannaccone (1992, 1998) or Wintrobe (2006) for overviews of how norms of various kinds can be encouraged (or exploited) in order to solve free-rider and coordination problems in organized groups. Most economists recognize the importance of incentive systems within organizations, but tend to focus only on pecuniary ones. See, for example, Holmstrom and Milgrom (1994).

a good reason for formeteurs to adopt off-the-shelf reward and recruiting systems. Although formeteurs can influence both technological and cultural developments, neither is completely within their control, because both are consequences of complex networks of social relationships and dynamics that are beyond the complete understanding or control of any single person or organization. The partly spontaneous and unintentional nature of productive internal and external cultures implies that new reward systems and new recruiting methods may have unintended consequences on an organization's ability to attract, motivate, and retain productive team members. For example, the evidence surveyed by Frey and Jegen (2001) suggests that increases in explicitly conditional forms of motivation often reduce (crowds out) self-motivation.

In principle, the unintended effects of changes in reward systems on intra-organizational culture can be positive or negative, but even if the unintended effects (prediction errors) are symmetrically distributed around zero, rather than biased toward undermining the organization's supporting culture, risk aversion on the part of formeteurs implies that fewer organizational experiments take place. Institutional conservatism in such cases is an entirely rational response to the problem of unanticipated consequences by risk-averse formeteurs (and their successors). "If it ain't broke, don't fix it."

Economic Support for Institutional Conservatism

Rational institutional conservatism is further supported by advantages associated with being conventional. Stable internal routines, theories, and norms can be passed on to successive generations of team members at a relatively low cost, as current team members teach new members the methods for getting along and succeeding within the organization. The use of routine off-the-shelf methods of reward and assignments of responsibility within an organization allows personnel to be easily shifted among teams within large organizations. It also allows new team members to be recruited from other organizations and employed with lower training and acculturation costs than is possible when differences among internal reward systems are large.

In settings in which a number of organizations compete to attract the services of team members, team members will naturally tend to join the teams offering the highest (risk-adjusted) rewards and exit from those providing the lowest (risk-adjusted) rewards. Organizations that offer too little to current and potential team members will not be viable, because they will not be able to retain or attract team members. Conversely, teams cannot promise to pay too much, because the system of rewards cannot be greater than the team's total production without reducing the viability of the organization. Competitive pressures, thus, reinforce other practical advantages associated with the use of conventional reward systems. The greater is the competition for team members, the narrower is the range of feasible reward systems.

Such economies of conventionalism reinforce tendencies for convergence of internal incentive regimes and provide additional support for institutional conservatism and stability. Together, the common interests of formeteurs and competitive pressures imply that very similar solutions to intrafirm incentive and governance problems tend to be widely used in culturally linked regions and applied for long periods of time.

The convergence and stability of reward systems do not, however, imply that every formeteur regards his or her organizational form to be the best that can be imagined or that formeteurs are extremely risk averse. Nor do they imply that the results are socially optimal in some sense. For example, excessive conservatism may be induced by a prisoner's-dilemma-like social dilemma that increases the stability of prevailing practices beyond optimal levels. Individual formeteurs may not be able adopt more efficient practices without losing team members or customers to their more conventional rivals, even though all formeteurs and team members would be better off with revised practices.

With or without such social dilemmas, however, it remains the case that formeteurs adopt the most cost-effective reward systems that are feasible for them, and that considerable convergence among reward systems tends to take place. Stable patterns of rewards thus imply that the anticipated cost of significant reforms exceeds their benefits for formeteurs, given prevailing practices and norms in the communities in which the organizations operate. Fishing clubs will use similar nets to catch similar fish in similar places. Pear-harvesting co-ops will use similar ladders and baskets. Cherry-picking firms will use similar harvesting techniques and pay similar wages to their employees based on similar performance criteria.

WHY ORGANIZATIONS HAVE GOVERNMENTS

Institutional conservatism and convergence do not imply that experimentation ceases or that organizations become completely rigid, although they do suggest that standing routines tend to be relied on, experiments tend to be relatively small, and the routines employed tend to be similar within organizations pursuing similar goals.

As external circumstances change, organizations that have routines for adjusting their team's production to take advantage of the new circumstances will tend to do better than organizations that do not. For example, changes in the location of fish or fruits caused by seasonal or long-term changes in weather may require fishing clubs, pear-harvesting cooperatives, and cherry-picking firms to relocate and/or change their methods of team production. Seeking new fish may require new fishing gear, new times of day for fishing, or new fishing strategies. Harvesting new fruits from new orchards may involve larger or smaller trees, more perishable types of fruit, or more travel. Changes in the supplies of particular ores or demands for particular metals may similarly induce blacksmiths and smelters to search for new sources of ore and to refine their alloys.

The fact that specific forms of team production become more or less viable as external circumstances change has a number of important implications about organizational design, one of which is relevant for the purposes of the first half of this chapter, and another that is important for the remainder of the book.

Regarding the first, dynamic circumstances provide another explanation for the use of complex reward systems. Multidimensional reward systems can be more easily adjusted to encourage personnel to shift among tasks than single-dimensional compensation schemes. There are more margins for adjustment, and it is less likely that all the dimensions of compensation are constrained by useful internal norms. The pear-harvesting cooperative and cherry-picking firm may provide long-distance harvesters with somewhat generous travel reimbursements (new shoes) or better equipment, or they may create new prizes for those who have walked the most miles in the service of their organization. Such rewards may encourage team members to volunteer for work in new locations without undermining other useful aspects of family-, seniority-, or loyalty-based reward systems.

Regarding the second implication, it bears noting that organizations with flexible reward systems can induce their teams to be more effective in new circumstances only if they have procedures for recognizing new circumstances and adjusting their methods of team production to take advantage of the new circumstances. A fishing club, pear-harvesting cooperative, or cherry-picking firm that simply returns to the same pond or orchards after all the fish and fruit are gone will simply not survive. They must also be able to recognize innovations in "best practices" in order to take advantage of innovations in reward systems and team production.

Organizations that are able to detect relevant changes in circumstances and make modest adjustments to their standing policies thus tend to be more successful than those that cannot. They survive in more environments because they are quicker to adjust to changing circumstances and better able to make adjustments than those without routines for recognizing new circumstances and for responding to those changes. *In other words, durable organizations have governments because the present is not entirely stable, the future is not completely knowable, and the best methods of team production vary with circumstances.*

Paradoxically, survivorship, institutional convergence, and rational institutional conservatism imply that organizations cannot be entirely rigid in the medium and long term, except in completely unchanging and understood circumstances.

ORGANIZATIONAL GOVERNANCE

The standing procedures for making policy decisions within organizations have attracted far less attention by economists and other rational-choice analysts than have the internal incentive systems analyzed in the first half of this chapter. For example, Williamson's widely read books and articles on corporate governance (1967, 1996, 2002) implicitly assume that the institutions for choosing policies are already in place, essentially automatic, and well functioning. The same can be said about Alchian and Demsetz's (1972) analysis of team production, Vicker's (1985) analysis of delegation, and Laffont and Tirole's (1993) game-theoretic analysis of relationships among firms and between government regulators and firms.

A partial defense of that neglect is that an organization's government is often an instance of team production and delegation. In most cases an organization's standing policies are jointly produced by several team members who have been delegated authority to make various policy decisions. Information is collected about internal and external circumstances, the information analyzed, alternatives evaluated, and decisions made. In only the simplest of organizations and circumstances is all this done by a single individual. As a consequence, those participating in organizational governance normally have artificial incentives that are largely determined by the organization's standing system of rewards, because many of the usual problems of team production have to be overcome to create an effective organizational government.

However, just as an organization is more than an incentive system, its government is more than just another team.

The outputs of an organization's government are very different from those of other teams. Its outputs are decisions that substantially create the organization itself and revise it through time. It determines whether teams will be organized to pick cherries, pears, or apples. Once teams are organized and production is under way, it determines whether to continue or not and whether to change direction or not. A pear-harvesting cooperative may switch to grapes or olives. A fishing firm may shift from fishing to shipping, and if it does so, the policy choices of its governing body will substantially determine which ships head to which port cities and who and what is on board its ships. The decisions of the ruling body of a regional government determine what will be taxed, who will collect the taxes, and also how future decisions about taxation will be made.

As a consequence, there are informational, bargaining, and collective-choice aspects to organizational governance that are absent or much smaller for other teams within large organizations.

Natural Organizational Governance

In most cases, formeteurs choose standing procedures for making and revising policies at the same time that they create a new organization because they recognize that their initial policy decisions are provisional, rather than final.

The "natural" first form of organizational governance is the one (implicitly) assumed by most economists and also by many political theorists. Formeteurs may simply retain their initial authority to make and revise all major policy decisions after their organizations are up and running. Such authoritarian decision-making procedures have many advantages for formeteurs and their organizations. Formeteurs often have a superior understanding of organizational possibilities, which justifies their initial investment of time and attention to assembling a team and devising methods for advancing particular goals. Formeteurs know their own goals better than others, and they are likely to have leadership skills that allow them to form and motivate groups at lower costs than others. Leadership skills often include a relatively large informational base and the ability to persuade others that it is in their interest to defer to the formeteur's direction.

However, there are cases in which sharing policy-making authority can improve organizational governance, and other cases in which limiting or sharing their policy-making authority can advance other formeteur goals. Voluntary transfers of policy-making authority are partly driven by informational problems that emerge as an enterprise increases in scale and complexity, and partly by other practical advantages that can be realized by shifting and trading authority within and between organizations. In the medium and long run, it is often in the interest of formeteurs to relinquish part or all of their initial control over their organization's policies.

For example, formeteurs of contemporary commercial enterprises often give up part of their control over their organization in exchange for investments by those who purchase voting shares. By going public, formeteurs become shareholders in, rather than owners of, their enterprise. Such trades of authority for money increases the resources available to their organizations, albeit at the cost of reduced control over their organizations. Similar transactions often took place between European kings and parliaments in the period between 1400 and 1900, as developed in Part II of this book. Analogous transactions also took place between local rulers and free towns in the late-medieval period. No threats of violence were necessary for such shifts of authority to occur.

The remainder of this chapter focuses on the informational advantages of governance based on the king-and-council template. It argues that informational problems are a sufficient condition for the emergence of divided forms of governance. Other advantages of divided governance and opportunities for trading policy-making authority within the King-and-council template are developed in Chapters Three to Six.

THE FORMETEUR-RULER'S INFORMATIONAL PROBLEMS AND INSTITUTIONAL SOLUTIONS

Consider the case in which a single formeteur initially chooses to run his or her organization as an autocrat. This is not the only possible type of formeteur or initial form of government, but it is a natural place to start, and it is widely assumed in rational-choice analyses of economic and political institutions. The formeteur is clearly in the best position to know his or her own interests and has a reasonably clear idea about how an organization can be created to advance those interests. As a single actor, he or she avoids the collective-choice dilemmas noted by Olson (1965) and the potential intransitivity problems of collective decision making noted by Arrow (1963).

Wintrobe (1998) argues that all such autocratic governments face several kinds of information problems, many of which are consequences of their control over organizational rewards and punishments.

First, an autocrat faces the same information problems as an ordinary person. An autocrat must decide how much information to gather about every dimension of choice and every causal chain that may affect his or her assessments of alternatives. He or she must decide which information sources are reliable and how much of the information gathered to share with others. A formeteur, however, has greater need for accurate information than other persons in his or her organization, because the scope of a formeteur's policy-making authority is initially much wider than that of other members of the organization. There are many alternatives that must be accurately assessed if he or she is to make policy decisions that effectively advance his or her own interests. In unstable settings, autocrats will also require useful information about changes in the internal operation of the organization and in the external environment in order to make effective use of the team assembled. The decision-making, recruiting, and incentive systems of the organization created may also be revised, as weaknesses and strengths are revealed, and as new opportunities arise through time.

Second, an autocrat confronts a series of information problems that are consequences of his or her authority to allocate organizational resources and to adjust the internal system of rewards. The information provided by others within the organization tends to be intentionally biased whenever there are potential benefits from manipulating the autocrat's assessment of alternatives or people within the organization. Personal careers can often be advanced by exaggerating one's loyalty and performance relative to other rivals within the organization. Apple polishers do not simply seek the boss's favor, but hope to profit from that favor. Wintrobe (1998, chapter 2) refers to this aspect of a rule maker's informational problem as the "dictator's dilemma."

Persons who assure the autocrat that he or she is right in every case may increase the ruler's confidence (and gain his or her ear), but they will not increase the accuracy of the ruler's policy decisions. The larger the organization and more complex the goals and operating environment, the more difficult such informational problems tend to be and the more costly are mistakes that could have been avoided with better information.

Why Well-Informed Formeteurs Benefit from Advisory Councils

Consider first a shrewd, fairly well-informed formeteur-ruler with unbiased expectations about the consequences of alternative policies and therefore about the relative merits of policy alternatives. Such formeteurs will not make systematic policy errors and will choose policies that maximize the (average) effectiveness of their organizations and, thereby, their own expected utility. Yet a formeteur, like any other person, will economize on information and devote his or her time and attention to collecting and processing information only up to the point where the expected marginal benefits equal its marginal cost. Statistical theory implies that the smaller the data set on which estimates are based and the less sophisticated and thorough the analysis, the greater the errors tend to be, other things being equal.

In most cases, the sum of the information possessed by an organization's team members includes much that is not and cannot be known by even a well-informed formeteur. For example, team members often know a good deal more about the specifics of production than the formeteur. Members of a pear-harvesting co-op or cherry-picking firm often know details about particular orchards or trees that the formeteur does not. Pears or cherries on the northeast side of particular trees may be juicier than those on the northwest side at some locations or during some times of the year. Taking account of this information would improve harvests and/or increase profits, although that information cannot be accessed directly by the formeteur.

In small organizations, useful information and recommendations may simply be collected from all team members. In larger organizations, an advisory council may be recruited by choosing members randomly from the organization's team (or citizenry). Such citizen-advisors are often less informed overall than the formeteur-ruler because such persons lack an encompassing interest in the organization. Advice from such councils, however, may still be useful because team members have different personal experiences and expertise.

Insofar as the information (samples) of the formeteur and members of the advisory council are independent of one another, their predictions about future events are also independent and may be approximately unbiased. There are many cases in which the unweighted average or median estimate of a group is more accurate than the estimate of the member with the largest data set. Elementary statistics implies that an appropriately weighted average of several unbiased estimates is nearly always a better estimator (more accurate) than any single estimate. This information-aggregating effect implies that a council of nonexpert advisors that makes recommendations on the basis of majority opinion or consensus can be a cost-effective method of assessing the merits of alternatives because it produces relatively accurate median forecasts and recommendations.[4]

4 This aggregation effect of the use of majority rule is often referred to as the jury theorem or Condorcet's jury theorem. Nitzan and Paroush (1985), Wit (1998), McLennan (1998), and Congleton (2007b) show that a council that uses majority rule to select recommendations tends to be far less error prone than individual members of the council. Large committees would make essentially no mistakes if individual members are even slightly more likely

In areas in which specialized knowledge is useful, the formeteur can improve the quality of the advice obtained by assembling a panel of especially well-informed individuals – experts – whose more complete understanding of the organization and its operating environment makes their forecasts less prone to error than the typical member of the organization. Such expert councilors may have a comparative advantage at gathering and processing information relative to other team members. They may simply have greater talent for assembling and processing information, or they may have devoted more time and energy to acquiring large information sets and skills for analyzing them. Their greater data sets and skills at analysis allow them to provide the formeteur with much more accurate assessments of the medium- and long-run effects of alternative policy decisions.

Some specialization in data collection and analysis may also be useful. For example, the formeteurs of the pear-harvesting co-ops and cherry-picking firms might send out orchard spotters to assess the quality of the fruit available at various orchards in the area on a particular day. A committee of experienced fruit harvesters may listen to the spotter reports and offer their informed opinions about which orchard is likely to provide the best harvest. Similarly, the formeteur-ruler of a trading enterprise that wants to establish a new trading post may direct his advisors to sample the opinions of well-traveled persons, and to recommend a few places where a trading post can profitably be established. The leader of a team of roving bandits may send out scouts to bring back information about the availability and cost of acquiring goods in new territories. His war council may use that information to make suggestions about where and when to launch the team's next raids.

Competition for Membership in Advisory Councils

The value of the information and advice produced by advisory councils will often be far greater than the cost of the advisory team's compensation because policy errors are costly and the reward systems for obtaining good advice are normally a combination of status, privileges, and money, roughly in that order. Many advisors will be pleased to provide free information

to be right than wrong in their recommendations and voted on the basis of their private information.

That consulting with a "council of wise men" can improve decision making is, of course, not a new idea. The idea that a committee of experts possesses more information than a group of ordinary people (who often possess more information than a single expert) is mentioned, for example, by Aristotle in book 3 of *The Politics*, which has been widely read for centuries.

to the formeteur simply because they value the approval and thanks of ambitious men and women. And, of course, advisory councils can be quite small, which tends to enhance the prestige associated with membership.

To increase the expertise of committee members, the formeteur may construct contests for council membership that reward analytical skills, policy-relevant information acquisition, and loyalty with relatively high status and/or salaries. Contemporary research suggests that such contests can be extremely effective methods for inducing investments in useful information and analytical skills. Compensation in the form of positional goods can be quite inexpensive for the proprietor, yet encourage substantial efforts by prospective councilors (Tullock 1965, Hirsch 1976, Frank 1985, and Congleton 1989). Even slightly higher salaries may induce a good deal of effort for similar reasons. Competition for modest pecuniary rewards is often quite intense. The sum of the investments by the purchasers of lottery tickets is normally greater than the sum of the rewards given out, which is, of course, what makes lotteries profitable (Tullock 1980, Hehenkamp et al. 2004). Moreover, being councilor to a successful formeteur may also produce new consulting opportunities as well as status through reputation effects.

As a consequence of all these considerations, the advisory council is one of the most widely used informational technologies. The duties of advisory councils normally include assessing the policy ideas of the formeteur and making suggestions about alternatives that he or she has not considered. The former implies that advisory councils have some veto authority over policy proposals, and the latter implies that advisory councils have some agenda control over the policies under consideration. In this manner, the use of advisory councils can be said to create an informal form of divided governance.

The Dilemma of Experts

Motivational problems for advisory council members are fairly limited in environments in which the proprietor is sufficiently informed about policy consequences to make his or her own unbiased estimates of the facts or policy consequences. In such cases, the formeteur-ruler can reject obviously manipulative estimates and recommendations by the council (and individual council members) as implausible outliers and punish the conspirators for their disloyalty, that is, for placing their own interests above his. A cherry spotter's claim that the "the cherry trees in the next village are three hundred feet tall with tons of cherries on every branch" can easily be rejected without traveling to the recommended village by a formeteur that knows something about cherry trees.

The motivation problems become more difficult as one shifts from settings in which the formeteur-ruler and councilors have small samples of essentially complete information to ones in which the formeteur and potential councilors all remain completely ignorant about some relevant dimensions or possible consequences. For example, the formeteur may not have traveled or studied extensively and so may be largely ignorant about orchards, trading posts, and rival bandits in other territories. His potential councilors may include individuals that have traveled more widely and know more languages, but even such sophisticated travelers will not have visited every orchard in every territory. Some kinds of fruit trees will remain entirely unknown. In such circumstances, a completely unbiased estimation about the best type of orchard or method of harvest may not be possible for the formeteur-ruler or his councilors (Congleton 2001a, 2007b).

Knowledge problems of this sort increase the potential advantage of additional information but also increase the risk of manipulation. To profit from the advisory councils in areas in which the formeteur-ruler is essentially ignorant, the organization of the council must overcome the "dilemma of experts," the difficulty of taking advice from knowledgeable persons whose information cannot be readily appraised by the person receiving it and that may be biased.

The dilemma of experts would not be a problem if members of the advisory committee were indifferent about the formeteur's subsequent policy and personnel decisions and so simply passed on their best advice, but this is not always the case. A few orchard spotters may prefer one kind of fruit or location to others. Bandit scouts and war councils may have grudges against particular communities or persons. Trading-post experts may have friends who own real estate in one of the areas of interest or prefer some climates to others. Such personal interests may induce advisors to provide overly optimistic assessments of some opportunities and overly pessimistic ones about others that are less personally advantageous.

In the previous "rational expectations" case, the formeteur had his own independent and unbiased estimates that could be used to reject opinions and advice that were clearly outliers. But in settings in which ignorance, rather than small samples, is the main informational problem, the formeteur can not make such estimates. Relatively short-term forecasts and expert advice can often be directly checked as events unfold, but during difficult times, even short-run decisions based on bad advice can be disastrous for an organization.

Beyond the Kitchen Cabinet: Advantages of Representative Advisory Councils

A common method of addressing the dilemma of the expert in settings in which significant formeteur-ruler ignorance exists is to assemble a small, loyal group of advisors – a council of loyal wise men – who have demonstrated that their interests are aligned with those of the formeteur, and whose recommendations on past matters have been sound. In small- and medium-sized organizations, such advisors might, for example, be assembled from the formeteur's family members, friends, and long-term employees whose interests are often well aligned with those of the formeteur. Such "kitchen cabinets," however, may exhibit considerable ignorance about matters beyond their own organization (or the royal court).

A council whose membership extends beyond the organization has informational advantages over "kitchen cabinets" because outsiders have a larger sample of information and include more kinds or dimensions of information than insiders could or would be inclined to assemble on their own. The more extensive information sets of councils of outsiders reflect their broader range of talents, interests, and experiences. Many of these informational advantages reflect systematic differences in backgrounds (education, profession, and/or family) that can be easily recognized by the formeteur, while others reflect chance events that provide outsiders with unique experiences and acquaintances (travel, talent, and friends) that cannot be so easily appraised.

The informational advantages of a council of outsiders, however, come at the price of greater motivational problems. In many cases, biased (manipulative) advice can reduce the effectiveness of outsider councils to levels below that of insider councils. This partly explains why "kitchen cabinets" are so common, especially in cases in which outside information is not particularly valuable or can be acquired without relying on outsiders.

In cases in which outside information is especially valuable and tends to be available only from outside experts, an advisory council that includes outsiders can provide more useful advice than a "kitchen cabinet," even if all problems cannot be completely eliminated. For example, both our illustrative pear-harvesting cooperative and cherry-picking firm may benefit from the advice of a panel of agronomists and marketing experts, even if their advice cannot be entirely trusted, because such persons have incentives to exaggerate their expertise.

One institutional method for reducing the agency problems associated with outsider councilors is to assemble "representative councils" with predictable biases. By including members with opposing personal interests, one hears arguments on all sides of an issue and can be reasonably assured that points of agreement are unbiased assessments. The members of such councils can be assembled, for example, by having various economic and ideological interest groups (regional authorities, guilds, landowners, banks, labor unions, clergy, and so on) propose members for the advisory council. The problem of manipulation (biased advice) can be further reduced by including insiders as well as outsiders on the advisory council, which allows outsider assessments to be evaluated by insiders before being applied. Such representative councils allow policy assessments to be based on a broader information base than possible from groups of insiders, while at the same time increasing the likelihood that the median or average of the analyses and advice given is well informed and unbiased.[5]

WHY WELL-INFORMED FORMETEUR PARTNERSHIPS EMPLOY A CHIEF EXECUTIVE

The informational problems of a formeteur-ruler and advantages of advice from committees suggest that organizations founded by small groups of formeteurs may be better able to make policy decisions than those founded by a single formeteur. Formeteur partnerships can function as a committee of experts by themselves; they can potentially draw on more information and use it more effectively than an otherwise similar single formeteur. It is thus not surprising that many organizations are founded by small teams of formeteurs who form partnerships of various kinds. (Our illustrative pear-harvesting cooperative may have been formed in this way.)

Even a small group of formeteurs, however, may not be able to realize their potential informational advantages, because the individual formeteur-partners lack a fully encompassing interest in their organization's operation. Each partner receives only a fraction of the organization's surplus or profits. As a consequence, each tends to underinvest in their joint enterprise. For

[5] Gilligan and Krehbiel (1989), Krehbiel (1991), and Banks and Weingast (1992), among others, provide a careful game-theoretic analysis of the informational aspects of heterogeneous committees and agencies. Although their main focus is essentially the opposite of that explored here, their analytical results are consistent with the arguments developed above, namely that advisory committees function best when all interests are represented. See Balla and Wright (2001) for a useful overview of this literature as it relates to advisory committees and for evidence that such representative advisory committees are used in contemporary governments.

The advice of such representative councils may still be problematic if the council as a whole has policy interests that differ systematically from those of the formeteur-ruler.

example, each member of a small pear-harvesting cooperative tends to be more interested in his or her own orchard's success than in the cooperative's overall production and profits. As a consequence, the partners collectively underinvest in the cooperative's activities, which reduces their partnership's ability to lower member costs and increase sales by negotiating with suppliers or running joint advertising campaigns.

Formeteur-partnerships cannot always solve all of their informational and managerial free-riding problems by simply ruling as a committee.[6]

A natural solution to the committee-government dilemma faced by formeteur-partners is to delegate responsibility for managing their organization on a day-to-day basis to a single person: a chief executive officer (CEO), senior partner, governor, high priest, or prime minister. Such CEOs directly participate in the day-to-day execution of policy and so acquire relatively complete and detailed knowledge of the process of implementing policy within the organization. The CEO's informational advantage allows him or her to understand the effects of alternative day-to-day policies better than other members of the partnership, and so he or she is able to make better-informed decisions. In this case, however, the king (CEO) will serve at the pleasure of the council (formeteur partners), who will retain considerable policy-making authority for themselves, including veto power over major initiatives.

The previous analysis of reward systems implies that the formeteur-partners will use cost-minimizing combinations of pecuniary and nonpecuniary rewards to align the interests of their chief executive officer's with formeteur interests. The effectiveness of that reward system can usually be improved by selecting CEOs who are relatively easy to motivate and have the talent to be effective managers. In other words, chief executives are chosen only partly for their managerial ability. Their norms and desire for approval, respect, status, fame, and financial resources are equally important because these reduce the cost of solving principal-agent problems.[7]

Selection procedures are also important because they can also induce competition for the post of CEO. Insofar as the selection process is sufficiently open and CEO compensation is sufficiently generous to produce

6 Such free-rider and agency problems partially explain the existence of partnership law, which attempts to assure that partners do their duties and receive what is properly due to them. Partnership law extends back to at least Roman times (Weber 2003).

7 Brennan and Hamlin (2000) discuss how selection can be used to find the right persons to fill positions in organizations in which monitoring is difficult and contracts are incomplete. Their discussion addresses problems in democratic design, but their logic clearly applies to other organizations as well.

competition for the post of chief executive, many talented individuals will invest in acquiring the skills and knowledge to be an effective CEO. The latter also provides some redundancy in advice and information sources, which further reduces monitoring costs for the council of formeteur-partners.[8]

For such reasons, organizations founded by small groups of formeteurs also frequently use the king-and-council template for organizational governance, although formeteur-partners will adopt a quite different initial distribution of policy-making authority than that used by a single formeteur. The council will normally retain broad policy-making authority, including complete veto power over major policy changes and also over changes in the organization's distribution of policy-making authority. They will also retain the authority to replace their current chief executive officer when selection errors are made and/or when their reward system fails to align the CEO's interests with their own.

Delegation to a King and Council by Very Large Groups of Formeteurs

When a large group of formeteurs (or organizations) forms a new organization, day-to-day management and considerable policy-making authority may be delegated to an organizational government for similar reasons.

It is very costly for the members of large cooperatives, stock companies, partnerships, and polities to meet and debate policy alternatives every time a decision has to be made. Such meetings are time consuming and inconvenient. Moreover, informational free riding tends to be a greater problem for large groups than for small ones. Consequently, one of the first collective decisions by the founders of a large cooperative or small town is normally to delegate significant policy-making authority to a cooperative or town government.[9] As in other organizational choices, there are templates for

[8] It bears noting that modern elections for presidents require candidates to reveal their policy preference, personal propensities, and managerial talents to the persons selecting them. Contests for the CEOs of large organizations are similar in many respects, although less public.

[9] Buchanan and Tullock (1962) use rational-choice models to explore how particular governmental structures might be selected by such large groups. The focus of their analysis is political governments, rather than organizations in general, but many of their results are relevant for the present setting. For example, their results on voting rules are clearly relevant for the large group of formeteurs setting. They do not mention the king-and-council template in their analysis, but they also suggest that divided governments (bicameralism) can be more likely to better advance common interests than undivided ones (unicameralism).

cooperative and town governance that have survived the test of time, and large groups of formeteurs will normally choose from among preexisting forms, rather than invent a new one from whole cloth.

For reasons similar to those developed for the single formeteur and small number of formeteur cases, large founding groups are likely to adopt some version of the king-and-council template: a chief operating officer and board of directors, a mayor and town council, a president or prime minister and a parliament. Such forms of government, which include meetings of the community of formeteurs as a whole, produce better policy decisions than others by solving a variety of informational and incentive problems and by reducing decision costs. In this case, both the king and the council are likely to be selected by the formeteurs through some process of collective choice (direct or indirect elections), and some veto power over the government will normally be retained by the founders.

In the large number of formeteurs case, the use of divided forms of the king-and-council template also tends to reduce losses from selection errors, that is, from the failure to select the best persons to serve as managers and monitors under an existing reward system. In undivided governments, a single mistake in selecting an organizational autocrat can clearly be very costly. By dividing policy-making authority between a king and a council, this risk is reduced because the policies adopted by such systems tend to be weighted averages of the institutionally induced interests of the king and council. The institutionally induced interests are consequences of the process through which the officials are selected and renewed, the reward systems in place, and the division of policy-making authority between them. Consultation and compromise will be necessary for major decisions within such divided governments, which tends to reduce errors.[10]

The use of the king-and-council template also improves error correction because it increases the likelihood that honest accounts of the organization's activities are made available to the entire body of formeteurs. On the occasions when they meet as a body, the founders may ask the council to report on the chief executive and the chief executive to report on the council. The natural inclination of the officeholders of each branch of government is to

[10] In commercial enterprises, the formeteurs are often modeled as shareholders, who are assumed to have a uniform interest. Within such large organizations, conditional contracts are also used to align the interests of CEOs with their formeteurs. See, for example, Gibbons and Murphy (1990) or Holmstrom and Milgrom (1994). That literature, while shedding a good deal of light on CEO compensation practices, tends to neglect divided governance within the firm and policy-making aspects of governmental decisions, although it acknowledges that contract "solutions" tend to be incomplete.

tout their own achievements and attribute all mistakes to the other. By combining the two reports, a reasonably complete overview can be achieved, albeit one with higher variance than would be ideal.[11]

Such informational and control advantages, reinforced by institutional conservatism, also explain why the king-and-council template is widely used to delegate authority within large organizations. A CEO may choose to create his or her own council of advisors. He or she may also delegate policy-making authority in particular policy areas to individual managers who are monitored and/or advised by specialized committees of experts. The number of advisory councils can also be adjusted, and specialized advisory councils of various sizes can be created to analyze particular subjects or policy areas. The result frequently creates hierarchical forms of organizational governance in which top levels constrain the choices of lower levels through specific delegations of authority and control over selection and reward systems.

OVERVIEW: FORMETEUR INTERESTS AND ORGANIZATIONAL DESIGN

This chapter has provided a theory of organizations that explains (a) why durable organizations have governments, (b) why most organizations use some form of the king-and-council template for governance, (c) why most organizations use mixed forms of conditional incentives to solve team-production problems within the organization, and (d) why internal incentive systems and organizational policy tend to be somewhat flexible at the margin, although (e) core policies tend to be fundamentally stable and similar among organizations. An organization's system of governance and its reward system tend to be stable because organizations tend to make better decisions and are better able to retain and train their teams when they have institutionalized their reward and governance systems. The analysis also demonstrates (f) that decision-making authority within an organization can be distributed in a number of ways and argues (g) that the initial division of authority varies systematically with the origin of the organization.

Single formeteurs are inclined to adopt king-dominated forms of the king-and-council template of governance, partly for informational reasons. They will have standing councils of advisors who make proposals for improving policy in areas of interest to the organization, which the

[11] Persson and Tabellini (1997), for example, demonstrate that divided governments tend to increase information flows to principals.

formeteur will consider and choose whether to accept or reject. Formeteur partnerships, in contrast, will tend to adopt council-dominated forms of the king-and-council template in which day-to-day decisions are delegated to their CEO, but the authority to veto major policy decisions is retained by the partners. More evenly divided forms of the king-and-council template may be adopted in cases in which organizations are founded by a large number of formeteurs.

As in other aspects of organizational design, formeteurs choose the institutions of governance based on their assessment of the performance of those institutions in other organizations about which they are familiar. The governmental templates that attract their interest tend to collect and use information relatively efficiently, and they tend to produce decisions that increase the viability of their organization while advancing formeteur interests. This is not to say that the templates for creating organizational governments are completely robust or advance formeteur interests perfectly. However, ineffective and nonrobust procedures for making policy decisions tend to disappear from the menu of governmental forms that attract the attention of formeteurs.

The analysis of the second half of Chapter Two suggests that informational advantages of the king-and-council template are sufficient to explain the use of this template for governance by a broad range of organizations throughout recorded history. Additional rationales for using the king-and-council template are developed in the Chapters Three to Five, in which long-term organizational viability and territorial governance are analyzed.

THREE

Organizational Governance in the Long Run

GOVERNING IN THE LONG RUN

All of the conclusions reached in Chapter Two about how formeteurs create organizations to advance short- and medium-term goals also apply to cases in which formeteurs attempt to advance long-run goals. Organizations created to advance long-term goals have to overcome the same recruiting, motivational, and adaptation problems, which imply that they will have recruiting, reward, and governance systems that are fundamentally similar in most respects. Formeteurs that found organizations to advance long-term goals confront similar problems, and many of their solutions will also be similar. Formeteurs of such organizations, for example, are likely to be aware of the difficulties of robust organizational designs. Thus, they are likely to pay even more attention to best practices when selecting governance and reward systems.

There are, nonetheless, significant differences between organizations designed to advance long-term goals and those expected to be short-lived. Perhaps the most obvious of these is that durable organizations will outlive their founders. In the long run, formeteurs will necessarily turn over policy-making authority to successors of one kind or another. It is also likely that procedures of governance and other standing policies will require somewhat larger adjustments in the long run than in the short run because unfamiliar (low probability and new) circumstances are more likely to be experienced in the long run. Other members of an organization's governing team (and their successors) will also need to be replaced.

Long-run solutions to the problems of governance consequently include standing procedures for replacing an organization's rule-making officials, as well as procedures for adjusting the standing routines of organizational decision making. The latter, it turns out, are constrained by advantages of stable, predictable governance in the long run as well as institutional conservatism. This chapter suggests that the king-and-council template provides a variety of natural solutions for many of the problems associated with governance in the long run.

DECISION COSTS, STANDING POLICIES, AND ORGANIZATIONAL RULE OF LAW

Organizational governments face a continuing stream of decisions to be made. Should we continue what we are doing or change? And if the latter, how so? Because not every problem or opportunity can be analyzed simultaneously, a common decision-making procedure is to group problems into relatively independent and separable subsets that can be dealt with one at a time. That is to say, decision makers tend to use an "other things being equal" methodology analogous to that which is widely used in natural science, engineering, social science, and history. After such problems sets are identified, they can be ranked from most important to least important (from those most likely to those least likely to affect formeteur interests significantly). This allows the time and attention of policy makers to be efficiently allocated among problem sets. Information is gathered and analyzed, as necessary, to rank both problems and alternative solutions for the problem class at hand. When this is done perfectly, the most important decisions are made first, the second most important second, and so forth.

If circumstances are stable and few mistakes have been made, past decisions will be left in place. They will need to be revised only when new problems emerge or new relevant information becomes available.

In this manner, sequential decision making by an organization's governing body tends to create a relatively stable set of policies and rules for the organization. Such policy decisions are normally enforced by the organization's usual procedures for reward and punishment. Rule followers are rewarded and rule violators are normally punished (or not rewarded). The policies and rules that remain in force for significant periods create an organization's standard operating procedures, its internal law of the land.

The stability of an organization's standing procedures and policy decisions is increased by many of the same considerations that support rational institutional conservatism for internal reward systems. Any hypothetical advantages from alternative rules remain abstract, untested, less studied, and so more risky. Moreover, changes in the standing rules will be resisted by those who had expected to profit from the existing routines, which increases the cost of changing the rules and further increases their stability.

Table 3.1. *Inducing Rule-Following Behavior*

Team member A	Team member B		
	Obey	Disobey	Exit
Obey	R^e, R^e	R^e, Z^e	R^e, X^e
Disobey	Z^e, R^e	Z^e, Z^e	Z^e, X^e
Exit	X^e, R^e	X^e, Z^e	X^e, X^e

The cell entries are the (expected) subjective payoffs for team members A and B for obeying or disobeying organizational rules and for leaving the organization.

Forward-looking formeteurs realize that predictability allows somewhat lower average rewards to be paid to risk-averse team members through time and also tends to reduce intra-organizational conflict over decision-making procedures and responsibilities.

Risk Aversion and the Economic Advantages of Stable Rules

Table 3.1 illustrates the economic advantages of stable rules and patterns of enforcement. Consider the effects of revising the organization's artificial reward system. Suppose that the standing rules initially specify that if a team member performs duty D, he or she is entitled to reward R, but if not, he or she receives punishment Z. If the team member decides to leave the team, he or she receives payoff X. In Chapter Two, following the rules was called "working" and disobeying the rules was called "shirking," which are plausible interpretations of choices to follow or disobey the rules that advance organizational (formeteur) objectives. A rule-following, behavior-inducing reward system has payoffs $R > X > Z$.

Instability and arbitrariness in rules, rewards, or punishments make the payoffs associated with following the rules stochastic, rather than certain. For example, suppose that, rather than certain reward R, there are two possible rewards for rule-following behavior, R_1 and R_2, which are received with probability P_1 and P_2 when duty D is performed. Similarly, rather than punishment Z, there may be penalties Z_1 and Z_2 received with probabilities F_1 and F_2. In such a case, it is anticipated long-term (average) rewards and punishments that matter, rather than the specific rewards and punishments, here $R^e = P_1R_1 + P_2R_2$ and $Z^e = F_1Z_1 + F_2Z_2$.

Risk aversion implies that even if the same average payments are received by team members, the subjective value of those rewards and punishments is lower than that of the original, completely predictable case. To further flesh out the illustration, suppose that the subjective value of reward R is $U = R^{(0.5)}$. Let $R = 100$, $R_1 = 50$, $R_2 = 150$, and $P_1 = P_2 = 0.5$. The expected subjective value (utility) of certain reward R is $(1.0)(100)^{(0.5)} = 10$. The expected utility of the stochastic system of rewards is $(0.5)(150)^{(0.5)} + (0.5)(50)^{(0.5)} = 9.66$. The average reward for the stochastic system has to be more than 5 percent greater than the certain reward to generate the same subjective value.

When rewards are arbitrary or unpredictable, it will cost more to generate the subjective rewards that are greater than punishments and that are subjectively greater than rewards available outside the organization. As rewards and punishments become less predictable, the net benefits of continued association with the organization becomes riskier and less valuable for risk-averse team members.

Formeteur arbitrariness is thus constrained to the subset of whims that help solve team-production problems or that have minor costs relative to the satisfaction obtained by the formeteur. Arbitrariness is acceptable to team members only if $R^e > X^e$, that is to say, only if the average reward for following the organization's rules is greater than that associated with opportunities outside the organization.[1] In nasty environments, exit may not be an attractive option, but it is still a constraint on the arbitrariness of organizational incentive schemes. Even a pirate ship eventually arrives at port. In this manner, the economics of reward systems and exit possibilities reduce arbitrariness within voluntary organizations. Risk aversion on the part of team members also implies that an organization's government cannot costlessly adjust the organization's rules to obtain modest short-term efficiency gains, because such adjustments tend to reduce rule-following behavior and increase recruiting and retention costs. The anticipated efficiency gains (or formeteur advantages) from reforms have to exceed the higher retention and recruiting costs associated with less predictable reward systems.[2]

1 Advantages associated with manipulating exit costs are discussed in Chapter Four for the case of territorial governments. Exit-cost-manipulating systems tend to increase retention at the same time that they increase the cost of recruiting new team members from outside the organization or territory of interest.

2 In cases in which errors are made in detecting disobedience, the expected payoffs will have a similar probabilistic structure. In this case, there will be some probability that an obedient team member will be punished (receive Z) rather than be rewarded. And there will also be some probability that a disobedient team member will be rewarded (receive R) rather than be punished. Monitoring also tends to reduce the cost of compensation systems. See Chapter Four.

Organizational Rule of Law

As the standing rules become well known throughout an organization, there will be an obvious distinction between day-to-day decisions made using standing procedures and revisions of the standing procedures and policies.[3] Insofar as the standing rules are generally believed to advance the interests of the organization, a widespread belief in the "rule of law" or custom as a norm might emerge among an organization's government and among its membership. Such ideas will be encouraged by the organization's leadership insofar as they increase organizational surplus or support their authority by, for example, reducing personnel costs or internal conflict.

Of course, organizational rule of law does not necessarily imply equality before the law in the sense used by modern legal scholars and liberal political theorists. Neither rewards nor punishments are likely to be uniform for all members of an organization. For example, senior members and relatives of the formeteurs may be subject to lower (or higher) standards of conduct and different punishments. Team members with greater exit costs or less-attractive external opportunities may be paid less for the same work than those with lower exit costs and better external opportunities.

Within large organizations, there are also asymmetries in policy-making authority. Policies made at higher levels of the organization bind others below them. In this manner, asymmetries in authority create a hierarchy in which one's "level" is determined by one's relative ability to impose rules on others in the organization. This is not to say that all rules are developed from the top down, but those at lower levels will necessarily have less influence over policy than those at upper levels.

Such unequal and asymmetric reward and punishment systems can nonetheless be systematic and rule based. They may be stable for long periods of time, because they advance the interests of law-abiding team members and forward-looking organizational governments.

A subset of a prominent organization's standing rules may also be incorporated into a community's civil law in places in which such rules are widely believed to increase efficiency, equity, stability, or justice. Trading posts, military bases, and monasteries often catalyze the formation of towns and cities. Colonial enterprises often create regional and local governments in order to advance their economic, military, and religious agendas. Many communities and regional governments were originally founded by

[3] Buchanan and Brennan (1985) argue that this is a key distinction between constitutional and nonconstitutional decision making.

organizations such as firms, military organizations, and churches. In such cases, the surrounding community's law is initially that of the founding organization(s).

CONSTITUTIONAL ORGANIZATIONAL GOVERNANCE: WRITTEN AND UNWRITTEN CHARTERS

Standing decision-making procedures and norms do not have to be written down to characterize an organization's government or reward systems, although this is often done in large organizations to increase predictability and reduce conflict. Written rules increase certainty for those subject to reward and punishment systems and decrease conflict by reducing the scope for disagreement about what the standing procedures really are.

Formeteurs adopt written rules in such cases not because they operate behind a veil of ignorance or necessarily believe in the rule of law as an abstract principle of justice, but for the practical reason that stable, well-understood procedures tend to improve the performance of their organizations and reduce their costs, just as written contracts that specify the terms and duties of agreements between independent persons and organizations tend to increase the value generated by such agreements. Without such standing rules and systematic rewards and penalties, the cost of team production would be higher, and organizations would lose productive team members to other organizations in which rewards and punishment are more predictable. Even pirate captains often use written contracts to attract and keep effective crews on their ships (Rediker 1989, Anderson and Gifford 1996, and Konstam 1998, Leeson 2007).

A written charter for an organization can be regarded as its constitution insofar as it describes the core procedures for making standing policy decisions and selecting members of its decision-making bodies, and describes how authority to make and revise policies is distributed. It bears noting that such core procedures and constraints are normally far easier to describe than are the many informal relationships that completely determine an organization's decision-making procedures. In cases in which such informal practices are also durable, stable, and significantly affect policy-making decisions, it may be said that large organizations have both written and unwritten constitutional rules. The fact that a written description is incomplete, however, does not imply that written rules have no effect on an organization's practices. It only implies that the de facto standing decision procedures and compensation systems are more complex than represented in writing.

Although there is a sense in which an organization is only as old as its charter, there is also a sense in which every charter tends to be far older than the organization described. Both the written and unwritten parts of an organization's charter normally include procedures and norms taken from organizational templates that proved successful in earlier times.[4]

AFTER THE FOUNDERS, THE PROBLEM OF SUCCESSION

At some point in time, every durable organization has to move beyond the period in which formeteurs dominate their organizational governments. In some cases, this may occur because the formeteurs decide to transfer all of their authority for making policy decisions to others so other matters can be focused on, such as founding other new organizations. In other cases, formeteurs may retain control until they become incapacitated because of illness, age, or death. Formeteurs do not live forever. In both cases, the transition from formeteur to successor governments is often a crisis point for organizations because effective governance often ends with a formeteur's departure. The formal rules were developed with the formeteur goals and talents in mind, and the supporting culture of the enterprise may have largely been based upon deference to the founder(s). The departure of the formeteur(s) thus tends to undermine both the governance and culture of an organization.

Solutions to Intra-Organizational Conflict Can Increase Succession Problems

Although durable organizations outlive their founders, it bears noting that durability in this sense is not always in the formeteur's interest.

A formeteur often becomes wealthy or widely respected as a consequence of his or her organization's success. Successfully solving team-production and governance problems often produces profits, prestige, and power. To the extent that these are largely consequences of successful standing procedures, others inside and outside the organization may attempt to obtain

[4] See, for example, Sterzel (1994) for a concise overview of the historical antecedents of contemporary administrative law and procedures in Sweden. Evidence of the importance of innovations in writing and record keeping is developed by Dudley (1991, 2000), who provides a historical and economic analysis of how informational technologies can affect the size and scope of territorial governments. Although his analysis focuses on bureaucratic reforms within territorial governments, his analysis of the importance of information technology clearly applies to other organizational bureaucracies as well.

those rewards for themselves by taking over the organization's government. The greater the rewards available to the organizational leaders, the more it pays to seek such high positions. Competition over who will rule an organization can be intense, but such internal competition is not always good for the organization, because it diverts the time and attention of formeteur(s) and potential rivals away from solving organizational problems. By doing so, it tends to reduce and/or consume a substantial part of the organization's potential surplus. Moreover, those engineering successful takeovers (and palace coups) normally replace the organization's top officeholders (those with the most policy-making authority), which usually includes the formeteur(s), as noted in Chapter Two.

Formeteurs naturally take the risk of being pushed aside and of losses from internal rent seeking into account when choosing their organizational designs. One organizational strategy used by many formeteurs is to make themselves irreplaceable. Opportunities for rivals to secure the experience and broad support necessary to become an organizational rule maker may be blocked in various ways. Potential rivals may be rotated among distant posts or banished from the organization when serious threats are detected. The responsibilities of other senior team members may be narrowed and routinized beyond the point of economic efficiency to make them easier to replace and also less able to replace the formeteur.

This method of maintaining control and reducing internal conflict makes the formeteur's policy-making experience unique within the organization and critical for the organization's continued success. In such cases, it will be widely understood by team members that replacement of the ruler would tend to reduce the effectiveness of organizational decision making. This further reduces support for possible rivals and increases opposition to such takeovers. It also reduces the leadership rents available to potential rivals. In this manner, organizational designs that create irreplaceable rulers tend to reduce unproductive conflict within the organization and increase the expected returns of those holding leadership posts.[5]

Unfortunately, while advancing formeteur interests, that particular solution also implies that a formeteur's departure or death tends to greatly reduce the efficiency of his or her organization. The death or exit of a founder in such cases tends to create an organizational crisis. It reduces the effectiveness of organizational governance and produces new conflict for control of the organization among possible successors. These effects reduce

[5] See Tullock (1987, chapter 2) for an overview of some of these strategies. See Hillman and Katz (1987) for a model of internal conflict over organizational rents.

the organization's ability to respond to new circumstances, diminish its surplus, and may also undermine the organization's internal culture by reducing cooperation among other team members.[6] It is for such reasons that many clubs, family businesses, small churches, and dictatorships disintegrate shortly after the founder's death or departure.

In contrast to many other governance problems, the irreplaceable formeteur does not have strong reasons to solve the resulting transition problems, although other members of the organization (and his or her heirs) may. Whether such formeteurs have interests that extend beyond their departure or death depends partly on their goals, partly on the nature of their organization's enterprise, and partly on the institutions in place.

Organizational Leadership Posts as Property

The simplest solution to the succession problem confronted by an irreplaceable formeteur is to simply appoint a successor shortly before his or her departure. Leaving the decision to the last moment reduces the risk of overthrow by a rival whose talents have been acknowledged by the organization's leadership. A similar appointment procedure can be used to replace loyal, productive members of a council as they depart.

Although there are advantages to making such decisions at the last moment, there are also advantages for announcing the procedures through which these decisions will be made before the decision is to be made. In such cases, persons who wish to be chosen will attempt to attract the formeteur's attention and favor. The rules of this succession game can be adjusted to assure that the formeteur receives good service and advice from a broad cross-section of talented persons within the organization. Well-designed contests may thereby increase the organization's effectiveness.

Under such procedures, the top leadership post of the organization effectively becomes the property of the formeteur. When the most productive supporter of the formeteur is appointed, the successor may be said to have bought the post in an "all pay" auction among insiders. When the post of king can literally be sold to the highest bidder – as is true of many commercial enterprises – leadership positions can be auctioned off to insiders and outsiders. Both types of auctions create incentives for otherwise

[6] The modern contest and rent-seeking literatures demonstrate that conflict in such circumstances will often consume the entire surplus of the organization (Tullock 1967). See Buchanan, Tullock, and Tollison (1980) or Congleton, Hillman, and Konrad (2008) for rational-choice research on how institutions can encourage or reduce unproductive conflict within a wide variety of settings.

self-centered formeteurs to create effective, durable organizations that address succession issues because both internal and external auctions allow the formeteur to profit today from the future effectiveness of the organization after he or she is gone.

Unfortunately, as noted earlier, it is not always possible to design contests for top positions that limit the efforts of contestants to productive activities that benefit the formeteur(s). In practice, rivals often compete with each other in a manner that reduces the effectiveness of the organization, as with attempts to destroy one another's reputations by spreading falsehoods, or with attempts to destroy the rivals themselves. Nor is it always the case that the formeteur's departure can be fully anticipated.

Robust procedures for replacing organizational leaders must account for surprise departures, for the possibility that unproductive competition for the leadership posts takes place, and for the leadership's interest in avoiding overthrows.

SUCCESSION WITHIN KING-AND-COUNCIL SYSTEMS OF GOVERNANCE

Within the king-and-council systems of governance, another method of addressing CEO-succession problems is possible. Namely, the council may be authorized to appoint successors. The entire council is unlikely to die or depart suddenly. The use of councils for such decisions also tends to reduce unproductive conflict when council members make decisions through majority rule (Congleton 1984). Council members also have substantial knowledge of the skills necessary for effective organizational governance, which may differ from those necessary to launch a palace coup. Similarly, replacement members of the council may be chosen by the remaining council members, the king, or they may be jointly determined.

In this manner, the king-and-council template allows an organization's government to be gradually renewed by those with the largest stakes in continuation of the organization and the most intimate knowledge of its operation.

Such arrangements have been common historically within a broad cross-section of organizations, including churches, commercial enterprises, and national governments. A council of cardinals selects the new pope, and the pope selects new cardinals. A board of directors hires a new CEO, and the CEO appoints (or nominates) new board members. A parliament or council of electors directly elects a king or indirectly determines them by specifying rules for succession. Kings often had the authority to appoint (or nominate) new council members, as with elevations to the noble chambers of parliament.[7]

Inheriting the Throne

In cases in which an organization's council cannot agree on a new CEO because of problems associated with internal factions that produce majority cycles, conflict among council members can also consume substantial resources (in some cases including assassination of rival council members). Such occasions of council indecision and conflict tend to reduce their organization's prospects for survival insofar as governance or continuity is important during the period of interest. In such cases, a more or less automatic method of selecting successors may prove superior to council deliberations.

A very common mechanistic solution to the transition problem is to make the formeteur's oldest son his successor. By avoiding organization-threatening conflict at times of transition, such dynastic organizations have more resources available to weather the storms that confront every long-standing organization. It also reinforces incentives for formeteurs (and their successors) to consider the long-term consequences of their decisions carefully, insofar as parents value the future prospects of their first-born sons and daughters.[8] Perhaps surprisingly, several cases exist in which a council representing noble interests voted to make the office of king hereditary, as, for example, was true in Sweden in 1544. The right of inheritance is another sense in which a formeteur may be said to own his or her organization.

It bears noting that, in most cases, successors chosen in this manner tend to be less talented than the organization's founders. Genetics suggests reversion toward the mean. However, successors can often be less talented than the organization's founders without significantly reducing the effectiveness of the organization, because relatively efficient governance and internal reward systems are already in place. Moreover, access to education and the formeteur's advisory council implies that the policy decisions reached by the formeteur's heirs will be nearly as well informed, if not always as well judged, as those of the formeteur.

[7] The British king's ability to appoint new members to the House of Lords, perhaps surprisingly, played an important role in early suffrage reform, as noted in Chapter Thirteen.

[8] See Buchanan (1983) for an analysis of disputes for inherited wealth and position. Usher (1989) and Tullock (2002) analyze dynastic governance in the context of nation-states.

It should also be noted that this form of secession has effects on the balance of authority within the king-and-council system. A less talented successor CEO tends to become (and should become) more dependent on his or her council of advisors. This dependence simultaneously increases the relative policy-making authority of the council and frees the heir to devote his or her time to activities that are of greater interest than that of managing his or her parent's organization. The new balance of authority tends to increase the long-term viability of the organization by improving governance.

That positions in organizational governments are often inheritable suggests that avoiding unproductive intra-organizational conflict over leadership posts is often more important than maximizing the talent of the persons with rule-making authority.

INSTITUTIONALLY INDUCED INTERESTS AND THE INSTITUTIONAL CONSERVATISM OF SUCCESSORS

As noted in Chapter Two, formeteurs normally decide which forms of team production will be engaged in, which reward systems will be adopted, and what the standing procedures for making organizational decisions will be. In the case of durable organizations, they will also choose procedures through which the offices of the organization's government are renewed through time. The members of a durable organization's successor governments thus tend to be selected by standing procedures and receive rewards from a stable system of pecuniary and nonpecuniary rewards. The officeholders chosen have standing tasks and duties that are supported by their organization's reward and recruiting systems. These systems provide incentives for the successors to make decisions that tend to increase the effectiveness of the organization's team production.

Although every member of an organization's government has a personal constellation of private interests, all members of the organization, including its governmental officeholders, have "induced interests" that are generated by the durable rules that characterize the organizations of which they are members. In this sense at least, a durable organization – or at least its government – may be said to have its own interests, the ones implied by the systematic effects of its standing reward and selection systems on both team members and organizational leadership. Social scientists take account of such induced interests when they characterize senior managers of commercial enterprises as "profit maximizers," democratic politicians as "vote maximizers," and persons in the mass media as "publicity hounds" or "fame maximizers."

Insofar as the standing procedures continue to advance the interests of top officeholders after the formeteurs depart, successors have interests similar to those of the founders. They will support the standing procedures of their organizations because they facilitate the ability to make policy, solve team-production problems, and reduce internal conflict.

In cases in which successors believe that they could not have created an equally productive organization by themselves, they will tend to be even more defensive of existing organizational routines than formeteurs. Successors tend to be loyal organizational men and women, because standing organizational reward and selection systems have long played an important role in their personal life plans.[9] In most cases, it is through their organization's standing procedures for reward and renewal that successors rose to leadership positions and so "earned" their income, policy-making authority, and status. Institutional conservatism, in this case also justifies their relatively high income, authority, and prestige.

Moreover, durability itself may become an asset for recruiting and motivating team members insofar as it suggests that team members can count on their promised rewards. Durability may be demonstrated to team members with stories, pictures, or statues of past organizational leaders and past organizational successes. Remembering and honoring the past tends to be important for the senior members of durable organizations for a variety of practical reasons.

AMENDING AN ORGANIZATIONAL CHARTER

To argue that stability has advantages for formeteurs and their successors is not to say that a durable organization's practices are completely rigid.

As noted in Chapter Two, all durable organizations have standing procedures that allow them to identify and respond to changing circumstances in a manner that advances organizational goals. That is to say, they have governments. However, completely rule-bound organization does not simply repeat today what it was doing yesterday; it uses standing procedures to

9 This characterization of organizational men and women differs from Whyte's (1956), but bears more than a passing resemblance. As in Whyte, it argues that the personal goals of individuals do not have to change for loyalty to the organization to develop. Rather, it is induced by the organization's incentive system and its success through time. In the present case, however, "organizational interests" are not limited to middle managers. Indeed, it may apply more to senior managers, who are often most tied to their specific organization's aims and survival because of specialization and their organization-specific knowledge of internal procedures and personalities.

respond appropriately to new developments. In the long run, the standing procedures for making policy decisions are also subject to modification. When other procedures have been demonstrated to work better than current ones, or when current ones fail, an effective organization will modify its rules to better advance formeteur and successor interests. Improved organizational governance increases productivity and reduces decision errors, which allows larger and more consistent rewards to be provided to team members through time. However, institutional conservatism implies that such modifications will be infrequent and tend to be modest in scale and scope.

The possibility of amendment is partly a consequence of succession. Each new generation of organizational leaders will have some ability to adjust organizational procedures in ways that benefit themselves. In many cases, this will be done through informal bargains reached among the officeholders in a manner analogous to that developed in Chapters Five and Six.

Formeteurs, however, also have interests in choosing organizational designs that are somewhat flexible insofar as they are able to profit from the future performance of their organization. Forward-looking formeteurs acknowledge that their organizational designs are not the best possible design for all possible circumstances. As a consequence, their core procedures will include formal and informal procedures for amending their organizational charters. Amendment procedures allow reforms to be adopted without requiring their organizations to be reinvented every time a change in governance seems advantageous. Such forward-looking organizational charters increase the value of organizational leadership posts for their successors and allow formeteurs to extract part of that value by encouraging productive forms of intra-organizational competition for positions of authority.

Forward-looking formeteurs with long-term goals will thus prefer templates for governance that include amendment procedures and governmental templates that can be adjusted at a variety of margins. The former allows reforms to be adopted as necessary; the latter allows them to be adjusted without reinventing the organization as a whole.

The king-and-council template includes a variety of margins for adjusting policy-making procedures. It also accomodates amendment procedures that are more restrictive than for day-to-day policy making. Amendments, for example, might require the assent of both the king and the council, whereas day-to-day policy making may only require decisions by the king. The procedures of governance within the king-and-council system can be adjusted to increase or decrease the scope of the king's or council's authority to make decisions. In policy areas in which the king and council exercise joint control, the division of authority can be adjusted in a variety of ways.

The balance of authority between the king and council, for example, might be adjusted to increase the speed of deliberation during times of crisis or to reflect changes in the talent and ambition of council members and kings. The procedures through which kings and councils are selected may also be adjusted when the goals of the organization change, the pool of potential government officeholders changes, or the methods of team production change, because of technological or ideological changes.

The king-and-council template can also be used to adjust the distribution of policy-making authority within an organization as it changes in size. The king-and-council template is scalable in the sense that it can easily be adjusted for use in large and small organizations. It is also nestable, which allows hierarchical systems of policy-making authority to be developed by delegating subsets of authority to lower levels of kings and councils. Regional offices and other subdivisions of a large organization may have their own CEOs and councils that make a variety of local policy decisions. The latter allows hierarchical governance structures to emerge based on the king-and-council template as the organization expands in size or scope.

The Advantages of Predictability Limits the Scope for Constitutional Reform

To say that some institutional flexibility helps organizations survive in the long run, does not mean that organizational designs are completely flexible. The benefits of predictable standing policies would be lost if an organization's procedures for choosing policies became totally unpredictable. To serve as rules of the game, an organization's decision-making procedures and informal norms have to be reasonably stable in the short and medium term. Consequently, even formeteurs who retain complete control over their organizations have good reasons to use their power of amendment infrequently. Constitutional self-restraint reduces uncertainty for team members, suppliers, and customers.

The advantages of predictable procedures together with the uncertainties associated with major reform proposals imply that proposed rule changes tend to be piecemeal, rather than whole cloth, and tend to be infrequently adopted in stable political and economic environments. Most charter amendments will address a particular class of problems and take for granted that most other standing rules will remain in force. For example, a business may change the voting rules within or number of persons on its board of directors without changing the rules for selecting directors and without affecting the relationship between the board and chief executive officer. A church may change its procedure for appointing ministers or priests without changing other management practices, religious doctrines, or the location and times of church services. A territorial government may change its suffrage rules or electoral procedures without changing other aspects of governance, such as the number of chambers in parliament, the relationship between the executive and parliament, or the organization of the bureaucracy.

In this, the usual process of governmental reform tends to be similar to that of normal science. The *ceteris paribus* methodology of normal science allows progress to be made one step at a time as theories are refined in fields and subfields of study. In the organizational context, the relative merits of governmental reforms (and their effects) also tend to be easier to imagine and analyze than are great shifts in organizational templates. An automobile company is more likely to change the models produced and methods of production than it is to suddenly reinvent itself by taking up spaceship design or deep-sea mining. Reforms and institutional breakthroughs that seem revolutionary when adopted usually appear relatively modest with the benefit of history's hindsight. Most practices remain unaffected by such breakthroughs.

A Digression on Contemporary Amendment Procedures

Consistent with the prediction that formeteurs have interests in stability and limited flexibility is the fact that the standing procedures for amending organizational charters and governmental constitutions tend to be substantially more difficult than procedures for changing day-to-day policies. For example, contemporary amendment procedures within democratic states normally require a broader consensus and longer process of review than is required to make day-to-day decisions. Article 5 of the U.S. Constitution requires amendments to be approved by a two-thirds majority of both chambers of the legislature and then approval by three-fourths of the state legislatures. Ordinary legislation requires only majority approval in both chambers of the legislature and acceptance by the president; state governments are not consulted. Article 15 of the Swedish constitution requires amendments to be approved by two successive parliaments separated by an election. Ordinary laws require approval by only a single parliament.[10]

Similarly, revisions to the charters of contemporary private organizations are normally constrained by civil law as well as by provisions of the charters themselves. In most cases, external approval is also necessary. For example, Section 11 of the charter of the American National Red Cross gives the U.S. Congress the sole power to amend its charter, although they may, of course, do so at the request of the Red Cross. International organizations, such as the European Union and United Nations, normally require ratification by all of their member states for changes in core decision-making procedures, but use various forms of majority rule for day-to-day decisions.

CONCLUSIONS: SOME COMMON PROPERTIES OF DURABLE ORGANIZATIONS

The analysis of Chapters Two and Three suggests that there are a mind-numbing number of design parameters to consider simultaneously when founding an organization. There are infinite varieties of reward systems, recruiting systems, and governance systems that can be imagined, and each combination of these systems tends to have different advantages and risks associated with them, which vary according to the goals to be advanced and the environments in which the organization will operate. If formeteurs knew the properties of every constellation of decision-making procedures and internal incentive systems and could perfectly predict the future, they would pick the one that most perfectly advanced their goals, that is, the most efficient organizational design. If, however, the range of alternatives is not

[10] The constitutional law of the United Kingdom is nearly unique in not specifying an amendment process that is more complex than that of ordinary legislation. The constitution of the United Kingdom consists of a series of laws with special status rather than a single document. Generally speaking, majority approval in the House of Commons is thus sufficient for both new constitutional provisions and new legislation. The latter makes it difficult to discern clearly the difference between constitutional and ordinary legislation. Yet as argued in section C, the latter is not uniquely a problem for the United Kingdom. Most political constitutions include core procedures and constraints that are enacted as ordinary legislation.

A modern curiosity for constitutional theorists is the current Swiss constitution. It includes many checks and balances on both ordinary legislation and constitutional revision. It specifies a *less restrictive* petition to force *ordinary legislation* to be passed by referendum (50,000 signatures; see Article 89) than to force a proposed constitutional revision to be subjected to direct referendum (100,000 signatures, see Article 120). A smaller minority can demand a referendum on ordinary legislation than for constitutional referenda. This implies that a greater supermajority is required for adopting ordinary legislation, without a referendum, than for adopting constitutional amendments.

entirely known, and if what is known cannot be fully analyzed at reasonable cost, formeteurs will realize that they can make a variety of mistakes when forming organizations and recruiting teams. In such cases, prudent formeteurs will choose their governance, recruiting, and reward systems from existing organizational templates known to function relatively well, and they will adjust them a bit at the margin for the purposes at hand. Knowledge and calculation constraints rule out perfect solutions by formeteurs.

This assessment of the problem of institutional design differs from the mathematical solutions characterized in the mechanism-design literature in several ways. First, it acknowledges the limited scope of the knowledge of formeteurs and also their limited time for appraising the alternatives they do know about. Second, the best institutional designs in the mechanism-design literature are often of the "ridge line" variety that require net benefits to be maximized at every instant, as for example, in Holmstrom and Milgrom (1994). In such cases, myopic and long-term analyses reach essentially similar conclusions about the best standing policies. Such solutions, however, characterize intertemporal optimization problems only under fairly restrictive mathematical assumptions; for example, when the objectives are concave, differentiable, and continuous, and the constraints are convex and continuous.

In the real world, one cannot always climb to the top of a mountain range by simply striking out for the closest ridge and following it upward, because not every ridge leads to the top. The jaggedness of mountains is a problem for both partially and fully informed theories of mountain climbing and trail design. In the real world, most trails that climb mountains head upward for the most part, but they do not usually follow ridge lines or rise at every point.

The properties of alternative institutional designs also tend to be a bit ragged (nonconcave) and discontinuous. Nonetheless, much of what has been argued about reward and recruiting systems in Chapters Two and Three is compatible with the microeconomics literature on organizational incentive systems and mechanism design. The types of mechanisms that continue to attract the interests of formeteurs and their successors will tend to solve the various internal incentive and recruiting problems analyzed in those literatures. Similarly, the analysis of organizational governance developed in these chapters is compatible with most contractarian theories of constitutional design and most analyses of institutionally induced equilibria in governing organizations. In cases in which formeteurs create an organizational government to which significant policy-making authority will be delegated, the institutions of governance will tend to reflect considerations similar to those analyzed, for example, by Buchanan and Tullock (1962). And it is possible that the profits of the organization will be distributed among formeteurs in a manner analogous to those described by Rawls (1971). Inequality among formeteurs may be tolerated only insofar as it increases organizational efficiency.

The processes through which those solutions tend to be developed and adopted, however, differ from those characterized in the mechanism design and contractarian literatures in that organizational designs reflect a long series of modest experiments by formeteurs and their successors through time, rather than a single optimizing choice by a well-informed, forward-looking entrepreneur or constitutional convention.[11] Instead, the designs and experience of previous generations of formeteurs are assessed by persons contemplating the formation of new organizations. The organizational designs chosen by previous generations of formeteurs produce the menu of organizational designs that attract the interest of contemporary formeteurs because those designs are known to have advanced formeteur interests in a wide range of circumstances in the past.

Knowledge problems and jaggedness do not imply that reaching the highest point in a mountain range is impossible or that hikers are necessarily walking on suboptimal trails. Rather it implies that identifying the top and finding the best trails to the top will be the result of trial and error by a long series of mountain climbers who learn from one another's innovations and mistakes. Although the best trail known at a point in time may not be the best that will ever be found, such trails may be used for centuries with only minor variations, as true of organizational designs. Similarly, the best trail will vary somewhat with the technology of transport and with the goals of those using them. The best foot trails, horse trails, and automobile trails share many properties but are rarely identical.

This does not mean that organizations are entirely products of history or technology. Each part of each organizational design on the menu of best practices is the result of past experiments and assessments by formeteurs about what works. In most cases, previous reforms of preexisting templates were undertaken with specific performance improvements in mind, and in cases in which the hypothesized improvements were realized, the reforms were not only kept but copied by other formeteurs and their successors.

The historical requirements for survivorship of organizational templates are largely determined by the interests of formeteurs. Only those

[11] See, for example, Williamson (2002) or Spulber (2008) for overviews of this extensive literature.

organizational designs that have advanced formeteur interests well enough to be copied by other formeteurs will be widely known or considered by them. Organizational experiments that fail to advance formeteur (and successor) interests tend to disappear from the menu of organizational designs – although they may continue in managerial mythology as instances of designs and policies to be avoided.

Some Common Features of Robust Organizational Governance

The common interests and problems of formeteurs imply that the templates for organizational governance that remain on the menu share a number of properties, a subset of which have been analyzed in Chapters Two and Three. First, every durable organization will have a body of internal procedures for making policy decisions that serve as its charter or constitution for governance. The standing rules normally specify the officeholders who participate in major decisions and the manner in which those officials interact to make decisions. The latter may include specific architectures for policy making that group and/or assign tasks to subsets of officeholders. The standing procedures of long-lived organizations also include rules for selecting and replacing officeholders and rules for amending the organization's charter.

Second, although the existence of an organizational government allows organizations to change policies every instant, and the existence of amendment procedures potentially allows organizations to reinvent their procedures of governance every day, durable organizations will not do so. Institutional conservatism is supported by the risk aversion of government officeholders and team members as well as various economic advantages associated with being conventional.

Durable organizations tend to have standing policies for recruiting and rewarding team members, because it is in the interests of most organizational governments to have predictable policies on these matters. The core procedures for making organizational policy decisions also tend to be stable, partly because of similar advantages associated with predictable policies, and partly because governance stability reduces unproductive internal conflict. Reward and governance systems are only adjusted in circumstances in which the benefits are expected to exceed the cost of lost predictability.

The reforms adopted tend to be piecewise, focused at solving particular problems rather than reinventing the organization. Such modest reforms preserve advantages associated with existing procedures and avoid unforeseen costs generated by large institutional experiments. Although many such changes may be proposed and evaluated, only a few will be adopted. Moreover, the standing procedures for governance are not developed anew for each new organization, but are largely copied from successful organizations of the past. In many cases, the standing procedures are written down in formal charters, compacts, or other similar documents to reduce uncertainty.

Third, the founding charters and constitutions of organizations favor formeteur interests because formeteurs normally draft their organization's founding documents. For example, the number of formeteurs that found an organization affects the initial division of authority within the organization's government, as noted in Chapter Two. Formeteur opportunities to profit from their organization, however, are constrained by the tasks undertaken, the environment in which their organizations operate, and the exit options of their team members. These limit the extent and kind of leadership rents that can be extracted from their organizations.

Fourth, the analysis predicts that successor governments tend to be more conservative than formeteur governments, because successors are more dependent on preexisting institutions for their positions of authority. Increased institutional conservatism, however, does not imply that durable organizations exhibit complete institutional rigidity, but it does imply that experiments will tend to be relatively small and that strictly organizational interests tend to emerge on the part of an organization's leadership. Durable organizations will exhibit considerable continuity in their procedures of governance and amendment, because continuity advances both the personal and institutionally induced interests of successive generations of officeholders with the authority to adopt constitutional reforms.

Fifth, the analysis demonstrates that the king-and-council template for governance can be used to address a variety of long-term governance problems. The king-and-council template provides several robust solutions for succession problems and also allows authority to be shifted between the king and council in a manner that can improve organizational decision making. The latter allows the distribution of authority to be finely tuned to take advantage of new circumstances and the talent and skills of formeteurs and their successors without changing the fundamental architecture of the organization's government. These advantages, in addition to the informational advantages discussed in Chapter Two, suggest that it will often be prudent for formeteurs (and their successors) to adopt forms of organizational government based on the king-and-council template. Of particular importance for the main purposes of this book is the subset of durable organizations that are or become territorial governments. When the above analysis is applied to territorial governance, it implies that governance will tend to be rule bound, but flexible, and that policy-making authority is likely to be shared in practice, rather than vested in a single person or committee. This contrasts with most models of dictatorship and democracy analyzed by political scientists and political economists. It also challenges the practical relevance of political theories that rely on or defend undivided sovereignty, such as Hobbes's (1651) theory of social contracts.

The next chapter provides an explanation for the emergence of territorial government and explores problems and opportunities that are unique to territorial governments. It and the next several chapters also explore the dynamics of territorial governance. The reforms of greatest interest for this volume are those that can account for the peaceful emergence of parliamentary democracy from organizations that are initially based on relatively autocratic forms of the king-and-council template.

FOUR

The Origins of Territorial Governance

Two meanings of the term "government" are common in English. One refers to the decision-making or policy-making part of a formal organization. Every club, nonprofit organization, and firm has a government in this sense, for reasons explained in the previous two chapters. These policy-making bodies devise and enforce rules for their team members in order to solve team-production problems and direct an organization's resources to specific purposes. The other meaning of the term refers to the subset of organizations that have extensive ability to impose rules on persons within a particular geographical territory. Chapter Four provides an explanation for how the former can become the latter.

All organizations can impose rules on their own team members because realizing the fruits of team production normally requires team members to perform certain tasks at particular times with particular persons in a particular manner. The range of behaviors that can be induced by organizations varies substantially, but many organizations exercise significant control over their members. An organization's management is often able to tell team members how to dress, when and what to eat, when and how to work, and even who their friends should be (other team members). The organization's management may induce team members to go on trips far away from families and friends (as with hunting clubs, commercial transport shipping, and military operations), via means and to settings that involve risks to life and limb. They may induce persons to sacrifice the necessities of life for a period – fasting and abstinence, for example, are often required for the members in religious organizations.

Many organizations can also impose rules on outsiders. Both suppliers and customers have to accept some rules in order to sell their products to an organization or purchase an organization's output: "Deliveries at the back"; "Sales of our products take place only on Saturday from 10:00–14:00."

Territorial governments are the rule-making, policy-making bodies of organizations that have a relatively great ability to impose rules on outsiders within a geographic territory.

This chapter provides a theory of the emergence of territorial governments as one of many productive organizations in an initially peaceful territory. The analysis draws from and extends the productive theories of the state found in the work of Aristotle (350 BCE), Montesquieu (1748), Nozick (1974), and Buchanan (1975). The general approach differs from other productive theories of the state by stressing the incentives of formeteurs and the gradual emergence of governments, as opposed to a sudden shift from anarchy to statehood through conquest or social contract. It also differs by pointing out that the ability to impose rules does not necessarily require the organization of force.

Organizations with monopoly power over critical services in a region can impose rules on many persons outside their organization. The ability of monopolists to do so, however, is constrained by the mobility of the persons ruled and the availability of substitutes.

Problems With Hobbes-Based Theories Of Territorial Governance

It seems clear that a Hobbesian (1651) "war of every man against every other" would not last very long in practice, because formeteurs would quickly organize teams for purposes of defense (and aggression), as noted by Montesquieu (1748). However, the Hobbesian low-income trap of war of every man against every man does not literally require conflict among individuals. The same logic applies for "wars of every tribe against every tribe," and "wars of every state against every state." Peace treaties are notoriously difficult to negotiate and enforce, so wars among organizations can easily be all-encompassing, perpetual, impoverishing affairs.

The Hobbesian approach explains why persons and organizations tend to fight and why they would want to escape from an all-consuming conflict, but the solution proposed by Hobbes seems to require an all-powerful world ruler, or at least a continental government, which we have never seen. The creation of military clubs cannot really explain how civil societies emerge in settings in which there is a good deal of natural conflict.[1]

1 See, Tullock (1972) for an early collection of rational-choice-based analysis of the emergence of the state from anarchy. Oye (1986), Garfinkel and Skaperdas (1996), and Stringham (2006) provide more recent collections. See Konrad and Skaperdas (2005) for a game-theoretic treatment of "protection services" and the emergence of coercive states in a setting without exit possibilities. See Congleton (1980) for an early discussion of how institutional reforms can reduce losses from conflict in Hobbesian settings.

It is more likely to be the case that somewhat prosperous communities emerge before, rather than after, territorial governance and warfare. If there is nothing worth taking, why invest in theft or conquest?

Prosperous communities are far more likely to emerge if conflict is initially limited, rather than all-encompassing, or if at least a few islands of relative tranquility exist. Some communities may, for example, be initially protected by natural barriers of one kind or another. After prosperous communities emerge, their relative prosperity provides formeteurs in other places with incentives to organize theft and conquest, but prosperity also provides resources for defense. The existence of "roving bandits" and similar organizations provides prosperous communities with reasons to organize themselves against such attacks.

The nonviolent theory of the origins of territorial governance developed in this chapter does not imply that military organization and violent conflict are irrelevant. Rather, it implies that local prosperity does not require an initial escape from the Hobbesian jungle, nor does it require an initial monopoly of organized violence, as argued by many political theorists, including most recently Olson (2000) and North, Wallis, and Weingast (2009). Warfare is likely to be induced by the relative success of early organizations, rather than their failures; but the resulting warfare cannot be all encompassing without eliminating the rationale for theft, conquest, and defense.

The approach and conclusions of this chapter are broadly consistent with the historical analyses of Spruyt (1994) and Ertman (1997), among others, who stress that nation-states emerged in the fifteenth, sixteenth, and seventeenth centuries as one of many organizational types through various coercive and noncoercive forms of competition. It is also consistent with Nozick's (1974) analysis of voluntary association within productive states, although no normative inferences are drawn from the present analysis. Territorial governments for the purposes of this book are simply organizations that have a relatively great ability to impose rules on persons outside their organization within a specific geographic area.

A DIGRESSION ON RULE BY STRONG MEN

Brute-force theories of the state often begin with discussions of "pecking orders," common in many animal groups, in which the biggest, strongest animal gains privileged access to food and sex. By analogy, it is often argued that in early human societies, a strong man simply uses his brute strength to dominate a group. He profits by taxing other group members who pay up to avoid being attacked. Such theories often note that the first human organization, the nuclear family, is often dominated by such strong men for decades at a time. The patriarch is often the physically strongest member of his extended family.

In less biologically based groups, the physically strongest man may also be a better formeteur than others because he can solve many internal enforcement problems directly by threatening to punish shirking team members. Such forceful leadership is evident in the mythic histories of famous kings of the past, from Odysseus to Arthur.

The critical weakness of the brute-force theories of the state is that organizational talent and physical strength are not necessarily correlated with each other. Thus, in many cases, it would be possible for the second- and third-strongest members of a group to organize a team of two or three and defeat the strongest man. Even a very strong man needs to sleep. Consequently, if the second-strongest man is a better organizer than the first, he will tend to emerge as the community's strong man, as might also the third- or fourth-strongest, and so forth.

Physical strength is not of central importance for leadership posts in large organizations, even in cases in which the organization is largely based on the ability to make credible coercive threats. Napoleon, Hitler, and Mao were not unusually tall or strong men, although they ran powerful coercive organizations. Once durable organizations emerge, the strong man is simply the pivotal decision maker within his or her organization's government.

A MODEL OF COERCIVE RULE OF COMMUNITIES WHERE EXIT IS POSSIBLE

An organization's ability to impose rules on insiders and outsiders makes the boundary of an organization less than perfectly sharp, although that distinction is a useful one for the purposes of this chapter and as a description of relationships between territorial governments and their residents for much of recorded history. A commercial organization's customers are not insiders, because they do not ordinarily participate in the firm's team production, although they clearly affect the viability of such organizations and indirectly affect their decisions. A religious organization's congregation participates in church services but does not produce the sermons or the doctrines being espoused. Similarly, community residents pay taxes and obtain benefits from their territorial governments but rarely participate in decisions about taxes or the production of government services. The distinction between insiders and outsiders is less sharp in contemporary democracies grounded on popular sovereignty, but there is still a clear distinction between those who directly participate in government decision making (elected representatives, the courts, and the bureaucracy) and ordinary citizens.[2]

Commercial, religious, and governing organizations can often impose rules on outsiders, but only within limits. Those limits are not consequences of the size of an organization. Very large, successful organizations are often created by energetic formeteurs, such as Henry Ford, Kiichiro Toyoda, Thomas Edison, Friedrich Krupp, Henry Dunant, Clara Barton, and the like. Such talented formeteurs can impose many rules on their team members, but relatively few rules on people outside their own organizations. Henry Ford once attempted to reduce his production costs by imposing a particular color on his customers at the height of his monopoly power. Ford's customers could purchase his automobiles in "any color they want, as long as it is black." Many of his potential customers preferred other colors and purchased automobiles produced by his less demanding rivals, and Ford's monopoly power quickly disappeared. The ability to impose rules on outsides is limited by the exit opportunities of outsiders, rather than organizational size or wealth.

Coercive Rule with Mobile Subjects

The essential logic for requesting that outsiders follow particular rules and for accepting such requests is represented in Table 4.1. It is sensible for an organization to make such requests of outsiders (that is, "please follow rule *D*") as long as the organization's surplus will be increased by the outsider's compliance ($\Pi - R > C > X$ or $\Pi - R > X > C$). The outsider-resident expects to receive benefit *R* if he or she complies with the demand, expects to receive benefit *B* if he or she does not comply, along with penalty *P*. He or she expects to receive $A - E$ if he or she chooses to leave the community, where *A* is the expected net benefits from residence in the best alternative community and *E* is the member's exit cost. The outsider-resident accepts the organization's demand (obeys rule *D*) only if the (long-term) reward *R* from

2 The concepts of popular sovereignty and social contracts emerged during the seventeenth and eighteenth centuries. These theories, in effect, make the entire community the true formeteurs of governing organizations, whose authority is delegated to them by the residents. Although there are very few cases in which community governments were formed in this way, the ideas of popular sovereignty and social contracts can affect the willingness of subject-citizens to resist arbitrary rules and to lobby for constitutional reform as developed later.

Table 4.1. *Payoffs for Formeteur-Ruler and Community Members*

	Formeteur	Resident
Community member accepts the organization's demand.	Π–R	R
Community member rejects the organization's demand.	C	B–P
Former community member emigrates.	X	A–E

doing so is greater than the alternatives of (long-term) noncompliance and exit, $R > B - P$ and $R > A - E$.

In perfectly ruled polities, the productivity of the rules enforced is always greater than the cost of enforcement, and the reward to community members is always sufficient to induce compliance. In such polities, community members always follow their government's rules because punishments are precisely targeted at community members that violate the rules. Residents remain in such communities because the rewards are greater than those in alternatives communities, net of exit costs. Such well-ordered communities are rare, however, because the information available to territorial governments is rarely sufficient for choosing only productive rules or for perfectly enforcing the rules chosen.

Nonetheless, the rules chosen and enforced have to advance organizational and community interests tolerably well, given the exit and cost constraints of territorial governments. Unless following community rules generates sufficient net benefits for residents, they will quietly depart for other communities with better or no governing organizations.

EXIT COSTS AND EXIT CONTROL

It bears, noting, however that exit costs are not entirely determined by the natural physical and emotional costs of relocating but are partly determined by the policies of governments.

Exit may be discouraged by encouraging the dissemination of information about hardships in other communities and about the dangers of travel to them. "You are lucky to be here, rather than there!" Information about hardships inside the community and about better alternatives may also be suppressed through censorship laws.

Exit costs can be directly increased by punishing exit with fees of various kinds. Organizations may attempt to damage the departing member's reputation by declaring that the person leaving "is a shirker," "has never done his duties," "has violated our trust," "is a thief," and so on. Exit may be illegal. There may be harsh punishments for even attempting to exit. Extreme examples of the latter include the fugitive slave laws common in all slaveholding societies, restrictions on peasant and serf mobility that were common in feudal Europe and Japan, and the Berlin Wall and "Iron Curtain" of the former Soviet Union.

Territorial governments that increase the cost of exit can reduce their rewards for compliance and/or increase their penalties for noncompliance without inducing mass exit by residents and team members, albeit at the risk of attracting fewer immigrants.

Exit costs are also partly a consequence of the entrance costs of other organizations and territorial governments. Because there are cases in which it pays to banish a person for shirking (as when $X > C$ in Table 4.1), it will be difficult for other organizations to judge whether a particular departure is a voluntary exit from a dysfunctional community or the banishment of a person for poor performance or criminal acts.

Other organizations will not want to include shirkers or criminals from other communities on their teams, because they increase the cost of team production without producing sufficient offsetting benefits. Similarly, regional governments will hesitate to allow immigrants of questionable character to resettle in their communities. Rule breakers increase enforcement costs and reduce the productivity of territorial rules. Productive rule followers would normally be welcome, insofar as they contribute to team or community output, but they may need to prove themselves before being accepted.[3]

In cases in which it is not easy to exit or join a given community, the calculus of remaining or becoming a resident will be based on the long-term average (expected) net benefits of affiliation relative to those available in other communities, net of exit costs. Governments of communities whose residents have relatively high exit costs can use relatively severe penalties to enforce their rules, even if alternatives outside the community are somewhat better than those inside.

Predictable Rules and Penalties

Whenever exit possibilities exist, there are limits to the feasible range of rules and punishments that can be imposed, as noted above. Exit

[3] Communities with labor shortages and little fear of shirkers thus may attract new residents by eliminating entrance fees or rewarding people for joining their community with citizenship and other "signing bonuses." During the medieval period, independent cities often rewarded serf immigrants with freedom from feudal duties after a period of residence. "City air makes one free" in such cases.

possibilities also tend to encourage accuracy in the imposition of whatever punishments are used.

Organizations and communities that routinely impose penalties on the wrong persons provide lower risk-adjusted net benefits for their team and community members than otherwise similar organizations with smaller errors or less severe punishments. The expected reward of following a community's rules falls to $[(1 - p)(R) + (p)(B - P)]$, when the probability of being wrongly punished, rather than rewarded, for following the rules is $p > 0$. Persons in such communities would leave for other communities when punishments are relatively severe $[(B - P)$ is below $(A - E)]$ and the probability of wrongful punishment, p, is relatively high.

This does not imply that arbitrary punishment is impossible, only that one community's error rate cannot be much greater than another's, net of exit costs, other things being equal. That is to say, punishment systems are constrained to fall within a band determined by exit costs and those used elsewhere.

A pirate ship captain can use more severe and arbitrary penalties at sea than while at port – denial of food and water or accommodation on the ship itself. However, unless the bounty is unusually plentiful, a harshly sanctioned crew will depart for other ships as soon as a port is reached. Similarly, communities whose residents face unusually arbitrary and harsh treatment tend to evaporate as residents (and team members), depart for other locations where punishments are less arbitrary and harsh, unless the rewards from continued association are also unusually great. The anticipated risk adjusted net rewards of continued association have to be kept above those of the available alternatives.[4]

Inequality before the Law

To say that community governments are constrained in their ability to use arbitrary and harsh punishment does not mean that the rules enforced will be the same for all community members or that the rules will be enforced in a uniform manner.

In many cases, a community's residents are heterogeneous in ways that affect a government's return from rules and enforcement. Some residents and some team members provide services that are more important for

[4] Even greater exit would occur under some asymmetric theories of behavior under uncertainty. Avoiding possible losses may be considered to be more important than obtaining possible gains.

their communities and organizations than others. Some residents and team members have better exit opportunities than others. The minimum acceptable combination of rewards, punishments, and punishment errors thus varies among community members, as does the extent to which territorial governments profit through their association with particular residents. In such cases, organizations will treat different residents or classes of residents differently because they cannot afford to overpay for compliance, nor can they afford to provide rewards below those required for retention.

As a consequence, unusually productive community members who could easily move to other communities will be more carefully treated (subject to less arbitrary punishment) and will receive higher rewards for their efforts (or be subject to lower taxes). A wealthy merchant may be subject to different rules and penalties than a wealthy farmer because the merchant is more mobile than the farmer.

TERRITORIAL MONOPOLY AS A FOUNDATION FOR COERCIVE RULE

Economists devote a good deal of their time to thinking about settings in which customers may acquire the same services from a variety of organizations and in which exit costs are very low. In such cases, no organization and no territorial government can demand a higher price for its services than any other, whether in cash or kind. In cases in which an organization provides an important, unique service, a much higher price can be charged, because in monopolized markets, customers must pay the price or do without.

Figure 4.1 depicts the pricing decision of a local monopolist that charges a uniform price for its services, modified slightly to take account of the possibility of exit. Here, one can imagine a water monopoly that controls the local irrigation network. If a farmer wishes to have food on the table next year, he must have a reliable source of water and so is willing to pay a high price to the local water monopolist. The highest possible uniform price reduces water user net benefits from a maximum of $A - E + \Pi + \Pi'$ to $A - E$, the level that could be obtained from alternative sources of the water in other communities. If the price is set any higher, the farmer would sell his land and move, although prices would have to be very high to induce abandonment of fertile farmland and buildings. In such cases, the quality and extent of fixed assets partly determine exit costs.

Monopolists are often said to extract "rents" (net benefits or profits) from their customers by controlling access to their services. The monopolist of

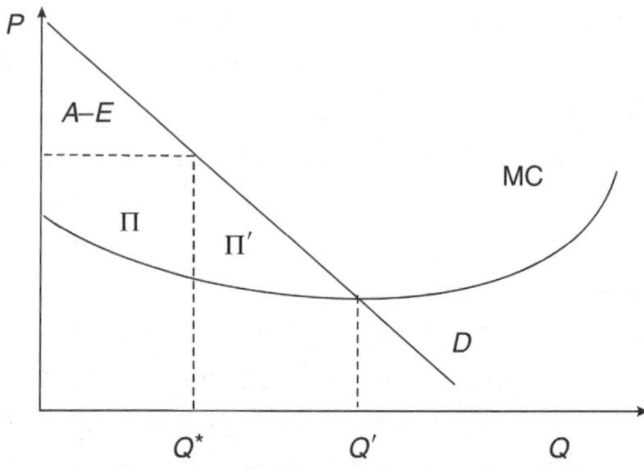

Figure 4.1. Monopoly profits.

Figure 4.1 can be said to have extracted monopoly rents (profits) equal to area Π from its consumers.

It bears noting that the rents extracted from consumers may involve more than a simply transfer of money from customers to the monopolist's treasury. In cases in which money economies are not well developed, a monopolist organization may find it useful to accept a combination of money, farm output, hours of work, and deference to the organization's leadership as payment for the monopolized services. Such pricing can generate significant improvements in the resources available to the water monopolist and in the psychic rewards associated with leadership positions in the organization. Deference, for example, may be valued greatly by the monopoly's leadership, yet it may not be directly purchased in markets.

It also bears noting that all-or-nothing offers and price discrimination potentially allow a monopolist to increase net receipts by up to the amount characterized by area Π′. In either case, the price paid for similar services varies among consumers. Some customers value the service more than others (have more inelastic demands), have less attractive exit alternatives, or can provide the water monopoly with especially valuable services. There may well be inequality before the monopolist's "law" when price discrimination is feasible.

Monopolists have a greater ability to impose rules on their client-customers than nonmonopolists because exit options are more limited. The logic of Table 4.1, however, implies that monopolists may have to reduce their money price and profit somewhat to compensate their customers for rule-following behavior. In such cases, imposing rules is profitable for monopolists only if the rules reduce production costs or increase demand enough to offset the cost of inducing rule-following behavior. Figure 4.2 illustrates the

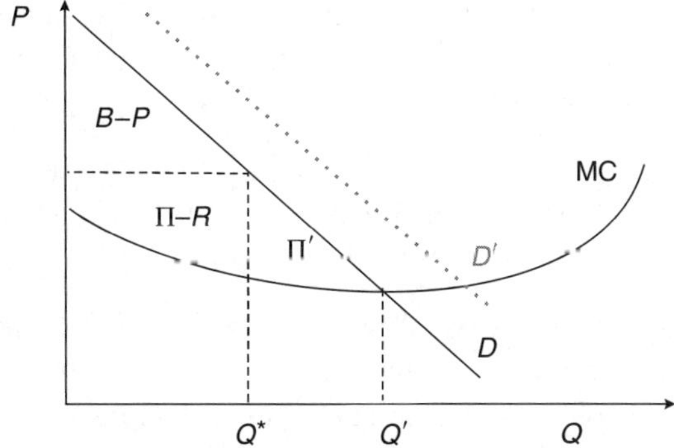

Figure 4.2. Monopoly gains from increases in regional income.

case in which the demand for services is increased by changes in the rules. Requiring orderly queues and refusing to bargain over posted prices may be said to increase effective demand by reducing transactions costs.

Note that the ability of a local monopoly to impose rules in such cases arises not from the exercise of military power (although some police power may be necessary to retain control of the monopolized service), but rather from their ability to deny access to a valuable service and the inability of their customers to easily substitute services from other organizations (exit). If a person fails to pay for water, he or she might face dehydration or starvation in the future. If a person fails to pay their dues to a defensive-wall cooperative, he or she may be banished from the walled community and so lose all to roving bandits.

In cases in which more than one organization has monopoly power in a territory, more than one organization will be able to impose rules on the residents of that territory. In addition to the water monopoly, there may be a salt or religious monopoly that can benefit from imposing a few rules on their client-customers.[5] By controlling the magnitude and mix of payments

[5] Even firms in fairly competitive markets can also impose rules on their customers: A grocery store or restaurant may demand suitable attire. A firm might exclude unruly customers who impose negative externalities on other customers or significantly increase production costs by disturbing the arrangement of inventory on shelves or other displays. In competitive markets, however, the rules must directly or indirectly benefit customers, or they would shop elsewhere. For example, limiting shopping hours must allow firms to provide their services at lower costs to the customers or to improve ambiance for their customers. Dress codes may similarly be imposed to create ambiance desired by a restaurant's customers.

Ease of substitution (exit), however, clearly limits the ability of rival organizations to impose rules on their customers. McDonalds, for example, could not require all of its customers to wear tuxedos when eating its hamburgers, although restaurants with monopoly power might be able to do so.

required for access to its services, the governing bodies of important local monopolies (and cartels) can exercise significant control over all who live in their service territories.

ENCOMPASSING INTERESTS, RENT EXTRACTION, AND THE RULE OF LAW

Economics implies that regional monopolists have incentives to increase the demand for their services through every method that increases their organizational surplus. Rent extraction can be increased, for example, by monopolizing several critical services, rather than just one. Rent extraction can also be increased by reducing the availability of substitutes by blocking the entry of rivals in various ways. Such methods for increasing rent extraction tend to make community members worse off by shifting the terms of exchange in favor of the ruling organization – although there are, as noted earlier, limits to a monopoly organization's ability to extract rents from its client-customers.

Perhaps surprisingly, there are also methods for increasing rent-extraction opportunities that provide additional benefits to a community's residents. For example, the demand for a monopolist's services can be increased by reducing transactions costs and increasing client-consumer income. Such effects give regional monopolists what Olson (2000) calls an "encompassing interest" in their communities' economic development. For example, a local monopolist may undertake or subsidize the construction of a network of roads to reduce production and distribution costs for all consumers and nonrival firms in its territory. Similarly, a regional monopolist may provide dispute resolution and other legal services because law and order increases local prosperity and the demand for its services.

Any public or private service that directly or indirectly increases net revenues for the monopolist may be provided.

On the Provision of Law and Order by Local Monopolists

It is interesting to note that dispute-resolution services can be provided at a relatively low cost by large regional monopolists because their rulings can be enforced by simply threatening to increase prices or deny services to those who fail to follow its rulings.

To produce dispute resolution services, a monopolist may delegate authority to an arbitration board and head arbitrator. A network of more or less permanent locations may be established and times scheduled at which disputes will be evaluated and judged by company arbitrator-judges. Again the logic of rational conservatism applies. It will normally be the case that the rules enforced by local authorities will be based on older successful bodies of law rather than invented whole cloth for each dispute or each community. The rules may be modified slightly for the cases or communities at hand, insofar as doing so increases the surplus of the monopoly organization.

Consistency can be assured by writing down the rules and allowing appeals of particular decisions that end with a single individual or committee, such as the governor (formeteur or successor) or supreme court. Such procedures also tend to reduce the risks associated with arbitrary treatment for much the same reason that written contracts reduce risks from relationships among organizations and customers. It clarifies what is expected and reduces the extent to which the rules may be changed after decisions based on them have already been made. Predictable, rule-governed enforcement systems tend to make retention of a community's residents easier for community rulers, although, for reasons already noted, equal protection of the law may not.

Deference to established laws and court decisions tends to reinforce institutional conservatism because the law in most countries is regarded as a long-standing collection of rules and procedures with a high degree of functionality and normative support. The long-standing rules that emerge from such procedures are often regarded as natural laws or rights. It bears noting that the earliest known written laws are from the Euphrates valley where governments were based at least in part on monopolized irrigation networks. These early laws are known because they were literally written in stone. The Code of Ur-Nammu was carved into tablets about 4,000 years ago and the Code of Hammurabi was chiseled into basalt a few hundred years later. Other codes from the same area include similar provisions, and these legal codes subsequently affected the standing rules of many other communities in the Middle East, including what became Jewish law (Finkelstein 1968–69).

Religious services were also among the core monopoly services provided by many ancient governments (Bailkey 1967). The monopoly power of state religions allows them to impose rules on believers and nonbelievers by espousing universal norms for behavior. "Thou shalt not …" When supernatural threats are believed, they can be a cost-effective method of encouraging compliance with the rules and also for reducing resistance to the decisions reached in court proceedings. Formal laws and norms are often enforced through religious court systems. Such courts were run, for example, by Catholic, Jewish, and Islamic churches through the medieval period.

When religious services are not directly provided by governments, religious monopolies are often supported by regional governments. The state-supported church, in turn, normally reciprocates by encouraging support for the government. Even today, the sovereign of England is the head of the Church of England, and holds the title "Supreme Governor of the Church of England."

Just as a consistent, predictable set of rules can increase an organization's viability by solving coordination and team-production problems, so can a predictable set of community rules (laws) increase the prosperity of a community. Stable sets of community rules can solve coordination and externality problems. They can reduce the extent and cost of unproductive conflict among persons and organizations in the community. They can also facilitate (and encourage) long-term planning by individuals and organizations by increasing expected returns and/or reducing the risks associated with capital investments and specialization.

The value added by law-and-order services is emphasized in the early-enlightenment contract theories of the state developed by Hobbes (1651) and Locke (1689) and in contemporary game-theoretic explorations of shifts from anarchy to civil society, as in Nozick (1974), Skogh (1982), and Volckart (2000). There is also a substantial body of empirical research in economics that links the provision of law-and-order services with increased national income.[6]

Providing such services tends to encourage the development of prosperous communities, which increases potential rent extraction for ruling monopolists by increasing the demand for their services.

MILITARY THREATS, RENT EXTRACTION, AND DEFENSE

As profits and deference are produced, rivals inside and outside the organization may attempt to take over the leadership posts in regional governments in order to enjoy the rewards associated with those positions. Such takeover efforts may include threats of violence.

Both formeteurs and their successors naturally take steps to avoid both internal and external overthrows. With respect to the latter, they will defend themselves, their organization, and their territory. They do so by organizing defensive teams and investing in defensive capital. The organization may fortify its offices and production facilities. The monopolist's team members

[6] See, for example, Keefer and Knack (1995, 1997) or Feld and Voigt (2006).

and customers may be encouraged to turn out and defend the organization's capital assets (the irrigation system, windmills, buildings, etc.).

An implication of the analysis of Chapter Two is that the cost of defensive teams can be reduced by encouraging militaristic norms (the warrior ethic) and other forms of loyalty (community patriotism) that tend to promote rule-following behavior, toughness, and a willingness to sacrifice for "one's" government and its community. Defensive teams, norms, and capital can also be used to drive up exit costs, which allow tougher penalties to be used to assure compliance with the rules adopted to promote the territorial government's interests.

Artificial and Natural Monopolies

The infrastructure and teams organized to provide defense can also be used to increase an organization's monopoly power.

Economists often distinguish between natural and artificial monopolies, and this distinction is of some relevance for the present analysis. There tends to be both a maximum and minimum efficient-sized service district for a given technology because the cost of the services varies with the technologies of production and distribution. Natural monopolies tend to emerge when there are significant economies of scale in production and a regional market is only large enough to support only a single efficiently sized firm. Similar monopolies may emerge when particular skills or natural resources are available from only a single source within the region of interest because of natural genetic or geological variation. Examples of services that exhibit significant economies of scale include irrigation systems, village defense, theology, dispute settlement, urban planning, education, sanitation services, and social insurance. Regional monopolies also occur when a single organization or cartel controls critical natural resources such as an artesian well or salt mine.

In contrast, artificial monopolies arise when an "entry barrier" is created that allows only privileged organizations or persons to provide particular services in the region of interest. For example, religious services, exports and imports, and military training are often monopolized by making rival organizations illegal. Such barriers to entry tend to induce competition to join privileged groups, which can further increase income, authority, and support within the privileged organizations and groups. The possibility that such barriers can be created or dismantled tends to induce competition for the government's favor, which can be a useful source of in-kind services for regional governments. Monopoly privileges may also be sold or rented to other organizations as an additional source of government revenue (Congleton and Lee 2009).

Artificial monopolies can be created in many ways. A monopolist's rule-making and dispute-resolution services, for example, can be used to enforce requirements that producers of particular products belong to specific clubs or families, or that they obtain special permits from the ruling organization. Monopoly power can also be increased by adopting and enforcing rules that reduce the viability of potential rivals (Lott 1990).

To help pay for fortifications and defensive teams, a monopolist may also rent out well-defended positions to persons in the community when military risks are significant. Indeed, providing community-wide defense services is another area in which monopolies may emerge. Persons whose life or property is at risk are willing to pay very high fees for access to a fortress or redoubt when external security risks are high because exit options are of little value at such times. Those seeking protection are willing to pay essentially any price, which may include promises of cash payments and other services in the future. The implied offer is essentially "your money or your life," although in this case, the monopolist offers a service, rather than a threat. The threat is produce elsewhere.

All these effects imply that a regional monopolist with military power will frequently have a greater organizational surplus than ones without such power. The organization of military force helps monopolists protect and extend their monopolized markets. The highest levels of dispute resolution are often run by the physically strongest organization in a given territory because there are economies of scale in making credible military threats. In such cases, "might" may literally be said to make "right." The confiscatory powers and credible threats associated with military power also make it easier for such organizations to obtain the resources required to sustain their team members and to weather temporary setbacks. Territories may be defended from other military bands and commercial rivals may be prevented from serving particular markets by closing them down through force of arms.

Military power thus tends to increase organizational viability in the short and medium term, as long as mass exodus is not induced and the cost of producing it is not too great.

Military Power and the Dissipation of Monopoly Rents

In the long run, however, success tends to intensify efforts to overthrow territorial governments. The greater are the local monopoly profits and the more prosperous is a given community, the more it pays rivals to invest in internal and external takeovers (Thompson 1974, Tullock 1974). Internal threats may undermine stable governance in the medium run, as noted in Chapter Three. External threats may cause a territorial government to be absorbed into another at great cost to its leaders and their communities.

The winner-take-all nature of external takeovers implies that when conflict occurs, it will generally consume substantial resources. To be prepared for wars of conquest requires significant investments in training, fortifications, and arms. The intense short-term nature of wars also tends to attract the full attention of the government, which tends to reduce its productivity in other areas. Monopoly fees and tariffs tend to rise and productive investments tend to fall as governments shift resources from peaceful to military purposes in order to resist the takeover efforts of rival organizations. Contest theory implies that essentially all of a regional monopoly's profits may be dissipated by such conflict, as in a rent-seeking contest (Congleton, Hillman, and Konrad 2008).

History suggests that such risks are not simply a matter of conjecture. There are many cases in which prosperous communities have been plundered by roving bandits and annexed by rival armies. The high cost of protracted contests are evident in the border conflicts of medieval and early modern Europe, which often took European kings and princes to the verge of bankruptcy (Ertman 1997, Ferguson 2002).

The all-encompassing nature of conflict during times of intensive border conflict helps remind us that military power is not likely to provide an explanation for the origin of civil society, although it does enhance the ability of regional monopolists to impose rules on persons outside their organizations.

Fortunately, the same natural barriers that increase regional monopoly power and increase exit costs also provide a good deal of free defense for many communities around the world. Natural defenses such as mountain ranges, deserts, rivers, and oceans simultaneously increase monopoly power and reduce threats from rivals, which reduces the need for military organization. Great empires have often been assembled by overcoming such national defenses, but the conquests did not create the prosperity that made empire-building a profitable activity.

CONCLUSIONS: AN EXPLANATION FOR THE FORM, BASIS, AND LIMITS OF TERRITORIAL GOVERNMENTS

The ability of territorial monopolists to impose rules on their customers increases their command over resources and thereby provides those organizations with additional resources that can be used to weather difficult times. This makes territorial governments unusually robust and durable organizations. Few organizations last as long as territorial governments, and those that do, such as religious organizations, often have similar monopoly powers and rule-imposing abilities.

Economies of scale in the core services of major territorial monopolies often require, or at least support, relatively large organizations. Territorial governments are often the largest organization within the territory of interest.

The rules enforced by regional governments, like those of other organizations, tend to be stable, but unequal. A rent-extracting regime has little interest in civic or economic equality for its own sake. Some persons are more important to an organization than others, and such persons may be privileged in various ways to encourage their participation in team production and/or residence in the community of interest. Opportunities to profit from price and rule discrimination and from the direct sale of market privileges imply that the prevailing rules will be substantially unequal.

In other respects, regional governments are predicted to be similar to other durable organizations. As true of other organizations, a mixture of pecuniary and nonpecuniary rewards and punishments, as well as local norms, will be used to solve the government's internal (and external) incentive problems. As true of other organizations, the architecture for making governmental policy tends to be drawn from preexisting templates, among which the king-and-council template is prominent. The balance of authority within that template will reflect the origin of the governing organization. If founded by a single formeteur, a good deal of policy-making authority initially will reside with the organization's chief executive – mayor, governor, or king – and somewhat less authority will tend to be available to its council – town council, cabinet, or parliament. If founded as an alliance of local residents or a confederation of regional governments, the council will tend to be the dominant policy-making authority and the chief executive officer will, for the most part, simply implement council decisions.

As true of other organizations, durable territorial governments are predicted to have standing procedures for making policy decisions and for replacing their leaders. Standing procedures for making policy decisions tend to remain in place because of the advantages that those rules have for government leaders and because of uncertainties associated with experimentation. As a consequence, the persons inhabiting the policy-making offices of durable organizations normally change more frequently than the core procedures of governance. As the English saying goes, "The king is dead, long live the king." (Even in cases in which an internal overthrow takes place, the preexisting procedures of governance will be retained for the most part.) Succession problems are often solved by allowing kings and/or councils to appoint one another, or through mechanistic succession based in family bloodlines.

However, regional governments are not free simply to take (or threaten to take) everything from those outside their organizations, if that which to be taken is produced by other organizations in the community, who may exit or refuse to comply. Moreover, a territorial monopoly that has its own interests at heart often has good reason to increase general prosperity, insofar as it profits directly or indirectly from greater demands for its services.

Relevance of the Theoretical Analysis for European History

These predictions are consistent with most historical accounts of regional governments in recorded history, which, it must be acknowledged, were written long after territorial governance and large prosperous communities emerged. Nonetheless, there is substantial evidence that durable governments had stable procedures of succession and stable public policies. There is evidence that privileges of various kinds inside and outside government were commonplace, and to a significant extent, were engineered by regional governments. Regional governments often monopolized important services such as water, salt, dispute resolution, and religion.

There is evidence that mobility was a concern for governments and a balm for community residents. Natural barriers thus influenced the course of political and economic development (Jones 2003). Very large migrations also occasionally took place to escape from governments with reputations for arbitrary rewards and harsh punishments. There is substantial evidence that the king-and-council template for governance was widely used.

It bears noting that many of the properties that allowed territorial governments to emerge remain commonplace in contemporary governments. Their rules are still backed by threats that include denial of services (banishment from the community) and threats to property, life, or limb. Monopoly services are still used as sources of revenue, and government is still based on the king-and-council template.

Of equal significance for the historical purposes of this book is that Chapter Four provides an explanation for the core architecture and policies of national governments in late-medieval Europe and Japan. National governments in Europe and Japan emerged in this period and so were relatively new organizations. In cases in which a single person can be said to have organized the amalgamation of the territories governed, the CEO of the subsequent government was usually dominated by the formeteur, as with the kings of England, France, and Sweden, as well as the Shogun of Japan. In cases in which the government was initially organized as a defense alliance, a council of formeteur representatives tends to be the dominant chamber of government. The Netherlands was founded in the sixteenth century as a defense alliance and initially had a relatively strong council (estates general) and weak executive (*stadhouder*). Similar histories and balances of authority are also evident in Switzerland and the United States.

Medieval laws also treated members of different classes of families differently. Nobles and royals had many privileges. European councils and parliaments were largely populated by "blue bloods," persons from wealthy and privileged families, many of whom held their seats in government as an inherited birthright. Many positions in the military and in the bureaucracy were also reserved for privileged families. Slave and serf families had restrictions that others did not. The members of families in between these extremes had intermediate privileges and restrictions.

A variety of barriers to trade and state monopolies existed within and among the medieval kingdoms. These were often used as revenue sources for the state of interest, as with tariffs and sales of monopoly privileges. By the end of the medieval period, the fiscal foundations of territorial governments began to shift toward tariffs and property taxes, which can be thought of as charges for defense services, although national and regional governments continued to have significant monopoly power over dispute-resolution services, transport networks, potable water, sanitation, law enforcement, and national defense.

Medieval governance was normally supported by a state church with monopoly power over religious and moral theory. "Deviant" ideas (new entrants) were discouraged by widespread norms of deference to religious and state authority. The authority of the medieval church and state were, after all, the consequences of divine intent. To challenge their authority was thus simultaneously blasphemous and traitorous. Informal religious and cultural sanctions were further buttressed by censorship and treason laws enforced in religious and state courts.

FIVE

Constitutional Exchange and Divided Governance

The theory of territorial governance developed in the previous chapters provides an explanation for the existence of territorial governments, why they tend to be rule driven, and why we rarely observe a ruler without an advisory council or a ruling council without a chief executive officer. It also explains why every government tends to have its own relatively stable law of the land and why that law will not generally be the same for all members of the communities ruled. The rules are partly informal (or spontaneous) and partly the result of conscious efforts to adopt and enforce polices that advance organizational interests and, more specifically, the interests of formeteurs and their successors.

To say that governments are constrained by the advantages of stable rules and their own institutional conservatism does not mean that the policy-making procedures and policies of governments are entirely static. Many persons inside governments will have some discretion to make informal adjustments to standing policies at the margins. Moreover, the core procedures of governance may be modified when reforms appear to be useful – that is, when amendments appear to benefit the members of the organization's rule-making bodies.

The authority to make policies and other rules is often divided between a king and a council, because some divisions of authority advance formeteur and/or successor interests. Chapter Two noted that the king-and-council emplate can be used to solve various information problems. Chapter Three suggests that the king-and-council template can also be used to solve a variety of problems associated with succession. This chapter argues that authority-sharing arrangements can also serve as a method for obtaining additional resources or services from persons affiliated with a territorial government, as a method of reducing losses from internal and external conflict, and as a method of obtaining preferred policy outcomes within already divided governments.

Chapters Five and Six also demonstrate that, together, divided government and the multidimensionality of policy and policy-making authority imply that reforms of standing policy-making procedures can be adopted through bargaining and exchange. Advantages that can be realized through particular divisions of policy making authority also suggest that changes in that distribution may be adopted voluntarily through formal and informal amendment procedures when circumstances change.

Within the undivided (unitary) hierarchical governments favored by Hobbes and many others, there are few opportunities for constitutional exchange, because by definition, only one formal assignment of policy-making authority is possible. The sovereign always retains complete control over policy. Even in such organizations, however, it is possible to reallocate delegated authority among offices to take advantage of the talents and interests of persons in the organization, although such changes formally require the approval of the sovereign and can be changed by the sovereign at will.

Within divided governments the degree of control and distribution of authority among policy areas can be varied among persons and centers of policy-making authority. For example, within the king-and-council template, policy-making authority can be divided between the king and council, policy-by-policy. The authority of individual council members can also be varied, for example, by using weighted voting, by giving subsets of council members additional agenda control, or by dividing the parliament into separate chambers with more or less veto and agenda control. These institutional variations create numerous possibilities for dividing up and shifting policy-making authority.

Specific divisions of authority have more or less predictable effects on policy outcomes, which justify the use of particular designs and also provide a possible basis for constitutional bargaining and reform. As in ordinary markets, it will at least occasionally be possible for policy-making authority to be reallocated among insiders in a manner that advances the interests of all those whose authority is changed.

This chapter analyzes gains to trade that can be realized by sharing policy-making authority and by reassignments of agenda control and veto power within the king-and-council template. It notes advantages and disadvantages for the parties involved in the constitutional bargaining and demonstrates that cases exist in which a reassignment of authority can advance the interests of all those at the bargaining table. The analysis focuses on standing territorial governments that have passed beyond their formeteur stage and so are led by persons who take the organization's present assignment of power as given. In such cases, the initial assignments of policy-making authority can be regarded as initial endowments of political property rights that can be traded, whether the status quo distribution of authority is characterized in writing or not. The result will often be forms of government that depart from the near polar cases of king-dominated and council-dominated governance.

SHARED SOVEREIGNTY AS A METHOD OF INCREASING ORGANIZATIONAL RESOURCES

The persons who have the authority to adjust an organization's standing procedures for making policy decisions are normally all insiders who occupy the highest policy-making offices within the organizations of interest. Insiders, as noted earlier, have many reasons to support the existing procedures and assignments of policy-making authority. However, this does not mean that they are opposed to all changes in the procedures through which their organization's policies are chosen, nor does it imply that they are always opposed to changes in the procedures through which high officials in their organization are selected. Institutional conservatism simply implies that they will be opposed to *most* such reforms and tend to prefer modest reforms to major ones.

A Market for "Power": Sharing Policy-Making Authority to Obtain Organizational Resources

Organizational effectiveness can occasionally be increased by trading policy-making authority for additional organizational resources. For example, in the case of our illustrative pear cooperative and cherry-picking firm, prospective team members with ladders or those who are especially adept at climbing trees may be more willing to participate in the annual harvests of these organizations if they have some veto authority over the use of the ladders or the trees to which they are assigned. Exit is, of course, always possible if they are misused, but risk of damages (broken ladders and legs) can be reduced by giving such valuable team members the right to participate in decisions regarding the use of their ladders and assignments to particular tree tops.

Similarly, a regional government that confronts external threats from pirates or Vikings may benefit from the use of commercial ships in defense of their communities. The owners of such ships, however, may be unwilling to allow their ships to be entirely subject to the command of the regional

Table 5.1. *Gains from Sharing Authority Game*

		Organizational leadership		
		No authority	Shared authority	Complete authority
	Complete authority	8, 10	–	–
Potential team member	Shared authority	–	10, 12	–
	No authority	–	–	6, 14

government. They might fear, for example, that the government would assign their ships to the most dangerous missions while holding the government's own ships in reserve. Granting the commercial ship owners some veto authority, or at least the ability to influence how their ships will be employed, may make them more willing to allow their ships to be used for regional defense.

Table 5.1 illustrates patterns of risk and rewards that can lead to authority-sharing bargains in such cases. The initial state is the one characterized by the upper-left-hand cell, in which the resource is entirely controlled by the potential team member. The organization's leadership is better off if it obtains complete control over the prospective team member's resources, rather than shared or no control (14 > 12 > 10). The prospective team member is better off with shared control than with complete or no control (10 > 8 > 6), because retaining complete control requires sacrificing advantages from team production. Giving up complete control, however, places his or her resources at greater risk than under shared control.

Both the organization's leadership and the prospective team member benefit from shared control in this case. There are gains to trade that can be realized by sharing policy-making authority in a fairly narrow range of the organization's activities. The organization has additional output (more pears, more cherries, or better defense), and the prospective team member profits from the advantages of team production while avoiding some risks associated with delegating control to an organization's leadership.

Similar gains from sharing authority may also exist when organizations or communities decide to merge their governments to realize economies of scale, diversify risks, or reduce transactions costs (Congleton, Kyriacou, and Bacaria 2003). In such cases, sharing policy-making authority allows the interests of the merging organizations or communities to be protected against rent extraction by the other, while the additional joint output or reduced risks make governmental officeholders better off. (Mutual advantages are, of course, necessary for a voluntary exchange of authority to take place at the level of organizations or governments.)

SHARED SOVEREIGNTY AS A METHOD OF REDUCING LOSSES FROM CONFLICT

Similar gains to trade may also arise in settings in which control over resources is disputed. Conflict over control of resources does not always involve violence or threats of revolution, but always tends to reduce organizational output and surplus by diverting time, attention, and other scarce resources from other productive activities. Losses tend to arise from both civil and noncivil conflict. Such losses are naturally taken into account when an organization is initially formed and when reward and governance systems are reformed through time, as was noted in Chapter Three's analysis of succession and overthrow problems.

The game matrix characterized in Table 5.2 characterizes an asymmetric contest in which two parties clash over the control of some policy, territory, theology, or ideology. The case of interest is one in which the weaker of the two parties is able to resist the stronger, and complete control is costly for the stronger party to implement. The Nash equilibrium of this game implies that both parties devote resources to the contest because each party's private payoff increases as it invests more resources in the conflict, other things being equal. The weaker party benefits from resisting the stronger party because resistance achieves a better result than unconditional surrender, which may simply be the pride of having resisted the takeover.

The Nash equilibrium implies that existing procedures for adopting policies are suboptimal for both the strong and weak parties. Eight units of resources are wasted in conflict at the Nash equilibrium [8 = (6 + 14) – (2 + 10)]. As in a conventional rent-seeking contest, both parties would be better off if they could alter the contest so that they achieve the same result without using so many resources in conflict.

One possible solution is to revise the rules of the game in a manner that changes the nature of the conflict in a manner that benefits both players (Buchanan 1975, Congleton 1980, North 1987). For example, the leader of a conquering army may exchange local autonomy to well-run communities in exchange for veto power over local foreign policies and tax (tribute) payments in order to avoid an expensive conquest. Alternatively, a new

Table 5.2. *Asymmetric Power Game*

		Stronger party		
		Little aggression	Moderate aggression	Intense aggression
Weaker party	Little resistance	6, 14	3, 16	0, 18
	Moderate resistance	7, 10	4, 12	1, 14
	Intense resistance	8, 8	5, 9	2, 10

council representing the interests of the weaker party might be formed and given limited control over future policy with partial agenda control or veto power (Congleton 2004b, 2007a). Or the weaker party may be given seats in an existing council and/or additional votes within that council. Insofar as conflict within political institutions tends to be less costly than on the battlefield (or within an organization's production teams), adopting such procedures tends be advantageous for both parties.[1]

An effective collective-choice mechanism does not eliminate all losses from conflict, but reduces its cost by inducing more civil forms of rivalry (Congleton 1980). Persuasion and coalition building may replace warfare on the battlefield or assassination and counter-assassination (Hobbes 1959, Bush 1972, and Buchanan 1975). The same logic also implies that changes in circumstances that create new conflicts may also induce changes in a preexisting distribution of policy-making authority. Modest procedural reforms do not require existential threats to advance the interests of pragmatic governmental leaders.

THE GEOMETRY OF DIVIDED AUTHORITY WITHIN KING-AND-COUNCIL GOVERNMENTS

Within the king-and-council template, policy-making authority can be shared in many ways, and control over particular policy areas can be subdivided in even more ways. For example, a person or committee might have

[1] See Congleton, Kyriacou, and Bacaria (2003) for an analysis of bargaining between central and regional governments.

complete control over specific policy areas and none in other areas. Control may be shared in some areas and complete in others.

Shared control may entail different assignments of veto power and agenda control over some or all policy areas. A person or committee may be said to have partial control if possessing veto power, but not agenda control, or when veto power and agenda control are distributed among several decision makers or centers of authority. Complete control over an area of public policy can be said to exist if a single decision maker or decision-making body has both complete veto power and agenda control in that area of policy. Such persons can choose which possibilities to consider and unilaterally decide whether to accept or reject them.

Constitutional gains to trade between the king and the council emerge when reassignments of agenda, veto power, or jurisdiction are mutually beneficial. Such gains can emerge entirely within the domain of policy assignments or may arise when money (tax receipts, for example) or other services are traded for authority.

There are two choice settings of interest. In some cases, the parliament or council may not have its own policy agenda. In others, it may. With respect to the former, Black (1948) and Arrow (1963) demonstrate that committees that choose policies using majority rule will not always be able to reach a final decision because of majoritarian cycles. With respect to the latter, there are cases in which council-member ideal points are identical, linear, or symmetrically arrayed, in which case the cycling problem will not exist, as noted by Black (1987) and Plott (1967). In such cases, the council will make consistent recommendations and consistently exercise its veto power. Such alignments produce "decisive councils," rather than nondecisive ones.[2]

Veto and Agenda Control with Decisive Councils

Consider, first, a near-polar case in which the king confronts a small, decisive council. An example of a "decisive" alignment of council preferences

[2] The cyclic majority problem can also be avoided through various institutional devices, as has been noted by Shepsle (1979), Shepsle and Weingast (1981), and Baron and Ferejohn (1989), among others. In cases in which cycle-majority (and the related majority-coalition instability) problems are avoided through institutions the analysis would parallel that of the decisive committee analysis below. The cyclic-majority examples indirectly suggest that an executive (king) may profit by blocking reforms that eliminate cycles or stabilize coalitions and so strengthen the council. Although there is considerable evidence that parliaments and royal councils are reasonably stable in their policy preferences, there is also evidence of cycling through time (as with tax reform) and also of executives playing factions against each other.

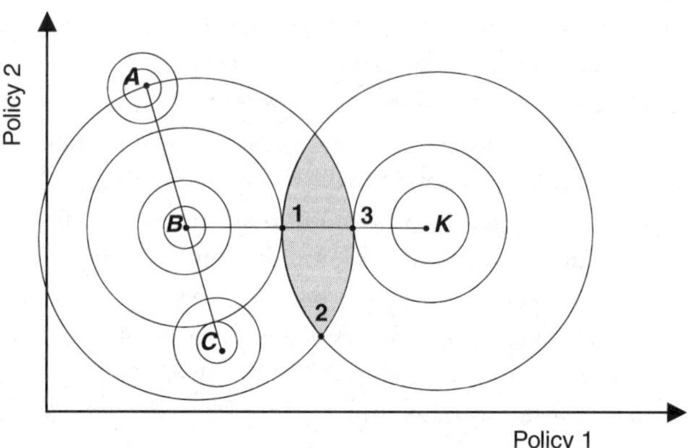

Figure 5.1. Effects of veto and agenda power.

is depicted in Figure 5.1, with the three committee members' ideal points lying on a straight line and denoted with the capital letters *A*, *B*, *C*. The ideal point of the king is denoted with the letter K. Assume that initially the king has complete control over both dimensions of policy and that the initial policy is thus his ideal point K.

The king is assumed to exercise complete control over two separate dimensions of policy and is considering transferring some veto power or agenda control to the council. Whenever political circumstances are stable, the king can shift either veto power or agenda control to the council at essentially no cost. Note that if the king gives the council veto authority and retains agenda control, he can propose K, which confronts the council with a "choice" between K and K. Because only K is possible, K continues as the law of the land, regardless of whether the council vetoes the policy or not. On the other hand, if the council is granted agenda control rather than veto power, the king can veto any proposal made by council to move away from K.

In stable times, retaining either agenda control or veto power is sufficient to protect the king from reforms that would make him worse off.

The other polar case is that in which a decisive council initially has both agenda control and veto power. In that case, the initial policy is *B* (the median council member's ideal point). In stable circumstances, a decisive council can also share policy-making authority with the king at little cost. Note that if the council gives the king (CEO) agenda control, the pivotal council member can use veto power to block any policy proposal by the king that makes the median council member worse off. On the other hand, if the council gives the king veto power and retains agenda control, it can simply propose that policy *B* be continued, and policy combination *B* will remain in place regardless of the king's veto, since B is also the reversion point.

Either branch of government's ideal point can be defended as long as it has either veto or agenda control and circumstances are stable in the sense that the policy preferences of high officials do not change during the period of interest. In stable settings, sharing power with the weaker branch of government is surprisingly inexpensive for the initially stronger branch. The willingness of the weaker branch to purchase authority from the stronger, however, would consequently be very limited in stable times, unless the weaker chamber expects more turbulent times to emerge in the near future.

Sharing Power with Decisive Councils in Unstable Times

During unstable periods, policy interests may change and power-sharing arrangements will affect the policy adjustments that can be made. Suppose that political circumstances change in a manner that affects officeholder policy preferences. A change of ideal points, for example, often occurs at times of succession, because policy preferences are not entirely induced by institutional factors. Scientific advance may also change policy rankings by producing new estimates of the consequences of policies. Technological advance may allow formerly impossible policies to become possible and necessary.

Suppose that prior to the change in circumstances, the status quo (reversion point) had been policy combination 2 in Figure 5.1, which should now be interpreted as the ideal point of the previously dominant branch of government. The ideal points characterized by the indifference curves of the king and council should now be interpreted as those associated with their new ideal points. In the absence of a veto by the weaker chamber, the stronger chamber will simply adopt its new ideal point as the official policy of the realm, K or B, according to which chamber is dominant. However, if the weaker chamber has veto power, it can now block such moves.

The policies that can be proposed by the agenda setter without being vetoed are identified by the shaded lens or football-shaped area. Note that the presumed status-quo policy combination 2 is preferred by the king to B, and by the median council member to K. In the new setting, the best result that a king with agenda control can achieve is policy 3, given the veto power of the council. In the converse regime, the best policy that an agenda-setting council can hope for, given the veto power of the executive, is policy 1.

In unstable circumstances, the consequences of alternative assignments of veto power and agenda control are no longer identical. The party with agenda control does better relative to the party with veto power in the illustration, although neither party is able to obtain their ideal policy.

These cases also demonstrate that policy tends to be more stable within divided forms of the king-and-council template than in polar forms because shifts in policy tend to be smaller. The geometry of Figure 5.1 implies that the policy shifts induced by political shocks are often smaller, and cannot be larger, than those which would have been adopted under either polar form of governance. (A movement from 2 to either 1 or 3 is smaller than a movement from 2 to either K or B.) Insofar as stable policies tend to promote economic growth by, for example, making the legal and regulatory framework more predictable, divided governments may help promote economic development in an uncertain world.

Veto Power and Agenda Control with Nondecisive Councils

Consider next the case in which the council is "nondecisive" in the sense that no pivotal voter exists. The geometry of Figure 5.2 illustrates a case in which the preferred policies of council members are such that they cannot make a final decision because of majoritarian cycles. Cycles of this sort are observable to those outside government as a lack of decisiveness. Such councils may be regarded as weak, factional, or disorganized. Every possible proposal can be defeated by some counter-proposal.

In such cases, it can be argued that only one division of agenda control and veto power is possible: nondecisive councils can exercise veto power but cannot exercise agenda control. Given a nondecisive council, the executive branch can use agenda control to obtain very good results for the king (or queen).[3] To see this, suppose that a political or technological shock has changed the ideal points of the council and/or king so that the status-quo policy is neither the ideal point of the king nor in the Pareto set of the council. For purposes of illustration, assume that the status quo is again policy 2, which is Pareto-dominated for council members by policies within lens-shaped area P. However, if the council uses majority rule rather than consensus to make decisions, a king with agenda control can propose policy 3, which will secure majority approval over policy 2.

[3] This point was first developed by Schap (1986), although his analysis differs somewhat from that developed here.

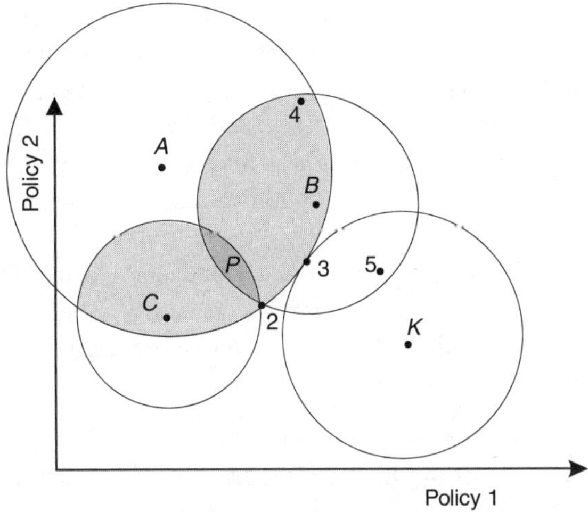

Figure 5.2. Agenda control with a weak council.

Policy combination 3 is a stable outcome only until the king can propose another policy. Indeed, the king can propose a series of policy proposals that allows his ideal policy combination to be realized – notwithstanding the veto power of the council (McKelvy 1976). In effect, the king plays the three council factions off one another, which occasionally require the king to sacrifice his own interests strategically in the short run, as with proposal 4 rather than 3, which allows the more desirable policy combination 5 to be achieved in the next round.

How long such governmental deliberations might take in real historical time is beyond the scope of the present analysis, but this possibility suggests that a strong, forward-looking king faced by a weak (nondecisive) council can offer veto power in exchange for council acquiescence on other pressing issues, or as compensation for service to the sovereign at a very low cost in both stable and unstable circumstances. Nondecisive alignments of council interests allow kings to use agenda control to achieve their own ends, perhaps surprisingly, without undermining the council's veto power over new policies.

Constitutional Barter

A forward-looking council can rationally make concessions to the king or provide extraordinary services in exchange for veto power or agenda control whenever they anticipate future circumstances in which the council will be both decisive and able to constrain the choices of the king. (Indeed, a council or parliament may modify its internal procedures to make it more likely to be decisive [Congleton and Tollision, 1999].) In the long run, such constitutional contracts can provide a future decisive council, however unlikely, with greater authority over public policy than even a hard-pressed king would have agreed to.

As will be seen in Part II of this book, such decisive councils did emerge in the eighteenth and nineteenth centuries, as new economic interests, new ideological interests, and new politically active organizations affected the policy preferences of those holding seats in parliament.

Constitutional Bargaining and Royal Secession

Another systematic source of drift away from executive control is variation in the talent, age, and planning horizon of kings and queens through time. The bargaining positions and constitutional interests of kings tend to vary during their time in office. The interests of young and old kings often differ because of age and energy, but also because of training, education, and experience. New sovereigns tend to depend more on the judgment of their advisors than experienced sovereigns; and they are also less familiar with the biases of their advisors and the negotiating techniques of their councils and parliaments. Young kings have worldviews that are shaped by their tutors rather than by past experience in real policy settings. Older kings may also rely heavily on their advisors when their health fails or their interest in day-to-day politics fades.

The vagaries of training, tastes, and genetics suggest that the talent and interests of successive kings and queens also tend to vary through time. (Substantial evidence exists of reversion toward the mean in the children of talented persons.) Countries thus can be fortunate or unfortunate in the persons who accede to the throne at times when major reform issues arise, as historians often emphasize.

In contrast, competition for membership in the royal council and parliament tends to be relatively open and intense, so the talent of councils and parliaments remains relatively high and constant through time. A disinterested or relatively untalented king may be out-bargained by his relatively energetic and talented prime minister and/or members of parliament. Even if an ambitious and talented king is able to recapture most of the authority given up by less engaged forebears, genetic trends produce a systematic drift away from direct royal control of public policy, other things being equal.

Executive councils (cabinets) and prime ministers are normally the direct beneficiaries of royal delegation during such periods, especially prior to the nineteenth century. Parliaments, nonetheless, indirectly benefit from genetic trends, insofar as executive councils are chosen from members of parliament, prime ministers need continued support in parliament to obtain the policies required to keep the sovereign's support. Parliamentary bargaining power also tends to increase in cases in which the next person in line for the crown is less than perfectly obvious because this allows the terms of the next elevation to be controlled by parliament. Parliaments never unexpectedly die, although important members may. Part II discusses several such cases.

Divisions of Authority through Time: Random Walk or Trend?

To this point, we have explored three possible settings in which policy-making authority may be adjusted through a process of constitutional exchange. At any moment in time, most such gains from trade will already have been realized because doing so advances the interests of most of the persons involved. New gains from trade may occasionally arise when technologies change, when ideology changes, when the persons occupying high office change, or when new military threats emerge.

Technological Shocks

Changes in the patterns of trade or warfare may affect the relative cost of maintaining control over the polity and also the extent of information needed to make good policy decisions. When economic development takes place in towns and cities, the greater population densities of cities allows industrialists, tradesmen, and laborers to more easily organize to resist and advocate public policies. Prosperous towns may also be willing to pay more for autonomy. Insofar as the parliament represents those interests more than the king, this tends to favor parliaments in constitutional negotiations. In some cases, it is cheaper to cede a bit more authority to local governments or parliament than to suppress local resistance. In others, increased payments from urban centers may more than offset modest reductions in central government authority. When technological advance reduces the cost of overcoming resistance or reduce urban wealth, royal authority tends to be favored. When the complexity of policy analysis increases, the value added by the advice of councilors tends to increase.[4]

Ideological Shocks

Changes in the positive and normative theories of governance can similarly affect the costs of control and/or willingness to pay for additional policy-making authority by changing the norms against which current institutions are assessed. Ideological shifts may also reduce the costs of organizing formerly unorganized groups in a manner that increases support for (or resistance to) particular reforms and policies. Moreover, as ideology increases in importance, councils are more likely to be decisive because liberal-conservative political spectrums tend to be fundamentally one-dimensional (Poole and Rosenthal 1991). As ideology declines in importance, councils are less likely to be decisive, which tends to increase royal control over public policy.

Genetic Shocks

A systematic source of drift toward council and parliamentary control of policy making is variation in the talent or planning horizon of kings. Insofar as competition for membership in the council and parliament is generally more open and intense than that for king – particularly in dynasties – the talent of the council and parliament tends to be high and fairly consistent through time. In contrast, the vagaries of training and breeding imply that the talent and interests of kings tend to vary considerably through time. Less ambitious or talented kings may simply allow a relatively talented council to make more and more policy decisions directly. A weak king may be simply out-bargained by a talented council or parliament. A farsighted or forceful king may not be able to fully recapture the authority given up by his weaker forebears, because of deference to tradition and precedent.

If technological, ideological, and genetic shocks occur randomly, the division of power between king and council would tend to resemble a random walk. During some periods, the executive will increase control over policy; during others, the council or parliament will gain authority as political shocks change the bargaining positions of king and council and the reversion points of policy. Through time, one would expect to observe

[4] Evidence of the importance of how technological developments may affect political organization is developed in Dudley (2000, 1991), who argues that informational technologies can affect the size and scope of national governments. Although his analysis emphasizes technological change rather than the use of advisory councils and parliaments, his analysis of the effects of information technologies is very much in spirit of that developed here.

all constellations of authority within a single polity, as has been the case in European history. Trends in constitutional exchange, however, require trends in constitutionally relevant shocks.

Institutional Conservatism of Territorial Governments as Shock Absorption

As monopolists, regional governments normally face far less competition for resources than most other organizations. This means that the incentives for governments to alter their decision-making procedures and reward systems tend to be somewhat weaker than for most other organizations – although formeteurs and their successors remain interested in reforms that improve the efficiency of their organizations insofar as this is likely to increase the expected rewards of office. The durability of regional governments also implies that more policy decisions are made by successors than formeteurs: successors tend to be relatively more dependent on existing procedures and routines for their positions of authority and so are less prone to experiment than are the organization's founders (formeteurs). The reforms that regional governments adopt, consequently, tend to be relatively infrequent and are relatively modest ones that advance insider interests, rather than great revolutionary reforms that advance the interests of outsiders.

A territorial government's relatively great control over resources implies that its top officials are subject to fewer exogenous shocks that can only be survived by adopting major reforms. Even in cases in which reforms are literally imposed by external military events, preexisting institutions and interests are rarely ignored. Terms of surrender are usually negotiated by losing governments, and, predictably, the terms of surrender tend to reflect the interests of the officials sitting around the negotiation table. In cases in which internal military events such as a civil war or coup d'état induce a change in government, preexisting templates for governance are normally retained rather than revolutionized: a change of leadership takes place rather than a wholesale change of institutions. Institutional conservatism is nearly as appealing for those taking over existing organizations as for those who inherit them.

Indeed, there are cases in which the purpose of a revolution is the restoration of older institutions. For example, England's medieval constitution was restored twice during civil wars of the seventeenth century, once after Cromwell failed to find a sustainable alternative, and once through force of arms to restore its former balance of authority, including parliament's long-standing veto power over taxes. The first is called the *Restoration* and the second is called the *Glorious Revolution*. (See Chapter Twelve.)

CONCLUSIONS: DIVISIONS OF AUTHORITY WITHIN THE KING-AND-COUNCIL TEMPLATE

A central claim of this book is that constitutional bargaining accounts for most of the reforms adopted in the eighteenth, nineteenth, and twentieth centuries that gradually produced Western democracy. Chapter Two suggests that the division of policy-making authority within organizations often begins with delegation: various day-to-day policy decisions are delegated to team members, who in large organizations may have limited authority to make rules that bind others. Chapter Five suggests that divided governments may also arise through constitutional bargains that increase the resources available or reduce the costs of conflict within or between organizations. Constitutional barter also may occur among insiders, as interests in particular policies or the relative talent of the council and king change through time.

Historians, political scientists, and economists often neglect the ebb and flow of authority within king-and-council systems and focus on the dominant part of government. They may, for example, ignore the existence of royalty after parliaments begin to dominate policy making or ignore parliaments and councils when dominant kings or queens occupy the throne. Partially because of such neglect, neither the possibility of constitutional exchange within divided governments nor the continua of policy-making authority have received much attention in the rational-choice-based political science and political economy literatures.

Indeed, even the properties of divided governments have largely been neglected. With respect to the latter, Schap (1986) and Carter and Schap (1987) demonstrate that an executive veto can affect the decisions of a legislature and policy outcomes in general. They also demonstrate that an executive veto can contribute to stability in policy choices. Persson, Roland, and Tabellini (1997) demonstrate that electoral feedback can induce a divided government to adopt policies that are more favorable to voters than would have been adopted by unified governments when candidates are not systematically different with respect to policy preferences. Dixit, Grossman, and Faruk (2000) analyze self-enforcing divisions of political or economic surplus between two parties within a democracy that interact repeatedly through time; they find that stable rules for dividing a nation's resources can emerge in a divided government that is entirely self-interested, but whose relative power shifts randomly through time.

These important lines of research, however, assume that the division of policy-making power is exogenous for the purposes of analysis. Taking institutions as given is a reasonable assumption for short- and medium-run analysis. Institutional conservatism, as noted earlier, implies that most policy making procedures tend to be stable for long periods of time. In the long run, standing procedures may be revised as external or internal conditions change, and the effects may be important.[5]

To entirely neglect relatively weak branches of government and the possibility of constitutional reform clearly understates their influence on policy in the long run, because the weaker branch of government may be able to use its limited authority to obtain additional authority in favorable circumstances. The advice of advisory councils has to be accepted now and then if serious advice is to be obtained. Prime ministers and cabinet members have to be delegated authority to be effective and so normally have some discretion to implement the instructions of their kings and/or legislatures (Niskanen 1968; Breton and Wintrobe 1975).

Focusing exclusively on the polar cases of governance also tends to make one forget that intermediate cases exist and that transitions from royal to parliamentary dominance can be gradual rather than sudden. Historians that focus on the dominant branch of government often give readers the impression that a major change always occurs when a formerly weaker branch becomes dominant. The present analysis suggests that such changes may occur from relatively minor shifts of policy-making authority, albeit ones sufficient to cause a particular historian to conclude that a new branch of government has become dominant. The intermediate cases provide a continuum through which small but significant reforms of government policy-making procedures can take place.

In practice, some specific constitutional bargaining settings and bargains are historically more important than others. One of the most important is taken up in the next Chapter, in which the origins and effects of parliament's "power of the purse" are analyzed.

[5] Even the *Federalist Papers*, a pioneering study of divided governance, focus on a particular division of authority without analyzing alternatives in much detail. A useful counterexample that is relevant for king-and-council models is Dicey's (1887) overview of the manner in which the powers of royal councils ebbed and flowed during the late middle ages and early modern period.

SIX

The Power of the Purse and Constitutional Reform

The theories of governance and constitutional bargaining developed in the previous chapters provide a rational-choice explanation for the general architecture of European governance, for peaceful reforms of parliament, and for the existence of divided governance. To more fully account for the transition to the contemporary architecture of Western democracy, however, requires analysis of specific aspects of governance: in particular, those dealing with fiscal authority and the manner in which members of parliament are selected. This is undertaken in the next three chapters. Chapter Six provides an explanation for the medieval power of the purse and analyzes how it can be used to obtain additional policy-making authority for parliament. Chapters Seven and Eight analyze possible reforms of election-based methods for selecting members of parliament.

Regional governments have the ability to impose binding rules and fees (taxes) on persons throughout their territories. Their ability to tax – perhaps unexpectedly – provides additional economic reasons for divided governance and additional opportunities for constitutional exchange. To analyze these possibilities, the models of Chapter Five are extended and developed in a more mathematical form. As a consequence, Chapter Six is a long and somewhat technical chapter. The prose provides the intuition behind the mathematics and helps explain the results. Examples from European history are again used to motivate the analysis.

ORIGINS OF THE MEDIEVAL PARLIAMENT'S LIMITED POWER OF THE PURSE

As a point of departure, again assume that a king-dominated form of the king-and-council template is in place: one-man rule with an advisory council. The council may be used as a source of information and advice, but it plays no direct role in policy formation. The king can collect any taxes that he wishes and spend the money as he sees fit without taking account of the policy interests of his advisors or others outside government. The ability to tax and spend as the king wishes creates problems analogous to those represented in Tables 5.1 and 5.2, although this may not be evident at first.

Territorial governments nearly always want additional tax revenue, but government cannot simply use its coercive authority to obtain additional revenues, because the size of the tax base is largely controlled by taxpayers. New tax collections may be resisted by, for example, working less hard, investing less, or exit. More militant forms of tax revolt are also possible. In such cases, allowing taxpayers some control over fiscal policy may allow additional revenues to be collected. Such constitutional bargains account for a particular division of authority between kings and parliaments that was common in late-medieval Europe. It turns out that that division of authority played a central role in the rise of parliament-dominated governance many centuries later.

Because this division of authority is historically so important in Europe and because a continuum of tax rates can be adopted, the fiscal problem and potential gains from sharing authority over tax policies are analyzed using somewhat more general mathematical models. For purposes of analysis, assume that the king and taxpayers have similar utility functions defined over their own private consumption, X, and two government services, guns, G_1, and butter, G_2. Both the king and taxpayers benefit from the public services provided. Their wealth is protected by the army and walls. They benefit from public services such as road networks, potable water supplies, and a royal court system. Such services increase private (nongovernmental) wealth and also enlarge the tax base. However, only the king directly benefits from his private consumption expenditures.

$$U = u(X, G_1, G_2) \tag{6.1a}$$

The king's budget constraint is determined by his own household wealth, W, which is usually considerable and the present discounted values of the taxes that he levies, T, which are used to pay for the cost of government services, $C = c(G_1, G_2)$, and his personal consumption, X. Using personal consumption as the numéraire good allows the royal budget constraint to be written as $T + W = X + c(G_1, G_2)$, or

$$X = T + W - c\left(G_1, G_2\right) \tag{6.2}$$

where c is a separable convex cost function of the two government services. Substituting for personal consumption yields

$$U = u(T + W - c(G_1, G_2), G_1, G_2) \tag{6.1b}$$

Differentiating with respect to the control variables T, G_1, and G_2 yields the following first-order conditions that characterize the unfettered king's preferred long-term fiscal policy:

$$U_{G_1} - U_x C_{G_1} = 0 \tag{6.3}$$

$$U_{G_2} - U_x C_{G_2} = 0 \tag{6.4}$$

$$U_x = 0 \tag{6.5}$$

The first two first-order conditions imply that the king sets public service levels so that the marginal utility of the service equals its marginal cost in terms of his diminished personal consumption of the private good. This implies that taxes will be collected until the marginal utility of his additional personal consumption falls to zero.

Credible Commitments and Constitutional Gains to Trade

Unfortunately, the marginal utility of consumption reaches zero only if the king has sufficient household and tax revenue to *achieve satiety in all goods.* ($U_x = 0$ implies that both U_{G_1} and U_{G_2} also equal zero at the utility-maximizing public policy.) Whether this is feasible or not depends on the king's preferences and the extent to which tax revenue can be squeezed from the kingdom. The tax base of the kingdom is clearly constrained by the wealth of the kingdom, which in most cases derives from the productive abilities and efforts of the king's subjects as well as the country's endowment of natural resources.

If the king's tastes are such that satiation does not occur within the feasible range of the kingdom's output, he will be disposed to tax away or otherwise extract the entire surplus of the kingdom. (The "surplus" is the total economic output of the kingdom above that required to retain its residents, which clearly requires at least subsistence levels of income for those producing the outputs taxed.)

Unfortunately for the king, if every subject in the kingdom expects all of their production above subsistence to be taken by the government, there is no private incentive to produce a taxable surplus and none will be produced.[1]

[1] This is intuitively obvious, and can easily be demonstrated. Consider a typical farmer-taxpayer whose utility is $U = u(L, Y)$ where $Y = (1-t)f(H-L, G_1, G_2)$, t is the marginal tax rate, f is the taxpayer's strictly convex production function of farm output, L is leisure, and H is the available hours in the day. $H-L = W$, the hours spent farming. Y can be regarded

To obtain the hypothetically maximal tax revenue, the king must essentially enslave the entire population of the kingdom. Exit must be blocked and a centralized system of command and control over all economic activities adopted. If neither generalized slavery nor central administration is a useful strategy – because they are inefficient, very expensive to implement, or impossible – the king's control over tax revenues will be less than absolute, even though he has complete control over tax instruments and rates.[2]

Granting Veto Power to a Council of Taxpayers

The possibility of peaceful tax resistance is sufficient to create an opportunity for constitutional exchange between a nearly all-powerful king and those who pay the taxes.

In exchange for a commitment to take only a specific fraction of the surplus, the subjects might agree to provide more tax revenue by producing more surplus. To make the promised tax system credible, the king may also promise to seek the approval of those taxed before increasing tax rates in the future. Institutionalizing veto power over new taxation helps make the promise of leviathan credible. For example, veto power might be vested in a tax council that represents the interests of (major) taxpayers.

The royal advantage secured by a standing tax council can easily be demonstrated. In the absence of a tax council with veto power, the process of taxation can be represented as a three-stage game. In the first stage, the king announces a tax rate; in the second, the subjects produce their output; in the third, the king collects the taxes. In a one-shot game, the king would announce a very low tax in period 1, but subsequently, take the entire surplus produced in period 3 regardless of the tax announced in period 1. Forward-looking subjects would anticipate the final confiscatory tax and produce no taxable surplus. Consequently, the king's tax revenue in period 3 would be zero in equilibrium.

Constitutional gains to trade are clear. Any tax institution that increases the expected after-tax income of taxpayers and produces additional revenue for the king makes all better off.

as income greater than subsistence income. The taxpayers work $H-L^*$ hours, and L^* is such that $U_L - U_Y(1-t)F_W = 0$. Note that given U monotone increasing, twice differentiable, and concave, whenever t = 100 percent, a corner solution emerges with $L^* = H$. If subsistence output, $Y = Y^s > 0$, is required to survive, maximal leisure is $L^* > H - f^{-1}(Y^s)$ for given G_1 and G_2.

2 Note that a lump-sum tax cannot be truly neutral when it is bounded by production of the taxable base and/or other exit possibilities exist. Farmers will produce a surplus only when the net of tax utility realized after tax is greater than that associated with subsistence and exit.

The creation of a council with veto power over tax increases is one such institution. It transforms the three-stage game into a four-stage game. In the fourth stage, the council may veto any increase in taxes announced by the king in period 3, causing tax rates to revert to those announced in period 1.[3]

In the four-stage game with a council veto over tax increases, an income-maximizing king, who is constrained to use particular tax instruments such as a proportional tax, will announce the proportional tax rate in period 1 that maximizes net tax receipts, given the productive propensities of his subjects. Because the revenue-maximizing tax rate is less than 100 percent, the subjects produce a surplus above subsistence, knowing that they will be able to keep a part of it, and the king collects taxes according to the announced tax schedule.[4]

It bears noting that *no vetoes will be observed* when the system is working smoothly; consequently, such councils may well appear to be toothless. Nonetheless, in the absence of the council's veto power over new taxes, both the king and the kingdom would have been substantially poorer. The mutual advantages achieved by this constitutional reform are clear. Moreover, once enacted, the king has incentives to abide by the new procedures.

The medieval tax constitution is surprisingly stable once in place because the institutional structure is (often) subgame perfect.[5] The king cannot formally reduce the veto power of the council without substantially undermining the tax base. For example, the king cannot simply add another stage to the game in which the king can accept or reject the council's veto. In such a game, an income-maximizing king would always be inclined to raise taxes in period 3 and then overturn the council's veto in period 5, taking the entire surplus. Production would again fall to near subsistence levels, and/or mass emigration might be induced; the taxable base would again approach zero.

Nor can the king occasionally renege on his assignment of veto power to the council by suddenly calling out the army, because his future tax receipts

3 Taxpayer utility always diminishes in t whenever tax receipts are increased to support additional consumption for the royal household. Given $U = u(L, Y)$ and $Y = (1-t) f(H-L, G_1, G_2)$, after tax utility can be written as $U^* = u(L^*, (1-t)f(H-L^*, G_1^*, G_2^*))$. The envelope theorem implies that $U_t^* = U_Y[-f(H-L^*)] < 0$.

4 An early economic analysis of the effects of alternative constraints on the royal tax base and choice of tax instruments is developed by Brennan and Buchanan (1977, 1980).

5 Tax rebellions, for example, are often consequences of efforts to add new tax bases or to increase taxes substantially on existing taxes. Such rebellions are not always violent, military affairs, but simply widespread refusal to abide by the new laws (Cohn 2004, Adams 1998).

would likely fall in future periods. Producers would simply discount the constitutional promise and produce less to be taxed in future periods, or they would emigrate to other communities where constitutional promises are kept. The anticipated interventions of the army or royal tax collectors thus increase the effective rate of taxation beyond the long-term revenue-maximizing rate.

The taxpayer response to confiscatory taxation – reduced production or exit – is credible as long as production is a costly activity for the subjects, exit is possible, and the king is not able to reduce his subjects to slavery.[6]

Medieval Tax Constitutions

It bears noting that this constitutional solution to the king's fiscal dilemma had many real-world counterparts in medieval Europe. To secure a more predictable or less costly tax-revenue stream, medieval kings often created councils or parliaments composed of major taxpayers and vested those councils with veto power over new taxes. Perhaps the most famous of these formal agreements is the English *Magna Carta* of 1215, which among other provisions established a representative council of 25 barons that made decisions via majority rule and had the power to veto new royal taxes. Similar political arrangements that formally vested veto power in councils representing major taxpayer interests were also adopted in France, Spain, Germany, and Sweden at around the same time. Palmer and Colton (1965: 31) notes that:

> Parliaments, in this sense, sprouted up all over Europe in the thirteenth century … The new assemblies were called *cortes* in Spain, *diets* in Germany, estates general in France, parliaments in the British Isles. Usually they are referred to generically as "estates," the word "parliament" being reserved for Britain, but in origin they were essentially the same. (Palmer and Colton 1995, 34)

In most cases, the parliaments or tax councils were codified in writing. They often included members that were elected via quite narrow electorates. The electorates consisted for the most part of major taxpayers. The parliaments normally had veto power over new taxation and powers to petition

6 I neglect many aspects of long-term continuous dealings to avoid the ambiguities of the folk theorem, which demonstrates that a wide range of equilibria are possible if one or both parties is able to make creditable commitments to particular intertemporal responses. Note, however, that the tax-council equilibria are consistent with the folk theorem. For example, if the taxpayers can make a creditable commitment to reducing their taxable surplus to zero, the behavior characterized above would be equilibrium strategies in infinitely repeated games as well.

the king for policy reforms, as in England, Denmark, France, Spain, and Sweden. Later kings and queens routinely signed accession contracts (as a condition of office) in which they promised to abide by the existing constitutional rules. These tax councils recognized the significance of their tax authority. During times of crisis, for example, they would normally extend taxes only for short periods, rather than amend the tax constitution to provide new permanent sources of revenues for the king.

Medieval councils and parliaments were amazingly durable, lasting for many centuries in most cases. Indeed, several medieval tax councils survive to the present in modified form as the parliaments of contemporary constitutional monarchies.

TAX VETO AUTHORITY AND PARLIAMENTARY AUTHORITY OVER EXPENDITURES

We next examine circumstances under which a king might voluntarily agree to cede some direct control over government programs to the council in exchange for new taxes. Such transfers of power *transform a tax council into a legislature.*

The analysis parallels that of Chapter Five, but takes explicit account of tax-revenue constraints and provides mathematical representations of the policy and constitutional equilibria. Four possible transfers of policy-making power from a strong king to a weak council are analyzed: (a) partial veto power over policy proposals; (b) complete veto power; (c) partial agenda control over policy proposals; and (d) complete agenda control. Only decisive councils are analyzed, which tends to overstate the cost of shifting legislative authority to the parliament, but allows gains and losses to be evaluated from the perspective of the pivotal member of parliament. The aim is to develop a mathematically tractable model of the market for power between the king and parliament.

Most of the conclusions turn out to be intuitively obvious, although the analysis demonstrates that there are many counterintuitive possibilities that need to be taken into account to reach them.

Constitutional Reform in Stable Political and Economic Circumstances

Suppose that the tax constitution developed in the previous section has been adopted, and the king initially retains complete authority over expenditure policies. A secure king with complete control over public policy will use his revenue to secure his ideal combination of public services, G_1 and G_2, and private consumption, X, given his veto-constrained tax revenue, T^0, and his household income, Y.[7] Substituting the veto-constrained tax revenue into his budget constraint, solving for personal consumption, and substituting the result into his utility function yields:

$$U = u\left(T^0 + Y - c(G_1, G_2), G_1, G_2\right) \tag{6.6}$$

which is an objective function with two control variables, G_1 and G_2, and two first-order conditions similar to those just described:

$$U_{G_1} - U_x C_{G_1} = 0 \tag{6.7}$$

$$U_{G_2} - U_x C_{G_2} = 0 \tag{6.8}$$

Together, the first-order conditions imply that the king's optimal policies are determined by his household income and the constraint imposed by the tax constitution: $G_1^* = g(Y + T^0)$ and $G_2^* = h(Y + T^0)$. As long as the king's personal income and the tax constitution are stable, these expenditure policies remain ideal as far as the king is concerned. The subjects may prefer more butter and fewer guns, or perhaps more of each with a less extravagant level of personal consumption by the king, but under the existing institutional arrangements, they have no authority to influence government-services levels. They can veto new tax rates and new taxes on currently untaxed activities, but they do not otherwise control the royal budget.

At this constitutionally constrained royal fiscal equilibrium, there may be additional unrealized potential gains from constitutional exchange. The council members may prefer a different combination of public services to that provided. If so, the tax council may be willing to exchange higher permanent taxes for a new pattern of expenditures. It is clear, however, that the king's agreement is not sufficient to achieve this fiscal bargain. The king may accept a permanent increase in tax revenue from T^0 to T^1 but fail to change public policies as promised. He may simply build a new wing on one of his palaces.

Granting the council veto power over *public* expenditure changes does not, however, necessarily secure the king's promise, because there are other

[7] It bears noting that tax revenue was often less important in the late-medieval and early-modern period than it is today. Other revenues sources normally provided more royal income than taxes per se. However, tax revenues were significant at the margin, and as demonstrated below were in the long run sufficient to produce major shifts in policy-making authority, especially in the nineteenth century when tax revenues became increasingly important sources of government revenue.

dimensions of royal expenditure, namely household expenditures. The king may accept the additional revenue but use it for private consumption, rather than to increase the desired public service(s).

Insofar as no new government-service levels are proposed, *the council has nothing to veto*. The same logic holds for agenda control for cases in which the king retains veto power. Here the council may propose a new pattern of expenditure, and the king may simply veto it, leaving the status-quo service levels unchanged, but increasing his personal consumption. Neither veto power nor agenda control is sufficient to secure the king's promise when existing public policies are already optimal for the king, particularly in circumstances in which the king retains complete authority over other policies. Consequently, as noted in Chapter Five, the king can offer veto power or even agenda control to the council in a stable political and economic setting at very low personal cost.

However, such partial transfers of policy-making authority would obtain little of value from the council, who would recognize that such procedural powers would have little effect on public policies as long as political and economic circumstances are stable.

THE VALUE AND COST OF PARTIAL AND COMPLETE VETO POWER IN UNSTABLE SETTINGS

Vesting the Council with Partial Veto Power

Political uncertainty increases the value of partial transfers of policy-making power to the council and the cost of such transfers for the king. Consider the case in which the king's ideal combination of government services changes from (G_1^0, G_2^0) to (G_1^K, G_2^K) and the council has secured partial veto power over changes in G_2, "butter." In this case, the king faces two constraints on his fiscal decisions, his budget constraint $T^0 + Y - c(G_1, G_2) = C$, and a new procedural constraint $W(X^c, G_1, G_2) - W(X^c, G_1, G_2^0) \geq 0$, where W is the utility level (welfare) of the pivotal council member, and X^c is the after-tax consumption of the decisive member of the council. Policy G_1 can be set to maximize royal utility, but any new service level for G_2 has to make the council better off than it would have been with the original service level G_2^0. (The superscript "0" denotes the status-quo policies. The superscript "*K*" denotes the king's new ideal point.)

The council will veto any new proposed for service G_2 that makes the pivotal council member worse off than he or she would have been at its current level (G_2^0). The king realizes this, of course, and only proposes public

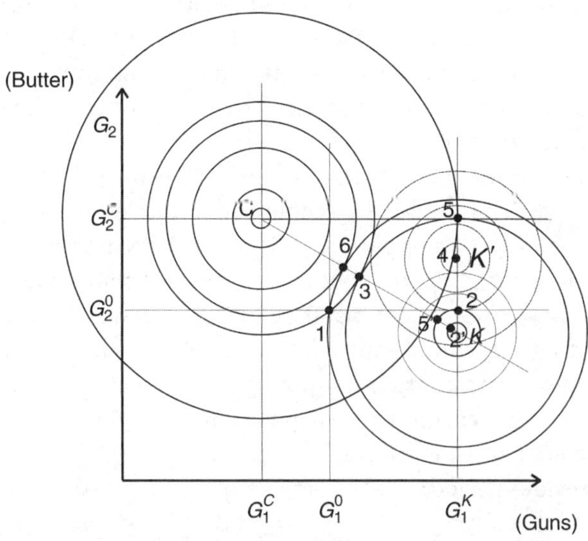

Figure 6.1. Veto and agenda control in the king-and-council template for governance.

policies that will satisfy the council in this sense. Policies that maximize the king's welfare, while preserving that of the council, can be characterized by differentiating the king's Kuhn–Tucker control function:

$$\begin{aligned} U = u\left(T^0 + Y - c(G_1, G_2), G_1, G_2\right) \\ -\lambda\left[W\left(X^c, G_1, G_2\right) - W\left(X^c, G_1, G_2^0\right)\right] \end{aligned} \tag{6.9}$$

The tangency solution requires G_1 and G_2 such that:

$$U_{G_1} - U_x C_{G_1} = 0 - \lambda\left(W_{G_1} - W_{G_1}^0\right) = 0 \tag{6.10}$$

$$U_{G_2} - U_x C_{G_2} - \lambda\left(W_{G_2}\right) = 0 \tag{6.11}$$

$$W\left(X^c, G_1, G_2\right) - W\left(X^c, G_1, G_2^0\right) = 0 \tag{6.12}$$

Figure 6.1 illustrates the effects of the council's veto power over G_2 in the $G_1 \times G_2$ plane. For purposes of the illustration, the pseudo-indifference curves of the king and pivotal council member are represented as concentric circles, as generally assumed in spatial voting models and in work that assumes quadratic-loss functions. It is similar to the figures used in Chapter Five for the decisive council cases, but in this case, the figures are used to illustrate some mathematical results, rather than being the engine of analysis. (Most of the mathematics appears in the footnotes.) The iso-utility lines are not conventional indifference curves in that effects of changes in public policies on the king's private consumption are implicitly taken into account. (Otherwise the indifference curves could not be concentric circles, given the assumption that the public services are goods with positive marginal utilities over the range of interest.)

Given values of T^0 and Y, the pivotal council member and the king have a wealth-constrained ideal policy combination that can be represented as the highest point of their respective utility mountains in the $G_1 \times G_2$ plane.[8] Given complete control over public policy, the ideal points C and K characterize the policy combinations that the council and king would select if they had no binding procedural constraints. These points represent the policies adopted under the polar forms of the king-and-council constitutional template. If the king has agenda and veto power over guns and butter, he adopts the policy combination labeled K.

If in a previous period, however, the king or one of his predecessors had granted the council veto power over one of the policy dimensions, the king may not be able to adopt his ideal policy combination. The council's veto power over G_2 implies that the king's new policy proposal has to make the pivotal member of the council at least as well off as he or she would have been with the status-quo level of the service over which they have veto power (G_2^0). In the case depicted, the king can only achieve policy combination 2, which is some distance from his new ideal. This policy combination is veto proof, because G_2 remains at the status-quo level, which leaves the council nothing to veto.

The mathematics of the tangency solution appears to suggest that the king can do a bit better than this by proposing a policy combination like 2′, which makes the pivotal member of the council as well off as he would have been at policy 2. However, both geometric inspection and the Kuhn-Tucker first-order conditions imply that 2′ is not feasible. Recall that the veto player chooses last. Consequently, policy 2′ would be vetoed by the council to realize a policy outcome that is a bit better than either 2′ or 2 from the point of view of the council, although worse than 2′ or 2 for the king. The king recognizes this and will propose policy combination 2, which is the best the king can achieve in this new political setting.[9]

8 The assumed trace of the king's utility function in the $G_1 \times G_2$ plane is $U = U^* - (G_1^K - G_1)^2 - (G_2^K - G_2)^2$, and that of the council is $U = U^* - (G_1^C - G_1)^2 - (G_2^C - G_2)^2$.

9 The Kuhn–Tucker conditions for this case can be derived from the following maximand:

$$K = U^* - (G_1^K - G_1)^2 - (G_2^K - G_2)^2 - \lambda\left[(G_2^C - G_2^0)^2 - (G_2^C - G_2)^2\right]$$

Granting the council veto power over G_2 can make the king a bit worse off in unstable settings, although this is not always the case. For example, had the king's preferred policy combination shifted to K', rather than to K, his new ideal policy combination, 4, would have been accepted by the council because policy combination 4 is preferred by the council's pivotal member to policy combination 2, the result if G_2 reverts to the status-quo level. Partial veto power can interfere with a king's policy-making power, but it does not constrain him in every case, even if his preferred policy is affected by new circumstances.

Vesting the Council with Complete Veto Power

As might be anticipated, the effect of granting the council veto power over both policy dimensions generally has a greater constraining effect on the king's ability to get his preferred policy than granting veto power over one dimension. Mathematically, the effect of granting the council veto power over both government policies is very similar to that above. The procedural constraint under complete veto power is: $W(X^c, G_1, G_2) - W(X^c, G_1^0, G_2^0) \geq 0$, and the Kuhn–Tucker first-order conditions describing the best feasible policy along the constraint becomes:

$$U_{G_1} - U_x C_{G_1} - \lambda\left(W_{G_1}\right) = 0 \tag{6.13}$$

$$U_{G_2} - U_x C_{G_2} - \lambda\left(W_{G_2}\right) = 0 \tag{6.14}$$

$$W\left(X^c, G_1, G_2\right) - W\left(X^c, G_1^0, G_2^0\right) = 0 \tag{6.15}$$

where (G_1^C, G_2^C) is the ideal point of the pivotal member of the council, labeled C in Figure 6.1. Differentiating with respect to G_1, G_2, and λ yields the following first-order conditions:

$$-\left(G_1^K - G_1\right) \leq 0 \ \text{ with } G_1 \geq 0 \ \text{ and } \ G_1\left[\left(G_1^K - G_1\right)\right] = 0$$
$$-\left(G_2^K - G_2\right) + \lambda\left(G_2^C - G_2\right) \leq 0 \ \text{ with } G_2 \geq 0 \ \text{ and } \ G_2\left[\left(G_2^K - G_2\right)\right] + \lambda\left(G_2^C - G_2\right) = 0$$
$$\left[\left(G_2^C - G_2^0\right)^2 - \left(G_2^C - G_2\right)^2\right] \geq 0 \ \text{ with } \lambda \geq 0 \ \text{ and } \ \lambda\left[\left(G_2^C - G_2^0\right)^2 - \left(G_2^C - G_2\right)^2\right] = 0$$

The first of the first-order conditions implies that $G_1{}^* = G_1^K$ or $G_1{}^* = 0$. Whether the constraint is binding or not, the king sets service level one equal to his ideal level, $G^K{}_1$, or equal to zero. The second of the first-order conditions implies that if $\lambda = 0$, then $G_2{}^* = G_2^K$ or $G_2{}^* = 0$. If the constraint is nonbinding, either the king sets service level one equal to his ideal or equal to zero. In the case in which the constraint is binding, that is, the threat of veto affects his policy options, $\lambda \neq 0$ and the third conditions imply that $G_2^C = G_2$. Consequently, there are just two equilibrium strategies for the king in this setting away from the lower bound. The king always sets $G_1^* = G_1^K$. If the veto power threat is not binding, he sets the veto constrained service at his ideal level, G_2^C, otherwise he sets service level 2 equal at the status-quo level ($G_2^C = G_2^0$).

Only the procedural constraint differs, and the constraint again may or may not be binding.

In many cases, however, granting the council veto power makes the king worse off relative to the unconstrained and partial veto power analyzed above. This possibility can also be illustrated with Figure 1. Given complete veto power, the council can now reject any policy combination that makes its members worse off than the status-quo ante. This implies that the king cannot choose a policy combination outside the decisive council member's iso-utility line passing through the status quo (G_1^0, G_2^0).

If the king's new circumstances lead him to prefer policy combination *K*, the best that he can achieve is policy combination 3, which is inferior to policy combination 2 for the king. Policy 2 is no longer feasible. The council would now reject policy combination 2 because they prefer the original combination of services to that offered. In the case in which the council is granted complete veto power, the council now constrains the king at *K*′, whereas, as shown above, he would not have been constrained by a council with partial veto power. The king will be blocked by the council's veto power in all cases in which his new ideal point lies further from the council's ideal than the status-quo ante.[10]

[10] The Kuhn-Tucker first-order conditions for king in this case are derived from the following KT maximand:

$$K = U^* - (G_1^K - G_1)^2 - (G_2^K - G_2)^2 - \lambda\left[(G_1^C - G_1^0)^2 + (G_2^C - G_2^0)^2 - (G_1^C - G_1)^2 - (G_2^C - G_2)^2\right]$$

Differentiating with respect to G_1, G_2, and λ, yields the following first-order conditions:

$$-(G_1^K - G_1) + \lambda(G_1^C - G_1) \le 0 \text{ with } G_1 \ge 0 \text{ and } G_1\left[-(G_1^K - G_1) + \lambda(G_1^C - G_1)\right] = 0$$

$$-(G_2^K - G_2) + \lambda(G_2^C - G_2) \le 0 \text{ with } G_2 \ge 0 \text{ and } G_2\left[-(G_2^K - G_2) + \lambda(G_2^C - G_2)\right] = 0$$

$$\left[(G_1^C - G_1^0)^2 + (G_2^C - G_2^0)^2 - (G_1^C - G_1)^2 - (G_2^C - G_2)^2\right] \ge 0$$

$$\text{with } \lambda \ge 0 \text{ and } \lambda\left[(G_1^C - G_2^0)^2 + (G_2^C - G_2^0)^2 - (G_1^C - G_1)^2 - (G_2^C - G_2)^2\right] = 0$$

The first of the first-order conditions implies that if $\lambda = 0$, then $G_1{}^* = G_1^K$ or $G_1{}^* = 0$. If the constraint is nonbinding, either the king sets service level one equal to his ideal or equal to zero. In the case in which the constraint is binding, $\lambda \neq 0$ and either the status quo is chosen, $G_1 = G_1^0$ and $G_2 = G_2^0$, or both policies G_1 and G_2 lie along the indifference curve passing through the initial policy position (G_1^0, G_2^0).

The second of the first-order conditions implies that if $\lambda = 0$, then $G_2^* = G_2^K$ or $G_2^* = 0$. If the constraint is nonbinding, either the king sets service level one equal to his ideal or equal to zero. In the case in which the constraint is binding, $\lambda \neq 0$ and the third constraint implies that either the status quo is chosen, $G_2 = G_2^C$, or both G_1 and G_2 lie along the indifference curve passing through the initial policy position (G_1^0, G_2^0). There are, thus, three possible equilibrium strategies for the king in this setting according to the location of the king's new ideal point. If the veto-power threat is not binding because his new ideal point

In such cases, a decisive council is clearly better off with complete veto power than with partial or no veto power. They cannot be worse off. The king would thus demand a higher price for complete veto power than for partial veto power, and the council would be willing to pay a higher price for complete than for partial veto power, particularly at times when the king's policy preferences are likely to change.[11]

PARTIAL AND COMPLETE AGENDA CONTROL

Granting the Council Partial Agenda Control

Another transferable policy-making authority by which gains from constitutional exchange may be realized is agenda control. Veto power allows the empowered party to determine whether particular departures from the status quo will be undertaken. Agenda control allows the empowered party to determine which departures from the status quo are considered. As in the case of veto power, the value of agenda control to the council depends on future changes in the king's policy preferences, as previously noted. Without changes in his policy preferences, the king can costlessly give agenda control to the council and defend the status quo by vetoing all proposed changes.

We next analyze the extent to which a partial transfer of agenda control constrains a king's future policies.

Given partial agenda control, the council will make the specific proposals that maximize its own welfare, given the king's veto power. Given agenda control over G_2, the pivotal member of the council will propose a level of G_2

is closer to the council's ideal than the original policy combination, he proposes service levels at his ideal levels (G_1^C, G_2^C). If the procedural constraint is binding, that is, proposing his ideal point would be vetoed, the king may choose a combination of G_1 and G_2 such that one of his iso-utility curves is tangent to that of the council's iso-utility line passing through the original policy combination. Alternatively, he may set both service levels at their status-quo levels (G_1^0, G_2^0).

11 Veto power is occasionally shared, as in the settings with multiple veto players analyzed by Tsebelis (2002), although this possibility is neglected in the present analysis. If veto power were the only policy-making authority available, such divisions would often lead to stalemates and worse in "zero sum" settings, as implied by Hobbes's (1651) analysis of divided sovereignty, and would more often produce conflict than opportunities for constitutional reform. Buchanan and Yoon (2000) discuss the problem of multiple veto powers in their piece on the "anti-commons." Tsebelis notes that fully rational participants in a government with multiple veto players will take the interests of other veto players into account to avoid complete deadlocks.

that maximizes his or her utility, given the veto power of the king and the king's choice of G_1.

$$W = w\left(X^c, G_1, G_2\right) - \lambda\Big[u\left(T^0 + Y - c(G_1, G_2), G_1, G_2\right) \\ -u\left(T^0 + Y - c(G_1, G_2^0), G_1^0, G_2^0\right)\Big] \tag{6.16}$$

The Kuhn–Tucker tangency solution requires:

$$W_{G_1} - \lambda\Big[U_X\left(-C_{G_2}\right) + U_{G_2}\Big] = 0 \tag{6.17}$$

while the king sets the policy that he fully controls, G_1, to maximize:

$$U = u\left(T^0 + Y - c(G_1, G_2), G_1, G_2\right) \tag{6.18}$$

which requires:

$$U_{G_1} - U_X C_{G_1} = 0 \tag{6.19}$$

given G_2. Policy combinations that satisfy both first-order conditions simultaneously are analogous to Stackelberg equilibria in noncooperative games.

The geometry of granting partial agenda control to a noncooperative council can be illustrated with Figure 6.1. Were it not for the veto power of the king, the solution to this policy-making game would resemble policy combination 5 in Figure 6.1, in which the king and the council secure their preferred level of the service over which they exercise agenda control. Given complete veto power, however, the king can do better than policy combination 5 by vetoing the council's proposed level of butter. The result in this case is policy combination 2, which combines the king's ideal level of guns with the status quo level of butter. The vetoer goes last in full knowledge of the proposal of the agenda setter.

Anticipating this, the council might be tempted to moderate its proposal for butter service levels, but no proposal that it makes above G_2^0 would be accepted by the king, and no service level below G_2^0 would lead to a better policy combination for the council than that of 2, because the king can keep G_1 at his preferred level (under the assumed geometry, this is a dominant strategy). In this case, granting agenda control to the council leads to the same policy as a grant of partial veto power to the council.[12]

[12] Again, gains to fiscal exchange exist at policy combination 2; however, in this case, the agenda setter cannot capture these potential gains to trade. If the council suggests the "butter" service level required for policy 5′, the king would accept this, but still opt for his preferred level of "guns." Under the procedural institutions in place, the gains from fiscal exchange would be unrealized.

This equivalence, however, is an artifact of the particular preference shift of the king. Had the king's ideal point shifted to K', policy combination 5 would have been veto proof, and agenda control would have made the council better off than partial veto power.[13] Policy combination 2 is a possible outcome under both institutions, but policy combination 4 is preferred by the king to policy combination 5. The pivotal council member, however, prefers policy combination 5 to policy combination 4. This suggests that king is somewhat worse off and the council is somewhat better off with partial agenda control than with partial veto power.

Vesting the Council with Complete Agenda Control

Granting complete agenda control to the council, while keeping complete veto power, makes the king worse off than granting complete veto power to

[13] The Kuhn-Tucker conditions for the council are derived from the following KT maximand:

$$K = W^{\star} - \left(G_1^C - G_1\right)^2 - \left(G_2^C - G_2\right)^2 - \lambda\left[\left(G_2^K - G_2^0\right)^2 - \left(G_2^K - G_2\right)^2\right]$$

Differentiating with respect to G_2, and λ, yields the following first-order conditions:

$$-\left(G_2^C - G_2\right) + \lambda\left(G_2^K - G_2\right) \leq 0 \text{ with } G_2 \geq 0 \text{ and } G_2\left[\left(G_2^K - G_2^0\right)\right] - \left(G_2^C - G_2\right)\Big] = 0$$
$$\left[\left(G_2^K - G_2^0\right)^2 - \left(G_2^K - G_2\right)^2\right] \geq 0 \text{ with } \lambda \geq 0 \text{ and } \lambda\left[\left(G_2^K - G_2^0\right)^2 - \left(G_2^C - G_2\right)^2\right] = 0$$

The first of the first-order conditions implies that if $\lambda = 0$, then $G_2{}^* = G_2^C$ or $G_2^* = 0$. If the constraint is nonbinding, the council sets service level two equal to its ideal level (or equal to zero if that is less than or equal to zero). In the case in which the constraint is binding, $\lambda \neq 0$, the second constraint implies that the status quo is chosen, $G_2 = G_2^0$.

The king's optimization problem is unconstrained for service level one and constrained by the agenda chosen by the council in stage one, which he can choose to veto or not. He chooses G_1 to maximize:

$$K = U^{\star} - \left(G_1^K - G_1\right)^2 - \left(G_2^K - G_2\right)^2$$

which requires:

$$-\left(G_1^K - G_1\right) = 0 \text{ or } G_1^K - G_1$$

The king sets service level one at his ideal level regardless of what the council chooses for service level 2. There are, thus, two possible equilibrium budgets in this setting according to the location of the king's new ideal point. If the king's veto-power threat is not binding, the council's proposes its own ideal service level for G_2, $G_2^* = G_2^C$. If the king's veto power is binding, the council proposes the status-quo level of service two, $G_2{}^* = G_2^0$. The seperability of spatial utility functions implies that the king always chooses his ideal level of service 1, $G_1^K = G_1$, and, given the above option, never vetoes the council's proposal.

the council. Given complete agenda control, the council would propose a policy combination that maximizes:

$$W = w\left(X^c, G_1, G_2\right) - \lambda\left[u\left(T^0 + Y - c(G_1, G_2), G_1, G_2\right) - u\left(T^0 + Y - c(G_1^0, G_2^0), G_1^0, G_2^0\right)\right] \tag{6.20}$$

The Kuhn-Tucker tangency solution for which requires:

$$W_{G_2} - \lambda\left[U_X\left(-C_{G_2}\right) + U_{G_2}\right] = 0 \tag{6.21}$$

$$W_{G_1} - \lambda\left[U_X\left(-C_{G_1}\right) + U_{G_1}\right] = 0 \tag{6.22}$$

At the tangency solution, the council chooses its utility-maximizing combination of guns and butter along the king's iso-utility line passing through the initial policy combination. Figure 6.1 illustrates the geometry of this solution with policy combination 6. Policy combination 6 is the most favorable of the policies examined for the council and the least favorable to the king. It is essentially the mirror image of the case in which the king had agenda control and the council veto power.

Given complete agenda control, *nearly all changes in the king's policy preferences make the pivotal member of council better off*. Moreover, the council can now assure the status-quo ante; so, changes in the king's preferences can no longer make the pivotal member of the council worse off. There are now three possible equilibrium strategies for the council in this setting according to the location of the king's new ideal point. If the king's veto-power threat is not binding, because his new ideal point is closer to the council's ideal than the original policy combination, the council proposes service levels at the pivotal member's ideal point (G_1^C, G_2^C). If the procedural constraint is binding and away from the lower bound (0,0), the council may choose a combination of G_1 and G_2 such that the pivotal member's iso-utility curve is tangent to the king's iso-utility line passing through the original policy combination. Alternatively, the council may set both service levels at their status-quo levels (G_1^0, G_2^0).[14]

[14] The Kuhn–Tucker conditions for council in this case are derived from the following KT maximand:

$$W = W^* - \left(G_1^C - G_1\right)^2 - \left(G_2^C - G_2\right)^2 - \lambda\left[\left(G_1^K - G_1^0\right)^2 + \left(G_2^K - G_2^0\right)^2 - \left(G_1^K - G_1\right)^2 - \left(G_2^K - G_2\right)^2\right]$$

Differentiating with respect to G_1, G_2, and λ yields the following first-order conditions:

PUBLIC POLICY OPPORTUNITY SETS WITH DIVIDED AUTHORITY

The mathematical analysis demonstrates that the range of policies that are feasible for the king varies with the division of policy-making authority. Overall, it is clear that more favorable policy outcomes are often obtained by the council in unstable settings as policy-making authority is transferred to it. However, the results do not produce a simple deterministic ranking of divisions of authority. Figures 6.2A and 6.2B illustrate the typical policy opportunity sets for the king under different power-sharing arrangements. Figure 6.2A illustrates the feasible set for complete and partial assignments of veto power to the committee. Figure 6.2B depicts the feasible sets of policy outcomes for complete and partial agenda control. Together, these figures allow the restrictiveness of the four assignments of policy-making power to be compared. The feasible sets are not convex, and the relationships of the feasible policy domains to one another are not immediately obvious.

Figure 6.2A depicts the range of policies that can be adopted under alternative assumptions about the council veto power. In the case of complete veto power, the council can block any move that will make it worse off than the status-quo ante (labeled policy combination 1). The range of possible policy outcomes under complete veto power consists of those policy combinations that lie inside the decisive council member's indifference curve through the status-quo policy. This is the shaded circular area in Figure 6.2A.

$$-(G_1^C - G_1) + \lambda(G_1^K - G_1) \le 0 \text{ with } G_1 \ge 0 \text{ and } G_1\left[-(G_1^C - G_1) + \lambda(G_1^K - G_1)\right] = 0$$
$$-(G_2^C - G_2) + \lambda(G_2^K - G_2) \le 0 \text{ with } G_2 \ge 0 \text{ and } G_2\left[-(G_2^C - G_2) + \lambda(G_2^K - G_2)\right] = 0$$
$$\left[(G_1^K - G_1^0)^2 + (G_2^K - G_2^0)^2 - (G_1^K - G_1)^2 - (G_2^K - G_2)^2\right] = 0$$
$$\text{with } \lambda \ge 0 \text{ and } \lambda\left[(G_1^K - G_1^0)^2 + (G_2^K - G_2^0)^2 - (G_1^K - G_1)^2 - (G_2^K - G_2)^2\right] = 0$$

The first of the first-order conditions imply that if $\lambda = 0$, then $G_1^* = G_1^C$ or $G_1^* = 0$. If the constraint is nonbinding, either the council sets service level one equal to its ideal or equal to zero. In the case in which the constraint is binding, $\lambda \neq 0$ and the procedural constraint implies that either the status quo is chosen, $G_1 = G_1^0$ and $G_2 = G_2^0$, or both G_1 and G_2 lie along the indifference curve passing through the initial policy position (G_1^0, G_2^0).

Similarly, the second of the first-order conditions implies that if $\lambda = 0$, then $G_2^* = G_2^C$ or $G_2^* = 0$. If the constraint is nonbinding, either the council sets service level one equal to its ideal or equal to zero. In the case in which the constraint is binding, $\lambda \neq 0$ and the third constraint implies that either the status quo is chosen, $G_2 = G_2^C$, or both G_1 and G_2 lie along the indifference curve passing through the initial policy position (G_1^0, G_2^0).

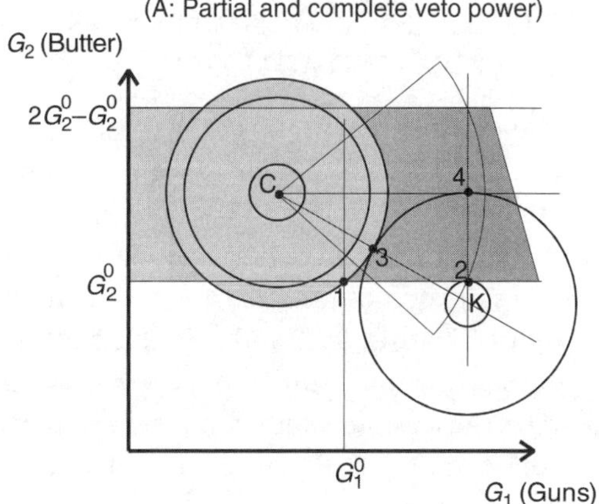

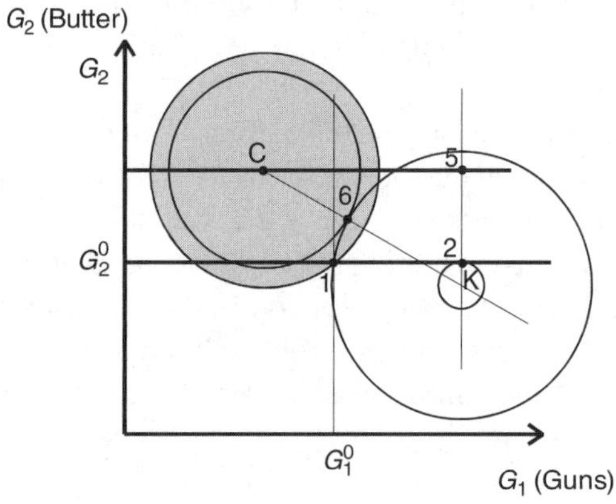

Figure 6.2. Partial and complete veto and agenda control in the king-and-council template for governance.

In the case of partial veto power, the council will also accept all such policies, but cannot block some policies that make it worse off. The council will veto any policy proposal made by the king in which the status-quo level of the service over which it exercises veto power is preferred to that of the policy proposed by the king. For the spatial-preference ordering assumed for the diagrams, this implies that only policies within the trapezoid are potentially acceptable. (The budget constraint of the king determines the upper bound of the trapezoid in the uncontrolled dimension.)

Figure 6.2B depicts the range of policies that may be chosen when council has various degrees of agenda control. In the case of complete agenda control, the council will only propose policies that make it better off relative to the status quo ante. (If no better alternatives are veto proof, the council proposes the status-quo ante.) Consequently, the range of possible proposals is limited to those within the council's indifference curve passing through the initial policy position. For the spatial preferences used in our illustrations, the feasible set is a circular shaded area similar to that shaded in Figure 6.2A.

The feasible policies under partial agenda control include that area plus other policy combinations that may emerge from the king's area of control given the council's proposals for the policy over which it exercises agenda control. The geometric and mathematical results imply that the council will either propose its own ideal service level or the service level of the status quo. Consequently, the range of policy outcomes that can arise under partial agenda control include the circular area associated with complete agenda control plus additional two line segments. The upper bound of the line segments in the uncontrolled dimension (G_1) is determined by the king's budget constraint.

The more restrictive the procedural constraints, the smaller average distances to the council's ideal point tend to be, and the larger they tend to be for kings.

THE DEMAND AND SUPPLY OF POLICY-MAKING AUTHORITY

We now characterize the willingness of the council or parliament to pay for additional control over public policy and the reservation price that the king or president requires for selling policy-making power.

The reservation price for the king to shift policy-making power to the council, and the reservation value to the council for shifts of power to the king can be assessed given a probability-density function that describes likely shifts in the king's preferences (or political circumstances) and the associated effects of alternative distributions of legislative authority on public policies. For example, if all the possible policy outcomes are considered to be equally likely in the long run, the council's reservation offer is least for partial veto power, followed by partial agenda control, then by complete veto power, and thereafter by complete agenda control. The king's reservation prices have the opposite rank order; the least binding will be offered at the lowest price in terms of new tax revenues (or other transfers from the council to the king). The marginal reductions in the feasible domain of policy become smaller as the legislative authority is shifted to the council, which suggests that the marginal cost of ceding additional powers to the parliament declines.

Let $j(G_1, G_2)$ be the probability function that describes the range of policies that the king may wish to pursue if not constrained, and let $k(G_1, G_2, R_i)$ be the probability function describing the range of policies that the king may wish to pursue under procedural restraint R_i. The domain of k is a subset of that of j.

The lowest offer that the king would accept to adopt R_i is O^{k*} such that:

$$\iint j(G_1,G_2)u\left(T^0 + Y^k - c(G_1^{**},G_2^{**}),G_1^{**},G_2^{**}\right) dG_1\, dG_2 \\ - \iint k(G_1,G_2,R_i)u\left(T^0 + O^{k*} + Y^k - c(G_1^{*},G_2^{*}), G_1^{*},G_2^{*}\right) dG_1\, dG_2 = 0 \quad (6.24)$$

Similarly, the highest offer that the council would be willing to make is such that:

$$\iint j(G_1,G_2)w\left(Y^c - T^0 - c(G_1^{**},G_2^{**}),G_1^{**},G_2^{**}\right) dG_1\, dG_2 \\ - \iint k(G_1,G_2,R_i)w\left(Y^c - T^0 - O^{c*} - c(G_1^{*},G_2^{*}), G_1^{*},G_2^{*}\right) dG_1\, dG_2 = 0 \quad (6.25)$$

where policies are set at the king's ideal for the cases of interest, as previously developed.

For bounded and continuous probability and utility functions, the implicit function theorem applied to equation 6.24 implies that lowest offer that the king will be willing to accept can be written as:

$$O^{k*} = s\left(R_i,\, T^0 + Y^k\right) \quad (6.26)$$

and, from equation 6.25, the highest that the council is willing to be make as:

$$O^{c*} = d\left(R_i,\, T^0 + Y^c\right) \quad (6.27)$$

As in ordinary markets the *exchange occurs when the reservation price of the party demanding more power exceeds that of the party that currently possesses the authority of interest*. For a wide range of probability functions, it is clear that the rank order of these prices will parallel the restrictiveness of the procedural constraints.

In polar cases, there may be no intersection of the demand and supply of authority curves, because the reservation price for transfers of power is too great for the other to pay. This case is illustrated in Figure 6.3 for king-dominated systems with curves D_0^C and S_0^K. In intermediate distribution of authority, as with D_1^C and S_0^K, the two curves intersect, and small shifts in supply or demand will produce constitutional gains to trade. In such cases, constitutional bargains that shift authority to the parliament may be reached by trading a broader tax base or other in-kind services to the king in exchange

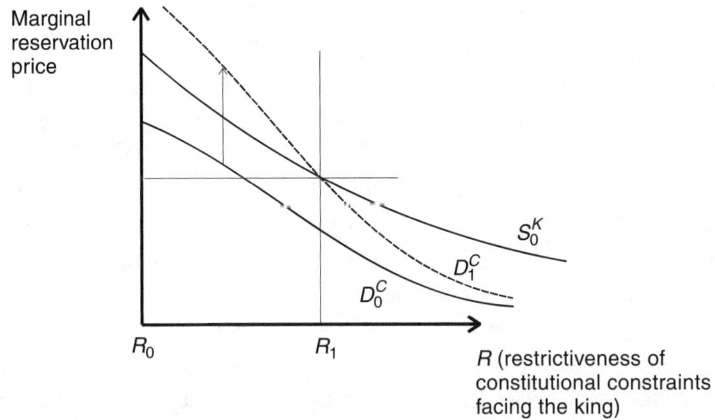

Figure 6.3. The market for policy-making authority.

for greater policy-making authority. The reverse occurs when the king purchases additional authority from the parliament.

For constitutional bargaining between the king and council to be mutually beneficial in many polar cases, there must be a fairly large shock of some kind to produce new gains to trade. For example, there may be a crisis that affects only one of the parties: the king may have urgent financial needs because of poor investments in royal enterprises, or he may face a new threat of piracy. In intermediate cases, any shocks sufficient to overcome institutional conservatism may generate new gains to constitutional exchange, which suggests that more constitutional reforms are adopted by intermediate forms of the king-and-council template than in the polar cases

Gains to trade may arise, for example, when there are changes in untaxed wealth or royal income. A decline in the king's wealth causes his reservation price for authority to fall.

$$O^{k*}Y^k = \left[\iint j(G_1,G_2)\,u_{Yk} - k\left(G_1,G_2,R_i\right)u_{Yk}\,dG_1\,dG_2\right] / -[U^e{}_{OO}] < 0 \qquad (6.28)$$

An increase in the council's wealth causes its reservation price for political power to increase.

$$O^{c*}Y^c = \left[\iint j(G_1,G_2)\,w_{Yc} - k\left(G_1,G_2,R_i\right)w_{Yc}\,dG_1\,dG_2\right] / -[W^e{}_{OO}] < 0 \qquad (6.29)$$

Constitutional exchange takes place when $O^{c*} > O^{k*}$.

The shift from D_0^C to D_1^C in Figure 6.3 illustrates how a change in demand for policy-making power can lead to a partial transfer of power from the king to the council. A sufficient increase in the reservation price of the council makes it willing to purchase additional policy-making power from the king at a price that the king is willing to accept. In the illustration, authority R_1 is transferred to the council, perhaps partial veto power over domestic spending.

Within the model, such constitutional exchanges may require amending the tax constitution. During a crisis, such shifts of authority may be temporary, as for example, new temporary veto powers may be exchanged for temporary increases in tax revenues.[15]

The king may also occasionally buy back some or all of the council's constitutional powers, in cases in which his wealth increases relative to that of the council. Even in peaceful and lawful political circumstances, the road to parliamentary democracy is not a one-way street, nor one that always leads to full parliamentary rule.

In the absence of systematic trends favoring one or the other center of policy-making authority, as discussed in Chapter Five, a random walk of power-sharing arrangements between king and council may arise as weather, disease, technology, and ideology change through time, with periods during which the council increases its power, and others during which the king becomes less subject to council vetoes and agenda control.

Increases in Parliament's Purchasing Power

Among the systematic trends observed in rapidly industrializing countries are those affecting the extent and distribution of wealth. Consider the effect of taxpayer income or wealth on the level of taxation allowed by a tax constitution. Suppose that the pivotal member of a decisive council knows the king's objective function, is assured of veto power over taxes, and knows his or her tax payments. The council thus knows that public services are set at $G^{1*} = g(Y + T^0)$ and $G^{2*} = h(Y + T^0)$ by the king under tax limitation T^0.

The pivotal member's ideal fiscal package, given the King's supply functions, would adjust the royal budget, T, to maximize:

$$U = u\left[Y^{c0} - s(T), g(Y + T), h(Y + T)\right] \tag{6.30}$$

[15] Constitutional exchange involving councils that represent other interests, for example, religious or ideological ones, may also engage in constitutional exchange. In such cases, the terms of trade may include metaphysical dimensions as well as tangible ones. For example, a religious council or chamber of parliament may exchange theological support for the king for tax exemptions.

where $s(T)$ is pivotal voter's share of the tax revenues paid. This requires:

$$-U_X s_T + U_{G_1} g_T + U_{G_2} h_T = 0 \quad (6.31)$$

This ideal tax may exceed that allowed by the current constitution, in which case, there are potential gains to trade, at least from the council's perspective. The ideal tax system provides revenues:

$$T^* = t(Y^{C0}) \quad (6.32)$$

and the pivotal council member's welfare is:

$$U^* = u[Y^{Co} - s(T^*), g(Y + T^*), h(Y + T^*)] \quad (6.33)$$

Whenever $T^* > T^0$, it can be said that parliament (the council) is willing to fund additional services and/or to pay for additional public policy-making authority. Equation 6.32 suggests that this willingness to pay is affected by the wealth of the groups represented in parliament. It is clear that as parliament's income increases, the willingness to trade tax expansions for service increases and/or additional policy-making authority increases:

$$T^*_{Yc}\left[-W_{XX^S T} - W_{C^S TT}\right] / -W_{TT}\,] > 0 \quad (6.34)$$

Given W concave and $s_T > 0$ and $s_{TT} >= 0$. The king's own welfare also increases with tax revenue:

$$U^*_T = U_X + U_{G_1} g_T + U_{G_2} h_T > 0 \quad (6.35)$$

Consequently, a sufficiently large increase in the wealth of those represented in parliament can produce constitutional exchanges in which the tax constitution is revised in exchange for policy-making authority. Thus, it is not surprising to see that several expansions of parliamentary control and/or suffrage occur at approximately the same time that income taxes are adopted in the nineteenth century in rapidly industrializing countries.

Parliaments are also willing to pay more taxes to secure additional control over public policy whenever uncertainty about the king's future policy agenda increases, because political insurance clearly becomes more valuable in such circumstances. This suggests that constitutional bargains will be more likely to be consummated towards the end of a king's life (term of office) or at the beginning of a new king's term. Similarly, the price demanded by the king tends to increase with his uncertainty about the future policy preferences of pivotal members of parliament. The greater variation in the policy preferences of members of parliaments in the early twentieth century evidently made constitutional bargains somewhat more difficult to reach in, for example, Sweden, Germany, and Japan.

Parliamentary Authority Does Not Imply Democracy

Insofar as parliaments represent more interests than the king, trends in constitutional exchange that favor parliamentary authority may be said to favor democracy, as often argued by economists and political scientists.[16] It bears noting, however, that parliamentary authority and the basis for membership in parliament are controlled by different laws, and that the procedures for adjusting the balance of authority between the king and parliament are different from those for changing the basis of membership in parliament.

Parliaments can gain authority without changing the basis for membership in its chambers. England and Sweden, for example, had periods of parliamentary rule in the seventeenth and eighteenth centuries, respectively. In neither case was there a major expansion of suffrage, although in the English case there were experiments with changing the basis for membership in parliament (see Chapters Twelve and Thirteen). Given the medieval qualifications for membership in parliament – nobility and wealth – it may be said that the rise of parliament often simply replaces autocracy with aristocracy.

Moreover, there is nothing about king-and-council governance, per se, that implies that the rise of parliament is inevitable or irreversible. Gains to trade between a parliament and a king or prime minister can also shift power from parliament to the executive during times of domestic or international crisis.[17] During such times, parliaments evidently believe that the executive's better information about the problems at hand lead to policies that better advance national interests. Such reforms are often intended to be temporary, but not always so.[18]

[16] In this sense, political liberalization and economic development are predicted to be correlated, as found in Paldam and Gundlach's (2008) analysis of contemporary transition data.

[17] Other possibilities also exist, of course. For example, Wintrobe (1998, chapter 11) develops a theory of the emergence of dictatorship as a consequence of democratic inaction. Kuran (1989) demonstrates how public opinion can rapidly switch from one preferred policy or form of political organization to another as a consequence of differences between public and private preferences generated by conformitive pressures. Mommsen (1995, 11–14), among others, suggests that the German Constitution of 1871 was adopted by Bismarck in large part to counter liberal and socialist lobbying groups that emerged in rapidly industrializing Germany.

[18] In some such settings, there may be a tendency to shift from one extreme to the other. In correspondence, George Tridimas notes that if the constitutional supply curve is "flatter" than the demand curve in Figure 6.3, the equilibrium (intersection point) is unstable in the sense that a series of myopic disequilibrium price adjustments is unlikely to converge to the equilibrium price. In such cases, an ever increasing (or decreasing) sequence of political bargains may continue until the vertical (or horizontal) axis is hit. The latter suggests that one of the two decision-making bodies tends to become all powerful. However,

Stability of the Medieval Division of Authority

Before 1800, periods of parliamentary control over public policy tended to be relatively brief, and there was a tendency to return to the medieval balance of authority. Charles II was invited by parliament to restore England's medieval constitution a year after Cromwell's death in 1658. The eighteenth-century "Age of Liberty" in Sweden was ended by Gustav III in 1772, partly through decisions of the Swedish Riksdag in response to a fiscal crisis. The Dutch republic had seen the rise of executive power in the eighteenth century, as the office of stadhouder became an increasingly regal post. In the second half of the eighteenth century, George III began reclaiming powers from the British parliament before being overtaken by health problems. The French Revolution of the late eighteenth century was reversed after the defeat of Napoleon, and a hereditary French sovereign was restored by the Congress of Vienna in 1815.

The long-run medieval equilibrium of king-dominated king-and-council systems of governance must have seemed as safe and sound as ever in 1815, except perhaps in the recently formed United States of America. And even there, the shift from the first U.S. constitution, the *Articles of Confederation*, to the second one can be interpreted as a peaceful shift of power from a council-dominated system – the Congress – to a mixed system with greater executive authority. The new constitution created the office of president and vested it with substantial powers. (For more on these historical cases, see the historical narratives of Part II.)

Yet in just slightly over a century, the long-standing king-dominated systems of governance disappeared throughout Europe. Parliaments rose in legislative and fiscal authority, and their members came to be chosen by increasingly broad electorates. Ancient tax systems based on land and tariffs were replaced with new ones based on income and manufacturing. Ancient economic systems based on monopoly privileges, family, and farming were replaced with far more open systems based on large-scale commercial and manufacturing enterprises. Ancient legal and political systems based on birth, status, and/or wealth were replaced by more uniform bodies of law that applied equally to all adult men and women.

The last two chapters can account for the increase in parliamentary authority and for the modernization of taxation in the nineteenth century.

insofar as the supply curve is "steeper" than the demand, as drawn, the equilibrium is stable. Small adjustments in the terms of constitutional trade move the constitution (assignment of policy-making authority) back toward the equilibrium levels characterized by the intersection of demand and supply in Figure 6.3.

For example, data for Great Britain assembled by Lindert (1986, table 1) indicate that the value of noble estates averaged £2032 in 1810 and had risen to £9,855 in 1875. Merchant estates averaged far less, £608, in 1810, but by 1875 had risen to £11,804, both in constant 1875 British pounds sterling. Other classes and occupations also had significant increases in wealth, although not as great as those of merchants or titled persons. The population of nobles was essentially stable between 1810 and 1875 (rising from 22,000 to 25,000), whereas the number of merchants, professionals, and industrial and building trades increased substantially (rising from 42,000 to 61,000 and from 638,000 to 2,835,000 respectively). The fraction of wealth controlled by those outside the noble and royal families increased substantially during the nineteenth century. The models of this chapter imply that the increase in nonroyal relative to royal wealth would create new opportunities for constitutional exchange favoring parliament in the nineteenth century.

In addition to being wealthier, nineteenth-century parliaments became more decisive and more difficult for kings (and queens) to manipulate. New liberal political and economic ideologies and associated political parties made parliaments more decisive and less satisfied with the status quo. Moreover, royal demands for revenues increased as the cost of competitive navies, armies, and palaces rose and revenues from tariffs declined. Ideological shifts (the rise of liberalism) also somewhat undermined deference to inherited authority inside and outside government, which further enhanced the bargaining power of parliament and somewhat reduced that of the king. All these changes favored constitutional reforms that shifted political authority from kings to parliaments.

To transform the medieval king-and-council template into a liberal parliamentary democracy, however, also required another series of reforms – ones that broaden the electoral base used to select members of parliament and increase competition for those offices.

In practice, the reforms that increased parliament's authority and expanded suffrage were not always adopted simultaneously, which suggests that these important series of reforms were caused by different factors. Nineteenth-century history thus suggests that a separate analysis of suffrage reform is necessary and appropriate. With this in mind, the next chapter demonstrates that several proposed explanations for suffrage expansion are inconstant with a rational choice approach. Chapter Eight develops a few others that are more constant with self-interest–based explanations.

SEVEN

Suffrage without Democracy

Before the nineteenth century, medieval parliaments represented the interests of major landholders: the church, nobility, and relatively wealthy merchants and farmers. Those sitting in parliament gained their seats through a mixture of heredity, appointments, and elections based on narrow suffrage.

The subset of the members that were elected to their offices often ran unopposed and represented, for the most part, locally powerful families. Those eligible to run for office often had to be relatively wealthy men, both as a formal condition of eligibility, and in order to be able to afford to attend meetings of parliament, because those holding seats in parliament were not directly paid for their services. There were no professional members of parliament, per se, although members with jobs in the capital city often invested considerable time and energy in parliamentary activities.

Parliaments met irregularly, as needed by the King, and only for relatively short periods. Not all members would attend the meetings called, because travel was difficult in those days and the issues were not always important, although in some cases proxy (weighted) voting was allowed for those not able to attend.

Kings would often reward persons who voted the "correct" way with positions in the national bureaucracy and/or appointments to their advisory councils. This enabled kings to know what parliaments were up to. It also enabled them to assemble a block of members whose interests were aligned with the king and who would reliably attend the meetings of parliament. Nobles and local governments often used similar practices. As a consequence, the men elected to the "commoner chambers" often represented noble or royal interests, although most did not hold noble titles.[1]

Such dynastic political systems tend to reduce political competition, which in some settings can promote economic development by reducing wasteful forms of political conflict, as noted earlier. The economic regulations that the medieval parliaments adopted (or accepted), however, also tended to reduce economic competition and innovation through various land and market privileges, and through restrictions on labor mobility. These restrictions created formal and informal economic property rights that were quite different from contemporary Western property law, at the same time that they tended to create substantial economic and civic inequality. Indeed, history suggests that medieval privileges and legal practices evolved to support royal and noble authority and to protect the economic rents of privileged families in a manner consistent with the theory of regional governance developed in the first chapters of Part I.

The next two chapters analyze possible rational-choice-based explanations for the stability of the procedures through which members of parliament were chosen and also for the major electoral reforms of the nineteenth century. The qualifications for casting votes in medieval elections varied among localities, but suffrage was normally limited to the wealthiest 5 to 10 percent of taxpayers. Elections for office were not through secret ballot, but normally through public, physical "divisions" (all those in favor of "x" stand over there) or by voice vote. Literacy was not extensive in the early days of parliament, and both paper and printing were expensive.

The models of Chapter Seven explain why medieval parliaments in which a significant number of members were elected did not automatically produce democratic rule. It demonstrates that neither rising income nor popular revolution are likely to induce an expansion of suffrage, even when suffrage law is entirely controlled by elected members of parliament. Chapter Eight provides an explanation for gradual suffrage reform based on shifts in ideological and economic interests.

A NARROWLY ELECTED PARLIAMENT'S DISINTEREST IN ELECTORAL REFORM

It is important to understand that a general disinterest in suffrage reform within parliament does not require royal veto threats, inordinate noble

[1] Local governments often had a more representative structure than national governments. City-states were often republics ruled by narrowly elected councils, rather than formally hereditary rulers. Farm villages often made local policy decisions at broadly attended town meetings.

or royal control over parliament, or extreme institutional conservatism, although these may also counter any impulse for suffrage reform that emerges. In most cases, parliaments were free to organize themselves without direction from the king (although not necessarily without royal interest or influence), and so royal support or opposition to electoral reform can be neglected in order to focus on parliamentary incentives for maintaining or revising existing suffrage law. The stability of medieval political-economic systems suggests that parliamentary systems are not necessarily destined to evolve from aristocratic regimes into parliamentary democracies.

It turns out that both the pivotal voter and the pivotal member of parliament are likely to be completely satisfied with the existing suffrage laws if they have only pragmatic policy interests. To see this, we need to analyze the kinds of policies that a narrowly elected parliament would favor; and given those policies, we also need to understand what preferences for suffrage laws look like at the level of the pivotal or median voter.

Voter Demands for Government Services

Given the medieval composition of parliaments, including their houses of commons a natural point of departure for analysis of suffrage reform is one in which the privilege of voting for representatives is defined by wealth or income.

Consider the following highly simplified model of parliamentary decision making under preexisting suffrage laws in a setting otherwise lacking medieval features. Suppose that citizens have preferences defined over private consumption, X_i, and a bundle of public services, G_i, that are uniformly available to all within the community, $U_i = u(X_i, G_i)$. Each citizen has an endowment of labor, L_i, and capital, K_i. National income, Y, is produced via constant returns to scale using labor and capital under technology, Z. This implies that national income can be represented as $Y = f(\Sigma L_i, \Sigma K_i, Z)$. In cases, in which markets are competitive, each person would receive his or her marginal product, with wage rate, $w = df/dL$, and return on capital, $r = df/dK$. In less competitive settings, wages would differ from marginal product. In either case, citizen *i*'s income can be represented as $Y_i = wL_i + rK_i$, and $Y = \Sigma Y_i$.

Let $C = c(G, Z)$ be the rate of transformation between private consumption good X and government service G. This implies that private consumption, X, can be characterized as $X = Y - c(G, Z)$. Assume that government services are funded with a proportional tax on income just sufficient to fund the service level demanded, $tY = C(G_j, Z)$. In this case, the citizen-voter will prefer the service level that maximizes:

$$U = u\left(\left(1 - c\left(G_i, Z\right)/Y\right)Y_i, G_i\right) \tag{7.1}$$

which requires service level G_i to be such that:

$$ux\left(-C_G/Y\right)Y_i + u_G = 0 \tag{7.2}$$

The implicit function theorem implies that the typical citizen's demand for government services is determined by:

$$G^* = g\left(wL_i + rK_i, Y, Z\right) \tag{7.3}$$

Each citizen demands services based on his or her endowment of labor and capital, the marginal product of those inputs, and national income. Because only the initial endowments of productive inputs vary by person in this model, it is the variation in the initial endowments that determines the distribution of citizen demands for government services.

The Median Voter Is Determined by Suffrage Law

Suppose that the frequency distributions of labor and capital are approximately independent and can be approximated with triangular distributions, with labor endowments distributed between 0 and maximal labor endowment, L_M, where $l(0) = 2/L_M$ and $l(L_M) = 0$, and capital endowments distributed between *0* and maximal capital endowment K^M with $k(0) = 2/K_M$ and $k(K_M) = 0$.

Figure 7.1 depicts a triangular distribution of labor endowments and labor-based incomes. The triangular assumption is not crucial for the present analysis, but does assure that voter interests differ somewhat and that median income is below average income, as tends to be the case in most observed income distributions, particularly in societies with little occupational mobility.

The distribution of income, Y_i, can be written as $Y_i \sim rL_i + wK_i$ within the domain of realized incomes.[2] The mean of this income distribution is $Y_A = (rK_M + wL_M)/3$ and its median is $Y_v = (wL_M + rK_M)(2 - \sqrt{2})/2$.[3]

2 The sum of two linear monotone decreasing functions is also linear and monotone decreasing.

3 The two triangular density distributions can be written as $F_L = (2/L_M - 2L/L_M^2)$ and $F_K = (2/K_M - 2K/K_M^2)$. Average income is denoted Y_A and can be characterized with:

$$Y_A = \int_0^{L_M} wL\left(2/L_M - 2L/L_M^2\right) dL + \int_0^{K_M} rK\left(2/K_M - 2K/K_M^2\right) dK$$

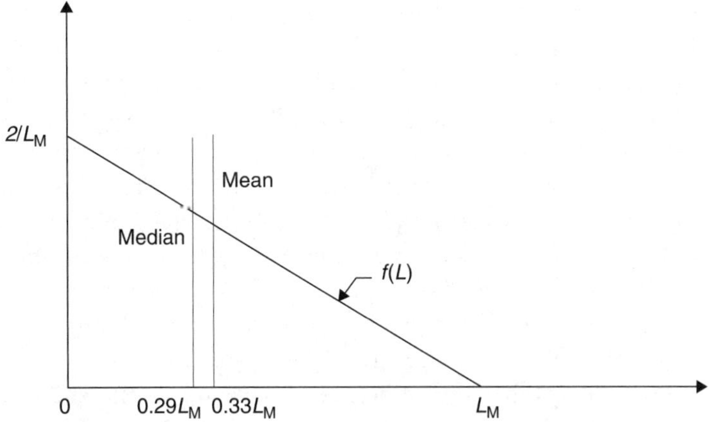

Figure 7.1. Distribution of citizen labor endowments.

In a polity in which all citizens are eligible to vote and a median voter exists, two-candidate or two-party competition for office tends to converge to the policy preferences of the median voter. In such polities, the median voter can be represented as the *citizen* with the median endowment of capital and labor.

The median voter is, however, not always the citizen with median endowments or income, because the distribution of endowments among potential voters may differ from that of the persons lawfully entitled to vote. In modern democracies, suffrage eligibility is determined by citizenship and age, with the consequence that the median voter is older than the median citizen. (Children and foreign nationals cannot vote.) For much of the history of parliamentary systems, eligibility to vote was determined by tax payments and/or land ownership, as noted earlier. In the medieval context, the median voter was generally a citizen with much greater income than that of the median citizen.

Because of such effects, suffrage restrictions tend to change the identity and service demand of the pivotal voter. The effects of income or tax qualifications for suffrage can easily be modeled. Suppose that citizens are allowed

or

$$Y_A = \left(rK_M + wL_M\right)/3$$

The medians of labor and capital distributions are $L_v = L_M(2-\sqrt{2})/2$ and $K_v = K_M(2-\sqrt{2})/2$, respectively, given the assumed triangular distributions. Median citizen income is, consequently, $Y_v = (wL_M + rK_M)(2 - \sqrt{2})/2$, where w and r again reflect the marginal product of labor and capital for the total employment of labor and capital. Note that $(2 - \sqrt{2})/2 = 0.2929 < 1/3$; median income is less than average income. Triangular distributions are skewed distributions with different modes, means, and medians.

to vote whenever their labor-based tax payment is greater than T^L or their capital-based tax payment is greater than T^K. Suppose also that the tax constitution limits taxes to a single rate sufficient to pay for government services, $t = c(G^*, Z)/Y$. Whether persons qualify as voters or not in this case varies both with their endowments of productive assets and the government service level. That is to say, citizen i can vote if his or her quality-adjusted labor endowment, L_i, satisfies $twL_i > T^L$ or if his capital endowment, K_i, satisfies $trK_i > T^K$, where t is the prevailing average tax rate, w is the typical wage rate, and r is the rate of return on capital. L_i can be thought of as the quality of citizen i's labor endowment, which varies with education, experience, and health. (Women could rarely vote before 1900.)

Note that it is possible to shift between tax-payment- and endowment-based suffrage laws without modifying the basic structure of the model. Given the prevailing national prices for capital and labor, citizens with a labor endowment greater than L^E, with $L^E = T^L/tw$, or with a capital endowment greater than K^E, with $K^E = T^K/tw$, are able to vote. Eligibility to vote in tax-based systems is partly based on endowments, partly on productivity (insofar as marginal productivity is reflected in wage rates and the return on capital), partly on the general price level, and partly on the level of taxation.

For the present analysis, assume that the economic determinants of wage rates and the rate of return on capital are stable. This would tend to be the case in economic steady states, and in short-run analysis, for which it is normally assumed that a constant supply of capital and labor is employed using a particular production technology.

Under these conditions and a triangular distribution of the endowments, L_v and K_v, the median holding of capital and labor will satisfy:

$$\begin{aligned} &\int_{T^L/tw}^{L_V} w\left(2L/L_M - L^2/L_M^2\right)dL + \int_{T^K/tw}^{K_V} r\left(2K/K_M - K^2/K_M^2\right)dK \\ &= \int_{L_V}^{L_M} w\left(2L/L_M - L^2/L_M^2\right)dL + \int_{K_V}^{K_M} r\left(2K/K_M - K^2/K_M^2\right)dK \end{aligned} \tag{7.4}$$

in which case, the median voter's income is:

$$Y_V = \left(w\left(L_M - T^L/tw\right) + r\left(K_M - T^K/tw\right)\right)\left(2 - \sqrt{2}\right)/2 \tag{7.5}$$

and he or she will demand service level:

$$G^* = g\left(Y_V, Y, Z\right) \tag{7.6a}$$

or

$$G^* = \gamma\left(L_V, K_V, T^L, T^K, Y, Z\right) \tag{7.6b}$$

Note that *suffrage rules partly determine government policies* by determining the identity of the median voter and the composition of parliament.

A Pragmatic Median Voter's Lack of Interest in Suffrage Reform

Suffrage laws in most polities can be modified through acts of parliament.

Equation 7.6b allows the present median voter preferences over suffrage law to be characterized with the indirect utility function:

$$U_v^* = u\left(1 - C\left(\gamma\left(L_v, K_v, T^L, T^K, Y, Z\right), Z\right)/Y\right)Y_v, \gamma\left(L_v, K_v, T^L, T^K, Y, Z\right) \qquad (7.7)$$

Differentiating equation 7.7 with respect to T^L and T^K and applying the envelope theorem allows the first-order conditions for the median voter's optimal suffrage laws to be characterized.

$$U_{vT^L}^* = \left(u_X C_G - u_G\right)G\gamma\gamma_{T^L} = 0 \qquad (7.8a)$$

$$U_{vT^L}^* = \left(u_X C_G - u_G\right)G\gamma\gamma_{T^K} = 0 \qquad (7.8b)$$

Equations 7.8a and 7.8b imply that the present suffrage qualifications T^L and T^K are *already optimized for the present median voter*. No other combination of wealth requirements for suffrage will generate a better service-tax combination for the pivotal voter, because the present value of G^* maximizes the median voter's welfare under the present electoral laws (and the assumed tax constitution). The median voter is completely satisfied with the existing suffrage law, S′, because that law made him the pivotal voter! Other things being equal, the present median voter is content to be the median voter and has no interest in enacting laws that will worsen policy by creating a new pivotal voter.

The use of majority rule to select members of parliament and/or within parliament for selecting policies does not by itself generate a political impulse for universal suffrage.

Economic Growth Cannot by Itself Induce Liberal Suffrage Reform

During periods of economic growth in societies with income- and tax-payment-based suffrage laws, the electorate tends to expand as capital is accumulated and government services expand because these tend to increase income, wealth, and tax payments, other things being equal. Technological advance further increases income by increasing the productivity of labor and capital, and in many cases, land as well. Wealth-based rules for suffrage consequently imply that a somewhat larger electorate and somewhat

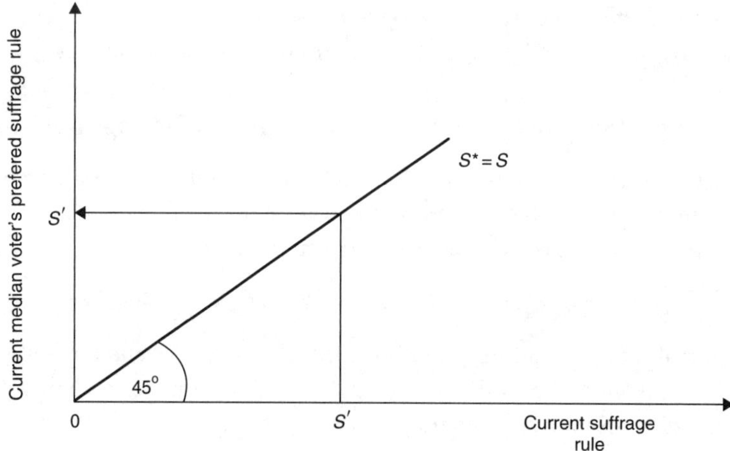

Figure 7.2. Median voter equilibrium for suffrage law.

new median voter tend to emerge in every election cycle during periods of economic growth (and also during periods of economic contraction).[4]

The direct electoral effect of economic growth on suffrage under stable tax- or income-based suffrage rules thus tends to make the present median voter somewhat worse off. After all, it is only by being the median voter that a particular citizen can realize his (or her) most preferred government service levels. Therefore, the median voter's desire to maintain his position as median voter is not entirely compatible with a stable set of tax- and wealth-based rules for voter eligibility in a setting in which wages or returns from capital increase through time.

Perhaps surprisingly, if the present median voter always had his (or her) way on suffrage reform, economic progress would tend to be associated with suffrage laws that gradually become *more demanding*, rather than less demanding, through time. A forward-looking median voter would be inclined to tighten the eligibility rules for suffrage by, for example, increasing the wealth or income requirements for electoral qualification so that he remains the median voter as economic growth takes place.[5]

[4] This purely economic route to suffrage expansion in periods of rapid growth can be as important as major reforms of suffrage laws. This method of obtaining suffrage was historically important in the United Kingdom and Sweden, where suffrage rates approximately doubled, largely as a consequence of income increases, rather than suffrage reform.

[5] There are a few historical cases in which suffrage reforms gradually introduced more restrictive qualifications for the right to vote. For example, in the years 1620–63, there was essentially universal free male suffrage for selecting the members of Virginia's colonial parliament (although restricted somewhat by a poll tax), after which suffrage was limited to "freeholders" and increasingly restrictive definitions of freeholder were introduced.

TAXATION THROUGH REPRESENTATION AS A MOTIVATION FOR SUFFRAGE REFORM

We next consider other factors that might induce suffrage expansion. The tax constitution implicit in the model used to this point allows the government to tax anyone that it wishes, although all taxpayers must be taxed at the same rate and upward revisions of that rate are subject to parliamentary veto.

Suppose instead that the tax constitution limited the tax base to those with the privilege of suffrage. That is to say, suppose that only those directly represented in parliament could be taxed. Such reasoning evidently played a role in the early European and American theories of representation, because only substantial taxpayers were given the privilege of voting and were eligible for positions in parliament, and those not represented were often not directly taxed. Similar logic also applies to settings in which territorial boundaries determine the tax base and electorate. If a group petitions to be included in a polity, it normally negotiates for representation and suffrage rights along with its new tax obligations. In such cases, suffrage rules simultaneously determine the identity of the median voter and the tax base available to the polity.

When a polity's tax base is affected by the degree of suffrage, the present median voter and his representative in parliament may have a practical fiscal interest in suffrage reform. The median voter's ideal suffrage level in this institutional setting can be characterized by modifying equation 7.1 to take into account the effect of changes in suffrage on the tax base Y. Let Y be redefined as the size of the income tax base, which under the assumed tax constitution is a decreasing function of the wealth or income-tax qualifications for suffrage, $Y = y(T^L, T^K)$. Changes in suffrage laws will generate a new median voter who will have different demands for public services and also for suffrage laws. The fiscal effects of the new median voter is accounted for by the implicit function describing G^* and in the cost-sharing rule through effects on the ratio of median income to national income Y^v/Y.

The present median voter's own income, Y^v, is not affected by changes in suffrage although his future tax price for government services is affected. The present median voter's preferred suffrage eligibility rule now maximizes:

$$U_v = u\left(\left[1 - C(G^*, Z)/y(T^L, T^K)\right]Y_v, G^*\right) \quad \text{with } G^* = \gamma\left(L_v, K_v, T^L, T^K, y(T^L, T^K), Z\right) \tag{7.9}$$

By 1736, the franchise was limited to white male Protestant freeholders (owning at least 100 acres of land) and who were twenty-one years of age and resided in the counties in which they offered to vote. See McKinley (1905, chapter 2). Similar reductions in the scope of suffrage were also common in the other colonies in the early eighteenth century.

which requires:

$$Uv_{T^L} = \left[u_X\left(-C_G/Y\right)Y_v + u_G\right]G^*_{T^K} + u_x\left[Y_{T^L}C(G^*)Y_v/Y^2\right] = 0 \qquad (7.10a)$$

and

$$Uv_{T^K} = \left[u_X\left(-C_G/Y\right)Y_v + u_G\right]G^*_{T^K} + u_x\left[Y_{T^K}C(G^*)Y_v/Y^2\right] = 0 \qquad (7.10b)$$

The first set of bracketed terms are the effects of increased suffrage restrictions on government services and the costs of those services; the second set of bracketed terms characterizes the effect of suffrage restrictions on the overall tax base.

Consider first the case in which the income of the new median voter is approximately the same as that of the present one. This case might arise, for example, when non-income-based requirements for suffrage are relaxed: another territory may join a confederation; suffrage may be extended to another group with similar income to those already entitled to vote; residency, race, or sex qualifications may be dropped. In such cases, the marginal effects of suffrage rules on G^* can be neglected because the new distribution of voters has approximately the same median voter, $u_X(-C_G/Y)\ Y_v + u_G = 0$. In that case, equations 7.10a and 7.10b imply that the median voter will expand suffrage until the *tax base is maximized*, which occurs at the point where $Y_{T^L} = Y_{T^K} = 0$. In such cases, essentially all taxpayers may be allowed to vote in this case, although not nontaxpayers.

In the case in which the income of the new median voter is expected to differ from the present one, service levels and tax rates will change as suffrage is adusted. In this scenario, the first-order conditions imply that the present median voter will trade off advantages from a greater tax base (lower tax rates) against marginal losses from changes in government services. Note that it is possible that no reform of suffrage laws will be adopted in such cases, in spite of the advantages of a broader tax base. The median voter's marginal losses from new service levels may be larger than his or her marginal tax savings from a somewhat broader tax base. Only if the anticipated tax savings more than offset marginal losses from suboptimal service will suffrage be expanded.

In the latter case, however, reforms may still be blocked. The present median voter may believe that all future median voters will prefer further expansion of suffrage and the tax base. In such cases, a "slippery slope" may be said to exist, and an initially small increase of suffrage might be gradually be expanded to include all taxpayers, as a series of suffrage expansions are adopted and ratified by successively poorer (or more liberal) median voters. Economic growth could play a role in such slippery slopes for suffrage reform, insofar as economic development increases the wealth and tax worthiness of relatively low-income citizens. Note, however, that a forward-looking median voter who felt that the associated path of fiscal packages was inferior to the initial one would want to block otherwise desirable suffrage reforms to avoid the slippery slope.

These tax-base explanations of suffrage expansion are internally consistent, but they depend on somewhat strong assumptions about median-voter expectations and the existence of a peculiar tax constitution under which only the enfranchised can be taxed. In most cases, breaking the link between tax payments and suffrage and simply expanding taxation without expanding suffrage would be broadly support by voters and within parliament. Changing the tax base would expand the potential scope of public services, salaries, and so forth for all those currently eligible to vote, without the undesirable policy effects of a new median voter and median representative.

Given this, most members of parliament would *vote to eliminate a suffrage-based taxation restriction*, so that nonvoters could be taxed without expanding suffrage. A suffrage-based tax constitution tends to be unstable.

Practical Difficulty of Fine-Tuning Electoral Laws

The rules that determine voter qualifications are usually more difficult to change than ordinary policies because they are quasi-constitutional in nature. This increases the stability of suffrage laws beyond that implied by the median voter's pragmatic interest in continuing to be the median voter.

The stability of suffrage law is further reinforced by the institutional conservatism of both voters and members of parliament. Political and policy uncertainty would clearly increase if election laws were routinely revised every time that parliament met. Thus, risk aversion among the members and their voters encourages stable suffrage laws, other things being equal. Stable electoral systems may be further supported by widely held norms that justify particular suffrage rules or which make tradition a desirable feature of political systems, especially among those already entitled to vote. Moreover, there are practical constitutional advantages to stable election laws, insofar as such laws reduce the ability of a temporary majority to capture parliament (Congleton 2003a).

In addition, the members of parliament normally have a private interest in preserving the laws that brought them to office. Political organizations may also resist reforms that destabilize existing coalitions of political interests in parliament or in electoral districts. Consequently, debate on suffrage issues is often extensive and normally runs through several parliaments.

For all of these reasons, the median member of parliament is normally inclined to resist changes in suffrage law, and in practice most proposals for reform are defeated. This does not mean that all members of parliament, all voters, or all citizens prefer the existing suffrage laws to all others. Differences in individual circumstances, tastes, and ideology cause many citizens to be dissatisfied with their government's present rules, including many who are entitled to vote. For example, voters with relatively large capital, land, or labor holdings usually prefer more restrictive rules. Voters with smaller endowments tend to prefer less restrictive rules. For such dissatisfied citizens, election-law reform can potentially generate a new median voter whose preferred policies are closer to their own.

PROTESTS, REVOLUTIONARY THREATS, AND SUFFRAGE REFORM

Given the absence of spontaneous political pressures for reform, those not represented in government may try to organize themselves to press for reform through persuasive means, and in extreme cases, to threaten a revolution against the present government. However, both effective suffrage reform supporting interest groups and democratic revolutions are difficult to organize and unlikely to be successful, because those whose interests are being advanced by the existing institutions of government are already organized in a manner that allows them to oppose such efforts.

Organizing a Peaceful, Persuasive Campaign

Politically active interest groups are formed for reasons similar to those of other organizations. There are economies of scale that can be realized by developing persuasive arguments, by organizing meetings of persons with shared interests, in lobbying members of parliament, and in organizing peaceful demonstrations that reveal the breadth of support for a given policy or reform. Formeteurs, thus, may attempt to form political organizations if they expect to profit from such organizations, either financially or by significantly increasing the likelihood of desired reforms.

Table 7.1 illustrates how rewards and penalties can be used to encourage and discourage individuals to join political organizations and public protests. The game to the left of the matrix is the "natural" assurance game of political organization. The game to the right characterizes how rewards,

Table 7.1. *Participating in, Organizing, and Opposing Mass Demonstrations*

	The assurance game for popular demonstrations		Organizational solution for popular demonstrations opposed by government		
	Potential protester B			Potential protester B	
	Protest	Stay home		Protest	Shirk
Protest (A)	3, 3	0, 0	Protest (A)	$3 + R - P, 3 + R - P$	$R - P, 0$
Stay Home (A)	0, 0	1, 1	Shirk (A)	$0, R - P$	1, 1
Exit (A)	1.1	1, 1	Exit (A)	1.1	1.1

The cell entries are expected utilities or net benefits that can be used to rank order the subjective payoffs for prospective protesters.

R, and penalties, *P*, can be created to encourage or discourage participation in the political organization. (To simplify the exposition, it is initially assumed that both rewards and penalties are realized with certainty.)

The potential gains from organization are four units in the illustration, (3 + 3) – (1 + 1). These unrealized gains imply a formal political organization can potentially be fruitful for its members and leadership. In the absence of governmental opposition ($P = 0$), rewards greater than one unit are sufficient to induce attendance at the organization's meeting or mass demonstration.

If, however, formeteurs can provide a reward of $R > P + 1$ in the "Protest Game," participants will find it to their private advantage to assemble at the designated time and place and participate in public demonstrations supporting suffrage reform or other policy changes. It is partly to increase *R* that political organizers often include music, food, rousing speeches, prayers, and other forms of entertainment at their meetings and mass demonstrations in settings in which expected penalties are small. The required coordinating reward decreases when the organized forms of political expression are enjoyable activities themselves, or if participation in large gatherings of persons who share important goals is satisfying or comforting for the participants.

Efforts to organize groups favoring major policy and procedural reforms are often opposed by the persons already represented in government, because such persons benefit from current policies. Their representatives can, for example, pass laws that create new penalties or increase existing penalties on political formeteurs and on those participating in public demonstrations in support of new policies. Most societies, consequently, have laws that regulate large public gatherings, and many have laws that regulate the formation of organizations with public-policy agendas. Even relatively liberal regimes may have rules on what can and cannot be published in newspapers and books, and what can and cannot be said at public and private meetings.

Table 7.1 illustrates why increasing punishments for organizing and participating in demonstrations tends to make such demonstrations more difficult to organize. The expected net benefits of participants falls which makes it more likely that they will free ride, rather than participate. As a result, mass protests are usually associated with governments that are already relatively liberal, because such regimes tolerate, rather than penalize, law-abiding interest groups and peaceful demonstrations favoring changes in existing policies. Peaceful mass demonstrations are also possible in cases in which non-liberal governments are already disintegrating (failing), because such governments are unable to impose significant penalties on large numbers of demonstrators.

Imposing penalties on peaceful demonstrators can be rationalized in a variety of ways. Additional law enforcement is often argued to be necessary for crowd control. Even well organized demonstrations find it difficult to prevent various sorts of thuggery. Consequently, even demonstrations in which most participants are law-abiding, often have a minority of participants who are unwilling to follow the organizer's rules or the country's civil law. Moreover, property destruction and fights tend to reduce the perceived effectiveness of the government's law-enforcement abilities, which diminishes the efficiency of its efforts to police other crimes. Imposing penalties on demonstrators can reduce both problems. Indeed, even minor penalties may be sufficient to discourage mass demonstrations of support or opposition to current public policies and institutions. Moreover, such penalties will not necessarily produce large numbers of convictions if they are credible, because relatively few protests will take place, and so few organizers or protesters will be punished.

Domestic pressures for reform thus can often be easily diffused by even relatively weak governments. The finite nature of the gains from policy reform implies that a finite expected penalty, P, exists that is sufficient to discourage all organizations of moderate men and women. In the case illustrated, a penalty greater than 3 is sufficient to discourage the formation of political organizations and would cause an organized group to disintegrate. Given $R < 3$ and $P > 3$, each potential protester finds him or herself better off free riding (staying at home) than protesting, regardless of choices made by others.

Repression and Revolution

The organization of a mass revolt tends to be much more difficult than organizing peaceful public demonstrations for several reasons. Revolutions against a well-organized government require a strong military organization in addition to convincing arguments, pamphlets, speeches, mass meetings, and petitions. The cost of organizing revolutionary movements also tends to be far greater in both the planning and execution stage, because revolutionary campaigns are likely to attract aggressive opposition from the existing government. The risks are larger for those favoring the status quo, and so the punishments meted out for organizers and participants tend to be much larger.

All these problems imply that formal organizations, such as revolutionary armies, will be necessary, except perhaps in cases in which the government to be overthrown is very poorly organized. Armies have long been more effective than mobs and other unmanaged groups a creating and implementing credible threats. This is, of course, why village law enforcement and national defense is normally an organized activity, rather than an unorganized activity left to spontaneous citizen efforts. Revolutionary armies can use threats of violence to solve internal and external free riding and coordination problems, as when persons who provide information to the existing government or fail to actively cooperate to advance the goals of the revolution are severely punished.

Revolutionary armies are, nonetheless, very difficult to organize. These difficulties can be analyzed using the revolutionary recruiting game characterized in Table 7.2. Assume that there are just two possible outcomes, the status-quo ante and the outcome of a successful revolution. The difference between a person's net benefits in the pre- and postrevolutionary state is their "stake" in the revolution. In principle, an individual's revolutionary stake can be positive or negative according to whether he or she expects to be better or worse off if the revolution succeeds.

One important difference between peaceful and revolutionary groups is the effect of organizational size on the probability of success. Even a single very persuasive author may directly change a lot of minds, but a single assassin can only change a handful of leaders. In robust governments, such leaders are routinely replaced as they die. No man or subset of leaders can be irreplaceable in a durable government, although policy formation may be temporarily disrupted as replacements are recruited and learn their new roles. Suppose that the probability of successful revolution is $F = (m/n)^{(1-g)}$, where m is the membership of the revolutionary organization, n is the

Table 7.2. *The Revolt Game for Constitutional or Policy Reform*

	Number of Revolters				
Strategies	0	1	2	m	All
Join Revolt	P, P	$(1/n)^{(1-g)}S + R - P$	$(2/n)^{(1-g)}S + R - P$	$(m/n)^{(1-g)}S + R - P$	$S + R$
Do Not Join	0	0	0	0	0
Exit	E	E	E	E	E

The cell entries are expected utilities, S is the net benefit of successful revolt, R is the reward of participating in the revolution, and P is the expected penalty associated with participation. E is the net benefit of moving to another community. In a community with a stable population, $E < 0$.

number of persons in the community at large, and g represents the government's ability to resist revolutionary pressures.

Even in this simple representation, the decision to participate or not is influenced by a number of considerations. To simplify exposition, it is assumed that all participants are risk neutral, which tends to favor the formation of revolutionary organizations relative to the assumption of risk aversion. If $(m/n)^{(1-g)}S_i + R - P > 0$, then individual i joins the revolt. This implies that for individuals with positive stakes in the revolt, there is a membership size, m^*, beyond which participating in the revolt increases expected utility for given stakes, revolutionary rewards, and penalties. If the organization is smaller than m^*, however, such individuals are better off free riding.

In the special case in which all persons have the same stake in the revolutionary outcome, $S > 0$, the game resembles the assurance game described earlier, because the result would be better than the status quo if everyone participates, and everyone would participate once the group reached critical size m^*. In such cases, either the entire society revolts or essentially no one does. It is, nonetheless, clear that an effective government can manipulate P and g to undermine revolutionary organizations even in such cases.

In settings in which the stakes vary within the community of potential revolutionaries, membership does not necessarily fall to zero for finite values of P and g. The smallest group that a person i will join is $m_i^* = (n)[(P - R)/S_i]^{1/g}$, which falls as stakes, S_i, organizational rewards, R, increase and increase with population, n, and expected penalties, P. Persons with very high stakes are often persons with strong religious and ideologically motivated policy goals in addition to pragmatic economic and political goals. Such revolutionaries may have very large stakes, indeed infinite ones, at issue. Such idealist-fanatics will join small, very risky, secret revolutionary associations, with almost no chance of success. Pragmatists with only economic stakes in changing government policies will not.

The ability of a government to discourage the formation of large revolutionary organizations is affected by a variety of resource considerations, including the size and discipline of its own military and law enforcement systems, as well as the internal support for the present government and support within the community at large (who may provide information about conspirators).

An effective government can often impose relatively large penalties (*P*) on revolutionary participants without inducing fear among nonparticipants (which tends to increase *S* and *E*) and without indicating that the group is relatively large (and thus, possibly, worth joining). Laws against treason can be aggressively enforced; rewards for providing the ruler(s) with creditable evidence of conspiracies will be high; commissions, rather than individuals, may be given responsibility for internal policy making (to minimize risks from internal defections); and potential rivals to present government leaders may be rotated or exiled in a manner that reduces opportunities for opponents to acquire support within or outside government. Spies can be hired to determine secret meeting times and locations.

The organization of small revolutionary groups can similarly be discouraged by imposing large penalties on political organizers and those discovered to have attended their meetings. The death penalty for conspiracy and treason has long been included among deterrents, which can discourage participation for all but fanatics. As long as the government is reasonably efficient and retains the loyalty of those charged with imposing punishments, it can increase expected punishments sufficiently to discourage the formation of most revolutionary organizations, even in high stake settings.

Such governmental strategies may also eliminate publicly organized political meetings and demonstrations. The lack of significant protests, in turn, may cause those who weakly support revolution to believe that support for the government is stronger than it actually is.

Some situations are at theoretically more conducive for revolutions than others. For example, a political or economic crisis can increase S_i to very high levels for many persons in the society of interest, which, in combination with a failing state, can induce large revolutionary groups to form rapidly, as argued by Kuran (1989) and Weingast (2006). Moreover, as Kuran (1989) points out, active public support may increase the perceived probability of success, *F*, and decreases the perceived probability of punishment, *P*, and thereby increase the size of reform movements. However, if such organizations are not able to generate enough resources to be self-sustaining, an initially lucky revolutionary group may disintegrate, as noted by Ferrero (2002).

Indeed, in many cases, potential formeteurs and potential members may simply emigrate from their home community, because their exit options are more attractive than those at home, $E > 0$. It is surprisingly common for revolutionary "leaders" to talk about revolution while safe in a relatively liberal foreign land, rather than to organize and conduct the required recruiting and military operations at home. As a consequence, expatriate communities often include many self-described radicals and revolutionary leaders, at the same time that the government under "attack" remains at peace. In cases in which a revolution does succeed against all odds, subsequent expatriate communities often include counter-revolutionaries, such as displaced kings and their retinues.

The organizational theories of Chapters Two and Three imply that a revolutionary army is unlikely to establish liberal democratic reforms in the rare cases in which revolutionaries are successful. Revolutionary formeteurs are usually charismatic individuals. Their organizational governments are often based on the king-and-council template, with a powerful executive and a small council of fellow activists. As true of other organizations, revolutionary formeteurs normally desire to retain control of their organizations after it is up and running. Moreover, their success against all odds clearly demonstrates that their leadership and their organization are unusually effective.

As a consequence, the leaders of revolutionary organizations are inclined to retain their relatively authoritarian prerevolutionary procedures for making policy decisions after they successfully take over. That is to say, revolutionists are inclined to be institutionally conservative after the civil war is won.[6]

[6] It bears noting that George Washington was not a revolutionary formeteur, but rather the agent of a council of colonial leaders, most of whom were representatives of elected colonial governments (state parliaments). The first national government of the United States simply constitutionalized the system used to orchestrate the war of independence. The individual member-state governments were also very similar to the colonial governments that they replaced (see Chapter Eighteen). George Washington continued to defer to both the national and state governments after the war was won.

The *Articles of Confederation* adopted in 1781 (somewhat before the war was over) was partly a mutual defense treaty among colonial-state governments. Article 1 states that "Each state retains its sovereignty, freedom, and independence and every power, jurisdiction, and right, which is not by this Confederation expressly delegated to the United States, in Congress assembled." Article 2 states that "The said States hereby severally enter into a firm league of friendship with each other, for their *common defence*, the security of their liberties, and their mutual and general welfare, binding themselves to assist each other, against all force offered to, or attacks made upon them, or any of them, on account of religion, sovereignty, trade, or any other pretence whatever."

A Digression on the Greater Feasibility of Palace Coups

A successful revolt tends to require relatively high stakes (high *S*), relatively high rewards (*R*), and relatively weak governance (low *g*). This suggests that small groups operating within government often have better prospects for changing governments than large groups operating outside of government, as argued by Tullock (1974, 1987).

Although the aggregate benefits obtained by replacing extractive or dysfunctional governments can be very large, only a few persons are likely to gain positions of authority (or wealth) in the new government. It is the smallness of the individual stakes of potential revolutions that makes revolutions relatively easy to discourage. The private advantages of participating in a palace coup, however, are normally far greater than those associated with a popular uprising. The smaller scale of internal conspiracies also makes them more difficult to detect and punish than larger external ones. Insiders can silently shift their support among competing factions on the basis of anticipated success, and secure greater expected personal benefits at somewhat lower expected cost.

Consistent with this analysis, there is a good deal of evidence that palace coups are organized more frequently and succeed more often than popular revolts (Bienen and Van de Walle 1989, Tullock 1987: 9). Such revolts normally maintain, rather than replace, most preexisting governmental institutions if they are successful.

RATIONAL CHOICE AND THE LONG-RUN STABILITY OF SUFFRAGE LAW

Overall, this chapter suggests that suffrage laws can be stable for long periods of time, whether they are broadly supported or not.

The stability of narrow suffrage laws for selecting members of parliament is not an accident. There is nothing inherent in majority rule that inclines voters or those elected to expand suffrage to new voters. A median voter with only pragmatic interests will prefer qualifications that maximize his or her influence over public policies. This support for the status quo is reinforced by the interests of those elected to office under the existing rules and institutional conservatism on the part of both those eligible to vote and those elected to office. The models demonstrate, perhaps surprisingly, support for the status-quo suffrage laws is not undermined by increases in median voter income. Those with the authority to adopt reforms will normally prefer that the status-quo procedures remain in place, because those procedures advance their personal and organizational interests.

Although this conclusion seems to suggest that only revolutions can expand suffrage, the chapter also argues that democratic revolutions are unlikely to occur and that successful revolutions are unlikely to promote democracy. Revolutionary groups are difficult to organize because of the usual free rider problems faced by all organizations and the active opposition of the government that revolutionaries hope to overthrow. In those few cases in which outsiders orchestrate a successful civil war against the existing government, the advantages of hierarchy, discipline, and secrecy in fighting such wars, together with institutional conservatism, tends to favor continuation of the revolutionary organization's own hierarchical methods for decision making, rather than the open and competitive ones of democracy.

Overthrows of governments by insiders are more common than those organized by outsiders, but in such cases, most of the old institutions are preserved, although the persons holding offices of authority are replaced. Palace coups are not constitutional revolutions. The leaders of insider groups that overthrow a preexisting government expect to profit from many of the same rules that benefited the leaders of the previous regime.

One can imagine cases in which those in office negotiate with revolutionaries in order to preserve most of their authority; however, this is not the only strategy for holding on to their offices of authority. The threat of revolutions can be reduced through repressive measures that make revolutionary organizations very difficult to create and manage. In medieval Europe, for example, new ideas and new organizations were routinely censored and those espousing them severely punished. Even mildly revolutionary (liberal) tracts were normally circulated and/or published elsewhere under assumed names or anonymously.

As states liberalize, censorship is gradually reduced, but one of the last area of censorship to be lifted is normally that with respect to political reform. Indeed, conservative states often punish all novel ideas as blasphemy or treason, unless governmental authority has been substantially undermined by failures of their own internal incentive and decision-making systems.

For existing suffrage laws to change, the policy interests of those with the authority to change the laws governing political participation must also change.

EIGHT

Ideology, Interest Groups, and Adult Suffrage

The analysis of the previous two chapters suggests that the rise of parliament and the expansion of suffrage are not necessarily connected with each other. There are many occasions on which parliaments may gain policy-making authority, without producing similar gains to trade between those eligible and not eligible to vote. Chapter Six suggests that changes in the distribution of income, new technologies of production (and destruction), and changes in the person holding the royal office may induce changes in the distribution of policy-making authority between the king and parliament. Chapter Seven suggests that those same changes would not produce a majority in parliament in favor of suffrage reform, because both voters and members of parliaments tend to prefer the existing election laws for pragmatic reasons.

Shifts of authority between a king and council, consequently, are predicted to be more common than changes in suffrage laws. Revolutionary threats and palace coups may also affect the balance of authority between the king and parliament, but are not likely to produce suffrage reform. Fear of revolution is likely to increase executive power, which may be used to discourage participation in politically active interest groups. Moreover, it should also be noted that parliaments may be elected by very broad suffrage without producing democratic rule, if parliament itself has little policy-making authority.

This chapter focuses on the possible roles that ideological norms and interest groups may play in suffrage expansion and contraction. That norms may influence behavior was discussed in Chapter Two, when analyzing composite incentive systems. In that chapter, it was shown that some norms can reduce various intra-organizational prisoner's-dilemma and coordination problems in a cost-effective manner, which induces organizations to use and encourage such norms.

The norms that are relevant for suffrage reform and other constitutional reforms emerge from normative theories that attempt to characterize proper behavior and institutions for large groups of persons. Such normative theories often characterize what might be called the "good society," and provide systematic methods for determining whether the present society can be improved or not. Economists use the Pareto principles for these purposes. Utilitarians use social welfare functions and contractarians use the veil of ignorance construction to characterize "the" good society for given groups and resources. Theologians use particular authoritative texts to make such assessments. The particulars of the normative theories used are not important for the purposes of this chapter, only that such norms exist, affect behavior, and may directly or indirectly affect assessments of who should be entitled to cast votes in elections for members of parliament.

How changes in such norms may induce changes in suffrage laws is examined in the first half of this chapter. Several of the most plausible routes to suffrage reform involve interdependencies between ideology, economic development, and politically active interest groups.

Insofar as norms may change and be changed, norms and normative theories may also encourage the formation of interest groups. Some groups may attempt to promote specific norms with the aim of changing politically relevant behavior. Other groups may be able to form only because norms or economic circumstances have changed in a manner that reduces their organization costs or increases their effectiveness.

As noted in Chapter Seven, organized interest groups with political agendas are not always tolerated, because they threaten the interests of those profiting from the status quo. Chapter Two, however, reminds us that the status quo is not always feasible, and so organizations have to be able to recognize and solve new problems and take advantage of new possibilities to survive in the long run. Consequently, toleration of (limited) internal debate can be defended on the pragmatic grounds that it increases a government's ability to identify advantageous reforms. Consistent with this analysis, most members of late medieval parliaments had the right of free speech during meetings of their parliament, although not outside those meetings.

In polities that tolerate even limited debate and dissent in parliament, formeteurs will often have an incentive to organizing groups that attempt to influence the opinions and interests of members of parliament. This may require small or large groups and may be accomplished in several ways. The strategies chosen depend on formeteur goals and circumstances. For example, interest groups may attempt to persuade office holders to change their ranking of policies or constitutional possibilities, or they may appeal to their pragmatic interests by promising various conditional rewards and making various conditional threats. The second half of Chapter Eight analyzes nonrevolutionary strategies through which organized groups of outsiders may be able to influence public-policy decisions made by insiders.

Shifts in suffrage relevant norms and in the relative strength of politically active interest groups may also produce new gains from constitutional exchange between the king and parliament, although these are not analyzed in the present chapter. Such effects, nonetheless, provide a possible explanation for the correlation between suffrage reform and shifts of policy-making authority between kings and parliaments in several of the case studies of Part II.

A DIGRESSION ON NORMS AND RATIONAL CHOICE

It is important to understand that rational decision making does not rule out norm-following behavior. Economists, for example, often focus on narrow self-interested behavior in models in order to analyze how relative prices and rates of return tend to influence individual behavior and thereby market outcomes. Norm-driven behavior tends to be neglected in such analyses, in part, because "tastes" (utility functions) are assumed to be stable over the period of analysis. When an economist concludes that a change in *X* causes a change in *Y*, other things being equal, among the other things implicitly being assumed constant are an individual's internalized norms. For many purposes, internalized norms can be regarded as "tastes" or preferences that affect a person's tradeoffs between various activities and products.

There are, however, several problems with this approach. First, norms may change through time in a manner different than one's taste for chocolate. In such cases, a model that takes explicit account of how norms affect behavior and change can shed more light on individual choices and behavior through time than models that subsume norms into tastes. Second, the taste-approach to norms also neglects a good deal of economic and socially important activity. A person's norms may produce opportunities that are unavailable to other person. For example, economists often analyze marginal product as if it were the result of genetic ability and knowledge about particular production methods. (The number of times that a person has to hit a nail to drive it home varies with a person's strength and hammering technique.) Marginal product on teams is, however, more complex than that description. For example, persons with particular internalized norms may be more productive in organizations than others lacking such norms, as developed in Chapter Two. Team members with the right norms will work hard whether monitored or not, because they have an internal work ethic or internalized norm of promise keeping. A private "golden-rule ethic" tends to internalize externalities, reduce losses from conflict, and encourage trust-based relationships. Recruiting persons with such norms, or simply an internalized norm of rule following, reduces monitoring and enforcement costs within organizations and in society at large and increases their effectiveness.

Moreover, broadening the use of particular norms can also be the principal aim of an organization, as true of groups practicing the same religion or philosophy and groups advocating narrow norms, as early scientific and temperance societies. Normative rules and theories that that are well aligned with economic interests are often culturally supported (e.g., encouraged among children), because the behavior induced by those norms tends to increase prosperity and reduce unproductive social conflict. Persuading children to adopt such norms is evidently one of the main tasks of parenting and formal education. Good students get their homework done on time, diligently, without cheating. Students are encouraged not to be trouble makers and are taught about proper behavior at the same time that they are encouraged to learn a bit about language, mathematics, and history. "Good work" means following the teacher's instructions for the task at hand. Similar lessons are taught at home, by religious organizations, and in most other formal and informal organizations.

This does not mean that every choice is determined by normative theories, nor does it mean that people have only normative aims. For most people in most social settings, normative interests are only a subset of the goals that individuals pursue, although this becomes obvious only in cases in which there is a conflict between normative aims and economic, political, or biological ones.

Rational-choice models can be used to shed light on the tradeoffs that influence decisions made and actions taken in such circumstances. To the extent that norms are internalized, it can be said that advancing normative goals directly increases utility. To the extent that advancing normative goals requires time and attention, there is clearly an allocative problem that can be analyzed using the standard tools from rational-choice models. In cases in which norms and economic interests are not perfectly aligned, there will be tradeoffs among normative and economic objectives, and even among the norms that might be applied in a given setting.

Time, attention, and other resources will be used to pursue normative goals, rather than that pragmatic ones, only up to the point where expected (subjective) marginal benefits equal expected marginal costs. Consequently, religious persons do not give all of their wealth to their churches, because religious goals are only one of many goals pursued by religious persons, and religious duties are only a subset of their many internalized duties. Such persons have to eat if they are to survive, and feel obliged to take reasonably good care of their children and loved ones. Similarly, persons with a strong ideological agenda are likely to turn out and provide support in favor of policy reforms that advance their ideological goals, even when doing so is likely to be punished, as noted in Chapter Seven. Only zealots, however, such as suicide bombers, advance normative agendas irrespective of personal costs. At the other extreme, only pure pragmatists are unaffected by normative theories.

Most men and women in civilized society trade off normative and pragmatic goals when making both day-to-day and long-term choices.

SOME MATHEMATICS OF PRINCIPLED DECISIONS WITH RESPECT TO SUFFRAGE

Tradeoffs between pragmatic and normative interests are very likely to affect a voter's and/or member of parliament's assessment of the optimal qualifications for suffrage. These tradeoffs can be analyzed by extending the model of the suffrage demand developed in Chapter Seven to take account of the effects of normative (or ideological) theories of suffrage.

For example, one can easily extend the model to analyze the suffrage laws preferred by a person who has internalized a universal suffrage norm. Such a person has a utility function that increases with the extent of suffrage, S, *other things being equal*. However, other things are not always equal, because changes in suffrage affects fiscal policies. Such tradeoffs between idealistic and practical interests will be reflected in voter preferences over suffrage law and public policy choices.

To see this, suppose that suffrage levels are again determined by tax thresholds, $S = s(T^L, T^K)$, that can be adjusted to generate any suffrage level, and that voters are interested in private consumption, public services, and the breadth of suffrage. Building on the previous model of the demand for suffrage, voters with an ideological interest in suffrage as well as narrower interests in personal consumption and public services prefer the suffrage qualifications that maximize:

$$U = u\Big(\big[1 - C(\gamma(L_v, K_v, T^L, T^K, Y, Z), Z)/Y\big]Y_v,\\ \gamma(L_v, K_v, T^L, T^K, Y, Z),\ s(T^L, T^K)\Big) \tag{8.1}$$

which can be characterized by the first-order conditions:

$$U_{T^L} = \left[U_X\left(-C_G\right)Y_v / Y - U_G\right]G^{\cdot}_{T^L} + U_S S_{T^L} = 0 \tag{8.2}$$

$$U_{T^K} = \left[U_X\left(-C_G\right)Y_v / Y - U_G\right]G^{\cdot}_{T^K} + U_S S_{T^K} = 0 \tag{8.3}$$

where $S = s(T^L, T^K)$ refers to the percentage of adults eligible to vote given thresholds T^L and T^K.

In the model depicted in equations 8.1, 8.2, and 8.3, the pragmatic-normative tradeoffs are characterized by the relative sizes of the marginal utility of personal income, U_X, public services, U_G, and the universal suffrage norm, U_S. Economic persons, with their narrow utility function, are pure pragmatists, because, by assumption, $U_S = 0$. The models used in Chapter Seven are thus special cases in which pragmatists determine suffrage levels.

The extended utility function allows us to model voters that philosophically favor universal suffrage but do not ignore other goals when casting votes. Applying the implicit function theorem to equations 8.2 and 8.3 allows the typical citizen's demand for voting thresholds to be characterized as:

$$T^{L*} = l\left(L_i, K_i, T^L, T^K, Y, Z\right) \tag{8.4}$$

$$T^{K*} = k\left(L_i, K_i, T^L, T^K, Y, Z\right) \tag{8.5}$$

where T^L, T^K are the existing suffrage laws that produced the present median voter and T^{L*}, T^{K*} are the new suffrage laws preferred by the present median voter.

Voters with ideological interests tend to disagree about the ideal suffrage law for reasons that are similar to their disagreements about other policies. They may have different economic interests at stake or differ in their assessment of the relative importance of personal consumption, public services, and normative goals (the ideal breadth of suffrage). The more important normative theories are for a voter's choice, the more idealistic or ideological that voter tends to be. The less important norms are, the more pragmatic that voter can be said to be. Voters may also disagree because they have internalized or applied different norms.

SUFFRAGE NORMS AND OPTIMAL QUALIFICATIONS FOR SUFFRAGE

In the absence of an ideological or normative interest in suffrage, as shown in Chapter Seven, the existing suffrage thresholds are optimal for the median voter. For a pragmatic median voter, $U_S S_{T^L} = 0$ and $U_S S_{T^K} = 0$, which implies that the first two terms in the first-order conditions are always satisfied, and his or her ideal fiscal package is provided, G^*.

In the case in which voters are influenced by norms and suffrage is initially less than ideal, however, $U_S S_{T^L} \neq 0$ and $U_S S_{T^K} \neq 0$, and there is a tradeoff between advancing normative and economic interests in suffrage qualifications. In such cases, equations 8.2 and 8.3 demonstrate that normative interests in suffrage create a suffrage-fiscal tradeoff analogous to that which was present in the "only voters pay taxes" case explored in Chapter Seven.

Voters that philosophically favor universal suffrage, but are not zealots, prefer suffrage qualifications that are more inclusive (lower) than those which optimize their fiscal package, but are less inclusive than required for universal suffrage. Extending suffrage produces marginal benefits from greater conformity with the voter's ideological norms, but also produces a marginal cost because taxes and government service levels shift away from more preferred levels.

The optimal suffrage rule for a voter influenced by norms favoring universal suffrage thus extends suffrage beyond that favored by an otherwise similar pragmatist, but only to the point where marginal benefits from broader suffrage equals its marginal fiscal costs. This is not necessarily hypocrisy. It simply reflects the fact that universal suffrage is only one of many goals for such persons.

Equilibria below universal suffrage may not exist, however, because they require the current median voter's suffrage norm to be satisfied: $T^{L*} = T^L$, and $T^{K*} = T^K$, which implies that the actual extent of suffrage is also ideal $S = s(T^{L*}, T^{K*})$. When a universal suffrage norm is widespread among voters, an equilibrium of this sort may not exist. Instead, a slippery slope may exist. Each successive median voter may want to expand suffrage a bit more, to include a few more persons in order to advance their theory of the good society. A series of suffrage reforms in the direction of universal suffrage would be adopted in such cases until a median voter is reached who considers the existing rules to be optimal, which in this case may require universal adult suffrage.

Of course, any median voter who recognizes the existence of a slippery slope, and who prefers the fiscal-suffrage law combination of the status quo to that associated with universal suffrage, might simply accept the status quo, rather than press for his or her preferred suffrage rule. The slippery slope provides an additional basis for institutional conservatism. This tends to make the slope toward democracy "sticky" rather than "slippery" if voters are forward looking – especially in settings in which fiscal policies under universal suffrage have never been observed.

Normative Support for Limited Suffrage

Universal suffrage, however, is not the only possible normative theory of suffrage, and it was not until the twentieth century that very inclusive suffrage norms became widespread among voters in the West. Prior to the twentieth century, it was more widely believed that all "qualified" persons should be entitled to vote. The qualifications thought necessary varied among persons, but generally included various attributes that increased the independence and quality of one's votes: education, wealth, experience, and residency. Here it bears noting that most persons in the West would be opposed to extending the right to vote in their national elections to five-year-old children or to noncitizens living on other continents. Nineteenth-century arguments against universal suffrage paralleled contemporary arguments against extending the vote to children. Children are not wise enough, educated enough, nor independent enough to cast meaningful votes.

Qualification-based theories of suffrage allow normative aims to vary significantly among voters (and nonvoters). Such normative theories also allow the possibility that norms (acceptable qualifications) may shift through time, as merit thresholds are revised in light of experience and shifts in ideology. Qualification-based theories of suffrage imply that all those who are properly qualified should be entitled to vote, but no others. They do not imply that the ideal qualifications are necessarily unchanging constants.

Analyzing the effects of qualification-based theories of suffrage on the suffrage preferences of voters requires their normative theories to be modeled more explicitly than was necessary for the universal suffrage norm. Suppose that a voter's ideal suffrage level is $S^* = s(T^{L*}, T^{K*})$, where T^{L*} and T^{K*} are the tax payments from labor or capital income that indicate sufficient independence to cast a meaningful vote. Normative goals are advanced when the difference between the real and the ideal thresholds diminish. The normative advantages of a more perfect suffrage law can be characterized as $\nu = n(|S^* - s(T^L, T^K)|)$ with $\nu|_{S^*-S}| < 0$. The effect of such normative theories on suffrage can be modeled by replacing function s with function n in the equation 8.1.

The first-order conditions for a voter's optimal suffrage law are similar to 8.2 and 8.3.

$$U_{T^l} = \left[U_X\left(-C_G\right)Y_v / Y - U_G\right]G^*_{T^L} + U_S V_{T^L} = 0 \tag{8.6}$$

$$U_{T^K} = \left[U_X\left(-C_G\right)Y_v / Y - U_G\right]G^*_{T^K} + U_s V_{T^K} = 0 \tag{8.7}$$

The effects of qualification-based suffrage norms on voter preferences, however, are less clear cut than a universal suffrage norm, because the tradeoffs depend on whether the existing laws are more or less inclusive than a voter's normatively ideal suffrage law. It is also interesting to note that some persons may now favor laws that are more inclusive than those considered philosophically ideal, because somewhat broader suffrage advances other pragmatic goals, including economic ones, through the policy changes induced by including additional voters in the electorate.

Under a qualification-based theory of suffrage, as opposed to universal suffrage, stable suffrage law does not require that the median voter be a pragmatist or concerned about a slippery slope. A stable suffrage law under a qualification-based norm occurs whenever the existing suffrage law is consistent with the median voter's normative theory $S = S^*$. At his or her normatively ideal suffrage level, the marginal utility of further suffrage reform falls to zero, $U_S S_{T^L} = 0$ and $U_S S_{T^K} = 0$, which implies that the median voter's regards the current law to be ideal. In this sense, it can be said that equilibrium suffrage laws are driven by normative theories, because only laws that exactly satisfy the median voter's normative theory of suffrage can be equilibria (in the absence of strategic voting).

Figure 8.1 illustrates the equilibrium pattern of suffrage that tends to emerge when either universal or qualification-based suffrage norms are widely accepted by those eligible to vote. The first reaction function, $s(S)$, depicts a universal suffrage norm, which tends to produce universal suffrage, a corner solution. The second, $n(|S^*-S|)$, depicts an interior solution of the sort associated with merit-based theories of suffrage (at the fixed points of functions s and n).[1]

Other functional forms are, of course, possible according to the normative theories employed and the distribution of those theories and the pragmatic interests of voters. There may be, for example, more than one equilibrium set of qualifications for suffrage (several fixed points of function n). Not all of such equilibria are dynamically stable, however, and it is interesting to note that external shocks in such cases may induce a series of myopic suffrage reforms that reaches a new equilibria through a series of discrete steps, rather than through a series of infinitesimal adjustments or great leaps, except in the neighborhood of the new suffrage-law equilibrium.

[1] The extent of suffrage as a percentage of the citizenry is always between 0 and 100 percent. Consequently, the continuity of functions s and n are sufficient to assure the existence of a fixed point. The fixed points characterize equilibrium levels of suffrage. In some cases, the fixed point may lie along the upper or lower bounds of S.

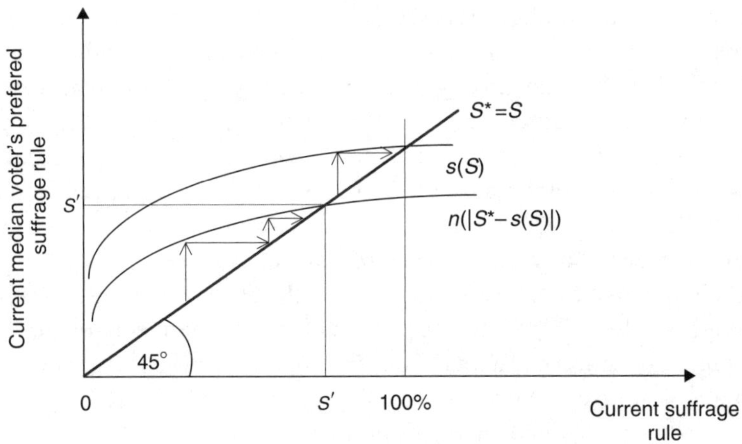

Figure 8.1. Median voter's preferred suffrage rule.

Equilibrium suffrage laws produce a median voter that prefers the existing law to all others.

Absence of an Income Effect on Equilibrium Suffrage Laws

At every suffrage-law equilibrium in Figure 8.1, the marginal utility of changing suffrage laws is zero, which implies that changes in the marginal utility of other goods and services do not affect the marginal rate of substitution between those goods and suffrage. When the median voter's suffrage norm is the actual law, changes in the median voter's income *will not* induce the present median voter to change the existing suffrage laws. (Recall that marginal rates of substitution can be expressed as a ratio of marginal utilities and that zero always equals zero.)

At a suffrage-law equilibrium, the present median voter remains entirely content with the existing pattern of law as his or her income changes, whether he or she is motivated entirely by pecuniary interests or takes account of ideological or other norms as well. Economic growth can change the rules governing suffrage by affecting the marginal rate of substitution between suffrage and other desired services *only at points away from the normative equilibrium*, where the marginal utility of suffrage reform is not zero.

Changes in the median voter's merit-based suffrage norms, however, can induce reform by changing the equilibrium, and can do so without necessarily leading to universal suffrage.

IDEOLOGICAL GROUPS, PERSUASIVE CAMPAIGNS, AND THE EXPANSION OF SUFFRAGE

Changes in normative theories may, in principle, occur idiosyncratically as individuals independently revise their theories in light of personal experiences, inspiration, or analysis. Alternatively, changes in norms may reflect events that affect a broad cross section of humanity. New evidence may undermine some preexisting normative theories while supporting others. A new continent may be discovered that undermines widely held flat-world theories that also characterize the good society. A new very persuasive book may be published that promotes a particular normative theory and/or challenges a widely held normative theory. A change in economic or political circumstances may favor persons with particular norms over others, which may induce many persons to revise their behavioral rules of thumb to better fit the times.

Norms and normative assessments may also change when organizations conduct persuasive campaigns. Suffrage campaigns may, for example, argue that more persons are qualified to vote than previously thought, or that fewer are. In general, persuasive campaigns operate by subsidizing the production and dissemination of information that demonstrates the relative merits of the preferred reforms and/or normative theories. Interest groups may sponsor or write editorials, pamphlets, and books; they may organize public addresses and meetings where information can be easily provided; or they may subsidize other organizations and persons that can do so.

Persuasive campaigns are educational in the sense that they change the knowledge base of voters and/or high officials, which changes relevant predictions about future events or changes the norms used to judge the relative merits of alternative policy proposals. The possibility of inducing electoral reforms, together with the effects that such reforms are expected to have on public policies, create incentives for proponents and opponents of reform to organize persuasive campaigns.

The advantages of scale and coordination imply that organized groups are often campaign more effectively than individuals or unorganized groups. With such organizational advantages in mind, the leaders of existing organizations may create special divisions to engage in a variety of lobbying activities for their organizations (firms, unions, sporting clubs, ideological interest groups, and so forth). Formeteurs may also create new organizations with the aim of influencing policy and constitutional developments.

Every country that liberalized its suffrage laws in the nineteenth century did so after long campaigns by groups organized to promote suffrage expansion inside and outside government. In many cases, persuasive campaigns evidently changed the norms of a broad cross section of voters and members of parliament.

A Model of Contributions to Suffrage Groups

The relationship between suffrage norms and support for suffrage groups can be analyzed with another minor extension of the model developed earlier. When election laws are stable, the current median voter and current pivotal member of parliament tend to be completely satisfied with the existing suffrage laws, so that $S^{v*} = s(T^{L*}, T^{K})$. In such cases, neither the pivotal member nor his or her supporters have an interest in supporting groups that advocate suffrage reform. They are completely satisfied with the status quo.

However, other voters and other members of parliament will be less satisfied with the status quo. Those who favor more liberal election laws have an interest in supporting pro-suffrage groups if there is a chance that suffrage groups can persuade the median voter to change suffrage norms. Those who favor more restrictive rules may similarly donate to groups lobbying for a more aristocratic electorate. Support for pro- and anti-suffrage groups provides dissatisfied individuals with a method of increasing their (expected) utility over the status quo whenever such groups have a reasonable chance of affecting suffrage policies.

Consider the case in which new suffrage level $S' > S_v^*$ is supported by a pro-suffrage group. Individual supporters make donations, D_i, to the suffrage group in order to maximize their expected utility:

$$\begin{aligned} U_i^e &= \left(1 - p(\Sigma Dj)u\left(X_v - D_i, G^v, n\left(\left|S_i * - S^v *\right|\right)\right)\right. \\ &\quad + p\left(\Sigma D_i\right)\left(uX_v - D_i, G^v, n\left(\left|S_i^* - S'\right|\right)\right) \end{aligned} \tag{8.8}$$

where $P = p(\Sigma D_j)$ is the probabilistic success function of the relevant suffrage group's efforts to change suffrage norms, D_i is citizen i's donation, and ΣD_j is the total of all individual donations. Under the usual Nash assumptions, the expected utility-maximizing donation satisfies:

$$-P_D U^0 + (1-P)\left(-U_X^0\right) + P_D U' + P\left(-U_X'\right) = 0$$

which implies that Di* approximately satisfies:

$$-P_D\left(U' - U^0\right) - U_X = 0 \tag{8.9}$$

Equation 8.9 and the implicit function theorem imply that an individual's contributions to the suffrage group can be written as:

$$D_i^* = d\left(Y_i, S', S_v^*, \Sigma D_j, Y, Z\right) \tag{8.10}$$

The effects of changes in circumstances on a particular individual's donations can be analyzed by differentiating equation 8.10 with respect to personal income and the donations of other persons.

$$\begin{aligned} Di^*_{Y_i} - &\left[P_D(1-\iota)\left(U'_X - U^0_X\right) - (1-t)U_{XX}\right] \\ &/\left[P_{DD}(U'-U^0) + P_D(U^0) + P_D\left(U^0_X - U'_X\right) + U_{XX}\right] > 0 \\ &\left(\text{given } U'_X - U^0_X \geq 0\right) \end{aligned} \tag{8.11}$$

and

$$\begin{aligned} D_i^*\Sigma D_j = &\left[P_{DD}(U'-U^0)\right]/-\left[\left(P_{DD}(U'-U^0) + P_D\left(U^0_X - U'_X\right) + U_{XX}\right] > 0 \\ &\left(\text{given } P_{DD} > 0\right) \end{aligned} \tag{8.12}$$

These derivatives imply that individual contributions increase as personal income increases and with the overall level of contributions if persuasive campaigns exhibit constant or increasing returns. Such comparative statics are commonplace in interest-group models of lobbying, although most such models do not account for ideological interests (Congleton 1991a, Olson 1965).

Insofar as persuasion and lobbying activities become more effective as more resources are devoted to them, other things being equal, the model of support for interest group activities implies that the probability of suffrage reform increases as supporter income and the effectiveness of suffrage organizations increase. The more effective suffrage groups are and the longer their campaigns, the more likely the median voter and the median member of parliament are to be persuaded to change their suffrage norms.

Industrialization and the Effectiveness of Suffrage Groups

There are several reasons that pro-suffrage groups tended to benefit from industrialization during the nineteenth century. In the nineteenth century, many employees and employers had similar economic interests and relatively liberal normative theories. Industrialization thus tends to increase the incomes of persons that benefit from economic and political liberalization more than it increases the incomes of persons opposed to liberalization. This change in relative income (and other liberal reforms) produces relatively better-financed and more effective pro-suffrage interest groups.

Reductions in censorship, technological innovation, and industrialization in the late eighteenth and nineteenth centuries also made interest groups more effective and thus more likely to be supported than had been the case in previous centuries. Many of the same improvements in coordination, communication, and transport that allowed economic entrepreneurs to assemble and manage large numbers of employees in many locations also allowed political entrepreneurs to assemble and coordinate the political activities of large numbers of individuals in many locations. The costs of organizing interest groups were further reduced by the urbanization associated with industrialization and by the habits of deference and rule following behavior commonplace within large organizations.[2]

As a consequence, the number of politically active groups increased throughout the nineteenth century. Many late-nineteenth-century, politically active interest groups had relatively narrow policy agendas in education, trade, public health, debt, and labor law. Such groups often had overlapping supporters and members, and many also supported modest (or radical) suffrage expansion. Consistent with the model developed earlier in the chapter, their memberships were not drawn entirely from the unenfranchised. They were often financed and led by those who could already vote, and who had normative and pragmatic interests in policy reform.[3]

Industrialization thus may have induced suffrage-expanding reforms, because it tended to increase the resources flowing to pro-suffrage groups relative to anti-suffrage groups at the same time that interest groups were becoming more effective. However, persuasive campaigns inside and outside government were not the only methods used by politically active interest groups to influence public policy.

[2] Locating firms close to one another tends to reduce the cost of transporting intermediate goods and providing specialized services to large enterprises and their employees.

[3] Suffrage movements throughout Europe during the nineteenth century became increasingly strong during the course of the century. Part II of the book suggests that increased support for electoral reform occurred partly for pragmatic reasons. For example, in England, the new industrial centers were underrepresented in Parliament, which made it difficult to press for economic policy reforms without first pressing for electoral reform. Industrialization in the nineteenth century tended to reinforce liberal ideological tides in other policy areas as well, such as education reform, reductions in internal and external trade barriers, and reapportionment. Similarly, suffrage groups were generally supported by the liberal and labor movements, each of which had a pragmatic interest in having suffrage extended to their members. Their success, however, was substantially dependent on the ideological effects of their persuasive campaigns. Only the persons that could vote and their elected representatives could adopt suffrage reform.

EMERGENCE OF POLITICAL PARTIES AND PARTISAN INTERESTS IN SUFFRAGE REFORM

When pro-suffrage movements succeed, politics gradually becomes depersonalized, because the number of voters increases and fewer voters personally know the candidates running for office. Voter assessments of candidates, therefore, become more indirect, as secondary sources of information substitute for direct knowledge. News accounts, pamphlets, the recommendations of knowledgeable persons, and gossip increasingly determine voter assessments of the relative merits of candidates.

These indirect sources of news can be manipulated (and augmented), which allows candidates and groups to conduct campaigns for office, rather than passively await election results once nominated. Candidate efforts to engage in persuasive campaigns exhibit the many of the same economies of scale that other persuasive campaigns do. And those same economies of scale imply that a single organization can organize campaigns for several candidates at a lower average cost than a single candidate can. Average campaign costs can be further reduced if the candidates supported have similar policy goals and sponsors, because similar arguments and speakers can be used to promote several candidates.[4] It is thus sensible for formeteurs to create organizations to orchestrate the political campaigns of candidates with similar policy agendas.

Through time, such political clubs may gain a reputation for supporting talented candidates with particular policy aims, which further lowers the cost of informing voters about candidates. Campaign organizations may also engage in a variety of loyalty-building and loyalty-promotion activities among voters, such as organizing parties and festivals at which candidates or their supporter's speak, particularly on or near election days. Simply being a speaker at such parties provides voters with useful information about the candidates. Indeed, parties and party affiliation can become electorally more important than the candidates themselves in settings in which electoral politics becomes a mass-marketing affair. Voters may increasingly use party labels as evidence of both candidate talent and policy positions. The joint reputation of past members of the club and the various networks of club members significantly reduce the difficulty and cost of having new candidates taken seriously by voters. Just as there can be

[4] There are other advantages in creating and joining organizations that promote candidates with similar ideological positions. Like-minded politicians may enjoy each other's company, may cooperate to get legislation of mutual interest adopted, and therefore may be inclined to help each other get elected to office.

guilt by association, there is also "reflected glory," as present party members gain some secondary reputation from great reforms of the past. Unaffiliated candidates face much higher informational and organizational barriers to mounting a successful campaign and so become less likely to enter or succeed in contests against organized party slates.

If the pool of partisan voters can be increased through suffrage reform, the political parties that expect to profit (or lose) from the new electorate have *organizational* reasons to support (or oppose) suffrage expansion in addition to the fiscal and ideological ones analyzed previously for voters. Appropriate electoral reforms may create a relatively strong base of future electoral support for political parties.

During the early and mid-nineteenth century, liberal parties generally pressed for suffrage expansion for both ideological and pragmatic reasons, while conservative parties defended the medieval order, with its 5 to10 percent suffrage, noble chambers, aristocracy, and state church. As suffrage reforms were adopted and further reforms became more likely because of ideological and electoral competition, conservative parties also became increasingly pro-suffrage. Indeed, "conservative" governments of the late nineteenth century would often initiate suffrage expansion in order to control the details of the reform. In such cases, partisan interests clearly trumped ideological ones. Toward the end of the nineteenth century, liberals were joined by social democrats in their efforts to expand suffrage. The fact that a political party's slate of recommended candidates must be elected to affect legislation implies that political parties must be sensitive to changing voter interests *and also to those of nonvoters who may one day be able to cast votes.*

The influence of organized political clubs (parties or factions) tends to grow as the number of votes required to win office increases and as parliamentary majorities become an increasingly important determinant of public policy.

SPECIALIZATION, LABOR UNIONS, AND SUFFRAGE REFORM

Another manner in which politically active organizations may influence policy outcomes involves direct trades of money or support for policy changes. Bribery, per se, is normally illegal, but several legal forms of conditional payments are possible for interest groups. For example, well-paid jobs may be provided for high officials and their family members in exchange for supporting the "right" policies. As mentioned earlier, the unpaid members of parliament often obtained positions in the bureaucracy from kings. In the nineteenth century, similar offers were offered by industrial interest groups, such as the railroad industry, who might provide members of parliament with well-paid positions on their boards of directors. The emergence of new wealthy persons and organizations increased the number of the persons in positions to trade money for votes during the nineteenth century.[5]

Instead of payments for services, interest groups can also threaten to withhold support or reduce an official's income in order to generate support for particular policies. When the threat is violence, this bargaining technique (extortion) is illegal; however, many similar threats are perfectly legal.

As industrialization takes place, specialization increases, and personal income becomes increasingly dependent on the availability of other complementary resources and the market demand for their employer's outputs. Farmers have always needed seeds, farm animals, and good weather. Farmers that ship their produce to market via railroads also need railroad engineers, efficient steam engines, well-maintained track, coal, water, and steel nearly as much as they need seeds and farm animals. The more specialized production becomes, the more interdependent are the incomes of persons engaged in production.

That interdependency allows organized groups to threaten to reduce the incomes of those outside the group by collectively withholding their purchases or inputs (labor or capital) from the market, as with boycotts, strikes, and strike threats. In this manner, industrialization allows relatively well-organized economic interest groups to use their exit options as threats to those needing their services.

Political Bargaining Using Strike Threats

Consider the following model of bargaining between the present median voter and a prosuffrage group with a credible strike threat. Recall that the rules governing suffrage determine the identity (total income) of the median voter, which along with the available tax base and cost of government services determines the level of government services. In the absence of a strike threat, the median voter under a given electoral set of rules (T^L, T^K) realizes after-tax consumption level $C^* = (1 - C(G^*, Z)/Y)(w(L_M - L_V) + r(K_M - K_v))(2 - \sqrt{2})/2)$ and government service level $G^* = C(L_v, K_v, T^L, T^K, Y, Z)$.

[5] Illegal bribes and threats were also used, although only at the margins, because laws against such deals existed and usually were enforced.

At suffrage equilibria, the suffrage laws maximize the welfare of the pivotal voter.

In the usual neoclassical model of competitive markets, production exhibits constant returns to scale, and each factor is paid its full marginal product. In such an economy, a strike threat has fiscal effects only. A group that temporarily withholds their factors of production from the economy suffers a loss in income, and nonstrikers suffer a reduction in the tax base, which causes tax payments to rise for nonstrikers, public services to fall, or some combination of the two. (Recall that Y is an argument in G*.) In an economy in which substantial specialization exists or in which there are increasing returns to scale, a group that withholds its factors of production from the economy may also reduce the incomes of nonstrikers by reducing the marginal product of fellow team members and of other firms that rely upon their outputs. (It is difficult to make automobiles without steel, steel without coal, and any of these without labor or transport.)

Note that fiscal effects, by themselves, allow such prosuffrage organizations to bargain with the enfranchised for electoral reform. Economic effects simply increase the bargaining power of such groups. In the absence of franchise reforms, the present pivotal voter will face higher taxes, lower government services, and reduced private consumption. In such cases, strike threats place the median voter in a situation similar to the case analyzed in Chapter Seven, in which the tax base is partly determined by suffrage levels. The pivotal voter will be willing to vote for the suffrage expansion requested by the strikers whenever the expected losses from more frequent strikes exceed those associated with extending the franchise.

If the present median voter's tradeoff between suffrage and fiscal stability is known beforehand, organized labor can select the probability of strikes that elicits the desired constitutional response. For example, they could choose a strike rate that will induce suffrage to be extended to union members, but perhaps not to peasants, persons on relief, women, or children. Contrariwise, given a menu of conditional strike probabilities from the prosuffrage interest group (as within a Grossman and Helpman [1996] model), the present median voter may adopt the suffrage reform that equates his or her expected marginal gains from increased income and tax-base security with the cost of the less appealing combination of government services that will be adopted by the new median voter.[6] Any constitutional

[6] Promises to reduce the probability of striking in the future are somewhat more credible for radical suffrage reforms than for minor reforms. Once universal suffrage is obtained ($T^L = T^K = 0$), no further increase in suffrage can be secured via strike threat.

bargain reached, however, depends somewhat on the particular sequence of offers and counteroffers that take place.[7]

During the late nineteenth century, there were a few occasions in the early twentieth century (in Sweden and Belgium) in which strikes played a significant role in negotiations to reduce tax and income thresholds for suffrage rights. Suffrage reforms in such cases were consequence of fiscal-suffrage bargaining between outsiders and insiders analogous to those discussed. Large-scale boycotts or strike threats, however, were not easy to organize for reasons noted in Chapter Seven and rarely affected suffrage law. Suppression of strikes, however, is more difficult in highly industrialized settings, because exit is always possible in market relationships and productive teams cannot be costlessly reassembled. There are many "choke points" in industrialized economies at which a relatively small organization can have large effects on several markets at once, as with railroad strikes in the late nineteenth and early twentieth centuries.

That labor unions and other interests groups may have effects on policies and constitutional reform does not mean that "class consciousness" plays a major role in such reforms. The interest group models of suffrage and other constitutional reforms developed in this chapter are not class based, but rather ideologically and economically based. Many interest groups can be organized that include members with quite different incomes, as is true of liberals, women, farmers, steel mill owners, and laborers in different industries. Such nonclass-based economic interest groups may have considerable effects on public policy, as with the contemporary American Association of Retired Persons (AARP) and the Organization of Petroleum Exporting Countries (OPEC).

In the case of nineteenth-century suffrage reform, however, the constitutional interests of *unenfranchised men* were *largely a result of their similar incomes*, because the electoral rules that interest groups wished to change were income or class based. Wealth- and income-based rules for suffrage discriminated against those who had relatively low income and wealth, and these are, of course, often used by sociologists as a method of defining socioeconomic class.

[7] Although satisfactory to the pivotal member of parliament, the existing suffrage laws are not necessarily Pareto efficient. For example, unrealized gains from political exchange may exist in equilibrium if transactions costs are significant. The unenfranchised might well be willing to pay enough to induce the median voter to change suffrage rules, but may be unable to raise the money to deliver the necessary side payment to alter the median voter's position on suffrage (recall equations 9.1 and 9.2).

If strikes are easier to arrange than side payments, the constitutional bargain achieved with a strike threat could generate a Pareto-efficient constitution, although it is unlikely to be one that is Pareto superior to the initial constitutional setting.

In the nineteenth century and most earlier periods, income, wealth, religion, and sex were all used to determine a person's civil status.

CONCLUSIONS: WESTERN DEMOCRACY AS A CONSEQUENCE OF CONSTITUTIONAL REFORM

We now have three groups of models that together provide explanations for the peaceful and gradual emergence of parliamentary democracy. The first accounts for the emergence of policy-making institutions and for the widespread use of the king-and-council template in organizational governance. When applied to territorial governance, the king-and-council template provides a continuum of governmental types and distributions of policy-making authority. The second demonstrates that within that template, the balance of policy-making authority tends to be relatively stable, although in some periods kings may gradually bargain away their authority in exchange for tax revenues and other support. The third suggests that the basis for membership in the parliament also tends to be relatively stable, although suffrage may be gradually expanded if the interests of pivotal members of parliament change. The latter tends to occur when policy-relevant norms or economic interests change. Such changes may be induced by interest groups that press for liberal economic and political reforms.

The analytical histories of Part I suggest that increases in parliamentary authority and the breadth of suffrage occur through substantially separate processes. The king-and-council template is because it solves a variety of information and succession problems. External and internal shocks that produce constitutional gains to exchange between the king and council may do so without generating parliamentary support for reforms of the rules through which members of parliament are chosen. Shifts in widely held normative theories can produce support for suffrage expansion without producing support for new constitutional architecture or new divisions of authority between the king and parliament.

Constitutions define political property rights for the king and the council and gains to trade tend to emerge when circumstances change. A king's need for new taxes may be greater than his wish for control over particular areas of public policy, and parliament's interest in additional authority in those areas may be greater than the opportunity cost of additional taxes. Similar gains to trade also emerge when the theories of governance of the king and pivotal members of parliament shift in the same direction. Similar bargains over suffrage law are less common, because nonvoters lack political property rights that can be traded to those who can vote.

Nonetheless, there are occasions when members of parliament may have an interest in changing the rules through which they come to office. Three such cases were explored in Chapter Eight. The first involved changes in the normative theories of governance that can induce the median member of parliament to favor electoral reform. Suffrage laws may also be reformed to advance the organizational interests of the political parties. Political parties that expect to obtain the electoral support of new voters may favor suffrage reform for entirely pragmatic political reasons. An organized economic group that can engineer a strike or boycott threat may also be able to bargain with existing voters over suffrage laws, insofar as they can reduce tax revenues or the incomes of persons already entitled to vote.

These three mechanisms suggest that democratization and industrialization tend to be associated with one another, because liberal economic and political reforms advance the economic interests of industrial entrepreneurs and their employees. Technological and sociological trends associated with industrialization may reinforce liberal trends, because interest groups become easier to organize as communication and transportation costs fall, as population densities increase, and as techniques for managing large groups improve.

Yardstick Competition and Exit Options as Liberalizing Factors

It bears noting that liberal ideas and industrialization are not the only factors that can produce pressures for political and economic liberalization within the models developed in Part I. Results also matter, insofar as these change beliefs about the relative merits of public policies or institutions for governance. As noted in Chapters Two to Four, the successful innovations of fellow formeteurs tend to be copied by others, and the exit options of team members and residents tend to constrain the strategies of formeteurs and territorial governments. Policies that increase the effectiveness of organizations are of interest to all potential formeteurs. Policies that increase tax revenues are of interest to most governments. Institutions and strategies for increasing parliamentary control are of interest to all members of parliament. Reforms that increase national income and/or induce inflows of labor and capital tend to advance both economic and geopolitical interests.

Such yardstick competition clearly played a role in the emergence of relatively liberal economic and political institutions in the seventeenth century. For example, as developed in Chapters Fifteen and Eighteen, labor and capital could choose among provinces in the Dutch Republic and among British colonies in what became the United States of America. Labor and capital were attracted to places with relatively open political and economic systems, because rates of return were higher and risks were lower in such places. In this manner, the success of liberal reforms in the Dutch provinces and in the English colonies induced trends in reform at the province and colonial levels of governance. Similarly, a century or two later, both yardstick and international competition encouraged liberalization in Japan during the late nineteenth century, as developed in Chapter Nineteen.

Constitutional, trade, and tax reforms of neighboring governments tend to be widely known, and successful ones are often copied.

The Gradual Emergence of Democracy through Peaceful Means

Overall, the models of Part I provide a schema for thinking about gradual, peaceful transitions to parliamentary democracy. The models suggest that sudden radical breaks with the past are not necessary for democracy to emerge from medieval parliamentary regimes, nor are class consciousness or civil wars necessary preconditions for liberal reform. Institutional flexibility, bargaining, and liberal interests are sufficient.

The models suggest that peaceful lawful constitutional reforms are possible, and that parliamentary democracy can emerge gradually as a series of constitutional reforms are adopted. This does not preclude intense debates or the use of extravagant rhetoric in politics any more than the usual economic characterizations of gains to trade in ordinary markets imply that trade among market participants always occurs quietly and dispassionately. What Tilly (2004) calls "contentious politics" is a predictable consequence of disagreements over reforms in which the stakes are high.

Revolutionary rhetoric was used by interest group organizers throughout the period of interest, but few truly revolutionary organizations were created. Such rhetoric evidently helped motivate members of many interest groups, but it was only a subset of the many factors that induced the long series of reforms leading to Western democracy.[8] It takes more than fiery rhetoric for voters and members of parliament to be persuaded that reforms should be developed and adopted. The intensity of many constitutional debates and associated revolutionary rhetoric with respect to constitutional reform is not usually evidence of revolutionary threats, but simply evidence

[8] As noted in Chapter Nineteen, the direction of causality does not appear to be unidirectional. As suffrage was extended in northern Europe, additional economic liberalization took place as well.

of the importance of particular reforms for politically active organizations and their supporters.

Part I has included illustrating examples from European history to demonstrate that the logic of governance and reform can account for many of the institutions and reforms that produced parliamentary democracy in Europe. The illustrations suggest that the models have some explanatory power, but mere illustrations are not sufficient to demonstrate that the models – or the general constitutional bargaining and reform perspective – shed significant light on the rise of Western democracy. If democracy emerged gradually through liberal reform, there should be many instances of such reforms, and most of the reforms adopted should be products of negotiation in which circumstances favored parliaments and/or liberal ideas. Suffrage reform should be associated with ideological shifts and politically active interest groups.

In order to determine whether these predictions are borne out, Part II provides a series of historical narratives written with the implications of the models of Part I in mind, and with a focus on constitutional developments. Additional statistical tests are undertaken in Chapter Nineteen.

PART II

HISTORICAL EVIDENCE ON WESTERN DEMOCRATIC TRANSITIONS

NINE

Setting the Stage: Philosophical, Economic, and Political Developments Prior to the Nineteenth Century

FROM AUTOCRACY TO DEMOCRACY WITHOUT REVOLUTION

Part I of this volume suggests that the king-and-council template is a robust architecture for governance. It is a template for governance that solves various information and succession problems and can be adjusted at many margins as circumstances change. Particular instances of it divide policy-making authority between the king (the executive) and the council (the parliament or legislature). Insofar as a particular assignment of policy-making authority is sufficiently stable that it can be taken as given by those holding positions within government, the officeholders know what their authority is, and what is required for policy decisions of various kinds to be made and implemented.

The initial division of authority advances the interests of the founding formeteur(s), and the political property rights thereby established provide the basis for both continuity in governance and constitutional reform.

Authority to participate in and to determine particular policy decisions can be traded directly or traded for support on critical issues or for new tax revenues. The bargains reached may be temporary or essentially permanent, but in either case the process of constitutional bargaining and exchange allow constitutions to be peacefully revised through time as circumstances change.

The analytical history demonstrates that technological shifts favoring industrialization and increases in the persuasiveness of liberal arguments can induce rational, generally self-interested men and women to adopt constitutional reforms that gradually produce parliamentary democracy. That conclusion does not imply that the West was somehow destined to democratize, as some have argued (Diamond 1999; Jones 2003). Nor does it suggest that the road to democracy is a one-way street. Rather, it suggests that chance innovations in technology, political theory, and economics, combined with preexisting institutions of divided government, can produce a gradual, peaceful, transition from king-dominated political systems to parliamentary democracy through a series of constitutional reforms.

The remainder of the book attempts to determine whether such political property rights and constitutional bargains can, in fact, account for the emergence of Western democracy.

Part II attempts to answer such questions as: Were the shifts in political authority from kings to parliaments and expansions of suffrage separate events? Were they largely peaceful and lawful, rather than consequences of civil war or obvious, credible threats of revolution? Were there new alignments of economic and political interests that emerged in the nineteenth century? Did groups inside and outside government lobby for more open political and economic systems, for equality before the law, and for suffrage expansion? Is there evidence of the acceptance of liberal political and economic ideas among political elites?

ORGANIZATION OF PART II

Part II of the book provides an overview of constitutional developments in the West from the late Middle Ages until World War I. A general overview is provided in Chapters Nine to Eleven and six case studies are developed in Chapters Twelve to Eighteen. Chapters Nine to Eleven discuss changes in ideas and interests that motivated reforms, especially those that favored liberal reforms of political institutions and economic regulations and promoted civil equality. The case studies of Chapters Twelve to Eighteen focus most of their attention on constitutional debates and the details of constitutional and policy reforms in the century between 1825 and 1925. Three of the case studies are natural applications of the models of Part I, and three of the cases are less natural applications, which turn out to be consistent with the models, but less obviously so. Chapters Twelve to Fifteen examine the British, Swedish, and Dutch transitions. Chapters Sixteen to Eighteen examine the German, Japanese, and American transitions. In all six cases, peaceful shifts of power between king and council were commonplace. In all six cases, similar economic and ideological pressures triggered similarly great transformations of governance and economic life in the nineteenth century, although transitions to parliamentary democracy were not always completed or stable once completed. Interests and ideas motivated the reforms, but the particular reforms adopted also reflected preexisting political institutions, local issues, and leaders.

The remainder of Chapter Nine sets the historical stage for the European transitions of the nineteenth century. It reviews the institutional starting point of the late Middle Ages and briefly chronicles the shift in production technologies that allowed new economies of scale to be realized in private organizations devoted to market activities (what economists refer to as firms), the emergence of liberal political and economic ideas, and their increasing relevance for public policy negotiations.

European history prior to 1800 suggests that there was nothing about European monarchical-parliamentary systems, Christianity, or Roman law that oriented European governance toward parliamentary democracy. Although European society was not entirely static in the Middle Ages, it was remarkably stable. Its political, economic, and religious institutions were largely self-replicating and supported stable hierarchical patterns of life and death based largely on family.

Chapters Two to Four suggest that stable societies are often dominated by institutional conservatism (for perfectly good reasons), and that any reforms adopted will provide additional support for existing arrangements, rather than undermining them. Such reforms may, for example, reinforce the authority and wealth of the state church or aristocratic and royal households. In some cases, however, policies that initially protect the status quo may lead to other reforms, as for example when law courts become more independent or when authority is shifted to those previously outside government in order to obtain additional resources or support during a time of war or other crises.

In late-medieval Europe, reforms for the most part reinforced the dynastic rule of royal families, rather than shifting policy-making authority from kings to parliament or to commoners.

AN OVERVIEW OF THE MEDIEVAL CONSTITUTION

The roots of many contemporary parliaments extend back to the medieval period and beyond. The present English Parliament extends back to the ancient Great Council (Magnum Concilium), which was composed of lay and ecclesiastical magnates. The Great Council met with English kings on affairs of the realm, including taxation. The *Magna Carta* of 1215 formally established a new, narrowly elected council of twenty-five barons to monitor and enforce implementation of that compact between the English king, church, and nobility.[1] The English Parliament emerged half a century

[1] The council of barons was formally empowered to protect "the peace and liberties we have granted and confirmed to them by this our present Charter." The rights of the *Magna*

later during the reign of Edward I, after a period of political instability. The early English Parliaments voted on tax matters, heard petitions from the public, petitioned the king to address various grievances, and occasionally impeached senior government officials (Lyon 1980, chapter 34).[2]

Similarly the parliament of Sweden (the Riksdag) evolved from the ancient Scandinavian and German institution of the *ting (ting, lagting*, or *althing*), which had powers similar to those of the Great Council. *Tings* were deliberative assemblies that met at regular intervals to settle disputes, pass sentences on law breakers, and elect kings. As such, *tings* combined aspects of modern judicial and legislative branches of government. *Tings* existed at both local and regional levels. As Sweden emerged as a state in the fourteenth century, a new Swedish council of state was established by law in 1319, when Magnus Eriksson was elected king, in exchange for oaths of fealty by the great men of the realm. That council had veto power over taxation and some policy decisions. At about the same time, a similar Danish council of state was established with veto power over war and some authority over new taxes (Danstrup 1947, 37).

The French Estates General also originated around 1300, at which time the king (Philip the Fair) called representatives from the nobility, burgers, and clergy to form a grand council, which was consulted on all major decisions. A smaller group composed of judges and lawyers (the Parlement) was also consulted on a more regular basis. The Estates General played a significant role in medieval France, but had only a minor role in the century of absolutism before the French Revolution (see Bély 1998, 33, 58, 62, and 75). During the century in which the Estates were not called, the various judiciary parliaments served as the main check on the king's authority.

Medieval European political institutions were very stable. Although the families that occupied the posts of greatest authority varied somewhat through time, as did the territories ruled by particular families, the main procedures of policy making fluctuated within a fairly narrow band.

King-dominated forms of the king-and-council template provided the core institutions of governance for nearly all of Europe for most of the five centuries before 1800. The various parliaments, national assemblies, and estates general were not self-calling during this time; they met only when the king wanted their opinion on some matter, or (more commonly),

Carta were gradually extended to include lesser landowners, merchants, and eventually the nonpropertied classes (Strayer and Gatzke 1979).

2 Tax revolts have occasionally led to significant shifts in policy-making authority. For example, the *Magna Carta* was obtained from King John as a consequence of a tax rebellion by an organized group of English barons.

wanted authority to collect additional tax revenues. Meetings in times of peace took place at irregular intervals, doubtless because kings found it difficult to obtain new revenues at such times. The number of meetings often increased in periods before, during, and shortly after wars, because at those times parliament's permission to collect additional taxes (subsidies) was more likely to be obtained. Such "war subsidies" were normally temporary in nature, which assured that the king had to call parliament back into session during long wars and as new international and domestic military action seemed necessary or advantageous.

Meetings of national and regional parliaments were normally called every few years, and after called, parliaments normally met for just a few weeks. Parliaments had the right to petition the king to address problems of regional or local concern, and most citizens had the right to petition members of parliament to bring such requests to the sovereign. Such meetings thus provided useful information about problems and grievances throughout the realm (kingdom, principality, barony, city).

The festivals associated with such special occasions also provided members of parliament with opportunities to arrange marriages among their children, to coordinate their opposition to particular royal policies, and to negotiate interregional trade agreements. Essentially all national (and many regional) policy decisions were made within the executive branch of government by the king and persons to whom he had delegated policy-making authority. This also tended to be true at the local level, where dukes, counts, and barons determined and enforced regulations concerning peasant life and also settled many legal disputes within their essentially personal, family-based domains.

In addition to noble-ruled territories – kingdoms, principalities, duchies, baronies, and counties – there were also independent free towns and cities, many of which had purchased their independence from local rulers. Many of these city governments used, by medieval standards, relatively liberal versions of the king-and-council template.[3] A town's mayor might be elected by the town council. The members of the ruling council might be elected by a relatively large number of voters, usually major property owners in the city. In some cases, larger, more representative assemblies were called for discussion of public policies. For example, many of the major cities and principalities of what became the Netherlands routinely called representative assemblies of nobles, guilds, churches, and commercial

[3] City governance often included a chief executive (mayor, magistrate, or burgomeister) and a council representing local religious and business interests.

interests. However, well-connected, wealthy families usually controlled the membership of both branches of local government, which made most city governments dynastic in practice, although not formally so.[4]

Titles, manorial assets, and personal wealth were assigned to particular families and passed on to heirs through durable civil laws governing inheritance and marriage. This was also largely true of seats in parliament, where noble families automatically received seats as a birthright, as was true in England, France, and Sweden. In cases in which the right to sit in parliament was not directly inherited by members of particular families, their greater access to education, government officials, and wealth allowed members of noble families to qualify more easily for the non-hereditary seats in parliament and for senior positions in the religious and commercial organizations represented there.

Family members who inherited multiple territories often had several parliaments in which to sit and/or to negotiate with. Kings, princes, and barons thus often spent considerable time on the road consulting with a variety of parliaments to assure their loyalty and to press for new subsidies from their subjects.

This pattern of rule by a king and parliaments representing wealthy families was the medieval constitutional template for Europe. Kings and kingdoms, princes and principalities, barons and baronies were largely determined by heredity and marriage for more than a thousand years. Somewhat similar institutions were present in other parts of the world, as in Japan and China, during the same period.

Medieval European governance could be said to be rule by blue bloods for the benefit of blue bloods. Although family rivalries and alliances were complex and often far from peaceful, the balance of economic and institutional interests was stable because of the importance of landownership as a source of wealth, the church as a source of ideas, and the practical interests of elites in defending the political institutions that helped to cement their privileged place in society. Institutional and intellectual conservatism was completely rational for such men and women.

Indeed, the paucity of the governmental alternatives analyzed by enlightenment scholars shows how narrow the range of governance was in Europe in the late-medieval and early-modern periods. Neither Hobbes, Locke, Montesquieu, Rousseau, Kant, nor von Humboldt took the time to analyze representative or parliament-dominated systems fully, in large part because they had never seen one operate. This intellectual

[4] See, for example, Pirenne (1925), Blockmans (1978), Tilly and Blockmans (1989).

constraint was reinforced by tough penalties for treason and by political and religious censorship at the time that they wrote. Many enlightenment scholars honestly thought that election-based representative systems were impossible, and others evidently pretended to think so, because to suggest otherwise risked the punishments associated with treason and/or royal disfavor.

Those few theorists who believed systems of popular government were possible and were brave enough to put their pens to paper (but often not their names) referred to two-thousand-year-old examples from classical Greece. For example, in the mid-eighteenth century, Rousseau imagined grand democratic constitutional conventions that would provide the basis for legitimate governance. He referred to ancient Greek and Roman assemblies in an attempt to argue that such assemblies and broad political participation were actually possible: "The people in assembly, I shall be told, is a mere chimera. It is so today, but two thousand years ago it was not so" (*Social Contract*, 1762, chapter 12).

Constitutional Bargaining within Medieval Governments

King-dominated forms of the template were common at both the national and regional levels, although these royal constitutions were not entirely static. There were, for example, a few unusual times, particularly toward the end of this period, in which parliaments gained significant policy-making authority. There were also periods in which kings, conversely, attempted to eliminate parliamentary authority.

An extreme case of the former occurred during the English Civil War of the mid-seventeenth century, during which a (rump) parliament elected on the basis of very narrow suffrage was in control of English policy making for about ten years. Another occurred during the middle of the eighteenth century, when the Swedish parliament became dominant for a half century during that country's Age of Liberty. At the other extreme, kings occasionally disbanded or ceased calling parliaments, as in Denmark and France in the seventeenth century, and to some extent in England in the two decades before and after its civil war in the mid-seventeenth century. The constitutional center of gravity, however, remained a dominant king and a relatively weak parliament for several centuries.

The balance of power between kings and their parliaments varied somewhat through time, but it usually returned to the medieval division of authority. Much of that balance and many of the changes were described in written constitutional documents.

In essentially every country and every independent duchy, there were long series of formal agreements that shifted power from kings to councils (or parliaments) and back again to kings, as well as many informal agreements. Formal documents often marked periods when parliamentary power was on the rise. For example, in 1414 the English King Henry V proclaimed that all new laws be adopted with the assent of both chambers of the British Parliament, a decision that was occasionally enforced by the British courts. In 1534 the British Parliament proposed and the king accepted rules for future accession to the sovereign. Similarly in Sweden, the first Riksdag Act was adopted in 1617, which required that the king consult the four estates before declaring war or forming alliances. In 1660, a protocol calling for the routine meeting of parliament was adopted, which made parliament a self-calling institution. In the years 1720–3, constitutional reforms led to a half century of parliamentary domination of policy making – from 1719 to 1772.

Similar fluctuations also occurred in late-medieval France and Denmark. The Estates General and the State Council became relatively more important when subsidies were needed by the sovereign, and less so during periods in which they were not. In these last two cases, however, the sovereigns were eventually able to circumvent the veto authority of their parliaments, which allowed periods of "absolutism" to occur in the seventeenth century. During these times, parliaments (estates) were not called, and new, less representative councils were created for advisory and administrative purposes.

Medieval history also suggests that shifts of policy-making power from the king to the council depended on the political environment in which new divisions of policy-making power are worked out. Bargaining is evident in that parliaments and kings both retained some authority over national policy, except perhaps once in Denmark during a period favoring the expansion of royal authority. Parliaments and estates-general continued to exist during the absolutist periods in France and England, although they were not routinely called into session. Only Denmark formally disbanded its parliament.

Such patterns of negotiation and reform were also present outside of Europe. For example, Japanese governance used various forms of king-and-council rule at national and local levels during its medieval (Edo) period. The Tokugawa shogunate period of 1603–1868 also includes a number of peaceful shifts of authority between the shogun and his council and between the central government and regional governments. During much of this period, the shogun gradually transferred authority to his council and the bureaucracy for day-to-day rule, and regional governments gradually secured increased autonomy (Mason and Caiger 1997, 215–16). The distribution of policy-making authority fluctuated somewhat, but shifted in the direction of council rule and regional autonomy.

Few political histories devote significant attention to the ebb and flow of political authority between king and council or king and parliament in the medieval period, although numerous illustrations from medieval England are provided in passing by national histories. Field (2002), for example, provides several examples for England. Examples from other parts of Europe are discussed in Ertman (1997) and Guizot (1861). The long-term stability of the medieval constitution provides a rationale for the neglect of temporary shifts of authority by historians, and it also demonstrates that there is nothing latent in constitutional monarchy itself that tends toward parliamentary democracy.

Relatively Weak National Governments

The governments of medieval nation-states were decentralized and federal in structure, and local rulers normally had considerable autonomy to regulate conduct within their own territories. In the period before the Protestant Reformation, the Catholic Church also exercised considerable political and economic influence and often had its own parallel court system for religious and family matters (Berman 2003). The central governments of early nation-states were rarely the only source of new laws and law enforcement.

Conflict between the center and periphery were common: the center attempted to shift authority from the regional governments to the center, and the periphery attempted to preserve local authority or expand it. The places where the central government gained authority through marriage, constitutional exchange, and military threats gradually became nation-states, such as England, France, Denmark, Portugal, Sweden, and Spain. The places where central governments were not as fortunate remained loose confederations, as in Germany, the Netherlands, and Switzerland.

The long-run stability and durability of medieval constitutions suggest that medieval governance advanced the interests of those represented in government tolerably well; otherwise, reforms would have been adopted.

Evidence of their success for privileged families is found throughout contemporary Europe. The palaces and castles of kings, nobles, and wealthy townsmen from the fifteenth, sixteenth, and seventeenth centuries are so impressive that they continue to attract tourists from around the world to nearly every independent polity of that period. Their scale, attention to detail, and setting demonstrate that wealth was concentrated in relatively narrow elites who could afford to employ large work forces for their own personal amusement. (Very few houses of ordinary persons remain or are of sufficient interest to attract international tourists, and few of today's wealthy could employ so many craftsmen for their personal amusement.)

ECONOMIC DISRUPTIONS TO THE MEDIEVAL EQUILIBRIUM

The stability of both centralized and decentralized late-medieval systems depended on the stability of blue-blood interests and opportunities, which affected bargaining within government and the marriage arrangements and alliances that determined relationships among governments. Around 1500, many of these blue-blood interests began to change, as understandings of religious, political, and economic life were revised and as new opportunities for commerce emerged. Luther and Calvin proposed new interpretations of biblical texts and new church rituals. New theories and experiments by men who would later be called political philosophers and scientists challenged long-standing claims about the normative foundations for governance and the nature of the physical world. New sea routes to Asia around Africa became feasible. Columbus's great miscalculation of the distance to Asia led to the discovery and European colonization of vast new lands in North and South America.

After 1500, medieval society in western Europe began to change, but slowly. It was not until the nineteenth century that radically new forms of political and economic life emerged.[5]

New Lands and Revenues from Abroad

The discovery of new territories and greater access to distant lands already known to exist created a number of new economic and political interests and coalitions.

Foreign territories were of interest to kings and queens for several reasons. First and most important, they potentially provided new sources of royal revenues that could be used to cement and extend their authority. Sales of royal land, monopoly privileges, and tariffs were all customary sources of royal income beyond the veto of parliament. New colonial

[5] See, for example, North and Thomas (1973) for an overview of gradual economic and legal reforms in the late-medieval and early-modern period. See Finer (1997) and Spruyt (1994) for overviews of the gradual centralization of policy-making authority during the late Middle Ages and the emergence of the nation-state.

territory and expanded commerce could also be used to expand royal support within parliament through land grants and appointments to posts in colonial governments.

In contrast to many other national policies, support in parliament for colonial investments was relatively easy to obtain. No new taxes were required, at least in principle, and a larger territory meant more opportunities for those whose interests were represented in parliament. Territorial expansion could also reduce the need for future royal subsidies. In addition to these economic and political advantages, amassing an empire might also be regarded as necessary for self-defense. If one nation did not act as the others did, it would be left behind economically, militarily, and culturally. Many of the colonial enterprises undertaken in the seventeenth century were sovereign companies, whose stockholders included nobles and other men and women of means who held seats or were represented in parliament.

Others outside government also had interests in colonial activities. Many merchants believed that larger territories would produce new business opportunities and profits. These, in turn, produced new opportunities for the middle class, as colonial enterprises needed both craftsmen and ordinary labor. Larger territories increased the scope of national markets, providing new opportunities for a broad range of people throughout the kingdom. Many citizens (and kings) evidently believed that national status was associated with the size of national territory. To be part of a great nation was widely accepted as better than being part of a minor nation, and thus territorial expansion was often broadly supported as a national aim in its own right.

Although it soon became clear that very few territories had gold for the taking, efforts to build empires were often popular (especially when successful) and remained so well into the nineteenth century.[6]

[6] This popularity provides indirect evidence of an imperial strand of European ideology that is essentially orthogonal to the liberal-conservative ideological spectrum. The aims were partially economic and political to be sure, but the arguments favoring such policies were often essentially "nationalistic"; that is, they argued that a "good society" is both strong and prosperous. This allowed more resources to be devoted to establishing trading posts and colonies than economics or military advantage alone could account for. National status and honor of the nation matter to many within a kingdom, partly for their own sake, and this together with desire for wealth and glory led wealthy nobles and commoners to invest in foreign enterprises and many less wealthy individuals to bet their lives on new opportunities in foreign lands. Evidently, most of these colonial ventures earned only meager financial returns for most investors. Indeed, many companies were rescued from bankruptcy by royal subsidies of various kinds.

However, the territory that could be brought under a national government's authority at reasonable cost was scarce. Conflict and escalating competition for potential colonial resources naturally arose. The empire-building game resembled a prisoner's-dilemma game under mercantilist rules. In most cases, the cost of the fleets and armies necessary to assemble and defend empires increased more rapidly than the revenues generated by the new territories. The technology of sea and land combat improved rapidly, as did their expense.

These increased costs, unexpectedly, tended to increase rather than diminish parliamentary authority; new taxes were often necessary, and parliamentary assent was required for new taxes under the medieval constitution. To avoid making requests for subsidies in the short run, royal land holdings at home and abroad were often sold off to nobles and freeholders. This tended to increase the resources of those represented in parliament relative to the king in the long run because royal investments abroad often earned below average returns. Public policy also became more complex as colonies expanded, which caused the national bureaucracy to increase in size and authority.

Thus, rather than freeing kings from the necessity of going to parliament for revenues, colonial enterprises often increased the importance of parliament's control over tax resources. As the importance of majority support in the parliament increased, kings were gradually forced to take parliamentary majorities more seriously. For example, they often used scarce royal resources to purchase marginal seats for their supporters and/or from pragmatists. Although election laws were not changed, nor many parliamentary procedures, pivotal members of majorities in parliament became more important.

Technological Innovations and the Expansion of Commerce

The same technologies that made war more costly – bigger and faster ships – made long-distance shipping cheaper and more reliable. If one could stay clear of pirates and warfare, more goods could be shipped greater distances more quickly and with less likelihood of loss. As the territories in which trade could take place expanded, new formerly unrealized (and unrealizable) opportunities for exchange arose internationally and domestically. The demand for better military hardware also induced a good deal of experimentation with metals and machining. Improved metallurgy allowed guns and cannons to become more reliable, more accurate, and more powerful.

These improvements were, in turn, taken up in various domestic industries. For example, the same advances in metallurgy and machining that made cannons more reliable and accurate were applied to create the early steam-powered mining pumps of Savery (1698), Newcombe (1712), and Watts (1769). The shift from wood to metal machine parts, the production of steam engines, and their new applications created new economies of scale in production. These caused new organizations and new industries to emerge. The steam engine also increased the feasibility of production away from the riverside cities and estates that had long dominated commerce. As new, more capital-intensive production methods were adopted (ships and water-powered looms, foundries, and machine shops), markets for skilled and unskilled labor increased, and the value of land away from major waterways increased.

New techniques in farming were also introduced in the eighteenth century. More productive crop rotations from Flanders and the Netherlands, improved plows from England, and new tilling methods and seeds were adopted, which increased farm output per unit of land and labor. Together, better farming techniques and transportation allowed larger populations and larger cities to be supported by fewer farmers. Complementary industries expanded while others declined, which further shifted the geographic and familial distributions of wealth and produced new alignments of political interests.

The new economies of scale in farming, textiles, mining, and metal working could not always be realized within existing late-medieval legal systems. Medieval rules and regulations included a wide variety of internal and external barriers to exchange, which limited the size of the market that an economic organization could serve, and thereby the size of those organizations. Many formal and informal rules would have to be changed if the new technologies were to be profitable. More complete transport networks would also be necessary to create broader and more integrated domestic markets.

New rules, new canals, and new highways would all require new legislation by national and regional governments. To the extent that members of parliament or those represented by them expected to profit from the new technologies, these same technologies also changed political interests in parliament, which in Europe gradually induced a good deal of legal reform.

An early and important example of such reforms involved changes in real estate law. Under medieval law, labor was often immobile, and most land holdings were illiquid and difficult to transfer. New rules and procedures gradually allowed "strip" farming to be replaced by what might be called "rectangular" or field farming, the normal pattern for contemporary farming. Compact parcels could be more economically fenced (enclosed) and plowed than the long, thin strip fields that were common in the medieval period. In the eighteenth and nineteenth centuries, new legal procedures were adopted to facilitate the assembly of unconnected strips of land into more contiguous and compact fields. The new enclosure laws also increased the fraction of land that could be transferred among persons through private purchases. Before the Industrial Revolution, about 90 percent of families were farmers or employees of farmers, so medieval real estate laws were significant impediments to commercial development.

Other long-standing legal impediments to trade included a variety of town and guild monopolies. Even toward the end of the eighteenth century, Adam Smith in *The Wealth of Nations* lamented the poor quality of workmanship within guild-dominated cities, which still had significant monopoly power within many geographical regions of England and Scotland:

> The pretense that corporations [guilds] are necessary for the better government of the trade, is without any foundation. The real and effectual discipline which is exercised over a workman, is not that of his corporation, but that of his customers. It is the fear of losing their employment which restrains his frauds and corrects his negligence. An exclusive corporation necessarily weakens the force of this discipline. A particular set of workmen must then be employed, let them behave well or ill.
>
> It is on this account, that in many large incorporated towns no tolerable workmen are to be found, even in some of the most necessary trades. **If you would have your work tolerably executed, it must be done in the suburbs, where the workmen having no exclusive privilege, have nothing but their character to depend upon, and you must then smuggle it into the town** as well as you can. (Smith 1776, chapter 10.)

As the Industrial Revolution literally gathered steam, it created new opportunities for many ordinary persons. New career possibilities and new urban lifestyles emerged with the adoption of new methods of production and distribution. Jobs at the new production facilities were largely outside the home (and farm) and could most easily be realized by moving close to those facilities. In this manner, factory production created new communities and caused old ones to expand. These new towns were culturally and economically less homogeneous than medieval villages because they were composed of persons from many villages, towns, and cities – and in some cases, from many countries.

The gradual reorganization of production made possible by technological and legal innovations also tended to change the interests of many ordinary and wealthy persons. It encouraged them to challenge traditional and religious conceptions of a "proper" (traditional) life on

Earth and to challenge the existing medieval system of economic regulation and property. The number of persons occupied directly or indirectly with manufacturing and commerce increased in the eighteenth century, although not enormously so as a fraction of the population, which expanded rapidly along with agricultural output.

Technological innovation and associated profit opportunities in the countryside and cities changed the interests of many of those already represented in national parliaments who could bargain with other members and with the king for desired reforms of public policies.

IDEOLOGICAL DISRUPTIONS TO THE MEDIEVAL EQUILIBRIUM

The philosophical foundations of governance became a major subject of inquiry at about the same time that foreign lands were discovered. This was not entirely a coincidence. The new colonies required new colonial governments, and their very newness meant that those governments could not be said to be grounded in ancient traditions and divine authority. Newness did not preclude the use of long-standing constitutional structures in the new territories, but the new colonial institutions could not be taken for granted, as God-given, natural, or simple historical facts. Partly for this reason, and partly because of political and intellectual changes associated with the late Renaissance and Protestant Reformation, scholars and practitioners developed new theories of the state.

The new theories grounded legitimate governmental authority in natural rights, sovereign duties, implicit constitutional contracts, and in some cases, elections and popular sovereignty.

New Political Ideas and Constitutional Debates

Perhaps surprisingly, some of the new political ideas were codified in European constitutional documents. For example, in 1581, conflict between the Dutch and their Habsburg governors led to a Dutch war of secession from the Habsburg territories (which had recently shifted its family headquarters to Spain). The Dutch declaration of independence (Act of Abjuration) articulates a theory of the state based on sovereign duties and natural rights, rather than tradition or unconditional deference to a preexisting divine order.

As it is apparent to all that a prince is constituted by God to be ruler of a people, to defend them from oppression and violence as the shepherd his sheep; and **whereas God did not create the people slaves to their prince**, to obey his commands, whether right or wrong, but rather the prince for the sake of the subjects (without which he could be no prince), to govern them according to equity, to love and support them as a father his children or a shepherd his flock, and even at the hazard of life to defend and preserve them. And when he does not behave thus, but, on the contrary, oppresses them, seeking opportunities to infringe their ancient customs and privileges, exacting from them slavish compliance, then he is **no longer a prince, but a tyrant**, and the subjects are to consider him in no other view...

So, having no hope of reconciliation, and finding no other remedy, we have, agreeable to the **law of nature in our own defense**, and **for maintaining the rights, privileges, and liberties of our countrymen, wives, and children**, and latest posterity from being enslaved by the Spaniards, been constrained to **renounce allegiance to the king of Spain**, and pursue such methods as appear to us most likely **to secure our ancient liberties and privileges**.

If the sovereign fails to live up to his duties, this document argues that the people ("we") have a natural right to replace the current sovereign with a new one. The Dutch were fortunate in their revolt, and a new Dutch republic was founded a few years later, which rapidly became one of the most wealthy and powerful nations of seventeenth-century Europe (Israel 1998, see also Chapter Fifteen).

During the next two centuries, many other proposed charters in Europe were grounded in similar theories. For example, about a half century later, a group called the Levellers proposed major reforms of England's medieval constitution in their *People's Agreement* (1647). The *People's Agreement* proposed a republican constitution for English governance based on popular sovereignty and civic equality, rather than sovereign duties.

(3) That the people do [should] of course **choose themselves a parliament** once every two years ... (4) That the power of this and all future representatives of this nation is **inferior only to those who choose them**, and does extend to whosoever is not expressly or implicitly reserved by the represented to themselves. ...**That in all laws made or to be made, every person may be bound alike** and that no tenure, estate, charter, degree, birth, or place to confer any exemption ... That **all laws ought to be equal**, so they must be good and not evidently destructive to the safety and well-being of the people. (Sharpe 1998, 94–5)

The *People's Agreement* mentions freedom of religious conscience and equality before the law as "reservations" by the people. Their conception of popular sovereignty is explicitly democratic.

In other petitions sent to Parliament, writers from the same group attacked monopoly privileges: "The **oppressive monopoly** of Merchant Adventurers and others do still remain to the great abridgment of the liberties of the people and to the extreme prejudice to all industrious people" (Sharpe 1998, 79). They also lobbied for improved judicial proceedings: "That ye will permit no authority whatsoever to compel any person or persons to answer questions about themselves or nearest relations" (Sharp 1998: 82). In these respects and several others, the *Agreement* may be regarded as the beginning of English debate on civic equality, a concept that would play a central role in policy debates and liberal political reforms for the next three and a half centuries.[7]

Academic Contract Theories of the State

Several scholars subsequently elaborated and deepened the Dutch and Leveller arguments. During the English Civil War, from the relative safety of Paris, Thomas Hobbes wrote a famous book, the *Leviathan*, which was published in England in 1651. Among many other carefully reasoned arguments, he explained why it could be in the self-interest of all citizens to delegate their power to a sovereign in order to avoid the calamities of life without law and order. Although his logic supported complete irrevocable sovereignty (1959, chapter 14), the argument was based on popular sovereignty:

> A COMMONWEALTH is said to be instituted when a multitude of men do agree, and covenant, every one with every one, that to whatsoever man, or assembly of men, shall be given by the major part the right to present the person of them all, that is to say, to be their representative; every one, as well he that voted for it as he that voted against it, shall authorize all the actions and judgments of that man, or assembly of men, in the same manner as if they were his own, to the end to live peaceably amongst themselves, and be protected against other men.
>
> From this institution of a Commonwealth are derived all the rights and faculties of him, or them, on whom the sovereign power is conferred by the consent of the people assembled.

Once a commonwealth is created, Hobbes argued that it could not be cast off, nor could the sovereign (whether a single man or representative assembly) be bound by a covenant (chapter 18):

> First, because they covenant, it is to be understood they are not obliged by former covenant to anything repugnant hereunto. And consequently they that have already instituted a Commonwealth, being thereby bound by covenant to own the actions and judgments of one, cannot lawfully make a new covenant amongst themselves to be obedient to any other, in anything whatsoever, without his permission.

[7] Several of the Leveller tracts also raised issues concerning the proper size of the welfare state. A proper welfare state "will provide some powerful means to keep men, women, and children from begging and wickedness, [so] that this nation may no longer be a shame to Christianity therein" (Sharpe 1998, 83).

And therefore, they that are subjects to a monarch cannot without his leave cast off monarchy and return to the confusion of a disunited multitude; nor transfer their person from him that beareth it to another man, other assembly of men: for they are bound, every man to every man.

Although Hobbes's theory of an irrevocable constitutional contract is both more abstract and conservative than the normative theories articulated in the Dutch declaration of independence and the Leveller's *People's Agreement*, it shares with them the idea that legitimate governmental power exists to advance the interests of those living within the commonwealth of interest. For Hobbes, the provision of law and order was sufficient to satisfy that requirement.

Hobbes's conclusions, were not, of course, universally accepted. Other enlightenment scholars challenged his doctrine of complete sovereignty and his theoretical approach to natural law (Berman 2003, 261–2).

John Locke (1689), for example, accepted Hobbes's use of abstraction and also accepts Hobbes's argument that individuals transfer their natural authority to the sovereign as a means of securing life and personal property (in both person and land) because these advance broadly shared interests within every community. Locke notes that the logic of social contracts also implies that some actions of a sovereign cannot be legitimate, because authority to make some kinds of policy decisions would never have been included in a voluntary social contract:

But though men, when they enter into society, give up the equality, liberty, and executive power they had in the state of nature, into the hands of the society, to be so far disposed of by the legislative, as the good of the society shall require; yet it being only with an intention in everyone the better to preserve himself, his liberty, and property (for **no rational creature** can be supposed to change his condition with an intention to be worse) **the power of the society or legislative constituted by them, can never be supposed to extend farther than the common good**; but is obliged to secure every one's property, by providing against those three defects above mentioned that make the state of nature so unsafe and uneasy. (*Second Treatise*, 1689, 310)

Locke thus adopts the Dutch perspective on sovereignty, possibly because he spent many years as a refugee in the Netherlands avoiding the sanctions of the British King James II.

Popular sovereignty and social-contract-based arguments were further developed in the eighteenth century by Montesquieu, Rousseau, Madison, and Kant, to name but a few of the next generation of political theorists. Similar reasoning was also applied by important legal scholars such as Blackstone (1765).

The new theories of legitimate rule-making authority gradually undermined existing justifications for the medieval constitution and, in the long run, provided logical foundations for what would become liberal political theory. In governments grounded in social compacts, all members of the community should be regarded as a government's formeteurs, and the delegation of policy-making authority to a policy-making body should be regarded as simply a means for advancing their common purposes. Legitimate government policy, from this perspective, is for the benefit of the community members, rather than for those holding the offices of government.

Theories of government based on divine will and ancient privilege gradually fell from use, at least among scholars.

New Economic Critiques of Medieval Economic Privileges

During the same period in which liberal theories of the state emerged, new liberal theories of economic welfare and growth were also developed. To some extend, the new economic theories were attempts to explain the increase in international trade and changes in the methods of production taking place at the time, but their analysis and conclusions were far more general.

Many of the early liberal theorists analyzed economic and political matters simultaneously. For example, seventeenth-century Dutch writers noted that prosperity may be impeded as well as advanced through government policies. La Court's (1662) widely read book analyzed the economic and political interests of Holland and suggests that centralized political power, in contrast to Hobbes's argument a decade earlier, undermines prosperity (chapter 9):

> However, this **excellent and laudable harmony and union in commerce**, fishing, farming, and manufacturing **may be violated**, even to the ruin of all the inhabitants, none excepted but courtiers and soldiers, and that by **one sole mistake in government, which is the electing of one supreme head over all these inhabitants**, or over their armies. For seeing such a single person for the increase of his grandeur, may curb and obstruct Holland's greatness and power…they **would weaken or lessen all such [productive] cities and impoverish the inhabitants**, to make them obedient without control.

Locke's theory of the state is partly based on the economic advantages of secure property rights. He also wrote on usury laws in 1691, analyzing the difficulty of writing laws to regulate loans and the undesirable consequences of many such laws.

In the course of developing his unusually complete theory of governance, Montesquieu (1748) in *The Spirit of the Law* also developed a theory of taxation, noting that government policies can harm, rather than benefit the general interest:

> The public revenues are a portion that each subject gives of his property, in order to secure or enjoy the remainder. To fix these revenues in a proper manner, regard should be had both to the necessities of the state and to those of the subject. **The real wants of the people ought never to give way to the imaginary wants of the state.**
>
> Imaginary wants are those which flow from the passions and the weakness of the governors, from the vain conceit of some extraordinary project, from the inordinate desire of glory, and from a certain impotence of mind incapable of withstanding the impulse of fancy. Often have ministers of a restless disposition imagined that the wants of their own mean and ignoble souls were those of the state. (Book 8, chapter 1)

The most complete analysis of the tension between prosperity and government regulation was undertaken by Adam Smith, who published his *Wealth of Nations* in 1776. His book directly challenged medieval ideas on wealth, international trade, and economic policy (mercantilism). Smith noted that specialization and capital accumulation were the main engines of economic growth, rather than a nation's stock of gold, and he argued that markets tend to work best when the formation of new business organizations is not blocked by monopoly patents, heavy taxation, inadequate infrastructure, or corruption. He argued that the government regulation of trade tends to reduce rather than increase prosperity:

> In the foregoing Part of this Chapter I have endeavored to show, even upon the principles of the commercial system, how **unnecessary it is to lay extraordinary restraints** upon the importation of goods from those countries with which the balance of trade is supposed to be disadvantageous.
>
> Nothing, however, can be more absurd than this whole doctrine of the balance of trade, upon which, not only these restraints, but almost all the other regulations of commerce are founded. When two places trade with one another, this doctrine supposes that, if the balance be even, neither of them either loses or gains; but if it leans in any degree to one side, that one of them loses, and the other gains in proportion to its declension from the exact equilibrium. Both suppositions are false. **A trade which is forced by means of bounties and monopolies, may be, and commonly is disadvantageous to the country in whose favor it is meant to be established**, as I shall endeavor to show hereafter. (Book IV, chapter 3)

Smith goes on to argue that a nation's capacity for making goods depends on its human resources, holdings of productive equipment, and land, rather than holdings of gold. The ability to produce desired goods and services from those holdings increases with specialization and roundabout production (the division of labor). With respect to the latter, Smith develops what might be called a popular sovereignty theory of economic development. He argues that self-interest tends to promote the welfare of all involved in market relations, without need for significant intervention on the part of a sovereign, but as if guided "by an invisible hand."

Although governments can provide useful public services such as roads and canals, contract enforcement, and national defense, Smith and other economic liberals argued that wealth was for the most part a consequence of the voluntary nature of market transactions. Monopoly privileges and most impediments to trade were completely unnecessary and often counterproductive.

Reasoned Argument, Rather than Revelation

Liberal economic and political theorists used similar types of arguments and reached similar conclusions about the kinds of reforms that should be adopted. For the most part, they relied on reason, abstraction, and examples from the physical world, rather than revelation, authority, or scripture as their main engines of analysis.

> **Natural right is the dictate of right reason** showing the moral turpitude or moral necessity of any act … and consequently that such an act is either forbidden or commanded by God, the author of nature. … Now the **Law of Nature is so unalterable**, that it cannot be changed even by God himself …Thus two and two must make four, nor is it possible to be otherwise … (Grotius 1625, book 1, chapter 1, 21–2).

That right and wrong were susceptible to reasoned argument implied that governance and governmental policies could be analyzed in a similarly reasoned, dispassionate manner.

For the most part, the early liberals regarded men (literally so, in most cases) to be equal participants in the political and economic communities in which they participated. Such persons were not necessarily equal in their talents or wealth, but should nevertheless, be equal before the law and constrained by those laws only insofar as common interests are advanced by them:

> But **every man**, when he enters into society, gives up a part of his natural liberty, as the price of so valuable a purchase; and, in consideration of receiving the advantages of mutual commerce, obliges himself to conform to those laws, which the community has thought proper to establish.
>
> And this species of legal obedience and conformity is infinitely more desirable, than that wild and savage liberty which is sacrificed to obtain it. For **no man**, that

considers a moment, would wish to retain the absolute and uncontrolled power of doing whatever he pleases; the consequence of which is, that every other man would also have the same power; and then there would be no security to individuals in any of the enjoyments of life. **Political therefore, or civil, liberty, which is that of a member of society, is no other than natural liberty so far restrained by human laws (and no farther) as is necessary** and expedient **for the general advantage of the public**. (Blackstone 1765, book 1 chapter 1)

The center of gravity in public discussion and in Europe's scholarly literature in the eighteenth century, nonetheless accepted most of the existing pattern of privilege as reflecting fundamental differences in family, talent, and nature. Conservatism in this sense, for example, was clear in the religion-based theories of Filmer (1680) and Bossuet (1709) and also in the rational-choice analysis of Hobbes (1651).

Moderates in the late eighteenth century, like conservatives, were skeptical of democratic reform, but generally accepted elements of both liberal and conservative arguments. For example, Burke suggests that people are not equal, although they should be equal before the law. However, it is entirely proper that these differences be taken into account when determining the right to vote or hold high office:

The occupation of an hair dresser, or of a working tallow chandler, cannot be a matter of honor to any person – to say nothing of a number of other more servile employments. Such descriptions of **men ought not to suffer oppression from the state**; but **the state suffers oppression, if such as they**, either individually or collectively, **are permitted to rule**. In this you think you are combating prejudice, but you are at war with nature. (Burke 1790, 139)

On the other hand, Burke also suggests that the right to participate in politics and production could be extended a bit beyond the current elites, whose privileges were based on the accomplishments of their ancestors, to include those who had proven their worth in the present:

You do not imagine, that I wish to confine power, authority, and distinction to blood, and names, and titles. No, Sir. There is **no qualification for government, but virtue and wisdom**, actual or presumptive. **Wherever they are actually found**, they have, in whatever state, condition, profession, or trade, the passport of Heaven to human place and honor …

Woe to the country which would madly and impiously reject the service of the talents and virtues, civil, military, or religious, that are given to grace and to serve it; and would condemn to obscurity every thing formed to diffuse luster and glory around a state. Woe to that country too, that passing into the opposite extreme, considers a low education, a mean contracted view of things, a sordid mercenary occupation, as a preferable title to command. **Every thing ought to be open; but not indifferently to every man**. (Burke 1790, 140–1)

In the nineteenth century, these ideological trends accelerated along with commerce and industrialization.

In the nineteenth century, the contract-based theories of the state gave way to utilitarian ideas about the good society, under which policies and institutions were not judged by their contractual foundation, but rather by whether they increased or decreased "society's welfare," defined as the sum of the happiness (utility) of all persons in a given society. Most contract theories had already reached similar conclusions, so there was less conflict among intellectuals during this transition than might have been expected.

Both contractarian and utilitarian arguments focused on the secular sphere of political and economic life and relied on rational arguments, rather than on appeals to tradition or religious doctrine, to judge the relative merits of policies and institutions. The utilitarian analysis of public policy and constitutional design reached conclusions that were similar to those of contractarian analysis, and they provided another methodology for extending the rationalism of science and mathematics into policy debates.

Although utilitarian arguments sound quite different than their contractarian counterparts, utilitarian arguments were also rational and inclusive and made use of scientific predictions. Policy A is better than policy B if it will (predictably) make more people better off than worse off. By explicitly including everyone's welfare (happiness or utility) into their calculations, utilitarian theorists further undermined arguments for special privilege and thereby tended to promote liberal reforms. If the proper aim of public policy is to maximize social utility, every person's welfare should be accounted for, not just that of privileged families.

Contractarian and utilitarian normative theories, together with the gradual shift in economic interests, induced an increasingly broad swath of literate society to accept the notion that (a) historical privileges of birth were somewhat excessive and that (b) broadening economic and political opportunities might improve their own circumstances as well as society's. (Many liberal intellectuals were not eligible for government office or entitled to vote in national elections at the time that they wrote.)

Religious Beliefs Narrow, Rather than Weaken

As censorship laws were relaxed during the eighteenth century, such arguments were widely disseminated and read by educated persons throughout Europe and North America. A century or two of philosophical and policy debates among conservatives, moderates, and liberals had sharpened arguments on all sides and made the arguments more rational and less grounded in custom and religion. (U.S. colonial history is a special case here, as there was relatively little censorship during American colonial days and much more freedom to experiment with alternative forms of religion and local government, as noted in Chapter Eighteen.)

The effect of such rational, secular analyses of public policy on religion, however, was not to reduce the extent or intensity of religious faith in the West, which remained high in the United States and in Europe throughout the nineteenth century, even as liberal democracy emerged. Instead, it reduced the scope of religion.

The Enlightenment did so in three ways. First, the Scientific and Industrial Revolutions diminished the range of phenomena that educated persons interpreted as miracles. Lightning became electricity, rather than the wrath of God, and more generally, weather became a meteorological (physical) phenomenon, rather than a matter of God's favor or punishment. This implied that prosperity in the countryside was largely determined by physical phenomena (hard work, smart planting, and good weather), instead of prayer, God-fearing conduct, or sacrifices (church contributions). Subsequent scientific progress in the nineteenth century in geology, biology, and social science further diminished the extent to which educated persons regarded the world to be static or the product of routine divine interventions. A nontrivial role remained for divine intervention in the new scientific theories, but it was clearly less active and less frequent in those theories than had been taken for granted during earlier times.

Second, and partly as a consequence of the first, the sacrifices considered necessary to achieve an afterlife declined. This did not make people less intensely religious, but it did make them somewhat more tolerant persons. Their neighbor's sins and beliefs became less important to their own perceived chance of an afterlife. Consequently, "mistaken persons" (both errant fellow travelers and believers of other faiths) were less subject to persecution for being under the influence of the devil.

Moreover, the idea that contemporary doctrines perfectly resolved all theological issues conflicted with the evidence of the Scientific Revolution and the Industrial Revolution, both of which demonstrated that continual improvement is possible and useful. No contemporary theory is perfect. Perhaps perfecting one's religious beliefs also required a bit of creativity and experimentation.

Third, the scope of religiously neutral activities increased. This was partly caused by economic and scientific developments, but also by adjustments to theology. New discoveries and economic developments suggested that many of life's routines were not God-given, and so change was not always a sin. Even though one's father and grandfather and great grandfather had all been farmers and all lived in the same village, it was possible to choose another career or move to another place without undermining God's divine order for life on Earth.

This transition was evident in the behavior of many famous persons during the enlightenment and in the pattern of migration taking place within Europe and the United States, as new urban centers emerged and great waves of emigration took place. Many good people – not simply the community's wastrels, sinners, and deviants – left farm villages for towns and cities. Career choices, investment alternatives, food choices, clothing choices, reading choices, and so on increased with the Industrial Revolution.

The expansion of commerce and increased mobility also caused religious theories to change in order to accommodate the new lifestyles, economic circumstances, and greater competition among churches and religions. A new career, it turned out, could be a "calling," something intended or required by God, even if such careers had never existed before. Such changes in doctrine also contributed to the expansion of the domain of religiously neutral activities and actions in the eighteenth and nineteenth centuries (Weber 1930, 72–6). Less of life was devoted to traditional religious activities by most religious persons, and fewer aspects of life were deemed to have sacred origin.

> The capitalistic [industrial] system so needs this devotion to the making of money, it is an attitude toward material goods which is so well suited to that system, so intimately bound up with the conditions of survival in the economic struggle for existence, that there can today [in 1904] no longer be any question of a necessary connection of that acquisitive manner of life with any single Weltanschauung. In fact, **it no longer needs the support of any religious forces, and feels the attempts of religion to influence economic life, insofar as they can still be felt at all, to be as much an unjustified interference as its regulation by the State**. (Weber 1930, 72)

In this sense, life in the West gradually became increasingly secular, even as Europe and the United States continued to be populated by very religious people. Indeed, for many people, the domain of religion gradually shrank to the point that religion became a field of metaphysics, rather than a guide for daily life.

As the religiously neutral domain expanded, support for religious tolerance also expanded. In the mid-nineteenth century, religious conditions for political office were generally dropped and the rights to worship extended throughout the West, at the same time that state churches were maintained and privileged through state laws.[8]

Western democracies and laws in support of religious tolerance emerged in very religious societies, although not ones in which religion was all encompassing. The expansion of the religiously neutral domain made it easier (and more routine) for persons of faith to interact with persons from other faiths (which in nineteenth-century Europe were mostly slightly different versions of Christianity). It also simplified the organization of new firms, cooperatives, and interest groups.

Normative Theories and Nineteenth-Century Constitutional Reform

During the same period, notions of equality before the law began to replace theories of family and royal privilege among educated people, including many prominent members of parliament. Such ideas were not entirely new, as for example, many had been developed by the Leveller movement in England during the seventeenth century. These liberal conceptions of the good society and good government, however, were more widely accepted by politically active persons and groups during the eighteenth and nineteenth centuries than during the seventeenth century.

In 1800, such views were still minority opinions, especially among members of parliament. They nonetheless motivated several generations of pamphleteers and interest groups that advocated eliminating trade barriers, expanding public education, freeing slaves, and expanding suffrage. By 1900, there were clear majorities among voters and within parliament that accepted all these formerly radical policies as essentially obvious and uncontroversial.

[8] Such freedom of religion (conscience) were not new in all parts of the West. They had existed, as previously discussed, in the many of the U.S. colonies a century and a half earlier and in the Dutch Republic three centuries earlier. In the United States, this principle became part of the national government's Constitution in 1783. See Chapter Eighteen. for a discussion of colonial American institutional innovations.

Although the *Union of Utrecht* called for religious tolerance, as did many of the Republic's early political leaders, tolerance was not always supported by provincial and urban governments. Nonetheless, local autonomy implied that a place could nearly always be found in the Netherlands where nonconforming religious practices and intellectual perspectives would not lead to arrest or banishment by local authorities. This was to a considerable extent a consequence of its decentralized political institutions. Chapter Fifteen provides a more complete discussion of the Dutch Republic.

NEW EVIDENCE THAT REPUBLICAN GOVERNANCE IS FEASIBLE

In addition to new political and economic theories, new evidence emerged that representative systems of government with dominant parliaments were feasible and could be successful. Several important political and economic innovations occurred in the late sixteenth and seventeenth centuries.

In the late sixteenth century, the provinces in the northern Rhine delta successfully fought a war of secession from the Habsburg Empire and created a very decentralized and divided government without a King – the United Republic of the Netherlands. In the mid-seventeenth century the English colonies of North America formed and revised a series of colonial and town governments. Most retained the traditional king-and-council format of England, but the colonial versions of the template included far broader suffrage and more powerful parliaments than in England. In a few cases, new governments were literally formed by social contract.

The Dutch Republic and the British colonies were surprisingly successful regimes that they attracted mass immigration and experienced substantial economic growth. A century of success by these relatively liberal forms of government undermined conservative claims that more inclusive, less centralized political systems were necessarily doomed to chaos and disaster.

The Dutch Republic in the Seventeenth Century

The Dutch republic had a relatively strong federal parliament (the States General) and a relatively weak chief executive (*stadhouder*) by the standards of the late-medieval, early-modern period. The republic's decision rules caused it to be a decentralized state. Its decentralized governance together with the region's long history of international trade generated competition among localities for the large inflows of new capital and labor attracted to the new Protestant state. Decentralization thereby favored the emergence of relatively open internal and external trade networks.

Decentralization also produced a relatively tolerant society in which religious and political ideas could be expressed that would have been punished severely in other countries. If not a liberal state in the modern sense, the United Provinces rapidly became a safe haven for nonconformist religious and political ideas. Its tolerance for most forms of Protestantism and relatively open markets attracted substantial immigration and produced rapid economic growth. Commerce and population expanded as hard-working innovators, capitalists, craftsmen, and scholars from throughout northern

Europe converged on the Netherlands.[9] Amsterdam became a metropolis, and many other Dutch towns became cities. New universities, newsletters, journals, and printing companies were founded (Dunthorne 2004; Goldie 1997, xii; Schwoerer 1990).

In addition to those seeking economic and religious opportunities, the United Provinces attracted individuals and manuscripts with controversial political and philosophical ideas (Dawson 1954). The French philosopher and mathematician, René Descartes, spent more than twenty years living and writing in the Netherlands. Somewhat later, in 1682, Ashley Cooper, the Earl of Shaftebury and organizer of the first national political campaigns in England (against the accession of James I), arrived in the Netherlands. Cooper was followed a year later by his young protégé, John Locke. Locke remained in the Netherlands for six years. He completed his first and second treatises during this period, as well as his work on religious tolerance. The influence of Dutch political theory and history seems evident in both of his *Two Treatises*.

In other cases, the controversial persons themselves did not seek refuge in the Netherlands, but their books were anonymously published at Dutch presses, rather than at home. Among well-known enlightenment political philosophers, Montesquieu, Voltaire, and Rousseau all at one time or another found it necessary to publish their work on Dutch presses (Dunthorne 2004). Hobbes, who chose refuge in France, rather than the Netherlands during the English Civil War, also found on his return to England that several of his later books could only be published on Dutch presses (Macpherson 1985, 21–2).

From an economic perspective, the success of the Dutch republic partly reflected its fortunate location at the mouth of the Rhine River, a gateway to southern Germany, northern France, and western Switzerland. As output and trade expanded inland, more products were imported and exported. However, its more open internal and external markets amplified the advantages of its fortunate location. Other port cities at the ends of other rivers also did well, but not nearly as well as Amsterdam. In this manner, decentralized

[9] Many of these immigrants were religiously motivated. Thousands of Protestants and nonconformists from the southern provinces (Belgium) moved to the Netherlands in the late sixteenth and early seventeenth centuries. Other nonconformists from throughout Europe followed, including thousands of Huguenots from France and several hundred English Puritans. Of course, not all the new immigrants were pleased with life in the Netherlands – half of the pilgrims on the Mayflower's voyage to New England were English Puritans who found life in Leiden unsatisfactory – but substantial immigration continued for many decades.

governance allowed a relatively tolerant and prosperous polity to emerge at the mouth of the Rhine River during the early seventeenth century.

The magnitude and breadth of immigration into the United Provinces demonstrate that Dutch political institutions and their associated tolerance and prosperity were well known throughout Europe. Thoughtful persons began to analyze the sources of its success. For example, the Dutch experience is referred to Montesquieu's and Smith's famous books. Indeed, Adam Smith regarded the Netherlands to be the wealthiest place on Earth in the late eighteenth century. (See Chapter Fifteen for more discussion of the Dutch Republic.)

Representative Government in the English Colonies of North America

Another series of interesting constitutional experiments took place along the east coast of what became the United States of America. Commercial colonies were established in Virginia and North Carolina. A series of religious enclaves were founded in New England by English Puritans. A Dutch commercial colony was established along the Hudson River that later became New York City and New York State. Proprietary colonies were established by William Penn (Pennsylvania) and Lord Baltimore (Maryland).

Although founded for different purposes, the colonies all required new governments, and to be successful, those governments had to attract significant immigration. Autonomous rule-making bodies were created for the commercial and sovereign ventures, because the colonies were too far away to manage directly from the home country and few formeteurs took the risk of living in the colonies themselves. Consequently, a good deal of authority was initially delegated to a colonial CEO to govern the new territories for the king or crown company.

In the case of the religious colonies, new organizations were created to provide local public goods such as law and order, to help assure the purity of their faith, and to help manage economic development and colony defense. Religious and other disagreements among community residents often induced exit, and subsets of disgruntled town residents would set off to form new villages with new governments.

In the context of the great wilderness confronting colonists, it must have been somewhat of a surprise that securing cooperation from the colonists, many of whom were investors or employees of the home companies, was not always easy. In most cases, the CEO's appointed by colonial formeteurs were augmented by including new appointed councils and then new elected assemblies. In this manner, a form of parliamentary government emerged in the North American colonies that was loosely based on the English template.

One of the first instances – and a striking one – occurred in 1619, when the Virginia Company established a bicameral parliament with one chamber appointed by the governor and the other elected by all freeholders (the House of Burgesses[10]). In Virginia's colonial circumstances, the usual property qualifications generated nearly universal male suffrage, rather than the traditional 5 to 10 percent suffrage. The elected chamber had the right to veto all new taxes and new legislation.

These "minor" changes to the English template – broader suffrage and new veto power over new laws – proved to be significant reforms of the king-and-council template for governance. It should be noted that the new Virginians were mainstream English men and women, not rebels or revolutionaries. They belonged, by and large, to England's established church, and many were from aristocratic families. They were not religious or political radicals.

The system of divided government characterized by the third Virginia charter protected middle-class interests (represented in the House of Burgesses) against those of the colony's elites (represented in the appointed council), as well as against crown company interests (represented by the governor), and vice versa. In this manner, the Virginia colonial template assured that new laws could only be adopted if they advanced general interests within the colony. The power of the popularly elected chamber did not end the rule of law or produce great transfers of wealth to the middle class, as often argued by conservatives of this time (and for the next three hundred years). Rather, it attracted wave after wave of new immigrants from Europe.

Other innovations of the North American colonies included rules supporting religious tolerance and freedom of the press. In the case of New Amsterdam, religious tolerance was simply a normal part of Dutch legal practices. The Dutch colony attracted religious refugees from the New England colonies whose demanding religious practices (often established or supported by elected officials) alienated those who had sought religious freedom in the colonies, rather than religious purity. Religious tolerance was also formally adopted by Lord Baltimore's Maryland colony as a method of attracting Protestants evicted from Catholic France and Catholics fleeing Protestant Princes elsewhere in Europe. Other colonies gradually adopted

[10] A burgess is a citizen or representative of a borough, town, or university.

similar institutions of governance, partly because it was evident that the Virginia rules produced policies that worked tolerably well, and partly because Virginia was successfully attracting new colonists. The definition of a freeholder varied somewhat through time and among the colonies. The southern colonies tended to have a somewhat higher property threshold for suffrage than the northern colonies. Virginia subsequently reduced suffrage by redefining the term "freeholder," but suffrage remained very broad by the standards of world history. (See Chapter Eighteen for a more complete analysis and description of the colonial governments that became the United State of America.)

The results were widely known in Europe, in part because commercial developers had incentives to make them known (and indeed to exaggerate their success). Liberal governance and religious tolerance was, along with access to virgin land, among the main selling points for life in the colonies. Analysis of the new institutions was also provided in letters written to friends and families from those who did reasonably well and from those who stayed a few years and then returned to Europe. About 10 percent of those who made the trip to the English colonies subsequently returned home to family and friends. Colonial charters and other documents were also translated into many languages for study by scholars, constitutional lawyers, and founders of new colonies.

Many colonists died in the early years, as farming techniques were adjusted for the new soils and climate. Nonetheless, the colonies grew rapidly and average income was very high, in large part because land was fertile and inexpensive (Brown 1955).

The success of the Dutch and North American experiments supported a variety of liberal ideas about governments and markets and undermined a variety of conservative claims about the existing divine institutional and legal order in Europe. To eighteenth-century liberals and many pragmatists, the experience of the Dutch republic and English colonies suggested that the "divine order" could be improved upon.

RESTORATIONS: FAILURES TO PRODUCE STABLE ALTERNATIVES TO THE MEDIEVAL SYSTEM OF GOVERNMENT

It bears noting, however, that not all liberal experiments proved to be durable or successful. For example, in the early eighteenth century, the unexpected death of a Swedish king provided an opportunity for its parliament to take nearly complete charge of governance for almost fifty years. Laws were passed that increased freedom of assembly and speech. Commerce initially expanded, but budgetary problems and inflation produced a political crisis toward the end of that period (Roberts 1986). Partly because of a macroeconomic crisis, a new, more assertive king was able to restore most of the sovereign's medieval authority (see Chapter Fourteen for more details).

There were also two cases in which civil wars were fought in Europe and major reforms of governance were temporarily implemented. These revolutions, however, produced only temporary changes in medieval templates for governance because the new institutions proved to be unstable. In each case, a series of major reforms quickly produced dictatorships. During the English Civil War of the mid-seventeenth century, governance passed from republic to Cromwell's dictatorship and back via the restoration to the old medieval constitution of England. (When the next two Stuart kings violated the medieval constitution again, intervention by William III and the Dutch army restored it again in 1689.)

In 1789, the French Revolution produced a series of major constitutional reforms that led to Napoleon's dictatorship in a period of eight years. Napoleon's army subsequently conquered much of Europe and ended many long-standing regional governments in Germany and Italy. He also reorganized and centralized the national governments of Switzerland and the Netherlands. Napoleon's empire, however, was ended by an alliance of monarchies that restored the medieval template and balance of authority in France and throughout his short-lived empire.

In these three cases, major reforms liberalized governance in the short run, produced dictatorships in the medium run, and restored medieval forms of the king-and-council template in the long run.

Major reforms are clearly not easy to design and implement. Indeed, in the two centuries prior to 1800, only the Dutch Revolt and American Revolution could be said to have produced durable liberal reforms of governance. During the eighteenth century, however, the Dutch Republic gradually centralized authority, formally adopted a hereditary executive, and so began to resemble its royal neighbors. Napoleon ended that experiment, and the Vienna Congress transformed what remained into a relatively traditional European kingdom. Liberal political institutions in America were more stable, but most of their procedures had been worked out well before its war of independence was fought and won (see Chapter Eighteen).

BY 1815, THE STAGE IS SET FOR LIBERAL CONSTITUTIONAL REFORM IN EUROPE, BUT NOT OBVIOUSLY SO

Even before Napoleon was defeated, the eventual victors organized a conference in Vienna to address international security and constitutional issues. Between 1814 and 1815, that conference substantially redrew the map of Europe, creating somewhat larger states in Germany and reducing Poland and Venice to dependencies (Nicolson 1946, chapters 11–12). The Venetian republic was merged into the territory of Austria. Republican governance in the Netherlands was replaced with a constitutional monarchy. The Swiss confederation was restored, but it was less stable than it had been and remained so for three decades.

After the Vienna conference, the king-and-council template must have seemed as secure as ever. Experiments with republican governance in Europe appeared to be over.

Economic and political liberals remained a minority even in academic circles (in most places) during the seventeenth and eighteenth centuries, partly because political censorship was still very common in Europe, but also because there were many scholars who favored the traditional scholastic approach. Moreover, the poor constitutional results of the French Revolution – both the terror and the dictatorship – could be used to counter liberal arguments favoring more open politics. As a consequence, life was often difficult for liberal scholars.

Moreover, the fear of revolutions similar to the French one had not induced kings to adopt liberal reforms after 1789 or 1815, as some contemporary revolutionary-threat theories of constitutional reform seem to require. Rather, such threats induced worried governments to reduce civil liberties. For example, the United Kingdom curtailed the right of habeas corpus, increased censorship, and outlawed seditious meetings in 1817. Similar, more restrictive laws were also passed on the European continent during this time and at others when revolutionary threats were feared by political elites.

Censorship tends to be toughest with respect to proposals for political reform, and so proponents of liberal constitutional reform had be very careful about how they presented arguments so as not to run afoul of penalties associated with treason or blasphemy. This is one reason why many famous German and French liberals were "fiction" writers, rather than social scientists or political theorists. Fiction provided liberal authors with a natural defense against treason: "It's just a story."

Rationalism and liberalism remained minority views until well into the nineteenth century, although they were gaining support within educated circles. Burke was much closer to the mainstream in England in 1800 than Locke or Bentham. Indeed, by the standards of that time, Burke could be regarded as a moderate liberal, which is why both contemporary liberals and conservatives can find useful quotes in Burke's writings and speeches.

With the benefit of hindsight, we know that conservative confidence in 1820 was misplaced. That same hindsight, however, also makes the next century of reforms seem more inevitable than it was. Commerce and innovation could have stalled, and the ideas of intellectuals and radical liberal reformers might have lost public and legislative debates to other more traditional ideas, as they had in the past and in other places such as China and Turkey. Governments might have become more king-dominated had colonization proved to be as profitable as kings had hoped, and had wars been less costly.

Previous centuries had not provided any strong evidence that European culture would produce parliamentary democracy. Christianity had been the dominant religion for more than a thousand years. The Protestant reformation had taken place nearly three centuries earlier, without producing obviously more liberal societies, except perhaps in the Netherlands. Although it can be argued that Europe had gradually become a relatively wealthy place by the standards of world history, life in Europe was not radically different or more prosperous than in other places with reasonably well-functioning governments. However, as a consequence of technological and ideological changes that were under way in the late eighteenth century, the post-Napoleon restoration proved unstable and was gradually overturned by a long series of reforms adopted in the century that followed. The fact that both old and new kingdoms adopted similar reforms suggests that a common series of shocks were systematically changing the political and economic interests of Europe's political elites during the nineteenth century.

In 1820, none of this was obvious. The constitutional decisions made in Vienna had restored the traditional template and balance of authority throughout Europe. New king-and-council regimes were created at the same time that others were restored. Similar king-dominated templates would be adopted later in the nineteenth century by Greece, Germany, Italy, and Japan. The constitutional decisions made in Vienna had "clearly" restored the traditional template and balance of authority throughout Europe.

TEN

Liberalism and Reform in the Transformative Century

THE GREAT TRANSFORMATION

Prior to 1800, life for the typical person in Europe had not materially changed for many centuries. Farming was the main occupation, as it had been for millennia. Social mobility was not impossible, but it was difficult because of legal, cultural, and economic barriers. Opportunities were largely determined by laws and customs that explicitly linked political and economic positions to families. Rule of law existed in most of northern Europe and in Japan, but somewhat different laws and rights existed for royals, nobles, peasants, serfs, and slaves, and also for men and women. A state-supported monopoly church provided religious services and a more or less uniform world view. Water, wind, and muscle were the dominant motive forces of economic production, as they had been for centuries.

Significant changes in ideas about the world had occurred in the centuries before 1800, as noted in Chapter Nine, and these changes had effects on the lives of an important subset of the relatively wealthy who engaged in international affairs, travel, and education. Such changes are part of the case for arguing that the transition in the West actually began well before the nineteenth century (North and Thomas 1973). New knowledge and ideas about the world, together with improvements in European ships, produced new opportunities for exploration and trade, which produced new trading networks as well as advances in philosophy, science, and art. Technological shifts on land were also evident during the late eighteenth century, as better techniques for using water and wind power increased the scale of efficient cloth and lumber mills. Better seeds and plows, together with new techniques of crop rotation and plowing, were also making existing agricultural land more productive. New highways and canals were being constructed to form somewhat more integrated regional markets.

These "new" technologies of trade, production, and organization, however, were not fundamentally different from those of past centuries. Most of the new technologies were simply bigger and better versions of the ones that they replaced, and many of the new laws simply codified or restored long-standing informal practices. Animal propulsion along canals and roads remained the principal engines of domestic trade and integration. Sails remained the principal engines of international trade. Buildings and bridges were constructed of bricks, stone, and wood, as they had been since Roman times. Nor were the organizations that carried out these tasks very different from those in past centuries. They remained largely based on family finance, management, and relationships – albeit augmented with non-family members who occasionally held positions of significance. Improved land and transport continued to be the limiting factors of economic production during times of population expansion.

The king-and-council template had long been in use in Europe, and its late-medieval formulation with a dominant king and a relatively weak parliament with veto power over taxes had been the norm for several hundred years. The process through which kings and members of parliament were selected was largely based on, and supported by, inheritance and family networks. Although there had been earlier periods in which the office of king had been an elective office, most European kings in 1800 had inherited their positions. Exceptions occurred, but for the most part, these were cases in which the previous king had died without (legitimate) children. Inheritance was also the basis for selecting the men that held seats in the noble chambers of parliaments. They were also usually first-born sons. Members of the other chambers of parliament were also often members of distinguished families who were often related to noble families in fairly direct ways.[1]

The changes in economic and political life that occurred in the nineteenth century were far larger and more fundamental than those that had occurred in the seventeenth and eighteenth centuries. Indeed, it is difficult to exaggerate the magnitude of the changes that took place in northern Europe, the United States, and Japan during the nineteenth century. It was a truly transformative century. This chapter and the next provide overviews

[1] It is clear that this method of solving the succession problem advanced the interests of elite families. It also allowed wealth and power to shift within a single dynasty, lawfully and peacefully. It also minimized unproductive conflict as discussed in Chapter 3. During times at which no heir to the throne existed, competition for succession often led to open warfare among elite families and their armies. The principle of first-born-male succession reduced this unproductive conflict over high offices at the same time that it cemented family wealth and authority.

of public-policy and constitutional reforms adopted over the course of the nineteenth century, what many today refer to as Westernization when applied to other parts of the world. More detailed historical accounts of constitutional reforms are provided in the country case studies of Chapters Twelve to Eighteen.

Technological and Ideological Trends and Innovations in the Nineteenth Century

In many cases, the nineteenth century simply accelerated and amplified changes that had been taking place in past centuries. For example, the money-based economy expanded as hiring oneself out for wages became an increasingly common method of securing personal necessities. Formerly novel methods of farming and organizing village life became the norm rather than the exception. Store-bought cloth and clothing gradually replaced homespun and homemade. Urban centers that had been growing slowly for centuries began expanding at an accelerating pace. Ancient cities such as Paris, London, Berlin, and Amsterdam grew larger than they had ever been in the past, as their medieval cores were surrounded by a rapidly expanding ring of nineteenth-century roads, canals, and buildings. Seaports expanded and long-standing highway systems were upgraded. Mining expanded as new uses for old minerals were discovered and refined.

In other cases, new trends were initiated as a series of new technologies, each with significant economies of scale, was introduced during the nineteenth century. New, relatively large organizations were founded to take advantage of the new technologies. Specialization among and within firms increased. Completely new occupations emerged, and literacy became an important factor in upward mobility for the middle class. New steam production and rail enterprises emerged. New occupations such as metallurgist, machinist, engineer, steam fitter, and steel driver also emerged.

Formerly expensive and exotic materials such as steel and aluminum became increasingly common building materials for machines, factories, urban buildings, bridges, and warships, as the cost of producing those materials fell. Steel became a major product, rather than an exotic specialty metal, after the Bessemer process was worked out in 1858. Aluminum became a significant material for manufacturing in the late nineteenth century after Hall worked out a process for smelting aluminum in 1886. The use of petroleum for lighting and heating took off in the late 1850s, a decade after Gesner developed a method for producing kerosene in 1846. Toward the end of the nineteenth century, other new power sources became available as practical motors using kerosene, gasoline, and electricity were developed. Elevators, bicycles, automobiles, trucks, and airplanes emerged as common modes for local transport in the early twentieth century.

Mechanical forms of propulsion supplemented and then largely replaced animal-based transport and manufacturing. Transport became faster, more reliable, and more comfortable within and between countries. The great mechanized systems of cloth and lumber mills were attached to steam engines, rather than water wheels or wind mills, which freed them from the uncertainties of weather and also allowed them to move away from streams and rivers. Instantaneous communication over long distances became commonplace within and between cities as telegraphs and telephones were invented and their networks expanded. Very few steam engines had been in use in the late eighteenth century, and no electric ones (Pomeranz 2000, chapter 2; Taylor 1951, chapter 5; Fulbrook 1990, chapter 5).

As rail and communication networks were developed, the points at which lines crossed became convenient places for trans-shipping and manufacturing. New towns and cities emerged as inland "port" cities. New commercial and industrial centers were also established at places where the new factories and mines were located. New cities emerged in the British midlands, the German Ruhr, and the American Midwest as transport networks improved and as industrialization and economic migration took place.

The new forms of transport and new materials made new forms of buildings, bridges, and roads possible, although it took some time for architects and engineers to fully exploit the potential of the new materials and new engines. New scientific fields also arose as chemistry, biology, geology, economics, political science, and sociology became subjects undertaken by specialists, rather than subfields of natural philosophy and physics. New organizations and new industries emerged to produce equipment for those enterprises and to undertake the large construction projects required for the new, more capital-intensive production methods.

Employment in a wide range of supporting industries grew. Most of the new opportunities for employment were in cities. As a consequence, wages were usually greater in towns and cities than in the countryside, which induced more people to move to towns and cities. The quality of urban life also improved gradually as water systems, central heating, street lights, and electricity became commonplace. Communication costs fell as printing presses improved and as telegraphs and telephones were invented and widely adopted. Commerce expanded to unprecedented levels. Ancient town walls were often demolished and their materials recycled to build new dwellings, shops, and factories as old towns and cities expanded.

By the end of the nineteenth century, many of the "ordinary" technologies and materials of transport, manufacturing, and communication were very different from those that had been the norm for many centuries or millennia.

Farming remained an important occupation, but in many cases farming itself had become a new industry. Western farmers served larger and more distant markets than in the past, using more capital-intensive methods of planting, harvesting, and storage. Refrigerated railcars were introduced in the second half of the nineteenth century, which greatly extended the range of many agricultural markets. The rural populations of Denmark, Germany, the Netherlands, and Great Britain fell from between 75 and 90 percent of the population in 1850 to between 50 and 60 percent in 1900 at the same time that population approximately doubled in size (Cook and Paxton 1978, chapter 10).

LIBERAL REFORMS AS PREREQUISITES FOR INDUSTRIALIZATION

This short overview suggests that technological innovations were central to the transformation of life in the nineteenth century. However, the uneven adoption of the new technologies within Europe and around the world suggests that more than product and production innovation was important. The advantages of new technologies were partly determined by the legal and political settings in which they were to be applied. Exploiting new economies of scale required access to large markets. Urbanization required new city boundaries and a somewhat broader array of public services to be provided. Many of the laws governing the use of real estate, internal monopolies, tariffs, and labor laws were controlled by national, rather than regional, governments. A broad range of reforms to medieval regulations and laws had to be adopted in order for the new modes of production to be profitable.

Even in England, often regarded as the most open of the eighteenth-century economies, Adam Smith noted that the rules of incorporated towns and trade associations created for the "better government of trade" had restricted competition, as noted earlier. The profits associated with new economies of scale created new political support for reducing local restrictions, improving transportation networks, the elimination of tariffs, and local government reform. Many persons inside and outside government in the late eighteenth and early nineteenth centuries also supported reform of political institutions in order to advance normative interests in more open societies. Other less idealistic persons believed that desired economic-policy reforms would be easier to adopt if the allocation and method of choosing members of parliament were changed.

Open support for reform of the national government was often illegal during this period, but as political censorship was reduced, advocates for such reforms organized politically active groups to make the case for economic and political reform inside and outside government. Many of the reforms adopted were liberal in the sense used in this volume. A wide range of reforms promoted civic equality; for example, political and economic opportunities became less dependent on family and wealth.

In what became the West, coalitions of pragmatists and liberal idealists were often sufficient to induce reforms of long-standing political procedures and economic regulations. The first reforms often increased support for further reforms by changing the net returns from political and economic opportunities, as with reductions in censorship and the enclosure laws. Such boot-strapping effects were reinforced by the success of many liberal reforms, many of which advanced general interests. The success of such reforms also weakened the case for institutional conservatism and encouraged the copying of the new "political best practices" by governments in other communities and countries.

Together, the extension of public education and the economic organizations founded to take advantage of the new technologies produced a new middle class that was largely composed of persons who had benefited from past economic and political liberalization. The new middle class tended to be more widely read, more widely traveled, and more often interested politics and liberal reforms than their parents had been.

Increasing support for reform was also evident within government. For the idealists in government, policy reforms provided convincing evidence that progress and improvements were possible in many areas of life. For many pragmatists, it became increasingly obvious that technological advance and economic growth generated profits, taxable resources, and national military power. Many wealthy landowners represented in parliament also invested in the new commercial enterprises or were themselves formeteurs of new economic enterprises. Many who became eligible to vote or to serve as government officials tended to support somewhat more open political and economic systems, because openness had allowed many of them to rise to high office. The interests of members of parliament and kings are not entirely determined by political institutions.

Laws governing what could be owned and inherited were changed in substantial ways. Land became an asset that could be more freely sold and more widely owned at the same time that government positions became less tradable and inheritable. Entrance into businesses was made easier by reducing the scope of local monopolies and guild privileges. Such reforms also allowed new technologies to be more easily adopted, and profitable innovations encouraged further efforts at innovation. Large enterprises were made easier to found and finance, as standing procedures for incorporation (often with limited liability) replaced procedures that effectively required separate acts of national legislation.

Economics, politics, and law became less family based, less hierarchical, and more uniform. Slavery was eliminated. Formal aristocratic privileges gradually disappeared, while middle class and peasant "privileges" expanded. Religious and wealth requirements for high offices gradually disappeared. Racial and sexual restrictions for suffrage and high office also diminished, but often later and more slowly.

Major reforms of national governance also occurred. Parliaments gradually became the most powerful branch of government as policy-making authority shifted from kings to parliaments. Parliaments also became less based on family and more based on electoral competition. The ancient noble chambers of most parliaments were gradually eliminated (or weakened) and were replaced with more representative chambers, albeit often ones that included many members from noble families. The breadth of the electorate used to select members of parliament gradually increased to unprecedented levels.

By century's end, a new form of government had emerged that was largely supported by a new consensus about the core features of a good society. That consensus is largely taken for granted in Western politics today, but it took more than a century to emerge and its proponents were not assured of success. The long series of liberal reforms in Europe did not occur spontaneously or through great revolutionary wars, but through gradual, thoughtful, carefully crafted, intensely debated, formal changes in law that reflected changes in the interests of those with the authority to adopt reforms through legislation.

In parts of the world where politics and public policies were not liberalized, the new technologies were much less widely employed, and where they were employed, they tended to be used less extensively, as in China and the Ottoman Empire. In most cases, this does not seem to have been a consequence of important differences in natural resources, wealth, or location, but rather of long-standing legal barriers and customs that reduced opportunities to profitably use the new technologies. In regions of the world that did not modernize, the conservatives won the policy debates within government, rather than the liberals. As a consequence, their internal and external trade barriers remained in place, and their privileged families continued to govern "their" relatively poorer countries.

Liberal Theories and the Direction of Reform in the Nineteenth Century

Political liberalism was grounded in normative theories that stressed the implicit contract basis of the state, a government's duty to ordinary citizens, and the importance of written constitutional documents and representative institutions as methods for encouraging governments to advance broadly shared interests. Economic liberalism was grounded in new models of economic development that supported open, competitive markets over tightly regulated and monopolistic markets, for largely similar reasons. The origins of these two important strands of liberalism often overlapped and reinforced each other, as noted in Chapter Nine. The arguments used by liberal proponents of economic and political reform in the late eighteenth and nineteenth centuries also overlapped to a considerable extent, and liberty, reason, and general welfare were often used as norms.

Consider, for example, a few passages from Adam Smith's widely read and widely translated book, *The Wealth of Nations* (1776). Smith's book was often cited by economic liberals in the nineteenth century. Many of his observations and arguments supported liberal constitutional reforms as well as economic reforms. He argued, for example,

> [Regarding liberties in the English colonies:] In every thing, except their foreign trade, **the liberty of the English colonists** to manage their own affairs ... **is secured in the same manner, by an assembly of the representatives of the people, who claim the sole right of imposing taxes for the support of the colony government**. The authority of this assembly over-awes the executive power [of their governors], and neither the meanest nor the most obnoxious colonist, as long as he obeys the law, has anything to fear from the resentment, either of the governor or of any other civil or military officer in the province. ... the executive power either has not the means to corrupt them, ... [and, consequently, their representative assemblies] are perhaps in general more influenced by the inclinations of their constituents. (Adam Smith 1776, *The Wealth of Nations*, Book IV, chapter 7.73)
>
> Regulated companies resemble, in every respect, **the corporations of trades so common in the cities and towns of all the different countries of Europe, and are ... enlarged monopolies** of the same kind. As **no inhabitant of a town can exercise an incorporated trade without first obtaining his freedom in the corporation, so in most cases no subject of the state can lawfully carry on any branch of foreign trade**, for which a regulated company is established, without first becoming a member of that company. **The monopoly is more or less strict according as**

the terms of admission are more or less difficult; and according as the directors of the company have more or less authority, or have it more or less in their power to manage in such a manner as to confine the greater part of the trade to themselves and their particular friends. (Adam Smith 1776, *The Wealth of Nations*, Book V chapter 1.96)

The legislature, **were it possible that its deliberations could be always directed**, not by the clamorous importunity of partial interests, but **by an extensive view of the general good**, ought upon this very account, perhaps, to be particularly **careful neither to establish any new monopolies of this kind, nor to extend further those which are already established.** Every such regulation introduces some degree of real disorder into the constitution of the state, which it will be difficult afterwards to cure without occasioning another disorder. (Adam Smith 1776, *The Wealth of Nations*, Book IV, chapter 2.44)

It is clear that Smith's analysis is grounded in the normative theories that had emerged in the previous two centuries. These paragraphs, among many others, support the advancement of general interests through public policies and constitutional design, rather than the interests of king, national glory, or state religion. These paragraphs also suggest that Smith favored both more open and representative political systems and more open and competitive economic systems. Similar arguments and policy positions were evident throughout the nineteenth century, partly because of Smith and other liberal scholars of that period, but also because experience with modest liberal reforms showed that more open and competitive political and economic systems could, in fact, advance broad common interests.

Another useful window into the argument and policy agenda of politically active liberals in the early nineteenth century is provided by John Stuart Mill's description of his father's hopes for political reform:

In politics, [he had] an almost **unbounded confidence in the efficacy of two things: representative government, and complete freedom of discussion**. So complete was my father's reliance on the influence of reason over the minds of mankind, whenever it is allowed to reach them, that he felt as if **all would be gained if the whole population were taught to read, if all sorts of opinions were allowed** to be addressed to them by word and in writing, and **if by means of the suffrage** they could nominate a legislature to give effect to the opinions they adopted. He thought that **when the legislature no longer represented a class interest, it would aim at the general interest**, honestly and with adequate wisdom; since **the people would be sufficiently under the guidance of educated intelligence, to make in general a good choice of persons to represent them**, and having done so, to leave to those whom they had chosen a liberal discretion. (J. S. Mill, *Autobiography*, 1873, chapter 4)

It also bears noting that the arguments of liberal theorists could often be used to build support for any liberal reforms favored by pragmatists, at least at the margin, because they argued that such reforms advanced broad interests, not simply those of would-be industrialists or privileged families. Support is easier to build for reforms that make most persons (or members of parliament) better off than for ones that simply make one individual or firm better off.

Trends in Liberalism and Reforms in the Nineteenth Century

Nineteenth-century trends in economic and political reforms throughout the West were remarkably consistent with trends in liberal political and economic theories. This was not because nineteenth-century Europe was populated by liberals or because liberals favored a specific program of reforms, but because there were a sufficient number of liberals in government who agreed about the *proper direction* of reform to influence the reforms adopted. Liberals generally favored reforms that increased civic equality by reducing hereditary and other privileges (and disadvantages) in economic life, the law, and politics.

Although liberals nearly always voted for modest expansions of civil liberties and modest reduction in special privileges when they were proposed, there was less agreement about how far such reforms should go. Consequently, policy debates among liberals were nearly as intense as arguments between liberals and conservatives.

It should also be noted that there was a trend in the mainstream liberal opinion during the nineteenth century. Only a few radical liberals explicitly called for the end of the medieval order in 1800. Instead, mainstream liberals favored modest reforms that opened political and economic life to somewhat more families. They favored the expansion of public education, reductions in censorship, and a gradual end to slavery. The mainstream liberal political agenda of 1830–80 favored somewhat more detailed written constitutions with a somewhat broader electorate that reached "down" to what today would be called the upper-middle class. Mid-century liberals also favored reduced tariffs, increased parliamentary control over cabinet ministers, and infrastructure expansion.[2] Only "radical" liberals such as John Stuart Mill favored (nearly) universal men's and women's suffrage or parliamentary dominance during the mid-century.

[2] Cabinet officials were often essentially above the law during the early nineteenth century, because they were servants of the king or queen, rather than ordinary persons. They were thus subject to royal mandates and administrative procedures. Liberals and others in parliament during the mid-nineteenth century often wanted cabinet ministers to be subject to criminal law and to parliamentary sanctions, rather than protected by royal privilege.

Liberal ideas about proper qualifications for suffrage became less grounded in property and tax payments during the century and somewhat more in education and self-sufficiency. This shift induced mainstream liberals to favor extending suffrage to middle-class professionals in the early nineteenth century; to most of the middle class in the mid to late nineteenth century; and finally, to nearly all adult men in the early twentieth century. The shift in opinion was partly the result of changes in norms for qualification. It was also partly induced by the expansion of public education, which had reduced illiteracy, and changes in economic opportunities that caused fewer persons to be servants or otherwise completely dependent on their employers. Practical political considerations also played a role, insofar as the party preferences of new voters were taken into account. Shortly before (and after) World War I, support for women's suffrage became mainstream as rationales for male suffrage was extended to women. In 1920, even moderates largely accepted Mill's formerly radical positions and in many cases supported greater civil equality than Mill had. Liberal positions that had been radical a half century earlier had become mainstream ones (see Chapter Eleven).[3]

Although there were trends in liberalism, there was always a spectrum of opinion. It is likely that the breadth of liberal opinion about specific reforms allowed liberalism to have a larger effect on day-to-day policy decisions during the nineteenth century than it would have had if liberals were all doctrinaire or radical. This allowed "conservative" legislation to be adopted by attracting the support of a few relatively conservative or moderate liberals in exchange for a few minor liberal reforms. Such forms of compromise and cooperation would not have been possible if liberalism had been a truly revolutionary movement with inflexible, radical goals.

A Long Series of "Minor" Liberal Reforms

The remainder of this chapter provides an overview of major reforms supported by liberals during the nineteenth century, many of which proved to be so durable that they are taken for granted more than a century after they were adopted. The main purpose of this part of the chapter is to demonstrate that liberalism affected many areas of public policy and that liberal reforms

3 This liberal-conservative classification scheme is not arbitrary, but reflects the labels that many reformers used for themselves, as well as party labels and platforms that were common in the second half of the nineteenth century. Conservatives opposed reform of the medieval order in the early nineteenth century. They too shifted ground during the late nineteenth century, as developed later.

tended to be gradual and were broadly sustained during the nineteenth and early twentieth centuries. Examples of reforms include reductions in censorship penalties, increases in support for public education, reductions in minor tariffs, subtle shifts in corporate and tort laws, and slight changes in electoral laws.

Other significant reforms were more radical, as with the elimination of slavery and major tariffs, significant changes in property and suffrage law, and formal constitutional amendments. However, even major reforms normally revised, rather than replaced, long-standing policies, laws, and procedures for adopting public policies. Many other examples could have been discussed, but the ones included are sufficient to show that broad liberal trends in policy reforms were evident during the late eighteenth, nineteenth, and early twentieth centuries throughout most of what came to be called the West.

For the purposes of this book, it is liberal constitutional reforms that are of greatest interest, but it is important to understand that liberalism was not exclusively a constitutional movement, although it had significant effects on the procedures of governance. The other reforms demonstrate that liberals were politically active and became increasingly influential during the course of the nineteenth century. It is also important to understand that the new liberal economic and political systems were created by a long series of reforms, many of which were quasi-constitutional, rather formal parts of constitutional documents.

THE END OF MEDIEVAL PROPERTY RIGHTS: ENCLOSURE AND FREE TRADE

Medieval Ownership and Strip Farms

Prior to 1750, most land in Europe was owned, but "ownership" involved quite different bundles of rights than it did in 1850. Noble families owned their estates in the sense that they managed them without external interventions, but they could not sell them without the king's permission. Within most estates, peasant farmers similarly owned their land in the sense that they farmed and controlled access to particular fields. Their fields, like those of their lords, were normally passed on to their children. Families could use their fields largely as they saw fit and block others from using them, but they could not easily sell or transfer their claim to the fields that they controlled.

The relationship between church-controlled lands, farmers, and peasants was similar to that of lords, farmers, and peasants. Families farming church fields had durable, if informal, property claims, and inheritance was an important source of their wealth and opportunity. Freeholders also existed, although they normally controlled less land than the royal family, nobles, and churches. Nonetheless, such freeholders were a large fraction of the non-noble elite and the middle class. Freeholder ownership was less encumbered and so more closely resembled today's property arrangements. However, these land holdings were also largely passed onto family members, because land was the most reliable store of wealth and income in the medieval period.

Many positions within local and national governments were owned in a similar manner. Nobles often held several titles as a consequence of marriage and inheritance. Such posts were inheritable and essentially family property. In some cases, family titles and positions could be sold, but only the least important ones. (Top posts in Catholic churches could not be routinely passed on to children, because of celibacy vows, but they were often passed on to other family members.)

In the medieval and late-medieval periods, land, titles, and positions were largely birthrights, rather than liquid assets. Servants and farmhands were often employed to help with household chores and field work, but they were largely paid in kind (room and board), rather than in cash for their services.

The rural landscape also physically differed from that which we are familiar with today. Medieval farmland was normally divided into hundreds of narrow strips of land, rather than into large roughly rectangular farm fields that typify the contemporary countryside. Peasant land holdings consisted of particular strips of land that were interspersed among the similar strips of fellow farmers. Strip farmers often lived together in farm villages and would walk out to their individual strips together. These narrow strip fields could not be fenced off at a reasonable cost because of their long perimeters, and a good deal of private farmland consequently consisted of "unenclosed" fields. Much of the farmland that was held by independent farmers was also in the form of strip farms.[4]

In addition to strip farms, other "wasteland" was often held in common and could be used by all persons living on the manor, farm, or village, including farmhands and servants without fields of their own. Access to

[4] Macfarlane (1978, 83–91) provides evidence that land titles were in principle transferable in England and much of Europe in the period before enclosure, but he acknowledges that land titles were for the most part inherited under rules of primogeniture. Land was rarely, for example, included in wills, and there were restrictions on transfers of land within manors. The so-called customary estates are those of interest for enclosure movements.

communal pastures, woodland, and gardens was normally tied to ownership of particular pieces of land and to employment on farms within the community. Such access-rationing systems helped avoid the "tragedy of the commons" by limiting use of communal property.

Strip farmers on manors had obligations to the owner of the manor (often a minor noble, who occupied the manor's grand house). Manorial obligations could be regarded as a form of property tax or rent, although manorial obligations were normally in kind, rather than in cash. Farming decisions were often made collectively at village meetings of various kinds, both on manor estates and among independent (but interwoven) strip farmers in the countryside.

The strip-field, three-class (aristocrat, farmer, and peasant) farming system had existed for centuries in much of Europe. The strip-field system of property rights was neither communal property nor private property according to contemporary definitions (Demsetz 1967), but addressed both commons and long-term resource management problems by creating residual claimant-owners.[5]

This long-standing system of land management and usufruct underwent major reforms in eighteenth- and nineteenth-century Europe in what can be considered the first of the major liberal economic reforms.

Enclosure as Liberal Civil Law Reform

Proponents of "enclosure" called for the consolidation of strip farms into contiguous fields to be independently owned by their freeholders. The advocates of enclosure in most cases were economic and political entrepreneurs who combined narrow economic interests with ideological ones. Enclosure entrepreneurs were paid to devise acceptable enclosure plans and to obtain permission to change the property systems, normally one village or manor at a time (Allen 1982; Blum 1981). They argued that land output could be increased by rationalizing the fields and that enclosure would increase the liberty of landholders by eliminating manorial duties.

The first enclosures required specific legislation be adopted by national parliaments, but this cumbersome process of reform was later revised to facilitate enclosure.

[5] Similar systems remain evident today in several nonindustrialized countries where property claims are still often based on informal traditions and historic use, and many farm fields are strips of land, rather than large contiguous rectangular fields. See, for example, Benneh (1973) or Ostrom (1991, 2005). See North, Wallis, and Weingast (2009, 77–87, 107–9) for a discussion of medieval land practices, title reform, and concentration of ownership in England.

Enclosure plans had four direct effects. First, the plans rationalized the medieval farming system by collecting the strip fields and communal lands into a few more or less rectangular fields that could be more efficiently farmed with the new plows and field rotation. This geometry also made fencing and hedge rows more practical, which indirectly provided the English name for this property reform movement. (The perimeters of the new squarer fields were much shorter than the original strip fields.) Second, the new fields were to be managed independently by individual farmers, rather than through collective village decisions of one kind or another. This often caused medieval villages to disintegrate as farmers moved out of villages to their fields and barns.[6] Third, the land was generally freed from familial restrictions on transfers of property, which allowed property to be shifted more easily among family members and from family to family, and thus increased the liquidity of this form of wealth. Fourth, most jointly used communal property (often wastelands, but also common wood lots, gardens, and pasture lands) was divided up and assigned to individual farmers, although small communal plots often remained after most land was enclosed.

All these changes increased economic efficiency and independence by reducing transaction costs and allowing economies of scale to be realized. The new property rights made land holdings a more liquid asset, which allowed persons who were more effective at farming to expand their land holdings more easily and allowed less skilled farmers to more easily sell off their holdings and relocate to towns and cities. After enclosure (privatization), agricultural experiments could also be undertaken one at a time by individual farmers without the consent of their village, which increased the rate at which better equipment and field rotations could be discovered. The new field system also reduced the cost of policing boundaries between neighbors by reducing the length and number of property boundaries.

The new field system of farming increased economic risks for many farmers because the new freeholders controlled a narrower distribution of soil types, sun exposure, and drainage. Enclosure also reduced the extent of informal village and family-based social insurance (Richardson 2005). Privatizing village holdings, especially the common "waste areas," also reduced the implicit wealth of nonowners (renters and servants) and

[6] A few villages chose to aggregate their strips into more or less triangular blocks with a common point at the village boundary in order to preserve their farm villages. Such enclosures created a star-like pattern of land holdings. See, for example, Allested or Nørre Højrup in Denmark.

small landowners, who previously had had more or less equal access to common grazing, gardening, and forest areas. These losses to servants and small landowners were, perhaps surprisingly, offset in the short run by an increased demand for labor to build enclosures and new roads and also to help improve and farm the newly enclosed areas (Allen 1982, Blum 1981).

The main economic advantage of privatization was evidently reduced transaction costs, rather than increased farm output.[7] The greater liquidity of land allowed entrepreneurial farmers to use their lands as capital for financing farm expansion and other commercial ventures. Land also gradually shifted from less efficient to more efficient farmers. Increased agricultural efficiency was evidently not often claimed by proponents of enclosure (Clark 1998; Pomeranz 2000, chapter 2). Villages composed of farmers also have strong incentives to maximize total farm output.

About 20 percent of English land was enclosed by parliamentary acts between 1760 and 1820 (Blum 1981). Similar enclosures and enclosure movements took place during the same period in Denmark, Sweden, Germany, and France (Pomeranz 2000, chapter 2; Blum 1981). Much of the remainder was held as royal land, as grants to families (nobles), and by churches, which could not easily be transferred permanently to others.[8]

The Political Procedures and Consequences of Enclosure

The enclosure acts themselves required political decisions and had political consequences. The enclosures required legislation to revise existing civil and customary law at the village level, as both use and transfer rights were redefined at the same time that land holdings were aggregated and communal properties were divided up among property holders. New property rights were established essentially one village at a time by passing private bills in parliament (for a relatively high fee).[9] At the local level, sufficient

[7] The extent of the agricultural advantages of enclosure is much debated within the economic history literature. Most studies, however, show that only relatively small agricultural productivity gains can be attributed to enclosure (Clark 1998).

The enclosures of this period evidently hold a special fascination for economic historians, in part because they shed light on the privatization campaigns of the late twentieth century.

[8] Noble titles and lands reverted to the king or queen when an aristocratic family died out. The king would subsequently grant the land and title to prominent supporters, often in exchange for loans and other services, or would sell it to freeholders to meet royal expenses.

[9] Among the costs of enclosure were solicitor and parliamentary fees, commissioner and surveyor fees, and the cost of fencing, roads, and drainage. The General Enclosure Act of

support of landowners had to be assembled, which required bargaining over the reassignment of rights to strips of land (and other claims). These negotiations determined the size and location of the new parcels and also affected the nature of local governance (Blum 1981).

Although cases existed in which smaller landholders pressed for reform, it was normally the large landholders that paid the legal fees associated with enclosure bills. Small farmers often opposed enclosure because of uncertainties associated with the process of consolidation (Blum 1981).

The first procedures for enclosure required unanimous agreement among the landowners and the passage of national legislation. Under these procedures, essentially all property owners had to anticipate gains from the enclosure plans, or parliament would not adopt the required legislation. Parliaments gradually reduced the requirements for unanimous support for enclosure plans by reducing the veto power of small stakeholders. In England and other countries, land-weighted supermajority voting gradually replaced unanimous agreement among property holders. In the late eighteenth century, if persons owning three-quarters of the land at issue wanted enclosure, parliament normally passed the desired bill; if not, the desired bill was rejected or tabled. In 1801, the required assent in England was reduced to majority rule. A commission would be appointed to undertake the consolidation, which reduced the transaction costs of enclosure but vested a good deal of authority in the commissioners. Parliament adopted about four thousand separate enclosure bills between 1760 and 1840.

Changing the formal procedures for enclosures to be accepted by parliament required assembling national coalitions in favor of the new procedures. Those opposed to enclosure legislation argued that there were no (net) economic advantages from enclosure and that the political risks associated with non-unanimity were too high. The opponents clearly lost the political debate, except in France, albeit slowly.

General enclosure acts were adopted in England in 1801 and 1845 to streamline and regulate the process of enclosure. Similar reforms to streamline enclosure procedures were adopted in other countries at about the same time. For example, enclosure reforms were adopted in Denmark (1769, 1781), Sweden (1749, 1757, 1783, 1803, and 1807), Prussia (1751, 1811, and 1821), Saxony (1834 and 1843), Hanover (1842 and 1856), Baden (1856), and France (1791, 1865, and 1919). Many of the new rules used

1801 reduced solicitor, parliamentary, and commissioner fees; this act established standing guidelines for enclosure procedures (Blum 1981).

land-weighted voting among local landowners to determine whether an enclosure petition was acceptable or not.[10] This created opportunities for significant redistribution among landholders and other stakeholders at the same time that it created a precedent for wealth-weighted voting on important local matters.

The timing and nature of enclosure legislation reflected a variety of factors, but the relative bargaining power of the groups represented in parliaments and in royal councils was clearly an important determinant (Grantham 1980; Blum 1981; Pomeranz 2000, chapter 2).[11]

By the mid-nineteenth century, persuasion and economic circumstances had produced a gradual shift of local property law that greatly extended national and regional markets for land throughout most of northern Europe. The number of freeholders initially increased, which together with new farming techniques produced the familiar rectangular geography of small- and medium-size farm fields that remain typical in contemporary northern Europe.

Enclosure affected the distribution of political authority as well as the geography and economics of rural Europe. The political relationships among a number of groups were affected: (a) the interests of relatively wealthy commoners (whose land rights were revised); (b) nobles (privileged families whose lands were not normally subject to royal taxation and who often exercised significant quasi-governmental control of "communal" lands); and (c) the central government (which stood to profit from increased taxes and fees associated with enclosure). In general, village governments and local aristocrats lost policy-making authority, and the central government and individual farmers gained.[12]

[10] See Helmfrid (1961) for a thorough overview of Swedish land reform and some remarks on Danish consolidation. In some cases, enclosures were augmented by royal shifts of land from nobles to commoners. See Grantham (1980) for a table of reform legislation and decision rules and for an extended discussion of French rules for enclosure, which required unanimous consent well into the nineteenth century.

[11] In England, the forty-shilling franchise also created a political incentive for broader ownership of land (Chase 1991).

[12] Surveys of French farmers indicated that they recognized the value of consolidating their land holdings, but these surveys also showed farmers opposed the creation of mechanisms for accomplishing this change against the will of individual landowners. It was not until 1919 that majority rule replaced unanimous agreement in French enclosure proceedings (Grantham 1980). A single landowner could enclose his or her own land, essentially without consulting his or her tenants. However, enclosures by large French landowners were evidently not very common. Voluntary enclosures continued to be the norm in France, even after the 1865 procedures were adopted. Private property (and customary law) was, in this sense, better protected in France than elsewhere in northern Europe.

Free-Trade Movements of the Nineteenth Century

During the early nineteenth century, another broad liberal movement emerged that supported the elimination of other internal and external trade barriers. As true of the aims of the enclosure movement, these reforms required political decisions to overturn long-standing regulations. In contrast to the enclosure movement, for which reforms could be adopted one village or city at a time, reducing international barriers to trade could only be adopted at the national level. The liberalization of international trade, however, could be adopted one product or industry at a time, which helps explain the variation in tariffs and timing of trade liberalization among products.

Support was sufficiently broad that large national organizations in support of more open trade emerged throughout northern Europe during the early nineteenth century. Examples include the Anti–Corn Law group in England and the Handelsvertragsverein and Kongress Deutscher Volkswirte in Germany, which undertook broad lobbying campaigns (Welby, Rea, and Murray-MacDonald 1908; Kindleberger 1975).

The proponents of free trade included merchant and industrial groups that expected to benefit from reduced tariff and nontariff barriers such as exclusive import or export privileges, and liberals opposed to special privileges (rents) generated for those protected. Contributions to the Anti–Corn Law League (which lobbied against agricultural tariffs in England) reflected employment in exporting industries that were likely to prosper from free trade in general and from reduced agricultural protection (Schonhardt-Bailey 1991).

The breadth of support required to adopt reforms, however, was generally broader than the membership of the groups in which economic advantages were concentrated. To assemble a broader coalition, the free trade groups used both ideological and economic-interest arguments in persuasive campaigns. Economic arguments in favor of free trade were augmented by mentioning advantages that liberals favored on (ideological) principle, such as broadening economic opportunities (Kindleberger 1975; Schonhardt-Bailey 1991, 2006).

> In 1838 a corn law league was founded, Richard Cobden and John Bright being its leading spirits. The league made an educational campaign lasting through several years, which ended in convincing the bulk of the Englishmen of the impolicy of protection. The Corn Laws were repealed in 1846, and by 1852 the protective duties were all gone. (Judson 1894, 231)

Mass politics had clearly arrived in the United Kingdom, in spite of the fact that suffrage for the House of Commons was still very narrow by twentieth-century standards.

On a broader scale, the league based its national network on an organizational strategy that joined the voter registration campaign with the league propaganda scheme. As league agents distributed propaganda tracts to every elector in 24 county divisions and 187 boroughs, these agents submitted to the league headquarters consistent and complete reports on the electorate in their districts. (Schonhardt-Bailey 1991, 47)

Schonhardt-Bailey argues that the eventual success of the Anti–Corn Law League reflected ideological arguments in Parliament and changes in the voting behavior of members of parliament, who increasingly saw themselves as representatives of their specific regional interests, rather than independent agents for themselves or England. Pivotal members of Parliament had evidently internalized some of the popular sovereignty arguments of liberal political theory: "Repeal appears to have gained passage as these MPs switched from voting more as trustees to voting more as delegates" (Schonhardt-Bailey 2003, 581). Average British tariff rates declined from 1820 through 1900 (Nye 1991).

The persuasive campaigns in England were unusually broad – indeed, national in scope – and their propaganda pamphlets combined a variety of arguments, including ideological campaigns, to persuade educated persons to favor the end of agricultural subsidies.[13] Not every country witnessed large-scale campaigns similar to those of the Anti–Corn Law League, but similar economic and ideological arguments were made in the parliaments and councils of essentially all Western countries during the late eighteenth and entire nineteenth century. Indeed, an international customs union for northern Europe was proposed in 1813 by the Prussian Chancellor K. A. von Hardenberg (Scott 1950).

The success of the economic liberals throughout Western Europe is evident in the tariff reforms of the late eighteenth and early nineteenth centuries. For example, Denmark adopted a comprehensive free trade act in 1797 (Danstrup 1947, 5). The Netherlands lowered tariffs to an average of 10 percent in 1822 (Kossman 1978, 35). Internal restrictions on trade were eliminated within Prussia through an internal customs union in 1818, which eliminated a variety of internal tariffs and taxes (Fulbrook 1990, 114–15). A similar customs union for the German Confederation (the Deutsher Zollverein) was established in 1834, partially as a consequence of internal

[13] It is possible this shift in perspective was a consequence of the petitions of the Chartist constitutional-reform movement, which was active during the same period and is discussed below. Pickering (2001) notes that "Gladstone recorded that '[Chartist] discussions very greatly increased the influence of popular feeling on the deliberations of the House,' although Gladstone did not entirely approve of that influence" (p. 388).

lobbying by economic liberals, although the new revenue-sharing mechanisms associated with external tariffs also generated substantial support among regional sovereigns. (Confederal tariff revenues were not subject to the oversight of the regional parliaments [Dumke 1978].) Swiss liberals negotiated a new federal constitution in 1848, which eliminated internal barriers to trade among cantons.

Indeed, tariffs on the continent were often reduced to levels below those of the United Kingdom. For example, trade-weighted French tariffs fell from about 20 percent in 1820 to about 5 percent in 1870 and remained well below average British tariff rates during most of the nineteenth century (Nye 1991). Between 1820 and 1860, U.S. tariffs fell from an average of 45 percent to an average of about 20 percent (James 1981).

The influence of the various nineteenth-century free-trade movements can easily be exaggerated. Although many liberals stressed the advantages of broad open markets, pragmatists preferred broad open markets only in cases in which they were likely to be personally advantageous; they preferred protectionist tariffs and other restrictions in other trade areas (Kindleberger 1975; Schonhardt-Bailey 1998; Nye 1991). The point here is not that liberal ideology – specifically that of laissez-faire economists – won the day, but rather that loose coalitions of liberals and economic interest groups emerged and pressed for broad internal and external trade reforms. These coalitions were sufficiently well represented in government to influence economic policy at the national level.

The free-trade movements of the nineteenth century were notable for their size, intensity, and success during the early and mid-nineteenth century. Tariff rates drifted downward on average during much of the nineteenth century in most of the countries of interest for the purposes of this book, but with many reversals, particularly near the end of the century.

Intranational barriers were also dismantled during this period and have nearly been forgotten by contemporary economic historians. Town monopolies were gradually opened to competition. The economic privileges of aristocrats and guild members were gradually diminished and then formally eliminated.[14] The ebb and flow of tariffs, however, demonstrates that liberals did not win the debate on international trade restrictions as decisively as they won the debate on internal trade liberalization.

[14] This asymmetry probably reflects the fact that foreigners do not vote in national elections. Resurrecting internal barriers to trade tends to affect other domestic parties in fairly obvious ways. The adversely affected groups armed with liberal arguments can thus normally organize to counter local pressures for protection in national and regional parliaments. This tends to increase the political stability of domestic liberalization. The effects of one

CIVIC EQUALITY

Many political issues were permanently settled during the nineteenth century, whereas others remain on the agenda today. Notable permanent successes include areas of civil law in which a variety of long-standing, family-based handicaps and privileges were reduced or eliminated. Such reforms usually required significant lobbying campaigns in which liberal ideas played leading roles in public and governmental discussions. Their success gradually increased civic equality in many areas of law, although some reforms were clearly more important than others.

Perhaps the most striking of the early reforms of hereditary entitlements were the laws that ended slavery in the West, an institution that had been in place since the dawn of written history. Other examples include the expansion of public education and laws that reduced religion-specific rights: rights to worship were extended to more religious groups, and religious requirements for high office were gradually eliminated. In many of these areas of public policy, it seems clear that shifts in norms, rather than changes in economic interests, were the principal motivations for reform.

Slavery and its Abolition in the Nineteenth Century

Although all stable societies are governed by laws that are routinely and consistently applied, the laws often distinguish among families in a manner that produces and protects significant differences in wealth and status. In medieval societies, some families had far greater authority and protection than the average. Others had far less than average. The clearest example of law-based antiprivileges were the laws with respect to slavery and serfdom, although there were many others in most countries.

These laws assured that the lives of some families were entirely subject to the direction of others, and that members of such families had few, if any, exit options. That such laws had long existed is equally clear. Slaves are mentioned in the Code of Hammurabi, written in Mesopotamia four thousand years ago. The Code of Hammurabi, for example, includes provisions that govern the sale, theft, and punishment of slaves. Slavery was discussed by Greek philosophers during their golden era. Many of the great monuments of Greek and Roman times were products of slave labor. Slavery was used in European colonial enterprises during the seventeenth and eighteenth centuries. Slavery was a highly profitable method of producing sugar, cotton,

nation's restrictions on another nation's prosperity are not directly represented in parliamentary debates, because foreign losers do not vote in member elections (although they may sponsor lobbying groups).

tobacco, and coffee in the tropical and semitropical colonies of the Western hemisphere (Engerman 1986). The slave trade was a significant source of profits for British, Portuguese, French, and Dutch traders.[15] Serfdom was more common than slavery in late-medieval Europe, and serfs had more legal protections than slaves, but serfs were also bound to particular manors by law and normally could not own real estate (Kahan 1973).[16]

Normative debates on slavery and serfdom are nearly as old as slavery and serfdom themselves. For example, in about 330 BCE, Aristotle argued that some persons should not be slaves, because it was against their nature. He also argued that slaves should have some prospect of liberation. (Both positions would have been relatively liberal ones for most of the next two thousand years.) On the proslavery side of the debate, appeals to history, necessity, and precedent were used. Such inequality was part of the "natural" or "God-given" order of things, after all.

The idea that some families or persons were destined to be slaves tended to be taken for granted.

"He is sometimes slave who **should be** master; and sometimes master who **should be** slave" [Latin: Fit in dominatu servitus, in servitute dominatus.] (M. T. Cicero, *Oratio Pro Rege Deiotaro (XI)* 46 BC).

European debate over slavery intensified during the eighteenth and nineteenth centuries, in part because of philosophical and theological innovations associated with the rise of liberalism and the enlightenment. It also intensified because several European countries had became more involved in the slave trade and slavery through their merchant fleets and colonial enterprises. As a consequence, a variety of normative arguments for and against slavery were developed during the sixteenth, seventeenth, and eighteenth centuries (Turner 1929).

The debate about the abolishment of slavery was not the one-sided affair in the eighteenth and nineteenth centuries that it would be today. Slave owners had clear economic interests at stake and were predisposed to defend slavery (and serfdom), partly as an economic necessity, but also an essential part of the natural order of human society.

Those opposed to slavery developed economic and ideological critiques of the economics, efficiency, and morality of slavery. For example, Adam

[15] Lovejoy's (1982, 483) estimates of the Atlantic slave trade suggest that the British shipped 2.5 million slaves, the Portuguese 1.8 million, the French 1.1 million, and the Dutch approximately 350,000 between 1701 and 1800.

[16] Such laws, however, were routinely violated when labor was scarce, at which time serfs might move among manors (North and Thomas 1971). A serf that successfully escaped his or her manor could become free if he or she reached a free town.

Smith (1776) and other economists argued that consenting labor always was more efficient than slave labor.

From the experience of all ages and nations, I believe that the work done by free men comes cheaper in the end than the work performed by slaves. Whatever work he does, beyond what is sufficient to purchase his own maintenance, can be squeezed out of him by violence only, and not by any interest of his own.

Indeed, the economic strand of the arguments against slavery was responsible for economics being labeled the "dismal science" by conservatives defending the institutions of slavery and slave ownership (Levy 2001).[17]

The civic-equality and social-contract strands of liberal political theories provided a variety of normative arguments in opposition to slavery. Locke's contention that there are some contracts that no person would ever voluntarily agree to also applies to slavery. That logic was used, for example, by the Pennsylvania Society for the Abolition of Slavery, who with the support of Benjamin Franklin, argued that administration of the new national constitution for the United States should be color blind:

These blessings [of liberty] ought rightfully to be administered, without distinction of color to all descriptions of people … that **equal liberty was originally the position, and is still the birthright of all men** influenced by the strong ties of humanity. (Excerpt from the February 2, *1790 PSAS petition*, Unites States Senate, Center for Legislative Archives.)

Such lines of argument also produced debates about the proper definition of persons. Were African or West Indian slaves really persons? Did they have souls? Could they make sensible, reasoned choices? Many pragmatists were also predisposed to argue against slavery on economic, moral, and nationalistic grounds, because their products competed with those of slave enterprises.

Few members of the groups involved in the public debates on slavery in Europe or the northern part of the United States owned slaves or directly competed with imports produced by slaves. Consequently, the main issues tended to be metaphysical and ideological ones for proponents of abolishing slavery. An antislavery tract by Clarkson (1786) helped energize the abolitionist movement in England (Drescher 1990), which was subsequently formally organized and effectively led by William Wilberforce.

Ideological and economic abolitionists solicited horror stories from travelers and others who had seen the dark side of slavery: the abuse, the

[17] It can be argued that the label stuck, however, because of Malthus's gloomy prediction about prospects for long-term increases in average income.

mortality rates, and the effects of the trade on the traders themselves. Those defending the status quo produced reports of the benefits conferred by slavery on the slaves themselves and on the quality and extent of their nation's merchant fleet (Heffernan 1973).

> The song and the dance, says Mr. Norris, are promoted [on slave ships]. It had been more fair, perhaps, if he had explained that word promoted. The truth is, that for the sake of exercise, these miserable wretches, loaded with chains, oppressed with disease and wretchedness, are forced to dance by the terror of the lash, and sometimes by the actual use of it. "I," says one of the other evidences, "was employed to dance the men, while another person danced the women." (W. Wilberforce speech in Parliament, 1789, *Hansard* 29, cols 45–8.)

The Abolitionist Society's abstract of evidence presented to the English parliament in 1791 focused nearly entirely on moral issues associated with slavery.

Within parliaments and royal councils ideological, military, and economic national interests were all debated (Drescher 1990). The moral (ideological) issues, however, trumped the other considerations in the context of the late eighteenth and early nineteenth centuries. As a consequence, a broad cross-section of Western parliaments adopted laws that gradually eliminated both slavery and the slave trade.

Liberal opposition to slavery was international in scope. In 1815, the participants of the Vienna Congress expressed their opposition to slavery. An international meeting of abolitionist groups was organized in London in 1840.

Slavery was eliminated state by state in the northern United States and country by country in Europe. For example, slavery was abolished by the Vermont state legislature in 1777, by Scotland in 1778, and by the state of Massachusetts in 1783. An act of Parliament in 1807 ended British participation in the slave trade, and slaves were emancipated throughout the empire by another act in 1833. Denmark's government abolished remaining mobility restraints on peasants in 1788 and began phasing out slavery in 1792. Denmark ended its participation in the slave trade in 1803 and banned slavery in its colonial territories in 1847. The Netherlands ended its participation in the slave trade in 1814 and emancipated slaves in its colonies in 1863. The Swedish government abolished slavery in 1843. The French banned participation in the slave trade in 1818 and emancipated slaves throughout its empire in 1848. The United States banned the slave trade in 1808 and slavery in the Southern states (after the Civil War) in 1865 via the Thirteenth Amendment to its Constitution.

In many cases, slave owners were compensated for the cost of slaves freed or the burden of emancipation was reduced by freeing only the children of existing slaves. For example, Pennsylvania adopted laws in 1779 that gradually phased out slavery by ending the hereditary basis for slavery. In Europe and in the northern states of the United States, parliamentary politics produced new laws that gradually overturned centuries of established precedent without revolutionary threats to Europe itself and only modest ones within their colonies.[18] Slaves could not vote and rarely revolted against their masters. Abolition of slavery in the Southern United States, however, was essentially imposed by the Northern states after the Civil War (see Chapter Eighteen).

Public Education Reform and Expansion

Public education has a long history in Europe; although for most of that history, it was provided by religious organizations, rather than governments, in the period after the Roman Empire collapsed. Priests at important cathedrals and monasteries founded most of the earliest public schools in Christian Europe. Assemblies of church officials also occasionally recommended support for public education. For example, in 529 the Catholic Council of Vaison recommended the establishment of village schools. In 800, a synod at Mayence required its priests to provide free schooling for local village and town children:

> Let them receive and teach these with the utmost charity that they might themselves shine as the stars forever. Let them receive no remuneration from their students unless what the parents through charity may voluntary offer. (as cited in Barnard 1874, 18)

The Catholic Church itself promised public education at its cathedrals in proclamations in 1179 and 1215. Martin Luther, who wrote on pedagogical theory as well as theology, recommended the establishment of schools in many of his communications with government officials.

Partly as a consequence of such highly regarded advice and partly as a consequence of shifts in political authority, many late medieval duchies and towns provided free education for local children. For example, public education systems were established in Saxony in 1560 and Hesse in 1565. Royal ordinances that established grammar schools in Denmark, Sweden, and England were adopted during the same period, in part to substitute for Catholic schools that were closed after the success of the Protestant

[18] Similar reforms gradually ended most legal aspects of serfdom throughout much of northern Europe during the same period. The final reforms often occurred in the nineteenth century.

Reformation in northern Europe.[19] Charitable schools in many large towns and cities were endowed by persons of wealth. Compulsory education was introduced as early as the seventeenth century by some local governments (Bernard 1874).

The result of several centuries of public education in Europe was an education system that emphasized religious training and that exhibited substantial variation from town to town in the quality and extent of the education provided. Elementary schools remained for the most part religious enterprises. Most universities were also heavily influenced by religious practices and theories, although their curricula had gradually increased their coverage of nonreligious subjects. For example, at Oxford University, monastic religious vows applied to the faculty, who could not marry and had to attend daily religious services through the first half of the nineteenth century (Morris 1978, 206).

In the late eighteenth and early nineteenth centuries, this almost completely decentralized, religiously oriented education system began to change in response to the lobbying efforts by reform groups. For example, a "society for the public good" was organized in Groningen in 1784 to press for public education and other reforms. Similar societies of teachers and "friends of education" were organized throughout the Netherlands and Belgium during the next three decades. Other educational lobbying groups were founded in France, Sweden, and Denmark (Bernard 1874). These organizations pressed for broader access, increased support, and more coverage of secular subjects in public education.

Such educational reform groups were not initially national in scope or membership, although in the long run they affected national as well as regional educational systems. At the beginning of the nineteenth century, in Bernard's words,

> a new era in popular education ... commenced by the formation of voluntary associations **to extend the blessings of knowledge, human and divine, to the great mass of the people**. (Bernard 1874, 725)

In countries that had such groups, parliaments recommended, and their kings accepted, a long series of public-education reforms that gradually broadened access to education, increased public funding, and reduced the religious focus of public school curricula. Early-nineteenth-century education reforms are noted by many historians. Major reforms include the

[19] The Protestant (Lutheran) duchies and countries closed most formal Catholic organizations, including their schools, after the treaty of Augsburg in 1555.

Dutch reform of 1806, French reforms of 1808 and 1833, the Prussian reform of 1809, the Danish reform of 1814, the Swedish reform of 1825, and the English reform of 1847. These were, of course, part of a long series of educational reforms that continued throughout the century and into the next.

For the most part, the new educational laws were liberal reforms that broadened access to education by (a) increasing public funding at local levels (often through unfunded mandates from the central government), (b) increasing funding and quality control for schools that trained elementary school teachers (often called "normal schools"), and (c) increasing inspections of individual schools (which were often very small) to assure more uniform curricula and teaching quality.

As in the case of tariff reform, it is easy to exaggerate the importance of liberal ideology, as opposed to liberal arguments, within the various educational reform movements. Firm owners, whether liberal or not, expected public education to reduce their training and labor costs, and they often supported public education for economic, rather than ideological or altruistic reasons. Liberal ideas and arguments were also used by nationalists that favored education reform as a method of nation building that would reduce regional and ethnic differences and increase identification with the central government. (The Prussian reforms are sometimes interpreted in this way.)

The policy debates themselves often used arguments and quotes from liberal scholars who advocated education reform and greater government support of education. For example, in Germany the educational theories of Locke, Rousseau, and Pestalozzi were often mentioned in reform pamphlets and editorials in support of education reform. In England, the educational positions of Smith, Bentham, and Malthus (who favored universal education) were often mentioned (Bernard 1874; Rorty 1998).

The secularization of education advocated by many liberal and radical reform groups was a major area of contention between liberals and conservatives in most countries during most of the nineteenth century. Indeed, educational reform issues sometimes played a significant role in constitutional bargaining, as in the Belgian secession from the Netherlands in 1830, and in the constitutional reforms adopted by the Netherlands in the mid-nineteenth and early twentieth centuries. Increased tax support for education in general, however, was somewhat less controversial, and public education budgets expanded throughout most of the nineteenth century.

Reorganizing various aspects of public education at national and regional levels did not instantly produce uniform universal education or equal opportunity, but it did gradually level the playing field for successive generations of children and adults by reducing the extent to which family determined education and thereby economic and political opportunities. The reforms also indirectly catalyzed future liberal reforms, because many teachers were liberals, and the secular part of the curricula stressed reasoning and observation. Consequently, the students became more independent readers and thinkers and were more likely to be exposed to liberal theories of government and economics than they would have been in church schools. Subsequently, many of the students earned higher incomes, because of the increased demand for literate and numerate employees in nineteenth-century commercial enterprises and government.

Laws Extending Religious Tolerance and Opportunity

Other efforts to promote civic equality during the nineteenth century addressed various formal privileges associated with religious affiliation. Religious tolerance had increased prior to 1800, in the sense that heretics were no longer routinely burned at the stake or banished from towns and kingdoms. Nonetheless, most states in Europe had official state religions. Membership in those churches was often a prerequisite for senior positions in government, and the leaders of those churches were entitled to seats in parliament and were often included in the cabinet. For example, the Anglican Church was entitled to appoint its own members of parliament in England (the lords spiritual). The Lutheran church of Sweden had its own chamber of the parliament with veto powers similar to those of the three other chambers. Indeed, all the estate-based parliaments included a separate chamber for church officials.

Most European central governments provided direct tax support for particular religious organizations (state churches). The Lutheran church was privileged in Denmark, Sweden, and Prussia; the Anglican in England; and the Catholic in France, Ireland, and Belgium.[20] Most of the American colonies had established churches or restricted worship to a subset of Protestant practices during the first half of the eighteenth century. Kings, queens, members of parliament, and high government officials all had to belong to and affirm the doctrines of their national church. The king of England could only be Anglican. The king of Sweden could only be a Lutheran. (Religious

[20] Subsequent debates on established churches gave rise to a favorite spelling word in English and American grammar schools: antidisestablishmentarianism, the position, for example, of persons who favored the continuation of established state churches (i.e., they were opposed to those favoring disestablishment).

qualifications for accession to the throne remain in many contemporary constitutional monarchies.)

Few religious organizations that lacked state support often could lawfully hold services. Catholics, for example, could not hold public services in most Protestant countries, and organized Protestant churches were illegal in most Catholic countries at the beginning of the nineteenth century. Such restrictions were broadly supported by most worshippers in their respective countries for doctrinaire reasons. They knew the "unique truth."

Naturally, the excluded religious groups opposed the laws that reduced their ability to hold services and proselytize. As restrictions on interest-group activity diminished and religious tolerance increased, national groups favoring reductions in existing theological privileges began to lobby for reform and repeal of their respective intolerant religious laws.

Religious groups were often already organized to provide informal (secret) religious services and so did not require the formation of new organizations to overcome team-production and free-riding problems. Their minority status, however, implied that persuasive campaigns based entirely on narrow self-interest were unlikely to produce new legislation by members of parliament holding essentially opposite views. Claims that "my church is the only true religion and should be allowed to hold services" would obviously be unconvincing to members of the state-supported religions. To be successful, a persuasive campaign had to appeal to the religious majority in the country of interest.

General liberal arguments favoring religious tolerance had been developed in the sixteenth and seventeenth centuries (Laursen and Nederman 1997), and these arguments were used and extended by the protolerance movements of the late eighteenth and nineteenth centuries. Among the most influential arguments against state churches and intolerance were those developed by John Locke in 1689, shortly before his return to England:

> [In the first place] whatever profession we make, to whatever outward worship we conform, if we are not fully satisfied in our own mind that the one is true and the other well pleasing unto God, such profession and such practice, far from being any furtherance, are indeed great obstacles to our salvation. For in this manner, instead of expiating other sins by the exercise of religion, I say, in offering thus unto God Almighty such a worship as we esteem to be displeasing unto Him, we add unto the number of our other sins those also of hypocrisy and contempt of His Divine Majesty.
>
> In the second place, **the care of souls cannot belong to the civil magistrate, because his power consists only in outward force; but true and saving religion consists in the inward persuasion of the mind**, without which nothing can be acceptable to God. And such is the nature of the understanding, that it cannot be

compelled to the belief of anything by outward force. Confiscation of estate, imprisonment, torments, nothing of that nature can have any such efficacy as to make men change the inward judgment that they have framed of things. (J. Locke, 1689, *A Letter Concerning Tolerance*, originally published in Latin while he was in exile in the Netherlands.)

In the first half of the nineteenth century, liberal arguments for religious tolerance were helped by the increased acceptance of other liberal arguments favoring more open political and economic systems and equality before the law. The hypothesis that ethical behavior could only be sustained under a single uniform religious doctrine was also increasingly challenged by successful experiments with religious tolerance. The Dutch Republic and several English colonies in North America were noteworthy in this respect. Protestant concerns about the efficacy of "Catholic conspiracies" also gradually diminished.

The stability and durability of intolerant laws over several centuries suggest that liberalization in the religious sphere of public policy was not easily accomplished, even by well-organized groups with intense interests in reform. Indeed, the result of many decades of religious warfare between Catholics and Lutherans in late-medieval Europe was not increased tolerance, but a patchwork of intolerant Lutheran and Catholic duchies. Without the rise of liberalism in the first half of the nineteenth century, it is very unlikely that nonconforming religious groups would have been able to induce reforms of intolerant laws, because it was only those already represented in parliament who could actually press for the desired reforms, and these were normally members of the state-supported church.

As a consequence of persuasive campaigns in favor of religious tolerance and for specific changes in religious qualifications, legal rights to organize churches were gradually extended to nonconforming Christians, Jews, and a few other religious groups. And religion-based legal barriers to participation in economic and political life were also gradually eliminated.

In 1828, the Test Act was repealed, which allowed Catholics in England to run for parliament and be appointed to high offices. Jews received similar rights thirty years later.[21] In 1835, Jews were given full rights of citizenship in Denmark and the right to work in the bureaucracy in 1848. The

[21] In addition to the Test Act, access to seats in parliament were controlled by the oath of office after 1534, which was very gradually expanded in the eighteenth and nineteenth centuries to allow Protestants, Christians, theists, and finally atheists to take the oath in good conscience. For example, after 1858, Jews could sit in Commons or Lords, but only if a special bill was adopted to exempt them from the Christian portion of the oath of office. This allowed Baron de Rothschild to sit in Commons in 1858. In 1860, the oath of

new Dutch constitution of 1848 guaranteed religious liberty for Catholics, and allowed the church to organize in its usual manner for the first time in two and a half centuries.[22] In 1849, religious freedom in Denmark was established (Danstrup 1947, 103). Freedom of religion was also proclaimed (again) in the second French Republic in 1848 and was adopted by the Swedish government in 1860. These reforms were significant shifts away from long-standing medieval doctrines and practices. Most such reforms proved to be quasi-constitutional in and would be taken as given for many decades at a time.

It bears noting that religion remained central to the beliefs of most persons in those societies and for most persons in parliament in the mid-nineteenth century. Support for greater civic equality in this important area of life did not require a radical weakening of religious beliefs on the part of those favoring and adopting it.

AN OVERVIEW OF CONSTITUTIONAL REFORMS AND SUFFRAGE IN THE NINETEENTH CENTURY

At the same time that liberal economic and civil-law reforms were being debated and gradually adopted, a variety of liberal constitutional reforms were also being proposed, debated, and adopted. The remainder of this chapter provides an overview of the series of constitutional reforms that gradually produced Western democracy in the nineteenth and early twentieth centuries. More fine-grained historical narratives and analyses are provided by the next eight chapters.

Many countries in Europe began the nineteenth century with their medieval form of government largely intact. For example, England began the nineteenth century with its five-century-old bicameral parliament, in which one chamber was based on noble birthrights and the other was elected on the basis of narrow suffrage (often with geographically disproportionate

office was modified so that such special bills were no longer necessary. In 1888 the oath was modified so that atheists, such as Bradlaugh, could affirm their commitment to the English constitution without also confirming their acceptance of a supreme divine being (Walker and Wood 2000).

[22] The new Dutch constitution extended religious liberties to Catholics, which was followed by the creation of five new bishopries by the Catholic Church in 1853. In this case, the leading parliamentary liberals were more tolerant than their voters. The Dutch extension of religious freedom *to organizations* produced a Protestant backlash and a governmental crisis. Although liberals were pivotal members of the government that adopted the new constitution, those supporting freedom to organize religious affairs were not (yet) a majority of the electorate in the Netherlands.

representation). Government officials were normally selected from the House of Lords, rather than the House of Commons. Sweden began the century with its two-century-old, four-chamber parliament with separate chambers representing nobles, clergy, townspeople, and farmers; the latter two chambers were elected on the basis of narrow suffrage. Its most powerful officials tended to be chosen from the noble chamber. Other countries continued with their unwritten (informal) constitutions in place, as could be said of Prussia and Denmark.[23] In much of continental Europe, the constitutional clock had been reset by the Congress of Vienna, which had promoted constitutional monarchy as the proper form of European governance.

Many of Europe's written constitutions in 1820, nonetheless, were relatively new and included modest departures from previous practices. The most recent Swedish instrument of governance, for example, had been adopted in 1809, and its rules for succession were revised in 1810. A relatively liberal Norwegian constitution was adopted in 1814. The Congress of Vienna caused new written constitutions to be developed for the new kingdom of the Netherlands and for the restored monarchy of France after the defeat of Napoleon. The new parliaments of the Netherlands and France adopted the British architecture, rather than the estate system. They were bicameral with elite, appointed first chambers and narrowly elected second chambers. The Congress of Vienna also required the duchies and kingdoms of the new German Confederation to adopt formal written constitutions (Nicolson 1946).

Many European sovereigns, nonetheless, had more, not less, authority in 1820 than they had had a few decades earlier, as in France, the Netherlands, and Sweden. (Indeed, the Netherlands had never before had a king). This could also be said of the monarchs of Italy, Germany, and Japan when their new national constitutions were adopted in the second half of the nineteenth century. George III of Great Britain spent much of his long term of office reclaiming authorities delegated to past cabinets and parliaments by his predecessors.

Although many constitutions were relatively new, there were long series of proposals for constitutional reforms during the nineteenth and early twentieth centuries. Many of the constitutional proposals attempted to advance liberal political and economic ends. Liberal proposals called for

[23] These countries had constitutional and quasi-constitional laws that, in principle, bound their sovereigns, but no single written document that could be referred to as their constitution.

more complete written constitutions that would force royal cabinets to rule according to the law. Cabinet officials, for example, should be subject to criminal law and/or be discharged by parliament for failure to execute existing legislation. Most liberal proposals also increased parliamentary authority over budgets and public policy. Many also supported (modest) expansions of suffrage and salaries for members of parliament. Others called for equal protection of the law, judicial independence, reduced censorship, and the use of secret ballots.

Most such proposals were rejected when they were first proposed, as is true of most proposed amendments in contemporary democracies (Rasch and Congleton 2006). However, enough liberal amendments were adopted during the century between 1825 and 1925 that the Western procedures of governance in 1925 were quite different from those of 1825. A long series of amendments had created Western democracy, more or less as we know it today.

Negotiations Rather than Revolutions

For the most part, proposals for constitutional reforms were developed by senior cabinet ministers and by members of parliament and their staff, although there are also instances in which external interest groups made detailed constitutional proposals. Notable among the latter were the English Chartist petitions of the 1840s and the Frankfurt proposal for a new German constitution in 1849.[24] The occasional large-scale public demonstrations in support of constitutional reforms were not usually associated with specific proposals and so only indirectly affected the constitutional reforms adopted during the century.

The particular reforms adopted depended on the interests – institutional, economic, political, and ideological – of the king, members of parliament, and other officials in the top levels of government. It was only such persons who were directly involved in negotiations and only such persons who could formally adopt constitutional reforms. Large-scale demonstrations, however, could affect the interests and relative bargaining power of high officeholders, even in cases in which no genuine revolutionary threats existed.

Support for the Chartist and Frankfurt proposals, for example, strengthened the hand of liberals in parliament by demonstrating that liberal

[24] The Frankfurt parliament at which the proposals had been worked out was authorized by the government of the German Confederation, although it followed on the heels of widespread popular demonstration for constitutional reform in 1848 (Koch 1984).

constitutional reforms were supported by a broad cross-section of persons in those two countries. This somewhat increased the persuasiveness of the case for reform, particularly among neutrals and opponents who accepted, at least in the abstract, the Hobbesian or Kantian justifications for central government authority. Insofar as normal commerce was disrupted by such demonstrations, affected pragmatists might also favor modest reforms as a method of reducing future demonstrations. To increase support among such pragmatists, the risk of future demonstrations, or even revolution, was often stressed by proponents in parliamentary debates.

It important to note that serious internal and external military threats were normally responded to with increased censorship and *reduced* civil liberties, rather than liberal constitutional reform. For example, the French government increased censorship and curtailed rights of assembly for three decades after the monarchy was restored. Similarly, in response to more or less peaceful (but not entirely lawful) mass demonstrations, the British suspended habeas corpus in 1817 and adopted the so-called Six Acts in 1819 in order to restrict political meetings by proponents of constitutional reform. The Acts increased censorship and allowed trials to take place without juries.[25] Danish censorship in the early part of the nineteenth century was so strong that a college professor was imprisoned for life in 1821 for simply "demanding" democracy. Proposals for constitutional reform (in print) were severely punished within the German Confederation for most of the nineteenth century, although not proposals for economic reform.[26]

Such repressive steps were not taken in response to obvious well-organized threats of civil war (the existence of revolutionary armies), but rather to suppress annoying dissent and reduce opportunities for organizing large public demonstrations in support of particular reforms.[27] The rhetoric of speeches given at the demonstrations often challenged the status quo, the authority of government officials, the justness of existing laws,

[25] The acts (a) forbade training persons to use arms, (b) authorized the seizing of arms, (c) expedited trials, (d) forbade assemblies greater than fifty persons for deliberations of public grievances, limited attendance at town meetings to freeholders, and essentially ruled out smaller meetings to raise funds for politically active interest groups, (e) forbade the distribution of many kinds of seditious pamphlets and allowed courts to confiscate them, and (f) extended censorship to small pamphlets containing political news or commentary. A good summary of the acts is available from Halévy (1987, 66–70). Condensed versions of the acts are available in Aspinall, Smith, and Douglas (1996, 335–41).

[26] See Fetscher 1980; Bély 2001, 89–91; Lee 1994, 22–3; and Jacobson 2000, 93.

[27] For example, the Six Acts were partly a response to mass meetings of liberals favoring repeal of the Corn Laws and constitutional reform, such as those that had occurred in Lancaster in 1818 (Halévy 1987, 59–60).

and occasionally used the term "revolution." Most of the various popular "uprisings" were peaceful mass demonstrations that posed no serious military threat to the rulers. Such demonstrations simply undermined claims by those in power that they governed for the good of their country and with the broad support of their citizens.[28]

The reforms proposed by such demonstrators were often significant, but could not be truly revolutionary if they hoped for success. For example, the proposal of the Frankfurt constitution called for a new, *stronger* central government with a hereditary king (kaiser) and a federal parliamentary government. It was rejected by leaders of the two largest and most powerful states in the federation, Prussia and Austria. And when told to disperse, most members and supporters of the Frankfurt assembly peacefully returned to their homes. The remaining militant minority was severely punished (often by death) for disobeying repeated orders to disperse. In Great Britain, the proposed constitutional reforms of the second Chartist petition (with more than three million signatures) were similar to those proposed by the Levellers two centuries earlier: universal male suffrage, annual elections, and payment of members of parliament. The Chartists also objected to corruption, high taxes, and payments to the established church.

Both the Frankfurt and Chartist proposals were formally proposed to government authorities, considered by them, and rejected. After failing to secure reforms, the Chartist movement peacefully disintegrated, as most members departed for other politically active groups.

> Understanding the centrality of petitioning in the Chartist experience highlights the fact that, with few exceptions, the **ideological horizons of the Chartists were constitutional**, and in this sense its decline owed less to extension of the suffrage than to the gradual fracture of the 'master narrative' of England's libertarian Constitution after 1867 (Pickering 2001, 387).

Large interest groups proposed lawful changes: reforms rather than revolution. Moreover, the reforms proposed by the Chartist and Frankfurt groups were moderate relative to the cumulative effect of reforms that were adopted in the decades that followed. Smaller reforms were more often acceptable to the existing authorities than major ones, as predicted by the models of Part I.

[28] Many such meetings were also illegal and could be said to be revolutionary in the sense that those at the mass meetings ignored laws governing such meetings and political speeches. Of greater practical concern to most European kings was the possibility that their armies would disobey orders or shift their loyalty from king to parliament or to the reformers.

Liberal Trends in Constitutional Reform

A series of modest constitutional reforms were adopted throughout most of what became the West in the nineteenth century. The various coalitions in support of reform represented similar economic and ideological interests and used similar liberal arguments to justify the reforms proposed. The possibility of assembling such coalitions had been made possible by gradual reductions in the king's or queen's ability to influence parliament. and the increasing cost of government services.

The pragmatist-liberal coalitions in parliament that supported reform obtained the required assent of their king or queen in large part because of the parliament's power of the purse. It was no longer possible to finance government entirely from traditional royal sources of revenue. The cost of government services had increased and customary tariff incomes had diminished because of the free trade legislation. These fiscal trends shifted policy-making authority from kings to parliament and created numerous opportunities for political bargaining along a number of policy and constitutional dimensions. The parliamentary tax bills, which used to simply supplement government revenues, had gradually become the main source of government revenues. This allowed stable coalitions in parliament to affect public policies by trading reforms for (often temporary) tax increases.

During the first half of the nineteenth century, majority coalitions in the elected chambers usually had to include a few liberals. During the second half of the nineteenth century, liberal political parties became increasingly successful in elections and so were often majority parties in their own right. As a consequence, constitutional gains to trade between kings and parliaments exhibited a liberal trend throughout the nineteenth century.

The increased stability of parliamentary coalitions was partly induced by reforms of suffrage law, as discussed earlier, and partly by the increased importance of parliamentary majorities. Party-line voting within parliament increased the bargaining power of parliaments relative to kings on budgetary matters by making it more difficult for kings to ignore parliamentary leaders. It also increased the value of members who were likely to be members of majority coalitions. Voters would naturally be more supportive of representatives who could "bring home the bacon" or adopt broad reforms that advanced their interests.

As party discipline increased, party leaders became increasingly important for kings and queens, who in previous centuries had dealt with parliaments that they could substantially control through patronage and appeals to historic loyalties. In previous centuries, supportive coalition leaders might, for example, be invited to sit in the cabinet, be granted a senior post in the bureaucracy, or be elevated to (or further up) in the nobility.

It bears noting that many of the interests advanced through intragovernmental bargaining were *institutionally determined*, but in a manner that allowed shifts in economic and ideological interests to affect policy. Members of noble chambers had reasons to oppose the king on issues that affected parliament's authority. Centralization tends to reduce noble autonomy, status, and income. Kings, in turn, often had interests in reducing the authority of nobles, who had for centuries been their main opponents in parliament.

The emergence of party government (cabinets occupied by leaders of political parties) was a significant change in the relative policy-making authority of kings and parliaments, although it was not codified in constitutional documents. Elected officeholders have institutionally induced reasons to take account of the economic and ideological interests of their pivotal supporters. Electoral competition had obvious effects on conservative parties, which became increasingly liberal in the second half of the nineteenth century by taking positions that would have been regarded as liberal or radical in the first half. These more disciplined political parties also helped coordinate election campaigns and thereby framed a good deal of the policy debates of that period. In many cases, all-or-nothing offers from a durable majority coalition could often obtain more from the sovereign on a variety of issues, including constitutional ones, than less aggressive bargaining tactics. By century's end, both conservatives and liberals were far less deferential to the king and to past traditions than they had been in 1800. By 1920, elections to parliament and the members selected were more important than kings and the nobility, far more so than they had been in 1800.

Liberalism and Suffrage Reform Movements

Wealth and property were broadly considered to be evidence that a voter could cast an independent and informed vote during the first half of the nineteenth century, but how much wealth was required for independence and the extent to which other qualifications might substitute for wealth were much debated among reformers. Many liberals argued, for example, that an expanding segment of the population had sufficient education and income to exercise competent and independent votes, as with lawyers, managers, merchants, and college professors. If qualifications could not be changed, they argued that representation should reflect current, rather than historic, geographic distributions of population and wealth. Suffrage reforms thus often adjusted the geographic basis of representation as much as, or more so than, the qualification for suffrage.

Suffrage expansion was both a cause and effect of bargaining within parliaments and between parliaments and the sovereign. Pragmatic interests often supported liberal electoral reforms because the new districts would shift representation in a manner that favored the new communities that emerged with industrialization, and because political parties hoped to build support from newly empowered voters. Liberals tended to benefit from middle-class electorates and increased political competition. Many in the middle class realized that they had benefited from the opening up of political and economic life, thus they often favored a bit more openness.

Electoral reform movements were therefore partly idealistic enterprises that sought to expand suffrage to qualified persons, and partly pragmatic enterprises that favored shifts of policy-making authority to persons more likely to support particular policy reforms. With both liberal and pragmatic ends in mind, a variety of organizations were founded to conduct persuasive campaigns in favor of suffrage reform.

Suffrage organizations were common throughout Europe in the nineteenth century, although the size of the movements and the timing of reforms varied among countries. For example, national organizations favoring the expansion of men's (and subsequently women's) suffrage were founded in Great Britain, the Netherlands, Sweden, Belgium, Denmark, and many of the kingdoms and duchies of the German Confederation. Similar movements arose in Italy and Japan during the late nineteenth century. In addition to organizations devoted to suffrage issues, other organizations of liberals often supported suffrage expansion, although their main focus was on trade liberalization, public education, religious tolerance, labor law, and so forth. Labor and social democratic parties formed at the end of the century also favored suffrage reform, in part because expanding suffrage would advance their main policy agendas (the reform of labor law and increased social insurance).

The persuasive campaigns in favor of suffrage reform and partisan interests allowed male suffrage to be gradually expanded through a series of small changes in wealth (or tax) and residency qualifications. These reforms often spanned a good deal of the nineteenth century. For example, the British suffrage rules were significantly altered in 1832, 1867, 1884, 1918, and 1928; they were indirectly expanded several other times. Dutch suffrage laws were altered in 1848, 1887, 1896, 1917, and 1919. Swedish laws were reformed in 1866, 1907, 1920, 1945, and 1971. French suffrage was extended in 1830, doubled in 1831, and expanded gradually by about 50 percent during the next decade and a half.[29] In most cases, the ability to vote in national elections was gradually extended to successively poorer and younger male cohorts up through about 1910.

Similar campaigns and arguments were later used to support the qualification of women for suffrage. Women's suffrage was widely adopted in the period just before and after World War I, often about a decade after working-class men were deemed qualified to case votes in national elections. Other excluded persons, such as those on poor relief or who had once been bankrupt, were gradually added to the electorate in the period between the World Wars in England, Sweden, the Netherlands, Belgium, and Japan.

Together, persuasive campaigns, partisan interests, and parliamentary bargaining produced suffrage expansion.

Complex Constitutional Bargains

Negotiation was rarely straightforward, and the constitutional bargains that produced universal male suffrage often required significant reforms of other election procedures, as elaborated in Chapter Eleven. For example, the proper use of votes to select representatives was often part of suffrage negotiations. In the mid- to late nineteenth century, negotiations often included proposals for wealth- or education-weighted voting. In the last stages of negotiation before World War I, conservatives often insisted on the adoption of proportional representation (PR) in exchange for their support of changes in the qualifications for participation.

Conservative party leaders of that period feared that the postreform elections would eliminate their parties, as liberals and social democrats shared credit for the last reforms. Proportional representation, consequently, was

[29] In France, universal male suffrage had been adopted during the first Republic in 1792; however, wealth-qualified suffrage had been restored along with the French monarchy after Napoleon was defeated. Under the restored French monarchy, suffrage was reformed a number of times, although in an illiberal direction at first. After 1830, suffrage was expanded several times through ordinary revisions of suffrage law and by changing the manner in which the existing qualifications could be satisfied. Wealth and tax revisions were dropped in 1848 after the monarch abdicated, although a variety of residency and similar qualifications made suffrage less than truly universal (Seymour and Frary 1918, chapters 17–18).

Major extensions of male suffrage also occurred in Prussia in 1848, and subsequently in the new German empire later in the century, where universal male suffrage was adopted well before parliamentary authority challenged that of the monarch (see Chapter Sixteen). (France is the only country in northern Europe where civil wars and civil disturbances played even a temporary role in liberal constitutional reform, as with its great expansion in suffrage in 1848.)

often adopted in the early twentieth century as part of constitutional bargains reached on adult male suffrage, as in Sweden, Denmark, the Netherlands, Belgium, and Germany (the Weimar Republic).[30]

LIBERAL POLITICS AND IDEOLOGY IN THE EARLY TWENTIETH CENTURY

During the first half of the nineteenth century, politics could be divided into conservative and liberal factions with roughly opposite positions on the importance of religious homogeneity, trade protection, privileged families, and family-based political institutions. Liberals disagreed about how far reform should go and the relative importance of particular reforms, but they all supported constitutional government and greater civic equality: rule of law both inside and outside of government, greater equality before that law, somewhat more open political and economic systems, and broader access to public education. This political agenda made liberals the "left wing" of European politics, because they challenged the long-standing medieval order supported by the "right wing."

The New Consensus

During the nineteenth century, a new consensus gradually emerged. By the end of the century, the entire political spectrum could be said to be liberal, apart from small groups at the extremes. The major political parties all supported constitutional government, with representatives elected via broad suffrage, equality before the law, and taxpayer-funded education. Many European liberals also supported (modest) taxpayer-funded income and health insurance programs.

The new consensus, however, did not require or imply that voters and their representatives had all become doctrinaire liberals. Instead, many voters were "small c" conservatives in the sense that they preferred the status quo, to other societies that they could imagine. Most voters and elected officeholders had begun to take their new political and economic institutions for granted and routinely used liberal arguments both to defend the status quo and to justify reforms. They were opposed to major restrictions

[30] PR electoral systems protect parties that expected only minority support in single-member districts under extended suffrage (at first, chiefly the conservative parties). Social democrats also supported PR because it reduces opportunities for gerrymandering designed to minimize the number of seats won by the parties supported by blue-collar voters (chiefly the social democrats and labor parties).

on economic and political life, supportive of parliamentary authority, and approved of the policies that had extended the franchise to previously excluded voters. Such "small c" liberal voters and members of parliament, often supported by industrialists and wealthy landowners, were often pivotal members of majority coalitions in the early twentieth century.

The new consensus emerged partly because of changes in ideology, partly because of changes in lifestyle, and partly because of previous reforms. In 1800, liberal members of parliaments had been a small minority that occasionally played pivotal roles in majority coalitions. A series of somewhat liberal reforms gradually broadened opportunities in markets, politics, the bureaucracy, and the military and indirectly helped to produce more liberal governments. The persons in high office were somewhat less often in those positions because of ancient family privileges; they were somewhat more often there because they were professionally qualified for high office and had risen to their positions by demonstrating that competence. Senior advisors within the bureaucracy, as educated men and women, were also increasingly exposed to and influenced by liberal economic and political theories.

The formally liberal political parties that emerged in the second half of the nineteenth century were formed after many significant liberal reforms had already been adopted and after liberalism had already become widely accepted by those eligible to vote.

Nineteenth-century liberals were never a single doctrinaire group. They were constantly splitting into new parties and merging into new associations and unions. Such splits occurred among left, middle, and right liberals as a consequence of disagreements over the proper extent of economic regulation, the proper extent of economic safety nets, the proper role of the state in education, and the relative merits of single-member districts and proportional representation. Those on the right formed new (more liberal) conservative parties and sometimes aligned themselves with older conservative parties. Left liberals often formed new "radical" organizations, and sometimes formed alliances with members of the labor movement. These left-liberals, in many cases, subsequently became the moderate leaders of the new social democratic parties.[31]

[31] See Luebbert (1991, chapters 3–4) for a careful historical analysis of the process through which the liberal movement splintered throughout Europe during the late nineteenth century and for a good discussion of liberal–social democrat coordination on elections and constitutional issues during the late nineteenth and early twentieth centuries. Gould (1999) analyzes the constitutional and policy effects of liberal parties and liberal ideas in France, Switzerland, and Belgium.

Although romanticized views of the past and future played roles in campaign rhetoric, none of the mainstream parties of 1900 proposed ending elections, shrinking suffrage, returning to manorial life, or doing away with industry and commercialization. Such positions were left to relatively small groups of arch-conservatives and angry socialists. Nonetheless, the rhetoric of the mainstream political parties often made their remaining policy disagreements sound like issues that threatened civilization itself.

This was partly because of electoral competition with fringe groups, and partly because relatively extreme rhetoric tends to capture disproportionate attention from newspapers and newspaper readers. For example, the mainstream conservative parties on the right often argued for a return to (limited) hierarchy based on new aristocratic interpretations of social Darwinism and romantic views of national experience in the past. Similarly, social democrats often gave speeches and included platform planks favoring radical changes in the distribution of property and in the nature of ownership.

However, when the "conservatives" won elections, few liberal laws were repealed. The new conservatives tended to reduce taxation and weaken labor union protections, rather than eliminating regulation, disenfranchising the working class, outlawing deviant churches, or otherwise attempting to re-create medieval life. They were right liberals, rather than medieval conservatives. When the "socialists" won national elections in the 1920s and 1930s, they similarly adopted only modest reforms. They expanded social insurance programs (previously adopted by liberal and conservative governments) and revised labor law, rather than nationalizing the means of production or engaging in wholesale wealth redistribution, as some of their speeches implied. They were left-liberals, rather than revolutionary reformers.

Disagreements remained on a number of important policy issues, of course, or there would not have been three major parties or a need for coalitions. Only groups on the far left and far right, however, pressed for fundamental reforms of the liberal economic and political system. The groups on the far left normally left the mainstream social democratic and labor parties to form their own, more radical organizations and parties in the early twentieth century, as with the communist parties of Sweden, Denmark, Germany, and Italy. The groups on the far right similarly abandoned moderate conservative parties to form new, more radical parties in the early twentieth century, such as Mussolini's fascists in Italy, Hitler's National Socialist Party in Germany, and similar parties elsewhere.[32]

[32] In contrast to the conservative and social democratic parties, when these more extreme right- and left-wing groups came to power, they did engage in fundamental reforms

The emergence of a new consensus about the institutions of a good society is another indication that a great transformation that took place in the nineteenth century. The good society of 1900 was based on individual merit rather than family heritage, open discussion of ideas rather than censorship, policy making by elected representatives rather than historic elites, and favored technological advance over tradition. Mechanistic interpretations of nature, as in astronomy, chemistry, and physics, became increasingly central parts of the world views of even very religious persons, and ancient institutions and traditional patterns of life became less central. The new status quo in the West was very liberal and rational by history's standards.

The typical universe of the average person had become larger and more secular, in part because public education and literacy was more widespread, in part because long-distance communication and transportation had become far less expensive and more reliable, and in part because of scientific advances during the nineteenth century. The mainstream parties and their supporters had considerable faith that technological innovation and other forms of progress would continue in all areas of life.

The Robustness of Liberal Reforms

Both the new Western world view and the new Western political-economic system proved to be quite robust, although not entirely so. A good deal of the support for the new liberal economic and political theories was the result of their success. More open systems of production and exchange had increased, rather than reduced, wealth throughout society. More open and representative systems of politics had not produced more erratic or radically more redistributive public policies than before, as predicted by early-nineteenth-century conservatives. Instead, they had produced attractive societies that attracted emigrants from around the world.

Institutional robustness was also partly a consequence of the piecemeal, empirical manner through which they had emerged. Liberal political systems had not been adopted as great quantum leaps forward induced by revolutions in the theory of governance. Instead, the institutional reforms of the nineteenth century were adopted over the course of a century, with considerable experimentation and experience. The new institutions of liberal parliamentary democracies were fine-grained refinements of ancient templates that had already stood the test of time, and the new systems of

of the liberal democratic political and economic systems that had emerged during the nineteenth century.

governance had emerged slowly enough that supporting political norms and policies had emerged along with them.

As a consequence, they were broadly supported. Few twentieth-century critics of nineteenth-century developments argued for reestablishing the old manor and guild system or for restoring ancient aristocratic privileges and slavery, although many seemed to have fond memories of those ancient societies and would often defend other aspects of their culture and traditions.

Economic progress continued through most of the twentieth century, although it was occasionally interrupted by business cycles and policy errors. Political liberalization also continued in most of the West, as remaining civic inequalities were challenged and gradually eliminated.

ELEVEN

Fine-Grained Constitutional Bargaining

The shift from king-dominated versions of the king-and-council template to liberal constitutional democracy involved two major changes: (a) increased policy-making authority for parliament and (b) the selection of members of parliament by broad electorates. It is important to understand that both changes were multidimensional and the product of fine-grained constitutional negotiations and reforms. At some points in time, minor parts of liberal reform agendas were accepted in lieu of major reforms. In other cases, secondary details were used to reduce the effect of what would otherwise have been major liberal reforms. Suffrage might be extended for local elections before national elections or vice versa. In all cases, bargaining over the details made constitutional reforms possible that would otherwise not have been adopted.

At every step in the transition to Western democracy, a variety of procedural details had to be addressed, and many of these were revisited and renegotiated from time to time during the nineteenth century. In most cases, it was well understood that secondary reforms would affect the future course of public policy, and so debate and analysis were often extensive. The bargains struck were subtle and typically revised a number of long-standing practices at the margin with specific ideological, economic, and political effects in mind.

The bargaining and cumulative effect of secondary reforms was broadly similar throughout the West. Parliament's veto power over new taxes, together with changes in technology and the rise of liberalism, gradually produced governments that were directed by elected leaders of political parties. In parliamentary systems, these leaders often held posts in what had formerly been royal executive councils, and which gradually became ministries or cabinets. The most important executive officials gradually became prime ministers and chancellors, rather than kings and queens. The number of chambers in parliament and basis for holding offices in them were adjusted. Suffrage was generally expanded, but new qualifications for suffrage and elected office were sometimes introduced, while others were reduced. Voting itself was transformed as voice votes and physical divisions of voters were replaced with counts of secret ballots. Weighted-electoral systems tended to be replaced by systems based on the principle of one person, one vote.

At the end of these negotiations, kings and queens normally remained part of the architecture for governance. Most were formally sovereign and retained significant formal authority, including the authority to veto new laws and to appoint top officials. In most cases, new laws continued to be issued by the king or queen (or in his or her name). However, these formal powers were often circumscribed by new liberal norms for governance under which the elected chambers would have dominant authority over public policy. As a consequence, control over domestic areas of policy had largely shifted to the elected chambers of parliament. Military and international affairs would follow in the next decade or two in cases in which they were not already controlled by parliament. Kings and queens, never the less, continued to live "like kings," with luxurious lifestyles, important symbolic roles, and significant influence over public policy.

These late nineteenth-century bargaining equilibria between the king and parliament often remained unwritten well into the twentieth century, at which point the sovereign's de facto authority was occasionally codified in new instruments of government, as in Sweden in 1975 and the Netherlands in 1983.

Although the cumulative results were remarkably similar, the specific terms of trade varied with the interests represented in parliament and with the idiosyncrasies and innovations of the leaders directly engaged in the negotiations. For example, long-standing first-past-the-post electoral systems were often, but not always, replaced with systems based on proportional representation in the early twentieth century. The extent to which reforms were codified in formal constitutional documents or adopted through legislation and informal changes in decision-making procedures also varied, even in cases in which reforms were broadly similar.

PARTISAN AND MASS POLITICS

National party organizations were rarely mentioned in constitutional documents prior to 1900, although they played increasingly important roles in policy decisions during the nineteenth century. The new roles played by the leaders of such political organizations were among the most important quasi-constitutional reforms of the nineteenth and early twentieth centuries.

Loose affiliations of politicians and their supporters have existed as long as nations have had parliaments, because assembling majorities from members of parliament with similar interests is easier than doing so from a random cross section of the persons holding seats in parliament. Both formal and informal organizations of members allow fewer persons to be directly consulted and fewer discordant interests taken into account when assembling majorities for a given vote. The leaders of such groups (factions) were thus useful for kings and queens and were often able to obtain royal favors for their members in exchange for support on matters of interest to the sovereign. In the medieval period, such groups were normally based on regional issues and family trees. After the Reformation, theological and ideological differences also played significant roles.

Majorities in parliaments (or tax councils) had long been required for kings and queens to obtain new taxes (supplements) from parliament. However, during the eighteenth and nineteenth centuries, such taxes became increasingly critical for the routine operations of government. Even peacetime expenses could no longer be paid out of the sovereign's standing income sources. Consequently, requests for new taxes (and the continuation of past subsidies) were made more often, and without claiming that the nation faced an emergency as was common in earlier periods.

To obtain more and more routine expansions of tax revenues, sovereigns required more and more reliable parliamentary majorities. This increased the importance of factions and faction leaders in parliament and also provided stronger incentives for members of parliament to join the stable coalitions that gradually became known as political parties. Such fiscal and legislative bargains favored members of organized groups over independents, which provided a reason to join such groups and for group members to defer to their leaders.

Membership in such standing coalitions also became increasingly important for obtaining seats in parliament. As suffrage expanded, political parties began to include large numbers of persons who were not officeholders or especially influential in their town or regional governments. Campaigns for the votes of even less politically engaged persons induced parties to become more ideological and issue oriented. Proposed reforms (and continuities) had to be communicated to large numbers of persons in a relatively short period through pamphlets and speeches, and there were economies of scale associated with persuasive campaigns in the new settings in which large numbers of voters needed to be induced to vote for candidates who were often initially unknown to voters.

More restrictive rules regulating the (direct) purchase of votes and the gradual introduction of secret ballots in the second half of the nineteenth century further increased the importance of organized persuasive campaigns. The new election laws made voter decisions less subject to local economic and cultural sanctions, which reduced the number of ways in which political parties could influence electoral outcomes. As a consequence, many of the old loose political affiliations were transformed into "political machines," that is to say, formal organizations with standing institutions for making policy decisions, sanctioning their members, and organizing persuasive campaigns for elected offices.

Such national political organizations rarely emerged whole cloth. National parties normally formed as local and regional political clubs joined forces for national campaigns. As a result, many early national parties had decentralized decision-making procedures. Indeed, they could be said to be coalitions of regional factions rather than parties. The stronger party organizations of the late nineteenth century often emerged from these older loose coalitions (court and country parties), as with the English Whigs and Tories and Sweden's Farmer's party. In some cases, new, more hierarchical organizations were founded to replace older associations of politicians and their supporters. For example, in the Netherlands, the (conservative) Anti-Revolutionary Party was formed in 1878, the Liberal Union in 1885, a social democratic party in 1888, and a Catholic party in 1895. In Sweden, a social democratic party was formed in 1889, a liberal party in 1900, and a conservative party in 1904.

The new political organizations had their own internal policy-making institutions (which were often based on the king-and-council template) and methods for sanctioning members. The leadership (governments) of these new, more disciplined organizations could negotiate in parliament and with the king more effectively than possible by the leaders of the older loose confederations, because they were more likely to be able to deliver the votes of their members. Nonetheless, the first national parties were not always self-sustaining, and in many cases, considerable exit and entry took place among parties and party members. The new parties succeeded by attracting members away from older organizations. (In a few cases, international meetings were also held with the aim of forming international political parties, although these usually remained loose affiliations in the period of interest.)

The leadership of successful national party organizations (the persons occupying offices in their party's governing bodies) played increasingly important roles in negotiations within parliament and between parliaments and kings in all Western countries during the nineteenth century. As a consequence, party affiliation and party leadership posts become increasingly important determinants of public policy and also of the persons holding seats in the executive cabinet and bureaucracy.

LIBERALISM AND THE DISTRIBUTION AND BASIS OF AUTHORITY WITHIN PARLIAMENT

Prior to 1800, most European parliaments were multicameral and organized on the basis of class and occupation. Each chamber normally had some veto power and some ability to propose changes in law to the king. However, it was usually the noble chamber that had the most influence over taxation and public policy. The sovereign was usually a member of the noble chamber, as a person with noble titles, and often attended their meetings. Nobles (and clergy) occupied the most influential positions in the royal cabinet, councils, and bureaucracy.

The influence of the nobility also extended to the other chambers of parliament. Many high officials of the state church were from noble families, partly because of their greater access to education, and partly because of family influence within the local church hierarchy and with the sovereign, who chose or nominated persons to the highest religious posts. The nobility also normally had significant influence within the directly elected chambers of parliament. In many cases, only relatively wealthy persons were allowed to sit in the elected chambers of parliament. Membership in parliament was not a full-time job, and members were not paid a salary for holding their office. Consequently, those elected to parliament were often close relatives of persons already represented in noble chambers or in their employ.

Some of the most important constitutional reforms of the nineteenth century involve shifts in the relative authority of the noble and commoner chambers of parliament. Many of these reforms were informal, as new procedural customs emerged. For example, the British House of Lords routinely deferred to the House of Commons on budgetary matters during the second half of the nineteenth century, although it (formally) retained the power to intervene with vetoes and amendments and had done so in the previous centuries. Others were consequences of formal amendments of constitutional and parliamentary charters. Among the most striking of these were cases in which a noble chamber was replaced with a new "first" chamber with electoral rather than familial foundations.

Bargaining over the Distribution of Parliamentary Authority

Many shifts in policy-making authority among (and within) the chambers of parliament were informal ones not codified in constitutional documents. They reflected short-term policy bargains within and among the chambers and between the king and parliament. Some parliamentary rights and procedures were obtained for all members of parliament; for example, freedom of speech (within parliament) and free passage to meetings of parliament were often granted to members of parliament. Others favored one chamber over another. For instance, the late-medieval English House of Commons often gained a bit of new authority from the king (or queen) on religious issues when royal interests could be advanced by doing so (Field 2002, chapter 2). Prior to 1800, however, shifts in the relative authority of the chambers were often temporary and/or small.

The noble chambers remained the most influential of the chambers of national parliaments in most times and places until the nineteenth century, when new trends in politics gradually shifted policy-making authority away from noble chambers and toward the elected chambers.

Informal changes in the relative influence of the chambers of parliament reflected changes in the importance of temporary tax legislation, elections, and political parties. Royal influence over the noble chamber was not very much affected by those factors, but electoral and bureaucratic reforms often reduced royal influence within the elected chamber. For example, majorities became more difficult to organize in elected chambers as traditional deference to the sovereign diminished, as political parties became more disciplined, and as royal powers of appointment diminished. Such changes reduced the sovereign's influence within the elected chamber relative to the noble chamber, in which royal powers of elevation could still be used to reward supporters and to add new supportive members when necessary.

The greater independence and decisiveness of the elected chambers required the king or queen to pay a higher price for support in those chambers. Moreover, more continuous negotiations with leaders in those chambers were necessary because party politics and national elections would often change the persons with whom they had to negotiate.

The outcomes of the negotiations with the elected chambers also had effects on the relative authority of the hereditary and elected chambers. The sovereign might, for example, accept advice from leaders of the elected chambers regarding appointments to the cabinet and bureaucracy, or with respect to elevations to and within the upper chambers in exchange for support on policy or tax issues. Such fiscal bargains allowed elected chambers to gradually become the main source of cabinet officials and also to obtain some influence over the composition of the hereditary chamber. Indeed, the threat of adding new members to the noble chamber was often sufficient to change votes in that chamber. (See Chapter Thirteen.)

Liberal ideological trends tended to support such shifts in authority by undermining the usual arguments for deference to nobles, who were often sophisticated, well-educated, well-traveled men and women. If government is or should be grounded in social compacts, or officeholders have the duty to advance the broadly shared interests of all persons in a nation-state, commonwealth, or empire, relatively greater deference to elected chambers is implied insofar as the elected chamber better represents those interests. After all, their officeholders are selected by all the people who are qualified to cast votes, rather than by those with fortunate family trees, birth orders, and marriages.

It bears noting that the noble chambers nearly always included a few liberal idealists (and pragmatists using liberal arguments) who favored significant economic and political reform and greater deference to the elected chamber. Kings, partly for that reason, also occasionally used liberal arguments to support liberal constitutional reforms. Kings and queens also had pragmatic interests in reforms that weakened their noble chambers, because noble chambers had been the main check on royal authority in past centuries.

Formal Reforms of Parliamentary Architecture

Parliamentary architecture tends to be very stable, although the number of chambers that parliament is divided into and the qualifications for offices in those chambers are clearly characteristics that can be bargained over. Varying the number of chambers, number of seats, and qualifications for seats in those chambers allows one to include or exclude particular interests from formal representation; and it also allows the interests represented to have more or less influence over particular policy decisions. In the early days of parliaments, such bargains were fairly common. For example, chambers representing the interests of relatively wealthy commoners were often added to ones representing nobles and high clergy in the thirteenth and fourteenth centuries. However, such bargains were rarely struck in following centuries. Both bicameral and three and four chamber estate systems of representation, once adopted, continued with only minor changes into the early nineteenth century in much of Europe.[1]

That constitutional negotiations in the nineteenth and twentieth centuries produced several formal reforms of parliamentary architecture is evidence that new interests and theories were affecting constitutional negotiations.

Several new bicameral parliaments were created in formerly authoritarian states and republics. For example, the post-Napoleon constitutional monarchies of France (1815) and the Netherlands (1815) consisted of a king and a new bicameral parliament with veto power over taxes and legislation and a limited right to remove cabinet ministers.[2] Denmark established regional assemblies that were elected by relatively broad wealth-based suffrage and subsequently vested those assemblies with veto power over regional taxation in 1841. This was followed in 1849 by the establishment of a national bicameral parliament in which the popular chamber was elected on a similar basis (Danstrup 1947, 94–103). Prussia adopted a new written constitution in 1850 with a bicameral parliament, largely in response to internal lobbying by Prussian elites and liberals, but partly in response to large middle-class demonstrations calling for a written constitution and a representative parliament.

A few long-standing three- and four-chamber estate-based systems were also transformed into bicameral systems. In cases in which the new bicameral systems were based loosely on the English model – with a noble chamber – they were often subsequently transformed into ones resembling that of the United States, in which an indirectly elected (federal) chamber representing regional governments replaced the noble chamber.

Many of these reforms were consistent with liberal political theory, insofar as political liberals wanted to place governance on an electoral and constitutional basis. However, it is unlikely that there were ever a sufficient number of liberals in parliament to adopt the reforms for strictly

[1] In the British case, the House of Lords included both nobles and clergy (the lords temporal and lords spiritual). The House of Commons included wealthy farmers and townsmen. The estate system included separate chambers for nobles, clergy, and commoners. Sweden had separate rural and urban chambers for its commoners.

[2] The constitutional charter of 1814 replaced the previous multicameral estate system with a bicameral one. In most respects, the charter established a fairly typical medieval constitution. Universal male suffrage was replaced with a narrow wealth-based (indirect) suffrage for a new Chamber of Deputies. The charter was proclaimed by Louis XVIII a year before Napoleon I was defeated at Waterloo in 1815. A good summary of the 1814 constitution is provided by Seymour and Frary (1918, 328–33). An English translation is available at: www.napoleon-series.org/research/government/legislation/c_charter.html. In 1830, some agenda control over legislation was obtained by the French parliament.

ideological reasons. Reforming the architecture of parliament required support by majorities in the old noble chambers as well as majorities in the other chambers, and it also required the support of the sovereign. This support was not easy to assemble, as evidenced by the stability of the parliamentary architecture in past centuries.

That bargaining occurred to obtain the necessary breadth of support in the noble chamber is evident in all the reforms adopted. The constitutional bargains often included liberal parliamentary architectures and foundations, but with many conservative structural details that reduced the effects of the new architecture. Such details were carefully worked out to obtain the necessary majorities in the various chambers of parliament and assent from the sovereign. For example, most nobles (including proreform nobles) could agree that they would prefer to retain offices for themselves. So the new first-chamber reforms normally included wealth criteria for electorates and for those eligible for seats in the new chambers. The latter assured that a majority of the officeholders in the postreform first chambers would be nobles or members of noble families. Qualifications for seats in the second chambers of reformed parliaments also normally included much higher wealth and/or tax-payment thresholds than required for voters. In a few cases, as in Prussia, wealth or tax payments also determined the distribution of seats in the directly elected chamber of parliament.

Such "secondary" details assured that relatively wealthy persons, not all of whom were nobles, would continue to exercise disproportionate influence over public policy after the reforms were implemented. In a few cases, the new first chambers also included persons who were appointed by the king or queen. This allowed sovereigns to obtain addition control over the new chamber (at the margin) and also assured that loyal nobles would retain their seats in the reformed parliaments.

In spite of efforts to preserve the preexisting balance of authority, the new parliaments had new institutionally induced interests. The nobles who remained in office were now either directly elected by voters or indirectly elected by regional government officials, who were themselves elected to office (for the most part). Family and occupation were no long sufficient conditions for office. As suffrage expanded and elections became more competitive, their interest in holding seats in parliament induced both noble and commoner members of parliament to pay more and more attention to their electorates and less and less attention to their family interests.

The pragmatic interests of first and second chambers (and their supporters) in obtaining greater authority over public policy remained essentially constant, because more authority is nearly always better than less authority. This suggests that the nineteenth-century trend in parliamentary reforms was the product of ideological trends favoring civic equality, which had gradually reduced the legitimate scope of authority that could properly be exercised by unelected members of parliament.

Liberal trends in the reforms of elite chambers of parliament continued into the twentieth century. In the period before War World I, Sweden eliminated the weighted-voting system used to select its elite regional chamber, which reduced aristocratic representation in that chamber. In 1913, an amendment of the U.S. Constitution replaced its appointed Senate (by state legislatures) with a Senate directly elected by state voters. In 1915, the United Kingdom revised its intraparliamentary rules so that vetoes of its noble chamber (Lords) could be overruled by the directly elected chamber (Commons). After World War II, France, Belgium, and the Netherlands also reduced the veto authority of their first chambers. Denmark (1953) and Sweden (1970) eliminated their indirectly elected regional chambers through constitutional reforms that created unicameral parliaments. In 1999, the British House of Lords became a largely appointed chamber, although a number of seats were reserved for nobles, who could elect ninety-two of their members to represent them in that chamber.

PARLIAMENTARY REFORM, PARTISANSHIP, AND THE AUTHORITY OF THE SOVEREIGN

Together, the emergence of more disciplined political parties and changes in parliamentary architecture also affected the balance of authority between kings and parliaments. Shifts from estate-based systems to bicameral systems reduced the transactions costs of intrachamber bargaining by reducing the number of chambers. Changing the basis of representation from class and occupation to elections produced policy interests that were more aligned across the chambers. The members of both chambers had to please a majority of voters, directly or indirectly. Such changes enhanced parliamentary bargaining power by increasing the likelihood that parliament-wide positions on reforms would emerge, which reduced the likelihood of the indecisive parliaments (unstable coalitions) discussed in Chapter Six.

The shift toward elected members also made long-term bargains between the sovereign and leading members of parliament more difficult to consummate, because leadership policy positions were increasingly determined by electoral competition and party politics, rather than royal favor. Therefore, leadership in the elected chambers changed with election results. This tended to increase the influence of the elected chamber in the context of the nineteenth century because it meant that elected chambers would have to be routinely consulted. This "turnover" effect also increased the influence of those entitled to cast votes in elections. Leaders of factions within elected chambers of parliament could not defer to the sovereign more than to their party and voters without undermining their influence and support.[3]

The policy and constitutional effects of parliamentary reforms often took many years to emerge, in part because reformed parliaments did not gain much, if any, additional control over public policy, and partly because a majority of the members of the prereform parliaments normally returned to office in the postreform parliaments. The latter allowed many informal practices and alliances to continue in postreform parliaments.

The status quo was further protected through restrictive amendment procedures and by royal authority to appoint the executive cabinet. These reduced the ability of liberal coalitions in the elected chambers to draft constitutional reforms. Indeed, a committee appointed by the king often proposed the first drafts of major amendments. Their compromises with liberals in the elected and noble chambers produced liberal, but authority-preserving reforms. Such reforms are, for example, evident in the new constitutions adopted after the unification of Italy in 1861, Germany in 1871, and in Japan's first written constitution in 1889. These new constitutions were clearly liberal in architecture, but conservative in their effects on policy-making procedures and outcomes.

Nonetheless, such reforms often changed the balance of authority within parliament and between kings and queens and parliaments in the long run. The postreform parliaments tended to have more closely aligned interests because of their electoral basis and the emergence of more disciplined political parties. In the context of the nineteenth century, the postreform parliaments were somewhat more liberal and more assertive than the prereform parliaments that they replaced. The minorities that had opposed parliamentary reform often lost their positions in the new parliament as a consequence of the reforms, and many of the losers would have been inclined to support traditional and royal policies.

These shifts, together with parliament's long-standing power of the purse, increased the "price" that parliament could charge the king for support of policies of royal interest. The resulting terms of trade gradually shifted more and more policy-making authority from kings to their parliaments. By

[3] This is not to say that deference to the king or queen is never rewarded. Gaining preferable treatment from the sovereign through loyal statements and actions can enhance a leader's influence within his or her party and support from voters. A (pragmatic) dual loyalty of this sort often proved very useful to party leaders in the nineteenth century.

1925, elected chambers of parliament dominated public-policy formation and noble chambers had vanished throughout northern Europe – except in England, where the influence of the House of Lords over public policy had been reduced to a shadow of its former self.

CHOOSING AMONG ELECTORAL SYSTEMS AND QUALIFICATIONS FOR SUFFRAGE

To create an electoral basis for parliament, it is clear that decisions have to be made about who will vote, how votes will be counted and used to select representatives, and how often elections will be held. Elections are not simply about counting votes. Both the scope of the franchise and proper electoral procedures seemed fairly obvious before 1800 and also after 1925, but they were not nearly as obvious during the nineteenth century. Members of parliament could be directly or indirectly selected by narrow or broad electorates. Men and/or women could be elected from geographic districts, economic classes, religious groups, political parties, and so forth. There could be one person elected from each electoral district or several. Elections could be held periodically or whenever it seemed useful for the king and/or parliamentary majority.

Medieval electorates usually consisted of the wealthiest 5 to 10 percent of the men in the kingdom, duchy, or city of interest. One or two persons would be elected from each urban or rural district. The persons nominated for national elective offices were normally selected by (and on the payrolls of) relatively wealthy families in the towns or counties who were often also local government officials. Elections were held infrequently because the sovereign called for new elections only as necessary, often just before an emergency meeting of parliament. Votes were normally cast by simply walking to one side or another at the place where elections were held (divisions) or through voice votes.[4] Because most electoral outcomes were essentially predetermined, voter turnout was normally very low. Many candidates for parliament ran unopposed.

Local sponsors had interests that were affected by national policies. They were legally permitted to influence how voters cast their votes in the relatively few cases in which more than one candidate ran for office. They might simply pay voters to turn out and vote for their nominee or threaten those

4 Votes on issues are still called "divisions" in England, because of this physical, locational method of casting votes. Such divisions are still occasionally used today, as in the English Parliament and in party caucuses in some states within the United States.

who voted against their candidates with economic sanctions of one kind or another. They might also invite those who voted for their nominee to special celebrations (parties) before and after votes were cast. Public voting (divisions and voice votes), small electorates, and low turnouts made it relatively easy to know who voted for which candidate. The representatives elected would attempt to obtain various favors from the king (grants, monopoly privileges, high offices, and elevations) and/or to oppose the efforts of others to obtain such favors.

During the nineteenth century, these long-standing electoral procedures were debated and adjusted at their margins many times. The debates included analysis of alternative electoral systems and alternative bases for determining who was qualified to vote. Should persons be allowed to vote in many districts or just one? Should one or more than one person be elected from each district? Should the right to vote be attached to land, community, residence, competence, or be available to essentially all adult citizens? Should all persons have the same number of votes, or should some persons have more votes than others? Should voting be done in public or in secret?

In general, liberal reformers (and parliamentary decisions) favored the expansion of suffrage, increased electoral competition, nomination by political parties, secret ballots, and standardized election periods. In the early twentieth century, liberal reformers favored one-adult-man-one-vote systems, and subsequently, one-adult-one-vote systems. Although we take most of their decisions for granted today, contemporary voting systems were not the only ones possible, and a number of other electoral procedures were temporarily adopted in the nineteenth century.

Debates Regarding the Proper Qualifications for Suffrage

A useful window into the mid-nineteenth-century election law debates is provided by the widely read and translated John Stuart Mill. His writing and speeches summarize and critique a variety of possible electoral reforms at the same time that they explain his "radical" views about the proper qualifications for suffrage and best methods for electing members of parliament.[5] Consider, for example, Mill's (1859, 1861) discussion of the

[5] Mill was born in London in 1806. He edited the *Westminster Review* in the 1830s and was well known for his contributions to utilitarian philosophy, economics, and liberal political philosophy. He worked for the British East India Company until 1858. Mill was also briefly elected to the House of Commons (1865–8). The terms liberal and radical are used by Mill himself in describing the policy and philosophical perspectives of the *Westminster Review*.

merits of introducing new educational qualifications for suffrage and for further reducing the wealth and income requirements for suffrage.

> If there ever was a political principle at once liberal and conservative, it is that of an **educational qualification**. None are so illiberal, none so bigoted in their hostility to improvement, **none so superstitiously attached to the stupidest and worst of old forms** and usages, **as the uneducated**. … (J. S. Mill, 1859, "Thoughts on Parliamentary Reform," *Essays on Politics and Society Part 2*, Toronto: University of Toronto Press, 16.)
>
> It is also important [however] that the assembly which votes the taxes, either general or local, should be **elected exclusively by those who pay something** towards the taxes imposed. **Those who pay no taxes, disposing by their votes of other people's money, have every motive to be lavish**, and none to economize.… I regard it as required by first principles, that the **receipt of parish relief should be a peremptory disqualification for the franchise**. He who cannot by his labor suffice for his own support, has no claim to the privilege of helping himself to the money of others. **By becoming dependent on the remaining members of the community for actual subsistence, he abdicates his claim to equal rights with them in other respects**. (J. S. Mill, 1861, "Considerations on Representative Government," *Essays on Politics and Society Part 2*, Toronto: University of Toronto Press, 129.)

Both these arguments would sound somewhat "conservative" fifty years later, but it should be kept in mind that British qualifications for suffrage in 1861 prevented middle- and working-class men from participating in national elections (see Chapter Thirteen). A shift from the existing tax and property requirements to a welfare or relief exclusion, even if combined with a modest educational requirement, implied a major expansion of suffrage at the time that Mill was writing.

As evident in Mill's arguments, mid-century debates on suffrage expansion focused on a person's ability to cast an independent, thoughtful, vote. Many of the arguments were ideological in nature, although empirical arguments were also used. For example, those favoring suffrage expansion often noted increases in public education and in the training and independence of skilled managers, technicians, educators, and artisans.

The outcomes of the nineteenth-century suffrage debates generally favored civic equality, although wealth qualifications for suffrage and seats in parliament continued to exist in most places throughout the nineteenth century and into the next. Other qualifications, such as education and literacy, were also debated and occasionally introduced. Each expansion of suffrage was argued to satisfy broadly shared norms about who was truly qualified to vote. Further expansion was always rejected (if, temporarily) because the remaining voters were thought to be too dependent on others or too poorly informed to cast a meaningful vote.

The opponents of suffrage expansion feared that large-scale redistribution of wealth and a general decline in the quality of national policies would be caused by allowing unqualified persons to vote. (It bears noting that age, sanity, and residency are still used as criteria for determining eligibility to vote.)

Alternative Procedures for Electing Representatives

Once it is determined who should vote, elections can be organized in a number of ways. For example, members of parliament may be selected on a geographic or occupational basis, elected one at a time from small local districts or in groups from large regional election districts. The election rules can be uniform throughout the polity or vary by district. The districts can be *more or less* permanent in size (as tends to be true of federal districts: states, provinces, *länder*, and so on) or may be periodically adjusted in response to changing political demands or population shifts (as in U. S. Congressional districts). District "size" can be measured by area, population, or a combination of the two. Laws may constrain districts to be more or less equal size, to include more or less equal numbers of voters, or to vote on the same day(s) or not.

Many of the electoral reforms in the nineteenth century were as important for their effects on the distribution of representatives among regions and the manner in which votes were used to select representatives, as for their effect on the number of persons entitled to cast votes. Liberals tended to favor geographic districts that elected approximately the same number of representatives per voter. Conservatives tended to defend the existing very unequally sized districts representing different numbers of voters, largely for pragmatic reasons (many were elected from such districts), but also because such districts tended to increase the range of interests represented in parliament.[6]

Late-nineteenth-century liberals disagreed about the number of members of parliament that should be elected from each district. Most liberals favored single-member districts, because this allowed representatives to be more easily rewarded or punished for performance (and because liberals often won such elections). A significant minority of liberals, however, preferred multiple-member districts with elections designed to increase the extent to which voter interests were represented.

[6] Prior to 1832, for example, fifty members of the British Parliament were elected from districts with fewer than fifty voters. These included several talented, but not broadly popular, members of Parliament.

Objections to single-member districts were based on early public-choice analyses of electoral systems. The critics of single-member districts noted that half the voters in single-member districts can select members of parliaments, and that policy decisions in parliament required the support of just half of the members elected. Consequently, parliaments based on single-member districts allow legislation favored by as few as one-fourth of the voters to be adopted (one-half of one-half).

Again, quotes from Mill can be used to illustrate the breadth of debate over electoral procedures for multiple-member districts in the mid to late nineteenth century:

> Assuming, then, that each constituency elects three representatives, **two modes have been proposed**, in either of which a minority, amounting to a third of the constituency, may, by acting in concert, and determining to aim at no more, return one of the members. One plan is that **each elector should only be allowed to vote for two, or even for one, although three are to be elected. The other leaves to the elector his three votes, but allows him to give all of them to one candidate**. (J. S. Mill, 1859, "Thoughts on Parliamentary Reform," *Essays on Politics and Society Part 2*, Toronto: University of Toronto Press, 18.)
>
> The object being that the suffrages of those who are in a minority locally, should tell **in proportion to their number** on the composition of the Parliament; since this is *all* that is required, **why** should it be imperative that their votes should be received only for some one who is **a *local* candidate? Why might they not give their suffrage to any one who is a candidate anywhere, their number of votes being added to those which he may obtain elsewhere?** Suppose that a comparison between the number of members of the House and of registered electors in the kingdom, gives a quotient of 2000 as the number of electors per member, on an average of the whole country (which, according to Mr. **Hare's calculation,** would be not far from the fact, if the existing electoral body were augmented by 200,000): **why should not any candidate, who can obtain 2000 suffrages** [votes] **in the whole kingdom, be returned to Parliament**? (J. S. Mill, 1859, "Thoughts on Parliamentary Reform," *Essays on Politics and Society Part 2*, Toronto: University of Toronto Press, 40–1.)

Mills analysis and others from this period demonstrate that those interested in electoral reform were aware that voters can vote for several representatives simultaneously and that a number of choices about how to use votes to select representatives were possible. Voters might cast only a single vote per representative office or district, or be free to distribute multiple votes among the candidates and districts throughout the country. Representatives may be selected through winner-take-all contests (plurality rule) or be selected *more or less* proportionately to the votes received from political parties (proportional representation systems). These proportions can be calculated from small or large regional (or national) election districts.

Debates about the relative merits of single-member districts and multiple-member districts were fairly intense among liberals in the late nineteenth and early twentieth centuries, with mainstream liberals tending to prefer single-member districts and radical (left) liberals, like Mill, preferring multiple-member districts.

The Fancy Franchise: Weighted Voting

In addition to determining who should vote, the size and location of electoral districts, and the number of persons that should be selected in each electoral district, there was also a good deal of discussion of the merits of weighted-voting systems, what their opponents in England termed "the fancy franchise." There were precedents for using such systems, as property-weighted-voting systems had been used during the enclosure movement and share-weighted voting was widely used by stock companies. Less explicit weighted-voting systems were also common, as with the extra representation given to university graduates of Cambridge and Oxford in the English parliament, and the ability of landlords to cast votes in every district in which they were significant taxpayers.

Given the qualification debates, it is not too surprising that many mid-century liberals favored weighted voting as a method of giving additional influence to "more qualified" voters in elections and public-policy decisions. Other supporters and opponents of suffrage expansion favored weighted voting as a method of reducing the policy shifts that would be produced by adding new voters to the electorate. Again, quotes from Mill serve to illustrate the scope of debate and the types of arguments used.

> The only thing which can justify reckoning one person's opinion as equivalent **to more than one, is individual mental superiority**; and what is wanted is some approximate means of ascertaining that. … Subject to some such condition, **two or more votes might be allowed to every person who exercises any of these superior functions. The liberal professions**, when really and not nominally practiced, imply, of course, a still higher degree of instruction; and wherever a sufficient examination, or any serious conditions of education, are required before entering on a profession, its members **could be admitted at once to a plurality of votes**. (J. S. Mill, 1859, "Considerations on Representative Government," *Essays on Politics and Society Part 2*, Toronto: University of Toronto Press, 131–2.)

Most proposals for a "fancy franchise" were defeated, although in a few cases, compromises between opponents and supporters of suffrage expansion temporarily produced weighted-voting systems, as in Sweden and Belgium.

Such explicitly weighted-electoral systems were normally adopted as part of a larger constitutional bargain. In 1866, Sweden adopted an indirect, wealth-weighted-voting system for its first chamber (and wealth qualifications for all members of parliament) as part of a constitutional bargain that replaced its old four-chamber system with a bicameral system grounded in elections (Chapter Fourteen). In 1893, Belgium adopted a weighted-voting system as a method of securing sufficient support for a major expansion of male suffrage. It allowed one vote for all men, two votes for each educated man, and three votes for each educated man of means. The Belgian system was used for a decade at the end of the nineteenth century. In both cases, the weighted-voting systems were used to increase support for a package of constitutional reforms to levels required by their formal amendment procedures.

In the end, however, arguments for civic equality prevailed, and one-man-one-vote systems for casting and counting votes were adopted throughout the West. The timing of these reforms varied, as did the final step to the one-adult-one-vote principle, but the principle of civic equality clearly influenced the parliamentary debates and negotiations that produced the final reforms.

Gender-Neutral Suffrage Law

The last major stage of suffrage reform in most places concerned the competence of women as voters. Women's suffrage was not an entirely new idea, as women had occasionally had the same rights of suffrage as men, as in Sweden (for unmarried women) and temporarily in the state of New Jersey in the late eighteenth century (see Chapter Eighteen).

Public and parliamentary debate about the appropriate qualifications for women usually followed behind those regarding men's suffrage, although in most cases, the arguments were very similar. The focus tended to be upon the independence and competence of women and on the extent to which their interests were already represented in parliament by the votes of others (in this case by the votes cast by their husbands). Again Mill serves as a useful window into the issues addressed and arguments used.

In all cases where a woman is *sui juris*, occupying a house or tenement, or possessed of a freehold, or is otherwise in a position which, in the case of a male, would amount to a **qualification, there is no sound reason for excluding her** from the parliamentary franchise. **The exclusion is probably a remnant of the feudal law, and is not in harmony with the other civil institutions of the country**. (J. S. Mill, 1859, "Thoughts on Parliamentary Reform," *Essays on Politics and Society Part 2*, Toronto: University of Toronto Press, 49.)

In the preceding argument for universal, but graduated suffrage, I have taken no account of difference of sex. **I consider it to be as entirely irrelevant to political rights**, as difference in height, or in the color of the hair. **All human beings have the same interest in good government; the welfare of all is alike affected by it, and they have equal need of a voice in it to secure their share of its benefits**. (J. S. Mill, 1859, "Considerations on Representative Government," *Essays on Politics and Society Part 2*, Toronto: University of Toronto Press, 135.)

In the middle of the nineteenth century, such arguments produced little support among male voters. In the period just before and just after World War I, however, such arguments found majority support among male voters, and suffrage laws were changed to eliminate gender as a qualification for suffrage.

Woman's suffrage was the largest single expansion of suffrage that took place in the reforms that produced universal suffrage. And, of course, it took place without a credible military threat on the part of women or their male supporters in parliament.

PARTISAN INTERESTS IN PROPORTIONAL REPRESENTATION

Voting-system reforms were often crucial parts of the constitutional bargains that produced essentially universal adult suffrage. Support for PR systems had existed for at least half a century among a subset of liberal idealists and political pragmatists, as evident in Mill's analysis. Support for PR systems among party leaders, especially conservatives, began to increase toward the end of the nineteenth century.

Electoral campaigns had become more impersonal, ideological, and partisan as electorates expanded. This caused parliaments to be increasingly organized along ideological and party lines, rather than based on elite family interests or distance from the capital. Conservative leaders (and conservative voters) feared that universal male suffrage would cause their parties to disappear in electoral systems based on single-member districts and plurality rule.

Duverger's Theorem and the Conservative Interest in PR Systems

The number of political parties that can be sustained in a polity is directly affected by the choice of electoral system. First-past-the-post democracies tend to have just two dominant political parties. One explanation for this is Duverger's theorem (1954), which implies that a center-right and center-left party can effectively block third parties from winning elections under plurality voting rules. Duverger suggests that parties will adopt such blocking positions, because political parties have an interest in limiting competition. Consequently, two is the natural number of parties in first-past-the-post (plurality) electoral systems. (Two, however, can become three or four in plurality systems if regional differences are sufficient to prevent true national parties from emerging, as might be said of the United States during the period of the so-called Dixiecrats or of contemporary France and Canada.)

The analogous entry-blocking configuration of a PR system allows many more *national* parties to coexist in equilibrium. According to Duverger's logic, the maximum stable number of parties in PR systems is determined by the participation threshold. If n is the minimum fraction of votes necessary for a party to receive seats in parliament, an alignment of party platforms in which each party receives just a bit less than twice the minimum ($2n$) will be stable, because no new party can enter and receive sufficient votes to qualify for parliament. If, for example, the participation threshold guarantees any party with 4 percent of the vote a seat in parliament, thirteen different political parties could be sustained in a party-platform alignment that blocked the successful entry of additional parties.[7]

The relatively large number of parties that could be supported under PR systems was well understood in the nineteenth century, as is evident in Mill's early analysis of PR and multiple-member districts. Members of parties that expected to place third or fourth in national elections had clear practical reasons to favor PR over plurality (first-past-the-post) systems.

In addition to increasing the number of parties, PR systems also tend to increase the influence of party leaders. Within PR systems, voters cast

7 Duverger's theorem applies to plurality-rule elections. If two parties locate somewhat to the right and left of the median voter, the assumptions of spatial-voting models imply that no new party can enter and win an election. (Two parties positioned exactly at the median voter's position would not be a blocking alignment, because an entry somewhat to the left or right of the median could secure a larger vote than either of the two parties.) This is one explanation for the number and position of major political parties in the United States.

The counterpart to Duverger's theorem in PR systems occurs when a sufficient number of equally sized parties position themselves so that no new party can enter and secure sufficient votes to participate in government. For example, thirteen equally sized parties would each receive about 7 percent of the votes under PR. Any new party that attempted to locate between two adjacent parties would receive at most one-fourth of the votes of two adjacent parties, 3.5 percent, which is insufficient for representation if the participation threshold is 4 percent, as it is currently in Sweden.

See Mueller (2003, 271–2) for a discussion of Duverger's theorem. Duverger's theorem evidently does not apply to all plurality systems, especially in countries with distinct regional differences in the pattern of voter preferences and party strength. Mueller (1996, chapter 10) notes that plurality vote systems do not always yield parliaments with two parties.

their votes for political parties, rather than candidates. The party leadership determines the persons who will be on their party lists and in what order, which allows party leaders to determine many of the persons holding seats in parliament and also allows them to discipline elected officials who fail to vote the party line. They can do so by simply moving "disloyal" representatives further down the party list. This is not to say that party leaders in first-past-the-post systems are without influence, but the party lists give party leaders additional tools in PR systems not available under first-past-the-post systems.[8]

As a consequence of such partisan interests, the properties of PR systems played a central role in many of the constitutional bargains worked out in the early twentieth century.

At the time that universal male suffrage was seriously considered in northern Europe, it was widely believed that liberals and social democrats would dominate political decision making after universal male suffrage was adopted. Conservatives feared that they would become permanent minority parties and would therefore be eliminated from national politics in electoral systems based on single-member districts. They were well represented in the parliaments that considered extending the vote to all men, and they often insisted on proportional representation systems in exchange for accepting nearly universal, adult male suffrage.

Mainstream liberals were split over PR, with most preferring single-member districts. Left liberals continued to support PR for more or less idealistic reasons, albeit reinforced by pragmatic interest in obtaining conservative support for suffrage expansion. As a consequence PR systems were often adopted by coalitions of left liberals and conservatives at the same time that universal adult male suffrage and other reforms were adopted in the periods just before and after World War I.

PROCEDURES FOR AMENDMENT AND CONSTITUTIONAL REVIEW STRENGTHENED

Formal procedures for amendment and review are included in most constitutional documents, and these amendment procedures tend to be

8 Some PR systems allow voters to vote for candidates as well as parties, but generally, order on party lists remains a defining characteristic of proportional rule. Sweden has recently adopted a limited form of preference voting. The revised election laws allow each voter to indicate a special preference for a single candidate by writing in his or her name on the ballot. The Swiss electoral system also allows voters to affect the order of candidates on party lists.

among the most durable parts of a constitution. Partly for this reason, the age of a constitution is often measured by the period in which its rules of amendment are followed, rather than by the period in which particular political procedures and constraints have been in place. By this measure, the Constitution of the United States is generally regarded to be more than two centuries old, although it has been amended twenty-seven times, most recently in 1992.[9]

The bargaining that preceded most constitutional reforms in Europe during the nineteenth century suggests that formal amendment procedures played a significant role in the bargains struck. Most formal amendment procedures in early nineteenth-century Europe required majorities in each chamber of parliament and approval by the king. To obtain the necessary breadth of support, constitutional reforms had to advance and protect a variety of interests in parliament at the same time.

Amendment procedures, although remarkably stable, were also occasionally modified during the nineteenth century. This was most often accomplished at the same time that other reforms were adopted. In some cases, amending the amendment process was an indirect consequence of other reforms. For example, Sweden's shift from a four-chamber parliament to a two-chamber parliament implied that only two chambers need approve subsequent reforms, rather than four. Other reforms made explicit changes to preexisting amendment procedures. Several mid-century constitutions included relatively demanding requirements for amendments, such as supermajorities within parliamentary chambers or popular referenda or a series of approvals by parliament, as in Denmark, Prussia, the Netherlands, and Switzerland.

These somewhat more demanding amendment procedures tend to support the rule of law insofar as constitutional stability is increased and/or minority protections are enhanced. Such reforms also tended to reduce the king's ability to renege on his past constitutional agreements by increasing the breadth of support required for amendments.

Judicial Independence, Constitutional Reform, and Constitutional Review

Amendment procedures tend to identify constitutional bargains that are largely self-enforcing, insofar as amendment procedures require broad

[9] See Chapter Eighteen for an analysis of eighteenth-, nineteenth-, and early-twentieth-century Amendments.

consensus for constitutional reforms to be adopted; however, no constitution is entirely self-enforcing.

As a consequence, courts and court-like proceedings have often played a significant role in constitutional negotiations, reform, and enforcement. During the medieval period, judicial matters were themselves often subjects of constitutional bargains, as nobles and kings often found that written agreements combined with judicial independence helped to make specific agreements about procedures and constraints more stable and less arbitrary. National courts also constrained the ability of local government officials to arbitrarily change the law by reinterpreting or unevenly enforcing national laws or the laws that delegated authority to local officials. The independence and authority of the judiciary (and juries) emerged gradually through a long series of quasi-constitutional bargains analogous to those described earlier for kings and their tax councils (Finer 1997, Berman 2003).

During the nineteenth century, the role of the courts was also subjected to normative analysis in much the same manner as other aspects of constitutional design. Liberals often supported the expansion of judicial authority into the political domain. For example, contractarians and many other liberals regarded constitutions to be contracts that formally delegate authority from the people to their governments. Consequently, they argued that the national courts should enforce those contracts in much the same manner that they enforce others.

During the eighteenth and nineteenth centuries, authority to appoint judges and senior government lawyers gradually shifted from kings to parliaments along with other policy-making authority. This indirectly increased institutional support for the "rule of law" over the "rule of man" because laws were also increasingly determined by the formal procedures of parliament, even in countries in which new laws remained *formally* royal mandates informed by parliament's advice. Constitutional laws, however, remained for the most part beyond the jurisdiction of national court systems, although the judiciary had long played significant roles in day-to-day governance and constitutional interpretation in several countries (Montesquieu 1748/1914; Berman 2003; Field 2002).

There were also broad changes in jurisdiction that made more of the national government actions subject to judicial review. For example, in the middle of the nineteenth century, the royal immunity of cabinet ministers was often reduced or eliminated. Cabinet ministers were made criminally liable for violating ordinary criminal laws and often for their failures to implement legislation adopted by parliament and accepted by the king or queen. New standing committees in parliament were created to review administrative decisions for constitutionality. The constitutional committees were often given authority to overturn executive (administrative) decisions deemed unconstitutional. In a few cases, supreme courts were created to review executive (administrative) decisions for constitutionality, although not usually parliamentary decisions.

These somewhat stronger procedures for constitutional review reduced the extent to which a written constitution can be informally amended (or ignored) by the executive branch and tended to further stabilize constitutional procedures and constraints. Constitutional review also promoted what might be called a constitutional state of mind, by reminding legislators and sovereigns that they too were constrained by the law.

In this manner, governance became more tightly constrained by written constitutional documents and formal constitutional amendments during the nineteenth and early twentieth centuries. Governments had always been rule bound, but in the West they became more formally so than they had been in previous centuries at the same time that they became more democratic and grounded in popular sovereignty.[10]

It is important to note, however, that most liberals favored limited judicial authority with respect to politics and constitutional review. Their reasoning paralleled that of Hobbes with respect to sovereignty. Constitutional bargains differ from ordinary contracts in that no outside agency can be powerful enough to enforce the terms of constitutional contracts without being powerful enough to supersede those contracts. A court and police force that is independent and strong enough to enforce bargains between parliament and the king would be strong enough to create their own rules. Such courts would tend to become the true government of a country, as might be said of the Sharia courts in some Islamic countries.

TENTATIVE CONCLUSION: CONSTITUTIONAL BARGAINING PRODUCED WESTERN DEMOCRACY

Overall, the general pattern of liberal reforms in nineteenth-century Europe is consistent with the constitutional-bargaining models developed in Part I. Constitutional bargaining was fine-grained, multidimensional,

[10] Congleton (1997, 2003) suggests that equality before the law and rule-based governance are especially important for democracies because it helps them avoid cycling problems. Shepsle and Weingast (1981) suggest that this also tends to be true for parliaments themselves, which provides an explanation for the existence of many of parliament's formal internal procedural rules. The latter were, however, for the most part enforced by parliamentarians, rather than the courts.

and continuous, as predicted. Most reforms were adopted using preexisting amendment or legislative procedures. The bargains exploited the broad menu of constitutional possibilities that exist within the king-and-council template. Most constitutional bargains produced modest reforms of existing procedures in a few policy or procedural areas at a time, rather than entirely new constitutions.

The bargains were carefully crafted and intentional, rather than spontaneous expressions of the "general will" or hasty attempts to deal with a specific crisis. In cases in which relatively large reforms were adopted, there were broad linkages among several constitutional issues that were bargained over simultaneously. Free trade reduced royal revenues, so negotiations to reduce tariffs were partly conditional on agreements about new revenue sources (often from income taxes). Universal suffrage was expected to undermine some political parties more than others, and so the last stages of male suffrage extension were often linked to weighted-voting systems or proportional representation.

Constitutional bargains were constrained by formal amendment processes and constitutional conservatism. As a consequence, the basic template for governance was retained and many of the formal procedures for adopting and revising public policies remained similar to those from previous centuries.

Most European governments in 1920 still consisted of kings and parliaments. Parliaments still deliberated and made recommendations to their sovereign concerning public policies, as they had since medieval times. In most places, laws were still royal proclamations as they had been for many centuries. Nonetheless, a series of modest reforms adopted between 1820 and 1920 had produced major changes in governance. The influence of privileged families was reduced, electoral competition for seats in parliament increased, and policy-making authority shifted to parliaments during the course of the nineteenth century. By the early twentieth century, kings had become duty bound to accept the "advice" of parliament.

Public policies in Europe, consequently, became better aligned with the interests of the typical adult members of their societies than they had been in the past. In this sense parliaments could be said to have been perfected, or at least improved, as institutions for selecting public policies by the reforms of the nineteenth century.

Liberalism and Technological Change as Catalysts for Constitutional Reform

In Europe, trends in constitutional reforms were catalyzed by technological and ideological trends. A series of technological innovation produced new cost-effective, capital-intensive modes of production with economies of scale. The new modes of production could not be profitable without changes in economic regulation. And in many cases, economic reforms were impossible without political reforms. The economic theories of liberals provided rationales for dismantling the internal and external trade barriers that prevented new economies of scale from being profitable.

Liberal political theories provided norms and an agenda for constitutional reforms that were well aligned with the economic interests of those wishing to profit from the new technologies and the new markets associated with them. Political liberals argued that public policies and constitutions should reflect the interests of all citizens, not simply those of privileged families. Governance should be grounded in written laws, rather than the whims of rulers. As suffrage expanded during the nineteenth century, the electorate became more and more liberal.

Liberal trends in reform were evident in a wide variety of policy areas in Europe during the nineteenth century, including constitutional ones, as noted in Chapter Ten. Civic equality increased as slaves and serfs were freed, censorship was reduced, public education was expanded, and privileged control over markets and politics were largely eliminated. Regulatory and tariff reforms reduced internal and external trade barriers, which allowed new economies of scale in production and organization to be exploited.

There were several boot-strapping processes at work. As barriers to entry in markets were reduced, new larger economic enterprises emerged, which in turn produced a new middle class of small businessmen, managers, technicians, and artisans. Liberalism gained support among the new upper and middle class because it provided a basis for understanding life in new, less traditional, more commercial, and more urban societies. A new, or at least extended, economic elite also emerged based on innovation, mass production, and commerce, rather than land holdings and family monopolies. By reducing ideological and economic support for representation based on class, occupation, and family wealth, liberalism also tended to support the political aspirations (power and status) of these upwardly bound persons and families. Education reforms also produced more literate societies that were more familiar with liberal ideas and proposals for reform.

Authority shifted from the elite class-based chambers of government to the more directly elected ones at the same time that economic and political life were opened to broader and broader subsets of the adult population. The basis of government shifted from privileged families and tradition to popular sovereignty and mass elections.

Economic and political liberalization were interdependent phenomena in Western Europe and Japan. Essentially no Western countries industrialized without also liberalizing their political systems, and essentially no countries liberalized their political systems that did not also industrialize, although the relative pace of economic and political reforms differed among countries. Although not products of consensus, both liberal policy reforms and constitutional amendments were for the most part peacefully and lawfully adopted. Liberal ideas were not products of the nineteenth century, but changes in economic and political conditions increased their relevance, appeal, and support.

Together continued innovation and the success of liberal economic reforms demonstrated that progress was possible. More open markets increased average and median income by encouraging technological innovation and other value-increasing forms of competition. Political competition in elections with broad suffrage tended to advance broadly shared interests. Shifts in the basis of authority from elites to ordinary citizens did not weaken national policies or produce major redistribution, nor did equality before the law eliminate incentives for excellence.

Constitutional Bargaining Is Evident, but Additional Evidence Is Needed

Chapters Nine to Eleven provide a good deal of evidence that the general pattern of reform in Western Europe is consistent with the bargaining theory of reform developed in Chapters Two to Eight. Bargaining within parliament and between kings and parliament is evident throughout European history. The constitutional bargains consummated were multidimensional, fine-grained, and for the most part adopted through lawful, deliberate standing procedures. There is evidence that the reforms reflected interests of those sitting at the table during constitutional negotiations and also evidence that those interests changed during the nineteenth century. There were many more reforms than mass demonstrations or credible threats of revolution.

Individual constitutional reforms were rarely forced but instead were largely products of bargaining and amendment procedures.

It is, however, one thing to argue that the broad sweep of political and economic history is consistent with a particular theory and another to argue that the details in nearly every case are consistent with that theory. As economic and political historians know, the details often undermine, rather than support, the broad brush.

To determine whether that is true or not of the present theory, the next seven chapters examine the constitutional histories of six governments in greater detail. The six case studies can be divided into three "easy" cases, in which the analytical history applies nearly perfectly, and three "hard" cases, in which constitutional bargaining, industrialization, and liberalism are present, but in which the results or timing differ from that implied by the analytical history.

The three easy cases are England (Chapters Twelve to Thirteen), Sweden (Chapter Fourteen), and the Netherlands (Chapter Fifteen). All of these countries began the nineteenth century with strong sovereigns, all had a series of modest constitutional reforms adopted peacefully, and all became parliamentary democracies by 1925. All of these countries continue to have royal families who formally head their national governments, and all three continue to use political institutions that were substantially worked out in the late nineteenth and early twentieth centuries. Norway, Belgium, and Denmark could also have been analyzed as relatively easy cases.

The three difficult cases are Japan (Chapter Sixteen), Germany (Chapter Seventeen), and the United States (Chapter Eighteen). These provide useful challenges and support for the theory. Japan is an Asian country that adopted a constitutional monarchy rather late (in 1889). Although not a European country, its constitutional reforms were nonetheless influenced by industrialization and liberal ideology. Japan was briefly a liberal democracy in 1925, in the sense that its cabinets were appointed from majority parties in parliament whose members were elected by universal male suffrage. Japanese governance, however, reverted to royal rule in the next decade, largely as a consequence of electoral pressures and constitutional negotiation. Germany did not complete its transition to parliamentary democracy, although it nearly did so as World War I ended. The government of the Weimar Republic formed after the war was substantially grounded on the parliamentary negotiations that took place during the last years of the second empire.

The United States has not had a king since 1776, although its present constitutional template resembles that of a constitutional monarchy, insofar as the president can be regarded as an elected king. Its lack of a hereditary sovereign, however, is not evidence that its transition to democracy was completely unique or revolutionary. The U.S. transition to democracy began at least a century before the United States emerged as an independent country. The reforms adopted by its colonial precursors were consistent with the constitutional-bargaining model developed in Part I and were surprisingly similar to the European experience in the nineteenth century. Moreover, in spite of its early start, the United States completed its transition to (formal) universal adult suffrage at about the same time as northern Europe with the ratification of its Twentieth Amendment in 1920.

Although constitutional negotiations in these six countries were undertaken independently, and the individual reforms were drafted by different groups of senior government officials at different times and places, the broad outlines of their constitutional debates, negotiations, and reforms were very similar. Technological advance, increased support for liberal ideas, and fine-grained constitutional bargaining with respect to budgets, parliamentary authority, and suffrage reform are evident in each case.

TWELVE

An Overview of British Constitutional History: The English King and the Medieval Parliament

Chapters Twelve and Thirteen focus on the constitutional history of the United Kingdom. This extended narrative is undertaken for several reasons. England emerged as a nation-state relatively early, which makes its particular institutional developments relatively free from the effects of regional entanglements, although not entirely so. This allows a long and relatively detailed account of its constitutional history to be told without accounting for nation building itself. Although times were often troubled and occasional civil wars occurred, the English king-and-council template for governance has remained in place for essentially eight hundred years.[1] The English case is also the one that is likely most familiar to readers, although few will have much detailed knowledge of its constitutional developments.

This is partly because England has never had a formal constitution or grounding law, and partly because historians tend not to focus much attention on constitutional developments. The written constitution of England consists of dozens of acts of parliament that define and redefine the basic

[1] England is the medieval name for the kingdom from which the United Kingdom emerged. Its formal name has changed several times to reflect changes in its territory.

The country's name was changed to the (United) Kingdom of Great Britain under the Act of Union of 1707, which ended Scottish independence and added members representing Scotland to the English parliament. (Scotland had previously had its own parliament, but the same men and women had been kings and queens of England and Scotland since 1602.)

The name was changed to the United Kingdom of Great Britain and Ireland after the Act of Union of 1801, which ended (temporarily) Irish independence and added Irish representatives to the British parliament. (Ireland had previously had its own parliament, although England and Ireland had shared the same sovereign since 1542.) Brittannia was the Roman name for England (and Wales) during the four centuries in which England was part of the Roman Empire.

The formal name of the country is presently the United Kingdom of Great Britain and Northern Ireland (since 1927), which reflects the secession of the Republic of Ireland in 1922.

architecture of the government: how the persons who come to hold power are chosen and the constraints under which they may lawfully operate. There is a large literature in the United Kingdom on the subject of constitutional law, although it is little studied outside that country or even acknowledged by scholars from countries with more unified constitutions. English constitutional law is augmented by an elaborate body of unwritten procedures, norms, and conventions that fills the spaces left by its constitutional legislation.[2]

The core procedures through which English (and subsequently British and United Kingdom) public policies are chosen have been remarkably stable through time, although they are a bit ambiguous at the margin, as is often the case in other countries as well. For example, the sovereign (arguably) continues formally to have the power to call and dismiss parliament, appoint ministers, and veto legislation, but informally the sovereign has deferred to the House of Commons on such matters for more than a century. The last formal veto of an act of parliament occurred in the early eighteenth century, although implicit royal vetoes continued into the nineteenth century.

What is unusual about the English constitution is not that it is a blend of formal laws and informal practices, but rather that none of its written documents characterize formal procedures of amendment.[3] The same procedures used to refine narrow, relatively unimportant rules and regulations are also used to adopt constitutional reforms. However, the lack of formal distinctions between constitutional and ordinary law has not noticeably sped up the process of reform, because constitutional conservatism is evident throughout English history (as is the use of hyperbole).

English history demonstrates both the robustness of governments based on the king-and-council template and the emergence of opportunities for constitutional bargaining. England's constitutional core remained extraordinarily stable for long periods of time. Its medieval constitution remained substantially in place for four hundred years, except for two decades in the

[2] It could be argued that Cromwell's *Instrument of Government* (IG) was a formal written constitution. Cromwell adopted it by 1653, but it never really described the fundamental procedures and constraints of English governance. Cromwell clearly had more power in practice than described by the IG, for example, when he rejected more than a fourth of the first parliament elected under its rules. Moreover, the IG was substantially revised in 1657, and governance under the amended "constitution" disintegrated shortly after Cromwell's death in 1658 (Morgan 2001, 375–7; Field 2002, 122–5).

[3] The terms "English" and "British" are used nearly interchangeably in Chapters Twelve and Thirteen because of the continuity of English forms and procedures. (It bears noting, however, that governance in the kingdoms of Scotland and Ireland were also based on the medieval forms of the king-and-council template.)

seventeenth century, with only minor reforms and counter-reforms. In the nineteenth century, this stability ended and parliamentary dominance was cemented into place. Its modern constitution emerged gradually between 1828 and 1928 and has been very stable since then. Table 13.1 at the end of Chapter Thirteen lists four dozen significant reforms of the procedures of British governance spread unevenly over the course of eight centuries.

Episodes of reforms of the written parts of the constitution are concentrated for the most part in five periods: (a) in the mid-fourteenth century, during which parliament took its medieval bicameral form: a House of Commons representing county and town governments and a House of Lords representing nobles and senior church administrators, each with veto power on taxes and legislation; (b) in the early sixteenth century, when a new national church was established and it and the church courts were brought under the control of the sovereign via acts of parliament; (c) between 1688 and 1702, when new parliamentary authority over budgets and taxation was obtained, and routine meetings of parliament emerged; (d) between 1825 and 1835, when the medieval electoral practices for selecting members of the House of Commons and local governments were reformed, partly at the behest of organized reform groups outside parliament; and (e) from 1910 to 1928, when universal suffrage was adopted and the House of Lords lost its absolute veto power.

The unwritten constitution also underwent substantial reform during the late eighteenth and early nineteenth centuries as royal deference to parliament increased, the use of the royal veto declined, the House of Lords increasingly deferred to the House of Commons on money bills, and cabinet governance emerged. The suffrage reforms of 1430, 1832, 1867, and 1884 were also significant changes in the manner in which governments were formed and disciplined. Recent membership in the European Union and modifications of the House of Lords also affect the core procedures and constraints of contemporary English governance. However, the essential architecture of its government (bicameral parliament with a royal executive) and its main procedures for selecting members of parliament, sovereigns, and public policies have been stable for centuries at a time.

Several striking examples of institutional robustness occur in the seventeenth century, as discussed later in this chapter, during which the medieval English constitution was stretched to the breaking point and then rebounded to its old medieval form several times. The great "reforms" of 1660 (the Restoration) and 1689 (the Glorious Revolution) can best be understood as reversions to England's long-standing medieval constitution.

Overall, the evolution of the English constitution provides a nearly perfect illustration of the manner in which new opportunities for constitutional bargaining arise and how reforms can take place without major effects on core procedures or constitutional architecture.

Instead of a cumbersome amendment process, the stability of the English constitution is a consequence of the political interests and institutional conservatism of members of parliament, who tend to be well served by the rules that bring them to positions of authority. Informal bargaining equilibria between parliament and the crown and other informal norms of governance are essentially sacrosanct. For example, after 1911, the written constitution could be modified at any time by a simple majority of the House of Commons, but no significant structural changes were adopted until 1998, when parliaments were reestablished in Scotland, Wales, and Northern Island, and in 1999 when the hereditary basis of membership in the House of Lords was substantially reduced, although not eliminated.[4] Although there is no formal distinction between constitutional reform and ordinary legislation, it is well recognized by members of parliament and voters that some changes in law are more important than others.

THE MEDIEVAL PARLIAMENTS OF CATHOLIC ENGLAND: 1200–1500

In the thirteenth century, a number of agreements were negotiated between the barons and the English king, the most famous of which was the *Magna Carta*, signed at Runnymede in 1215. As often the case in English constitutional history, the immediate problem underlying constitutional reform was tax revenue. In exchange for an agreement by the barons to pay more taxes in the present, in 1215, King John negotiated and accepted in writing a variety of terms, including the right of a jury trial by one's peers and the right of a council of barons to reject future increases in taxation. The medieval baronial council characterized in the *Magna Carta* and its veto power over new taxes established the legal foundation of the medieval parliament.

[4] The new parliaments are essentially regional assemblies. Scottish, Welsh, and Irish members continue to sit in a single national parliament. The rules for membership in the House of Lords have been revised several times in the past half century. Lifetime memberships in this chamber (nonhereditary peers) were created in 1958. The number of hereditary peers eligible for voting in the House of Lords was reduced to ninety-two in 1999.

The possibility of eliminating the House of Lords all together has recently been seriously debated, and various alternatives to hereditary membership voted on in Commons (McLean, Spirling, and Russell 2003). Of course, debate about the proper role of the House of Lords has a long history. Indeed this chamber was eliminated for about a decade, along with the sovereign, during the English Civil War (1649–60).

The agreement was not entirely self-enforcing, and the authority of the baronial council had to be reaffirmed several times. These reaffirmations occasionally required civil war between the barons and the king, as in the mid-thirteenth century.

The council of barons became an essentially permanent part of English governance after "the provision" was adopted in Oxford in 1258, which also extended its authority somewhat by allowing it to appoint a few government officials.[5] During a subsequent military confrontation of the baronial council and the king, representatives of counties and towns were invited to participate in baronial meetings and the name "parliament" came into use.

Simon de Monfort (the Earl of Leicester) invited four knights from each county to join the barons in a parliament in 1264. Two representatives from the major towns (boroughs) were invited to the second Montfort parliament in 1265, which became the basis for the House of Commons. King Henry III eventually won the civil war against the Montfort and his barons, although the king was held as Montfort's prisoner for a short period. Broad support for Montfort's broader assembly, however, caused it to become standard English practice after 1295 (Field 2002, 48; Ransome 1883, 64–71).

As a consequence of a series of bargains between the crown and the barons, the authority of baronial councils on tax matters continued, and parliaments continued to be called by Henry III's son Edward I.[6] Inviting prominent commoners to meetings of the baronial councils, "knights of the shire and burgesses," also became routine. These parliaments voted on new tax proposals, heard petitions from the public, petitioned the king to address various grievances, and occasionally impeached senior government officials (Lyon 1980, chapter 34). Although town and county leaders (burgesses and knights) were not always called to meetings of the nobles,

[5] The council of barons included senior church officials and nobles with very large land holdings. Even before the *Magna Carta*, the Constitutions of Clarendon had accorded baronial status to the Catholic Church's archbishop and bishops in 1164.

Essentially, the Constitutions of Clarendon described procedures for establishing jurisdiction on legal matters and for appeal. According to Clarendon, the top appeal from both the ecclesiastical and the king's courts (which both considered criminal matters, murder, and the like) were to end with the king, rather than with the pope in Rome. (Appeals to Rome, however, were restored in relatively short order, although revised again four centuries later under Henry VIII.)

[6] Richardson (1928) provides convincing evidence that the term "parliament" and some of parliament's duties were imported from France. The precursors to the English parliament are, however, far older than the use of this term. Previous national assembles include the Witan and Witenagemot, imported from Germany after the Romans left, and the Grand Council (Magnum Concilium) from the twelfth century (Ransome 1883, 6–9, 52–4).

after 1295, they were routinely called to the meetings that considered tax increases. Edward I called forty-six parliaments in thirty-five years.

The familiar bicameral architecture of the English parliament emerged in the fourteenth century. After 1341, nobles and church leaders began meeting separately from the town and county representatives. The barons of the upper chamber normally met with the king directly and consequently had the power to initiate legislation of various kinds as well as to negotiate with the king on his requests for new taxes (subsidies). The lower chamber was the inferior body at this point and was not routinely consulted about new legislation, although it was routinely consulted on tax matters (Field 2002, 50–4; Lyon 1980, 52–3).

The authority of the baronial council and parliament over taxation was essentially self-enforcing because tax assessments were fairly general and so affected essentially all nobles. The barons had common interests and these, together with their combined military force in the Middle Ages, made it difficult for the king to reduce the baronial council's veto over taxation. On other policy issues and less important constitutional issues, however, the alignment of baronial interests was less complete, and their powers were more limited. For example, members of parliament never had complete freedom of speech within parliament during the medieval period, although it was often asked for and temporarily granted by the crown. In other periods, kings and queens often punished outspoken "radical" members of the House of Commons, and they did so with the approval of other factions in the Commons.

During the early fifteenth century, the House of Commons petitioned the king for a more uniform (and less corrupt) method of choosing local representatives. Three long-standing election statutes were subsequently adopted in 1413, 1429, and 1445 (Stephenson and Marcham 1938, 276–7). The 1413 law required that all county and borough representatives be residents of the communities that they represent. The 1429 law characterized suffrage rules for electing county representatives to the House of Commons. County suffrage was based on "a freeholding to the value of 40 shillings by the year at least above all charges." This enfranchised about 5 percent of the male population of the time, which tended to increase slowly through time with inflation and economic growth.[7] The 1445 law required that town representatives have a similar status (sufficient wealth to be a knight) and specified that

[7] The very gradual doubling of male suffrage in the next four hundred years is a testimony to the power of Malthus's model of population dynamics before the Industrial Revolution.

In century before the Great Reform, the county electorates, under the forty-shilling rule for parliamentary elections, still entitled just 5 percent of the population (Fields 2002, 62,

two representatives should be selected from each borough. Representation was not uniform throughout the kingdom, however, because no effort was made to construct boroughs of equal size.

These laws, which established procedures and qualifications for the House of Commons, are of particular interest because they remained essentially unchanged for four hundred years. They are also noteworthy because national suffrage and representation was relatively broad by the standards of the fifteenth century. The members of both chambers of parliament were either wealthy individuals or in the employ of such persons. Members were not paid a salary for serving in parliament until 1911. Members of the House of Commons were elected from electorates of very different sizes, often with quite different nomination procedures and election rules (Stephenson and Marcham 1938, 276–7; Lyon 1980, 542–3; Field 2002, 62).

For the most part, the late-medieval English parliament was a consultative body on matters other than taxation, a broad sounding board for royal policies, and a source of information about regional problems. Parliaments met when called by the king and were dismissed when the king thought they had met long enough or when the king accepted the parliamentary petitions for redress (whichever came first). Parliamentary sessions were normally relatively short meetings lasting two or three weeks. The longest session in the fourteenth century was the Good Parliament of 1376, which lasted for ten weeks. English kings had the power to overrule parliament on essentially all matters of law except new taxes.

The influence of the early parliaments varied considerably. During times of peace, they could use the standing royal income sources to avoid unpleasant discussions with the parliament over parliamentary status and authority. During times of war, however, the kings needed additional subsidies and would routinely call parliaments to request additional tax revenues. These temporary taxes were not freely given even in times of crisis. For example, Henry V granted the House of Commons veto power on legislation as well as taxation in 1414, at a time when war with France was pending and obtaining new taxes was of great importance (Lyon 1980, 605; Field 2002, 65; Morgan 2001, 228).

Parliament could often influence policies on trade, religion, and economic policy in exchange for temporary increases in royal tax revenues. At occasional peaks of power, parliaments might also be delegated

141, and 167). This suggests that the distribution of wealth remained as concentrated at the start of Industrial Revolution as it had been four hundred years earlier, although it had shifted somewhat among elite families.

significant oversight responsibility. There were also cases in which parliaments were instrumental in replacing an errant king and/or in confirming a successor when the sovereign died without legitimate children. At such times, kings would often accept parliamentary conditions for accession. For example, in 1310 the parliament appointed a committee of twenty bishops and lords to oversee the kingdom's finances. In 1399 the English parliament sentenced former King Richard II to lifetime imprisonment in the Tower of London, in large part for violating the medieval constitution. The throne was declared vacant, and Henry IV was installed in his place.[8]

Such peaks of parliamentary authority, however, were rare and usually short lived. During the Catholic period, kings (and their executive cabinets) were the primary center of policy-making authority within the governments of England.[9] Medieval parliaments were normally of tertiary importance. They were not self-calling. Neither the House of Lords nor the House of Commons had its own permanent meeting place until 1512 and 1549 respectively. Before that time, space for meetings was made available by the king, usually in his palace at Westminster (the site of the present Parliament).[10] Indeed the term House of Lords was not used to describe the noble chamber until 1544 (Field 2002, 69). The second most powerful organization in England in this period was usually the Catholic Church, rather than parliament.

The church controlled very large land holdings, had its own court system, and was directly represented at court and within the parliament. The "lords spiritual" (bishops, abbots, and priors) often formed a majority of the House of Lords during this period, and senior church officials were often among the king's most important ministers.[11] The church hierarchy could use the power of the pulpit to mobilize public opinion throughout England

[8] This was not a peaceful change of office, but was engineered by a group of barons lead by Henry while Richard II was away in Ireland. Nonetheless, the calling of a parliament to accept Richard's resignation, sentence him to life imprisonment, and approve the accession of Henry IV revealed that parliament had become a source of legitimacy and approval by English elites (Morgan 2001, 220–2, Ransome 1883, 85–6).

[9] Executive councils analogous to cabinets had long been used by kings for advice and for administrative and judicial purposes under such names as the Curia Regis and the privy council.

[10] It was also not until the sixteenth century that the respective chambers began keeping careful records of their meetings. Parliamentary records begin in 1510 for the House of Lords and 1542 for the Commons, respectively (Fields 2002, 69).

[11] By the end of the fourteenth century, the House of Lords had become largely hereditary and consisted of the "Lords Temporal," composed of the top five ranks of the nobility (Duke, Marquess, Earl, Viscount, and Baron) and the "Lords Spiritual" from the top three

and could also negotiate for new privileges and discreetly protect those that it had previously obtained behind closed doors at court. For hundreds of years, the Catholic Church was the only large organization within England that was substantially beyond the control of the king(s) of England, although that was soon to change.

Although parliaments had nontrivial influence on taxes and legislation in the fifteenth century, the sovereign could usually influence how votes would be cast in both chambers. English sovereigns controlled appointments to several hundred relatively well-paid positions of authority throughout the kingdom that could be used to increase parliamentary support in various ways. Kings could also influence elections to the House of Commons by appealing to national interests and by rewarding local elites who controlled seats in Commons. Kings could determine the membership and rank in the House of Lords through elevation. During the fifteenth and sixteenth centuries, about a fourth of noble families were replaced each generation.

Between patronage and occasional threats, an ambitious king could usually "manufacture" a compliant parliament.[12]

PARLIAMENT AND THE PROTESTANT REFORMATION: 1500–1625

The next two centuries were turbulent times intellectually, socially, and politically, as the Catholic universe underwent major revisions. With the discovery of the New World, the physical world that Europeans had "known" for centuries had to be revised substantially. The new continents of North and South America as well as the new southern sea routes to the East became new domains of European economic and political conflict for the next three or four centuries.[13] The balance of military power and

ranks of the church (Bishop, Abbot, and Prior). See the "History of the House of Lords," www.parliament.the-stationery-office.co.uk/pa/ld199798/ldbrief/ldhist.htm.

12 In most cases, replacement was necessary because a family lacked legitimate heirs; in others, replacement was a consequence of punishments that stripped families of privilege. Clearly both, but especially the latter, gave a king considerable power over the House of Lords. The total number of nobles was fairly stable during this period, ranging between fifty-five and fifty-seven (Field 2002, 67).

Kings would also occasionally threaten and/or pack the House of Commons. For example, in 1398, Richard II once surrounded the meeting place of parliament with archers, with bows drawn and ready to shoot. The power to incorporate new towns and counties was used by Henry VI to add fifty-three persons (of the two hundred seventy-seven) to the 1447 House of Commons.

13 At first, the new discoveries were simply interpreted within the existing frame of reference. Columbus (1492) insisted that he had found a new Western route to the Far East. However, his discoveries were reinterpreted by other explorers in the years following his famous

economic wealth changed with control over the new territories and sea routes. Revolutions of the spiritual and intellectual worlds also occurred at about the same time. The movable-type printing press developed by Gutenburg in the previous century brought the thoughts of Aristotle, Luther (1507), and Calvin (1534) to all who could read, and their interpreters brought their ideas to all who would listen.[14] By the century's end, the work of Copernicus (1473–1543), Galileo (1564–1642), and Kepler (1571–1630) had also begun to produce a new physical universe and, perhaps more important in the long run, a new scientific method that two or three centuries later would produce the technology for a new civilization (Margolis 2002).

By middle of the sixteenth century, there was no longer a single unified church in Europe, and no longer were European political and economic interests concentrated within the northwestern corner of the great Euro-Asian land mass. All this led to a good deal of military conflict, which was often good for parliaments throughout Europe, although it was not good for Europe itself. Conflict is expensive, and the winner-take-all nature of warfare tends to induce escalation in the resources committed to individual battles and to wars as a whole. The kings and queens of Europe were increasingly in need of additional tax revenue, which induced English kings to call parliaments more frequently to vote on tax proposals and to lend their support to new secular and religious laws.

In turn, parliaments often asked for and received various "privileges" such as freedom from arrest during parliament sessions. Parliament also obtained its own permanent meeting place in the sixteenth century. Many other constitutional and quasi-constitutional bargains were also consummated during the sixteenth century.[15]

voyages. And his new route to the Far East became the new Western continents. Perhaps the most famous of these revisionists was the Medici bank representative Vespucci, who declared the western lands to be a "new world" (*mudus novus*) after several voyages. In honor of his controversial conclusion, and perhaps because of his control of the substantial Medici financial assets, his first name, Americus, began showing up on maps of the New World shortly thereafter.

[14] Criticism of Catholic doctrines and church behavior had, of course, long existed in Europe, among both educated elites and illiterate peasant churchgoers. However, the grumbling of a few intellectuals and nonconformists on doctrine and various critical assessments of the behavior of church leaders did not produce a powerful mass movement until shortly after 1500.

[15] The Houses of Lords and Commons received permanent space in Westminster Palace in 1512 and 1550 respectively, albeit after a fire induced the king to move to other quarters (Field 2002, 69).

Constitutional Exchange during the English Reformation

English kings and queens often accepted recommendations of parliament in policy areas in which royal and parliamentary interests were closely aligned. In such cases, acts of parliament helped legitimize royal policies that might otherwise be controversial and also created precedents for broader parliamentary authority. For much the same reason, Henry VIII used several acts of parliament to secure control over the Catholic Church and its resources in England during the English reformation. These acts indirectly expanded the English parliament's authority over religious matters at the same time that they reduced that of the Catholic Church.

The first recorded majority vote in the House of Lords occurred in its consideration of the 1532 Act in Conditional Restraint of Annates, which ended payments to Rome by clergy appointed to public offices (benefices). Parliament's Act of Appeal (1533) made the sovereign the highest court in the land, ending appeals to Rome by ecclesiastical courts.[16] The Act of Supremacy (1534) made the sovereign the "supreme head in earth of the Church of England called Anglicana Ecclesia." The Bill for Dissolution of the Lower Houses (1536) closed the smallest monasteries and confiscated their assets for the king. In 1539, a similar bill closed the larger monasteries and allowed Henry to confiscate their assets as well. The Statute of Six Articles (1539) codified Henry's theological dicta for the new Anglican Church. Insofar as Henry VIII "deferred" to these acts, he had implicitly recognized a substantial expansion of parliamentary authority.

Henry VIII's interest in church reform was partly personal, a desire for divorce that could not easily be approved by the Catholic Church, and partly economic, his government needed resources to fight wars and reward supporters. The church had enormous assets within England – perhaps more than Henry's. Taking over the church also advanced his constitutional interests by providing him with more complete control of English governance and society. The church, its judicial system, properties, doctrines, courts, and pulpits had been largely beyond his control. Its lands could be used for revenue and as a manner of extending his control over parliament.

[16] This jurisdictional dispute was a long-standing bone of contention for the sovereign regarding the church. For example, similar authority had been sought long before in the Constitutions of Clarendon adopted in 1164. The church negotiated with King Henry II on this matter for many years, eventually inducing the king to reverse his position over the course of a decade (Morgan 2001, 144–5; see also the *Catholic Encyclopedia*). The rapid spread of the Protestant revolution throughout Europe prevented the church from obtaining similar results in the sixteenth century.

The parliament's interests were less than perfectly aligned with those of the sovereign in this case because the Catholic bishops and senior abbots had long been members of the House of Lords. However, most "temporal" members of parliament (the nobles without senior church positions) had an interest in expanding the domain of parliamentary authority and in finding tax sources other than their own property and income; and many also sought to reform the church itself. The latter is not to say that a majority in the Houses of Commons or Lords were Protestants in the modern sense of the word, but rather that the problems of corruption and doctrinal inconsistencies within the church were widely acknowledged, if not widely discussed (because of fear of being punished for heresy). Moreover, many of the temporal members of parliament would have anticipated their subsequent acquisition of monastic lands from the king and their relatively advantaged position in subsequent parliaments. Most of the members of the House of Commons and the temporal lords thus had economic and political interests in "clerical reform" that paralleled those of Henry VIII. Two-thirds of the monastic lands acquired had been sold, rented, or given away by 1547, and three-quarters by 1558. Much of the sovereign's newly found wealth was devoted to military ventures. Much of the remainder was dispensed as patronage to Henry's supporters (Morgan 2001, 285; Field 2002, 68).[17]

In addition, parliament obtained advantages in the long run that Henry VIII did not fully anticipate. By asking the parliament to ratify the laws reforming the church, Henry not only had expanded the scope of parliamentary authority, but implicitly had elevated parliament's statute law above all others. The English Church was reformed by formal acts of parliament, rather than divine revelation or royal fiat. After the reformation, parliament continued to be consulted on religious matters. For example, Edward VI induced parliament to pass the first (1548) and second uniformity (1552) acts, which made English, rather than Latin, the language of the Anglican Church, and it also required church attendance. Queen Mary

[17] In a few cases, nonetheless, Henry found it necessary to threaten pivotal members of parliament to bring them into line on important votes (Morgan 2001, 283). For example, in a private meeting with a prominent member of the House of Commons, Edward Montague, King Henry reportedly took Montague by the ear and said "Get my bill passed by tomorrow, or else tomorrow this head of yours will be off."

The royal threat was not entirely credible, in that the courts might have decided otherwise, but it was not an idle threat. The king often induced parliament to pass bills of attainder against unpopular political opponents and reluctant public servants who forfeited their life and property to the sovereign as penalty for treason (such as disloyalty to the sovereign). The bill was passed the next day (Field 2002, 70).

subsequently induced the parliament to reinstate the links to the Papacy, reinstate laws against heresy, and repeal much of Reformation law, which parliament did, albeit with the proviso that monastic lands not be restored. (The latter suggests that parliament was not at this point entirely motivated by religious interests.) Mary's heresy laws were rigorously enforced and at least 287 persons were burned at the stake (Morgan 2001, 298–9). Elizabeth I subsequently reestablished royal supremacy and full Protestant worship through acts of parliament in 1559.

These acts changed the fundamental relationship between the church and the state in England and also changed the perceived importance of parliamentary decisions throughout the country. Religion was a very important part of life in medieval Europe. The members of parliament expected to play a significant role in religious controversies from that point on, and did so. The balance of interests represented in the House of Lords was also affected by the Reformation. After 1539, there were fewer lords spiritual, because only the bishops and archbishops of the new Anglican Church were members of the House of Lords. The "Lords Temporal" formed a secure majority in the House of Lords *for the first time.*[18]

In other respects, the post-Reformation parliament was similar to what it had been in Catholic times. The domain of parliament's authority had expanded somewhat, but the parliament's main area of authority remained taxes. Its basis for membership was not fundamentally altered, although fewer church officials were included in the House of Lords. Its authority over public policy remained grounded in medieval documents, precedents, and informal customs and norms. The king continued to determine when parliaments would be called and when they would end. As a consequence, the timing of sessions of parliament tended to reflect the state of government finances. The House of Lords remained the most important chamber.

Ongoing Fiscal Bargaining between King and Parliament

The English government was largely "self-funding" during times of peace, relying on income from royal lands (which had expanded because of lands taken from the Catholic Church during the Reformation) and tariffs. Additional revenue beyond the control of parliament could be obtained by

[18] With the closing of the monasteries, the abbots and priors ceased being members of the House of Lords. Prior to 1539, the lords spiritual had often been a majority in the House of Lords at meetings of parliament. www.parliament.the-stationery-office.co.uk/pa/ld199798/ldbrief/ldhist.htm

selling monopoly privileges in what would otherwise have been competitive markets. Royal appointments were also often for sale. Parliament-approved tax receipts accounted for less then 10 percent of royal income during this period. Revenues from royal companies and colonies were also beyond the control of parliament.

Kings and queens independently increase their revenues by changing their policies with respect to sales of monopoly, government positions, and by investing in colonial enterprises. Towns, guilds, and entrepreneurs sought and received privileges to be exclusive producers of goods and services, and they often paid for their privileges. Oxford and Cambridge, for example, had long held monopolies for higher education. Such monopoly privilege and tariffs, naturally, made the many goods and services more expensive than they otherwise would have been. Monopolies in Elizabeth's time included such products as iron, transport of leather, salt, ashes, vinegar pots, lead, whale oil, currants, and brushes.

Queen Elizabeth's new marketwide monopolies were especially costly and unpopular. She had monopolized previously competitive markets and as a consequence prices for many ordinary products increased. Public demonstration opposing the Elizabethan monopolies occurred, and "antitrust" petitions were submitted to Elizabeth by parliament to revoke the monopolies. The queen was evidently persuaded that she had gone too far and eliminated several of her most burdensome monopoly "grants" (Field 2002, 89; Ransome 1883, 118–20).

This economic reform demonstrates that public demonstrations could indirectly affect public policies. Elizabeth's revoking of monopoly privileges reduced and implicitly limited her traditional revenues. Parliament's role in ending the most burdensome monopolies also demonstrates that parliaments were beginning to believe that they could circumscribe traditional sources of royal revenues as well as taxes.

That parliaments in the early seventeenth century were still called for the most part so that a king or queen could obtain additional revenues is suggested by many histories of England. Some fairly detailed accounts of the bargaining in the early seventeenth century are included in Rabb's (1998) biography of Edwin Sandys.

> [In 1610 the] members of **parliament had been recalled, so far as the government was concerned, for one reason and one reason alone: money** …
>
> In the end the members of parliament accepted the king's assurances and decided to "proceed notwithstanding." They now wanted confirmation of the adequacy of their offer, and also a more concrete set of proposals **outlining what the king might surrender in return**. (Rabb 1998, 140, 149)

Sandys can be regarded as an early liberal member of parliament. Sandys was involved in the repeal of Queen Elizabeth's monopolies and subsequently in the management of the Virginia Company that established England's first colony in North America. Rabb's biography of Sandys discusses several instances of fiscal bargaining between the king and House of Commons during his time in parliament. For example, Chapter Six provides a fairly detailed analysis of fiscal-policy bargaining that took place in 1610, as King James I requested new taxes to pay for the suppression of a rebellion in Ireland. Other less detailed accounts of fiscal bargaining can be found in most histories of England.

The Constitutional Political Economy of England in 1603

The late sixteenth and early seventeenth centuries were times of relative prosperity. The age of the shopkeeper emerged as village stores augmented the ancient marketplaces as places of local commerce. A small middle class of merchants, professionals, and successful farmers began to emerge below the nobility. A small leisure industry emerged, which allowed playwrights such as Shakespeare to take up the theater as a full-time occupation. The largest manufacturing industry was the decentralized production of homes, barns, and sheds. Population grew more rapidly than economic output, however, with the result that real wages fell for low- and moderately skilled labor. Food prices increased about twice as fast as wage rates (Morgan 2001, 329).

There were still ongoing theological disputes and tensions within the reformed English Church. Many of these doctrinal disputes were politically important, because of the lack of separation between church and state in England after the reformation. There were, for example, many debates in parliament over what types of church services should be permitted within England. The English Church was relatively tolerant during most of this period and allowed a broad range of services to be held, including those by nonconforming Protestants and Catholics.[19]

Religious disputes, tax revolts, international affairs, and economic growth had produced a modest increase in the authority of parliament, largely through constitutional bargaining. However, the royal family remained by far the wealthiest and most powerful in the kingdom. They had veto power over all parliamentary proposals and complete authority over many areas

[19] The Church of England was relatively tolerant during this time, as indicated by its official name, the Catholic and Reformed Church of England (Morgan 2001, 352).

of public policy. As head of government, they controlled about a thousand senior appointments in the national and regional governments. They also controlled the largest military force in England. Together their wealth and constitutional authority meant that the king (or queen) had a dominant influence over most policy decisions. They continued to rule, for the most part, through their own hand-picked great and privy councils.

The members of the House of Lords were the first-born male children of privileged families and senior members of the Church of England (who were also often from noble families). Members of the House of Commons were elected by about 5 to 10 percent of the wealthiest men in the kingdom under somewhat heterogeneous local election laws.

Kings and queens also had their own advisory and executive councils (great councils and privy councils) that were chosen from the nobility, church, and elite commoners. Many of the royal advisors thus were distinguished members of parliament. The presence of such persons in the executive indicated that their interests were well aligned with those of the king or queen. It did not demonstrate that parliamentary authority had penetrated into the executive. Other members of parliament whose interests were less important or less well aligned with the sovereign's were largely ignored. Short meetings of parliament were called, as necessary to request new taxation and occasionally to pass desired legislation or to affirm the accession of new kings and queens.

There was neither a large standing army nor an organized police force outside major cities. Local militias – small forces maintained by noblemen and the king – existed, rather than national ones. Volunteers marshaled by local leaders, rather than salaried civil servants, provided many local public services. The local county gentry largely determined local services and implemented parliamentary tax and regulatory policy. Day-to-day governance remained largely a local matter until the twentieth century.

Overall, the routines of English medieval governance and economic life were remarkably stable, although they would soon be challenged by constitutional conflicts that arose during the seventeenth century.

COLLAPSE OF THE MEDIEVAL ENGLISH CONSTITUTION AND ITS RESTORATION: 1625–1660

In the early seventeenth century, the medieval constitution of England was stretched to the breaking point by the Stuart kings. The proximate cause of constitutional distress was tax revenue, but this time negotiation with parliament failed to find a mutually agreeable solution. To circumvent parliament's veto over new taxes, James I and his successor Charles I greatly expanded the practice of selling public offices, benefices (local church positions), and monopoly privileges, and they also increased customs duties and tariffs.[20] In addition, the Stuarts made extensive use of "forced loans" and "ship's money" as sources of royal income.[21] Many of the new revenue sources appeared to be taxes in disguise, and others violated long-standing constitutional law and precedent. The latter were regarded as unconstitutional new taxes by many in parliament (and by the courts), but these objections were largely ignored by the sovereign.

When Charles I came to office in 1625, he wanted to finance a war with Spain and France. This required expanding government revenues and creating a national army, which induced him to call parliament three times during his first five years. In exchange for more tax revenues, the parliament demanded a return to the medieval constitution. Parliament wanted the fiscal and judicial practices of James I reversed and refused to provide subsidies of the magnitude that Charles I requested. In 1628, the parliament submitted the *Petition of Right*, which formally listed grievances against the king and sought to have Charles I affirm constitutional practices that parliament argued had been in place since the *Magna Carta*.

The Duke of Buckingham, acting on Charles I's behalf, attempted to pack the House of Lords by selling peerages to his supporters in order to obtain a favorable decision on government revenues.[22] The numbers of peers more than doubled from fifty-five in 1603 to one hundred twenty-six in 1628. James I and Charles I also applied harsh and somewhat arbitrary punishment to those who violated their mandates, using royal courts in a manner that violated long-standing procedures and norms of the English court system. Charles refused to accept parliamentary petitions of grievances, and after 1629, did not call another parliament for more than a decade.

Instead, he raised money from other sources. In many cases, Charles I simply began enforcing laws that had fallen into disuse in a manner that

[20] In 1623, James I accepted parliament's *Statute of Monopolies* which greatly reduced but did not eliminate the ability of the crown to sell monopolies. For example, monopolies for "technical improvements" and restrictive corporate charters could still be sold (Price 1913, 35–42).

[21] Ships money was a demand for money from port cities that would evidently be collected from ships as increased fees for port services. For parliament and its supporters, the constitutional issue was whether this was a tax or not. If it was a tax, then parliamentary approval would have been necessary (Cross 1914, 466; Morgan 2001, 313).

[22] Buckingham was impeached in 1627, but Charles dismissed parliament to end the proceedings (Field 2002, 99). Buckingham was subsequently murdered in 1628 (Morgan 2001, 349).

produced significant revenues from fines (as with the Royal forest laws). His more extensive collection of Ship's Money, however, extended an old practice for new purposes. English kings had customary rights to request Ships money from coastal communities that did not provide ships for national defense. Charles I attempted to collect ships money from all communities, not just coastal ones. His fiscal innovations allowed him to balance the budget without parliamentary subsidies after the war with France and Spain was over. Naturally, questions about the constitutionality of some of the royal income sources, as well as the burden of the new royal revenue sources, tended to undermine Charles' support within parliament.

Charles I's religious policies also reduced his support among Protestant members of parliament, especially Puritans. At his request, archbishop Laud tightened control of church practices and doctrine and forbade some of the practices used by nonconforming Puritan churches. Some forms of recreation, such as archery and Morris dancing, were also forbidden on Sundays. Puritan suspicions of papist conspiracies were reinforced by Charles' marriage with Henrietta Maria of France (a Catholic) and also by his alliances with Irish and Scottish Catholics to suppress the rebellious Presbyterian Scots.

Together, his violations of the medieval constitution and religious policies caused political, economic, and religious opposition to intensify in many of the groups and regions represented in parliament. When parliament was finally called again in 1640 to help finance and ratify the settlement with the Scots, not only was parliament's bargaining position unusually strong, but its opposition to royal policies was also unusually strong. The Stuart neglect of the long-standing English constitution had created a major constitutional crisis.

The 1640 parliament met in mid-April. A majority of parliament was willing to finance the war in Scotland, but in exchange insisted on a return to the medieval constitution, as had the previous parliament more than a decade earlier. The House of Commons complained about religious innovations, the sale of monopolies, ships duties, the expansion of royal forests, military charges, the violation of civil liberties, and his failure to call parliament into session for more than a decade.[23]

The House of Commons petitioned the House of Lords for a joint meeting, which was agreed to. Constitutional grievances were again voiced, but

[23] A list of claims against Charles I can be found in the *Journal of the Commons, II, 10f.* Excerpts from the proceedings of the Short Parliament can be found at www.constitution.org/sech/sech_095.htm.

no actions were taken. The king argued that all his policies were necessary for the safety of the nation and dismissed the "short" parliament on May 5, 1640. The two all-or-nothing offers made by parliament were tabled, rather than resolved through negotiation and constitutional exchange.

In November of 1640, parliament was again summoned, partly at the insistence of the Scots, who refused to accept a peace settlement unless it was ratified by parliament. This time, parliament was able to press for and obtain formal agreements with Charles I that affirmed the power of parliament. Much of the new legislation simply formalized long-standing medieval practices, but significant constitutional reforms were adopted. For example, the new legislation included the Triennial Act (no. 27: 144), which required parliament to be called at least once every three years and allowed parliament to be self-calling if no royal writs were forthcoming after three years. A subsequent act (no. 30: 158) prevented the king from unilaterally dissolving parliament.

These two acts made sessions of parliament autonomous of the sovereign for the first time in English history, and the latter was the constitutional basis under which parliament continued to meet throughout the English Civil War. (The "long" parliament did not formally dissolve itself until 1660.) In exchange, parliament passed and the king accepted the Tonnage and Poundage Act (no. 31: 159), which legitimated retroactively many of the "ship money" charges used to finance governance by James and Charles and extended them into the future, *but only for two months*. This freed James from various legal challenges to his past revenue sources, but it also made future royal solvency somewhat more dependent on parliamentary majorities (Gardiner 1906, vol. iii).

The king's authority to intervene directly on legal matters in the secular and religious courts was eliminated by acts that eliminated the Star Chamber and High Commission (no. 34 and 35). The consequent reduction in prosecutions for treasonous matters unleashed a torrent of popular pamphlets (Field 2002, 106). The use of ships money to finance the expansion of the navy was subsequently repealed (no. 36: 189), which increased parliament's future authority over public policy by reducing royal revenues. Supermajorities in parliament favored the reforms of 1640–1.

CONSTITUTIONAL BARGAINING FAILS AND THE ENGLISH CIVIL WAR BEGINS

To this point, it can be argued that the constitutional legislation of 1640–1 simply reclaimed and formalized authority that parliament had had or at least claimed to have at its various peaks of power during the previous three hundred years. It formalized the long-standing practice of summoning parliaments every few years, reestablished a more independent court system, and affirmed parliament's veto over new taxes and other tax-like revenue sources. After the Civil War had run its course and the crown was "restored" to Charles' son, Charles II, this is also approximately where English governance found itself in 1660. Similar rules were adopted again in 1689 at the accession of William and Mary. In this sense, one could argue that there were three restorations of England's medieval constitution during the seventeenth century.

The robustness of the medieval constitution, however, was not obvious in 1641. Tensions between parliament and king escalated rather than diminished in spite of the agreements reached. The "long parliament" and Charles I continued to maneuver for control of public policy and subsequently for control of the army. As parliament attempted to reduce the sovereign's authority to less than its traditional medieval levels, support, especially in the House of Lords, dwindled and the parliament split into "royalist" and "parliamentary" camps. Their disagreements about the proper balance of authority escalated to open civil war in 1642.

The royalist minority withdrew (and was subsequently excluded) from the parliamentary sessions in Westminster as the military phase of the Civil War began. Departure of the royalist members, chiefly from the House of Lords, reduced the parliament by about half its original numbers. Many of the royalists joined the king's parliament that met in Oxford in 1644; although, the king's "mongrel parliament" met only once (Field 2002: 110). Constitutional negotiations between Charles I and the Westminster parliament continued throughout the Civil War, but no agreements could be reached about the major constitutional issues.

Parliament won the war, which produced many years of radical constitutional experimentation by the parliament. Charles I was tried for treason by the Westminster parliament. The majority of the antiroyalist members, who made up the post–Civil War parliament, found for treason and favored execution, but a minority thought that execution would overturn the constitution and favored a less radical solution. To advance revolutionary aims, the majority decided to exclude the moderates from parliament. This new "rump" of the original long parliament sentenced Charles to death in 1649, eliminated the House of Lords, and declared England a commonwealth.[24]

[24] In December 1648, Colonel Pride reduced parliament by excluding 110 members (arresting forty and barring seventy others). The resulting rump parliament was essentially purged of

The execution of Charles I must have appeared to be an irreversible "reform" to the republican majority of the much-reduced parliament. The execution of Charles I made it impossible for the excluded members of parliament (the previously excluded royalists and the recently excluded moderates) to rally to the king and restore the monarchy.

The details of the Civil War and much of the parliamentary politics during the war are largely beyond the scope of this book, in that they clearly violated long-standing constitutional practices and failed to have lasting institutional effects on English governance. The failure of the king and parliament to find a compromise, nonetheless, serves as a useful illustration of how divided governments can produce civil war when uncompromising factions emerge that are willing to violate standing procedures and norms. (It was partly this failure to come to terms that led Thomas Hobbes (1651), writing in the safety of France, to insist that nations should have only a single sovereign authority.) The failure of parliament's constitutional experiments to produce a stable government provides a useful illustration of the difficulty of engineering major reforms of governance.

The Agreement of the People of 1649, a Liberal Constitutional Proposal

The next decade was truly a revolutionary period. After Charles I's execution, the rump parliament attempted to draft a republican constitution. Their negotiations were influenced by new theories of governance that had emerged in the years before and during the Civil War. The most influential of which was the Agreement of the Free People of England, a surprisingly modern social contract (1649) supported by one of the first English constitutional interest groups, the Levellers. The agreement was written, widely disseminated within England, and actively supported two years before Hobbes finished his famous work on the social contract in 1651, and more than four decades before Locke finished his treatises on government in 1689.

The Agreement of the People was written by four men while imprisoned in the Tower of London. It was evidently based partly on earlier proposals. It proposed a series of radical liberal reforms to English governance,

moderates. The new rump parliament included only about a sixth of the original 1640 parliament. A majority of this radical rump voted for the king's execution. The rump majority included less than a tenth of the original 1640 parliament (Morgan 2001, 370, 372). In 1649, Charles was beheaded for constitution crimes (treason). The excluded group is likely to have included many who were originally in the "anti–Charles I" majority of the 1640 parliament, given the reduced attendance at parliamentary sessions.

essentially a new constitution. Article I states that "the supreme authority of England shall reside" in a new four hundred member unicameral parliament, with paid members and representation "proportionate to the respective parts of the nation." Article II states that the "major voices" of parliament will be supreme ("shall be concluding to this nation") and that more than half the members to parliament will be elected. The elected members will choose the speaker of the parliament. Article III requires that all governmental officials be accountable to law and parliament.

Article VIII specifies annual elections for elected members of parliament. Article IX lists the duties of government: (a) foreign policy (peace and commerce); (b) maintenance of "our lives, limbs, liberties, properties, and estates"; and (c) raising money, extending freedom, redress of grievances, and promoting prosperity. Article XI specifies that "all privileges or exemptions of any persons from the laws, or from the ordinary course of legal proceedings, by virtue of any Tenure, Grant, Charter, Patent, Degree, or Birth, or of any place of residence, or refuge, or privilege of Parliament, shall be henceforth void and null; and the like not to be made nor revived again." Articles XVIII and XIX call for reducing regulation of international trade. Article XXI calls for limits on the death penalty and the payment of damages to victims.[25]

The supporters of the agreement became known as the Levellers, because most argued for the end of social privileges. (A few also argued for a major redistribution of wealth through land reform.)

The Leveller proposals and other controversies during the period of the republic are important for subsequent English constitutional developments. This is not because they succeeded, which they did not, but because they focused on issues that continued to play central roles in the constitutional debates of England and much of Europe for the next two centuries. Indeed, it can be argued that most of their constitutional proposals were gradually adopted in the following two and a half centuries, although very few of their proposals were adopted in the seventeenth century.[26]

[25] A complete copy of this surprisingly modern proposal for a social contract can be found at: www.constitution.org/lev/eng_lev_07.htm.

[26] The proposed social contract was widely circulated within England and must have been known to Thomas Hobbes, who sat out the Civil War in France, where he wrote his famous book, *Leviathan*, published in 1651, in which he articulated a new social contract theory of governance.

The tone of the Hobbes's governance chapters defending an all-powerful sovereign suggests that Hobbes believed that England would have been better off with the French form of monarchy, which was in a relatively autocratic phase, although he hedges a bit by allowing the possibility of an all-powerful parliament. Hobbes's proposed covenant (chapter 17)

The Failure of the "Rump" Parliament and Cromwell's Republic

Instead of placing procedural and policy constraints on itself, as recommended by the Levellers, the rump parliament gradually transferred all remaining political authority to a new executive council of state through a series of acts adopted in the next four years. Oliver Cromwell, the Lord General of the parliament's army evidently decided that this process of constitutional reform was too slow and corrupt – or perhaps, not sufficiently responsive to his advice – and dismissed the rump parliament (by force) in April 1653.

Cromwell proposed a new parliament composed of 140 worthy persons to be selected by local Protestant church congregations (Field 2002, 122). Eight months later, in December 1653, Cromwell announced that he would rule via a new written *Instrument of Government* (IG: no. 97: 405).

Cromwell's new constitution did not break entirely with the long-standing architecture of the English medieval parliaments, but it did change many of its core procedures. The government of the new commonwealth was to be composed of three major branches: (a) the Lord Protector (a lifetime position analogous to a king to be held by Cromwell), (b) an advisory privy council (effectively a royal cabinet), and (c) a unicameral parliament. A four-hundred-man parliament was to be elected and meet every three years. It would remain in session for at least five months. Suffrage (for men) required wealth greater than two hundred pounds (which limited suffrage to the landed gentry). Parliament would initiate all legislation (subject to Cromwell's veto) and would be called on in times of emergency to vote new taxes. When parliament was not in session, the council and Lord Protector would rule. During times of peace, taxes would be sufficient to maintain a thirty-thousand-man army and a naval fleet, and would also provide two hundred thousand pounds per year for administrative purposes.[27] There was to be freedom of worship for Protestants.

Members of the privy council would hold their seats for life. As vacancies arose on the privy council, the parliament would send the protector a list of six names from which the Lord Protector would choose a replacement. The constitution also included a supreme court. All acts of government could

states that citizens accept an oath like the following: "I authorize and give up my right of governing my self *to this man, or to this assembly of men*, on this condition, that thou give up thy right to him and authorize all of his actions in like manner."

(Note that Hobbes allows for the possibility of a republican government with a supreme parliament, "this assembly of men.")

[27] Cromwell's proposed thirty-thousand-man army was about ten times that normally supported in times of peace. Charles II kept a standing army of just three thousand (Morgan 2001, 378).

be challenged in court to determine whether they violated the *Instrument of Government*. The disposition of troops would be jointly controlled by the Lord Protector and the parliament if parliament was in session, or by the Lord Protector and council if not. Evidently, the constitution could be amended through ordinary acts of legislation (no amendment process was mentioned).

Of course, the problem with such a constitution is that if the Lord Protector is sufficiently powerful to impose it unilaterally, he cannot be bound by its rules. This was evident even before the procedures of the new instrument of governance could be implemented. In 1654, following the very first election for parliament under the new suffrage rules, Cromwell excluded 120 elected members he considered hostile to his regime (Gardiner 1906, part V; Field 2002, 123).

Those allowed to take their seats petitioned Cromwell for additional constitutional reforms. Their proposals attempted to make the new government more closely resemble that of England's medieval constitution. In 1657, parliament proposed reinstating the office of king (to be held by Cromwell), which Cromwell refused. They also proposed that the Lord Protector be able to appoint his successor, which Cromwell accepted. They also recommended the creation of a second chamber of parliament (of lifetime peers) to be appointed by the Lord Protector. Cromwell accepted that proposal as well. Cromwell named his son Richard to be his successor and began filling the new elite chamber with loyal Puritan supporters. (Subsequent peers would have to be approved by the existing members of the new house of peers, which would have limited somewhat the opportunities of future kings to assemble a loyal house of peers.)

The process of replacing members of the privy council was also changed to give the Lord Protector, rather than parliament, control over the initial proposal, with veto power in the council and parliament. The elected chamber also gained the right to accept or reject its own members.

The End of the English Republic and the Restoration of Charles II

Overall, it is clear that the 1657 amendments enhanced Cromwell's already considerable authority under the original *Instrument of Government*. It is also clear that the *Instrument of Government*, both before and after amendment, was never a constitution – a document that describes durable procedures for making rules. Its procedures were never fully implemented and did not survive Cromwell's death in 1658.

Although Cromwell's son did temporarily inherit the position of Lord Protector, and he did call for a new parliament; the new parliament met in 1659 for just three months before being (unconstitutionally) dismissed. The authority of the commonwealth subsequently disintegrated in the face of a widespread tax revolt. The new English commonwealth had lasted just six years.

As an alternative to the dysfunctional government, the old rump parliament was reassembled, but then dismissed by the army. In a quest for legitimacy, the surviving members of the more inclusive long parliament were summoned. The old long parliament met, lawfully dissolved themselves, and called for new elections under the rules adopted in 1641, ignoring nearly two decades of constitutional experimentation. The newly elected parliament called for the restoration of the monarchy in the person of Charles II and the restoration of the principle of hereditary succession.

Negotiations with Charles II were undertaken and the result of that bargaining is evident in the 1660 *Declaration of Breda*, which is Charles II's statement of the conditions under which he would "return" to the throne. It includes a clear statement of the divine right of kings: "We can never give over the hope, in good time, to obtain the possession of that right which *God and nature hath made our due*." It also promises to exempt most persons from royal retribution. There was to be a restoration of rights and a free and general pardon (with exceptions to be determined by parliament): "The restoration of *King, Peers and people to their just, ancient and fundamental rights*, we do, by these presents, declare, that we do grant a free and general pardon, which we are ready, upon demand, to pass under our Great Seal of England." Only those who signed his father's death warrant were punished (Morgan 2001, 178). Principles of religious tolerance were to be supported (through an act of parliament), and a royal commitment was made to pay the army its (overdue) past wages (which partly accounts for the military's interest in the Restoration).

And because the passion and uncharitableness of the times have produced several opinions in religion, by which men are engaged in parties and animosities against each other (which, when they shall hereafter unite in a **freedom of conversation**, will be composed or better understood), we do declare a liberty to tender consciences, and that **no man shall be disquieted or called in question for differences of opinion in matter of religion**, which do not disturb the peace of the kingdom; and that we shall be **ready to consent to such an Act of Parliament**, as, upon mature deliberation, shall be offered to us, for the full granting that indulgence. …

We do further declare, that we will be ready to consent to any Act or Acts of Parliament to the purposes aforesaid, and for the full satisfaction of **all arrears due to the officers** and soldiers of the army under the command of General Monk.

By the end of 1660, English governance had returned to its medieval constitution and England's short period of radical constitutional experimentation was over.[28] After two decades of constitutional experimentation, the medieval English constitution was restored.

The Civil War demonstrates the difficulty of major constitutional reforms and also the robustness of England's medieval parliamentary institutions. These, as well as the losses of the Civil War, provided empirical foundations for the constitutional conservatism of many future English voters and political theorists.

FROM RESTORATION TO GLORIOUS REVOLUTION 1660–1689

As part of the negotiations with parliament, all parliamentary acts between August 1641 and the Restoration were annulled, which implied that all the royal properties sold off during the Civil War would be returned to Charles II and his supporters. This, together with the sovereign's traditional access to customs duties, which were affirmed by the 1661 parliament, meant that Charles II could rule without summoning parliament to raise taxes during times of peace. Charles II proclaimed and subsequently promoted a modest extension of freedom of religion, although he also accepted parliament's Test Act (1673), which restricted government offices to Anglican Protestants.

Legislation adopted prior to August 1641, however, had limited some royal revenue sources and eliminated the royal high courts (Star Chamber and High Commission), which meant that Charles was somewhat less autonomous than his father had been, or at least claimed to be. In this respect too, it could be claimed that a restoration had taken place. Charles II's powers of taxation and legislation were not substantially different from those of kings and queens before 1600. He could still call and dismiss parliament at his convenience, subject to the new three-year constraint, and he could still rule by fiat in policy areas other than taxation and those determined by common law.[29]

His return to the monarchy, however, was negotiated by an old and new parliament reconstituted under the medieval rules. Parliament's role in

[28] Breda also dates the beginning of the reign of Charles II from the death of his father twelve years before. "Given under our Sign Manual and Privy Signet, at our Court at Breda, this 4/14 day of April, 1660, in the *twelfth year of our reign*." The full text is available at www.constitution.org/eng/conpur105.htm.

[29] At the time of the Restoration, the Triennial Act was revised to eliminate the "self-calling" of parliament, but the sovereign remained legally obligated to call parliament at least once every three years (Gardiner 1906, vol. III).

those negotiations had implicitly changed its role in government, at least in the minds of many of its members.

After his accession, Charles II pursued the usual political interests of kings. Although he followed the letter of the law with respect to the Triennial Act, elections were avoided altogether for most of Charles's regime by keeping the very royalist 1661 parliament (the Cavalier Parliament) in session for eighteen years without calling for new elections (Morgan 2001, 381). Patronage was used at all levels of government and across all groups to elicit support (Morgan 2001, 379). The long-standing election laws of 1430 were undermined by transforming many borough charters into corporations, which allowed borough members of parliament to be appointed by a handful of town officials, often replacing broader election processes. Less loyal but malleable members of parliament were bribed (Field 2002, 128). The search for new revenues beyond the control of parliament continued unabated.[30]

Toward the end of Charles II's reign, it became clear that Charles's brother James, a Catholic, would be the next in line to the throne because Charles did not have any legitimate children. That prospect produced what many historians regard to be the first nationwide political campaign in England. The Earl of Shaftesbury, a proponent of parliamentary supremacy, formed a political alliance that attempted to pass legislation to block the accession of James to the crown.[31] When Shaftesbury proposed the Exclusion Act in the House of Commons, Charles II simply dissolved the parliament (on three separate occasions). Many members of parliament, particularly in Lords, also opposed excluding James in the House of Lords because it would have broken the long-standing English practice of hereditary succession by adding new religious requirements for accession to the throne (Morgan 2001, 383).

Shaftesbury's efforts demonstrated that an organized group of members of parliament could affect national elections, a lesson that was not forgotten. Their campaign also produced durable party labels that continued to be used for two centuries. The proponents of exclusion came to be called Whigs. The opponents of exclusion came to be called Tories. The "party" labels for the pro and antiexclusion voting blocks were coined as insults by their respective opponents. The term Whig was slang for a group of

30 In return for French subsidies, Charles promised in the secret Treaty of Dover to abolish parliament and provide King Louis XIV the English sovereign after his death (Field 2002, 127). Evidently, King Louis was unfamiliar with recent English history.

31 The length of Charles's first parliament was unprecedented, which had inadvertently allowed more stable political coalitions and leadership to emerge in parliament.

crazy Scottish Presbyterian rebels, and Tory was slang for the papist outlaws of Ireland (Field 2002, 128). A few Whigs were, in fact, Presbyterians, although they could not yet be Scottish. The union with Scotland did not take place for half a century (in 1707). Tory members of parliament were, of course, Anglican Englishmen, rather than Catholics. Members of parliament could not be Irish until the union in 1801 and could not be Catholic until the Test Acts were repealed and the Act of Catholic Emancipation was adopted in 1829.

The Whigs generally opposed Charles II, supported religious toleration for Protestants only, and sought to increase the power of parliament relative to the sovereign. The Tories supported Charles II, the rule of law, established religion, and the hereditary rules of succession.[32] After it was clear that Shaftesbury had lost, he fled to the Netherlands in 1681, followed soon after by his middle-aged protégé, John Locke, in 1683.

James II inherited the crown after Charles I's death in 1685. Like his brother, James received customs duties for life by an act of parliament. But unlike his brother, James II proceeded to rule without parliament, violating the modified Triennial Act (Field 2002, 128). He also exacerbated religious tensions by promoting centralization and a more tolerant, but anti-Anglican policy agenda. For example, he called in town charters and rewrote them to advance the cause of Protestant nonconformists and Catholics. Three-quarters of the local justices of the peace were sacked and replaced with Protestant dissenters beholden to the king (Morgan 2001, 385). A large standing army was organized in which Catholic officers were prominent. Full religious liberty was declared (for Catholics and Protestants), and Anglican clergy were instructed to read his declaration at their services.

Whether James's policies were benevolent efforts to increase religious tolerance, a campaign on behalf of James's fellow believers, or a papist conspiracy, they were clearly policies that made the local elites and dominant religious communities worried about worse things to come.[33] The local gentry and nobles were well organized, as were mainstream Protestants.

[32] The exclusion act would have undermined the "divine right of kings" doctrine. If passed, sovereignty would have depended on criteria adopted by parliament, as well as birth, which would have increased the power of parliament. These constitutional arguments also partly determined the language rationalizing William and Mary's accession to the sovereign in 1689.

[33] Both Charles II and James II were sons of Charles I. Their mother, Henrietta Maria, had been a princess of France. Upon his brother's accession to the crown, James became Duke of York and Duke of Albany (in Scotland). There is evidence that James had raised money from the French king to supplement his revenues in the absence of parliamentary revenues.

And although neither group had an army at their disposal on this occasion, they did have contacts with someone who could potentially raise an army and who had an indirect claim to the throne, namely, Willem III, *stadhouder* of the Netherlands (who would subsequently be known as William III in English history).

In 1687, William III published a letter disapproving of James II's religious policies, but promising not to intervene in England unless he were invited to do so by leading Englishmen. The letter was published and evidently was well received within Protestant circles in England. As the Protestant daughter of the present king, James II, from James' first marriage, William's wife, Mary, was next in the line of succession to the crown after James II, as long as there was no male heir.[34] In 1688, seven prominent Protestant leaders (including five members of the House of Lords, both Whigs and Tories) invited William to drive James II from office in order to protect Protestantism and Mary's claim to the throne. (Parliament, per se, could not extend an invitation, because it had not been called to session since James II had acceded to the throne.)

WILLIAM III, THE DUTCH STATES GENERAL, AND THE ENGLISH PARLIAMENT 1688–1689

William III was not, however, a king with sovereign power, nor did he literally have his own army. William was a middle-aged man, a member of the most distinguished family in the Netherlands, and *stadhouder*, rather than king, of the Netherlands. He was the third stadhouder from that family since the independence of the United Provinces of the Netherlands had been won a century earlier. As stadhouder, William/Willem had considerable authority over the Dutch army, but he had little authority over the navy, which would be needed to transport the Dutch army to England, and he had no budgetary authority to finance the invasion.[35]

[34] Mary was the daughter of James II and his first wife, Anne. William III also had family ties to the English sovereign, as the grandson of Charles I. He and Mary were cousins. The soon-to-be-deposed James II was his uncle (Morgan 2001, table of descendants, appendix).

Perhaps more important for the future of English constitutional developments, however, was the fact that William III was the middle-aged patriarch of the distinguished Dutch Orange-Nassau family, a family that had long been influential in the Netherlands because of the family's implicit claim to the office of *stadhouder*. (William III is Willem III in Dutch histories.)

[35] For more constitutional details of governance in the United Provinces of the Netherlands, see Chapter Fifteen.

To invade England, William had to persuade the Dutch States General that such an invasion would advance Dutch interests. William noted that England had taken the French side in the previous war during the reign of Charles II, which had nearly ended Dutch independence. Another war with France was thought likely in the near future, which would again threaten the survival of the Dutch Republic. William argued that if he could secure the English throne, English resources would support the Dutch, rather than the French, in the next war. This would greatly improve prospects for the Netherlands. The States General were persuaded and agreed to fund William's English strategy.

A Dutch armada carrying twenty thousand troops arrived in England on November 5 (Claydon 2002, 28). A much larger, if much less experienced, British army marched to meet the Dutch invasion. The forty-thousand-man British army folded in disarray after several high-level defections, which led James II to reconsider his plans, retreat, and subsequently flee to France. William and the Dutch army marched essentially without further opposition to London, arriving on December 18. William ordered the remaining members of the English army to leave London, and they did, which placed the city completely in the hands of William and the Dutch army.

The London members of the House of Lords met on Christmas Day 1688 and asked William to take charge of government (Field 2002, 130). They also authorized him to call a "convention" parliament (Claydon 2002, 63). A convention parliament, composed in the usual medieval manner, met in early January 1689. On January 27, the parliament resolved that James II had broken the contract between king and people and had vacated his office (Field 2002, 130). After more internal negotiation and evidently a threat by William to return to the Netherlands with the Dutch army if not offered the crown (Claydon 2002, 63), parliament offered the crown to both William and Mary on February 13, 1689 in an act of parliament that has come to be known as the English Bill of Rights.

Both the offer of the crown and the conditions under which the crown would be accepted were clearly negotiated within parliament as well as between parliament and William and Mary. The reign of William and Mary is the *only time* in which England had two sovereigns.

The Bill of Rights addresses several issues simultaneously. The first part of the Bill of Rights describes why James II was no longer king, even though he was alive and well in France. In short, he had violated the constitution, and, moreover, had "abdicated the government and the throne [is] thereby vacant." The second part lists powers that the previous kings had "pretended" to have, including the power to impose taxes without parliamentary assent and to create their own law courts. These, it was stated, had no basis in long-standing constitutional law. (Many of these grievances had been claimed about previous kings as well, as noted earlier.) The second part lists various rights – the right of free speech in parliament, the right to bear arms for self-defense, the right to a fair and speedy trial by jury – and suggests that "for redress of all grievances, and for amending, strengthening and preserving the laws, Parliament ought to be held frequently." (Most of these rights had been claimed by parliaments since the fourteenth century. It could thus be said that section two tries to reset the constitutional clock back to August 1641 once again – this time, by nullifying the innovations of Charles II and James II.)

The third part offers the crown (of England, France, and Ireland) jointly to William and Mary and provides for a new order of succession. Although this was the only time that England has had two sovereigns, no rationale for this exceptional provision is provided by the text.

The fourth part reaffirms the Test Act, and essentially extends the Test Act to the sovereign for the first time. From hence forward, Catholics and those married to Catholics were excluded from the throne, and moreover could not sit in the parliament. This ruled out the lawful return of James II to the throne (which parliamentary Whigs had previously tried to block with their Exclusion Act) and also reduced Protestant fears about Catholic conspiracies.[36]

Overall, the Bill of Rights reasserts parliament's long-standing rights and only slightly extends them. Indeed, the striking thing about the Bill of Rights is how few new powers or restrictions are listed. Apart from ruling out future Catholic kings and providing for a dual monarchy, very little new is adopted. This is acknowledged in the document, which states that parliament "do pray that it may be declared and enacted that **all and singular the rights and liberties asserted and claimed in said declaration are the true ancient and indubitable rights** and liberties of the people of this kingdom." The conservative nature of the Bill of Rights was evidently necessary to secure broad support within the Houses of Commons and Lords for the act as a whole. Parliamentary records indicate that many members continued to support James II's claim to the sovereign, and many others wanted long-standing constitutional practices be continued. They clearly remembered the failures of Cromwell's Commonwealth, three decades earlier. Most members of parliament favored continuation of as much of the

[36] A complete copy of the English Bill of Rights can be found at: www.constitution.org/eng/eng_bor.txt.

medieval constitution as possible under the circumstances. Consequently, the provisions in the Bill of Rights cover familiar ground. It simply codified fundamental laws that had been accepted by parliaments and kings for much of the previous four centuries. Only a minority of the recorded debates seemed interested in a "glorious revolution."

To obtain the protection of the Dutch army, the crown was offered to both William and Mary, not to either Mary or William alone. To obtain the crown, William and Mary agreed to rule in accordance with the laws of the land, including those enacted by parliament and accepted by the sovereign – as had been promised many times before in English history at times of accession.

Although the medieval English constitution remained in place, the parties in power and their circumstances were substantially different than they had been in the past. This, more than the English Bill of Rights, affected the course of public policy and constitutional reform for several decades by creating new opportunities for constitutional exchange.

THIRTEEN

Constitutional Exchange in the United Kingdom

CONSTITUTIONAL EXCHANGES AND THE GLORIOUS REVOLUTION: WILLIAM III AND THE PARLIAMENT

From an early age, William (Willem) III had been educated in the fields most useful for a future *stadhouder*: in military matters and strategies for negotiating with a sovereign republican government (Claydon 2002, 15). During his adult life, William had become very good at building support within the provincial governments and in the States General. This was necessary in the context of the Dutch constitution (see Chapter Fifteen) because the provinces – rather than the *stadhouder* – were sovereign and had veto power over both budgets and legislation. The office of *stadhouder* was normally combined with that of captain general, which made the *stadhouder* responsible for the army and one of the most influential persons in the Netherlands.

By the time that *stadhouder* Willem III became William III, King of England, he was a middle-aged man with substantial experience in military leadership and in bargaining with parliament. He was not, as kings of England tended to be, long destined to the throne and used to royal deference throughout his life, although he belonged to a very distinguished and powerful Dutch family and was married to the daughter of James II.[1] As stadhouder, William III was used to dealing with several parliaments to obtain funds for his executive responsibilities, especially for national defense, as national security was the primary charge of the Dutch stadhouders (Claydon 2002, 25).

1 Willem-William III had an indirect claim to the English sovereign as the son of Willem II of the House of Orange (who died when Willem III was very young) and Mary Stuart, the daughter of King Charles I. Willem married Mary (the daughter of James II and thus also the niece of Charles II) in 1677 at the age of twenty-seven (Claydon 2002, chapter 1).

From approximately 1580 until 1790, the Netherlands was organized as a confederation of provincial governments, which themselves were often organized as confederations of local governments. The office of *stadhouder* was, in principle, an appointed rather than hereditary position, and a regional rather than a national position. In practice, however, the provinces always chose their *stadhouder*s from the Orange-Nassau family and only one or two family members were appointed stadhouders. Filling the office of *stadhouder* was not automatic, and the office was left empty several times in Dutch history. For example, it had been left empty for two decades after the death of William III's father, Willem II. Overall, this balance of authority was nearly the opposite of the English sovereign's historical relationship with parliament. Essentially unanimous support within the States General was necessary to obtain national resources for the Dutch army, and this could not be taken for granted.[2]

In 1689, as *stadhouder* of most of the Netherlands and as king of England, William III continued to have the security of the Netherlands and its conflict with France very much on his mind. He was, consequently, very interested in resources for war with France and was willing to bargain with parliament to obtain those resources. This is not to say that William was less interested in authority and wealth than previous kings, nor that war with France was not in England's long-term interests, but William III – as opposed to Charles II or James II, who had often been allied with France – was very concerned about French power and was used to working within constitutional constraints to advance his interests in a manner that previous Stuart kings were not.[3]

[2] The confederal structure of the Netherlands indirectly gave the city of Amsterdam a veto on national tax requests. Amsterdam had the largest tax base of any community in both Holland and the Netherlands. The province of Holland generally used unanimous agreement to pass major tax and military bills (Claydon 2002, 24–5). The province of Holland had similar veto power in the national States General. For more details about Dutch governance in the Republic, see Israel (1995). An more detailed overview is also provided in Chapter Fourteen.

[3] For example, in 1672, William refused King Charles II's (his uncle's) offer to press for his elevation to the king of Holland as part of a peace settlement with France. He refused, in part because the offer involved a smaller Netherlands, and in part because "his countrymen were more attached to their liberties than they would be to any royal ruler" (Claydon 2002, 19).

Shortly afterward, in gratitude for its liberation from the French, the elites of the province of Gelderland offered William III the sovereign office of duke, rather than the appointed office of *stadhouder*, which would have ended that province's republican form of government. Several other provinces complained that a Gelderland Dukedom would undermine the Dutch constitution. William, perhaps with greater aims in mind, refused the elevation to duke and accepted the lesser post of *stadhouder* (Claydon 2002, 23).

William's crown also depended more on parliamentary support than had recently been the case because James II and his wife Mary had stronger hereditary claims to the throne. William, consequently, was more interested in parliamentary good will and was more willing to trade royal prerogatives for tax revenues than previous English kings.

The 1689 parliament, in contrast, was more self-assured and independent than the one that had restored the Stuart monarchy and also more interested in shoring up its own authority. The announcement of French support for James II's effort to recapture the English and Scottish thrones increased parliamentary interest in supporting William's campaign against France. James II was unlikely to be as generous as his brother had been after the Restoration three decades earlier.

Opportunities for constitutional exchange between king and parliament were, consequently, the greatest they had been since the *Magna Carta* was signed four and a half centuries earlier. A deferential, rule-following, and resource-hungry king with urgent duties abroad confronted a parliament anxious to expand its control of public policy. The constitutional bargains struck over the next dozen years were pivotal events in English and Dutch history. William's success with the parliament is evident in the enormous funding that parliament provided him for his war with France. The tax base was expanded and tax rates were increased. Tax receipts more than doubled over those of James II, rising from two million to more than five million pounds in 1694 (Claydon 2002, 125–6). Expenditures rose even more rapidly, with the consequence that British debt expanded to unprecedented levels (North and Weingast 1989), accomplished in part via the Dutch method of earmarking some taxes for debt service and repayment (Stasavage 2003).[4]

Central government employment tripled in size from four thousand under James II to twelve thousand under William, while the British army and navy approximately doubled in size during the nine-year war with France (Claydon 2002: 25–6). The long-term geopolitical success of William's "English strategy" is also obvious.[5] The British had been inclined

4 Interest paid on foreign debt fell significantly during William's reign, evidently in large part because of the adoption of Dutch practices (Stasavage 2003, 74–7; 2002, 126–31), which facilitated the large-scale borrowing necessary to fund a good deal of the great military expansion. It also bears noting that Dutch financiers were more willing to purchase English debt, given that England now had a Dutch king.

5 His interest in bringing England to the Dutch side in its contests with France dated at least back to 1677, when he arranged to marry Princess Mary, who was at that time second in the line of succession after her father (Claydon 2002, 23–4).

to intervene on the French side under Charles II and James II, but after William III, English efforts to contain French influence continued for three centuries (Morgan 2001, 402). The Netherlands survived as an independent country.

The price paid for parliament's support in the nine-year war with France (1688–97) was also clear. The Coronation Act of 1689 required the sovereign to "solemnly promise and swear to govern the people of this Kingdom of England … according to the statutes in parliament agreed on, and the laws and customs of the same." In exchange, William and Mary obtained the traditional sovereign revenues for life. The customary revenues were, as ever, too little to support large-scale military campaigns, and taxes for war required the support of parliamentary majorities. Such taxes were normally extended for short periods, between one and four years, as they had been in the past.

In 1694, a new Triennial Act was passed, which (again) required parliaments to be called at least once every three years, but this time required new elections at least once every three years. The Triennial Act, together with the parliament's short-term tax policies, required more frequent elections to the House of Commons, which made the House of Commons more independent of the sovereign and somewhat more dependent on voter support. No longer, could a king lock in an especially supportive parliament by keeping it in session for more than a decade, as Charles II had done immediately after the Restoration.

Parliamentary audit and increased parliamentary control over expenditures were the result of precedents established by William in his effort to win the trust of parliament on military matters and thus obtain more resources for his French campaigns (Claydon 2002, 73–7; Reitan 1970). Parliament's power of the purse was strengthened early in William's administration when he relinquished several of the questionable revenue sources used by Stuart sovereigns for most of the previous century. Resistance at this point would have undermined his efforts to fund military campaigns (to pay the Dutch and English armies) and to build a more powerful British navy to confront France on the continent and abroad.[6]

The power of the purse had always provided parliament with some indirect control over the military, but parliamentary involvement in military matters expanded greatly during William III's period in office. This was perhaps most apparent following the peace of Ryswick in 1697, when the

[6] William himself spent the summers of the eight-year war on the continent leading military campaigns against the French.

British army was reduced to less than a third of William's request, about an eighth of its peak during the nine-year war with France. Parliament had always been unwilling to finance standing armies during times of peace as a curb on royal power. In 1699, parliament induced William to disband his trusted Dutch guards (Claydon 2002, 146–52).

Parliament's greater budgetary authority was also expanded by a new division of funding responsibilities that emerged during and after the war with France. William III's revenue stream had always been more uncertain than even that of the previous Stuart kings. This was largely because of the nature of wartime finance in parliamentary systems and his interest in rapidly expanding it, but also a consequence of the manner in which he and Mary had come to the crown. They had essentially inherited James II's standing revenues, rather than formally obtaining new ones on accession. Instead of pressing for a resolution of his finances in 1689, William pressed for new military funding. After a decade of negotiation, permanent (lifetime) revenues were finally secured after the conflict with France was settled. In 1698, the Civil List Act provided William III with permanent revenues for domestic (nonmilitary) expenditures (Reitan 1970). Military expenditures henceforward would be paid for with a separate budget.

It bears noting that William's domestic budget was somewhat larger than accorded previous kings, although it included the new caveat that only tax revenues up to seven hundred thousand pounds per year could be used for royal purposes. Revenues beyond that could only be used by the king with parliamentary permission. This prevented William and his successors from profiting from economic growth, as previous kings had, and also limited the sovereign's ability to maintain a standing army, the responsibility for which was entirely shifted to parliament for the first time (Reitan 1970). Revenues for support of the military in times of peace continued to be granted only for relatively short periods, as they had been in most past periods, but the parliamentary "subsidies" became the entire budget of the English army, rather than subsidies in the contemporary and medieval sense.[7]

Had government expenditures not increased so much, the income from royal properties together with the customs revenues for life might have been sufficient to fund peacetime governance, as two million pounds had been sufficient a decade or two before. In the new fiscal environment, royal

7 Charles II and James II had received permanent revenues that were about twice as large as William's, but included funds for routine military expenditures. The Civil List Act reduced the king's fiscal responsibilities and allowed for a somewhat more comfortable private life, but also greatly reduced his ability to shift resources among government services (Reitan 1970).

incomes were far below that required for peacetime government finance. This, together with the new method of financing the army, made William and his successors far more dependent on parliamentary tax bills, whether at peace or at war. The bargaining power associated with the governmental purse was now continuous, rather than available only during times of war.

In 1701, William also accepted the Act of Settlement. This act did not affect William but was to bind his successors. The first part of the act affirms Princess Anne's position as next in line to the throne and greatly elevated the German Electors of Hanover in the line of succession. (William and Mary had no children.) Anne was Mary's sister, another daughter of James II, and was married to the brother of the king of Denmark at the time of her accession. Her successor, George I of Hanover, was her second cousin, the great grandson of James I. George was the closest Protestant relative of Anne. There were more than fifty closer relatives, but all were Catholics.

The second part of the act is of greater constitutional interest because it changed the rules for succession, imposed a number of new restrictions on future sovereigns, and increased judicial independence. For example, it required future kings and queens to "join in communion with the Church of England." This new religious requirement was more restrictive than required under the 1689 Bill of Rights. Mary, who died in 1694, would have been eligible for the sovereign under the new rules, but not William. William was himself Protestant and satisfied the 1689 requirements, but he was brought up in the Dutch Reformed Church, which was more Presbyterian than Anglican (Claydon 2002, 99). The Act of Settlement also forbade future kings (from other lands) from engaging in wars outside England without the permission of parliament and prevented all future sovereigns from leaving "the domains of England, Scotland, or Ireland without the consent of parliament."

The Act of Settlement also elevated the privy council (the cabinet of this period) somewhat and specified that "no persons born out of the kingdoms of England, Scotland, or Ireland … shall be capable to be of the Privy Council, or a member of either House of Parliament." The latter ended the centuries-old custom by which the king was automatically a member of the House of Lords, which reduced the ability of foreign born kings, such as the German born George I and George II, to monitor and negotiate directly with members of the House of Lords.

The Act of Settlement also reduced royal opportunities for influencing the parliament by declaring that "no person who has an office or place of profit under the king, or receives a pension from the Sovereign, shall be capable of serving as a member of the House of Commons." (This last provision was subsequently weakened by the Regency Act of 1706, which required new elections for members of parliament (MPs) who became sovereign employees. This was a much milder restriction because elections at the time were rarely contested.) In addition, the settlement increased judicial independence by giving senior judges lifetime appointments during good behavior: "judges' commissions be made *quamdiu se bene gesserint*..." That is, subject only to parliamentary impeachment.

By the time of William's unexpected death in 1702, the formal and informal constitutions of England had been rewritten to increase parliamentary independence and control over governance.[8] Parliaments could meet regularly – with or without royal invitation – and electorates, however small and elite they might have been, routinely judged their representatives at least once every three years. Parliament's power of the purse had been increased by shifting more control over revenue sources to the parliament – many of which had previously been independently claimed by kings – at the same time that the size and cost of governance expanded beyond the royal household's remaining standing revenues. Bureaucratic inertia favored parliament in this case.

The precedent of audit and earmarked budgets reduced the sovereign's discretion to use tax receipts as he might desire and further reduced opportunities for a king to buy support in parliament. Freedom of speech and petition opened up the domain of public discussion on a variety of matters that previously might have been deemed treasonous and punished accordingly. The judiciary was more independent than it had been in past centuries.[9]

Royal Authority after William III

It was not necessarily the case that these late-seventeenth-century precedents and unvetoed acts of parliament would continue to bind future queens and kings. All English constitutional changes were reversible: the 1706 Regent Act undid reforms of parliament adopted by the 1701 Act of Settlement. A clever king who obtained a supportive parliament could, in principle,

[8] William, the heroic military leader of many campaigns, died from injuries sustained after falling off a horse.

[9] In this, it could be argued that William achieved his stated goal, announced on October 10, 1688 just before the invasion in his *Declaration of Reasons*: "a free and lawful parliament ... and securing to the whole nation the free enjoyment of all their laws, rights, and liberties under a just and legal government." The complete text of William's declaration is available at www.jacobite.ca/documents/16881010.htm.

repeal or amend any of these acts through majority votes. Precedent is to a significant extent in the eye of the beholder. Just as many routine disputes under common law are based on disagreements about what the law is, so were many of the constitutional disputes between parliaments and kings in previous centuries. Moreover, then as now, there is no formal procedure in England through which constitutional violations can be set aside.

Although it is often written that the Glorious Revolution created parliamentary governance in England, royal power did not disappear with the Bill of Rights or with the death of William III, and parliament had long participated in governance. The last sovereign to veto a parliamentary decision formally after it was passed by majorities in both houses was William's successor, Queen Anne, who vetoed the Scottish militia bill in 1707. However, she was not the last to affect the course of public policy in the small or large. The division of power between king and parliament had clearly shifted from king toward parliament between 1689 and 1702, but to another intermediate point, rather than from one extreme to the other.

The sovereign continued to have and exercise the power to appoint and dismiss ministers, call and dismiss parliament, and directly affect the composition of parliament through town charters and elevation to the nobility. The power of royal patronage, although reduced by the budgetary and audit practices implemented during William's reign, continued to be a useful method of influencing the behavior of members of parliament. Although there were many patrons who employed members of parliament, the king or queen was by far the largest patron. Queen Anne had one hundred "placemen" in her parliament (Field 2002, 141). A third of the House of Commons was on the executive payroll during George I and George II.

The necessity of parliamentary permission to obtain new tax revenues in combination with new constraints on royal finance and greater expenses indirectly increased the importance of political parties and the leaders of those parties after William III's constitutional bargains. Insofar as a particular leader could deliver a large number of votes, they could bargain directly with a king or queen.

It must be acknowledged, however, that kings and queens were often the most important of "parliamentary" leaders. Sovereigns had the ability to create "court majorities" in the Houses of Commons by bargaining with prominent local families that controlled seats in the House of Commons, by employing members in the executive, and by simply appealing to voters. Such residual authority provided kings and queens with a good deal of control over public-policy decisions and naturally reduced the need for explicit vetoes.

That royal veto power continued to exist in the century after Anne's 1707 veto became obvious in 1801, when Minister Pitt's powerful cabinet resigned over the king's threatened veto of the cabinet's proposed Catholic Emancipation legislation (Hill 1996, 157). Indeed, the most important of the electoral and parliamentary reforms of the nineteenth and twentieth centuries, the election reform of 1832 and the Parliament Act of 1911, occurred in large part because of threatened interventions by two kings in support of constitutional reforms desired by majorities in the House of Commons.

THE BALANCE OF AUTHORITY BETWEEN BRITISH SOVEREIGNS AND THEIR PARLIAMENTS IN THE EIGHTEENTH CENTURY

Several significant reforms of the written constitution were adopted during the first decades of the eighteenth century that affected the balance of authority between the sovereign and the parliament. The Scottish Union Act of 1707 brought Scotland firmly into the England sphere of influence by abolishing the Scottish parliament and formally linking the crowns of Scotland and England. Forty-five new seats were created in the House of Commons for Scottish town and county representatives and nine new noble seats for the House of Lords. A revised property qualification for the House of Commons was adopted in 1711. County representatives (knights) had to have six hundred pounds of income per year, and town representatives (burgesses) three hundred pounds per year. The Septennial Act of 1716 revised the Triennial Act and extended the maximum length of parliament from three to seven years, reducing what little electoral competition there was and by most accounts increasing royal authority by strengthening the effects of patronage.

To some extent, these constitutional reforms can be interpreted as "ordinary" partisan majoritarian politics, in that the reforms were intended to advance Tory or Whig political objectives or royal ones. For example, the Scottish Union was adopted by a Whig majority, and the new Scottish members subsequently voted with the Whigs. The Tories supported the new property qualification of 1711 to reduce part of the Whig electoral support, as the Tory base of support was in the upper middle gentry (Field 2002, 143; Hill 1996, 51). The Septennial Act of 1716 allowed an existing Whig parliament to be extended without an intervening election and provided it (and George I) with four more years to use patronage to cement the Whig faction's control of parliament.

After the Septennial Act, the written rules of the national political game remained stable for more than a century, but the unwritten procedures of governance continued to be revised to take account of the rising cost of governance and a century-long sequence of foreign kings.[10] Many of these informal revisions were indirect consequences of the new budgetary circumstances of the sovereign. As the size of governance increased well beyond the sovereign's own revenues, parliamentary subsidies became essential for day-to-day governance (Mathias 2001, 39). The short-term tax bills passed by parliament, in turn, necessitated annual meetings of parliament and cabinet ministers who could deliver majorities in both the Houses of Lords and Commons.

The use of ministerial councils was an ancient royal management technique, but in the eighteenth century, the need for ongoing parliamentary majorities substantially reduced the range of ministers that could be hired (or fired) by the sovereign. The king or queen remained the principal, but more and more authority was delegated to his or her agents. The ministers, in turn, became increasingly independent of the sovereign because their authority was increasingly based on the extent of their support in the two chambers of parliament. It became commonplace for the sovereign's top minister to be a member of parliament who could deliver reliable majorities.

The reliance on a single parliamentary leader to craft majority support through policies and royal patronage, as with Walpole and Pitt, helped established organizational patterns and norms that allowed the modern office of prime minister to emerge. Once selected, these early "prime" ministers would be allowed to dispense the sovereign's patronage (jobs) to increase support for the sovereign in the parliament.[11]

The use of a parliamentary prime minister to create and manage majorities in the House of Commons and Lords also gradually led to cabinet governance. As the scope of government increased, and sovereign interests

[10] William III (1689–1702), George I (1714–27), and George II (1727–60) were foreign by birth. Anne (1702–14) had lived in Denmark with her husband for nearly twenty years before her ascension to the throne. George III (1760–1820) was born in Britain, but evidently spoke English with a German accent, doubtless because he had a German-speaking mother, father, and wife.

[11] Walpole (1721–42) is often regarded as the first prime minister. He had the support of both George I and George II, and used both parliamentary and royal patronage to his and the sovereign's mutual advantage.

The Whigs essentially excluded Tories from government positions. On the other hand, it was the Whigs' superior access to foreign credit as well as the latent Jacobism of many Tories that initially predisposed George I to favor Whig ministers (Field 2002, 146; Hill 1996, 59, 77).

focused on foreign policies and expanding the empire, more domestic policy decisions were turned over to the royal council of ministers. Cabinet governance in its modern sense, however, did not emerge until well into the nineteenth century.

This was partly because disciplined, well-organized political parties had not yet emerged. Parties in the eighteenth and early nineteenth centuries were loose coalitions of members with common interests, rather than disciplined national organizations that crafted platforms and provided substantial electoral support. British politics in the eighteenth century was not characterized by the competitive elections and intense electioneering that are the hallmarks of modern democracies. Many borough elections and most county elections were uncontested and were substantially controlled by local elites (O'Gorman 1989, 334). In 1761, for example, only four of forty county elections were contested, and only forty-two of two hundred three borough elections (Field 2002, 143).

Indeed, the number of seats controlled by local elites expanded during the eighteenth century as the number of "nomination" boroughs in the House of Commons increased from about sixty to more than two hundred during the course of the century. It also became increasingly common to purchase nominations, which became more valuable as the authority of parliament increased. The price of a seat in the House of Commons was bid up from one thousand pounds to five thousand pounds over the course of the eighteenth century (O'Gorman 1989, 13, 21). Local elites who sold "their" seats would deliver the necessary votes and/or prevent opposition. (A few such seats were simply attached to ownership of particular pieces of land.) These nomination seats allowed kings and queens to exercise significant influence over the composition of parliament because only a relatively small number of local sponsors needed to be influenced.

Royal influence within parliament was also strengthened by their authority to elevate families to noble ranks. This allowed kings and queens to affect the composition of the House of Lords and to influence members of both chambers of parliament, many of whom sought noble titles and/or elevations for themselves and their sponsors. Patronage affected the distribution of persons who would actually attend meetings of parliament by providing a subset of both Lords and Commons with paid positions based in London.

Consequently, kings and queens throughout the eighteenth century were normally "blessed" with parliamentary majorities whose interests were well aligned with their own interests. George I and George II preferred Whigs to Tories – in part because of Tory support for James II and James III's claims to the throne – and sure enough, Whig majorities were had by George I and II.

George III was less partisan and less predisposed toward Whigs, and the Whig dynasty fell (Field 2002, 136–7, 146,149).

This royal influence on the composition of parliament continued well into the nineteenth century. George IV (1820–30) was known to favor Tories and managed to have a Tory majority in parliament – partly because he expanded Lords from 339 to 400 members (Field 2002, 164). William IV (1830–7) was known to favor Whigs, and the Tory majority was replaced by a Whig majority in the election that followed his accession to the crown (Pugh 1999, 48; Lee 1994, 58–9).

In 1800, parliament had more control over public policy than it had ever had before, but the British sovereigns retained considerable direct and indirect control over public policy.

POLITICALLY ACTIVE INTEREST GROUPS IN LATE-EIGHTEENTH- AND EARLY-NINETEENTH-CENTURY ENGLAND

Toward the end of the eighteenth century, a series of economic, technological, political, and ideological shocks began to transform the still largely medieval lifestyles and political outlooks of British commoners and nobles. International and intranational trade expanded rapidly during the eighteenth century, reflecting agricultural innovation, declining transportation costs, and population growth (Mathias 2001, 66–7, 88). English turnpike and canal systems expanded dramatically from the mid to late eighteenth century, which helped create a more integrated domestic economic market (Morgan 2001, 428–9, 483). Prosperity in northern Europe, improved ship designs, and expanding international trade networks (which were only partly a consequence of Empire building) increased trade worldwide (Mathias 2001, 87–8).

New large-scale techniques for spinning thread and weaving cloth led to major new manufacturing centers (Mathias 2001, 243–5), and the Industrial Revolution was literally beginning to gather steam with Watt's modifications of Newcombe's engine in 1774 and 1781 (Morgan 2001, 480). Expanding commerce and population growth caused new urban centers to emerge and older commercial centers to grow larger. Large-scale manufacturing became increasingly more commonplace and less tied to particular cities as trading networks expanded and became denser.

In the second half of the eighteenth century, reduced transportation costs and somewhat less intrusive censorship allowed a broader and more rapid dissemination of news and opinion, which led to a more truly national political system. For example, newspapers became commonplace during the eighteenth century, which increased knowledge of national and international political controversies and scandals. The (London) *Times* began publication in 1785. A number of influential books were published in the late eighteenth century by thoughtful men also helped stimulate interest in liberal economic and political reform. Adam Smith's (1776) *An Inquiry into the Nature and Causes of the Wealth of Nations* provided a thorough attack on the monopoly practices of previous centuries and defense of free trade and specialization, which helped to energize economic liberals for the next two centuries. Jeremy Bentham's (1789) *Introduction to the Principles of Morals and Legislation* challenged the customary foundation of law and suggested that laws and institutions should promote the greatest happiness to the greatest number. Edmund Burke's *Reflections on the French Revolution* (1790) argued that major institutional reforms, particularly revolutionary ones, were unlikely to improve long-standing institutions. Paine's rebuttal the following year, *Rights of Man and of the Citizen*, focused additional attention on individual rights and civil liberties, as opposed to family or aristocratic rights.[12]

A variety of organized groups took up the cause of parliamentary reform at the end of the century: The Society for Constitutional Information (1791), the Friends of Universal Peace and Rights of Man (1791), the London Correspondence Society (1792), Friends of the People (1792), and Sheffield Association (1792). These were largely middle-class groups, but their memberships extended into parliamentary elites and the working class (Lee 1994, 16; Hill 1996, 150–1, Pugh 1999, 22–3). These groups organized large-scale and more or less peaceful demonstrations and petition drives that promoted reform rather than revolution. Petitions and mass demonstrations became more common in the early nineteenth century.

Earl Grey, who was a member of Friends of the People, sponsored a series of parliamentary reform bills beginning in 1793. Such proposals revealed that significant support for electoral reform already existed, but not enough to adopt the proposed reforms. Grey's proposals attracted yes-votes from about 25 percent of the members of the House of Commons (Hill 1996, 233).[13]

[12] All three books were widely read and translated. They continued to be widely read and cited throughout the nineteenth century and are still on college reading lists today. Locke's book was an immediate best seller, selling two hundred thousand copies in 1793 (Field 2002, 156).

[13] Some three decades later, Grey became prime minister in more favorable circumstances and finally passed a bill very similar to his early proposals. (He served in the House of Lords at the time, inheriting the family title after the death of his father in 1807. See www.spartacus.schoolnet.co.uk/PRgrey.htm for a short biography.)

The new middle and upper-middle classes continued to be excluded from political life by the wealth requirements for suffrage and seats in the House of Commons. The 1711 property qualifications for the House of Commons also prevented middle-class and poor Anglicans from sitting in Commons (until 1859). The Test Act of 1673 prevented dissenters and Catholics from seeking parliamentary office (until 1829). Population shifts had further reduced the representativeness of borough governments, to the extent that it had ever existed.

Interest in parliamentary reform, of course, was not a new phenomenon in England. Parliamentary reform had been seriously debated in England at least since the Leveller's "Agreements" of 1647 and 1649.[14] However, the late-eighteenth-century revolutions in America and France had renewed interest in civic equality, suffrage reform, and the proper assignment of seats across the country.). Groups of men and women organized to increase their own wealth through collective bargaining and also to achieve political reforms. Many joined or supported groups that lobbied for expansion of suffrage and reapportionment (Pugh 1999, 22; Mathias 2001, 334).

Interest in reapportionment was largely a consequence of the new factory-based production of textiles in northern England, where new urban centers emerged that were underrepresented in the House of Commons. The new industrial centers of Manchester, Birmingham, Leeds, and Sheffield were among the seven largest cities in England, but they had only county representation (two members of parliament) in Commons. There were also several places where relatively large communities had gradually disintegrated through time without affecting their representation in parliament. Forty-nine two-member districts existed with fewer than fifty eligible voters (Field 2002, 142). Industrialists organized groups such as the General Chamber of Manufactures and petitioned parliament for favorable economic policies and also reforms of parliament (Morgan 2001, 482). Reapportionment was also supported by many politically active liberal groups of the time, in part because many liberals lived in the underrepresented parts of the country, but also because they favored greater civil equality.

[14] Grey's 1792–97 bills, however, were not the first late-eighteenth-century efforts at reforming the rotten boroughs. Reform bills had been offered even before the French Revolution. In 1785, Pitt had proposed shifting seats from smaller boroughs to larger ones in his reform bill, which included compensation for the "owners" of the small borough seats. In that case, as in 1797, George III was opposed to reform and helped marshal opposition to the bill (Hill 1996, 145). Grey's 1792–7 efforts were largely opposed by his own party, as Pitt's interest in reform had disappeared after the French Revolution (Hill 1996, 50–1).

Curtailing Political Interest Groups

Although free speech had been obtained for members of parliament by the Bill of Rights, political speech remained circumscribed outside the parliament. For example, Thomas Paine had to flee the country for France in 1792 (or face trial for sedition) after Pitt condemned his "monstrous doctrine" (Pugh 1999). Paine's critique of monarchy was unacceptable political discourse in England at that time.

When the first French Republic declared war in 1793, England shifted to a war footing and curtailed civil liberties to quell demonstrations in favor of constitutional reform. The Treasonable and Seditious Practices Act and the Seditious Meeting Act were passed in 1793 by large supermajorities. Treasonable practices included the transport and publication of writing opposed to the constitution. (Paine's publisher was sentenced to a year and half in jail for selling *Rights of Man*.) The Habeas Corpus Act was suspended in 1794.

Meetings of more than fifty persons were allowed only with magistrate approval. Moreover, large demonstrations in opposition to the Seditious Meetings Act were themselves considered to be seditious and broken up. In 1799, correspondence societies and trade unions were banned under the Corresponding and Combination Acts (Lee 1994, 19; Field 2002, 157). These political "gag acts" as well as medieval laws defining treason were used to prosecute reform, antiwar, and labor organizers, which postponed large-scale efforts to promote constitutional reform until well after the war with Napoleon ended in 1814. Rumors of revolt and revolutionary plots were abundant during the late eighteenth and early nineteenth century.[15]

Not all organizations were affected by the antisedition acts or the new restrictions passed in 1819 (the Six Acts). For example, "friendly societies" continued to flourish as did reform-oriented local newspapers. In 1801, about seven hundred thousand people belonged to such local-service and insurance clubs. By 1815, membership approached a million, and by 1830, about one in four males were members of such societies (Gerrard 2002, 169). The Masons also continued to expand their membership and influence.

After the Napoleon's defeat and the restoration of the French monarchy, most of these laws were repealed or weakened, which allowed reform groups to be organized again. During the following decades, well over one hundred politically active groups organized mass meetings, petition drives,

[15] See Field 2002, 156–62; Pugh 1999, 22–4; Hill 1996, 155; Lee 1994, 54; Morgan 2001, 486–8; and Holmberg 2002.

and demonstrations; they issued pamphlets and lobbied ministers behind the scenes (Hamer 1977, 8; Lopatin 1999, appendix). Correspondence societies provided links between the clubs with shared interests, including public policy (Lee 1994, 54; O'Gorman 1989, 312).

Such groups sponsored large-scale demonstrations and petition drives. For example, in 1816, more than four hundred petitions favoring the abolition of the income tax arrived in parliament (Hill 1996, 176). Although the economic and antitariff efforts were successful, the constitutional-reform movements were not. Indeed, parliament responded to large-scale constitutional reform demonstrations with legislation curtailing such groups, the Six Acts of 1819, rather than reform. Jury trials lessened the effect of these laws in that juries would not very often convict those charged or apply maximal sentences. The Treason Act of 1351 still defined seven offenses as high treason, including various assaults on the royal family and "levying war against the king within his realm or adhering to his enemies." The terms assault and war could be given nonviolent interpretations (Holmberg 2002).

Most public gatherings that pressed for reforms were peaceful, but the reform movement naturally induced the formation of antireform groups, which intensified verbal conflicts and occasionally led to violence. The language of politics often tends to be hyperbolic and emotional, and although there was no counterpart to the American or French Revolutions in the United Kingdom, there were outspoken demonstrations and petition drives that focused attention on constitutional issues.[16] The repeal of the 1799 Combination Act in 1824 also allowed local trade associations and unions to organize.

CONSTITUTIONAL BARGAINING AND THE "GREAT REFORM" OF 1800–1835.

The bargaining models developed in Part I of the book imply that constitutional exchange is most likely to be observed during unsettled times because the economic and political interests of kings and parliaments are also unsettled in such times and the value of modest increases in authority increases. It further predicts that constitutional bargaining will be multidimensional and that tax reforms will often be associated with the bargains struck. The

[16] No coordinated uprisings or attacks on government buildings or persons took place. Indeed, it was often quite the reverse, as in the Peterloo "massacre" in 1819 when eleven persons were killed at a parliamentary reform assembly by a cavalry charge during a very large but evidently peaceful meeting at St. Peters Field in Manchester. The speakers were arrested, as were the newspaper reporters who wrote up accounts of the meeting and cavalry charge (A nice overview is provided by: http://en.wikipedia.org/wiki/Peterloo_massacre.)

analysis also predicts that constitutional bargaining will be more commonplace than constitutional reforms and that organized groups will play a role in those negotiations. Such predictions are largely borne out by the course of constitutional reform in England during the nineteenth century.

The British Parliament in 1830

In 1830, the House of Commons included about 270 seats (of 658) from "nomination boroughs," in which a very small number of persons could select a candidate for the House of Commons who would (usually) run unopposed (Lee 1994, 57–9; O'Gorman 1989, 26). Seats in the House of Commons were disproportionately allocated to the south. Cornwall with a population of three hundred thousand elected forty-two members of parliament, while the county of Lancastershire, with a population of more than 1.3 million, elected just two members. Southern electorates were often even smaller than these numbers suggest, as for example Old Sarum's electorate consisted of just eleven voters.[17]

The least representative boroughs had suffrage rights that were attached to particular pieces of property, "burgages," which could be assembled under a single ownership, and which in a few cases allowed a single person to select a member of parliament. Others were selected by very small electorates, as with the "rotten" borough of Sarum. At the other extreme were towns (boroughs) in which all freeholders or all taxpayers were entitled to vote (O'Gorman 1989, 21–33). Overall, about 10 to 12 percent of the adult male population were eligible to vote, and the typical voter was surprisingly middle class. For example, Garrard (2002, 26) reports that the electorate in 1830 was composed as follows: landed gentry (13.6 percent), merchants and manufacturers (5.8 percent), retailers (20 percent), skilled craftsmen (39.5 percent), semiskilled workmen (19.2 percent), and those employed in agriculture (6.4 percent).

Partisan Interests in Reform

Neither of the mainstream parties favored a wholesale redistribution of seats or universal suffrage, but many Whigs favored a reallocation of seats

[17] It is interesting to note that the Pitt family owned much of the real estate and voting rights in Old Sarum in the eighteenth century. Their Sarum real estate entitled them to nominate two members of parliament. Members of the Pitt family thus often sat in parliament during this period. They sold their lands in Old Sarum during the nineteenth century. The price paid was said to be sixty thousand pounds, which suggests that the value of seats in Commons had risen to nearly thirty thousand pounds.

and revisions of borough suffrage rules. The Whigs had long been a liberal reform coalition by the standards of the early nineteenth century (Hill 1996, 178). For example, the Whig coalition had long opposed restrictions on freedom of the press and supported free trade, including repeal of the Corn Law Act of 1815. They also opposed laws forbidding Catholics and dissenters from holding public office; and had proposed several parliamentary electoral reform bills. Of course, reapportionment and suffrage reform were politically easier for the Whigs to support, because the preponderance of the reallocated seats would come from conservative (Tory) districts. Of the 270 nomination districts most likely to be affected by reform, only 70 routinely returned Whigs (Lee 1994, 57).[18]

Liberal arguments and lobbying campaigns gradually persuaded a majority of the electorate that reform was inevitable and may have also influenced the sentiments of a future king. George III died in 1820 and was seceded by his son George IV, who died in 1830, and was seceded by his brother William IV. William had served in the House of Lords and generally supported the Whigs during his time there. The election associated with William IV's accession returned a proreform Whig government later that year, thanks in part to William IV's support for Whig candidates (Phillips 1992, 18–21).

The new Whig government proposed a suffrage reform bill that called for a substantial reallocation of seats, uniform rules for the election of borough MPs, and a substantial expansion of suffrage. However, that proposal was defeated narrowly in the House of Commons at its second reading. Twelve hundred petitions were presented to the 1830 parliament in support of suffrage reform (O'Gorman 1989, 310).

Reform Tactics

Earl Grey asked the new king to call for new elections and parliament was dismissed. The ensuing campaign focused largely on suffrage reform and returned a large Whig majority to the House of Commons. Grey's coalition received 71.1 percent of the votes cast in Great Britain (Rallings and Thrasher 2000, 3). In thirty-five of the forty county elections, the Whigs took both seats. Of the 187 Tories elected, 90 percent came from districts

[18] Although completely isolating pragmatic and ideological interests is beyond the scope of the present paper, it is clear that the relative importance of the House of Commons and of the liberal factions within Commons (and their continental counterparts) increased as suffrage expanded. This provided some members with pragmatic political reasons to support greater openness in politics.

that would lose their seats if the Whig reforms were adopted (Hill 1996, 193). This time the reform easily passed in the House of Commons, but a majority of the House of Lords opposed the reforms, 199 to 158.

The rejection of reform by the House of Lords led to scattered riots, a few of which were targeted at peers and bishops who had opposed reform. It also induced a middle-class tax revolt and bank boycott. The unenfranchised middle class (widely) withheld taxes and withdrew funds from the banks. As a consequence, the Bank of England's reserves fell by 40 percent (Hill 1996, 195).

After the defeat in the House of Lords, Grey's ministry resigned, and William IV encouraged the formation of a minority Tory government. When this failed, he invited Grey to return to government and agreed to create forty-one proreform peers, if necessary, to assure passage of the Reform Act (LeMay 1979, 32). Correspondence between the king and Earl Grey reveal concerns about royal property claims and assurances that royal property claims would not be challenged by parliament (Grey 1867, 9–14.) A third reform bill, slightly modified to please the House of Lords, again easily passed the House of Commons. Electoral support for reform, the modifications, the external pressure, and the royal threat to create new Whig lords induced a majority of the House of Lords to accept the reform.[19] The king accepted the bill, and the first substantial reform of election laws in four hundred years took effect.

Reforms of the House of Commons

The great reform approximately doubled the electorate to about 20 percent of adult males by broadening the franchise in most boroughs. All households with property holdings rated at ten pounds per year were entitled to vote in boroughs. County roles were expanded to include fifty-pound renters as well as the forty-shilling householders already enfranchised under the medieval suffrage law of 1430. (There were twenty shillings to the pound.) One hundred forty-three seats were taken from the smaller

[19] The conservatives (Tories) could thus continue to control one house of parliament even if the liberals (Whigs) would win the next several elections for the House of Commons. Had the conservatives in the House of Lords failed to pass the electoral reform, and subsequent elections returned a liberal majority, the pace of subsequent constitutional reforms is likely to have been much faster. The liberal coalition did win the next three elections, but lost in 1847. Between 1830 and 1885, liberals won eleven of thirteen elections. The modifications implied that fewer seats would be shifted from England to Scotland (six) and Ireland (five).

boroughs, including one hundred twelve from towns and villages with populations under one thousand that previously had their own members of parliament. Sixty-five seats went to the new industrial centers, sixty-five more to county representatives, and the remainder were redistributed among London, Scotland, and Ireland.[20]

The great reform did not eliminate the over-representation of the south relative to the north, radically expand suffrage, or end patronage, but it did make patronage less decisive in future elections and increased electoral competition and representation in the new industrial cities (Lee 1994, 61). Before 1820, it was rare for even a third of the English elections for seats in Commons to be contested (Lang 1999, 19). After the reform, it was rare for less than two-thirds of the English seats in Commons to be contested (McLean 2001, 90). The 1832 reforms also changed the basis for representation within the House of Commons from more or less equal representation of boroughs and counties to a system based on electorate size (Jennings 1961, 13).

Many members of parliament continued to draw salaries from royal appointments and from other wealthy individuals and interest groups. Indeed, industrialization had created new groups who were in a position to support and reward MPs. An extreme example of this occurred in the mid-nineteenth century when a large number of the members of parliaments served on the board of directors of major railroad companies. Parks (1957) notes that "of the 815 M.P.s who sat from 1841–47, **145 were railway directors** ... in 1867 there were 179 ... as a result railway bills poured through Parliament." Members of parliament did not receive a salary for their services to the central government until 1911 (Machen 2001, 102).

The new industrial interests and new urban centers were now better represented, as were the interests of what might be called upper-middle class. This, together with more competitive elections, tended to make the House of Commons a more liberal body, whether seats were occupied by Whigs or Tories. Liberal interests were evident in education reform (1833),

[20] Lang (1999, 31–7) provides a nice overview of the details of reform. He reports that the 1832 reforms increased the electorate (those actually voting) from about five hundred thousand to about eight hundred thousand of a population of twenty-six million. All such numbers, however, are estimates, as many votes in small districts were cast through physical means, rather than paper ballots: voice votes, counting of hands, and the like. The electorate increased as a consequence of economic growth, inflation, and tax increases. Turnout was, however, evidently not particularly high, except for a short time after the reforms. The number of votes cast actually shrank from about eight hundred thousand in 1837 to about five hundred seventy thousand in 1859 (Craig 1977).

the abolition of slavery (1833), poverty law reform (1834), child labor acts (1833, 1842), and trade liberalization (1846) (Morgan 2001; Floud 1997).[21]

Increasing the number of seats in Commons held by representatives of the industrial districts also made pivotal members of the House of Commons more interested in industrial development than before. Trade policies were liberalized (as noted earlier), monopolies reduced, and the free-trade zone of the empire expanded.

Innovations and economies of scale in manufacturing gave British manufactures a cost advantage in many markets, which generated large trade surpluses and capital inflows. As a consequence, per capita income grew four times faster in the years 1830–50 than it had in the previous century (Pugh 1999, 36). Suffrage also expanded during this period because more persons met the property and income requirements of the 1832 reforms.

PARTY CABINETS AND PARLIAMENTARY RULE IN THE MID-NINETEENTH CENTURY

Reapportionment, redistricting, and the expansion of suffrage had significant effects on the distribution of authority between the king and parliament, even though the reforms only directly affected the House of Commons. Before the reform, the majority of the English members of the House of Commons ran unopposed. Before 1832, it was rarely the case that more than a third of the seats were contested (Lang 1999, 19). Much broader election campaigns were subsequently necessary to obtain seats in Commons. Although those elected to office were still often from the landed elite (Pugh 1999, 82), they had to be responsive to local economic and political interests to hold office (Schonhardt-Bailey 2006). This made parliamentary majorities in the House of Commons more difficult for kings and queens to engineer than they had been in most past centuries.

In addition to the indirect effects of suffrage reform and electoral competition, the sovereign's control over public policy was also reduced by other reforms that indirectly affected negotiations between the king and

[21] It bears noting that liberal arguments were more often utilitarian than natural-rights oriented or libertarian during this period. For example, those supporting education reform and factory acts generally recognized that reducing child labor would increase education levels (although some factory owners had their own schools for children) and thereby improve child welfare in the long run, even if it reduced their family's liberty and income in the short run.

(Adults that competed for the jobs held by children would have pragmatic reasons to reduce child labor, but few of these were represented in parliament under the suffrage laws of nineteenth-century England.)

parliament. For example, Curwen's Act of 1809 made the sale of seats in parliament illegal. Many sources of royal income were phased out, and a new income tax was phased in. The protectionist Corn Laws were repealed in 1846, which somewhat reduced the income of the large landholders, including the king. It also eliminated tariffs on six hundred articles and reduced them on five hundred others, which reduced one of the most important sources of executive income.

As part of the bargains used to reduce tariffs, "temporary" income taxes (in a series of three-year tax bills) were introduced (Edwin 1914, 138–142; Lee 1994, 81). Together with increased commerce and industrialization, this implied that more and more of the government's revenues were provided by temporary tax bills that had to be renewed to keep it up and running.[22] It bears noting, however, that the use of the income tax for public finance allowed government budgets to increase. Government expenditures rose from about 133 million pounds in 1856–7 to 143 million pounds in 1859–60 (*Historical Statistics of Europe 1750–1988*).[23]

The king or queen continued to appoint cabinet ministers, but the appointments were increasingly constrained by parliament's budgetary authority at the same time that the scope of royal patronage and other sources of influence over members of parliament were reduced. New cabinets could be appointed, but they could not govern without parliamentary support, and there was less that the sovereign could do to persuade members of parliament to vote the "right" way. By refusing to approve new taxes

[22] The expanding potential tax base is evident from all accounts of this period. For example, data for the English experience are developed by Lindert (1986). Lindert's table 1 indicates that the value of noble estates averaged £2032 in 1810 and rose to £9,855 in 1875. Merchant estates averaged £608 in 1810 – far less – but had risen to £11,804 in 1875, both in constant 1875 British pounds sterling. Other classes/occupations also had significant increases in wealth, although not as great as that of merchants or the "titled persons." Overall, it is clear that the fraction of wealth controlled by those outside the royal family increased substantially during this period. The population of nobles was essentially stable between 1810 and 1875 (rising from 22,000 to 25,000), while the population of merchants and professionals, and members of the industrial and building trades increased substantially – rising from 42,000 to 61,000 and from 638,000 to 2,835,000, respectively. Similar changes in the distribution of wealth and occupation were under way in much of Europe, although in most cases, the expansion of commerce and industry came later than that in England. (Increases in parliamentary power also occurred somewhat later.)

[23] It was only after the Queen's acquiescence on Gladstone's appointment that the income tax came to be regarded as a permanent tax (Seligman 1914, 166). However, it should be acknowledged that the need to keep government up and running also constrained parliamentary tax policies because voters and their patrons demanded it. In 1875, Gladstone campaigned on a promise to abolish the income tax, and he and his liberal allies were soundly defeated (Seligman 1914, 172–3).

and other policies, parliament could essentially shut government (and the royal household) down during times of peace as well as war.

The cumulative effects of the restrictions on royal revenues and adjustments to elections laws were increasingly evident in the policy bargains reached between the sovereign and parliament. That parliament had become the dominant policy-making body, rather than simply execising authority in areas of little interest to the sovereign, had become undeniable by 1858.

In that year, the liberal government headed by Palmerston resigned and was replaced with a minority Tory government preferred by Queen Victoria. New elections were called, but unfortunately for the queen, her favored conservative (Tory) coalition lost the 1859 elections. Queen Victoria did not care for Palmerston, whose liberal coalition had won the election, and she reappointed the conservative Derby to the office of prime minister. Her preferred prime minister, however, could not assemble a majority to pass legislation or taxes. Given the necessity of parliament's continuing financial support, Victoria grudgingly accepted Palmerston and subsequently Gladstone in 1860 (Pugh 1999, 96).

In this manner, a long series of minor constitutional bargains had gradually produced a parliament that was independent from the sovereign and had essentially complete control over legislation and taxation. Consistent with the analysis of Part I, a series of constitutional and quasi-constitutional bargains had gradually increased parliament's control of public policy. In the British case, the nineteenth-century reforms were joint consequences of liberalism and industrialization, which were themselves partly consequences of earlier reforms. Liberalism provided a reform agenda that helped motivate politically active groups and gradually reduced barriers to internal and external trade and induced fiscal and electoral reforms. Industrialization changed the distribution of wealth between the sovereign and parliament and created new potential tax bases.

The new procedures for selecting the cabinet and prime minister were not formally codified in constitutional documents or new legislation. Indeed, communications between parliament and the queen remained formal and deferential.[24] Nonetheless, after 1860, the cabinets were party based and reflected electoral results in the House of Commons. This transfer of policy-making authority from king and queen to parliament and from Lords to Commons took place without significant internal revolutionary threats and

[24] Victoria's role in government did not end in 1858. That she continued to play an advisory role, especially in foreign policy, is evidenced by a steady flow of very deferential letters to Victoria from Palmerston and his successors.

without substantial democratization of politics. Only about 20 percent of adult men could vote in 1860.

Universal suffrage did not emerge for another half century, which suggests, as implied by the analytical history of Part I, that parliamentary authority over public policy and the degree of suffrage are generated by substantially independent mechanisms. The predicted ideological and partisan basis of suffrage expansion is evident in subsequent reforms of suffrage.

THE GRADUAL EXPANSION OF SUFFRAGE DURING THE NINETEENTH CENTURY: THE SECOND REFORM OF 1867 AND THE THIRD REFORM OF 1884

A number of groups pressed for suffrage and constitutional reform during the nineteenth century. Some of these groups were quite large and well organized. Among the most prominent groups was a group that lobbied for a written constitution, universal male suffrage, the secret ballot, free trade, and the reform of the Poor Laws. The Chartists organized large public demonstrations and produced several large petitions in favor of their constitutional reform agenda. However, they failed to obtain sufficient support in parliament for their reforms, in part because some prominent members of the movement threatened law and order, which induced a conservative backlash.

Interest in suffrage reform and the secret ballot, however, did not end with the disintegration of the Chartist movement as other groups organized and pressed for suffrage extension and ballot reform. Suffrage extension bills were introduced by "radical liberals" in 1852 and 1854 but were defeated by overwhelming, but diminishing, majorities (Smith 1966, 29). However, voter interest in reform was sufficient to induce the conservative members of parliament to take up the reform issue, and in 1859, the conservatives introduced a reform bill (Smith 1966, 41), partly with the aim of protecting conservative interests in the face of "inevitable" reform.[25]

New regional reform organizations, with roots in the Chartist and Anti-Corn Law leagues, added to the pressure in the 1860s (Smith1966, 29, 39–40, Park 1931). A new Reform Union was formed in the northern industrial

[25] In May of 1859, Disraeli argued in the House of Commons that parliamentary reform had become a pressing matter of public policy. "Thus Parliamentary Reform became a public question, a public question in due course of time becomes a Parliamentary question; and then, as it were, shedding its last skin becomes a Ministerial question. Reform has been for 15 years a Parliamentary question and for 10 years it has been a Ministerial question" (quoted in LeMay 1979, 180). Disraeli's remarks clearly imply that interest groups may directly establish an issue as a "public question" and indirectly establish an issue as a ministerial issue.

centers by radical liberal politicians, merchants, and prominent reformers in 1864 to press for liberal reforms, including the secret ballot, a return to triennial parliaments, making seats in the House of Commons proportional to borough and county populations, and broadening the franchise to include all males not on poor relief. They emphasized the universality of the interests advanced by their programs, citing Mill and Gladstone, rather than class-based arguments (Cowling 1967, 243–52).[26]

A new Reform League was founded in London in 1864 by middle- and working-class activists. Its funding came from lesser lords, industrialists, and from the Trade Council. It promoted a similar constitutional agenda, but used somewhat more aggressive and radical language to promote reform (Cowling 1967, 246, 248). In 1865, the London Working Men's Association was formed largely from members of the trade unions to campaign for expanded suffrage, including lodgers not on poor relief (Cowling 1967, 247). These three groups organized numerous talks in medium-size towns and cities throughout England. Their members included journalists as well as elected politicians and so their views were widely reported in the press throughout the country.

After three decades, constitutional reform was again part of the mainstream political agenda. There is evidence that changes in taxes were part of the bargaining over suffrage. Consider for example this excerpt from a letter from Palmerston to Queen Victoria on January 27, 1861:

> If Mr. Gladstone were to propose a democratic budget making a great transfer of burdens from indirect **to direct taxation**, and if, the Cabinet refusing its concurrence, Mr Gladstone were to retire, the Conservative Party would **give the [Queen's] Government substantial support** except in the case of the Government wishing to take an active part in war against Austria. ... by the end of that time [of Conservative governance] the country, it might be hoped, would be prepared for a **good and real Reform Bill** ...

The Second Electoral Reform of 1867

In the 1865 elections, there was a changing of the guard as a new generation of members entered the House of Commons and leadership posts were

[26] Gladstone normally argued for a limited expansion of suffrage to include those "fit" to participate in national politics. For example, in the House of Commons in May 1864, he suggested that "every man who is not presumably incapacitated by some consideration of personal unfitness of political danger is morally entitled to come within the pale of the constitution. [That is to say,] fitness for the franchise, when it shown to exist – as I say that it is shown to exist in the case of a select portion of the working class – is not repelled on sufficient grounds from the portals of the Constitution by the allegation that things are well as they are" (quoted in LeMay 1979, 184).

passed on to a new generation of leaders. Earl Russell, with the assistance of Gladstone, formed a liberal reform government, with the support of Whigs (right liberals), liberals, and radicals (left liberals).

Early in 1866, Russell proposed a major reform expanding the national suffrage laws substantially beyond that of 1832, although less than advocated by many reform groups. The Russell-Gladstone reform bill obtained a slim majority in the House of Commons on its first reading – one that was much smaller than anticipated because of large-scale defections among Whig MPs (who by the standards of this period were right liberals). The bill failed on its second reading (after amendment) in the face of conservative and Whig opposition. Parliament was recessed, and during the recess, the Reform League and Working Men's Association organized large-scale demonstrations in favor of expanding suffrage throughout the country, including several large and occasionally disorderly demonstrations within London (Cowling 1967, 11–12; Smith 1966, 135, 160).[27]

The Russell cabinet resigned without requesting new elections, and the queen asked the leader of the conservative opposition, Derby, to form a new government. A new cabinet was formed in 1867 with the assistance of Disraeli. The new government was a right-of-center coalition of conservatives and conservative Whigs in the House of Commons (the "Cave" faction of right liberals). As in 1832, there was again royal support for suffrage reform. In her speech to parliament and in subsequent letters to Derby, Queen Victoria insisted that electoral reform should be addressed by the new government (Smith 1966, 135).

The Disraeli reform proposals were in some respects more liberal than those rejected in the previous year, but they were crafted at the margins to benefit conservative electoral interests in light of demographic research (Machin 2001, 65).

Three suffrage issues were addressed by the Derby-Disraeli reforms: extension of suffrage for national elections, a modest redistribution of

[27] One of the demonstrations is often referred to as the Hyde Park Riot. The "riot" began as a peaceful march, although it included an unlawful trespass in Hyde Park and some destruction of park property. The police tried to disburse the twenty-thousand-person crowd, at which point a riot ensued. The police were rebuffed with sticks and stones. Several dozen demonstrators and policemen were injured in the fray. One policeman subsequently died from injuries. The cavalry was called out and the crowd disbursed.

The demonstrators were not politically motivated, surly, revolutionists – the demonstrators played games and climbed trees throughout the park. Both the demonstration and police efforts to disburse the demonstration took place within sight of Disraeli's apartment, which may have contributed to the demonstrators' influence. Mrs. Disraeli reported that "the people in general seem to be thoroughly enjoying themselves" (Smith 1966, 129–31, 135).

boundaries and seats in the House of Commons, and suffrage extension in the towns (boroughs) for local elections beyond that for national elections. (a) The borough franchise was expanded beyond the level sought by the liberals to include renters (who might be influenced by their conservative landlords). *Renters* of twelve-pound properties were to be eligible to vote in the boroughs, and residency requirements in the towns and villages were reduced from three years to one year. Ownership requirements for suffrage in the counties were reduced from fifteen pounds to twelve. (b) The boundaries of boroughs were expanded to shift liberals to towns from county electorates, where suffrage remained subject to a higher property restriction. Only thirty seats from the smallest districts were redistributed, and only about half went to boroughs. After a good deal of debate and amendment, the bill was passed by a coalition of radical liberals and conservatives over the opposition of mainstream liberals, who objected to the conservative biases in Disraeli's bill.[28]

The second reform bill of 1867 nearly doubled the electorate, increasing it from just more than a million in 1866 to just under 2 million in England, and from 1.35 million to 2.48 million in the United Kingdom as a whole (out of a population of 30 million). The secret ballot was introduced in 1872.

The wealth and tax thresholds for voting were lowered more in the boroughs (town and urban districts) than in the counties. Borough electorates rose from 600,000 to 1.43 million, while those in the counties rose from 758,000 to just over a million (Smith 1966, 236). Although the borough seats became more representative in the sense that a broader cross-section of society could vote, boroughs did not have representation in the House of Commons that was proportional to their populations. The nineteen largest boroughs with a combined population of 5 million returned forty-six MPs, while the sixty-eight smallest boroughs with an aggregate population of 420,000 returned sixty-eight MPs, a twelve to one difference in citizens per representative. The ratio of citizens per member of parliament between the largest and smallest district was about 250:1 (Smith 1966, 240).

The "advanced" (left) liberals from the industrial midland and northern boroughs had obtained increased suffrage, but not increased representation, while the country gentry were protected from a substantial increase in electoral competition. About one in eight persons living in boroughs

28 One of the many proposed amendments that was rejected was sponsored by J. S. Mill, who attempted to replace the word "man" with the word "person" throughout the suffrage bills, which would have expanded suffrage to women. Mill's women's-suffrage proposal received only seventy-three votes in support (Smith 1966, 204).

were eligible to vote after the reforms, but only about one in fifteen persons residing in counties.[29] The conservative advantage in the counties was evident in subsequent elections (although they won majorities in Commons only in 1874). In 1874, the conservatives received 38.32 percent of the votes cast in England and Wales, which elected 154 MPs. The liberals received only about 1 percent fewer votes, 37.39 percent, but elected only 101 MPs (Smith 1966, 225).

The expansion of suffrage further increased the importance of partisan organizations for election campaigns and, consequently, also increased party discipline, which pushed British politics and parliamentary voting patterns toward their modern partisan forms. In 1860, only about 58.9 percent of liberals voted with their party leaders in the cabinet, and only about 63 percent of conservatives routinely opposed them. By 1881, 83.2 percent of the liberals supported their party leaders on critical votes, and 87.9 percent of conservatives. Party-line voting reached the 90 percent level in both parties in the following decade (LeMay 1979, 178; Stephens and Brady 1976).

The Third Electoral Reform of 1884–1885

The reform act of 1867 reduced, but did not eliminate, the disproportionate representation that had long characterized the House of Commons. Together with the wealth-tax requirements, the distribution of seats in the House of Commons allowed the landed gentry to retain disproportionate influence within government, although the importance of land holdings per se decreased. Electoral districts were rooted in historic town-county divisions, and larger towns and counties had multiple representatives (normally two or three) elected simultaneously in district elections. The House of Lords continued to be populated by nobles and senior church officials.

Moderate and left-liberal organizations continued to lobby for further extension of suffrage and more proportionate representation. In the late nineteenth century, they were joined by labor unions, whose policy agendas normally included support for suffrage expansion.

In 1884, the liberal government of Gladstone proposed a significant increase in the franchise by placing county voters under the same rules

[29] The expansion of suffrage in Scotland and Irish counties was passed in separate bills in 1868 and was more substantial, although the final fraction of voters was smaller than in England and Wales, one in twenty-four and one in twenty-six respectively (Smith 1966: 239). These ratios include women and children.

adopted for the towns in 1867. The conservatives were opposed to this reform unless it was combined with a redistribution of members to protect their seats. There were speeches throughout the country on the issue, and the queen encouraged conservative and liberal leaders to find a compromise. As had always been the case, assembling simultaneous majorities in a liberal House of Commons and conservative House of Lords was a nontrivial task that required a good deal of negotiation, bargaining, and compromise (Chadwick 1976, McLean 2001, 79–83; Machin 2001, 94–102).

In the end, a compromise was worked out in which two separate bills would be adopted (one extending the franchise and one redrawing electoral district lines and reallocating seats). The second reading of the redistribution bill took place in the House of Commons on December 4, 1884, and the franchise bill passed Lords on December 5 (Chadwick 1976, Machin 2001, 97).

A variety of possibilities had been discussed before the final agreement, including a shift to single-member districts, proportional representation, and women's suffrage. But these more radical reforms were rejected in favor of more modest reforms. The proposed redistribution bill was read in the House of Commons in December 1884, and the boundaries, which were partially settled by bargaining among leaders, would be finalized by a boundary commission in early 1885. The boundary commission's proposal would be voted on in the House of Commons soon after the report was made (Chadwick 1976; Machin 2001, 97).

The new districts were to be linked to population, rather than historical town and county boundaries. There would be more single-member districts, although multiple-member districts were retained. For the first time, new districts were developed on a more uniform basis for Scotland, Ireland, and England. Towns with populations less than fifteen thousand would be merged into county districts. The voter ratio between the largest and smallest districts shrank to 8:1, one-thirtieth of their previous ratio.

The 1884 suffrage bill extended suffrage in the countryside without much affecting the urban electorate, which enfranchised a broad cross-section of the rural middle and working class. The redistribution of seats (mostly accomplished by creating new seats) gave somewhat greater weight to urban voters in subsequent parliaments. The electorate again nearly doubled in size to about 5.5 million voters (Machin 2001, 97). About two-thirds of adult men had the franchise – essentially all male heads of households that met residency requirements.

Many of the new rural voters were culturally conservative and supported the expansion of the British Empire during this period, which gave conservative parties considerable support within the newly enfranchised middle class (McLean 2001, 100–1). The reforms of 1885, together with disagreements within the Liberal coalition on "home rule" for the Irish, shifted control of the House of Commons to conservatives for most of the next two decades.

Few significant constitutional reforms were proposed in the next two decades, although universal male suffrage and freer trade remained goals for many liberal reform groups. The British women's suffrage movement and the labor movement became more politically active and effective towards the end of the century. A new labor party was added to the mix of liberal and conservative coalitions, and an Irish coalition labored for greater independence (home rule), although relatively few labor MPs were elected before 1918. (Liberal and labor parties coordinated their campaigns for several elections prior to 1918.) Smaller groups lobbied for proportional representation.

PARLIAMENTARY DEMOCRACY EMERGES 1906–1928

British politics at the end of the nineteenth century was very different from that at its beginning. The shift to parliamentary dominance was essentially complete, with partisan cabinets and with the center of parliamentary authority increasingly in the elected chamber of parliament. Suffrage had expanded from less than 10 percent of adult males to more than 60 percent. The electoral reforms had made British electoral politics more competitive and the House of Commons more representative of the average person's interest than it had ever been before. Corruption and vote buying had been reduced by several pieces of legislation, including the 1883 parliamentary elections (corrupt and illegal practices) bill. Political parties had emerged as increasingly modern and disciplined organizations, although they had not entirely taken their contemporary form.

The distribution of election districts was more equal than in the past, although there were still a large number of relatively small districts. The larger districts selected several MPs simultaneously. Graduates of the major universities also had plural votes: they could vote for university representatives and in any district in which they met wealth and residency requirements. Wealthy persons had plural votes: they could vote in any district in which they met wealth and residency (property) requirements. About 10 percent of the electorate had plural votes (Morris 1921, 10). Overall, English suffrage was comparable to many others undergoing liberal reforms in the late nineteenth century, although a few countries had implemented somewhat more extensive suffrage (for example, France, Germany, and the United States).

The hereditary House of Lords retained veto power on legislation, which tended to bias legislative results and constitutional reforms in conservative directions. The sovereign formally retained considerable authority, but most of it had long been informally ceded to parliament. The sovereign, however, as a popular, well-informed participant in political life, could influence policies through public statements, access to the elites in the Houses of Lords and Commons, and contacts with other European sovereigns and influential families. The sovereign also retained the right of elevation through which new member of Lords could be created, which gave the king or queen an indirect veto over the House of Lords – although one that could not be exercised routinely. The latter had played a role in the reforms of 1832 and would again play a role in constitutional reform in 1911.

In 1906, the liberals won parliamentary elections to an extent not seen since 1832, based partly on constitutional issues. Four hundred liberals were elected, which, along with the support of forty members of labor and eighty-three Irish nationalists, gave them a large supermajority in the six hundred seventy–member House of Commons. The House of Lords, however, with a large conservative hereditary majority continued to oppose liberal legislation and constitutional reforms, such as ending plural voting in the counties (which tended to favor conservatives).

In 1909, the House of Lords vetoed the budget for the national government, after several decades of deference to the House of Commons on budgetary matters (LeMay 1979, 189–192; Machin 2001, 129). The bill included new taxes on inherited wealth and introduced the principle of progressive taxation, which directly threatened conservative and aristocratic interests (Lang 1999, 137–8). This was not the first House of Lords veto of legislation passed in the House of Commons in the twentieth century, but it led to new elections and a series of major constitutional reforms. The most important of these was a major reduction in the authority of the House of Lords, which cleared the way for many of the major reforms that followed.

As in 1832, the king supported liberal proposals from the House of Commons by threatening to add liberals to the House of Lords until the measure passed.

The 1911 constitutional reform reduced the influence of the House of Lords from an absolute veto to the ability to temporarily block bills favored by the House of Commons (for up to three years). Although this compromise did not completely end bicameralism, it ended nearly five centuries of formal equality between the Houses of Commons and Lords on legislation, and it created a new, very asymmetric bicameralism that assured the dominance of the House of Commons.[30]

By removing a long-standing veto player with predictable conservative interests, this constitutional reform potentially opened the door to many other reforms, although such reforms did not immediately take place. Minor reforms such as the end of plural voting were vetoed (delayed) by the House of Lords for the next few years, while others such as women's suffrage were delayed within the House of Commons (Morris 1921, 85–117).

World War I naturally caused public and parliamentary attention to focus on foreign affairs, rather than constitutional reform issues. Constitutional issues, however, had not entirely disappeared from the agenda of parliament. The term of the 1910 parliament had been extended beyond the normal limit because of its role in managing the war. This allowed the House of Lords to play a significant role in the constitutional negotiations. The Lords ability to delay proposed reforms meant that some reforms could not be adopted by the first "long parliament" of the twentieth century without their consent.

A broad package of constitutional reforms was introduced at the end of the Great War, the details of which reflected a good deal of bargaining among liberal and conservative party leaders during the war (Morris 1929, 113–99). The Representation of the People Act of 1918 included another major expansion of suffrage, another redistribution of seats in parliaments among districts, and a reduction of plural voting (to a maximum of two members of parliament). Essentially all adult men over the age of twenty-one, except those on poor relief or with criminal records, and women over the age of thirty were to be entitled to vote. The proposal more than doubled the electorate, increasing it from eight million to more than twenty-one million voters (Morgan 2001, 592).

Proportional voting for the seats in the large, urban, multiple-member districts was finally rejected as a compromise between the Houses of Lords and Commons (Machin 2001, 146). Perhaps surprisingly, the number of university seats in the House of Commons was increased from nine to fifteen, and graduates from several relatively new universities were given the

[30] It bears noting that such interparliament conflicts had been less frequent before 1866 because the House of Commons had been less liberal and more members of that chamber had been members of noble families, on noble payrolls, or supported by them in other ways (Sack 1980).

right to cast votes for university seats, which were normally conservative at that time (Morris 1921, 197–200).[31]

CONCLUSION: PARLIAMENTARY DEMOCRACY IN THE U.K. EMERGED THROUGH CONSTITUTIONAL BARGAINING AND REFORM

The English parliament emerged in the fourteenth and fifteenth centuries from earlier forms of the king-and-council architecture. During most of its first three centuries, parliamentary power ebbed and flowed with the king's need for new tax revenues and the bargaining skills of parliamentary leaders. Only the veto power on new taxes continued essentially uninterrupted. Other protections and powers were obtained by various parliaments and then were lost or ignored according to the interests and ambitions of the king or queen of the day. Parliaments were called and dismissed by the head of the royal household and were normally called only when he or she needed additional revenues (subsidies) from parliament. Medieval parliaments, consequently, met irregularly and for relatively short periods. The power of the medieval English parliament was nontrivial, but very limited by contemporary standards.

A gradual shift of policy-making authority from the king to the parliament began at the end of the seventeenth century during the reign of William III. This was nearly a century earlier than in most of the other countries focused on in this book and reflects unusual opportunities for constitutional exchange between William III and parliament in the decade after William and Mary's accession to their royal offices. These changes and a series of somewhat disengaged sovereigns in the first half of the eighteenth century allowed parliament and cabinet ministers to gain additional authority.[32]

[31] The parliamentary seats for Oxford and Cambridge Universities date to the thirteenth century when Henry III granted these towns monopolies in higher education (Brooke, Highfield, and Swaan 1988, 56). Their monopolies ended in the early nineteenth century when a handful of new universities were founded, as with University College in London (1826), King's College London (1829), and the University of Durham (1832). Several polytechnic universities were founded in the late nineteenth century. (Five other universities existed in Ireland and Scotland.)

[32] Queen Anne (1702–14), whose succession was an unexpected consequence of the 1689 Bill of Rights, which elevated her above her father and brother, had lived in Denmark with her husband for many years before inheriting the crown, was not trained for leadership, and often suffered from ill health. The first two Hanoverian kings, George I and II (1714–60) were, like William, foreign born. George I spoke German rather than English at court, and was as least as interested in political developments in Hanover and the Holy Roman Empire as in the United Kingdom. George III controlled the course of policy on many occasions. However, he was mentally ill and incapacitated during several periods of his long reign (1760–1820).

Trends in the Eighteenth and Nineteenth Centuries Favored Parliament

The center of policy-making power did not shift back to the sovereign as it had on previous occasions. Instead, parliament continued to bargain for and obtain additional authority over public policy.

Relatively stable political factions of MPs emerged in both chambers toward the end of the seventeenth century as noted in Chapter Twelve (Hayton 2002; Hill 1996, chapter 2), but these voting blocks did not account for the whole of parliament, nor were these voting blocks organized in the contemporary manner. Relatively few elections were contested, MPs were unpaid, and MPs attended parliament more or less at their convenience. Being a member of parliament was not a full-time salaried position.

The lack of party discipline and professionalism, along with the preponderance of uncontested elections, allowed patronage to affect the balance of power in parliament and between the king and parliament (Field 2002, 140–1). Kings, for example, continued to have significant influence over electoral outcomes to the House of Commons. The Whigs rose to power after George I's accession to the sovereign, largely because George only appointed Whigs to senior positions in government. The Whigs remained largely in control until George III's accession in 1760. George III was less favorably disposed toward partisan politics in general and to Whigs in particular than his grandfather and great grandfather had been. Under George III, the Tories assumed power for the first time in fifty years.[33] Neither the party system nor cabinet governance had yet emerged.

Nonetheless, the sovereign could not always control electoral outcomes or the members elected. Shifts in the composition of the House of Commons somewhat limited the king's choice of ministers and thereby affected the ordinary course of public policy. Men like Walpole and Pitt who could deliver majorities in parliament (using the king's patronage) became powerful and influential statesmen.[34]

Trends favoring parliamentary authority continued and strengthened during the nineteenth century. A series of reforms to suffrage law, tax law,

[33] In his words, George III wanted to "put an end to those unhappy distinctions of party called Whigs and Tories by declaring that I would countenance every man that supported *my* Administration" (quoted in Hill 1996, 105–6). He proceeded to appoint his nonpartisan tutor, the Earl of Brute to be his chief minister. The king, true to his word, subsequently appointed men who would put king over party, both Tories and Whigs, to posts in his administration (Hill 1996, 106).

[34] The term prime minister was coined with Robert Walpole in mind; however, this title was not meant as a compliment, but as an insult composed by Walpole's enemies (Field 2002, 145).

and to the national bureaucracy made the House of Commons substantially independent of the sovereign at the same time that the interests represented in Commons became more commercial and liberal. Shifts in finance, new demands for government services and reform, and the need for reliable majorities in parliament induced kings and queens to appoint members of the leading parties of the House of Commons to posts in the executive cabinet. As a consequence, effective control of domestic policy and foreign policy gradually shifted from the King and House of Lords to the House of Commons.

Independence of Suffrage and Parliamentary Authority

It is important to note that from 1689 to 1860, parliament's authority expanded without significantly expanding suffrage. This demonstrates that it is possible to have parliamentary rule without highly contested elections or broad suffrage.

The determinants of suffrage reform in England clearly differed from those that determined the balance of authority between kings and parliaments, as hypothesized in Chapters Seven and Eight. Groups outside of government pressed for electoral and other reforms, as had often been the case in previous centuries, but the nineteenth-century interest groups were more successful than previous centuries. New technologies for organizing and coordinating demonstrations were available, new economic and ideological support for suffrage expansion had emerged, and as suffrage expanded, political parties became more disciplined and elections became more competitive. These changes made constitutional bargains on representation and suffrage possible.

Constitutional Bargaining, Rather than Revolutions

The constitutional bargains struck reflected the political interests of those engaged in negotiations, which were partly induced by preexisting political institutions and partly by changing ideological and economic interests. The interests represented in the House of Commons and in the House of Lords

Evidently, Walpole appeared to be too deferential to George I and II. Walpole was not, of course, the first minister in English history to have had a great effect on English public policy, but he was the first to do so in the post–William III era when parliamentary majorities played a more important role in policy formation. Robert Walpole led the majority in the House of Commons from 1721–42 and is often regarded as the first Prime Minister of Great Britain.

changed as industrialization took place and as liberal ideology penetrated into the highest levels of government.

Many lobbying groups pressed for liberal economic and political reforms through petitions, mass demonstration, and electoral support. There were, however, no credible or immediate threats of revolution. Indeed, concerns about revolutions normally caused repressive, rather than liberal, measures to be adopted. Institutions were not ignored or destroyed by revolutionary constitutional negotiations, but rather were reformed a little at a time using standing procedures for intragovernmental negotiation and reform.

There is evidence of compromise and bargaining in every reform. Most reforms were modest and most remained in place for several decades at a time. A long series of reforms achieved through patient (and shrewd) bargaining gradually allowed parliament to obtain essentially complete control over public policy. Cabinets became increasingly determined by the electoral outcomes and majority parties in the House of Commons. Suffrage gradually expanded, and by 1930, was essentially universal.

Most of these reforms took place at approximately the same time that they were occurring in the other European kingdoms, largely between 1825 and 1925 – a period in which manufacturing and commerce replaced agriculture as the main source of wealth and in which liberal ideas and reformers favored increasingly open political and economic systems.

Table 13.1. *Major Constitutional Developments in English Constitutional History*

Date	Event	Description
1215	*Magna Carta*	Establishes right to jury trial and Council of Barons (including bishops and abbots) with veto power of new taxes.
1265	Montefort Parliaments	Invites four knights from each shire (county) to his first parliament. Two burgesses from every major town are also included in his second parliament.
1414	Equality of Commons and Lords	Proclamation of Henry V that laws be adopted with the assent of both the Houses of Commons and Lords.
1429	Election Law Statute	Forty-shilling franchise established in the shires (counties), allowing 5 percent of adult males to vote for shire representatives to the House of Commons.
1445	Election Law Statute	Boroughs to have two elected representatives each, who must be residents and possess the wealth of a knight (or squire).
1489		Court decision holds that legislation requires the assent of both the Houses of Lords and Commons.
1533	Act of Appeals	Appeals by ecclesiastical courts to the pope eliminated, which makes the sovereign the final level of appeal in both secular and religious courts.
1534	Act of Supremacy	Sovereign becomes head of English Church (rather than the Pope), creation of Anglican Church.
1534	First Act of Secession	Parliament passes and the king accepts rules for future accession to the throne. (The rules were suggested by the king.)
1536	Bill for the Dissolution of the Lessor Houses	Dissolution of smaller monasteries with all their assets turned over to the sovereign. Abbots and priors are subsequently removed from the House of Lords, ending the majority of the "Lords Spiritual."
1536	Union of Wales and England	English law extended to Wales; 24 Welsh MPs join parliament.

(*continued*)

Table 13.1. *(continued)*

Date	Event	Description
1641	First Triennial Act	Parliament to be called at least once every three years, will be "self-calling" if the sovereign fails to issue writs.
1641	Act Against Dissolution	Forbids the king from unilaterally dissolving parliament.
1642–60	Civil War and Commonwealth	Period of parliamentary rule (by a subset of the 1641 parliament) followed by the authoritarian rule of Cromwell.
1660	Breda Proclamation	Restoration of parliamentary monarchy: England returns to constitution of August 1641 (prior to Act Against Dissolution).
1664	Second Triennial Act	Requires parliaments to be called at least once every three years, but eliminates the self-calling provision.
1673	The Test Act	Forbids Catholics and dissenters (mostly Presbyterians and Puritans) from holding public office.
1689	Bill of Rights	William and Mary offered joint sovereignty, right to jury trial affirmed, right of free speech in parliament affirmed, forbids a standing army in peace time, and excludes Catholics from the sovereign.
1694	Third Triennial Act	Modifies the previous Triennial Act. A meeting of parliament is required at least once every three years, and the maximum duration of parliament is set at three years.
1689–1702	Precedents of William III	Annual tax bills, earmarked taxes, earmarked budgets, audit of sovereign accounts, parliamentary consultation on military and foreign affairs, Bank of England is established.
1698	Civil List Act	William III obtains additional tax sources for life, but caps the new revenues at £700,000/year, beyond which the approval of parliament is required.
1701	Act of Settlement	Advances the Hanovers in the line of succession (as the nearest Protestants), future kings and queens can only leave Great Britain with permission from parliament, MPs are forbidden from being on the royal payroll.

1706	Regency Act	Provides for a regent council after Queen Anne's death, naturalized all Protestant Hanoverian successors. It also weakens the 1701 provision regarding MPs on the royal payroll. MPs may now take paid positions, but must stand for reelection after taking a new position.
1707	Union of Scotland and England	Scottish Parliament abolished, 45 Scottish members join the "English" House of Commons and nine elected peers join the House of Lords.
1711	Property Qualification Act	County representatives to the House of Commons (knights) required to have 600 pounds of income per year and town representatives (burgesses) 300 pounds per year.
1716	Septennial Act	Modifies the Third Triennial Act, by setting the maximum duration of parliament at seven years.
1801	Union with Ireland	The Irish Parliament is abolished, 100 Irish MPs join the "English" House of Commons, and 32 new peers join the House of Lords.
1828	Repeal of the Test Act	Allows Catholics and dissenting Protestants to run for office and hold appointed positions in government.
1829	Catholic Emancipation Act	Allows Catholics to sit in Parliament.
1832	Great Reform Bill	Major electoral reform affecting the House of Commons: the borough franchise is made uniform, the franchise doubles from 10 to 20 percent of male voters; and many seats are redistributed from very small boroughs to the new industrial centers and counties.
1833		Slavery outlawed in the British Empire.
1835	Municipal Corporations Act	Replaces 178 unelected corporate borough governments with elected town councils. Extends local franchise to all male taxpayers with a three-year residency, mandates poor relief.
1859		Repeal of wealth qualification for members of parliaments.

(*continued*)

Table 13.1. *(continued)*

Date	Event	Description
1867	Second Reform Act	Approximately doubles franchise for parliamentary elections by extending the vote to all male property owners; redistribution of seats; expansion of borough boundaries; ends requirement of new elections for members of parliament who take or change posts in the government.
1869	Municipal Franchise Act	Extends right to vote in municipal elections to women taxpayers.
1872	Ballot Act	Secret ballot introduced for parliamentary elections.
1883	Corrupt Practices Act	Places limits on election expenditures by candidates according to a schedule that varies by size of electorate.
1884	Third Reform Act	Extends the franchise to occupants (renters) of properties worth more than 10 pounds per annum.
1885	Redistribution of Seats Act	Reallocates seats and divides most of the remaining two-seat boroughs to establish single-member districts.
1911	Parliamentary Act	Eliminates the House of Lords' veto power (House of Lords can only delay legislation for two years). It also revises the Septennial Act so that the maximum term of parliament is limited to five-year terms, members of parliament receive salaries for the first time.
1918	Fourth Reform Act: Representation of the People Act	Universal suffrage for men older than 21 and for women older than 30 (with some minor residency restrictions); all polls to be held on the same day; free postage for candidate mail associated with elections.
1918	Redistribution Act	Increases the size of the House of Commons, formally adopts principle of equal-size districts, and redistributes seats accordingly.
1922	Irish Free State Act	Irish Parliament reestablished, Irish MPs no longer called, except those from Northern Ireland.
1928	Equal Franchise Act	Women's suffrage put on same basis as men's suffrage (21 years of age).

1948	Representation of the People Act	The remaining two-member constituencies are eliminated (12), as are the university seats; more seats are redistributed.
1949	Parliament Act	Delaying ability of House of Lords further reduced to just one year for legislation.
1958	Life Peerage Act	Provides for the creation of life peers and allows women to sit in the House of Lords.
1973		United Kingdom joins the European Union, confirmed by national referendum in 1975 (67.2 percent yea).
1981	Representation of the People Act	Disqualifies those serving prison sentences of more than 12 months in the United Kingdom from serving in the House of Commons.
1998	Registration of Political Parties Act	Political parties are required to register names (to prevent attempts to confuse the electorate).
1999	Devolution of Powers	Substantial decentralization of policy making to Wales and Scotland. First elections to the "new" Scottish Parliament and Welsh Assembly.
1999	House of Lords Act	Restricts the number of hereditary memberships in the House of Lords to 92.

Sources: Morgan (2001), Field (2002), Rallings and Thrasher (2000), and Stephenson and Marcham (1938). See also *A Brief Chronology of the House of Commons*, House of Commons, 2002.

FOURTEEN

The Swedish Transition to Democracy

SWEDEN'S WRITTEN CONSTITUTIONAL HISTORY

Swedish constitutional history is in many ways similar to that of England, although its international entanglements and its evolutionary path differ somewhat from the English case. Sweden originated as a relatively small kingdom in the early fourteenth century at about the same time that its first constitutional documents were drafted (Helle, Kouri, and Jansson 2003, 401–2, Weibull 1993, 18–22). At its territorial peak in the seventeenth century, its domain included lands in present-day northern Germany, Poland, Russia, the Baltic states, and Finland. Norway was ruled by the Swedish king during most of the nineteenth century. Although not a small country today, Sweden is much smaller now than it was in past centuries. Its constitutional laws, perhaps surprisingly, have been more stable than the territory governed and may be argued to be among the oldest in the world.

It bears noting that usage of the term constitution in this book differs somewhat from that used by many Swedish legal scholars. "Constitution" is normally translated into Swedish as grundlag (foundational or grounding law). Under that definition, there was just one Swedish constitution during the period of greatest interest for this book. Sweden's 1809 grounding law remained in place from 1809 until 1975. However, the Swedish constitution consists of several written laws and customary procedures with special status, rather than a single foundational document, if by constitution it is meant the core procedures through which public policies and top policy makers are chosen. Under that definition, the Swedish state may be said to have operated under at least four different constitutional systems from

1809 to 1975 because its core procedures for choosing public policies and members of parliament underwent four major reforms.[1]

The "new" constitution of 1809 was a relatively liberal document with clear medieval antecedents as shown in the first part of this chapter. That constitution reaffirmed parliament's veto power over taxation and specified formal procedures for constitutional amendment. It included a four-chamber parliament based on the estate system, with noble, clerical, town, and country chambers.

The nineteenth and early twentieth centuries included two periods of major reforms and many other periods in which minor reforms were adopted. The Riksdag Act of 1866 changed the architecture of parliament from a four-chamber assembly to a bicameral one grounded in elections. Major electoral reforms were adopted in 1907 and 1920 that produced universal male and women's suffrage. Another significant reform occurred in 1970 when the two chambers of the Riksdag were merged into a single chamber, although that reform is beyond the scope of the present chapter.[2] Other unwritten reforms also occurred as the balance of public policy-making authority shifted from the king to the parliament in the late nineteenth and early twentieth centuries.

Although Swedish governance was not always bound by its constitution, Sweden's rules for creating laws and amending its constitution have been followed for nearly seven centuries. Table 19.1 lists more than two dozen constitutional reforms adopted during that period.

Origins of Swedish Constitutional Law

The evolution of Swedish governance is generally clearer than that of England because more of its constitutional reforms are formally codified in written constitutional laws.

During the Middle Ages, several territorial governments in Scandinavia were gradually merged into three kingdoms through wars of conquest

[1] That collection of constitutional rules specified that Sweden was governed jointly by a king and Riksdag and also characterized routine royal succession. Under a single instrument of government, Sweden went from a substantially unelected parliament with four chambers to a two-chamber parliament elected with wealth-weighted voting in 1866, universal male and female suffrage under proportional representation in 1909–20, and a unicameral parliament in 1970. These reforms were accomplished by amending the other parts of what is referred to as the Swedish constitution in this chapter (the Instrument of Government, the Riksdag Act, and electoral law).

[2] See Congleton (2003c) for an analysis of Sweden's twentieth-century reforms.

and arranged marriages: Sweden, Norway, and Denmark. The early kings of Scandinavia were normally elected at formal meetings called variously *tings*, *lagtings*, and *althings*, which can be considered precursors to modern parliaments. Indeed, the contemporary Danish parliament is called the Folketing or Folketinget: the people's *ting*. Medieval *tings* were deliberative assemblies that met at regular intervals to settle disputes, pass sentences on law breakers, adopt laws, and select kings. *Tings* thus combined aspects of modern judicial and legislative branches of government.[3] There were local, regional, and national *tings*. Once elected, however, a king normally retained office until his death, although kings were occasionally replaced for extreme malfeasance of their duties.

Contemporary Sweden's constitutional law may be said to have begun at a national *ting*. In 1319, after a twenty-year period of considerable turmoil and mayhem, Magnus Eriksson, the son of Duke Erik, was elected at a national assembly at which, according to the *Rhymed Chronicle*, "both the commons and privileged estates had assembled to elect a king." Magnus Eriksson was only age three and was evidently selected as part of a compromise to restore order and reduce conflict over the top posts in government. It was agreed that governmental decisions would be made by a council representing major noble families who initially served as regents and would later form the royal council after Magnus came of age. The regents (royal council) promised to govern by rule of law and observe due process, and they committed the new king to the same procedures. The regents also committed the king to impose new taxes only after consultation with the royal council (Helle et al. 2003, 401–9; Weibull 1993, 22).

Helle, Kouri, and Jansson (2003, 702) refer to the agreement that formalized Eriksson's election as the Swedish Charter of Liberty. Weibull (1993, 22) refers to the agreement variously as the Letter of Privilege and as the Swedish *Magna Carta*. The dates and details mentioned for this period (and many others) vary a bit among historians. The precise details of Eriksson's accession are less important for the purposes of this book than his subsequent creation and use of a national legal code.

Here and in several other places in the historical narratives, I apply what might be called the law of the blind men and the elephant. When several historians describe the same events in different ways and/or similar events at slightly different dates, I assume that they are all essentially correct.

The Letter of Privilege of 1319 was less an agreement between a king and council than an effort by the Swedish elite to constrain their still very

[3] Petersson (1994, 6) briefly describes these early collective decision-making bodies.

young sovereign. However, the "privilege" became accepted as the law of the land and can be regarded as the first Swedish constitution (Weibull 1993). The king's authority was also constrained by local governments and by international alliances in future years, such as the Hanseatic League and Kalmar Union, and by complex family relationships within northern Europe.

Standing tax revenues from land, many of which were paid in the form of produce, had been fixed in the previous century. There were also excise taxes on copper and obligations for nobles to provide military service to the kingdom when called upon (partly in exchange for tax exemptions). Magnus Eriksson made Stockholm the official port city of Sweden, through which all foreign trade was to pass. This made tariffs and similar payments easier to collect and also made Stockholm the main commercial and political city of Sweden (Helle et al. 2003, 333–4).

Royal income, however, was relatively small, and a good deal of day-to-day financing took the form of loans against future income. The loans were partly from the Catholic Church and partly from noble families in northern Europe (Helle et al. 2003, 407–8). Loans were evidently easier to obtain than new taxes from the council.

Approximately thirty years after the Letter of Privilege, King Magnus Eriksson promulgated a new unified legal code for the entire kingdom (the Land Law). The new legal code was a synthesis of the best practices in Scandinavia and served as the foundation of Swedish law until the nineteenth century. Eriksson's Land Law created a uniform criminal and civil law for the kingdom as a whole, specified judicial procedures, and included constitutional provisions, which included and extended the promises made on his behalf in the 1319 charter.

The constitutional provisions of Eriksson's Land Law stated, for example, that the king "shall be true and faithful to all his subjects and he shall not harm anyone poor or rich, except according to law and after legal process." It called for a royal council to be selected (by the king) that would consist of twelve Swedish nobles and seven native-born church officials who would serve on the council for life (Upton 1998: 1–2, Helle et al. 2003, 700–1). The royal council would have veto power: "in the future no laws should be given to the common people without their [the council's] aye and good will" (Wigmore 1912, 21). It further states that new taxes would be negotiated with delegations of the provinces and that subsequent kings would be elected by such assemblies (Helle et al. 2003, 701).[4]

[4] Similar civil codes and more or less representative constitutional structures had been adopted by Denmark (Jydske Law) and Norway (Laws of Gula-thing and Jonsbok) in

The main provisions of Eriksson's land law were repeated many times, as for example in Kristoffer's code ratified in 1442 (Weibull 1993, 22). A new official text was printed and distributed in 1608 (Upton 1998, 2). In this manner, Swedish governance became grounded in written documents that remained in force for centuries at a time.

EMERGENCE OF THE SWEDISH PARLIAMENT

Eriksson's Land Law codified the practice of calling for assemblies of nobles, church officials, and regional governments, but it did not create a formal architecture for such assemblies. This emerged gradually over the course of the next two centuries.

A series of Swedish national assembles were called during the fourteenth and fifteenth centuries to address tax issues and to elect sovereigns (Bellquist 1935; Helle et al. 2003, 701–2; Sawyer and Sawyer 1993, 95–9). These assemblies were initially similar to *tings* in that they were arranged at times of religious and commercial festivals to increase participation. The latter suggests that national assemblies during this time were not considered to very important, possibly because central governments were not considered to be very important. Governance was quite decentralized during the late Middle Ages.

The most important of the early Swedish assemblies occurred in 1388 when it met and elected Margrethe of Denmark to be the next Swedish sovereign, a few years after Eriksson's death. In 1389, Margrethe arranged to have the crowns of Denmark, Norway, and Sweden placed on a single head (that of her grand nephew, Erik), which began the period of the Kalmar Union (1389–1521). The Kalmar Union was formally a period of joint sovereignty, rather than a merger of the three countries (according to Swedish and Norwegian accounts). The national laws and councils of Sweden, Denmark, and Norway remained distinct, as was normally the case during periods of joint sovereignty in Europe.[5]

the century before (Wigmore 1912, 17–20). An early-fifteenth-century (illustrated) version of Eriksson's national law code can be found at the library of Uppsala University (on parchment).

5 Queen Margrethe was related to the Swedish royal family through marriage to Magnus Eriksson's son, Håkon. Magnus Eriksson had been sovereign of Norway as well as Sweden during most of his lifetime.

The transition from Erisson to Håkon to Margrethe was not a simple or uncontested one, although it was consistent with the rules of inheritance in Scandinavia at the time, and it was ratified by a Swedish national assembly as required under Eriksson's Land Law (Sawyer and Sawyer 1993, 69–75).

Sweden's Land Law thus remained in place, as did most national, regional, and local governmental institutions, including its royal council, which was largely populated by Swedes. Accession charters normally required the Danish kings to consult with the three councils of state and to call their parliaments. Assemblies of regional governments continued to be called in Sweden to deliberate on new taxes and royal succession. Such meetings occurred, for example, in 1396, 1441, 1448, 1520, 1521 (Sawyer and Sawyer 1993, 71–9).

The specific institutional form that emerged for meetings of the Swedish national assembly evidently reflected Danish practices. The Danes distinguished among the "estates" (groups that had their own legal rights), and Danish government included a national parliament of the estates, which had been called the Riksdag since 1241 (Helle 2003, 680; Wigmore 1912, 547–8).

Secession from the Kalmar Union

Disputes between the Danish sovereign and the Swedish and Norwegian councils did occur and occasionally rose to the point of armed revolts (usually over taxes).

In 1435, the usual centralization disputes of this period led to a rebellion in Sweden. The leader of that rebellion, Engelbrekt, called a meeting of nobles, clergy, burghers, and peasants in Arboga. The four groups met separately and each initially had equal veto power. They agreed to carry through the decision of a majority of the chambers and agreed to support Engelbrekt in his negotiations with the Danish crown. They also elected Engelbrekt and Knutsson protectors of Sweden. Subsequent negotiations (and a bit of military resistance) formally increased Swedish autonomy in 1438 and temporarily produced a Swedish king in 1448. Sweden's succession from the Kalmar Union, however, was not acceptable to the Danish king (Toyne 1948, 86–9; Sawyer and Sawyer 1993, 76).

A few decades later, a war of succession took place. Hansaeatic support for Sweden was enlisted against the Danes. The centralization contest between Sweden and Denmark was finally resolved in Sweden's favor during the first decades of the sixteenth century, after the Danish army lost a series of battles.

In 1523, the leader of the Swedish war of secession was elected king of Sweden by the Riksdag (at Strängnäs). Gustav Vasa, although bound by the procedures of the Land Law, acted rapidly to buttress his authority.[6]

[6] Norway remained under the Danish sovereign until the end of the Napoleonic period when the king of Sweden also became king of Norway.

Sweden's territory expanded as lands were taken from Danish rule and added to Sweden's. As the Swedish territories expanded, the national *tings* were replaced by formal gatherings of the four estates: the nobles, burghers (town leaders), clerics, and peasants (non-noble landowners).

In this sense, it could be said that the Swedish Riksdag (as a four-chamber national parliament) and the kingdom of Sweden emerged more or less simultaneously. Parliament (the Riksdag) was called principally to deal with tax issues and successions. Most of the kings accepted accession charters drafted by the Riksdag at the time they came to office, which normally committed them to rule lawfully and constitutionally while obliging their subjects to abide by the law. The four-estate architecture of the Swedish parliament continued until 1866.

Day-to-day governance was also based on the king-and-council template. The king continued to appoint and consult with a council of state, whose members were chosen from among the most powerful families in Sweden. The council of state (Riksråd) met far more often and exercised greater influence over day-to-day policies than Sweden's parliament.

The balance of policy-making authority among the king, council of state, and Riksdag fluctuated somewhat during the next two centuries, although the king remained the dominant figure in national politics during most of this period. The king had veto power over the recommendations of the Swedish parliament and council, and he could normally engineer support in the parliament and council for policies of interest to him.

The Shifting Balance of Authority

During periods in which kings were away (or were minors), the council of state would rule Sweden in the king's name. In other periods, kings would delegate more or less authority to their councils according to their personal interests on matters of state and policy agendas.

In 1527, King Gustav Vasa with the support of the parliament ended Catholicism in Sweden, making Lutheranism the official state religion with himself as head of the Swedish Lutheran Church. As in other places, Sweden's Protestant Reformation transferred control of a good deal of real estate from the Catholic Church to the king. This, as elsewhere in northern Europe, reduced the need for royal subsidies from the parliament and increased the king's ability to reward personal loyalty. Both effects increased pragmatic support for the reformation within the parliament (Toyne 1948, 130–4).

In 1544, sovereignty was made formally hereditary for the house of Vasa, which greatly reduced the parliament's control over succession. It also eliminated the parliament and council's ability to draft accession charters, which further reduced parliament's influence within the government for the next fifty years.

In 1594, however, there was no direct Vasa heir, and the council and parliament intervened to determine who would rule.[7] The parliament elected a new sovereign and required the new king (Sigismund) to accept an oath of accession, which among other conditions specified acceptance of Lutheranism. Sigismund accepted, and the next several kings also accepted accession charters and took oaths of office (*konungaforsäkran*) at the time of their accession. (The religious condition for accession was introduced in Sweden approximately a century before it was introduced in Great Britain.)

An especially restrictive oath of office was negotiated in 1611 under which the seventeen-year-old Gustav Adolphus pledged not to "make laws, declare war or peace, or form alliances without the estates' and council's consent, and not to impose any new taxes without first consulting with the council" (Weibull 1993, 40). It was in Gustav Adolphus's reign that the first formal Riksdag Act was adopted (in 1617). It affirmed the legal requirement that the king consult the four estates before declaring war or forming alliances. In 1650, the parliament secured veto authority over all new laws (Toyne 1948, 156–60; Roberts 1986, 4). In 1660, a protocol calling for the routine meetings of the parliament was adopted, which gave the Riksdag a more independent standing.[8]

As in other places, accepting a parliamentary veto reduced but did not eliminate the sovereign's control of public policy. Patronage, customs of royal deference, elevation, and land grants could be used to align the interests of members of the council of state and parliament with those of the royal household. The king's army could also be occasionally employed to threaten and punish those who opposed royal policy, although not arbitrarily. As a consequence, shifts of policy-making authority from the parliament to the executive branch normally reflected the skill of a particular king and his advisors, rather than new laws, and so were not always codified in formal documents.

7 An early Swedish contract theory of the hereditary monarchy was developed by Erik Sparre in 1590 (Roberts 1986, 64).

8 A series of other reforms were adopted at more or less at the same time. Positions in the council of state (Riksråd) were henceforth limited to nobles. Five major departments of government were also organized, including ones for the chancellor, treasury, admiralty, the marshal, and high steward. Schools were also established for noble children, and a pathway for talented commoners into the low nobility was established. A meeting place for nobles was established in Stockholm (Riddarhuset). The courts were reorganized and the law more uniformly applied (Toyne 1948, 156–60).

A very public example occurred when Karl XI took office in 1675. After a fifteen-year regency with considerable evidence of mismanagement by his five regents and the council of state, Karl asked the lower chambers of the parliament (the burghers and farmers) to investigate the regents and council of state (who were largely from major noble families). The lower chambers found against the regents and directed that essentially all countships, baronies, manors, and other estates owned by the guilty parties revert to the sovereign (*reduktion*). The penalty eliminated the fortunes of many of the most influential families in Sweden. Karl XI used the proceeds of land sales and grants to reduce debts, increase his support, and finance his relatively efficient government.

Karl XI elevated many loyal senior bureaucrats and army officers to the nobility after the *reduktion* had reduced the number of the old aristocratic families in that chamber. Many of the new nobles had little personal wealth and so depended entirely on their positions in the military and bureaucracy for their incomes, which provided the king with additional influence in the noble chamber (Roberts 1986, 4–6). The new nobles were relatively more likely to attend and vote in the noble chamber of the parliament because most lived and worked in Stockholm. Consequently, they tended to dominate proceedings in the noble chamber.[9]

Karl XI also created a new, more efficient Swedish bureaucracy, which could regulate and interpret laws but not, in principle, adopt new laws without parliament's approval. Riksdag approval, however, was somewhat easier to obtain with the support from the new members of the noble chamber (the Riddarhuset) and other members of parliament employed in the bureaucracy. A late medieval king did not have to resort to threats of violence to affect parliamentary decisions.

During times of war, the parliament and council often gave kings temporary authority to impose new taxes for a few years at a time during a period of war. In 1693, the parliament extended the royal taxing power again, but this time for "the period of crisis." The absence of an explicit time limit essentially freed Karl XI, and subsequently Karl XII, from parliamentary fiscal constraints because wars and other "crises" were commonplace at this period.

The result was a nearly absolutist period of Swedish governance. Indeed, Karl XII, perhaps inspired by British precedents, never called the parliament into session. National debts rapidly increased, as Swedish resources

9 Elevation also evidently allowed Karl XI to save money on bureaucratic and military salaries (Roberts 1986, 73–5). (Karl is sometimes translated as Charles by English historians.)

were consumed in a variety of unsuccessful military campaigns, in spite of the king's new freedom to raise taxes. Parliament's fiscal mistake had greatly reduced its bargaining power.

The unexpected death of Karl XII in 1719 reversed the tide of events favoring royal authority because Karl XII died without children.

THE AGE OF LIBERTY, 1720–1771

The absence of a clear heir (together with the army's support for the parliament) provided the parliament with the opportunity to choose the next king. Army leaders had declared that they would not take an oath to a king not elected by parliament. There were two natural alternatives, Karl Frederick of Holstein, the grandson of Karl XI, and Ulrika Eleonora, the sister of Karl XII.

Negotiations with the two potential sovereigns were undertaken with restoring the medieval constitution and enhancing the parliament's authority in mind (Roberts 1986, 6–7, 30, 60). As a consequence of those negotiations, Ulrika Eleonora accepted an oath of office (accession charter) that included the promises of no taxation without parliament consent, freedom of election for the three representative chambers (those representing farmers, townsmen, and church officials), and the right of free speech in the parliament (Roberts 1986, 60, note 9). These privileges had been granted to Swedish parliaments in previous times – although they had been largely ignored during the reign of Karl XI and Karl XII.

Additional opportunities for constitutional bargaining arose when the new queen attempted to have her husband Frederick (the landgrave [duke] of Hesse) elected King. The result was a new constitutional regime characterized by three documents negotiated by the parliament and accepted by the queen and her husband: (a) a new Instrument of Government (Grundlag, 1720), (b) Frederick's Accession Charter (1720), and (c) a new Riksdag Act of 1723. The new constitutional documents reestablished and strengthened the parliament's control of legislation and taxation.[10]

Under the new constitutional regime, the Riksdag would meet for three months every three years, and all new laws required majority approval in three of the four chambers. New taxes required support in all four estates. A "secret committee" composed of fifty nobles, twenty-five clerics, and twenty-five burghers served as the agenda maker for legislation in the parliament.

[10] In 1734, a new civil code was adopted to update existing civil law, although it and the new Instrument of Government remained grounded in Eriksson's Land Law.

A similar committee had formerly dealt with sensitive foreign-policy issues (secrets), but was now given responsibility for developing policy proposals and monitoring the cabinet (council) and the courts. The farmer's estate was excluded from the committee.

All nobles had the right to participate in their chamber, with the consequence that it was the largest of the four chambers, although normally nobles from distant provinces without business in Stockholm skipped meetings and votes.[11] Members of the lower three chambers were generally selected via elections of various kinds, often through wealth-weighted voting and/or indirect elections (Roberts 1986, 70). The burgher representatives were often appointed by town councils, and in many periods, the majority of the town representatives were burgermeisters (mayors). The farmer representatives were often appointed by local county governments, which were often dominated by large landowners, in part because of weighted voting. The clerics were elected by their fellow clerics, with fairly broad participation during much of their history. Weighted voting, indirect elections, and variation in local eligibility for suffrage continued until the early twentieth century.[12]

The combination of agenda control and veto authority gave the Swedish parliament far greater authority over legislation than it had possessed in previous centuries. However, the reformed council of state (Rådet) remained important during the Age of Liberty. It issued rules when the parliament was not in session, which it was not for thirty-three months of every three-year cycle.

Members of the council were selected by the king from a short list of candidates (normally three) recommended by the parliament. Council members could not sit in the parliament. The king served as the council's president and had two votes (of eighteen). He also had the ability to settle ties. The nomination lists, however, provided the parliament with significant agenda control over the selection of ministers and other advisors of state for the first time. The parliament could also impeach individual ministers (Roberts 1986, 82–9; Weibull 1993, 53). The council's major rulings had to be affirmed at the next meeting of the parliament, although this often

[11] Nobles could also appoint representatives to sit in their seats and occasionally sold this privilege (Verney 1957, 25).

[12] Suffrage in the towns was possible for all resident burghers who paid taxes, but votes were weighted in proportion to their financial contributions. Suffrage for the peasants was similarly constrained by land ownership and independence, and votes were often weighted by land holdings (Roberts 1986, 70). There were no national suffrage laws at this point. Instead, the towns made up their own rules, which varied somewhat throughout Sweden.

proved to be a difficult task, because the council and the parliament often disagreed about how "major" a given ruling was (Roberts 1986, 82).[13]

Although suffrage was limited by significant wealth qualifications, elections were often competitive.[14] This, together with the benefits of coordinated voting in a parliament with decisive policy-making authority, caused political parties to emerge (the "hats" and the "caps"), first as coalitions of representatives with shared interests, and then for purposes of national political campaigns.[15] The early political parties affected parliamentary decisions, including its suggestions for membership on the council of state, which allowed party leaders to indirectly control a broad range of governmental decisions.

Royal power did not completely disappear, as is sometimes claimed, but was greatly diminished in importance from 1720–72. Sweden did not become a republic. Formal control of the executive remained with the king, and a broad cross-section of members in the parliament held appointed positions in the bureaucracy of one kind or another, which gave the king some leverage over the parliament. The king's ability to use patronage, however, was far from complete, because many administrative positions were lifetime appointments reserved for nobles alone. Leadership positions in the army were also limited to nobles. Frederick I's ability to intervene in governmental affairs was further reduced by his inability to speak Swedish and by his lack of standing relationships with influential Swedish families.[16]

Frederick I died in 1751 without (legitimate) children. He was followed by Adolf Frederick, who ruled from 1751–71, and who took office under a similarly restrictive accession charter and constitutional rules.

[13] Parliament and the secret committee instructed the council on a variety of matters including foreign policy, monetary, and fiscal policies. The council was the fiduciary agent of the estates, but they had little control over the council while they were not in session (Roberts 1986, 82–6).

[14] Fregert (2009, 5) reports that only a few percent of the population belonged to the noble, clergy, and burgher estates. Suffrage for the much larger peasant estate included between 20 and 30 percent of the adult male population. Elections were made more direct, and qualifications for suffrage more uniform in the parliamentary reforms of 1866.

[15] The "Hats" are sometimes regarded to be the Swedish equivalent of the English Tories (who often had French support), and the "Caps" as Sweden's liberals (who often had Russian and occasionally English support). There were a number of politically important English, French, and Russian international intrigues at this time, which are neglected to focus on constitutional developments. See Svanstrom (2008, 210–50) for a somewhat dramatic presentation of them.

[16] After 1723, the Frederick I was reported to devote most of his energy to hunting and romance rather than governance (Nordstrom 2000, 108).

Constitutional negotiations continued under Adolf Frederick with revised amendment procedures adopted in 1766 and a reduction in state censorship. The freedom of the press acts of 1766 eliminated prepublication censorship except for religious materials. It remained a crime, however, to publish material attacking the king, the estates, or the Lutheran Church (Roberts 1986, 106). A Swedish enclosure movement began the mid-eighteenth century, followed by organizations that lobbied for suffrage reform (Roberts 1986, 138, 144, 208).

Economic Problems and the End of the Age of Liberty

The parliament was able to bring the budget into balance and to pay down the war debts of Karl XI and XII during the first twenty years of the Age of Liberty. However, it was not able to keep the budget in balance in the long run. This occurred partly because of the separation between budget and tax decisions, but mainly because of participation in two expensive international wars. Deficits increased during most of the second half of the Age of Liberty (and continued to expand after it had ended). Toward the end of the period of liberty, fiscal crises were commonplace, inflation was high, a severe recession was under way, and army salaries were not always paid on time or at all.[17]

Adolf Frederick was succeeded by his eldest son Gustav in 1771, who became Gustav III upon his accession at the age of twenty-six. The Riksdag continued trying to find agreeable institutional reforms to address the government's fiscal problems, but it could not find a compromise that would satisfy the four chambers of the parliament and the king, as required for constitutional reforms. Under the 1766 amendment procedures, all four chambers had to support constitutional reforms.

Partly because of Riksdag's failure to deal with Sweden's economic problems, parliamentary dominance of public policy came to an end shortly afterwards. In 1772, with the poorly and irregularly paid army at his side, Gustav III "suggested" constitutional reforms that increased royal authority over public policy. The parliament "accepted" Gutav's reforms by acclamation with armed troops assembled outside (Roberts 1986, 206; Svanstrom 2008, 253–5). Although many of the members of parliament favored a

[17] A careful description of the budgetary process and economic conditions during this period is provided by Fregert (2009). His figure 3 plots nominal and real Swedish government debt for 1719–76. It implies that much of the new debt between 1745 and 1776 was monetized, leading to inflation. Attempts to reverse the inflation and bring the budget back into balance, in turn, induced a recession and another fiscal crisis.

stronger monarchy, it is clear that the king's implicit threat changed many votes.

Gustav's 1772 Instrument of Government reversed the tide of political liberalization, although at first it could be said to have simply restored the medieval balance of authority. Under the revised constitution, the king regained his former authority to appoint members of the council of state and to call and dismiss parliament. The Riksdag ceased to be self-calling, but it retained its veto over new taxation and legislation. No new taxes, laws, or wars could take effect without the consent of a majority of the four estates. Indeed, the Riksdag's power of the purse was initially enhanced somewhat by its new control of the Swedish national bank, the Riksbank (Fregert 2009). Trade and freedom of the press were also somewhat liberalized through reforms adopted in 1774.

Gustav's intervention in 1772 was evidently quite popular, given the economic circumstances of that time. Stockholm was said to be filled with a "tumult of rejoicing" after the new Instrument of Government was adopted (Roberts 1986, 204).

Significance of the Age of Liberty

Sweden's Age of Liberty is important for the purposes of this book because it affirms several predictions of Part I. First, the more liberal constitution of 1720 was not invented whole cloth, but rather reformed preexisting Swedish political institutions. The new division of policy-making authority was the result of bargaining, rather than revolution. The shift in policy-making authority from king to parliament resulted from queen- and king-specific agreements in the form of accession oaths and constitutional reforms negotiated with (potential) sovereigns. The king-and-council template remained in place, although the balance of authority shifted from one nearly polar case to the other. The age of liberty demonstrates that substantial shifts in constitutional authority can occur peacefully within that template when the bargaining power of the parliament increases relative to the king (and vice versa).

Second, as in England after its civil war and during the first half of the nineteenth century, the Swedish Age of Liberty demonstrates that parliamentary domination of policy formation is not necessarily accompanied by major expansions of suffrage. A Swedish suffrage movement began to gather momentum in 1769, but the estates, if anything, were inclined to increase the requirements for membership in the parliament, rather than reduce them (Roberts 1986, 208–10). Electoral reform is not always in parliament's interest.

Third, the English civil war and Swedish age of liberty demonstrate that liberalization in Europe did not require the inspiration of the French or American Revolutions. Many Swedish policies reflected liberal ideological goals as well as economic and partisan ones in this period. Although pragmatic interests were arguably more important than liberalism, the torrent of political pamphlets published during the Age of Liberty (partly a consequence of reduced censorship) demonstrated that liberal ideas had already begun to affect the political theories and norms of Swedish intellectuals, voters, and politicians. Eighteenth-century constitutional debates included arguments favoring a free press, due process, and separation of powers in the 1760s (Roberts 1986, 61, 106–8).[18]

Fourth, the relatively poor fiscal policies of the parliament in the second half of this period suggest that parliaments, like kings, have tendencies to spend more than is raised through taxes. National debt fell somewhat during the first decade or two of parliamentary rule but rose substantially during its later period, particularly during the hat government. The national debt, however, rebounded between 1757 and 1765, largely because of participation in the Pomeranian war, but also because of peacetime extravagance (Roberts 1986, 19–20). Indeed, the fiscal problems were so severe that the government lacked the means to pay interest on the national debt and salaries for the army and bureaucracy, which created the support necessary for Gustav III to end parliamentary rule. Parliamentary rule by itself does not assure fiscal responsibility.

Fifth, the Swedish and English experiences suggest that the political influence of kings who do not speak the national language tends to be smaller than that of sovereigns who are able to undertake their own direct negotiations with parliament, the bureaucracy, and the army. As a consequence, more authority tends to be delegated to ministers and, indirectly, to parliament. The English and Swedish parliaments gained authority under two German-speaking kings and lost authority when a native speaker returned to the throne (George III and Gustav III). This suggests that bargaining ability as well as institutions affect the balance of authority between kings and parliament.

[18] It is an exaggeration to say that all of Sweden's constitutional reforms and public policies resulted from domestic pressures during the sixteenth and seventeenth centuries. Sweden had long received subsidies from France and England in exchange for participation in continental wars. Partly for that reason, war and international alliances had absorbed much of Sweden's governmental time and treasure since the Protestant Reformation. Adolf Fredrik's accession to the throne in 1743 as successor to Fredrick I (who died without heirs shortly after his queen) was clearly influenced by international considerations as well as domestic ones (Roberts 1986, 31).

Economic and Other Political Developments in the Eighteenth Century

The Swedish economy began gradually industrializing and internationalizing in the eighteenth century, as in much of Europe. A Swedish East India Company was established in 1731, which helped produce a new silk industry. Water-powered equipment for metal working was invented by Polhem, and the Celsius thermometer by Anders Celsius in the mid-eighteenth century. Botany was placed on a rational, scientific foundation by Linnaeus, who also revised the Celsius thermometer by making one hundred degrees the boiling temperature of water and zero its freezing point, reversing Celsius's initial mapping of temperatures into numbers. New Royal Academies of Science and Literature were founded. Copper and iron industries, which had prospered since the sixteenth century, grew more rapidly as new uses for metals were developed.

Steam engines were introduced by Triewal in the late eighteenth century. However, land reforms and the first railroads were not completed until the mid-nineteenth century (Roberts 1986, 139; Verney 1957, 22). Consequently, economic life in 1800 for the most part reflected its medieval foundations. Mercantilist policies continued to affect internal and external trade. Rural trading was constrained to favor specific market towns, many guilds retained monopoly privileges, and exports of silver and gold were controlled (Roberts 1986, 137, 165, 208).

THE 1809 INSTRUMENT OF GOVERNANCE

The 1772 Instrument of Government had essentially restored the medieval constitution. It did not attempt to return to the nearly polar case of Karl XII. Parliaments were routinely called and passed legislation and tax bills. The tax base was expanded to include noble estates, which had previously been largely untaxed. Royal successions, however, continued to be far from routine as infertility and unexpected deaths remained commonplace for the royal family as well as commoners. European entanglements continued to influence Swedish foreign and domestic policies. Swedish governance, nonetheless, remained fairly stable for nearly forty years, although trends in those years favored royal authority.[19]

[19] Gustav III's Act of Union and Security of 1789 attempted to secure somewhat greater authority for the king by reducing the independence of the nobility. It abolished noble privileges with respect to taxation and high office. It also established a new supreme court

Governance during the second half of the Age of Liberty, with its high debt, inflation, and even famine, had undermined support for parliamentary rule, but not parliament's interest in greater authority. Another dispute over succession to the throne in 1809 provided the Swedish parliament with another opportunity for constitutional renegotiation.[20] The Riksdag was again in the position of selecting a king (or two in this case). Accepting a new constitution was made a condition for occupying the Swedish throne. A revised grundlag (Instrument of Government, IG) was quickly adopted by the Riksdag and accepted by the new king, Karl XIII, as a condition of his accession.[21]

The 1809 Instrument of Government was, of course, not entirely new.[22] It specified the traditional architecture for Swedish governance: a constitutional monarchy with a king, a council of state (cabinet), and a four-chamber parliament. It also described a distribution of authority between the executive and the parliament that was still very much in the executive's favor, although less so than under Gustav III's 1772 Instrument of Government. For example article 4 stated that: the *king alone* should govern the kingdom in accordance with the provisions of the constitution (IG).

The constitution, however, did constrain the sovereign. The king was forbidden to deprive "anyone of life, honor, personal liberty, or well being unless he has been legally tried and condemned" (article 16). Other provisions

and reduced parliament's control over legislation and the declaration of war, although it preserved parliament's veto over new taxes. The act was accepted by the clergy, burgher, and farmer chambers, but rejected by the noble chamber. Gustav proclaimed the act to have come to force nonetheless.

His unconstitutional overruling of the nobles chamber on this and subsequent tax decisions is said to have led to his assassination in 1792 (Weibull 1993, 73–5; Ward et al. 1909, 780–2; Grimberg 1935, 314).

20 Gustav Adolf IV was deposed by a broad coalition of army officers and government officials (many of whom were members of the Riksdag). His heirs were declared disqualified for the throne in March 1809. The overthrow of Gustav was quickly ratified by the Riksdag, and the constitution of 1809 was drafted while negotiating with successors (Weibull 1993, 76). This "parliamentary" coup d'état occurred partly because of Gustav's failures in warfare (through which Finland was lost), partly out of concerns for his mental competence, and partly by his neglect of constitutional governance. (A few years later, the Vienna Congress granted the Swedish sovereign the Norwegian crown [from Denmark] in compensation for losing Finland to Russia.)

21 Karl XIII was the brother of Gustav III, who was relatively old and childless. At essentially the same time that Karl XIII was chosen to be Gustav IV's successor, his successor was also chosen, but surprisingly, from well outside Swedish royal and noble circles. Karl XIII's successor was to be Jean-Baptiste Bernadotte, a commoner who had risen to high military office in France during its revolutionary period (Marshall). He took the name Karl XIV when he became king of Sweden and Norway in 1818. Bernadotte renounced Catholicism and converted to Lutheranism to qualify for the throne. However, he never learned to speak Swedish.

22 A translation of the 1809 Instrument of Government can be found in Dodd 1909, 219–59. The article numbers referred to are from that translation.

restored the medieval balance, which had shifted in the king's favor during the past few decades. The king was bound to consult with his cabinet on most matters, including the declaration of war. He was also obliged to consult with parliament on matters of taxation and budgeting:

> The **ancient right of the Swedish people to tax themselves** shall be exercised by the **Riksdag alone** (article 58) … **No general tax**, of whatever name or character, **may be increased** without the consent of the Riksdag, the duties on imported and exported grain alone excepted nor shall the king lease the revenues of the state, or establish any monopoly for the benefit of himself and the crown or of individuals and corporations (article 60). … **All taxes voted** by the Riksdag, under the headings mentioned in the preceding article, shall be collected **until the end of the year** within which the new taxes are to be voted by the Riksdag (article 61).
>
> It devolves upon the Riksdag, after examining the needs of the treasury, to vote supplies to meet such needs and also to prescribe the special purposes for which separate items of appropriation may be used… (article 62).

Members were granted freedom of expression during meetings of parliament, and interference with a member's efforts to attend sessions of the Riksdag was punished severely (article 110).[23] The king retained the authority to appoint the council of state and retained substantial executive discretion to implement public policy as he and his council saw fit.

Beyond these relatively traditional medieval authorities and privileges, the Riksdag gained the authority to censure individual members of the king's cabinet, although not to remove them from office. The council was no longer entirely protected by royal immunity. The 1809 Instrument of Government also guaranteed routine meetings of the Riksdag of three months in duration (articles 49 and 109) and assured annual meetings through a one-year limit on royal tax authority (article 61). The Riksdag thus gained greater control over taxes and the budget than in any previous period except during the Age of Liberty. All royal acts had to be countersigned by the council of state.

Three other fundamental laws completed the constitutional core of Swedish governance: a new Riksdag act, a revised law of succession, and a revised press act were given explicit constitutional status (article 85). Fundamental laws were to be interpreted literally (article 84). Procedures for amending the fundamental laws required the consent of two successive sessions of the Riksdag and the king (article 82).

[23] Anyone, including ministers or other high officials, who forcibly interfered with a member of parliament's efforts to dispatch his duties was deemed guilty of treason. The mandated punishment for treason required that the guilty person's right hand be cut off, their bones broken on the wheel, and then executed. In addition, the treasonous party's properties were forfeited to the sovereign (Verney 1957, 23).

It was under the 1809 Instrument of Government that Sweden made its transition from monarchy to parliamentary rule and democracy during the nineteenth and early twentieth centuries. By coincidence, a major technological innovation occurred in the same year that also helped shape economic and political developments in the nineteenth century. The first Swedish factory using steam was founded in Stockholm by an English mechanic (Samuel Owen) in 1809 (Grimberg 1935, 339).

Sweden's gradual transition to parliamentary democracy in the nineteenth century required neither palace coups nor popular revolts, although many peaceful demonstrations took place. Rather, changes in underlying political and economic circumstances led to a series of constitutional bargains that made the Riksdag a more effective advocate of its institutional and partisan interests. This, together with the rise of liberal ideology, industrialization, and emergence of more disciplined political parties, gradually transformed Swedish governance into a modern parliamentary democracy.

The major reforms of the nineteenth and early twentieth centuries affected the organization of the Riksdag, election law, and the extent of civil liberties, rather than the existence of Sweden's constitutional monarchy. Major reforms were adopted using formal constitutional procedures for amendment. Minor reforms were adopted as ordinary legislation.

CONSTITUTIONAL BARGAINING PRODUCES A NEW BICAMERAL RIKSDAG IN 1866

In most respects, the constitutional history of Sweden after 1809 is consistent with the transition models of Part I. Policy reforms were commonplace, and there was a clear liberal trend in the pattern of reforms. Public demonstrations were also commonplace, but there was little if any real threat of revolution.

Liberal pressures for reform were immediately evident in the period following the adoption of the 1809 Instrument of Government. The estates themselves were modified as representation in three of the four estates was extended to include new groups. In the 1820s, the clergy estate invited new members from the major universities and from the Swedish Academy of Science. In 1830, the burgher estate added industrialists to its long-standing guild-based membership. In 1845, suffrage for the farmers' estate was expanded to include (non-noble) owners of tax-exempt land and was further expanded in 1863 to include middle-class property owners.[24]

[24] Representatives for the farmers' estate were indirectly elected at the county (*härad*) level by electors selected at churches; only Lutherans were allowed to vote until 1860. Only

Other significant procedural and public policy reforms were also adopted. In 1830, parliamentary debates were made public. In 1842, compulsory education was introduced. In 1846, King Oscar I abolished the guild system (by decree).[25] In 1860, a law of religious toleration was passed. Jews with sufficient property acquired the franchise in 1865. Numerous proposals for the reform of the Riksdag were also introduced, including demands for unicameral (1830) and bicameral parliaments (1840 and 1851), with memberships based on elections, rather than occupation. However, none secured the necessary approval of all four estates.

A consensus for placing parliament on an electoral basis was present in the farmers' and burghers' estates, and support for other reforms of parliament had been increasing in the noble chamber and council of state, as liberal economic and political ideas and industrialization gained ground during the first half of the nineteenth century. However, no proposals for parliamentary reform gained broad enough support to be adopted. To revise the Riksdag act, majorities in all four existing chambers and acceptance by the king were required.

In 1859, the accession of Karl XV changed the noninstitutional interests of the king and his cabinet, which provided new opportunities for constitutional negotiations. New men were appointed to the royal cabinet, including Baron Louis de Geer, who became minister of justice and chancellor. De Geer was a long-serving senior bureaucrat, a member of a successful industrial family, a noble, and also a moderate liberal interested in parliamentary reform.[26] In 1863, Chancellor De Geer proposed a new, more liberal organization of the Riksdag.

Much of what De Geer proposed had been suggested before, but there was greater support for political liberalization in the 1860s than in previous periods, and his reforms were more carefully crafted to acquire the support needed for constitutional amendment. De Geer proposed that the old

tax-paying farmers could participate in these elections, and no representative could be from other estates or in the employment of the sovereign, which eliminated nobles, burghers, clerics, and bureaucrats from the farmer estate (Verney 1957, 29–30). Such restrictions did not apply to the other estates, who often served in the army or bureaucracy.

25 Oscar I was the son of Karl XIII. He came to office in 1844 with the death of his father, who had lived well into his eighties. Oscar was a well-educated, relatively liberal man in the years before he assumed the throne. He initially chose his advisors from the liberal party, although he shifted toward the conservative party toward the end of his rule (Grimberg 1935, 330–1).

26 The institutional details in the rest of this chapter are for the most part from Verney's (1957) careful political history of the Riksdag in the nineteenth century. Grimberg (1935), Metcalf (1987), and Grofman and Lijphart (2002) also provide useful institutional details.

four-chamber Riksdag be reorganized into two chambers: a first and second chamber. All members of the reorganized Riksdag were to be elected for fixed terms of office, although new elections could be called during the terms by the king. The first chamber would have one hundred twenty-five members with relatively long terms of office (nine years), and who would be relatively old (older than thirty-five years) and relatively wealthy, and would not receive a salary, but would live on their own means. The second chamber would have one hundred ninety members with relatively short terms of office (three years). Membership in the second chamber was to be less restricted and more directly elected than that in the first chamber.

Chancellor De Geer managed to achieve the required level of consensus in the farmer, burgher, and noble chambers by proposing an indirect wealth-weighted-voting system for the first chamber based on existing appointment procedures for selecting representatives in the farmer and burgher chambers, and a more direct franchise for the second chamber. The interests of the clergy were also taken into account. A new church assembly was to be formed in which national church matters would be decided by the clergy without being subject to veto by the other estates (Verney 1957, 64).

The new one hundred twenty-five–seat first chamber was designed to protect the interests of the wealthier members of the three secular chambers. Its seats were reserved for men with substantial property. Only six thousand persons were eligible for seats in the first chamber, and in 1863 most of those lived in Stockholm. There were no residency requirements, so that those living in Stockholm could run for office in whatever province in which they might expect sufficient electoral support. Members of the first chamber were to be elected indirectly by twenty-four provincial councils in a manner roughly analogous to that of the U.S. Senate at that time.

The influence of wealthy Swedes in elections for the first chamber was reinforced by a striking feature of mid-century election laws for the provincial councils. All tax-paying citizens could vote in elections for provincial councils, including independent women. However, votes for provincial councils were weighted according to a schedule of tax payments. A person in the highest tax category might cast as many as five thousand votes. A similar system was used in towns, where persons in the highest tax categories could cast up to one hundred votes (Verney 1957, 50, 91). The weighted-voting system often allowed local elections to be determined by a handful of wealthy men or women. In 10 percent of the districts, the weighted votes of just three or four voters could be decisive (Verney 1957, 91; Särlvik 2002, 333). Election by provincial councils, nonetheless, implied that local interests could not be entirely ignored by their representatives.

And, although many nobles would secure offices in the first chamber, eligibility was now defined by wealth or tax payments, rather than family heritage per se.[27]

The interests of upper-middle-class farmers, burghers, and liberals were advanced by De Geer's proposed second chamber. Majorities in the farmers' and burghers' chambers had long favored somewhat broader suffrage and a reduced role for the nobility in the Riksdag and government. Members of the second chamber were for the most part directly elected for three-year terms. One hundred thirty-five seats were allocated to rural districts and fifty-five to town districts. Voter eligibility, however, was more restricted for the direct elections of members of the second chamber than for the indirect elections for the first chamber.[28]

Voters for second-chamber elections had to be males (Lutherans), eligible to vote in local elections, and had to satisfy national eligibility requirements in addition to local ones. There were three national eligibility qualifications for suffrage: paying taxes on one thousand riksdaler of real estate, renting six thousand riksdaler of real estate (for a period of more than five years), or paying taxes on more than eight hundred riksdaler of income a year. Given the Swedish economy at the time and its associated distribution of wealth and income, the electorate for the second chamber was less than half that of the first chamber. The second chamber's electorate consisted for the most part of successful farmers, bureaucrats, small businessmen, doctors, and lawyers.

Eligibility for seats in the second chamber, however, was less restricted than for the first chamber. Representatives simply had to be older than age twenty-five and eligible to vote in the local elections. The latter implied that representatives to the second chamber also had to meet minimum tax-payment constraints (article 19), but the lack of national standards implied that eligibility for seats in the second chamber was much broader than that for the first, and that it varied somewhat according to local assessments and tax laws.

[27] Weighted voting by the members of parliament themselves had previously been possible. For example, Anders Danielsson of West Gothland had once been chosen to represent twenty-seven districts and so had twenty-seven votes in the farmer's chamber, one-fifth of the votes in that chamber (Grimberg 1935, 327–8).

[28] Särlvik (2002, 332–3) notes that local voting districts were initially allowed to use either direct or indirect elections. A majority of districts used indirect election in the early years, but these were gradually phased out. Multiple member districts for major cities also existed during this period. All these details were, of course, matters worked out among the interests already represented in the chambers. About 20 percent of adult males had the right to vote for members of the second chamber.

Elections were to take place every three years (article 15) and meetings of parliaments were to be annual. Terms in the first chamber were to be nine years, a third of which would stand for election every three years. Terms in the second chamber would be three years. Salaries were paid to members of the second chamber, but not the first. Disagreements among the chambers regarding fiscal matters would be determined by a joint vote, which the second chamber was likely to dominate because it had 50 percent more members.

Ownership of real estate was given preference in the new suffrage rules for parliament because De Geer, as true of many nineteenth-century liberals, believed that ownership of real estate gave a man a greater stake in the country (Verney 1957, 52–3). To vote in elections for the second chamber, it was sufficient to pay taxes on one thousand riksdaler of real estate, which was only one-eightieth of that required for eligibility for membership in the first chamber. Satisfying the voter income requirement required payment of taxes on eight hundred riksdaler of income, which was one-fifth of that required for seats in the upper house (articles 6 and 14).

The king's acceptance of the proposal was made more likely by the fact that the reorganization of the Riksdag did not directly affect his power. The king retained powers of veto and initiative, and laws continued to be published and issued in his name (articles 79–82, see Verney 1957, 52–8). The king was also promised a somewhat increased budget (Verney 1957, 156) and the authority to appoint the ministry and the speakers of the two chambers. The first chamber would also be reliably conservative, although royal influence over it was likely to diminish because noble government officials (senior bureaucrats and military officers) without property were not likely to be returned to office.

Noble support for the proposal was increased by the wealth requirements for seats in the first chamber and the weighted-voting system of the provincial councils. These made it likely that many of those already sitting in the noble and burgher estates would obtain seats in the reformed Riksdag (Verney 1957, 50–2, 89). It also increased support among non-noble industrialists (iron mongers and miners) – who favored economic liberalization – by reducing the influence of the petty nobility and allowing them to obtain seats in the upper chamber (Verney 1957, 32, 77–82).[29] Majorities in

[29] De Geer was such a person. Baron Gerard Louis De Geer (1818–96) was the son of a wealthy landowner, who had risen to the ministry through a distinguished legal career and, of course, family connections.

the burgher and farmer chambers had long favored reforms along the lines proposed by De Geer.

In late 1865, after four years of public and private debate, votes were taken in each of the chambers. The proposal passed easily in the farmer and burgher chambers, where similar proposals had long had success. The final outcome would not be known until after the noble chamber voted, where previous proposals had failed. The noble chamber accepted the proposal 361 to 294. The clergy quickly followed.

After the last four-chamber parliament had completed its work in June 1866, the king signed the Riksdag Act, and the parliamentary reforms negotiated by De Geer became law. After ratifying the reforms, the king declared:

> "We end today not only a memorable session, but a whole era in the history of the Swedish people, an era that is measured in centuries."

As a consequence, as Verney notes, "Some of the pomp and ceremony left Swedish life. The heralds and trumpeters appeared for the last time and Ministers ceased to ride in their colorful robes to the State opening of Riksdag" (Verney 1957, 78).

The parliamentary reforms were significant reforms of Sweden's long-standing medieval system of governance. Although suffrage was still very restrictive, and only men of wealth could sit in the first chamber, membership in the chambers of the new Riksdag rested on elections for the first time, rather than a noble family heritage, appointment by the king, or membership in particular economic and religious organizations. The changes indirectly made future reforms more likely, because it increased parliament's decisiveness. The Riksdag had somewhat greater tax and legislative authority than in the past (except during the Age of Liberty), fewer chambers had to be consulted, and the interests of members in the two chambers were somewhat more aligned than before.

1866–1906: POLITICAL SUPPORT GROWS FOR EXPANDED SUFFRAGE

Support for further liberalization of Swedish governance existed within the Riksdag and also within a number of politically active interest groups around the country. However, the remaining constitutional reform issues were somewhat less clear cut for liberals than those in many other countries, and support for further reform was not initially very great among the new officeholders. Suffrage eligibility for the elections to the provincial councils was very broad by the standards of the nineteenth century, although the effect of relatively broad suffrage was reduced by weighted voting, which in turn produced relatively low turnouts. The voting districts for the second chamber somewhat favored the towns, which somewhat favored liberals. Rural districts required forty thousand residents to send a representative, whereas town districts required only ten thousand residents (Verney 1957, 52). Although this was not equal representation, it was relatively equal by mid-nineteenth-century standards.

The main liberal constitutional reform issues were, consequently, not simple ones such as suffrage expansion or unfair districts, but rather opposition to weighted voting in the first chamber and support of suffrage expansion in the second.

Besides blunting liberal criticism, the 1866 reforms also weakened the link between economic and political liberals. Sweden's new industrialists no longer had to press for expanded suffrage or reapportionment to influence internal and external trade policies (as in England). As wealthy men, they were eligible to sit in the first chamber and could also disproportionately determine its membership by casting weighted votes for the provincial councils. Because apportionment was relatively fair and somewhat biased in favor of liberals, political liberals also had institutional interests that worked against suffrage reform in the second chamber.

Proposals for reform of the second chamber were likely to be popular among middle-class liberals who could not vote, but less so among upper-middle-class and wealthy liberals who determined the members of the second chamber. Reform of the first chamber's rules would be supported by many members of the second chamber, but few in the first.

Moderate liberals and conservatives were satisfied with the reforms, as were the most active economic interest groups of that time. As a consequence, the new suffrage rules proved to be quite stable for the next forty years, although there were minor reforms. Economic growth, higher taxation, and changes in municipal voting rules gradually increased the municipal electorate from 20 to 34 percent of adult males between 1870 and 1902 (Dodd 1909, 233).[30]

30 The size of both chambers, for example, tended to increase through time. In addition, the number of members in the second chamber varied somewhat, as communities could merge for the purposes of elections to meet population requirements; consequently, the number of representatives in the second chamber varied with population growth and community interests in merging to form electoral districts. In 1894, it was agreed to limit the number of seats in the first chamber to two hundred thirty and those in the second to one hundred and fifty (Verney 1957, 109).

Economic Development

The period after the 1866 reform of the Riksdag was one of rapid economic growth and industrialization, punctuated by recessions. Major new firms were founded. The mining, timber, and banking industries were reorganized. A railroad system was constructed to connect the major cities. Water-driven saw mills were replaced with steam-driven mills. A paper industry emerged. Farmland expanded with the completion of the Swedish enclosures, which increased food production and freed labor for other purposes. New industries in explosives, matches, chemicals, and telephones were founded. Exports of manufactured goods and raw materials expanded. Population and average income increased (Magnusson 2000, chapters 5–6; Heckscher 1954).

Industrialization and changes in transportation had direct effects on the employment, location, lifestyles, and welfare of most Swedes. Economic growth accelerated in the years 1896–1912 as new industries expanded. At the beginning of the nineteenth century, about three-quarters of the population resided in agricultural districts. By 1910, the agricultural sector accounted for less than half of the Swedish population. Swedish lifespans and population levels increased as per capita income nearly tripled during the late nineteenth century. In 1850, only about 10 percent of Swedes lived in cities; by 1950, more than half did (Heckscher 1954, 214–15).

By these measures at least, governance by the wealthy was better for industry and for most Swedes than governance by nobles had been. It should be noted, however, that this was also a period in which Swedish emigration, especially to the United States, was very large.[31]

Politically Active Interest Groups

The policy goals and size of Swedish interest groups in the late nineteenth and early twentieth centuries were affected by the same technological changes that induced changes in economic scale and organization in industry. Greater income and wealth provided more resources for all individual

[31] Heckscher estimates that real per capita national income increased nearly threefold in 1861–1914 (1954, 260). Heckscher also notes, however, that beginning around 1880, the money wages of farm laborers fell dramatically (258) in part because of imported agricultural products. This would have increased real wages in other sectors, which is consistent with the increase in the population of Sweden and average longevity. However, it also evidently induced many tenant farmers and farm laborers to seek their own personal farms in the United States.

pursuits, including politics. The concentration of workers and firms within cities reduced the cost of organizing labor unions and producer cartels. Technological innovations, such as the train, telegraph, and telephone, reduced the cost of coordinating activities within cities and across the nation as a whole in those industries that remained diffuse, such as iron works and timber. The new industries and the new organization of work often created new, or at least more obvious, common economic interests. In economic terms, industrialization in Sweden caused the benefits of many kinds of collective action to rise and their costs to fall.

Liberal movements and other movements on the left grew faster than their conservative counterparts. This was partly because the liberal and labor movements advanced middle-class and working-class interests, two subpopulations that were rapidly expanding as a consequence of industrialization and increased commerce. The latter was partly a consequence of previous reforms, insofar as liberal economic reforms in the first half of the nineteenth-century Sweden (and elsewhere) had increased economic growth and development. Reducing economic privileges from the medieval period allowed new technologies to be adopted more rapidly and specialization to increase, which raised average income, as predicted by most economic theories.

At the same time that empirical support for economic liberalism was accumulating, there was also additional evidence that more open political systems do not necessarily produce policy disasters, as many conservatives had predicted. Budgets, if anything, tended to be better controlled by representative parliaments than kings. Many government services became more widely available. These developments, together with increased numbers of middle- and upper-middle-class families, increased support for liberal economic and political systems and reduced support for many long-standing medieval institutions. A variety of politically active groups inside and outside of government pressed for market and educational reforms, reduced alcohol consumption, and also for suffrage expansion and trade liberalization.[32]

In areas in which industrialization produced new problems, parliaments and interest groups generally attempted to solve those problems with new policies and organizations, rather than with a return to the medieval order. Some problems and solutions were more extreme in Scandinavia than in more populous countries. For example, increases in the scale of the efficient

[32] As in many other counties of Europe, the high tide for free trade occurred in the middle of the century when most Swedish tariffs were repealed. Toward the end the century (as in 1888), however, protectionist tariffs had been reintroduced for many commodities, and free-trade movements reemerged, although they were less successful in the late nineteenth century than they had been mid-century.

production of goods and services generated more monopolies in Sweden's relatively small economy than in larger or more open economies. The favorable prices engineered by monopolists and cartels, in turn, were often countered by the creation of new Swedish organizations, such as cooperatives, that could provide services at lower cost to their members (Strode 1949, chapter 12).

Late-Nineteenth-Century Swedish Liberals

Liberalism has a long history in Sweden, but interest in liberal ideas broadened during the nineteenth century at the same time that liberal support for openness and civic equality increased. Heckscher attributes much of the rise of liberalism in the middle of the nineteenth century to writings by Bastiat and Swedish liberals such as Hans Forssell and J. W. Arnberg. He also notes that the creation of the Nationalekonomiska Föreningen (National Economic Society) in 1877 provided a useful forum for liberal businessmen and senior civil servants (1954, 263). Verney (1957, 137) notes that J. S. Mill's *On Liberty* and writings by Hedin were influential among the leadership in the new liberal political organizations in the period after the 1866 Riksdag Act. He also suggests that the founding of the Verdandi, a student organization, increased the dissemination of liberal ideas.

As in other countries there was not a single unified liberal movements but rather a variety of groups that largely agreed about the direction for reform and disagreed about the extent to shifts in that direction were important or useful. Most liberals agreed that the public interest could be advanced by more open economic and political systems and greater civic liberty. And these points of agreement reduced organizational costs for various liberal reform groups and trade associations. Utilitarian and natural-rights-based arguments generated support for liberal reforms among the well educated, many of whom could already vote, although groups varied in their support for specific proposals.

The liberal view of economics implied that innovation, increased production, and perhaps free trade were ends in their own right and socially important engines of progress (Heckscher 1954, 214). The liberal view of politics implied that the purpose of government was to advance shared interests, such as equality before the law and economic progress. Public education should be universal, and all those who were capable of casting independent, well-informed votes should be able to do so.[33]

[33] An analysis of the policy consequences of a limited franchise can be found in Wicksell's analysis (1896) of the effects of government policies on the working class, who were at that

It bears noting, however, that the liberal reform agenda in Sweden was a moving target, as elsewhere. During the second half of the nineteenth century, the center of gravity of Swedish liberalism became more radical, as was true in much of the rest of Europe. Self-described liberals increasingly favored nearly universal suffrage, industrial regulations to increase market competition, and modest social insurance.

Late-Nineteenth-Century Swedish Economic Conservatives

Institutional and social conservatism are common perspectives among persons who are content with the existing order. In the late eighteenth and early nineteenth centuries, this perspective led many persons to support the medieval order. In the late nineteenth century, such conservatives defended the 1866 reforms, the end of serfdom, and the liberalization of trade. Conservative political theorists and politicians often recounted past glories, but few late-nineteenth-century conservatives wanted to reverse the reforms of 1866 or return to a feudal society. Conservatism in the late nineteenth century was not an explicitly class-based ideology, nor an entirely static worldview, although it did tend to favor the status quo.

By the end of the nineteenth-century Swedish conservatives had gradually adopted policy positions that were not so different from those of early- and mid-nineteenth-century liberals. Many conservatives thought that the economic reforms of the 1850s and the 1866 political reforms had worked quite well, although many believed that trade liberalism and reduced censorship had gone a bit too far in some cases.

As in the case of liberals, there were pragmatic as well as ideological reasons to take a conservative stance with respect to public-policy and constitutional issues. Those favoring cultural and political conservatism because of respect for cultural evolution, national religious beliefs, and history were joined by those who profited from existing arrangements and those who were simply risk averse about constitutional experimentation. Antiliberal arguments were taken up by many industrialists who had previously favored the liberal reform agenda but profited from protectionist measures in the late nineteenth and early twentieth centuries. For example, Swedish cartels in sugar, milling, and oleomargarine were able to obtain significant (and profitable) protective tariffs in the early twentieth century (Heckscher 1954,

time ineligible to vote in Sweden. His analysis suggests that the taxes paid by the working class, whose interests were not directly represented in the legislature, generally exceeded the value of services they received from government (see Wagner 1988, 159).

263). In the late nineteenth century, the Farmers' Party shifted from relatively liberal to relatively conservative positions on many policy issues. For example, the Farmer's Party opposed suffrage reform in the 1880s because they realized that the newly enfranchised would include fewer landholders from rural districts than earlier in the century. The new middle-class owned houses rather than farms (Verney 1957, 110). The party also shared protectionist interests with many large landholders and industrialists because imports from Russia and North America had reduced prices for Swedish farm products.

Social Democrats in Late-Nineteenth-Century Sweden

Another important political group emerged in the late nineteenth century to the left of mainstream liberals. Many were simply the radical liberals of their day, a new generation of left liberals with relatively strong interests in civic equality. Such persons pressed for universal suffrage, greater support for public education, and changes in the civil code to increase the symmetry of bargaining between firms and labor. They tended to oppose cartels and other barriers to trade. In addition to Sweden's left liberals, there was also a smaller group that thought private property was less an engine of growth than a device through which privileged persons secured unfair advantages in political and economic life. A significant subset of the latter was influenced by Marx's ideas about social evolution, conflict, and economic justice.[34]

The left also included pragmatists. It was widely recognized that advancing labor-union interests would be easier if middle- and working-class interests were directly represented in the Riksdag. Labor unions thus often pressed for suffrage reform at the same time that they lobbied for labor-law reform and social insurance. Unions of different trades in different industries also agreed on a number of policy issues. They often favored limited work weeks, social insurance, and increased safety regulations. Their shared policy interests led to the formation of nationwide organizations in the late nineteenth century, including a new Social Democratic Party.

Many of the most radical leaders of the Social Democratic Party promoted public ownership of the means of production. However, its mainstream leaders, such as Branting and Lindahl, could be regarded as left liberals, rather than revolutionaries, who favored the reform of capitalism

[34] A good overview of the ideas and norms that shaped the outlook of moderate socialists is provided in Castels (1978), who analyzes the social democratic movements that swept through Europe in the early twentieth century.

and extension of suffrage, as opposed to radical reforms. That mainstream social democrats were left liberals, rather than radical socialists, became obvious when the social democrats became the dominant party after World War I.

Suffrage Movements, Parties, and Reform

Suffrage expanded slowly during the nineteenth century as economic development and government growth took place. Income and taxes rose without substantial changes in electoral law.

The gradual increase in the importance of the Riksdag and in the number of voters required to win seats created new benefits for partisan organizations, and new political parties were gradually organized after 1866. The first to organize were the farmers, who dominated the second chamber for the first twenty or thirty years after the 1866 reforms. A Social Democratic Party emerged out of the suffrage and labor movements in 1889. A new Liberal Party was organized in 1899 when coalition of more or less like-minded members of the Riksdag organized over dinner at Tattersall's restaurant, many of whom were also involved in the suffrage movement.[35]

Nationwide economic organizations such as labor's Landsorganisationen (LO) were organized partly with the support of the social democrats in 1898. Industry's employer association, Svenska Arbetsgivarföreningen (SAF), was organized with the encouragement of the Conservative and Liberal Parties in 1902 (Heckscher 1954, 136, 235). A new conservative party was formed in 1904 (the National Election League). Both labor and industrial economic interest groups hoped to profit from reforms that increased their party's control of public policy.

Pressure for economic and suffrage reform was provided by left liberals elected to the Riksdag and by various interest groups and unions that lobbied in favor of suffrage reform outside government. For example, in 1890, a Universal Suffrage Association was founded with support among liberals and social democrats. A petition in support of suffrage reform with 364,000 signatures was presented to the Riksdag by liberals in 1898. Most strikes were conducted to advance negotiations with specific firms or industries over wages, workweeks, and working conditions. However, the Swedish

[35] Verney (1957, 98–9) discusses an earlier and less formal liberal party, the New Liberal Association, organized in 1868 just after the parliamentary reforms were adopted. It was, however, unsuccessful in its legislative aims and disintegrated in the next two years. The Farmer's Party was evidently much more successful in its early forms (1867), partly because it was based on membership in the old farmer estate.

labor movement occasionally organized large public demonstrations in support of specific public-policy reforms, including two very broad strikes in 1902 and 1909 that supported suffrage and labor-law reform (Strode 1949, 172).[36]

Representation of the unenfranchised in the Riksdag was initially undertaken by left liberals elected to the second chamber by upper-middle-class voters and the odd industrialist with sympathies for left liberal ideas. As the center of gravity of liberal thought shifted leftward during the late nineteenth century, their previously radical ideas became mainstream.

Together the gradual shift in liberal opinion and public demonstrations in favor of suffrage expansion caused electoral reform to return to the mainstream constitutional reform agenda. A series of proposals for electoral reform were made in the second chamber, especially after 1900. For example, in 1902, Prime Minister Boström proposed extending the vote for members of the second chamber to all taxpayers at the same time that a Swedish income tax was enacted (Steinmo 1993, 64). This was followed by proposals by his government and others in the second chamber for various forms of proportional representation and for extended suffrage in 1903 and 1904 – all of which were blocked by the first chamber.[37]

Norway's secession in 1905 further increased dissatisfaction with the incumbent parties, officeholders, and current institutions.

The liberal coalition continued to gain members in the second chamber in the early twentieth century, and its leader, Staaff, was invited to become the prime minister in 1906. He accepted and brought four fellow liberals to the ministry (the other six ministers were nonpartisan administrators). This led to a torrent of legislative proposals and several proposals for constitutional reform. The proposed constitutional reforms were again defeated in the first chamber (one lost one hundred two to eighteen) in part because the king refused support the bill in the first chamber.

36 The *New York Times* (June 22, 1902) and some other references report that the strikers had been promised universal suffrage for the 1904 elections, but universal suffrage was not adopted until several years later.

37 Although the policy goals of many activists in the Social Democratic Party and the labor movement differed from that of mainstream liberals, there was significant agreement among liberals and social democrats on constitutional reform issues.

This was evidently because many of the most influential Swedish social democrats were left liberals rather than radical Marxist reformers. Here, one may note that Hjalmar Branting, the son of a prominent university professor who became the leader of the social democrats and helped organize the 1902 strike, opposed bloodshed, and favored an evolutionary approach to reform. "It will take longer by evolution, but not so long as it would take to undo the destruction of property and spirit a revolution would bring" (quoted in Strode 1949, 171).

The first chamber generally opposed further liberalization of Swedish politics because the proposed reforms would reduce the influence of those represented in the first chamber or the first chamber itself. Reform clearly required a more sophisticated constitutional bargain than the one(s) proposed by Staaff.

1907–1920: ANOTHER ROUND OF GRAND CONSTITUTIONAL BARGAINING

After the failure of his reform bill, Staaff resigned as prime minister, and conservatives were invited to head the government (without an intervening election). Prime Minister Lindman proposed several reforms of the voting procedures by which members were selected for the two chambers of the Riksdag. Lindman's reforms were partly motivated by the broad support for expanding suffrage in the second chamber (as evidenced by the general strike of 1902 and liberal reform proposals) and partly by the conservatives' concern that expanded suffrage would end their influence over governmental decisions.

First, Lindman proposed that the franchise be expanded by reducing the property requirements in a manner that would double the franchise for the second chamber (from five hundred thousand to one million). This modification would allow nearly universal male suffrage. Second, he proposed that the weighted-voting system used for selecting members of the first chamber be moderated (maximum votes were reduced from five thousand to forty). Third, he proposed that proportional representation be introduced for elections to the first and second chamber. The method used for the first chamber would be "double proportional representation" in which the provincial councils would be elected using PR, and their votes would select the members of the first chamber using PR. Under the proposed D'Hondt rule, which favored the largest party, double PR would help preserve the conservative dominance of the first chamber, even with the reduced weighted-voting system.[38] Fourth, he proposed that PR also be adopted by the committees within the Riksdag. The term of office for the first chamber was also to be

[38] Under the D'Hont system, seats are allocated as follows: (a) the party with the most votes gets a seat, (b) that party's vote is divided by two and the party with the largest vote (after that division) gets a seat, (c) that party's vote is divided by three and the party with the most remaining votes gets a seat, and so forth until all the seats are filled. After the 1920 reforms, this electoral system worked to the benefit of the social democrats, because they had normally received the most votes. See Särlvik (2002, 342–5) for a careful analysis of this effect.

reduced from nine to six years, and wealth requirements for seats in the first chamber were reduced from eighty thousand to fifty thousand krona.

As in 1866, the proposals were carefully crafted to obtain support in each of the chambers of the Riksdag and the approval of the king. Proportional representation was seen as a method for minority parties (such as the conservatives in the first chamber) to retain influence in the Riksdag after reductions in weighted voting and expansion of the franchise. The broadened suffrage appealed to liberals and farmers in the second chamber who were divided on PR. (Most liberals favored the continuation of plurality voting in single-member districts.) There was only a single social democrat holding office at that time, and he favored an end to weighted voting.

Lindman's compromise satisfied demands for universal male suffrage but protected the interests of conservatives in both chambers with PR and weighted voting. The king's interest in reform was increased somewhat by a proposed 25 percent increase in the budget for the civil list and by the fact that his powers would not be altered. After several rounds of intra-parliamentary negotiations and compromise, Lindman's final proposal was passed ninety-three to fifty-two in the first chamber, and one hundred twenty-eight to ninety-eight in the second in April of 1907. It was ratified in 1909 after an intervening election, as required under the 1866 amendment procedures (Verney 1957, 154, 167–9; Weibull 1993, 113; Svanstrom 2008, 417–18).

These reforms set the stage for the emergence of more disciplined political parties in the years to come. Proportional representation gave party leaders direct power over their members in the legislature by allowing the leadership to control who would be on party lists and thereby who could potentially be in the Riksdag. The expanded franchise also created a new electoral base by which the social democrats would shortly come to dominate Swedish politics, although in the short run, both liberals and social democrats gained from the reforms. The liberals won the 1911 election.

Party Governance Emerges

Sweden was neutral during World War I, although its military budgets for national defense were increased. In 1914, the king made a speech that supported conservative proposals for further expanding the military budget, which the present liberal–social democratic coalition opposed. The king's speech, however, violated the custom that had emerged in the late nineteenth century. The "proper" method through which a king's interests should be presented to the parliament was indirect, through his cabinet, rather than through speeches by the king himself. The king was supposed to remain in the background of parliamentary debates, above the fray.

The liberal ministry resigned in protest of the king's more direct intervention. Elections in 1914 returned a conservative plurality to the second chamber. In spite of the conservative victory, the king's speech and the ministry's reaction is often regarded as the last time that a Swedish king publicly participated in parliamentary debate (Verney 1957, 190).

The shift to parliamentary dominance of policy was essentially complete, but not to party government. The king continued to exercise some discretion in his appointments to the cabinet, although these were increasingly determined by the electoral outcomes. For example, the king selected a moderate conservative civil servant, Hjalmar Hammerskjöd, to be prime minister in 1914, rather than a leading member of the majority party in parliament.

In 1917, conservatives lost the election, and the king accepted the recommendations of the majority liberal–social democratic coalition of the second chamber. The new cabinet had a liberal prime minister (Edén) and social democrat as finance minister (Branting), both from the second chamber.[39] This coalition is said to mark the beginning of party government in Sweden, although Swedish kings had long paid attention to electoral results.

(This routine of deference to the majority parties in the second chamber was not formally incorporated into constitutional documents until 1975.)

Universal Suffrage

The liberal–social democratic coalition government pressed for additional constitutional reforms as World War I ended, and those reforms completed the transition to parliamentary democracy.

Between 1918 and 1920, the franchise was further expanded as property restrictions for voting were eliminated and women were granted the franchise. Voters still had to be taxpayers of sufficient age, but most other restrictions were eliminated. Persons who were on relief or bankrupt, however, were not eligible to vote until the suffrage reforms of 1945 (Verney 1957, 215). The weighted-voting system modified ten years earlier was

[39] The social democrats had held more seats in the directly elected second chamber than the liberals since the 1914 elections. After the 1917 elections, their lead was eighty-six to sixty-two in the second chamber. Liberals, however, held more seats in the indirectly elected first chamber. It was during the 1917 election that the far left broke from the Social Democratic Party and formed their own coalition, which was about a sixth as large as the mainstream party.

eliminated, although differences in the electoral method and wealth qualifications for the first chamber remained. Members of the first chamber continued to be restricted to the very wealthy until 1933 (Verney 1957, 215).[40]

The resulting more disciplined and more broadly representative bicameral Riksdag became the chief architect of public policy in Sweden for the next fifty years.

The social democrats emerged as the dominant political party in Sweden. For most of the twentieth century, that party could be regarded as a left liberal party in that it continued to favor democracy and open markets, even as it attempted to reform the latter. The party's economic advisors in the late 1920s included Erik Lindahl, Gunnar Myrdal, and Bertil Ohlin (Steinmo 1993, 83–6; Verney 1957, chapter 10). The more radical members of the labor movement departed in the 1920s to form their own party.

THE EVOLUTIONARY NATURE OF THE SWEDISH CONSTITUTION

Most of Swedish constitutional history from late-medieval times until 1918 can be regarded as a bargaining contest between the Riksdag and the king in which their bargaining positions and strengths shifted back and forth over the centuries. Peaks in parliamentary powers were often marked by formal revisions to the instruments of governance, as in 1617, 1634, 1660, 1720, and 1809. Kings occasionally regained power through constitutional reform, as in 1680 and 1772, and also by playing the estates off one another. At times of maximum royal authority, the powers of the Riksdag were rather limited, although the king-and-council template remained in place. The flexibility of the king-and-council template, together with the lack of an effective constitutional court, meant that day-to-day governance reflected the particular personalities, talents, and circumstances confronted by those in government, as often stressed by political historians.

After 1809, the flexibility of the king-and-council template remained evident, although constitutional negotiations exhibited a clear liberal trend for the next century. In the nineteenth and early twentieth centuries, the Swedish parliament was reformed a number of times in a manner that indirectly changed the bargaining equilibria between the king and parliament

[40] The first chamber remained indirectly elected by provincial councils. The terms of office also differed, although these were modified by the 1918–20 reforms. Members in the first chamber retained office for eight years, and those in the second chamber for four years (Verney 1957, 248).

and also the selection process for members of the king's executive council (ministry).

The trend in constitutional reforms can be explained as a joint consequence of the rise of liberalism and industrialization. Economic reforms preceded political reforms in Sweden, insofar as education reform, free trade, land reform, and the extension of religious tolerance were well under way before the reform of the Riksdag in 1866. These reforms demonstrate that political liberalism had penetrated the aristocracy and king's inner circle, as well as the towns and rural districts during the early nineteenth century. Pressures for reform diminished after 1866, in part because so much had been achieved in 1866, and in part because of the institutional interests produced by the procedures of the reformed Riksdag. Further industrialization, however, continued to empower liberal and labor-based interest groups, who gradually persuaded the Riksdag to undertake additional reforms of suffrage. Together formal and informal reforms of Sweden's procedures of governance produced parliamentary democracy shortly after World War I.

This path of reform in nineteenth-century Sweden is consistent with the analytical history developed in Part I of the book. The king initially remained the dominant figure in public-policy formation, he but could not neglect parliament, because he needed an overall majority in the joint vote to assure that budgets would pass. The Riksdag gradually accumulated authority after the 1866 reforms through its control of taxation and public budgets, gaining complete control early in the twentieth century. Leaders of significant coalitions within the second chamber were often invited to be consulting ministers (Verney 1957, 134).

Fine-grained negotiations and compromise (constitutional exchange) among the king, the parliament, and the executive council are evident throughout Sweden's transition to parliamentary democracy.

The peaceful and lawful nature of Sweden's transition to parliamentary democracy remains evident in the medieval roots of its contemporary architecture. After 1925, the king and Riksdag continued to have roles in policy making, but the balance of policy-making authority had essentially reversed itself over the course of a century or so of constitutional bargaining. The king's authority had become largely advisory and ceremonial, as might have been said of the relatively weak parliaments during most of Sweden's medieval period.

The balance of authority over public policy in 1925 emerged as a consequence of informal shifts in bargaining equilibria associated with changes in the Swedish parliament and the balance of interests represented there, rather than through an explicit constitutional reform. It was not until 1975 that the bargaining equilibrium that emerged between the Swedish parliament and king in the first decades of the twentieth century was finally written down in new constitutional documents. It bears noting that the 1975 Instrument of Government continues to assign minor authority to the king (who, for example, presides over special sessions of the Riksdag [*Instrument of Governance*: Chapter Five, Article 1]) and continues to characterize the rules of royal succession.

It also bears noting that the 1975 constitution, in contrast to the 1809 Instrument that it replaced, begins with what might be regarded as a liberal statement concerning popular sovereignty, civic equality, and the constitutional basis of Swedish governance:

> All public power in Sweden proceeds from the people. Swedish democracy is founded on the free formation of opinion and on universal and equal suffrage. It shall be realized through a representative and parliamentary polity and through local self-government. Public power is exercised under the law. (Holmberg and Stjernquist 1996, 65).

Table 14.1. *Major Constitutional Developments in Swedish Constitutional History*

Date	Event	Description
1319	Letter of Privilege	Binds the sovereign to govern by rule of law, promises due process, and allows new taxes to be imposed only after consultation with the royal council.
14th century	Magnus Ericsson's Land Law	Provides for the election of a king, describes his duties and the election and functions of the members of the council of state.
1389	Kalmar Union	Common kingdom of Sweden, Norway, and Denmark established, each with their own parliament and council.
1442	Kristofer's Law	New Royal Charter, a revision of Eriksson's law.
1523	End of Kalmar Union	Gustav Vasa elected king by the Riksdag after successful war of secession from Danish sovereign.
1527	Protestant Reformation	Protestant Reformation initiated by Gustav, the king becomes head of the new Swedish (Lutheran) Church, Catholic Church properties are confiscated.
1544	Succession Pact	The office of king becomes a hereditary right of the House of Vasa.
1594	Accession Charters reestablished	After the end of the House of Vasa, Swedish kings return to signing an accession charter before taking office in which they promise to govern constitutionally. (All future kings and queens sign one, except Charles XII.)
1617	First Riksdag Act	Formally establishes the four-chamber system of parliament with veto power over new laws and taxes.
1634	First Instrument of Government	Clarifies and extends the Royal Charter and form of government.
1660	Swedish Triennial Act	The Riksdag is to meet every three years and parliament becomes self-calling.
1680	Instrument of Government Revised	Parliament exempts Charles XI from many provisions of the Instrument of Government, although Riksdag retains its veto power on new taxes.

Date	Event	Description
1719	Succession Pact Revoked	Following the death of Charles XII without heir, the Riksdag revokes the hereditary foundation of the monarchy, and Queen Christina accepts the new procedure.
1720	Second Instrument of Government	Reestablishes constitutional monarchy, with greater authority placed in the Riksdag, laws to be approved by the council of state, its members selected by the king or queen from lists prepared by Riksdag.
1723	Second Riksdag Act	Formalizes internal procedures of parliament and establishes a procedure for removing council ministers ("ministerial responsibility" established).
1766	Ordinance for the Liberty of Printing	Eliminates prepublication censorship (except for religious books) and includes rules regarding access to government documents, amending the act requires agreement by two successive parliaments (the act has constitutional status).
1766	Ordinance for the Better Execution of Laws	The justice chancellor henceforth to be appointed by parliament, rather than the king, a formal amendment process for constitutional law is adopted, constitutional amendments require approval by all four chambers of two successive parliaments and the king. Many reforms of the bureaucracy are adopted.
1772	Reform of the Second Instrument of Government	Gustav III negotiates a shift of authority from the Riksdag and council to the king. Legislative authority is to be shared between king and the Riksdag. The Riksdag ceases to be self-calling but retains veto power on taxes and new legislation. The king has veto power on legislation and can impose new taxes if the country is attacked.
1789	Act of Union and Security	Gustav III obtains further authority over the council of state and Riksdag, a new court of appeals is established, of which the king is a member and casts two votes.

(*continued*)

Table 14.1. *(continued)*

Date	Event	Description
1809	Third Instrument of Government	Reestablishes the Riksdag's authority on legislation and taxation and provides the Riksdag with new budgetary authority.
1810	New Succession Act	Sovereign is again made a hereditary office, with the new Bernadotte line.
1840	Cabinet Act	Government administration organized into departments, and heads of departments become ministers in the government's cabinet.
1860	Religious Tolerance Act	
1866	Third Riksdag Act	Four-chamber medieval parliament is transformed into a two-chamber elected parliament (the first chamber elected via wealth-weighted voting); the first chamber is indirectly elected by regional governments and the second is directly elected by voters; national election law replaces district-level laws.
1907–09	Lindman's Electoral Reforms	Reduces weighted voting for the first chamber, lowers wealth restrictions for elective office, adopts PR for electoral colleges of both first and second chambers and for parliamentary committees.
1920	Edén-Branting Suffrage Reforms	Essentially universal and equal suffrage for men and women becomes the rule for both the first and second chambers, a system of direct PR is adopted for the second chamber.
1969	Fourth Riksdag Act	The two-chamber parliament is merged into a single, directly elected chamber based on PR.
1975	Fourth Instrument of Government	Unified constitution adopted that combines elements of previously separate constitutional laws into a single document; the sovereign's diminished policy-making authority is explicitly described.

Sources: Holmberg and Stjernquist (1995), Verney (1957), Roberts (2002).

FIFTEEN

Constitutional Reform in the Netherlands: From Republic, to Kingdom, to Parliamentary Democracy

In contrast to the kingdoms of the United Kingdom and Sweden, the constitutional monarchy of the Netherlands does not extend back to the middle ages. The Netherlands has not always been a kingdom, nor part of some other kingdom, as might be said of Norway and Belgium. From the late sixteenth century until the late eighteenth century, the *Republiek der Verenigde Nederlanden* (United Provinces of the Netherlands) was a relatively liberal federation of seven sovereign provinces. Its territories consisted of the northern lowlands of the Rhine, and its national policies were jointly selected by a committee of provincial representatives and a *stadhouder*. The *stadhouder's* autonomy was greater than that of contemporary prime ministers and presidents, but his authority was less than that which kings normally had during the seventeenth and eighteenth centuries.

That the kingdom the Netherlands is relatively new makes the lowland kingdom a very useful addition to the present study because it demonstrates that relatively peaceful transitions to democracy within parliamentary systems do not require a long history of negotiations between kings and their parliaments or a deeply rooted, long-standing, authoritarian regime to rebel against. The first half of Chapter Fifteen provides a short history of the Dutch Republic and the origin of the kingdom of the Netherlands. The second half of the chapter focuses on its nineteenth-century transition to parliamentary democracy.

The period of the Dutch Republic is of interest because its success helped stimulate and support the work of enlightenment scholars and played important roles in the constitutional developments of the United Kingdom and United States. Its scholars included such influential men as Grotius, Spinoza, La Court, and Mandeville. Many well-known scholars from other less tolerant countries also spent time in the Netherlands in the seventeenth century, and many others published their books and pamphlets at Dutch printing houses. William III, King of England, was *stadhouder* Willem III of much of the Netherlands for many years before obtaining the British crown. As noted in Chapter Twelve, the Republic sponsored the Dutch invasion that made Great Britain's Glorious Revolution possible. The Dutch Republic's confederal government was also used as a model during constitutional deliberations in the United States (Riker 1957, Congleton 2008).

The Kingdom of the Netherlands *(Koninkrijk der Nederlanden)* was established in 1815 as part of the reorganization of Europe worked out by the great powers in Vienna following their victory over Napoleon and his French army. In spite of its relatively short experience as a kingdom, the evolution of Dutch parliamentary practices in the nineteenth century parallels those of the long-standing British and Swedish monarchies. As in the other kingdoms, constitutional bargaining and a series of agreements gradually shifted policy-making authority from the king to the parliament. A series of electoral reforms adopted during the same period caused members of parliament to be elected on the basis of increasingly broad suffrage.

The Dutch case demonstrates that the European path to parliamentary democracy was not rooted in deep evolutionary pressures within constitutional monarchies, but rather was a consequence of increased support for liberal reforms that emerged in the nineteenth century. Increases in commerce and industrialization helped to energize politically active liberal, commercial, and labor groups in the Netherlands during the nineteenth century. The Dutch case also demonstrates the durability and flexibility of the king-and-council template for governance.

SETTING THE STAGE: THE EMERGENCE OF THE DUTCH REPUBLIC

Recorded history in the Low Countries begins when the Roman Empire reached the place where the great central European river (the Rhine) enters the North Sea. Julius Caesar made the territory south of the main channel of the Rhine part of the Roman Empire in 57 BCE. The Romans did not go significantly north of the Rhine, and so their primary fortress cities and commercial centers were along its southern shores. Those territories remained Roman for more than four hundred years, until the empire began to disintegrate along its frontiers in the early fifth century. Consequently, Latin and French influences are far stronger south of the Rhine (contemporary Belgium and the southern Netherlands) than in the north, where Germanic and Frieslandic influences dominate. In this respect and many others, the

Rhine played an important role for the peoples of the Low Countries and elsewhere in Europe.

The Rhine did not only divide the future Netherlands from the future Belgium, but created important economic opportunities. Fishing and commerce were important economic activities for the Rhinish lowlands from very early times. The Rhine is central Europe's most important gateway to the North Sea and the Atlantic Ocean. Its large delta includes many channels through which the Rhine reaches the sea, which provided many potential harbors for transshipping goods from central Europe to other parts of the world, including England, Scandinavia, western France, and northern Germany. In this manner, the geography and geology of the Rhine created commercial and cultural ties with Germanic Europe and the sea ports of northern Europe.

The marshy nature of the delta and its relatively long coastline with the North Sea, however, created problems as well as commercial opportunities. Floods were commonplace and dry land was scarce. The marshlands isolated the coast somewhat from the mainland and reduced its agricultural productivity at the same time that commerce and fishing encouraged independent political and economic communities to develop. Towns often built hills and dikes to protect themselves from floods and storm tides. Villages and towns also joined forces to build protective larger dikes to protect settlements and existing farms and to drain marshland to create new farmland. These joint enterprises promoted the formation of loose regional associations of local governments.

These collective efforts to cope with the Rhine delta, in turn, produced specialized knowledge of flood control, drainage, and maritime enterprises. The soft and flat delta lands made expansion of the natural waterways relatively easy, and the same efforts could simultaneously produce more arable (dry) land for agriculture and reduce transport costs. An intricate maze of canals gradually developed, which were the most efficient method of transporting goods and people to market in the centuries before the invention of the steam engine.

By the time the various territories of the Rhine's delta found themselves (largely) in the hands of the Duke of Burgundy in the early fifteenth century, they were among the most urbanized areas of Europe. Their fishing and commercial fleets were among the largest in the world, and their cities among the most prosperous (Israel 1998, 113–16; Barker 1906, 23–5).

Governance at that time was largely in the hands of local town councils and noblemen, as was true of much of continental Europe in that period.

There was no national or regional government, although continental institutions existed: the Catholic Church and Holy Roman Empire. Most of the larger provinces had their own ruling aristocrat and parliaments (provincial estates), and most towns had their own mayors and town councils.

The seventeen provinces of the Low Countries did not form a single autonomous polity or administrative area in the late middle ages, although many belonged to the Burgundy family, whose territories more or less followed a southern branch of the Rhine (the Meuse) from present-day France to its delta. A loose regional government for the lowlands was first established by Duke Philip the Good of the House of Burgundy when he called for a meeting of the States General in 1464. Representatives from all of the provincial and town governments assembled, mostly for the purpose of being advised by Philip, who was attempting to centralize control over his far-flung properties. The States General met when called by Philip and only for as long as the meeting advanced Philip's purposes. In this respect, the Burgundian States General was similar to other parliaments during this time period. It was a consultative body with very little policy-making authority (Israel 1998, 21–2).

In addition to the States General, the Burgundy family created the office of *stadhouder* (provincial governor). The Burgundian *stadhouders* for the Rhine's lowlands were initially chosen from the southern (Belgian) nobility who had the wealth, connections, prestige, and education to be effective representatives of Burgundian interests in the lowlands (Israel 1998, 23). The *stadhouder*s normally had power of appointment (or at least agenda control) for major regional offices and served as arbitrators of major disputes within their territories. In this manner, a somewhat unusual form of the king- and-council template, with an assembly of local governments and governor, became the regional government of the Rhine's lowlands.

The authority and influence of the Burgundian *stadhouder*s varied through time as the centralizing efforts of the Burgundian administration ebbed and flowed. During times when local provinces obtained greater autonomy, as in 1477, *stadhouder*s were constrained by their respective provincial parliaments, which had veto power over new taxes and significant power over the creation and implementation of new laws. During such times, the provincial parliaments of the Burgundian period were routinely consulted about laws and appointments, and they occasionally vetoed Burgundy appointments of *stadhouder*s and bishops. During periods of increased centralization, the formal authority of *stadhouder*s increased, and the regional governors could use their power of arbitration and appointment to advance Burgundian interests in the provincial governments and town councils (Israel 1998, 25–6).

The Great Privilege

It was marriage and inheritance law that produced the great family-ruled domains of continental Europe during the late Middle Ages, although this process of amalgamation was not without problems and was often reinforced by territorial armies.

Philip's properties were inherited by his son, Charles the Bold, in 1476. Charles was killed the following year in a battle with the Swiss (in January 1477), who opposed Burgundian efforts to further centralize political authority. Rule of the Burgundian properties thus shifted to Charles' daughter Mary in 1477 (Israel 1998, 27). Shortly after coming to power, Mary found herself under attack by the French king, who disputed her claim to the Burgundian territories. Women could not always inherit noble titles and lands under French law. In desperation, Mary negotiated the Great Privilege with her provincial governments in exchange for their help in the conflict with the French king.

The Great Privilege granted Burgundian towns and provinces veto power over new taxation and war and also gave the cities the right to refuse payment of taxes for which they had not voted. The privilege also granted provincial courts priority on legal matters and allowed the States General in the Netherlands and their provincial counterparts to meet on their own accord (Barker 1906, 39–40). This authority was very rare among the medieval compacts of the day. Most other national assemblies met only when called by the local sovereign (normally a baron or count in the English terminology).

The self-calling provisions of the Great Privilege gave the provinces, cities, and regional parliaments considerable autonomy, which increased their ability to resist usurpation of their powers of governance.[1] From that point on, the States General exercised significant authority over the regional public policies of Belgium and the Netherlands. Many of the veto powers and procedures, and even the location of governance (Den Haag), specified in the Privilege continued in place for several hundred years. Indeed,

[1] The Great Privilege applied to most of the other principalities of the Burgundy domain, which at the time included parts of northern Italy and Switzerland, as well as a large area of modern-day France. The Burgundian holdings were greatly diminished in number and importance when the French king, Louis XI, took over the main Burgundian holdings later in 1477. Many other holdings of Burgundy (outside of France) were rescued by Mary's marriage to Duke Maximilian of the powerful Habsburg dynasty (who later became the Holy Roman Emperor Maximilian I). In one intervention, Maximilian sent his army into Belgium, winning an important victory over the French at Guinigate in 1479, which preserved the Netherlands as an autonomous region.

it could be said that the representative States General established by Philip the Good in the mid-fifteenth century continues to this day in both the Netherlands and Belgium, albeit in much-modified form.

The Habsburgs and the "Spanish Netherlands"

Support for Mary against the king of France increased after she issued the Great Privilege, but not enough to turn back the French army. Fortunately, Mary was betrothed to an important member of the Habsburg family, a man who would become the emperor of the Holy Roman Empire. Maximilian sent his father's German troops to Mary's defense. The Habsburg armies prevented the Burgundian properties outside of France from coming under the control of the French king.

In this manner, through marriage, the territories that would become the Netherlands became part of the powerful Habsburg family's domain. A subsequent series of marriages brought the German and Spanish crowns to a single head.

Mary's son, Philip the Handsome, married Joanna of Castile, and their son Charles subsequently inherited the Spanish throne (from Isabella and Ferdinand) in 1516. It is for this reason that the prerevolutionary Netherlands are often referred to as the Spanish Netherlands.[2] The same young man, Charles, subsequently became emperor of the Holy Roman Empire through his grandfather Maximilian in 1519.[3] Thus, through little of his own doing, but as a consequence of a very good genealogical tree, Charles V became the ruler of one of the largest empires ever assembled, an empire that included much of Europe and most of South America.[4]

[2] The Habsburg family held numerous duchies throughout Europe, but their main holdings were centered around present-day Austria. After the Dutch revolt, the part of the lowlands that remained under Habsburg control (present-day Belgium) came to be called the Austrian Netherlands.

[3] As national states emerged and the Holy Roman Empire declined, the Austrian branch of the Habsburg family provided the hereditary kings of Austria and subsequently the emperors of Austria. As such, they remained among the most influential families in Europe until the twentieth century. For an account of the Habsburgs influence on German history in the nineteenth century, see Chapter Sixteen.

[4] Charles V was born in Ghent in 1500 and became the king of Spain at the age of sixteen. Charles V ruled until 1556, when he abdicated and retired to a monastery in Yuste, Spain, turning the Habsburg territories over to his son Philip II. Charles V was born in the Low Countries, spoke Dutch (Flemish), and continued visiting the Netherlands even after assuming his position in Spain and subsequently the Holy Roman Empire. (Charles V is known as Carlos I [and Carlos V] in Spain, Karel V in the Netherlands, and Karl V in Germany. The English name is used in this case to reduce confusion as the historical

The Protestant Wars, Centralization, and the Dutch Revolt

It is clear that resistance to the centralizing efforts of the House of Burgundy took place throughout the Burgundian territories and that resistance occasionally produced open warfare. For example, as noted earlier, Charles the Bold was killed in 1477 during an attempt to retake Lorraine after it had resisted Burgundian efforts to centralize policy-making and tax authority. After Mary's Great Privilege was adopted, local governments in the lowlands continued to defend their new formal tax and legislative veto authority, which made it very difficult for the Habsburgs to finance and govern their lowland territories. The Habsburgs, naturally, attempted to renegotiate and weaken the Great Privilege. The local governments naturally resisted those efforts. In some cases, negotiation failures led to pitched battles, as for example when the Hoeksen party of Holland launched military campaigns against Burgundian-Habsburgian authorities in the early 1480s.

These long-standing political centralization conflicts were reinforced by religious ones in the sixteenth century. Luther's famous Ninety-five Theses were "nailed" to the Wittenberg church door at approximately same time that Charles obtained the Spanish and German crowns. Luther's critique of church practices and reinterpretations of biblical tests, together with other protests against Catholic practices and corruption, greatly intensified the long-standing decentralization conflicts throughout much of Europe.[5]

The eventual Dutch revolt was largely a consequence of conflict between local elites and the Habsburgs regarding the extent of local control over taxes, appointments, and religious practices. The Habsburg territories had been Catholic for centuries, but the new Protestant doctrines stressing independence from the centralized religious authority of Rome were very appealing for those already favoring decentralization, as well as for those Christians who questioned various aspects of Catholic religious practices. Such views were common in the Holy Roman Empire and northern Habsburg domains. Lutheran and Calvinist doctrines, consequently, found

analysis shifts across national boundaries. Charles V was of international importance, rather than a national leader.)

[5] This is the mythic version of events. There are no eyewitness accounts of this famous event. Most scholars now believe that it never actually happened. Rather, Luther evidently mailed or presented a letter to the archbishop of Mainz and Magdeburg in October of 1517 that objected to various church practices (particularly the recent increase in sales of indulgences) and also presented his Ninety-five Theses, which reinterpreted biblical texts. This letter and other works came to the attention of church authorities in Rome, who insisted that he recant, but Luther refused. He was declared an outlaw in 1521 and was hunted by troops of Charles V for many years.

many supporters in the lowland territories, especially in the provinces north of the Rhine's main channel. Religious and centralization conflicts intensified and were often bloody in northern Europe.

In an attempt to end the war, Protestantism was legitimized within the Holy Roman Empire by the Religious Peace of Augsburg in 1555. The Augsburg treaty allowed three hundred local rulers (dukes and barons) to choose between Lutheranism and Catholicism for themselves (and implicitly for all of their subjects). The treaty did not end religious tensions in Europe, but it did allow Protestant princes and barons to openly support Protestant beliefs within their domains, to suppress Catholic ones, and to gain control over Church properties. Traditional local political autonomy was henceforth augmented with significant religious autonomy throughout the Holy Roman Empire.

The treaty of Augsburg advanced Protestantism in the northern lowlands more than in the south, because the leading families of the north were more closely linked to German noble families (or held German titles themselves), who largely declared themselves Lutheran. This was, for example, true of the Nassau family, which ruled the Barony of Breda, a province in the center of the Rhine's lowlands.[6]

Charles V's son and successor, Philip II, attempted to reverse both areas of local autonomy after he assumed the Spanish crown in 1556 by aggressively suppressing local tax resistance and Protestantism.[7] Partly in response to these policies, in 1566, Protestants throughout the Netherlands stormed Catholic churches, destroying images of Catholic saints. Philip II sent an army to restore order and to increase his control of appointments and policy making in the Rhine's lowlands. His first efforts focused on the south, where Protestant doctrines and their supporting organizations were largely suppressed, although the cosmopolitan city of Antwerp remained an important center of Calvinist thought.[8]

[6] The Orange territory, with its associated rank of prince, was inherited by the Dutch Nassau's Willem I from a somewhat distant French branch of the family in 1544. Willem was appointed *stadhouder* of several of the major lowland provinces (Holland, Zeeland, and Utrecht) by Philip II in 1559 at the age of twenty-six.

[7] Charles V abdicated in 1556, and the Habsburg properties were divided between Charles V's brother and his son. Austria and other properties in the Holy Roman Empire went to Charles' brother Ferdinand I. Spain, Naples, Burgundy, and the Netherlands went to his son Felipe (Philip II). The Spanish branch of the Habsburg family died out in 1700 and produced the war of Spanish succession (1701–14).

[8] Calvin (1509–64) himself was the son of a French attorney, educated in Paris, and lived in the French part of Geneva, Switzerland for much of his life. The French-speaking elites of the southern lowlands would have found his writings much more accessible and congenial than Luther's German.

By bringing the Spanish inquisition to the Netherlands, Philip II increased resistance to Habsburgian rule among Protestants throughout the lowlands. His execution of eighty "rebellious" nobles in the south in 1568 alienated much of the aristocracy and made it clear that Philip II was not interested in compromise. By forcing a 10 percent sales tax through the States General in 1569 to finance his efforts to restore (his) law and order, the last in a long series of Habsburg tax increases to finance the suppression of Protestants, Philip II also alienated pragmatic businessmen and farmers who would otherwise not have been interested in politics or civil war. These policies made it clear that Philip II would not defer to local aristocratic families or respect long-standing rights and privileges of autonomy.

The Constitutional Foundations of the United Provinces of the Netherlands

In 1579, the seven northern provinces met in Utrecht and formally created a mutual defense alliance against Spain. Open warfare with the Habsburgs had occurred for at least a decade. For example, the important Spanish siege of Leiden had occurred in 1573–4. The treaty of Ultrecht thus could be said to have formalized military relationships among the provinces that had already successfully resisted the Spanish for a decade; however, it also provided the basis for future policy decisions.

Article 1 united the seven provinces as if a single province and also assured the provinces and cities their historic privileges. Article 2 permanently bound the provinces together in a mutual defense alliance. Article 9 affirmed the core procedures of the Great Privilege, which had been much contested by the Habsburgs. It specified that new general taxes and declarations of war and peace required the unanimous consent of the provinces. Other national policies would be determined by a majority of provincial votes. Article 13 provided for religious tolerance in accordance with the pacification of Ghent (recently negotiated in 1576). The provinces were free to regulate religious matters, provided that everyone remained free to exercise their religion. Articles 9, 16, and 21 specified that the *stadhouder*s were to arbitrate differences among the provinces on matters of general interest and on matters of constitutional law (Barker 1906, 99–100; Rietbergen 2002, 84).

Negotiations with the Spanish continued to be fruitless, and thus on July 26, 1581, the States General adopted the Dutch declaration of independence (the Act of Abjuration). The line of reasoning developed in this pre-enlightenment document is surprisingly similar to that developed by Locke a century later and also to that crafted by the committee of Jefferson,

Adams, and Franklin in Philadelphia two centuries later (Congleton 2008).

The Dutch declaration espouses a theory of limited government, includes a list of grievances, and mentions the natural and ancient rights of man. The Act of Abjuration uses the "necessity" of escaping from tyranny as its justification for secession:

> As it is apparent to all that **a prince is constituted by God to be ruler of a people, to defend them from oppression and violence as the shepherd his sheep**; and whereas God did not create the people slaves to their prince, to obey his commands, whether right or wrong, but rather the prince for the sake of the subjects (without which he could be no prince), to govern them according to equity, to love and support them as a father his children or a shepherd his flock, and even at the hazard of life to defend and preserve them. And **when he does not behave thus, but, on the contrary, oppresses them, seeking opportunities to infringe their ancient customs and privileges, exacting from them slavish compliance, then he is no longer a prince, but a tyrant**, and the subjects are to consider him in no other view …
>
> All these considerations **give us more than sufficient reason to renounce the king of Spain**, and seek some other powerful and more gracious prince to take us under his protection; and, more especially, as these countries have been for these twenty years abandoned to disturbance and oppression by their king, during which time the inhabitants were not treated as subjects, but enemies, enslaved forcibly by their own governors …
>
> So, **having no hope of reconciliation, and finding no other remedy, we have, agreeable to the law of nature in our own defense, and for maintaining the rights, privileges, and liberties of our countrymen, wives, and children**, and latest posterity from being enslaved by the Spaniards, been constrained to renounce allegiance to the king of Spain, and pursue such methods as appear to us most likely to secure our ancient liberties and privileges.[9]

The first and third excerpts provide an early theory of natural rights and of limited governance a century before Locke's *Two Treatises on Government* was published in 1689.

The second of the three excerpts demonstrates that the Dutch were initially reluctant to form a completely republican government without a prince or king at the helm. However, no king or queen accepted the proffered throne – most likely because of the military and economic costs associated with doing so. At the time of the Dutch revolt, the Habsburgs were the most powerful family in Europe, and Dutch success was by no means assured.[10]

[9] The translation of the Act of Abjuration is taken from Thatcher (1901, 190–99) as modified by Jerome S. Arkenberg, www.fordham.edu/halsall/mod/1581dutch.html.

[10] Nonetheless, England and France often supported the Dutch revolt, along with a number of Lutheran princes from Germany. This was more likely done to reduce the power of the Habsburgs than for religious reasons. France was ruled by Catholics in this period.

Instead, existing Burgundian institutions were modified to serve as a national government.

The military force raised by the northern principalities and led by Willem the Silent (of the Orange-Nassau family) succeeded in pushing the Spanish army out of the north, and temporarily from much of the southern lowlands.[11] The southern half of the Rhine's lowlands (Belgium) was subsequently subdued by the Spanish and remained in Habsburgian hands for another two centuries, but a new independent republic was established in the northern half of the Rhine's delta.

THE GOVERNMENT OF THE DUTCH REPUBLIC 1581–1795

The successful and somewhat fortunate Dutch war of secession allowed the procedures specified by the Union of Utrecht and its Act of Abjuration to become the constitutional core of national governance in the United Provinces of the Netherlands for the next two hundred years.

In combination with the Great Privilege, the Utrecht treaty favored those represented in the provincial governments, which were often controlled by representatives of the major urban centers.[12] The requirement of unanimity for new taxes helped keep the central government small, and the broad consent required for other policies made nationwide laws and projects difficult

[11] Willem I was himself a complex and interesting figure. He was a favorite of Charles V, who had appointed Willem to the office of *stadhouder* to represent Habsburg interests in the Netherlands. However, Willem defended the autonomy of the Dutch provinces against Charles V's son (Philip II), who attempted to centralize authority and crush Protestantism in the Low Countries. At first he did this peacefully through his office as *stadhouder* and, after his lands were confiscated by Charles V, through open warfare.

Willem was a member of a Lutheran family, although he was himself an avowed Catholic – until he joined the Dutch revolt. In 1573, he converted to Calvinism. The conversion to Protestantism allowed him to lead and energize most of the religious and secular groups that opposed Spanish rule of the Netherlands. (The political convenience of his conversion suggests that Willem's religious beliefs were a bit flexible at the margin and served practical, perhaps more than spiritual, ends.)

Willem's leadership of the Dutch resistance naturally attracted the attention of Philip II, who posted a twenty-five-thousand-crown reward for Willem's assassination in 1580. When Willem was assassinated in 1584, however, Philip refused to pay the assassin's family (Barker 1906, 107–9). Willem's highest noble title, "the Prince of Orange" was derived from his family's control of a principality in Catholic France. Willem the Silent is often referred to as Willem I, the first *stadhouder* of the United Provinces of the Netherlands.

[12] Seven provinces could vote in the States General: Holland, Zeeland, Utrecht, Friesland, Groningen, Overijssel, and Gelderland. Holland was the most populous, wealthiest, and most influential of the seven. The states of Brabant, Vlaanderen, and Linburg were governed by the States General as spoils of war for many years. Drenthe could not vote in the States General, but exercised a degree of provincial sovereignty (Rietbergen 2002, 84).

to adopt and implement. In practice, seven provincial assemblies were sovereign and governance very decentralized. The provincial assemblies and city governments had essentially complete control over local government finance, public services, and regulation.[13]

The provincial assembles were composed of representatives from city governments and from the countryside. The cities were normally represented by persons appointed by their town councils (*vroedschap*, "wise men"). In many cases, city councilors served for life, and their replacements were selected by the remaining city council members. The countryside was normally represented by the local nobility. The specifics varied somewhat by province, but in many cases, the urban representatives dominated deliberations at the provincial level. For example, in the large and prosperous province of Holland, the cities appointed eight of the nine members of the provincial States General (Barker 1906). Together, the provincial systems of representation and need for broad consensus at the States General, allowed the cities, especially Amsterdam, to have considerable influence over the policies of the national government.

After the Dutch independence, *stadhouders* were appointed by the provincial governments, rather than by the States General. Given the autonomy of the provinces, one might have expected each province to appoint a unique *stadhouder*. However, rather than seven *stadhouders*, as might have been expected, only one or two persons held the office of *stadhouder* at a time. The same person(s) was (were) normally appointed captain(s) general of the Dutch army throughout the Netherlands. (The Dutch navy was normally controlled by the other person[s].)

Although not formally a hereditary office, *stadhouders* were always chosen from the Orange-Nassau family. The northern provinces chose their *stadhouders* from one branch of the family, and the southern provinces from another, until that branch ended. This occurred in part because of tradition. Orange-Nassau family members had often been appointed *stadhouders* in Burgundian and Habsburg times. Support for Orange-Nassau family members also reflected the important roles that the family had played in the Dutch war of secession and in subsequent wars with France. It also bears noting that the family's wealth and past influence over appointments provided it with a base of support within the provincial assemblies.

[13] In addition to the States General, a National Assembly was created by the 1581 declaration of independence. Its decision-making procedures and representation were very similar to that of the States General. However, it met very infrequently and is therefore neglected in the present overview (and by most historians).

As a consequence, the Orange-Nassau family was the most influential family in the Netherlands, although it had far less control over public policy than truly royal families had at this time.[14]

As in any divided government, there were often disagreements between *stadhouders* and the States General on matters of national policy. These reflected to a significant degree institutionally induced differences in their interests. As national leaders, *stadhouder*s had a more encompassing interest in national unity, centralization, and development. As leaders of the army, *stadhouders* were especially interested in military expenditures, although less interested in spending money on the navy. The provincial members of the States General represented local political and commercial interests. As agents of local elites, provincial governments were less interested in national policies, generally opposed to national taxation, and more inclined to support profitable navy and capital projects than army salaries (which might well be used to increase centralization). The States General thus tended to support decentralized authority, naval power, and peace treaties.

With respect to the latter, they did so partly because they believed that war was costly and bad for commerce and partly because war increased the power and prestige of the *stadhouder(s)*. As a result, peace treaties were often accepted over the objection of the *stadhouder*, and military budgets were normally smaller than the *stadhouders* desired. For example, the twelve-year truce of 1609 was adopted by the States General over the objection of *stadhouder* Prince Maurice (Rietbergen 2002, 80).

Nonetheless, during national emergencies, the States General was willing to finance both the navy and army, often by selling bonds that were backed by new earmarked taxes (Stasavage 2003). About 90 percent of the Dutch Republic's national budget went for national defense during their eighty-year war of secession with Spain (Ferguson 2002, 41). National defense was often a matter of life and death for the Republic. At such times, the *stadhouder* was a very important man, even if he was neither sovereign nor the main locus of policy-making authority within the Netherlands.[15]

[14] Toward the end of the republican era, the position of *stadhouder* was formally made a hereditary position. Willem IV became the first hereditary *stadhouder* of all the provinces in 1747. He was shortly thereafter succeeded by his son, Willem V, who served as the last *stadhouder* of the republic from 1751–95 (Rietbergen 2002, 160).

[15] The title Prince of Orange is taken from an ancient French territory and title (prince) acquired through inheritance in 1515. The title was more prestigious than other Nassau titles (which included baron and count) and became part of the Nassau family legacy, even after the province was taken over by the French king in 1672. The Nassau family already had substantial holdings in the Rhine's lowlands and had served as provincial *stadhouders* in the fifteenth century.

After the death of Willem II in 1650, the office of *stadhouder* was left empty for twenty-two years in the south.[16] A new *stadhouder* was finally appointed in 1672 during a time of grave military threat from a French-English alliance. The French were repelled, but the risk from France and its English ally was not eliminated.

Subsequent Dutch geopolitical strategy played a pivotal role in English history, as noted in Chapters Twelve and Thirteen. After securing permission to invade England from the States General, Willem III led a successful invasion of that country, which induced James II to flee to France. As a result of negotiations with the parliament in 1689, Willem III became the king of England (as William III) and held both the offices of *stadhouder* and King of England until his death in 1702.[17]

Even as king of England, the long-standing *stadhouder* preference for the Dutch army over the Dutch navy continued to influence William IIIs military policies. In the ensuing war against France, William III used the Dutch army on land and the British navy on the sea. The latter subsequently made the British navy the unchallenged leader on the world's oceans, which in the long run undermined Dutch commercial international interests and promoted British ones – a sensible strategy for a *stadhouder*.

Economic and Political Effects of Decentralization

The decentralized control of public policies by local urban commercial elites, together with a mobile and well-trained work force, contributed to Dutch prosperity. Contemporary mercantilist theories and practices were less binding in the Netherlands than in other European countries because of its long-standing orientation toward international trade, and because its decentralized governance generated competition among localities for the large inflows of new capital and labor, which favored those with relatively open internal and external trade networks. Together these produced rapid economic growth, which encouraged further immigration by increasing economic opportunities for immigrants relative to those available elsewhere in Europe.

Economics was not the only reason for the influx of persons and capital into the United Provinces of the Netherlands. If not a liberal state in the

16 Willem II's son, Willem III, was born the week after his death. Willem III was only twenty-two when he was appointed *stadhouder* for the other provinces in 1672. Two of the seven provinces had appointed *stadhouders* during this period, Groningen and Friesland, but from a northern branch of the Nassau family.

17 More details are provided in Chapters Twelve and Thirteen. Willem III had been invited to intervene in English politics by several prominent members of parliament.

modern sense, the Dutch Republic was a relatively safe haven for nonconformist religious and political ideas. Although the Union of Utrecht called for religious tolerance, as did many of the Republic's early political leaders, tolerance was not always supported by provincial and urban governments. Local autonomy, however, implied that a place could nearly always be found in the Netherlands where nonconforming intellectual perspectives and religious practices would not be contested by local authorities. As a consequence, thousands of Protestants and other nonconformists from the southern provinces (Belgium) moved to the Netherlands in the late sixteenth and early seventeenth centuries.

A similar immigration from throughout Europe followed, including thousands of Huguenots from France and several hundred English Puritans. The population of the United Provinces grew rapidly, and commerce expanded as innovators, capitalists, craftsmen, and scholars converged on the Netherlands. Amsterdam became a metropolis, and many other towns became cities. New universities, newsletters, journals, and printing companies were founded. European liberals of this period thus found the Netherlands useful places to work and to have their work published.

Unfortunately for the Republic, the rapid growth of wealth generated by its internal tax competition, relatively free trade policies, and tolerance of political and religious nonconformists attracted the interest of the Dutch neighbors. Moreover, its borders and coastline were normally poorly defended during times of peace because provincial autonomy allowed the provinces to free ride on the provision of national public goods, including national defense. This tended to exacerbate the military crises of the next two centuries (Barker 1906, 181–2, 364–5, 379–83). A low-level war with Spain dragged on for eighty years with periodic major engagements, and the Spanish war was subsequently replaced with British and French conflicts.

CONSTITUTIONAL SIGNIFICANCE OF THE DUTCH REPUBLIC

National governance in the Dutch Republic was based on an intermediate version of the king-and-council template in which the balance of authority shifted as military threats increased and diminished. Two centuries later, such divided governments would be fairly common, but in the seventeenth century, this form of government was extremely unusual. In the Netherlands, national assemblies often had dominant authority over public policy, especially during times of peace. This was also true at provincial and local levels of governance, where provincial and town councils, rather than kings (dukes or barons), had extensive control over public-policy decisions. Votes were counted in the various regional and national assemblies, although those who held office were not broadly elected in the modern sense. There were no popular elections.

The Republic provided useful evidence about parliamentary governance, the effects that voting rules can have on parliamentary decisions, how very decentralized systems of governance operate, and about the effects of relatively open trade and relatively great religious tolerance. The supermajority and unanimity rules of the national government reduced its ability to impose taxes and regulations on the provinces. As a consequence, most fiscal and regulatory decisions were made at the provincial and city-government level. The supermajority provisions of its national policy-making system, also made the Republic a fairly rigid system of governance in which its component parts were difficult to reform. Toward the end of the republican period, there were true revolutionary pressures, as the proreform "patriots" pressed for liberal constitutional changes that would change the basis of representation within the local and national assemblies, while the antireform "Orangists" successfully defeated their proposed reforms in the assemblies (and once or twice on the battlefield).

Decentralization itself tended to produce relatively liberal economic policies and a relatively open society. Inflows of capital and labor tended to increase prosperity, and competition for capital and labor tended to favor provinces with relatively few trade barriers and restrictions on immigration. Although, the Republic was not dominated by liberals, there were many economic liberals, such as La Court, who played significant roles in the more successful provincial governments. Competition for labor and capital also tended to favor provinces with relatively liberal policies with respect to censorship and religion.

Dutch interest in the enlightenment and its associated political and economic reform agenda was relatively broad by the standards of the seventeenth century. Several famous Dutch scholars are mentioned at the beginning of this chapter and several are quoted in Chapter Nine, but there are many other examples. For example, consider this passage in praise of rationality taken from a piece written by Jacob Hendrix in 1582:

> A **free mind**, in which an unrestricted intellect governs, **can see and observe** … **what is honest, profitable, righteous, lawful**, proper, possible, feasible, and necessary … the mind inflamed by the fire of passion **cannot** judge rightly in private nor in common matters (Van Gelderen 1993, 169).

Dutch readers and publishers were interested in liberal ideas and willing to print books and pamphlets that discussed radical reforms of king-dominated systems of governance. Many influential books about political theory and constitutional design were published at Dutch presses, often in Latin during the seventeenth century, but also in many other languages. Elsewhere such books were likely to bring death penalties or long jail sentences to their publishers, rather than profits.

Proponents of enlightenment and liberal ideas were also somewhat freer to write and publish their theories in the Republic than elsewhere in Europe. Descartes spent two decades working in the Dutch Republic. John Locke spent five years in the Netherlands as a political refuge, where he completed his influential work on governance and religious tolerance. The safety of such persons, however, was largely a consequence of its decentralized political institutions, rather than widespread liberalism or tolerance per se.[18]

In the eighteenth century, scholars from other countries often used the experience of the Dutch Republic to motivate or illustrate general theories, as in Montesquieu's (1748) chapter on decentralization and Adam Smith's (1776) discussion of the benefits of trade liberalization. Dutch references and illustrations were also used during the Constitutional Conventions that led to the founding of the United States of America (Congleton 2008).

REVOLUTIONARY TIMES, 1795–1814: THE BATAVIAN REPUBLIC, FIRST KINGDOM, AND THE FRENCH EMPIRE

Most historical accounts suggest that centralization within the Republic increased during the second half of the second century because a single *stadhouder*, Willem IV, was appointed for all of the Netherlands in 1747 during another war with France, and the office was made formally hereditary. Partly for this reason, ideological competition and interest in constitutional reform intensified between Dutch liberals and conservatives at the national level.

A large, loosely organized, relatively liberal political-reform movement called the "patriot movement" emerged in the second half of the eighteenth century. The patriot movement began as a series of loosely affiliated reading societies that debated and pressed for Dutch constitutional reform. As true of other liberal movements of the eighteenth century, the members of the patriot movement often quoted and referred to such English political theorists as Locke, Price, and Priestley in their pamphlets and arguments for reform, in addition to their Dutch predecessors. Thomas Jefferson

[18] See Israel (2002) and Van Bunge (2003) for careful surveys of Dutch contributions to the European enlightenment.

occasionally met with leaders of the patriot movement during his tour of office in Paris. In the second half of the eighteenth century, a few patriot groups acquired arms and trained in military operations, as did, for example, the Free Corp (Israel 1998, 1136).

However, both peaceful and revolutionary efforts were largely unsuccessful until the French army provided additional support shortly after the French Revolution. In 1795, with help of the French army, the patriots induced Willem V to leave for England on January 18, and a mild Dutch counterpart to the French Revolution took place. Although much less bloodshed was involved, the patriot revolution also demonstrated the difficulty of radically reforming political institutions.

After Willem V's departure, the patriots organized a constitutional convention to write a new national constitution and found a new government, the Batavian Republic. The States General called for elections to a constitutional assembly in January 1796. Elections to the constitutional assembly were based on essentially universal male suffrage. All men older than twenty, in favor of popular sovereignty, and not on poor relief could vote for representatives to the constitutional assembly. This was very broad suffrage for its day.

Constructing an acceptable new constitution at the special assembly required much negotiation and bargaining, but finally, a federal constitution with sufficient support emerged from the assembly. As required for those espousing popular sovereignty, the proposed design was placed before the public in a direct referendum. Unfortunately, the proposed constitution was rejected in the referendum of August 1797.

The constitutional assembly resumed meetings and negotiations, and several more months of fruitless constitutional renegotiation followed. Finally, in January 1798, the French ambassador assumed the leadership of the constitutional assembly and dictated a unitary constitution with separation of church and state, broad male suffrage, and abolition of guilds, feudal duties, and the slave trade. This French proposal for a unitary state was accepted in a referendum in April 1798.

Although the new Batavian Republic was somewhat more stable and more humane than its French counterpart of that period, its constitution was also revised several times in a manner that tended to concentrate policy-making authority. For example, in 1801, the Batavian constitution was reformed to concentrate executive power in a small committee. Two years later, in 1805, it was reformed again to centralize executive power in a single person.

Later in 1805, the Batavian Republic was replaced by the first Kingdom of the Netherlands, as Napoleon appointed his brother Louis to be king. This, too, proved to be unstable. In 1810, the Netherlands became part of the French empire with the annexation of the Netherlands by Napoleon.

THE KINGDOM OF THE NETHERLANDS: 1815–1848

The Congress of Vienna and the Kingdom of the Netherlands

After the great powers had defeated Napoleon in 1813, the son of Willem V, Prince Willem, arrived in the Netherlands from England and with English support. A new constitution was quickly drafted by supporters of the House of Orange. It called for a new States General that would be a unicameral parliament to be appointed by regional governments. The old office of *stadhouder*, however, was replaced with that of king, which would have much-enhanced authority. As a consequence, Prince Willem was crowned King Willem I, rather than *stadhouder* Willem IV, by the new States General on March 15, 1814.

At roughly the same time that Willem was taking power in the Netherlands, the great powers held a Congress in Vienna to redraw the map of European governance with an eye to major power interests and to the future security and political stability of Europe. The great powers (England, Prussia, Russia, and France) agreed to merge many small polities into larger ones, ending the independence of many long-standing polities and creating new ones. The Holy Roman Empire was replaced by the German Confederation. Bavaria was elevated to a kingdom. Switzerland was reestablished. Venice lost its six-century-long independence and became part of the Habsburg domains. The Vienna Congress also placed Norway and Sweden under a common crown, transferring Norway from Denmark to Sweden; it formally placed "Swedish Finland" and part of Poland under the Russian sovereign.[19]

It was by no means clear at the time that the kingdom of the Netherlands would include the former Habsburg territories to the south, what would become Belgium in 1830. Many evidently believed that those lands would revert to Austria. Willem I, however, lobbied for incorporation of the southern provinces into the Netherlands and was successful. On July 31, 1814, Willem I and his government took over the administration of the south. (The Vienna Congress shifted parts of Spain and Italy to the Austrian sovereign to compensate the Habsburgs for the loss of their Belgian territories.)

According to the terms worked out between the House of Orange and the great powers in Vienna, the north and south were to be equal parts in a new unitary state, the details of which were to be worked out by the new

[19] The Vienna conference also encouraged the great powers to continue their alliance, which indirectly created a pan-European diplomatic forum, the Concert of Europe. Both the alliance and concert helped to reduce European tensions during the remainder of the nineteenth century.

Netherlands' States General and king (Kossman 1978, 109–11). A constitutional commission with twelve members from the north and twelve from the south undertook the task of refining the new constitution. Negotiations between northern and southern representatives show that a variety of interests, including liberal ones, were represented in the constitutional convention. It established a new bicameral States General with the first chamber based on nobility and royal appointments for life, and the second selected by provincial governments. The north, unlike the south, with its republican history lacked a proper nobility, although it had many influential and wealthy families, several of which held noble titles in the Netherlands or elsewhere. Willem I predictably "solved" the problem of northern peers by elevating his most prominent supporters to the new noble chamber.

The second chamber was a federal chamber composed of fifty-five members from the north and fifty-five members from the south, each elected by their respective provincial governments (Rietbergen 2002, 124). The provincial governments were modeled after the French system and were organized on the basis of the three medieval estates: the nobility, the towns, and the rural class. Representatives for the town and country were indirectly elected by urban administrators and county electoral colleges. One third of the members of the second chamber stood for election every year (Van Raalte 1959, 2). Suffrage rules for the urban administrators and for the county electoral colleges were based on tax payments and were much more restrictive than under the short-lived Batavian Republic. Only about 80,000 Dutchmen and 60,000 Belgians were entitled to vote out of populations of about 2.4 million and 3.4 million respectively (Kossman 1978, 113; Maddison 2003, table A-3A).

The bicameral parliament had formal power to veto proposed budgets and intervene on budgetary matters. However, until 1840, budgets were normally proposed only *once every ten years*, which left day-to-day governance almost completely in the hands of the king and his ministers. The constitution called for all routine peacetime expenditures to be part of a decennial budget. Of course, the king and parliament occasionally disagreed about what was routine. Extraordinary budgets were approved one year at a time (Van Raalte 1959, 2).

The new constitution was a king-dominated form of the king-and-council template. It included many provisions that were similar to those of other constitutional monarchies based on late-medieval negotiations, although never before present in the Netherlands. The king's appointment of the members of the first chamber, together with his control of ongoing government policies, gave King Willem I considerable control over public policy.

He and his ministers ruled largely by royal decree for most of his reign (Rietbergen 2002, 124; Van Raalte 1959, 2).

Amendments to the constitution had to be approved by majorities in the first and second chambers and formally accepted at a meeting of the provincial states and by the king. The former prevented the king from simply adopting new constitutional provisions by fiat, and the latter protected the king from usurpation by the parliament. (No formal provision for constitutional review was provided.)

Belgian Secession of 1830

Equal representation in the second chamber was consistent with the Vienna mandate for equal participation in the new unified national government; however, the south naturally felt shortchanged by this compromise. Those living south of the Rhine (Walloons and Flemish) outnumbered those from the north (Dutch) by more than 30 percent.

A variety of policies implemented by Willem I during his first fifteen years further alienated the south. Dutch was gradually introduced as the official language of the southern courts and government (1819). The language of civil service and governance became predominantly Dutch, which excluded many educated Belgians from government service. Although Dutch (Flemish) was widely spoken in the south, most educated Belgians were from French-speaking households and trained at French schools. A new system of public primary schools was established in the south, which competed with the long-standing Catholic system, which now had to be certified by national governmental authorities. In 1825, all Latin schools founded without government permission were closed (Kossman 1978, 127). These policies increased literacy in the south, but also increased Catholic reservations about the new union with the north.

By actively trying to "bring the south into the north," Willem raised suspicions among lay Catholics and French-speaking aristocrats that their lifestyles and wealth were threatened by the new regime. Many intellectuals and businessmen in the south believed that they were being held back by northern policies. A liberal Belgian petition movement gained momentum in the late 1820s, which advocated freedom of education, a free press, and personal liberty. Petitions were distributed by politically active groups, signed by hundreds of thousands, and presented to the States General.

The king and his ministers essentially ignored the petitions, because by constitutional law, such documents were irrelevant, and taking formal account of them would have implicitly changed the constitution. A right to petition would have provided direct participation for citizens and politically active groups, rather than the indirect one allowed by the constitution.

In 1830, an economic downturn produced large numbers of bankruptcies, falling wage rates, and unemployment in the south, which further increased discontent. By the end of 1831, a series of working-class demonstrations, resistance by liberal and Catholic interest groups, and mistakes by Willem I and his ministers led to southern secession. Willem objected to the secession both militarily and diplomatically, but the secession was supported by the French and British. In 1831, a new Belgian constitutional monarchy was formed under Leopold I, a Bavarian duke who had fought against Napoleon.[20]

Many of the same considerations that led to the Belgian secession and to a new, relatively liberal Belgian constitution were soon to induce major reforms of the Dutch constitution.

Reforms of 1840: Ministerial Responsibility and the Rule of Law

In 1839, Willem I formally acknowledged the secession of Belgium, which required revising the 1815 constitution because the southern provinces no longer required representation. The constitution of 1815 prevented the king from modifying the constitution by decree, which gave the parliament a chance to renegotiate some of the procedures of governance. The second chamber had also recently vetoed the king's proposed ten-year budget. The Belgian secession had shifted the full burden of the Netherlands' debt back on the northern provinces and reduced tax receipts.

The fiscal problems faced by the king increased the parliament's bargaining power with respect to constitutional reforms, as predicted by the models of Part I, and as it often had in other systems in which parliament held the power of the purse (Kossman 1978, 162–4, 182). Several liberal proposals for reform of the constitution had already been made and rejected. The second chamber refused to accept the current budget proposal unless some recognition of ministerial responsibility was incorporated into the constitution (Van Raalte 1959, 4).

Both the king and the first chamber were initially opposed to constitutional reforms beyond those necessary to take account of the Belgian secession. However, there were new constitutional gains to trade because of changes in the composition of the first and second chamber and the new

[20] During the Burgundian period, all residents of the territories of the Netherlands had been referred to as Belge in French or as Belga in Latin. However, by 1830 the term Belge indicated residents of the southern Netherlands alone (Kossman 1978, 118).

fiscal conditions. After additional negotiation and bargaining, several liberal amendments were adopted by supermajorities in both chambers in September 1840.[21]

The 1840 reforms eliminated the ten-year budgetary cycle and required that all departments submit two-year budgets. In addition, every future decree by the king had to be countersigned by a minister, and royal ministers could be prosecuted if they were suspected of violating ordinary or constitutional law. The requirement that decrees be countersigned by ministers by itself would not have affected the king's freedom of action very much, insofar as he retained complete control over appointments. The fiscal and immunity reforms, however, increased the king's need for ongoing support within parliament.

Previously, both the king and his servants were above the law, and there was no penalty that the States General or the courts could impose if the king or his ministers ignored constitutional law or ordinary legislation. After the reforms, the responsible minister could be fined, jailed, or executed, which made ministers more responsive to parliament (and the constitution) than before, and which indirectly reduced the king's power of decree. Equally important, the king would also require routine support in both chambers of the Dutch parliament to keep tax revenue flowing to "his" treasury. These reforms ended the era of royal governance in the Netherlands by shifting Dutch governance to an intermediate form of the king-and-council template.

Willem I abdicated shortly after the reforms were adopted to pursue an unpopular marriage. His son, Willem II, took office in October 7, 1840 (Kossman 1978, 180; Van Raalte 1959, 4).[22]

THORBECKE'S CONSTITUTIONAL REFORMS OF 1848

In 1839, a professor of history at Leiden University wrote *Comment upon the Constitution*, a book criticizing the 1815 Dutch constitution. In his book, Professor Johan Thorbecke argued in favor of broader suffrage, the parliamentary appointment of ministers, and other liberal reforms. A second edition was published in 1843 that took account of the 1840 amendments

[21] The amendments included approval by a meeting of the second chamber augmented by representatives of the provincial states.

[22] Willem II had had a rather non-Dutch childhood. During the French period, he lived in Berlin, where he received a Prussian military education, and later lived in England, where he attended Oxford University. He served in the British army in 1811 at the age of nineteen as aide de camp of the Duke of Wellington. He married Anna in 1816, the sister of the Czar of Russia.

but advanced similar arguments. Thorbecke's work was typical of liberal books, pamphlets, and newspaper articles that addressed constitutional issues at that time. Thorbecke, however, was not simply an academic theorist, but also a respected member of the second chamber of the parliament. In 1844, Thorbecke proposed a series of constitutional reforms. His proposals were rejected, as many other proposals for liberal reforms had been rejected over the years.

A few years later, King Willem II also became interested in constitutional reform. On March 16, 1848, in an often quoted conversation, Willem II reported to a group of diplomats from the major powers that "from being very conservative, he had in the course of 24 hours become very liberal." This statement was used to introduce his new strategy of constitutional reform as a method of maintaining the position of the House of Orange, which he described in some detail at the same meeting (Van Raalte 1959, 16). The king's new interest in liberal constitutional reform is often attributed to the demonstrations that swept across much of Europe in 1848, especially in Paris and Bonn.[23] These events surely influenced his constitutional strategy somewhat, although it was not the first time that he had proposed constitutional reforms, and it bears noting that demonstrations in the Netherlands were not especially widespread.[24]

The king's hand was not forced, but it seems clear that Willem II now believed that some liberal reforms were unavoidable and sought to control their course. In early 1848, his ministers proposed twenty-seven amendments to the Dutch constitution. Liberals and moderates in the second chamber favored more liberal economic and administrative reforms than proposed by the king's ministers, while Catholics wanted more religious

[23] In 1848, a series of large, but mostly peaceful demonstrations favoring constitutional reform took place in many parts of Europe. For the most part, the demonstrations were illegal, and in this sense, revolutionary, a term often used by historians to describe the events of 1848, although there was little bloodshed. There was, however, little evidence of revolution in the Netherlands. The Kingdom of the Netherlands, like much of Europe, was in economic distress, but there were no large-scale riots or takeovers of government buildings. Some 16 percent of the Dutch population were on poor relief, which suggests that a welfare state was already present in the Netherlands and may have reduced the urgency of those suffering from economic distress. Peaceful demonstrations, nonetheless, made it clear that support for liberal reforms was rising in the Netherlands, as in other European countries, particularly among the middle class.

[24] Eighteen years earlier, Willem II had proposed to his father that Belgium be granted a "separate administration" as a possible method of reducing Belgian opposition to the Orange sovereign, after negotiating with Belgian liberals. An emergency session of the States General was called by Willem I, which voted in favor of such reforms, but they were too little and too late to overcome pressures for Belgian secession (Kossman 1978, 153). This experience without doubt also influenced Willem II's thoughts and decisions in 1848.

freedom than proposed (Kossman 1978, 183–8). A majority in the second chamber thus rejected the proposed reforms, and the royal ministers resigned (Van Raalte 1959, 5).

In pursuit of more viable proposals, Willem II appointed a constitutional commission headed by Professor Thorbecke on March 17 and solicited a new cabinet under the leadership of Count Schimmelpenninck. Count Schimmelpenninck agreed to lead the reform cabinet under three conditions: (a) that he could select the other members of the cabinet, (b) that the new cabinet would review the proposed reforms of the Thorbecke commission, and (c) that the king would accept significant constitutional reforms. By accepting Schimmelpenninck's conditions, the king accepted what many regard to be the first ministerial government in Dutch history (Van Raalte 1959, 17).

Given Thorbecke's published work and his proposals while in the second chamber, the constitutional commission's recommendations were predictable. They would be more substantial than those adopted in 1840 and proposed by the king's ministers, but not as radical as many outside parliament favored. Thorbecke did not believe in radical reform, but rather in evolutionary reform. Moreover, his reforms had to be adopted constitutionally, which required majority support in the two chambers of parliament and among the provinces, and the support of the king. Thus, predictably, his proposed 1848 reforms were modest, relative to the French or Dutch constitutional experiments of the late eighteenth century.

Thorbecke submitted three carefully crafted reforms for approval on April 11. First, he proposed a major reform of the bicameral States General to place it on electoral foundations. In effect, the old first chamber of nobles would be eliminated. The confederal second chamber would become the new first chamber. A new, directly elected chamber would become the second chamber. The federal chamber of the States General would have thirty-nine members and be indirectly elected by the provincial governments. The new second chamber would have fifty members and be directly elected from single-member districts under restricted suffrage (Van Raalte 1959, 57). Members of the second chamber would serve four-year terms, and elections for half the members would be held every two years. Members of the first chamber would serve for nine years. A third of its members would stand for election every three years. Budgets were to be annual, rather than biannual. Sessions of both chambers were to be open to the public (Van Raalte 1959, 5–6).

Although the elections would determine essentially all of the members of parliament, the proposed electorate for the new second chamber was slightly *reduced* relative to that of second chamber that it replaced. The new, more uniform tax requirement reduced the franchise from perhaps ninety thousand to seventy-five thousand out of a population of three million (Kossman 1978, 194). Qualifications for suffrage at provincial and national elections were to be determined by the same law. Moreover, eligibility for seats in the two chambers was still restricted to Dutch elites. For example, to be eligible for membership in the first chamber, an individual had to belong to the highest category of taxpayer, which made about one thousand taxpayers eligible (Van Raalte 1959, 5). Such rules helped attract support from members of the first chamber, many of whom would expect to be elected to a seat in the new first chamber. The tough eligibility rules for seats in the new first chamber implied that a majority of the current peers would be "reelected."

Second, the principle of ministerial responsibility was taken a step further than in the 1840 reforms. Thorbecke proposed that parliament be able to dismiss cabinet ministers as well as punish them for illegal or unconstitutional actions. The king's other prerogatives were left unchanged, except that the Dutch colonies would no longer be treated as the king's royal property (reducing his non-parliament-based income and colonial authority). The king remained free to appoint his ministers, veto legislation, dismiss parliament, declare war, elevate persons to the nobility, and call for new elections for each chamber. To compensate for this reduction in authority, royal income was increased and guaranteed (by section 2).

Third, freedom of assembly, worship, and the press were guaranteed by the new constitution, as was funding for public education. The former assured Catholic support for the new constitution in the second chamber, because it meant that the Catholic Church would be free to organize bishropries for the first time since the sixteenth century. Increased support for public education reduced opposition from Protestants and increased support among moderates, because tax revenues would support education in church-run schools as well as secular ones (Kossman 1978, 291).

Overall, Thorbecke's proposed constitutional reforms shifted additional policy-making authority from the king to the parliament, slightly changed the membership of the parliament, and moderately expanded civil liberties. It provided electoral foundations for the Dutch parliament in a manner that made the reforms acceptable to majorities in the first and second chamber.

The ability of parliament to dismiss ministers meant that the ministers were no longer entirely agents of the sovereign. Indeed, ministers became increasingly responsible to parliament during the next two decades as new bargaining equilibria emerged. The elimination of the old chamber of appointed lifetime peers also diminished the king's influence within parliament, because the Dutch peers had been chosen in large part because of their loyalty to Orange interests. Nonetheless, the king retained far more control of public policy under the 1848 constitution than his *stadhouder* forebears had possessed in the days of the Dutch Republic. Netherlands remained a kingdom; the king could veto laws, appoint governments, and dismiss the parliament.[25]

Willem II found this moderate shift of authority to be an acceptable compromise with politically active liberals. The king pressed the first chamber peers into accepting elections. Liberals, moderates, and Catholics, with the king's support, provided majorities for the Thorbecke proposals in the second chamber, which in turn were accepted by the king. In this manner, negotiation and bargaining, rather than revolution or pressing revolutionary threats, produced a major reform of the constitution of the kingdom of the Netherlands. After 1848, the kingdom of the Netherlands had an elected parliament with significant authority over public policy for the first time.[26]

Willem II himself never experienced the effects of the 1848 reforms. In 1849, shortly after swearing in the new Thorbecke cabinet elected under the new rules, Willem II died unexpectedly, and his son, who was far less favorably predisposed to reform, became King Willem III.

The Gradual Emergence of Cabinet Governance, 1848–1868

The 1848 reforms were not a liberal revolution or coup, but rather a bargain worked out among all politically active groups with the support of the king.

[25] Other liberal provisions are scattered throughout the 1848 constitution, including rights of due process (articles 151 and 156), the requirement of warrants to enter private property or read personal mail (articles 158 and 159), freedom of association (article 9), freedom of the press (article 7), and freedom of religion and religious association (articles 167, 168, and 169). The new constitution also included central government responsibility for poor relief (article 193) and reformed local and provincial governance. For example, town governments would consist of a locally elected council whose president would be selected from among those proposed by the king (Article 143).

[26] The constitutional and national assemblies of the Batavian Republic (1796–1805) were also elected (and on the basis of broader suffrage rules, although Orangists and federalists were initially excluded). Thus, it could be said that for the second time in Dutch history, the Netherlands had an elected parliament.

However, the Batavian Republic was not fully independent in that it was subject to French monitoring and intervention (Kossman 1978, 91–7; Rietbergen 2002, 118–19). It also bears noting that the authority of the new parliament, although larger than it had ever been within the kingdom of the Netherlands, remained below that of the States General of the Dutch Republic for several more decades (Van Raalte 1959, 6).

As might be predicted, the reforms had relatively small, short-term effects on the authority of the Dutch political elites, although it did affect the distribution of policy-making authority among those groups and between the parliament and the king, perhaps more than anticipated. Between 1848 and 1877, more than a third of the four hundred ten men who became members of parliament were from families with noble titles. Of the one hundred different cabinet ministers, eighty-one came from noble or patrician families. Most of the other members and ministers were from the successful business and professional strata of Dutch life. (The latter had played a role in the old Dutch Republic and in the provincial governments, but had been less influential in the kingdom.) The overwhelming majority of the men elected to the new parliaments had law degrees or training in the law. It was clearly a government of relatively wealthy, well-connected men (Kossman 1978, 273–4).

Although parliament could dismiss individual ministers for nonperformance, it was not clear how far their authority over the cabinet extended. For the first twenty years after the 1848 reforms, cabinet ministers continued to serve at the pleasure of the king, including the two Thorbecke cabinets of 1849 and 1862. For example, in 1853 Thorbecke dutifully resigned when the king (and much of the country) openly disapproved of his liberal policy with respect to Catholics, although his ministry continued to have majority support in the second chamber (Van Raalte 1959, 18). This suggests that Thorbecke believed that the king's power of appointment and dismissal was not significantly reduced by the constitutional reforms.

On the other hand, there were practical limits to the king's power of appointment under the new budgetary arrangements. The power of the purse granted to the second chamber in the constitutions of 1840 and extended in 1848 allowed parliament to exercise veto power over the policies of ministers and their ministries – as long as a particular parliament could maintain electoral majorities. The importance of parliamentary support for ministers became very evident in 1868, when parliament vetoed the proposed budget of the Foreign Affairs Ministry over a policy dispute on Luxembourg. The cabinet offered to resign, but the king refused their resignations, arguing that parliament had unconstitutionally interfered in the government's execution of foreign policy.

The king called for new parliamentary elections and campaigned for a more supportive parliament. Nonetheless, the electorate selected a parliament that supported parliament's right to criticize and sanction ministers and their policies. The newly elected parliament again vetoed the proposed budget of the recalcitrant ministry of foreign affairs. The king reluctantly accepted the resignation of his cabinet and appointed a new cabinet that was more respectful of parliamentary advice (Van Raalte 1959, 20). After 1868, the sovereign routinely chose ministers from the major parties in the parliament.

Although arguably designed by liberals, the new government was not significantly biased in favor of liberal coalitions. The governments elected under the 1848 constitution alternated between liberals and conservatives, with liberals holding power a bit more often than conservatives. Suffrage was far from universal, although it gradually expanded as the economy grew in the decades before the next series of constitutional amendments.

DUTCH LIBERALISM AND POLITICAL COMPETITION IN THE NINETEENTH CENTURY

Nineteenth-century Dutch liberals were not Cartesian system builders, but rather were generally skeptical of such all-encompassing theories. They were evolutionists, while being skeptical of evolutionary theorists (Kossman 1978, 259–64, Stuurman 1989).

Mid-century liberals normally agreed about the direction of constitutional and quasi-constitutional reforms but disagreed about ends that reforms should achieve and did not often cooperate in their persuasive campaigns. What might be called right-of-center liberals sought suffrage of "competent" persons, reductions in trade barriers, and very little more. Centrist liberals pressed for educational reform, the abolishment of slavery, and a somewhat greater extension of suffrage, largely because of a more generous notion of competence. Left-of-center liberals (radicals) supported very broad suffrage, major educational reform, child labor laws, and a shift of tax instruments from excise to income taxation.

The liberal magazine *De Gids* (the guide) was founded in 1837 and played an important role as a forum for ideas, criticism, and advocates for reform(s). Thorbecke was by far the most important Dutch liberal during the following three decades, because he was simultaneously an important liberal theorist and three times the prime minister, in addition to being the author of the 1848 constitutional reforms.

Their opponents for most of the century were conservatives whose loyalties were not to an ancient kingdom and church, but rather to religious and cultural norms from the past. Conservatives remained skeptical of the usefulness of further political liberalization at each point in the series of reforms that gradually produced liberal parliamentary democracy in the Netherlands. Conservative groups also included former liberals who thought that reforms had gone far enough, members of economic interest groups opposed to free trade, and pragmatists who generally benefited from the status quo. (Von der Dunk 1978, Kossman 1978, 275–7).

During the late nineteenth century, radical liberals became increasingly influential within liberal groups in the Netherlands, as elsewhere. For example, the Gids was challenged in 1874 by the new, more radical Vragen des Tijds (Issues of the Day). As in other parts of Europe, the center of gravity in Dutch liberalism shifted toward increasingly open politics and markets and equal protection of the law. Conservatives also drifted to the left, as the previous generation's radicals became the next generation's conservatives.

Political Parties

Political parties during most of the nineteenth century were loose affiliations of persons and small groups who could agree on the merits of particular reforms and/or politicians. Suffrage was very narrow, and it was not until it expanded toward the end of the century that disciplined political parties emerged. In 1878, the Calvinist antirevolutionary (conservative) party was founded. The Liberal Union was founded in 1885, and the Social Democratic Labor Party was founded in 1894.

The new parties were formally organized, but their members remained open to new alignments and organizations. For example, the most conservative members of the antirevolutionary party broke away in the 1890s to found the Christian Historical Union Party. A few years later, the Liberal Union split into centrist liberals and the right-of-center Union of Free Liberals (which subsequently rejoined the Liberal Union in 1921). The left-of-center radicals left the Liberal Union in 1891 to form the Liberal Democratic Union (VDB). The left-of-center liberals in the VDB worked with the social democrats for universal suffrage. (The VDB subsequently joined the social democrats in 1946.) A similar split occurred among social democrats and Marxists in the first part of the twentieth century (Van Raalte 1959, 10; Kossman 1978, 338–47, 515; Skillen and Carlson-Thies 1982; Sap 2000, 35–7; Rietbergen 2002, 134).

Most Dutch voters, of course, were not driven entirely by liberal ideological considerations or party politics, but rather were influenced by them at the margin, as suggested by the models developed earlier. That is to say, most Dutch voters and politicians were pragmatists with dispositions for or against liberal reform.

Liberal Policy Reforms

Significant liberal policy reforms were adopted during Thorbecke's first and second periods of office. Policy-making power was decentralized somewhat in the municipality laws of 1850 and 1851, and local excise taxes were replaced with direct taxes. Policies protecting Dutch shipping were eliminated. Internal and external protectionism was dismantled as tariffs were reduced in 1854 and export duties eliminated in 1862. New, higher burgher schools, which focused on science and modern languages, were introduced by Thorbecke in 1863 (Kossman 1978, 414).[27] Slavery was abolished in 1863 (Rietbergen 2002, 134).

In 1860, the rail network begun under Willem I was extended. New canals and dikes were built. International trade expanded rapidly, partly because of the free trade regimes adopted in the Netherlands and elsewhere, and also because of the increased income associated with new production technologies and more open markets. Foreign trade increased by 179 percent during the 1850–73 period. The increased exports were initially largely agricultural, but cloth and clothing followed as the factory approach was more broadly applied. Textile and agricultural production expanded. The Dutch population grew rapidly in the second half of the twentieth century (Kossman 1978, 264–5).

The most difficult and controversial of the mid-century reforms was expanding the freedom of association to include the religious organizations of Catholics and Jews.[28] This was guaranteed by the constitution of 1848, but not fully implemented until 1853, when the Catholic Church established bishopries in Utrecht, Haarlem, Breda, Roermond, and Hertogengosch. A subset of Protestants responded with petitions and sermons predicting a new inquisition, censorship, tyranny, and so forth – in short a return to the days before the Dutch revolt nearly three centuries earlier. Although not all Protestants were outraged or participated in demonstrations, the king's response was to ask Thorbecke to resign as prime minister, which he did, as noted earlier (Kossman 1978, 282). The liberal majority of the second

[27] By all accounts the educational reforms and those that followed in the 1870s were very successful, as most graduates of the higher burgher schools went on to university training. Indeed, four won Nobel prizes in the early 1900s (Willink 1991).

[28] Jews and Catholics had long been worshipping in the Netherlands, but privately in secret churches, rather than openly, as had the Protestants before the success of the Dutch war of secession. Catholics were elected to the second chamber and provided important support for Thorbecke's constitutional reforms in exchange for his support for extended rights to organize churches (Kossman 1978, 193, 278–9).

chamber, however, pressed on with liberal reforms under new leadership. (Thorbecke did not regain the prime minister's office until 1862.)

Suffrage Movements

From the perspective of the twenty-first century, Thorbecke's failure to extend suffrage, rather than reduce it, seems odd, but it should be kept in mind that his proposal had to be accepted by the persons presently holding offices in parliament and the king. Moreover, universal male suffrage had never been used to select a national government, except very briefly during the period of the French Revolution, where the results were not widely admired. Under Thorbecke's law, suffrage expanded as personal income increased and tax payments satisfied the qualification thresholds. Suffrage also expanded somewhat as taxes were raised. These factors by themselves gradually increased the electorate to 122,000 persons in 1887, about 14 percent of adult males (Kossman 1978, 351).

Early- and mid-nineteenth-century liberals favored allowing all appropriately qualified (independent and thoughtful) men to vote. Thorbecke's 1850 election law used direct tax payments to determine whether one was qualified or not, with thresholds for the countryside that were somewhat lower than for urban areas. This law was similar to many others in Europe at the time and was adopted by a relatively liberal government. It enfranchised about 10 percent of the adult males (Kossman 1978, 194).

As educational reforms were adopted, literacy increased. As innovation and economic growth took place, average income and tax payments increased. The latter directly increased suffrage, as discussed earlier, but also caused additional debate on the proper qualifications for suffrage. Many liberals began to think that universal suffrage would emerge gradually as education and economic opportunity expanded and increasingly more people qualified as independent, thoughtful voters.

After the parliamentary reforms of 1848, support for expansion of suffrage gradually increased, and several political organizations devoted to suffrage reform were organized. In 1876, an association called the Algemeen Stemrecht (universal franchise) was created by the Dutch left. In 1879, the Comite voor Algemeen Stemrecht was founded by left-of-center liberals. Other groups were founded by socialists, labor unions, and liberals in 1880, 1881, and 1882. These groups launched persuasive campaigns aimed at a broad cross-section of the existing and potential electorate. A women's suffrage league was founded in 1894. Intellectuals wrote books that predicted near utopian results from universal franchise. Many of the political parties founded in the late nineteenth century also pressed for suffrage expansion. By the century's end, social democrats, radical liberals, liberals, and a good many conservatives supported essentially universal male suffrage.

If sociological political theorists are to be believed, the existence of such mass movements should automatically induce rapid changes in suffrage law. However, universal suffrage was not obtained for nearly two generations. Those who already had the right to vote had to be persuaded to extend suffrage to others.

Suffrage Reform in 1887 and 1894

A new round of constitutional negotiations was launched when a conservative government commission proposed a series of twelve constitutional amendments in 1883. These did not generate the required level of support, and the proposals were withdrawn. They were revised and resubmitted in 1885, but again there was too little support. After a year of negotiations, new elections were called in June 1886. The result was a small liberal majority in the second chamber and another round of constitutional bargaining. This time terms for constitutional change were found, and in 1887, a package of eleven provisions were passed, including suffrage reform, a slight change in the size of the two chambers, and a provision for subsidizing Catholic Church schools (Blok 1912, 504–6). New elections were called, as required by the amendment procedures adopted in 1848, and the required support was obtained in the (largely) reelected parliament.

The new suffrage laws eliminated the tax-payment threshold. Suffrage was granted to all male heads of household aged twenty-three or older who showed "signs of fitness and social well-being," with "fitness" to be defined by parliament through new election laws. The standard of fitness chosen, approximately doubled the electorate from 14 to 28 percent of the electorate (Kossman 1978, 350; Ogg 1918, 226; Blok 1912, 505).

Conservatives expected to benefit (and did) from an increased turnout of middle-class religious voters. Catholic and Protestant political parties after 1888 were often partners in government, as controversies over religious doctrine were put aside to advance shared policy objectives, especially subsidies for religious schools. Together they passed an educational reform bill in 1889 – long opposed by liberals – that allowed free schools (religious schools) to pass on one-third of their costs to the national government (Kossman 1978, 354).

Debate over election law continued and various proposals were made to further extend suffrage by left liberals. In 1893, Tak van Poortvliet proposed allowing all persons who could read and write and who were self-supporting to be eligible to vote. That proposal, however, was too large of an expansion for moderate liberals and conservatives at that time and was withdrawn. A few years later, suffrage reform was taken up again, but this time more successfully by a coalition of moderate liberals and conservatives. Von Houton's 1896 reforms of Dutch election law redefined fitness in terms of modest tax payments (one guilder), savings, rental payments, income, residency, and other measures of a man's ability to vote rationally and independently. Suffrage doubled to about 47 percent of the male population.

Consistent with the models developed in Part I, these reforms reflected changes in the beliefs of pivotal voters and pivotal members of parliament – as well as a bit of political pragmatism on the part of parties who expected to benefit from reform. Although left liberals had long supported universal suffrage, moderate liberals did not believe that poor or uneducated citizens were capable of exercising the franchise with sufficient competence to be given the vote.

Moderate and right-of-center liberals controlled the largest block of seats in the late-nineteenth-century parliaments, and so it was they (and their religious party opponents) who actually determined whether new suffrage laws would be adopted, rather than left liberals, the suffrage movement, or unenfranchised voters. Suffrage continued to increase gradually, reaching 60 percent by 1910, as education and wealth expanded and as election laws were reinterpreted (Kossman 1978, 361; Ogg 1918, 527–30; Blok 1912, 509).

These electoral reforms did not produce a "capture" by one of the main political coalitions, as might be predicted by an entirely opportunistic model of suffrage law. Government continued to shift among conservative, liberal, and left-liberal coalitions in the early twentieth century. Indeed, two decades of suffrage reform gradually allowed the Social Democratic Party (SDAP) to become a significant party in parliament.

ELECTORAL REFORMS OF 1917–1922: PR AND UNIVERSAL SUFFRAGE

The elections of 1913 returned eighteen social democrats, thirty-seven liberals, and forty-five conservatives to the second chamber. The left-liberal coalition had both adopted platforms that favored universal male suffrage and a new social-security system. The social democrats, however, refused to participate in government with the liberals, and as a compromise, a "nonpartisan" cabinet was accepted under the leadership of van der Linden.

In 1915, Prime Minister van der Linden initiated a new round of constitutional bargaining with the nonpartisan, three major party-coalition, as World War I was taking place. Three major reforms were negotiated and adopted through normal legislative and constitutional procedures in 1917. Male suffrage was made essentially universal. The first-past-the-post election process was replaced with a PR system. The school-funding provisions of the 1848 constitution were modified to allow full funding of free (religious) schools by the federal government.

All three parts of the package of reforms were necessary to generate the support necessary to amend the constitution. Without PR, the smaller parties feared being eliminated from parliament when universal suffrage was adopted. In the Dutch case, liberals insisted on PR as a method for saving seats for the three liberal parties that held seats at that time. Without constitutional provisions for educational-funding guarantees, the conservative religious parties feared that expanding suffrage would end taxpayer support for religious schools. The secular left had routinely opposed financial support for the religious schools. The social democrats accepted such funding, however, because they were unlikely to have significant control over other public policies unless suffrage was expanded. Together, the guaranteed funding for religious schools and PR produced sufficient liberal and conservative support for the package of reforms to be adopted (Kossman 1978, 555; van Raalte 1959; 20–3; Lijphart 1968, 98–104).

The logic of universal suffrage was extended to include women in 1922 when near universal women's suffrage was added to that of men. (If men were all competent to vote, surely women were as well.)

As expected, the parties of the left became relatively more important after universal suffrage was adopted; however, they did not become the dominant coalitions, as in Sweden. In the Dutch case, the post-World War I electoral rules benefited the religious parties and conservatives, rather than social democrats or liberals. Most of the new male and female blue-collar voters split between the Christian Democratic Party and Social Democratic Party, but the religious parties initially attracted more votes from the newly enfranchised. As a consequence, center-right coalitions of the religious parties formed the government in 1918, 1922, and 1925. Similar center-right coalitions continued to win the votes of conservative and moderate Dutch voters for several decades, although the liberal parties did not disappear.

Social democrats were not routinely invited to majority coalitions formed by other parties until after World War II. They became the largest party in 1960. Liberal political parties, as expected, lost seats after the 1917 expansion of suffrage. The 1918 elections using PR supported seventeen political parties in the second chamber, but the number of liberal members fell from forty to fifteen. Indeed, Dutch liberal parties lost ground with nearly every increase in suffrage, which suggests that liberal interests in suffrage reform tended to be ideological, rather than partisan, although pragmatic interests clearly affected their constitutional-bargaining positions and votes on how suffrage expansion would be implemented (Kossman 1978, 556–7).

In contemporary Netherlands, social democrats alternate with Christian Democrats as the "first" parties in left- and right-of-center coalition governments. Labor headed the cabinet from 1994–2002. The Christian Democrats headed the government from 2002–10. Liberal and conservative parties remain, among many others, and often participate in center-left and -right coalition governments.

CONCLUSIONS: INTERESTS, ECONOMIC DEVELOPMENT, AND REFORM 1815–1920

The Dutch transition to parliamentary democracy reflected opportunities for constitutional exchange that emerged during the course of the nineteenth century. As in Sweden, there were three major periods of reform. The first, in the years 1813–16, established a new Kingdom of the Netherlands, with a relatively powerful king and relatively weak and narrow parliament. The second, in the years 1840–8, created an electoral basis for governance by replacing the noble chamber with a directly elected chamber. The third, in the years 1917–22, adopted universal suffrage and proportional representation. Although the Netherlands remained a constitutional monarchy, control over public policy gradually shifted from kings and queens to the parliament during the nineteenth century.

As in England, the transition to parliamentary rule was faster than the transition to universal suffrage. Thorbecke's 1848 constitutional reforms formally shifted power from the king to parliament by giving it a stronger power of the purse and indirect control over ministers, but the same reforms reduced, rather than expanded, suffrage. Most of the shifts of authority from kings and queens to parliament were products of the new bargaining equilibria produced by Thorbecke's reforms. Royal office-holders in the second half of the century retained formal authority to dismiss ministers, but support from majorities in elected parliaments was difficult to obtain without deferring to leaders of majority coalitions. Consequently, cabinets were increasingly populated by leaders of major political parties in the directly elected chamber of parliament, and the king or queen increasingly accepted the recommendations of their cabinets.

Suffrage reform began several decades later (in 1887) and reflected ideological shifts and partisan interests within parliament. The qualifications for suffrage and for elected office were often revised as parts of carefully negotiated packages of constitutional reforms. For example, the reforms that produced universal male suffrage in 1917 also included a shift to proportional representation and reforms of educational funding. As predicted by the theory of constitutional reform developed in Part I, the reform packages reflected the institutionally induced interest of the negotiators and addressed several issues at a time. The reforms were nonetheless incremental, rather than revolutionary.

Perhaps surprisingly, the relatively liberal republican past of the Netherlands played almost no role in the constitutional developments of the Netherlands during the nineteenth century. Earlier liberal successes during the republic meant that the Netherlands began the nineteenth century with relatively more open trade, relatively greater religious and intellectual tolerance, and perhaps broader support for liberal ideas than elsewhere, but they did not produce a legacy of political institutions or politically active interest groups. The Netherlands did not return to its confederal structure with strong cities and provinces and a weak central government. The office of *stadhouder* was not re-created or reinvented.

The pattern of nineteenth-century reform was very similar to that of other constitutional monarchies affected by liberal tides and technological innovation. The royal office did not disappear, as might be predicted by other theories of constitutional change. Indeed, contemporary Dutch kings and queens retain significant formal authority. The Dutch constitution of 1983 states that each of the chambers of parliament may be dissolved by royal decree (article 64) and that the prime minister and other ministers shall be appointed and dismissed by royal decree (article 43). Article 74 states that the king shall be the president of the council of state and that the heir apparent is entitled to a seat on that council. The council is to be consulted on legislation and may draft general administrative orders.

Nonetheless, the bargaining equilibria that emerged as parliaments became more decisive, and as the power of the purse became more important, were remarkably stable. As a consequence, kings and queens continue to remain in the background on most policy debates. In that and many other respects, the formal and informal constitutional bargains struck by the liberal movement of the nineteenth century arguably created both the mainstream Dutch politics of the twentieth century and the core procedures of governance through which it determines contemporary public policy.

Table 15.1. *Major Constitutional Developments in the History of the Netherlands*

Year	Constitutional or political event
58 BC	Roman empire reaches southern edge of the Rhine. In what will come to be called the Netherlands, a series of fortress cities and trading posts are established, many of which remain today.
1450	States General created for most of the Netherlands by the Burgundy provinces.
1477	Mary's letter of preference grants the States General the right to veto taxes and meet as they wish, without being called by a king or queen.
1579 1581	The Union of Utrecht formalizes the alliance of Protestant provincial governments and provides constitutional foundations for collective decisions by the Seven United Provinces. Provinces have the right to appoint their own *stadhouders*, and a different *stadhouder* is appointed in the north than in the south, although both are from the House of Orange.
1650–72	First *stadhouder*-less period in Holland and several other southern provinces.
1672–02	Office of *stadhouder* reestablished, Willem III takes office and drives the French out.
1702–47	Second *stadhouder*-less period: after Willem III's death in 1702, no *stadhouder* is appointed in the south.
1747	Office of *stadhouder* reestablished. Willem IV is from the Friesland line of the House of Orange and becomes the first *stadhouder* for all of the Netherlands. Willem IV drives the French out.
1793	The French declare war on *stadhouder* Willem V, who flees to England in 1795
1798–1801	Batavian constitution adopted with a unicameral parliament elected under broad suffrage. The constitution provides for freedom of press and association, freedom of religion, independence of judges, and separation of church and state. It also formally eliminates guild privileges and feudal duties.
1801–06	Napoleon replaces the Batavian constitution with a more authoritarian system, with R. J. Schimmelpenninck at its head.
1806–10	Kingdom of the Netherlands created with Louis Bonaparte as king (Napoleon's brother).
1810	Netherlands temporarily becomes part of France.
1813–16	Kingdom of the Netherlands established; a new constitution is drafted with a bicameral parliament with a more or less noble chamber and a federal chamber. Its territories include present-day Belgium.

Year	Constitutional or political event
1830	Belgium secedes and secures independence in 1831. Its new constitution is finalized in 1839 and causes constitutional issues to be revisited in the Netherlands.
1840	Constitution reforms increase parliament's power of the purse by shortening the budget cycle from 10 to 2 years and introduces ministerial responsibility.
1844	Thorbecke (a law professor at the University of Leiden) proposes nine constitutional reforms shortly after coronation of Willem II, but they fail to receive a majority in the lower house.
1848	King Willem II proposes constitutional reforms, but these fail, and his cabinet resigns. A new constitutional commission is created on March 17 (headed by Johan Rudolph Thorbecke). Peaceful demonstrations take place in Amsterdam for constitutional reforms.
1848	Thorbecke proposes major reforms of the Dutch constitution: a compromise between liberals and House of Orange supporters is reached, with support of King Willem II.
	Parliament is placed on an electoral basis. The new first chamber becomes a federal chamber (essentially the existing second chamber) The new second chamber is to be directly elected by about 10 percent of male adults; it controls the budget.
	Members of the first chamber are elected for nine years (one-third of members elected every three years). The second chamber is elected for four years (and increasingly dominated by liberals).
1848	Freedom of press, association, and right of petition established through legislation.
1849	King Willem II dies, Willem III becomes king, and Thorbecke becomes prime minister. He has poor relations with the new king who threatens Thorbecke with the gallows.
1853	Thorbecke resigns at Willem III's request after Protestants protest the return of Catholic bishops to the Netherlands for the first time in 200 years (under the new freedom of association rules). Religious parties gain seats in the next election.
1868	Parliamentary power becomes more extensive as a consequence of bargaining over the budget; ministers now clearly require significant parliamentary support as well as support by the king.
1870	A liberal party is founded.
1869	Anti-Revolutionary Party (conservative coalition) is founded by Kuyper

(*continued*)

Table 15.1. *(continued)*

Year	Constitutional or political event
1880	New socialist parties started in the 1880s, although they did not have significant representation in parliament. They are firmly linked to the labor and social democratic movements.
1887–94	Parliamentary reforms: expansion of male suffrage to 27 percent of adult men. First chamber now includes 50 members and second chamber 100 members. Reforms in 1894 extend suffrage to about 50 percent of male voters. (Willem III dies in 1890 and is succeeded by his daughter Wilhelmina, who rules until 1948.)
1891	Special meeting of Anti-Revolutionary Party (conservatives) to address labor issues. Catholic parties are encouraged to pay more attention to labor by pope encyclical 1891.
1900	First national unions are organized and a major strike occurs in 1903. In response, the government tries to reduce the power of unions, but fails. There are Christian and secular unions closely related to the Christian Democratic Party and Social Democratic Party.
1917–22	Major constitutional reforms adopted in a complex constitutional exchange.
	Universal male suffrage, PR for second chamber, first chamber remains indirectly elected by provincial councils, but with no minimum wealth threshold for chamber seats. First chamber to have six-year terms, with half elected every three years (in 1980 went to four-year terms). Educational funding for religious schools is adopted in exchange for support of other parliamentary reforms.
1922	Women's suffrage is adopted. Support for religion-based political parties increases.
1938–72	Minor constitutional reforms.
1940–46	German occupation, government flees, no election until 1946.

SIXTEEN

Germany: Constitutional Negotiations in an Emerging State

INTRODUCTION: GERMAN DECENTRALIZATION AND SOVEREIGNTY

The next three historical narratives are less obvious applications of the king-and-council model of constitutional reform. Two are cases not usually associated with gradual democratization, Germany and Japan. The other case is often considered a revolutionary state, the United States of America, although as shown in Chapter Eighteen, parliamentary democracy had substantially emerged at the colonial level well before its war of secession. These more problematic cases help to test the generality of the theory of constitutional reform developed in Part I, a theory that is intended to explain more than the successful nineteenth-century democratic transitions of a few European constitutional monarchies.

The first of the difficult cases to be examined is Germany. The history of Germany in the nineteenth century is usually told with an eye on the twentieth century, a century in which German foreign policy led to two continental wars of mass destruction.[1] That such a fate lay ahead was not evident to observers at the beginning of the nineteenth century, nor was it inevitable. Indeed, observers in 1820 would have been surprised by this prediction. Germany had a very weak central government in the decades before, during, and after Napoleon's invasion of the Holy Roman Empire in the late eighteenth century. The empire was less a government than a loose association of independent city-states and duchies linked by language, religion, and commerce. There was clearly a German culture during this period, but the existence of a German government was debatable.

[1] See Blackbourn and Eley (1984) for further analysis of how this assumption, as well as French and English comparisons that emphasize bourgeois revolutions, has led many historians astray.

Germany's constitutional development in the late nineteenth and early twentieth centuries was marked by the formation of a new more centraled German state, and its (partial) transition to parliamentary democracy was affected by an unusually large number of military events as well as liberal shifts in ideology and economic development. As a consequence, this chapter differs somewhat from the previous historical narratives. It discusses more military events (although briefly) and also spends more time discussing "regional governments" than the other chapters. Many of the predictions concerning links among liberalism, industrialization, and the rise of parliament hold for the larger German duchies, such as Württemberg, Baden, Hanover, and Bavaria. Liberal influences are also evident in Prussia's development in the late eighteenth and early nineteenth centuries.[2]

In the German case, the nation-state formed incrementally along with its constitution. Partly as a consequence of this, much of its constitutional negotiation concerned centralization, rather than parliamentary reform. A centralized government with the power to tax did not emerge in Germany until 1871, and this government was formally the result of a series of treaties among the duchies, although it was catalyzed by military events that took place in preceding decades. The division of policy-making authority tended to shift from the member states toward the federal government, as civil and military codes were standardized and as central government services expanded toward the end of the nineteenth century into new areas such as social insurance.

Government leaders in Prussia played leading roles in the military events that led to the treaties and in the drafting of the constitutional treaties themselves. As a consequence, Prussia's government receives disproportionate attention in the first half of this chapter, as it does from most German historians. Military threats and regional politics clearly played major roles in the design of Prussia's constitution as well, although liberalism, constitutional bargaining, and institutional conservatism are also clearly evident.

[2] The term duchy is used to describe a broad cross-range of small, essentially independent territories that were formally parts of the Holy Roman Empire, not all of which were ruled by the German equivalent of a Duke (herzog, landgrave, markgraf). The lesser Germany polities were not formally duchies, because their territories were too small for that grand status, although they were normally ruled by a hereditary aristocratic family.

The true German duchies were relatively large territories, such as Württemburg, Baden, Hanover, and Bavaria. A few of the late-medieval duchies survive to the present day as independent polities, as with Luxembourg, Monaco, and Liechtenstein. Dozens of much smaller German polities also existed. Other terms such as state or *länder* are also used by English historians when describing members of the various German confederacies, although such terms fail to reflect their relative importance or the hereditary nature of most of their chief executives.

SETTING THE STAGE: THE HOLY ROMAN EMPIRE AS THE FIRST GERMAN CONFEDERATION

The Holy Roman Empire is said to have begun when Otto was crowned emperor by the pope in 962. At its peak in 1200, the first German confederation included modern Germany plus large parts of Austria, Switzerland, the Netherlands, the Czech Republic, and northern Italy. The king (emperor) of that confederation was an elective office, although participation in elections was very limited. The electoral college established in 1356 consisted of just seven electors who represented the major regions of the empire, the boundaries and method of inheritance of which were codified at the same time (by the Golden Bull). The elections normally took place in Frankfurt, and the pope normally crowned the emperor in Aachen, although Rome was not normally part of the empire. Nuremburg was the (first) site for the confederal assembly of the empire.[3]

Governance in the Holy Roman Empire functioned at two levels. At the level of the central government, representatives from several hundred independent cities, duchies, and church territories participated in imperial meetings at major cities in the empire, beginning with Nuremburg. These imperial assemblies can be regarded as the parliaments of the Holy Roman Empire (Reichstage or confederal diets). They were consulted on such matters as taxation, war and peace, marriage, and religion. The independence of the duchies was assured by constitutional laws adopted in the sixteenth century. These implied that imperial policy consisted of agreements (treaties) among the member states and imperial "advice" from the central government (rather than enforced edicts).

At the local level, sovereigns met with their own assemblies of important families and organizations (*landtage*) where local public policies and constitutional matters were bargained over. These assemblies often had veto power over new taxation and normally could propose new legislation. In some cases, policy-making authority was divided between the duchy

[3] What the English would refer to as dukes, barons, and counts were essentially independent sovereigns in the German confederation, rather than part of a well-ordered aristocratic hierarchy. German titles reflected the size of the territories ruled, rather than their position in the hierarchy.

This de facto independence of duchy rulers within the Holy Roman Empire is what made the Protestant Reformation in Germany possible. The local sovereigns simply ignored the kaiser's support for the Catholic Church and countered his military efforts to impose (restore) order with their own military efforts to resist Habsburg efforts to centralize authority. The Thirty Years' War combined religious and political centralization conflicts into a single bloody war throughout much of Europe.

parliaments and sovereigns, resulting in a form of divided governance termed a Ständestaat (Fulbrook 1990, 26–7; Holborn 1959, 25–36).

As in the previous cases, the tax veto power of national diets, duchy estates, and town councils caused the distribution of policy-making authority to shift between the relevant chief executives and parliaments as fiscal circumstances varied and as interests in authority were affected by relative wealth, emergencies, and theories of the state. In federal and confederal systems, opportunities to trade tax revenues for political authority may also emerge with respect to the distribution of policy-making authority between central and regional governments. For example, large towns and cities often negotiated for and received freedom from duchy regulations and taxes (Holborn 1959, 25–6).

During military crises, authority tended to shift in favor of the central government because the demand for central government services increases. Conversely, during times of peace, local autonomy tends to increase for relatively wealthier provinces, because the demand for central government services falls and value of local autonomy increases.

The Constitutional Exchange within the Holy Roman Empire

From 1438 through 1806, Habsburg family members were routinely elected to the office of Holy Roman Emperor by seven hereditary electors. This essentially hereditary claim to the thrown allowed the Habsburgs to increase centralization somewhat, although the duchy and city governments resisted those efforts and remained largely independent. The independence of the duchies was very evident during the Protestant Reformation, during which large parts of the empire took the Protestant side, while others, including the Habsburg territories, took the Catholic side in both religious debates and open warfare. When the end to the religious wars was negotiated in 1648, local rulers received new authority to determine the religion of their territories. (The treaty of Westphalia also formally recognized the independence of the Netherlands and Switzerland, both of which had seceded from the empire in the previous century.)

During the seventeenth and eighteenth centuries, warfare and the shifts in commerce from overland routes to the Atlantic tended to reduce the relative wealth of inland duchies relative to those on the sea coast and also tended to reduce the relative wealth of those represented in parliament relative to royal families. The economies of most noble estates and many urban trading centers grew relatively slowly in this period, although revenues from customs and associated excise taxes increased. This tended to increase the authority of the inland dukes relative to their parliaments, and the governments of the coastal provinces relative to the central government.

Several duchy parliaments gave up much of their veto power over budgets and legislation in this period. For example, the Prussian parliament gave up much of its effective veto power through tax reforms in 1653 and 1667, which increased standing tax revenues and allowed the king of Prussia to maintain an army even during times of peace (Fulbrook 1990, 77).

In the late eighteenth century, the economic tide reversed, and parliaments increased in importance at the same time that their policy interests shifted in a somewhat liberal direction. For example, in 1801, Bavaria introduced freedom of religious conscience and compulsory education and, in 1807, ended or at least greatly reduced its internal tariffs. In 1808, the Bavarian nobility traded new taxes for greater influence over parliament. Similar constitutional bargains with parliament were concluded by the Prussian government in 1810–12, partly as a consequence of Prussia's (initial) losses to Napoleon's armies.

The highly decentralized governance of the first German confederation remains physically evident today in the very large number of small German cities and towns with royal architecture and local defense structures: medieval palaces, formal gardens, castles, and remnants of city walls. In more centralized states, such structures tend to be concentrated around the national capital and territorial boundaries, as in England, Sweden, and France. It should also be noted that there are relatively few parliamentary buildings in old German towns, which suggests that the baronial diets met relatively infrequently in government buildings designed for other purposes. That local government and church revenues were substantial is evident in the magnificent buildings that survive in even relatively small duchies. In republics, such as the United Provinces of the Netherlands, the public buildings and official residences from that period tend to be more modest in appearance and size.

Decentralization in the German confederation was substantially reduced, although not eliminated, during the nineteenth century as consequences of warfare, treaty negotiations, and constitutional bargaining.

THE VIENNA CONGRESS AND THE (SECOND) GERMAN CONFEDERATION 1815–1867

Napoleon's invasion of the Holy Roman Empire in 1792 defeated a series of German regional armies over the course of fourteen years, including the Prussian army and Austrian armies in 1805–6. In 1806, with his army defeated and induced Emperor Francis II (of the Austrian Habsburgs) to give up leadership of the Holy Roman Empire, at which point the empire-confederation was essentially disbanded (Holborn 1964, 371–2, 387–91). In these circumstances, new taxes could be traded for new legislative authority, as in Bavaria in 1808 and Prussia during the period 1810–15.

In the territories conquered by Napoleon's army, the French induced a variety of legal and constitutional reforms. Many of these increased centralization. Smaller autonomous states were merged into larger ones with more centralized policy-making authority. In southern and central Germany, Napoleon also created a new federation, the Confederation of the Rhine, with a somewhat more centralized government than that of the former Holy Roman Empire. A new civil law (the code Napoleon) was introduced that eliminated some feudal privileges. Napoleon also induced the Confederation of the Rhine to secede from what remained of the Holy Roman Empire.

Many of these steps also tended to increase commerce by reducing barriers to trade. The amalgamation of territories and governments reduced the number of borders at which tariffs could be collected. The new civil code somewhat simplified commercial law and reduced local privileges.

Napoleon's good fortune in war ended with his Russian campaigns in 1812, where a very cold Russian winter defeated and decimated the French army. A few years later, the remainder of the French army was dispatched by a royal alliance of the English, Prussian, Austrian, and Russian armies. Defeat of Napoleon's army produced new possibilities for constitutional exchange within and among the major and minor duchy governments of the former Holy Roman Empire. Many of the institutions and theories of duchy governance and security had changed during the Napoleonic era.

In 1815, a congress of major and minor participants in the Napoleonic wars was held in Vienna. As a consequence, a very large number of governments played a role in the results and signed the treaties negotiated there. However, most of the most important negotiation was undertaken by the "council of five" major European governments. The council of five included Great Britain, Russia, Prussia, Austria and, surprisingly, France. Several of the Vienna Congress's geographic decisions and one of its constitutional decisions are especially important for German constitutional history.

First, the Congress merged many of the smaller polities of the old Holy Roman Empire into new, larger ones. In many cases, it simply accepted mergers worked out by Napoleon. After the mergers induced by Napoleon and the Vienna Congress, the number of independent German polities was reduced from more than three hundred to forty-two. Four were independent city-states and thirty-eight were autonomous duchies, including five territories that formally became German kingdoms: Bavaria, Prussia, Württemberg, Hanover, and Saxony. Second, Prussia, as one of the great powers, gained new territory along the Rhine (including Cologne), which significantly increased its population and economic resources, and which moved its economic and political center of gravity toward the West.

Third, and constitutionally most important, the Vienna conference established a new German confederation (Deutscher Bund), loosely based on the old Holy Roman Empire. Its constitution was negotiated by the German committee of the Vienna Congress. The leading members of that committee were Austria, Bavaria, Hanover, Prussia, and Württemberg.[4] Negotiations took nearly a year, and the final draft was proposed by Baron Wessenburg (a member of the Austrian delegation) and accepted by the committee (Nicolson 1946, 196–99). The negotiations and constitutional bargains accepted reflected the fact that the new constitution required the support of all the major duchies and kingdoms to be implemented.

The new government consisted of a confederal diet, council of state, and prime minister. Each of the member states selected a representative to the confederal diet who acted as an ambassador, rather than as an independent representative to a German assembly. There was no German citizenship in 1820. The confederal diet used a weighted-voting system to make decisions. The largest states had four votes each, while the other members had one or two votes (for a total of sixty-nine). Policy decisions in the diet required two-thirds majorities (Ogg 1918, 195–6).

The new confederal government, like the old, lacked significant power to raise taxes, although it was charged with the defense of Germany from internal and external enemies (Renzsch 1989; Fulbrook 1990, 101). The former implied that national resources could be used to defend member state governments from overthrow and internal dissent.

In addition to the diet, there was a council of state. The council was a relatively small "subdiet," analogous to the college of electors within the Holy Roman Empire. Eleven of the largest duchies had one vote each. Smaller states were grouped into six clusters that each shared a vote (for a total of seventeen votes). Austria was entitled to appoint the president of the council and diet (article 5), which gave Austria's Habsburg family and its

[4] Representatives from many other German duchies were also present in Vienna and were consulted regarding the constitutional architecture of the new German confederation. Representatives from Saxony (which lost 40 percent of its territory to Prussia), Hesse-Darmstadt, Luxemburg, and Holstein were also included in the final round of negotiations. Representatives of the major free cities were also admitted (Nicolson 1946, 197–9).

chancellor, Prince Metternich, additional influence insofar as the diet president had significant agenda control. Metternich is often regarded to be the chief architect of the confederation's policy. The new German confederal government met in Frankfurt, Germany.

Article 2 of the treaty founding the new confederation declares that the aim of the confederation is to maintain "the **external and domestic security** of Germany and the independence and inviolability of the individual German states." German politics in the first half of the nineteenth century, consequently, remained very decentralized. Armies were controlled and staffed by the duchy governments, and only a small fraction of total government expenditures within the confederation's territory was controlled by central government decisions.

Austria's relatively large influence in the new confederal government reflected the active role that its ministers played in the Vienna negotiations, rather than force of arms.

The Constitutions of the Member States: 1815–1867

Several new duchy constitutions were developed after 1815, partly to adjust existing duchy procedures for the new territories governed, partly to reestablish local policy-making procedures after Napoleon's defeat, and partly because the confederal treaty adopted in Vienna required the members to adopt a written constitution (article 13).[5] Many others were reformed or had been reformed in the period just before Napoleon's defeat. In both cases, the results reflected the interests of those participating in the constitutional negotiations.

During the late eighteenth and early nineteenth centuries, liberal political and economic theories were accepted by many in Germany, including university students and nobles that were members of royal advisory councils. Liberal theories and arguments were thus evident in constitutional and policy debates inside duchy parliaments. A few "enlightened" duchy rulers also pushed for liberal reforms in parliament using ideological, economic, and military arguments. Liberal and national arguments often complemented each other in nineteenth-century Germany. After Napoleon, external threats were also taken more seriously, which provided a national defense rationale for reducing internal trade barriers that discouraged industrialization.

[5] The requirement for written constitutions was clearly a compromise with German and Austrian liberals at the meetings in Vienna.

These pre–Vienna Congress factors were reinforced by liberal provisions of the confederal constitution, which included provisions for all citizens to be able to enter the civil service (rather than only nobles), freedom for all citizens to migrate and purchase land within the confederation, and equal rights for Christian churches (Holborn 1964, 446). Greater openness (reduced exit costs) would also have somewhat constrained duchy and local government decisions. As a consequence, the reforms of duchy constitutions in the early nineteenth century tended to be in liberal directions.

For example, Baden's constitution of 1818 included a lower chamber of parliament elected under wealth-based suffrage. Bavaria's constitution of 1818 included a bicameral parliament with a noble chamber and an elected chamber selected largely on the basis of wealth-based suffrage, although an eighth of the seats were reserved for noble landlords and another eighth of the seats for the clergy. Württemberg's constitution of 1819 included a unicameral parliament representing the three estates (church, town, and country) that had considerable veto power over new taxes and legislation. Such relatively strong, although far from dominant, parliaments were fairly common for the German duchies in the early nineteenth century (Möckel 1979, 261–5; Ogg 1918, 275–81).

The four city-states (Hamburg, Lübeck, Bremen, and Frankfurt) had republican governments based on a mayor-and-council format. Three of the city-states had bicameral parliaments. Their second chambers were directly elected via wealth-based suffrage. Members of the first chamber were elected by the second and served as the city's ruling council, although both chambers had authority over legislation and taxes. A mayor (burgomeister) would in turn be selected by the ruling council as its chairman. The city councils had control over executive and administrative appointments and played central roles in determining public policies (Moraw 1989, 117; Ogg 1918, 280–1).

Liberal constitutional reforms slowed after 1819 as consequence of confederal decisions in Karlsbad, which reduced freedom of press and curtailed liberalism at German universities. However, modestly liberal constitutional reforms continued to be considered and adopted. For example, in 1831, Saxony replaced an estates-based parliament with a two-chamber parliament; one chamber represented the old estates and the other was directly elected using wealth-based suffrage. Hanover adopted a relatively liberal constitution in 1833. There is also evidence of liberal influences in Bavarian constitutional developments (Ogg 1918, 275–81).

In mid-century, it seems clear that liberal political coalitions often affected duchy and confederal German policies. This is not to say that liberals dominated constitutional or policy debates, but rather that the outcomes negotiated in duchy parliaments were affected by their interests at the margin. Conservatism was also clearly evident in the duchy constitutions throughout the nineteenth century. The old political institutions were not replaced by liberal ones; instead, a few liberal reforms were introduced. In cases in which relatively large liberal reforms were introduced, the details often protected the interests of those involved in negotiations: wealth-based suffrage protected the interests of those already in government at the same time that the reforms advanced liberal ideas about the use of elections for choosing government officials.

Institution-induced interests and the rationality of institutional conservatism do not change very much as the size of one's territory changes.

These conservative interests were buttressed by the central government's responsibility for defending aristocrat dominated forms of king-and-council governance. The old duchy institutions were largely restored, adapted to their new territories, and modernized, rather than rewritten whole cloth (Caldwell 1997, 17; Schmitt 1983, 19–21).

LIBERALISM IN NINETEENTH-CENTURY GERMANY

As in other parts of Europe, there was a significant body of political and economic liberal thought in late-eighteenth- and early-nineteenth-century Germany. As usual, there was no unique liberal position, but rather a broad range of arguments, persons, and organizations that supported reforms that would increase equality before the law and/or support more open politics and markets.

For example, Immanuel Kant's 1793 essay "On the Relationship of Theory to Practice in Political Right (Against Hobbes)" provides a statement of liberal principles of political economy that places him as a moderate within the liberal spectrum of his time. Kant argued that a civil state is based on popular sovereignty, civic equality, and liberty:

> The **civil state**, regarded purely as a lawful state, **is based on the following a priori principles: the freedom of every member of society** as a human being, **the equality of each with all the others as a subject**, the independence of each member of a commonwealth as a citizen.
>
> No one can compel [a person] to be happy in accordance with his conception of the welfare of others, for **each may seek happiness in whatever way he sees fit**, so **long as he does not infringe upon the freedom of others** to pursue a similar end which can be reconciled with the freedom of everyone else within a workable general law – i.e. he **must accord to others the same right as he enjoys himself**.

These were the core beliefs of political liberals throughout the West. On the other hand, Kant, like Hobbes, grants the sovereign a monopoly on legitimate coercion and does not accept citizen's right of rebellion. "For he alone is not a member of the commonwealth, but its creator or preserver, and he alone is authorized to coerce others without being subject to any coercive law himself."

Whether Kant believed the latter was compatible with the former is not totally obvious. Although more liberal than appreciated outside of Germany, Prussia was not a liberal state at the time that Kant wrote (nor was France or England at the time Hobbes wrote a century earlier). In proclaiming limited sovereignty for his own sovereign or arguing in favor of a citizen's right to rebel when a sovereign violates the "a priori principles of a civil state," Kant would have been liable for state sanctions up to and including those associated with treason. Even an important philosopher knows when to curb his pen.[6]

The political writing of Kant's colleague Von Humboldt appears to be somewhat less inhibited in its advice to sovereigns. Von Humboldt was a very successful member of a recently elevated noble family. He had served as a Prussian minister and diplomat, was active in the founding of the University for Berlin, and had been involved in constitutional negotiations at the Congress of Vienna. Von Humboldt's provides a natural-rights-based critique of Kant and argues that the sovereign's main duty is to promote liberty, human development, and happiness:

A State, then, has one of two ends in view; it designs **either to promote happiness, or simply to prevent evil**; and in this latter case, the evil which arises from natural causes, or that which springs from man's disregard for his neighbor's rights.

If even to behold a people breaking their fetters asunder, in the full consciousness of their rights as men and citizens, is a beautiful and ennobling spectacle.

It must be still more fair, and full of uplifting hope, to witness a prince himself unloosing the bonds of thralldom and **granting freedom to his people**, – nor this

[6] Kant's *Critique of Pure Reason* is sometimes used to classify him as conservative or anti-enlightenment scholar. This classification, however, appears to use today's political spectrum (or at least that of the late nineteenth century), rather than the spectrum of liberalism that existed in 1800. In the eighteenth and nineteenth centuries, political liberals generally criticized the existing aristocratic order, which was largely based on family privilege and status, and pressed for reforms that broadened opportunities. Intellectual liberals, however, tended to defend the use of reason.

Kant's critique of reason is not theological or historical, but rather a carefully crafted (rational) argument that attempts to demonstrate that reason has limits, which in 1800 would place him along side of such late-eighteenth-century moderate liberals as Edmund Burke. The methodology of the critique is liberal, as are many of its conclusions. To place excessive confidence in the power of reason is itself irrational and often tends toward illiberal ideas and institutions (Hayek 1989).

as the mere bounty of his gracious condescension, but as **the discharge of his first and most indispensable duty**. (Von Humboldt [1792/1851] *The Limits of State Action*)

Von Humboldt arranged to have the *Limits of State Action* published after his death (1835). It wasn't published until 1851, many decades after it was written (in the 1790s).

Liberals often rose to high posts in government, as had Von Humboldt in the first half of the nineteenth century and Eugen Richter in the second half (Raico 1990). Despite the difficulty of publishing books and editorials or organizing demonstrations in favor of constitutional reform after the Karlsbad Decrees of 1819, there were occasionally large illegal demonstrations favoring liberal reform. For example, in 1832, twenty-five thousand persons assembled at the Hambach Festival for music and making political speeches in favor of popular sovereignty, freedom of the press, and republican forms of government (Fulbrook 1990, 109).

There is also evidence that German conservatives gradually adopted more liberal theories of government as, for example, is suggested by the manifesto of the Prussian Free Conservative Party in 1867:

Absolutism has a glorious history in Prussia. Nowhere else in the entire world has this system of governance left a more indelible monument than in this state: the accomplishment of absolute monarchical power. But **the time of absolutism is past**. Today, it would destroy what it once brought into existence with creative force. Our people, like all civilized nations of this age, do not just need **a rightful share** in the **determination of their destiny** for their own satisfaction; the monarchy itself requires the cooperation of the people in order to fulfill its lofty mission. Only the crown of a free nation is due our monarch; **his throne rests most securely on the will of free men**.

Liberal Economic Reforms in the Early Nineteenth Century

Economic liberals were generally more successful than their political counterparts in Germany during the nineteenth century, because it was generally easier to build coalitions favoring internal and external trade liberalization than for constitutional reform. Fewer institutional issues need to be addressed by proponents of economic reforms and censorship laws often do not apply to regulatory debates. Trade liberalization also tends to advance the interests of those who expect to invest in or work for the larger economic enterprises that larger markets permit. By increasing the tax base, manufacturing expertise, and rates of technological innovation, industrialization also makes possible larger, better equipped armies and navies.

Liberal economic reforms also can be more easily reversed than constitutional reforms if they don't work out as expected.

The success of economic liberals is evident in a wide variety of reforms adopted during the late eighteenth and nineteenth centuries. For example, Prussia ended serfdom in 1807, reduced the tax preferences of nobles in 1810, and ended many aspects of the feudal estate in 1811. It ended internal tariffs in 1818. In 1828 Bavaria and Württemberg created a free trade zone (customs union). The states of Saxony, Hanover, and Brunswick created a commercial union. In 1833, a new customs union (*Zollverein*) was created and joined by most of the member states of the German confederation (Fulbrook 1990 112–13). The various customs unions did not eliminate all intraconfederation trade barriers, but did substantially reduce those barriers.

By mid-century, a number of politically active regional and national groups lobbied for liberal economic reforms. For example, in 1846, a German Free Trade Union was formed in Berlin by a group of businessmen led by John Prince Smith. By 1851, some thirty societies were affiliated with Smith's Central Association for Free Trade. Gatherings of proponents of free trade also occurred in Frankfurt in 1857. A similar gathering took place in Gotha in 1858, where free traders and leaders of the cooperative movement founded a new Economic Congress, which lobbied for free trade and other regulatory reforms for two decades. Proponents of free trade were also directly represented in national and regional parliaments, as in 1870, when Smith himself was elected to the lower chamber of the Prussian parliament (Henderson 1950).

As a consequence of the activities of these groups, a broad range of German tariffs were reduced during the middle of the nineteenth century. Public investments in transport infrastructure that were advocated by liberals were also undertaken. For example, the first railroad (between Nuremberg and Furth) was established in 1835, followed by many others, including one between Leipzig and Dresden in 1837. New roads were built and old roads were paved. Canal networks were extended and steamboats began to operate on the Rhine (Fulbrook 1990, 113–14). Such reforms allowed a larger, more integrated, German market to emerge as commercial organizations and trading networks expanded to take advantage of economies of scale in production, reduced shipping costs, and greater specialization.

As noted earlier, support for liberal economic reforms is often pragmatic. That is to say, one does not have to become a political liberal to accept the economic case for ending medieval protections and promoting industrialization. In the sphere of economic policy, as Olson (1993) argues, sovereigns (and their officials) have an interest in promoting economic growth – as long as it does not place their sovereignty at risk. Indeed, many economic liberals argued that national security required economic liberalization. Nonetheless, there is evidence that economic liberals contributed to the economic policy debates and often drafted the reforms.

On the same [liberal] **principle** is to be explained the Edict of September 14th, 1811, which abolished the old prohibitions against the division of landed estates. On the **same principle** hereditary serfdom was abolished, and an effort made to regulate all forced services. **On the same principle** all trades were thrown open, all **monopolies of sale at particular mills and inns were abolished**, and "all props of idleness," as Hardenberg puts it, done away. The guarantee for the new birth of the State [of Prussia] was sought, not in the artificial protection of the economically unfit, but in the development of the powers of the fit. **That policy has borne the most splendid fruits**. (Bretano 1894, 76–7)

Although support for liberal economic reform tends to differ somewhat from that for liberal political reforms, economic reforms often have political consequences. Increasing freedom for the serfs and other farm laborers tends to weaken the landed aristocracy by reducing their local authority and their net income from farming. Reducing the monopoly power of guilds and privileged towns weakens old urban centers relative to new ones. Reducing tariffs makes other taxes and parliamentary majorities more critical for funding government programs. Industrialization tends to produce a broad middle class that in the nineteenth century tended to support political liberalization and politically active liberal groups.

Censorship Limits Public Support for Liberal Political Reforms

The efforts of political liberals in Germany were less successful than those of economic liberals, in part because debate on constitutional issues was limited by a variety of censorship and public-assembly laws. The members of the confederal diet in Frankfurt represented, first of all, the political and economic interests of the sovereigns of their respective duchies. To curtail popular demonstrations favoring liberal political reforms, the confederal diet adopted a series of national laws beginning with the Karlsbad Decrees of 1819, which forbade political gatherings, strengthened censorship, and discouraged the provincial diets from exercising "too much" power. The Karlsbad Decrees of 1819, for example, included the following provision:

Every Confederal state is answerable – not only to the parties directly offended, but also to the whole of the Confederation – for the published writings appearing under its supervision, hence for all [publications] included under the main provision of § 1,

insofar as the dignity or security of other Confederal states is thereby injured, [or] **the constitution or administration of the same attacked.**

The central government had little ability to enforce such laws because the member states were essentially sovereign entities, but the new laws provided duchy governments with a convenient rationale for suppressing ideas and groups that threatened their political and economic interests.

Historians often attribute these repressive policies to Metternich, who presided over the confederal council and diet for three decades. However, it seems clear that censorship was one of the few areas in which the duchy leaders could find agreement. Local enforcement of the confederal laws varied somewhat. For example, Baden allowed somewhat greater freedom of the press than the other duchies through its implementing legislation (Fletcher 1980). But, in general, the censorship laws and related strategies to reduce press autonomy were well enforced and had a lasting effect on political developments in nineteenth-century Germany.[7]

Harris (1987, 441) estimates that less than 1 percent of published pamphlets and books in Germany during the years 1848–71 can be classified as political, and much of what was published was done so anonymously. A freedom-of-the-press law was finally enacted in 1874, but even then the effects of press freedom were reduced by Bismarck's use of the Guelph Fund to hire reporters and support newspapers that reported favorably on government policies and officials and opposed Bismarck's political opponents and their arguments.[8]

During the first half of the nineteenth century, political censorship was reinforced by remaining internal trade barriers. Fetscher (1980, 379) notes, for example, that trade barriers prevented newspapers from realizing economies of scale. The price of the Seeblatter doubled as the newspaper left its town of publication (Konstanz) for other parts of Baden, and it doubled again as it crossed state boundaries. "Increases of 500–600 percent were not uncommon when several state borders had to be crossed."

Liberal political ideas did not vanish from the minds of liberals with time to think about politics, nor did constitutional issues totally vanish from public discussion and demonstrations, as in Hanover in 1837 and Baden

[7] Similar laws were, of course, also adopted in other countries in the early nineteenth century to suppress demonstrations for constitutional reform, including England, as noted earlier.

[8] Censorship at the national level was greatly reduced in 1874, although editors could be tried for publishing controversial material. The censorship that remained was largely targeted at socialists for the rest of the century, even after the Social Democratic Party regained its status as a legal organization in 1890.

in the years 1837–44. The German censorship laws simply forced most liberal political and constitutional discussions underground or relegated them to side discussions in organizations created for other purposes and at informal gatherings. Moreover, reporting on parliamentary debates was largely free from censorship, which allowed relatively far-reaching debates on political reforms to take place through the publication of speeches made in national and duchy parliaments. And, of course, it was also possible to smuggle books and newspapers into Germany that were printed elsewhere.

In general, the censorship laws made it far more difficult for political liberals to lobby for reforms. Supporters of economic liberalization could more easily organize and disseminate their arguments, because publications supporting economic reforms did not directly violate censorship law. They did not

> **threaten or violate the integrity of the German Confederation**, the integrity and security of the individual confederate states, the maintenance of freedom and inner peace of Germany, **or aim at a democratic alteration of the Bund**. (Paragraph 10 of the 1840 censorship ordinance, from Fetscher 1980, 385)

Efforts to lobby for economic reforms could be done in public through small organized groups, at universities, and in newspapers without violating prohibitions on political gatherings and political publications.

Political parties could be organized and campaigns for elective office on liberal economic policies. Liberal politicians and groups could publicly support liberal economic reforms, but could only publicly support political reforms, such as German unification, which did not threaten the confederal government or directly undermine specific duchy governments. Many economic and political liberals were elected to the state parliaments on such platforms. In contrast, open support for greater parliamentary power or extended suffrage would have violated censorship and other confederal laws.

Indeed, a subset of liberals believed that political centralization would induce liberalization of the duchy governments, because of their successes in 1833, 1867, and 1871, and so they evidently promoted German nationalism as a strategy for liberal reform.

A Digression on the Rationality of Civil Disobedience in 1848

Confederal censorship and laws governing association tend to reduce public debates about constitutional reform because they create risks (expected penalties) for the expression of one's true opinions, as discussed in Chapter

Seven. Kuran's (1989) more dynamic analysis notes that the need for public expression and risk aversion varies among persons within every community. Consequently, the individuals that speak out and the times when this occurs also tend to vary a good deal among people and places. He also argues that the personal risk associated with the public expression of "private truths," tends to fall as the number of people expressing similar beliefs in public increases. In this way, a sudden wave of public demonstrations can be generated through a snowball effect as successively less intense and/or more risk-averse proponents of change join others who are already voicing dissent. Unlawful and other risky private beliefs are publicly expressed only when the risks from doing so are small.

Kuran's theory, in conjunction with German censorship, provides a plausible explanation for the reform demonstrations in Hanover and Baden. It also provides an explanation for the demonstrations in support for constitutional reform that took place between 1847 and 1849, when large number of persons in Germany (and in many other parts of Europe) turned out for large-scale demonstrations favoring liberal political reforms of various sorts.

Outside of France and Austria, the 1848 demonstrations were more or less peaceful, although larger than had previously been experienced. Such public assemblies were revolutionary in the sense that they were illegal and novel in most places, although they were not revolutionary in the sense of being large-scale, violent armed rebellions.[9]

The demonstrations in Germany in 1848, as in most other countries, favored a variety of economic and political reforms, but liberal ones dominated their constitutional proposals according to most historians. Demonstrators pressed for governance via rule of law, written constitutions, and expanded parliamentary powers (restoration of estate powers) and broader suffrage. Radical liberals insisted on universal suffrage, expansions of education, greater poor relief, and redistribution of wealth through land reform. Some groups, it should be acknowledged, also lobbied against economic liberalism – against external free trade and for a restoration of the old internal trade barriers.

[9] In Austria and France, considerable violence – as opposed to civil disobedience – occurred. Violence emerged in Vienna and the eastern parts of the Austrian empire, which induced Metternich to resign (at the diet's request) and leave for safer ground in London. It also induced the aging Habsburg monarch to support constitutional reform. Violence also occurred in France, where a moderate king abdicated out of fear of a new French Revolution, which paradoxically led to a less constitutional form of government (that of Napoleon III).

In the political circumstances of 1848, it was not clear to duchy rulers whether what they observed was a precursor to revolution and overthrow, or simply evidence of broad support for constitutional and economic reforms. Most had never seen significant public dissent before because such assemblies and their sponsoring organizations were illegal and because of the personal advantages of law-following behavior when such laws are well enforced.

In response to the demonstrations, the duchies often replaced a few cabinet ministers with liberal leaders from their parliaments. The new cabinet members were able to bargain directly with other policy makers for liberal policy and constitutional reforms. Such negotiations often produced constitutional bargains that included liberal reforms. For example, several duchy parliaments regained or enhanced their medieval rights of veto over taxation and legislation.

Serious, high-level discussion of reforms was accepted by most demonstrators as success, and most demonstrators headed home to await reforms. Demonstrators who continued their civil disobedience, however, were forcibly dispersed – with many deaths in Prussia.

A Constitutional Convention in Frankfurt: May 1848–1849

The most important of the high-level discussions in Germany took place in Frankfurt, where the confederal diet authorized a constitutional convention to meet and to propose reforms of the confederal constitution. Representatives to the constitutional convention were elected, although qualifications for suffrage included wealth or tax-payment thresholds, as was the case for the duchy elections for their lower chambers. Turnout was small, and the result was an assembly composed largely of upper- and middle-class liberals. The constitutional convention had the power to propose reforms, but not to adopt them (Fulbrook 1990, 119).

The participants engaged in serious discussions and constitutional negotiations. A doctrine of fundamental rights was published on December 28. A rough agreement for a constitutional monarchy for Germany with an elected parliament and ministry responsible to parliament emerged early in 1849. A new German crown was offered to the king of Prussia in late spring by the convention. Other territorial issues were also addressed, but less successfully. For example, whether Germany should include the Polish parts of Prussia or the German-speaking parts of Denmark and Austria was never really settled. These involved religious and cultural divisions as well as geopolitical issues, and stable compromises could not be found. Many other issues also remained unsettled.

Unfortunately, the king of Prussia refused the constitutional bargain offered, and without Prussian support, little could be achieved at the confederal level. In the end, it proved far easier to agree that constitutional reform was necessary than to agree on specific changes, even within a single political movement. The constitutional conference ended in May with little effect on confederal governance (Fulbrook 1990, 120–1).

Nonetheless, the conference itself was an important constitutional event for Germany because it was the first directly elected body for Germany as a whole.

The Frankfurt conference is important for the purposes of this book because it provides a rare window into mainstream liberal positions on constitutional issues and demonstrates that constitutional negotiations are difficult, especially major reforms. It also shows that revolutionary threats do not always induce major constitutional reforms. If large-scale demonstrations were always sufficient to induce major reforms, the German confederal government and the duchy governments would all have been substantially liberalized, but this was clearly not the case. Instead, a few modest reforms that shifted governance in a somewhat liberal direction were adopted here and there.

THE PRUSSIAN CONSTITUTION OF 1850

The most important of the duchy constitutional reforms was adopted in Prussia, where the constitution of 1848 replaced a traditional estates-based assembly that had been worked out during the 1840s. In 1850, the 1848 constitution was further modified, although not entirely in a liberal direction. In all three cases, standing procedures of amendment were observed. Prussia's constitutional reforms were drafted with the king's support and subject to a royal veto. The 1850 constitutional reforms also had to be acceptable to those represented in the Prussian parliament, especially liberals, given the previous reform and the recent protests. The 1850 constitution thus included a large number of liberal constitutional features, although they were implemented in a manner that successfully protected preexisting political interests (Caldwell 1997, 17).

The reformed constitutional monarchy included a bicameral parliament with veto power over taxes and legislation (Caldwell 1997, 16–17). With respect to tax authority, it could be said that Prussia's new constitution approximately restored its medieval tax constitution. Regarding the organization of parliament, however, there were significant innovations. The upper chamber for the most part represented the interests of the ancient estates.

It was made up of noble heads of household, city and university representatives, church officials, and assorted lifetime appointments by the king. The new lower chamber was directly elected through essentially universal male suffrage, as insisted on by the radical liberals in the mid-century. Cabinet ministers were answerable to parliament, but only for constitutional infractions. The king retained control of the army and foreign policy.

Prussian qualifications for suffrage were the most liberal in Europe at the time. However, the manner in which representation was determined from the votes cast was far less liberal, and was unusually effective at preserving the preexisting distribution of political authority within Prussia. In other parts of Europe, the right to vote was determined by minimum tax payments, as was also the case in most German duchies that held elections in 1850. In the Prussian constitution of 1850, however, it was representation, rather than suffrage, that was determined by tax payments. The wealthiest taxpayers, who paid one-third of Prussian direct taxes, received one-third of the seats, the taxpayers paying the next third of direct taxes received a third of the seats, and the remainder elected the last third (Fulbrook 1990, 126; Ogg 1918, 257–60).[10]

This economic-class-based system of representation made it possible for the king of Prussia and the aristocracy to accept essentially universal male suffrage without ceding significant political authority to the poor or middle class. A supermajority of the elected seats were determined by a small minority of German voters. Suval (1985, 233) reports, for example, that in 1888, after nearly four decades of industrialization, 3.6 percent of the electorate determined the first third of the seats, 10.8 percent determined the second third, and 85.6 percent determined the last third.[11]

The liberal cast of the 1850 Prussian constitution was not an accident, nor a fraud. It was not written in surrender to the demands of those engaged in the demonstrations, as might have been expected by revolutionary theories of constitutional reform, but negotiated among persons already holding offices in the Prussian government. The negotiations included conservatives, pragmatists, and liberals, but the balance of interests at the table naturally favored conservatives (those opposed to political liberalization).

[10] A similar three-class representation system was also used in most municipal elections within Prussia. In approximately four thousand municipalities, one or two very wealthy persons controlled one-third of the seats in the municipal assemblies (Ogg 1918, 259).

[11] Participation also tended to be smaller in elections for seats in the poorest third (14–30 percent) than for seats in the wealthiest third (40–60 percent), as might be predicted by rational-choice models of electoral turnout. See Koch (1984, 382) for a table of eligibility and participation in earlier Prussian elections.

The new architecture clearly protected the interests of those who had determined public policy in Prussia under its previous constitutions at the same time that it modestly advanced liberal aims. The nobility expected to control the upper chamber and the top-third of the second chamber. Moderate liberals were generally in favor of less-than-universal suffrage at this point, but expected to be well represented in the middle third of the elected chamber. Radical liberals and early social democrats were pleased to have suffrage extended to the working class and expected to be well represented in the lower third of the elected chamber.

Constitutional bargaining in Prussia continued for the rest of the century: liberals pressed for greater authority for the elected chamber and greater parliamentary control over ministers at the same time that many conservatives favored weakening the elected chamber. However, few reforms were accepted, and there was no clear liberal trend to the reforms until early in the twentieth century. This was in part because the constitution of Prussia already satisfied many liberal design criteria. It was also, of course, because the first chamber advanced the interests of those previously represented in Prussian government who had little interest in reform.

The Prussian constitution was formally a law adopted by the sovereign, as true in most constitutional monarchies at that time. This created a variety of legal and practical issues about whether a king could simply revoke a constitution, which enhanced his government's bargaining power with the parliament. Members evidently feared that if they pressed the king too hard on reform, he would simply revoke the constitution.[12]

The architecture of Prussia's 1850 constitution turned out to be important for the future of Europe, not because it was widely copied, but because the Prussian government that emerged under it played a pivotal role in German politics for the next seventy years.

GERMAN UNIFICATION AND A NEW FEDERAL CONSTITUTION, 1866–1871

The German confederation's procedures and policies were not very much affected by the "revolution of 1848," and continued more or less as before, with relatively few policy decisions being made by the confederal

[12] Kings often threatened to revoke "their" constitutions during the nineteenth century, although none were carried out. In long-standing parliamentary systems, institutional conservatism tended to make such threats less credible. The plausibility of such threats also diminished as the fiscal changes increased the bargaining strength of parliaments in the late nineteenth century.

government. The next three decades of constitutional reform in Germany were consequences of geopolitical tensions and wars between Austria and Prussia, the two largest and most powerful of the member states, rather than liberalism and industrialization.

In 1866, a disagreement over the governance of a largely German-speaking duchy taken from Denmark in 1864 further polarized the confederation and led to a brief Austro-Prussian war. The military aspects of those wars are beyond the scope of this volume, except insofar as they affected constitutional developments.[13] Prussia unexpectedly won the war with Austria and enlarged its territory by annexing several of the defeated Austrian allies in the north. The duchies of Hanover, Hesse-Kassel, Frankfurt, and Nassau became parts of Prussia, as did the former Danish duchy of Schleswig-Holstein.

Prussian territory after the war included most of present-day northern Germany and part of present-day Poland. This made Prussia by far the largest of the German duchies. Prussia's victory over Austria also implied that Prussia was also militarily the strongest member of the German confederation. The new balance of military power and political influence in Germany created new constitutional gains to trade.

The Constitution of the Northern Confederation: 1866–1871

The Prussian government encouraged the remaining independent northern duchies to leave the old confederation, as it had done, and to join a new northern German confederation. A draft of a constitution for the new Northern Confederation was proposed by the Prussian government, and negotiations were undertaken among potential members. Membership in the new confederation was voluntary, but constitutional negotiations and internal deliberations regarding membership were undertaken in the shadow of the recent Prussian annexations.

To be adopted, the new confederal treaty had to account for the interests of its potential member states, which would require advancing the interests of duchy rulers and majority support by their parliaments. Partly for this reason, the proposed federal constitution of the Northern Confederation was loosely based on the proposals of the Frankfurt convention, and it satisfied a number of liberal design criteria for constitutional monarchies. The architecture of the new constitution, however, was designed with Prussian, rather than liberal, interests uppermost in mind.

13 See Bueno De Mesquita (1990) for a rational-choice and statistical analysis of the Austro-Prussian war.

The new government would consist of a sovereign king (initially referred to as the president of the federation), a council of ministers appointed by the king, and a bicameral legislature. The king appointed the council without parliamentary review, although the chancellor was subject to parliamentary oversight (although he did not require its support). The members of the federal chamber of the parliament (Bundesrat) were appointed by member-state governments and had the power to initiate and veto all legislation. In this, the new federal chamber was similar to the diet of the German confederacy that it replaced. Voting in the federal chamber also used weighted voting. Member votes would be weighted roughly by population. Prussia held seventeen of forty-three votes in the federal chamber. Most other member states had only one or two votes (Renzsch 1989: 20–1).[14]

The second chamber (Reichstag) was new and of greater interest to liberals. It was directly elected in single-member districts by essentially universal male suffrage and had veto power over taxes and legislation, although no formal power to initiate or amend legislation or budgets. (Men older than twenty-five years old who were not on poor relief or in bankruptcy could vote.) The electoral districts reflected historic community boundaries within the member states, and most districts initially represented about one hundred thousand voters (Suval 1985, 228).

Secret ballots were used, and voters could cast votes only in a single district.[15] Electoral competition was clearly evident in most districts after the confederal treaties were ratified. Of the two hundred ninety-seven elected representatives, two hundred thirty-five were from Prussia, twenty-three from Saxony, and three from Hesse with similar or lesser numbers for the rest of the small duchies. A large number of groups obtained seats. The king (who would be Prussian) retained control of military and foreign policy.

Although the new constitution satisfied many liberal criteria for governance, Prussia's control of the executive branch and its large representation in both chambers of parliament effectively made the Northern Confederation an extension of the Prussian government. It had a Prussian king, who was inclined to appoint Prussian ministers to the council and other senior posts

[14] Prussia included twenty million of twenty-five million of the confederation's residents after its expansion, and thus Prussia was in this sense *under*represented in the Bundesrat (Koch 1984, 110). Except for Prussia, the voting weights simply continued those of the German Confederation. This was also the case for the southern duchies when they joined in 1871, with the exception of Bavaria, which received six votes (Ogg 1918, 217–18).

[15] An English translation of the Electoral Law for the Reichstag of the North German Confederation (May 1869) is available from the *German History in Documents and Images* project.

in the confederal government. For example, Wilhelm I appointed Bismarck to be chancellor and selected only Prussians as cabinet ministers. Prussia's representation in the federal chamber allowed it to effectively control the federal council. Even in the elected chamber, Prussian interests were likely to be decisive because of its relatively large population, although the interests represented were not necessarily the same as those of the Prussian government.

The particular Prussian interests that would be advanced were largely determined by its 1850 constitution, which gave a relatively narrow cross-section of wealthy Prussians decisive control of both chambers of the Prussian parliament and the king control over its ministry.

Bismarck's proposed constitution for a Northern Confederation was sent to a popularly elected constitutional convention at about the same time that Prussia formally withdrew from the German Confederation in June 1866. In August, a treaty of confederation was laid before the remaining northern duchies and independent cities. Liberals secured significant economic and procedural changes, including the right of the elected chamber to call the chancellor before it to defend government policy and veto power over the entire budget, as opposed to just the domestic budget (Hudson 1891; Koch 1984, 106–10; Feuchtwanger 2002, 152–7).

Formal procedures of ratification took place in the new member states, and the result was ratified by the new confederal parliament (Hudson 1891). Prussian approval was assured by the recent military victory over Austria, which increased Bismarck's popular and royal support and, thereby, the Prussian parliament's inclination to accept Bismarck's proposed constitution.[16]

The extent to which the implicit threat of further annexation was decisive for the other member states can be assessed by examining the constitution itself, which is less one-sided than one might expect. Bismarck had clearly designed the constitution to secure support within the Prussian parliament and assent by potential members. Nonetheless, his proposed draft was rejected and significant amendments were incorporated during the first meetings of the confederal parliament in 1867. Liberal members of the

[16] It is interesting to note that the Prussian parliament opposed the war. Consequently, budgets for the war with Austria were not approved by the parliament, as required under the 1850 constitution. Instead, Bismarck used money appropriated for other purposes to fund the war and began efforts to sell some national railroads. His success in the war, however, produced ex post facto support for his Danish and Austrian policies and also divided the liberals in the elected chamber. This in combination with a few concessions to moderate liberals allowed his military budgets to be approved retroactively in 1867 (Stern 1977, 20–95).

new Reichstag lobbied for and secured amendments that broadened and strengthened the powers and privileges of parliament:

> Reichstag **members were granted legal immunity**, the **press was guaranteed the right to report Reichstag speeches regardless of content ...** time tables for elections following a dissolution were accepted ... Reichstag ratification of certain types of treaties and ... real power over federal taxing and spending were adopted. (Mork 1971, 65–6)

In the years that followed, the right to publish Reichstag speeches allowed public debate to take place on many controversial issues, in spite of continued censorship of books, newspapers, and universities. Laws guaranteeing freedom of movement within the confederation were adopted in 1867. Equal civil rights, specifically those related to political office and participation, were extended to members of all religious groups in 1869. A common northern market emerged.

The 1871 Federal Constitution of the German Empire

The Northern Confederation's constitution formed the foundation for Germany's future constitutional development, because the southern duchies joined the Northern Confederation a few years later. Austria remained outside the new confederation.

German unification was widely supported among nearly all groups, including conservatives, liberals, radical liberals, progressives, and moderate socialists. Access to northern markets was of interest to southern industrialists and bankers. The militant policies of Napoleon III had also increased the benefits from affiliation with a larger, more powerful polity. New treaties of association were negotiated, and the results were codified in a slightly amended constitutional treaty in 1871. In this manner, a new federal German state (with twenty-five states) became a reality, rather than a dream of nationalists.[17]

The 1871 federal constitution of Germany was based on that of the Northern Confederation, which in many respects was among the more

[17] The Prussian king initially served as its president and hereditary ruler of the Northern Confederation, rather than its king (or kaiser). The executive office of the Northern Confederation was not a royal one, to which local rulers owed fealty. That changed in 1871 when the southern duchies joined. However, obtaining the new title required some negotiation. For example, the Bavarian king received a cash side payment in compensation for transferring some of his authority to the emperor. There were also some special provisions for Bavarian autonomy (Koch 1984, 108–12, 119–21).

The title emperor was necessary because several of the duchies were ruled by kings. The name of the confederation was also formally changed to the German Empire (Deutsches

liberal constitutions in Europe at the time. The federal chamber, the Bundesrat, as in the Northern Confederation, consisted of representatives of the member states (duchy and free city) and were appointed by those governments. A (roughly) population-weighted-voting system based on the voting weights in the Confederation was used in the Bundesrat. Prussia again had the most votes (seventeen of a total of fifty-eight), Bavaria the second most (six), and the rest of the duchies and cities between one and four votes each. Because duchies were normally ruled by king-dominated forms of the king-and-council template, the Bundesrat tended to be populated by nobles, although it was not formally a noble chamber. (The fact that no salaries were paid to members of either chamber also tended to limit members to relatively wealthy persons, although no wealth restrictions were included.) The Bundesrat was self-calling in that a request by one-third of its members required the king (kaiser) to call it into session.

The directly elected second chamber, the Reichstag, was selected on the basis of unusually broad suffrage using a secret ballot, and the distribution of votes among the duchies was based on population, rather than wealth or class, as in Prussia. National suffrage was not only broader than most of the duchy parliaments, it was broader than most of Europe in 1871. Electoral districts initially included about one hundred thousand voters each. The Reichstag had veto power over budgets and legislation. The Reichstag was also self-calling, and if dismissed by the king, new elections had to be held within sixty days and a new meeting held within ninety days. Ministers could be called for questions, but could not be formally sanctioned by the Reichstag, except for constitutional violations. Criticism from this chamber, nonetheless, often induced ministers to resign, as in 1867, 1869, and 1872.

Selection of the German chancellor and control over Germany's military and foreign policy were retained by the king (who was simultaneously king of Germany and Prussia). This responsibility was important because the main duty of the central government was initially national defense, foreign affairs, and the promotion of internal free trade, all of which were controlled by the king and his appointed council of state (Mork 1971, 67–8; Stern 1977, chapter 9; Koch 1984, 122–7; Ogg 1918, 217–24). All other laws were also formally royal proclamations, but new laws had to be approved by both chambers of the parliament and countersigned by the chancellor.

Reich, rather than Norddeutscher Bund) by the 1871 constitution, after the elevation of the Prussian king to German emperor (kaiser). The term king is used in the text to maintain consistency, and the new government is often referred to in the text as the third Confederation rather than the second empire.

The constitution also included provisions for German citizenship, a national currency, railroad development, and government finance (via indirect taxation). It also standardized commercial and military law and specified that all persons were subject to seven years in the army, including three years of active duty. Amendments to the constitution required a three-quarters supermajority in each chamber of parliament. This implied that constitutional reforms could be blocked by fourteen (of fifty-eight) votes in the Bundesrat, which gave Prussia veto power on constitutional reforms, because it had seventeen votes. Constitutional reforms favored by Prussia, however, required supermajorities of the weighted votes from the other duchies in the Bundesrat and also a majority in the Reichstag.

The difficulty of formally amending the federal constitution locked in the core policy-making procedures and fiscal constraints of the central government and some aspects of its military organization. Constitutional stability was further reinforced by the stability of Prussian-elite interests and Bismarck's ingenuity at forming majority coalitions in the parliaments of the next two decades.

Changes in the basis for representation of either chamber were not very likely to be adopted, nor was it likely that ministerial responsibility could be formally introduced.[18]

Politics in the Third German Confederation

The federal government's pan-German policies and national assembly created incentives for new pan-German political organizations to be formed. For example, it was at the first meetings of the Confederal Reichstag that national political parties began to take shape. A National Liberal Party was established on February 27, 1867. A Catholic Center Party formed in 1871, a Social Democratic Party was formed in 1875, and a Conservative Party in 1876 (Blackbourn 1998, 264–9).[19]

The early political parties were often loose affiliations of regional organizations that were prone to disagreements on specific policies, especially those with different regional effects. German liberals, for example, had

[18] An English translation of the constitution of 1871 is available from the *German History in Documents and Images Project*.

[19] The Social Democratic Party was banned during the years 1878–90, although its members were able to stand for election to the Reichstag and were elected (Blackbourn 1998, 412–13). Previous to this campaign against the socialists, Bismarck had launched a campaign against the Catholics, especially the Jesuits, who were banned from Germany. Some 1,800 Catholic priests were jailed or exiled during that earlier campaign. While social democrats were banned, some 1,500 persons were imprisoned (Blackbourn 1998, 262–3).

already become divided about Bismarck's constitution for the Northern Confederation, and divisions among right, center, and left liberals continued through the rest of the nineteenth century. Disciplined national political parties did not emerge for two decades, as loose alliances of fellow travelers on the right, middle, and left frequently formed, divided, and reformed during the next several decades (Mork 1971, 64; Koch 1984, 140–7; Schonhardt-Bailey 1998). This reduced subsequent liberal influence on policy and constitutional developments in the federation. (Moreover, many of the constitutional issues on which late-nineteenth-century liberals could have agreed were already incorporated in the constitution.)

Absence of Constitutional Reform during the Bismarck Era

Bismarck's constitution proved durable and relatively stable. During the late nineteenth century, kings in other parts of Europe began to give up their formal powers of appointment and control of foreign affairs in negotiations with parliament on budgetary matters. This did not happen in the new federal government of Germany, partly because of the particular alignment of interests within Prussia, partly because of the stability of the Prussian constitution, and partly because of Bismarck's extraordinary ability to use divisions in the Reichstag to create temporary majority coalitions in support of his government's policies (often by exploiting fears associated with imaginary international and internal crises).

The king, his chancellor, his ministry, and the rulers in other duchies had very similar views on how to advance their interests, which reduced opportunities for constitutional reform. In Bismarck's words:

> We would **have succumbed to a parliamentary rule in the past 17 years**, if the princes [duchy rulers] **had not stood firmly by the Reich** … the opposition in the parliament would be much reinforced if the present solidarity of the Bundesrat came to an end and Bavarians and Saxons made common cause with Richter and Windtorse. It is therefore the right policy for your highness [Wilhelm II] to address yourself in the first place to your princely cousins. (Letter from Bismarck to Wilhelm II just before his accession in 1888, quoted in Feuchtwanger 2002, 241)

The absence of constitutional reforms does not imply that the elected chamber failed to exercise influence on policy, nor that influence could not potentially be used in constitutional bargaining. Parliamentary influence is evident in economic legislation of direct interest to liberals and in a variety of other matters, including military ones.

For example, Schonhardt-Bailey's (1998) statistical analysis of role-call voting in the Reichstag demonstrates that economic and partisan interests affected votes on tariff policies. Tariffs increased in 1879, diminished in the years 1891–94, and subsequently increased again in 1902. Internal and external tariffs were reduced during the period in which liberal coalitions were important, even though these were important revenue sources. As the free-trade coalition splintered and pragmatists lost confidence in the merits of free trade (or acquired economic interests that trumped their ideological inclinations), tariffs rose.

It was normally effective politics rather than institutional design or threats that allowed Bismarck to have his way in the Reichstag. "Anti-liberal" restrictions were adopted by the Reichstag by his more or less conservative coalitions. For example, a substantial weakening of the Reichstag's veto power on the military budget was engineered by Bismarck, who persuaded a majority of its members to accept a seven-year budget cycle for defense appropriations (about 90 percent of the central government's budget at that time), rather than face new elections in 1874 on the "wrong side" of the national defense issue (Mork 1971, 70–3; Feuchtwanger 2002, 187–8).[20] Restrictions on political participation were accepted in 1878, when the Social Democratic Party was temporarily banned from politics.

This political ingenuity is also evident in Bismarck's last major reform, the social-security program passed in 1889 with the encouragement of the new King Wilhelm II. As a master at building majority coalitions by exploiting national security concerns, Bismarck naturally used a national security argument to support federal old-age pensions:

> I will consider it a great advantage when we have 700,000 small pensioners drawing their annuities from the state, especially if they belong to those classes who otherwise do not have much to lose by an upheaval and erroneously believe that they can actually gain much by it. (Quote taken from Riminger 1968, 414)

German social-insurance programs were thus adopted over the objections of most liberals and social democrats with the support of Catholic centrists and nationalist conservatives in the Reichstag.[21] The new social-security

[20] Feuchtwanger (2002, 188) argues that "Bismarck was not sorry to see a compromise emerging, for a perpetual [military] budget would have weakened his position against the generals and made him that much less indispensable, as the only man who could manage the Reichstag."

[21] Although universal suffrage allowed social democrats to run for office, socialists were generally blocked from political assemblies and did not have many votes within the Reichstag at this time (Fulbrook 1990, 133–4; Koch 1984, 384–5). The left-of-center parties, however, evidently voted against their own constituents' interests in an effort to keep a unifying issue for future campaigns (Riminger 1968, 414–15).

program in combination with national-health and disability insurance adopted in 1883 and 1884 created the most extensive liberal welfare program in Europe at that time, although they were modest programs by today's standards.

The durability of the basic structure of Bismarck's social-welfare program with its "pay-as-you-go" financing made it quasi-constitutional in nature, and it is one of the few Bismarck's constitutional innovations that survives to the present in Germany and elsewhere.[22]

Constitutional Bargaining Intensifies after Bismarck: 1890–1918

After the death of King Wilhelm I at the age of ninety-one in 1888 and the departure of Chancellor Bismarck at the age of seventy-five in 1890, the nearly invisible shift of policy-making authority from the king to parliament that had occurred during Bismarck's tenure of office became more apparent.[23] In the post-1890 period, the chancellor's term of office was much shorter than before because the new chancellors could not replicate Bismarck's genius for coalition politics. For example, Chancellor Caprivi's term lasted only from 1891 to 1894, and his resignation was in part induced by a failure to obtain Reichstag approval for an army reform bill in 1892. Chancellor Hohenlohe's government lasted a bit longer, six years (1894–1900), because he was more successful at building coalitions in the Reichstag (Sammlungspolitik). However, following a number of crises, Hohenlohe retired in 1900. Bülow

[22] This is not to say that Bismarck's only long-term impact was on social-welfare programs. His constitutional innovations continued to be important factors in German politics for the next four decades and also, affected Japan's late-nineteenth-century constitutional design.

Also, his aggressive mode of domestic politics also tended to promote polarization and reduce trust within Germany, which made constitutional compromise more difficult. In Richter's (1890) words: "… existing confessional differences were exacerbated, on the one hand, through the battle over church policy, carried out by way of the police and criminal regulations, and on the other hand, through the chancellor's attitude toward the development of the anti-Semitic movement. The rampant growth of interest parties, striving ruthlessly to exploit state authority at the expense of the general good, can be attributed to the policy of protective tariffs and to the kind of agitation for protective tariffs that the chancellor personally called for and fueled. The incitement of the parties against each other, the suspicions cast upon people's patriotism, and the denial of patriotism to any political dissident all result from a press corrupted by the Guelph Fund" (*Freisinnige Zeitung*, no. 68, March 20, 1890).

[23] There was a short reign by Friedrich III in 1888 between that of Wilhelm I and Wilhelm II, but Friedrich died within a year of his accession to office. Wilhelm II was the son of Friedrich III, who was the son of Wilhelm I. Eighteen eighty-eight is, for that reason, sometimes referred to as the year of three emperors, as the German sovereign passed from father to son to grandson.

remained in office for nine years, from 1900 to 1909. However, budget deficits increased as conservatives refused to raise taxes to support Wilhelm II's military buildup. Bülow subsequently resigned in 1909 when his coalition in the Reichstag disintegrated over fiscal reform. His successor, Holleweg, also struggled to find a stable coalition of support for expanding military expenditures. In 1912, the social democrats became the largest party in the Reichstag, which made progovernment coalitions even more difficult to assemble (Fulbrook 1990, 142–3).

The turnover of chancellors in 1890–1912 suggests that Bismarck's success came from effective coalition-building strategies that his successors lacked. Indeed, it could be argued that Germany's entry into World War I was partially a method of circumventing parliament – in that the king had complete control of military and foreign policy during emergencies. There is considerable evidence that the Reichstag's power of the purse became more important after Wilhelm I's death and Bismarck's retirement.

That liberal influence remained present in the Reichstag is evident in a number of policy reforms adopted. Coalitions of economic liberals and progressives, often supported by Wilhelm II and the social democrats, were able to press for reforms that eliminated remaining feudal and mercantilist restrictions, abolished usury laws, established a legal basis for corporations, reduced restrictions on the free practice of crafts, removed restrictions on travel within Germany, and reformed the judiciary. Freedom of parliamentary debate and freedom of the press were broadened.

Constitutional Gains to Trade

The final step to parliamentary democracy in Germany required a substantial increase in parliament's authority over public policy, rather than suffrage expansion, in contrast to the other countries analyzed in this book.

An increase in parliament's authority does not necessarily require ideological support, as tends to be the case for suffrage reform. Nor does an increase in parliament's authority require formal constitutional reforms. It is sufficient that the royal government becomes increasingly dependent on majorities in parliament to advance the king's agenda, whatever that agenda might be. In Germany, however, the usual liberal fiscal bargains could not be obtained because Wilhelm II was not willing to accept ministers from the Reichstag's majority parties.

There were a variety of proposals for the reform of the German Confederation's constitution, but no ingenious liberal was able to find a proposal that provided sufficient advantages for support of the king and three-quarters of the national parliament. There were proposals for proportional representation, ministerial responsibility, and women's suffrage, although nearly all were rejected. Members of the parliament were, however, paid salaries following a 1906 amendment to the constitution.

Constitutional reform proposals were somewhat more successful in the duchies. For example, suffrage was liberalized in Bavaria, Baden, Hesse, and Württenmberg by reducing or eliminating wealth restrictions for suffrage and changing from indirect to direct representation. Weighted voting was introduced in Hamburg and Hesse as part of the price of extended suffrage. In Saxony, suffrage was expanded, although a wealth-weighted representation system was introduced (Suval 1985, 232–3, 240; Blackbourn 1998, 409–10). In Prussia itself, significant reforms of local government were adopted, which reduced noble (Junker) hereditary rights, with the support of Wilhelm II, who elevated a sufficient number of distinguished liberals so that the local government reforms could be approved in the noble chamber (Mork 1971: 67–68).

The Final Steps to Parliamentary Democracy: 1918–1920

Constitutional negotiation at the national level continued through World War I, and significant reforms were finally accepted by the king towards the end of the war, although it is not entirely clear whether a constitutional bargain was truly concluded or not.

In late 1918, the conservative war cabinet resigned, and a new moderate chancellor was selected (and ratified by a parliamentary vote). Chancellor Prince Max von Baden proposed constitutional reforms including the reform of suffrage (ending the three-class voting system of Prussia), ministerial responsibility to parliament, and control of the armed services by civilian government. These were accepted by Wilhelm II in October. The October reforms were very popular among liberals and social democrats, who organized rallies and speeches to celebrate their success throughout Germany. However, parliament also insisted that Wilhelm II abdicate in favor of one of his sons, but he refused (Fulbrook 1990, 157; Orlow 2008, 95–6).

As constitutional negotiations were being finalized, the king left Berlin to consult with his loyal generals. This was regarded as an act of bad faith and called into question whether the constitutional reforms accepted in October would be implemented. A constitutional coup was feared by reformers. Partly because of Wilhelm II's apparent failure to abide by his constitutional bargain and partly because of the disintegration of central government authority as the war ended, an even more radical series of reforms were adopted in the next few weeks.

The king's trip to his generals produced large-scale republican demonstrations by the moderate and far left throughout Germany. Local rulers accepted republican demands and resigned their offices, beginning with the king of Bavaria on November 7. In the following two days, most other duchy rulers abdicated in favor of their parliaments, although the duchy bureaucracies remained largely in place. Wilhelm II subsequently abdicated from Germany's imperial office on November 9, although he did not formally give up his Prussian crown until November 28 (Orlow 2008, 106–7).

After Wilhelm's resignation, there was no longer a German king or council of state with veto power over reforms, which provided new gains from constitutional exchange among members of the parliament. Chancellor von Baden resigned on November 9, after transferring his office to the social democratic leader of the Reichstag, the largest party in the Reichstag. This was done in a somewhat extra-constitutional manner, because parliament was not in session at the time and so could not provide the new chancellor with the vote of confidence required by the October reforms (Orlow 2008, 106).

A transitional government was formed based on constitutional proposals accepted by Wilhelm II before his abdication. Representatives to a new Reichstag (National Assembly) were elected in January of 1919, and members of a new Bundesrat (Committee of the States) were appointed by the *länder* governments. The government (council of ministers) was appointed by a majority coalition of the new National Assembly, which was a center-left coalition of social democrat, liberal, and center party members under the leadership of the social democrat Friedrich Ebert.

The new government called for a formal constitutional convention, which took place in the small city of Weimar.

The Weimar Republic

The first drafts of what became the Weimar constitution were prepared before the elections for the constitutional assembly took place.

Hugo Preuss, a left liberal, was given the task of writing a constitution a month after Wilhelm II's abdication. His draft constitution was discussed at length within the provisional government by members of the Reichstag and by a few distinguished scholars, including Max Weber. Those early drafts were subsequently revised in negotiations at Weimar, where among other changes, the office of president was strengthened. Approval required majorities in the National Assembly, the Committee of the States, and by transitional government (Kolb 2004, 17–19). There was no longer a king or royal council of state to veto proposed reforms.

The proposed constitution adopted reflected institutional conservatism in that it was largely based on the template of Bismarck's federal constitution, although it included a much stronger Reichstag, a weaker federal council (the Bundesrat was replaced by a Reichrat), and an elected president, rather than a king or hereditary president. The president was elected with a fixed term, but nonetheless had essentially royal powers during emergencies. He could appoint ministers, dissolve parliament, call new elections and national referenda, and rule by emergency decrees during times of crisis. The cabinet was responsible to parliament and could serve only with continued majority support.

The electoral basis of the Reischstag was changed in two ways: proportional representation was introduced and suffrage was extended for the first time to women. The constitution was approved after several months of negotiation and bargaining on August 11, 1919.

The new constitution created a government dominated by parliament and grounded in elections with universal adult suffrage. The formal transition also was largely constitutional and lawful, although governance in Germany was neither peaceful nor orderly in the period in which constitutional reforms were negotiated, nor entirely so in the years that followed. As in many other countries, central government's authority to use income taxation for revenues was adopted at the same time that other constitutional reforms were adopted as part of a constitutional bargain.

The governments of the former duchies, now *länder*, also became republics after their governments had resigned. The *länder* retained considerable local fiscal and regulatory authority under the new constitution, although the central government had somewhat greater powers to tax than before.

In this manner, constitutional negotiations, often in the shadow of wars, made Germany a parliamentary democracy, although a republic, rather than a kingdom. It is interesting to note that the Weimar reforms of the German parliament were broadly similar those being adopted elsewhere in Europe at about the same time.

The Weimar Republic survived as a parliamentary democracy for only fourteen years, after which it was captured and then effectively overthrown by the National Socialist German Worker's Party in early 1933 and 1934 by exploiting its emergency powers provisions. Whether the Weimar constitution's failure was an inevitable event or a matter of bad luck, as believed by this author, is beyond the scope of this book. It seems clear, however, that the lack of continuity in political institutions and leadership at the national and *länder* levels, together with significant errors in the Weimar constitution, contributed to the failure of the new German republic. These, together with the breakdown of law and order associated with the radicalization of German politics, paradoxically allowed Hitler to argue for and obtain emergency powers for his chancellorship in 1934, and subsequently to end competitive politics and constitutional governance in Germany for more than a decade. Hitler's use of the Weimar Republic's provisions for emergency power (after 1934), demonstrates how quickly supra-constitutional authority can reverse a century of liberal progress.[24]

It is interesting to note that with the death of Hitler in 1945, the Weimar constitution essentially returned to force, as specific enabling acts expired and the offices of chancellor and president became separate again. Given this, it is not surprising that the "new" postwar constitution for West Germany is broadly similar to the Weimar constitution in its bicameral architecture and in much of its language, although its various emergency powers provisions (article 48) were eliminated (Koch 1984, 315–17, 340–3).

CONCLUSIONS AND OVERVIEW

Overall, German constitutional history from 1815 through 1925 is largely consistent with the models developed in Part I. Although military events were unusually important factors as catalysts for constitutional negotiations and development, the constitutions adopted were negotiated by members of parliaments, councils of state, and kings, rather than imposed by victorious

[24] Hitler was appointed to the post of chancellor in January 1933 as the leader of the largest party in the Reichstag, having overtaken the social democrats in the 1932 elections. Emergency legislation was adopted in February, reducing freedom of the press and assembly, and new elections were quickly held, which increased the number of seats held by Hitler's coalition in the Reichstag. A temporary "enabling law" was passed in March by two-thirds supermajority in the Reichstag, as required for constitutional amendments. Articles 1–3 of the new "law for the recovery of the people and the Reich from suffering" formally allowed the government to adopt new laws through unconstitutional procedures. (English translations of the title and details of the act vary somewhat.) For example, the act explicitly allows the Reich government to adopt fiscal policies without parliamentary review (Koch 1984, 306–11).

In 1934, following the death of President Hindenburg, the posts of chancellor and president were formally merged instead of holding new elections for president as required under the constitution. The creation a new executive position, Führer, was a major constitutional reform, although it was adopted without formally amending the constitution. Hitler was appointed to the new position which combined executive authority with emergency powers. That enabling act, perhaps surprisingly, was renewed by the Reichstag in 1937, as required by the time limit included in the original act. It was the unconstitutional merger of the presidency and the chancellorship that effectively ended the Weimar Republic.

armies or drafted by leaders of mass demonstrations. There were clear constitutional trades and compromises in each successive reform and constitution. There were also liberal trends. Suffrage and civil liberties expanded. Party competition and a relatively free press emerged by the end of the nineteenth century.

The importance of parliamentary majorities also tended to increase as national budgets increased and more disciplined national parties emerged, especially in the two decades before World War I. Internal liberal and economic pressures were sufficient to end feudalism and produce relatively liberal trade regimes internally and externally. Economic life in Germany became more urban, commercial, and industrial during the nineteenth century.

Suffrage reform and the extent of parliamentary authority were essentially independent phenomena in Germany, as predicted by the analysis of Part I. Liberal pressures for constitutional reform were sufficient to obtain very broad suffrage at a very early date. Universal suffrage expansion was part of a complex constitutional bargain, as elsewhere, but it came well before parliament gained dominant authority over public policy. To obtain the necessary support from conservatives required accepting other constitutional details that reduced the potential effects of broad suffrage on public policy. Indeed, parliamentary dominance never completely emerged in the third German Confederation (second Reich). In this respect, the German case can be said to be the converse of the British case, where parliamentary dominance emerged several decades before universal suffrage was adopted.

This outcome was partly caused by the particular persons involved in the negotiations between kings and parliaments in nineteenth-century Germany. German and world history might have been very different if Wilhelm I had accepted the proposal of the Frankfurt convention, or if Bismarck had been less adept at forming majority coalitions, or if Wilhelm II had engaged in a bit of constitutional bargaining with his parliament a decade or two before World War I. Only in late 1918, after several important veto players disappeared, were significant reforms of parliament adopted.

The bargains struck at Weimar demonstrate that Germany's elected parliamentary leaders were affected by many of the same ideas, interests, and constraints as parliamentary leaders elsewhere in Europe. The Weimar constitution also reflected institutional conservatism, liberal theories of governance, and constitutional bargaining. As a consequence, the reforms adopted at Weimar after Wilhelm II's abdication were very similar to those adopted by other European countries at approximately the same time.

SEVENTEEN

The Japanese Transition to Democracy and Back

INTRODUCTION

The first four case studies might lead readers to conclude that there was something unique about European culture that made it "ready" for parliamentary democracy in 1820. The king-and-council template had long been used for European governance and provided numerous opportunities for peaceful constitutional reform. Liberalism can be regarded as the political reform agenda of the enlightenment, a European intellectual development. Many of the most important technological innovations of the eighteenth and nineteenth centuries were worked out in Europe. Overall, it might be argued that European ideas and institutions made Europe uniquely ready to shift from autocracy to democracy without revolution.

The theory developed in Part I is, however, not a theory of European transitions. It suggests that similar ideas and opportunities for constitutional bargaining will exist in other societies in which broadly similar institutions are in place and trends in constitutional-bargaining opportunities favor liberal reforms. The last two case studies demonstrate that the European transitions were not unique.

Chapter Seventeen focuses on Japanese constitutional history in the nineteenth and early twentieth centuries during which parliamentary democracy emerged in Japan and then receded.[1] As in the European cases, the king-and-council template of governance was widely used in Japan for governance at national, regional, and local levels. Constitutional negotiation and exchange were also commonplace in its medieval period, although, as in Europe, there were no liberal trends in the constitutional bargains

[1] This chapter is based on research presented at the 2006 meeting of the Japanese Public Choice Society, where many helpful comments were received. Thanks are especially due to comments by Professors Yokoyama, Oeda, and Suzuki.

negotiated. During the late nineteenth and early twentieth centuries, liberal trends in economic and political reforms emerged for reasons similar to those in Europe. Coalitions that favored economic and political liberalization were in positions of sufficient authority to bargain with others in government and obtain modest reforms.

Insofar as liberalism and many of the new production technologies were imported to Japan from Europe, it can be argued that the enlightenment also influenced the course of economic and political reform in Japan. However, the reforms were not entirely caused by European technologies and liberalism. The same liberal ideas, technologies, and supporting evidence were also present in Korea and China, for example, but they did not induce similar reforms in those countries during the late nineteenth or early twentieth centuries.

The Japanese case suggests that new economies of scale in production and the penetration of liberal ideas produce liberal constitutional reforms only in settings in which constitutional exchange is possible and in which the interests of those favoring industrialization and liberalization are reasonably well represented in government. This was not true of China and Korea, or in European countries that failed to liberalize. The Japanese experience of the 1930s also demonstrates that liberal constitutional reforms can also be undone through constitutional bargaining and counter reforms when a liberal tide recedes.

SETTING THE STAGE: RULE-BASED GOVERNANCE IN THE SHOGUNATE ERA 1603–1853

The early history of Japan exhibits alternating periods of centralization and decentralization of policy-making authority. Periods of centralization were often marked by warfare as regional rulers resisted the efforts of those attempting to create a stronger central government. During the sixteenth century, a long series of such wars occurred between the emperor's forces and those of the daimyo (roughly the equivalent of dukes in English nobility). The wars ended with the success of the emperor's commanding general, his shogun. The negotiated settlement at the end of the war produced a relatively stable system of governance that lasted for more than two centuries.

There were several unusual features of the system adopted. The shogun evidently believed that new oaths of fealty to the emperor and shogun after the wars would not eliminate future civil wars and wars of secession. Games of conflict tend to be social dilemmas, rather than coordination games, so incentives to renege on peace agreements nearly always exist. To bind local rulers to their promises to defer to the shogun required an enforcement device of some kind. In other places, peace treaties and oaths of fealty are reinforced by maintaining a large national army, but this tends to be expensive and produces other risks for government leaders. The shogun devised a safer and less expensive solution.

The peace agreement required each daimyo to spend at least one year in two in Edo (present-day Tokyo). Their families were required to reside in Edo during the periods in which the daimyo was away. This residency-hostage system reduced the likelihood of revolt in several ways. The residency requirement reduced the daimyo's day-to-day control over their territories, which made it more difficult to organize rebellions and also tended to make regional governance more law-based. The hostage requirement reduced the daimyo interests in wars of secession by assuring that strong sanctions would follow from such revolts. The residency requirements also caused a good deal of the attention and resources of the daimyo (and their advisors) to be invested in the usual status-seeking and rent-seeking activities of capital cities. Such games would tend to increase deference and active support for the shogun.

The peace treaty, however, was not simply imposed on the losers. Policy-making authority was not simply vested in the shogun and emperor, but remained divided between the central government (shogunate) and the regional governments headed by the daimyo. In exchange for their oaths of fealty and half-time residences in Edo, the daimyo retained the authority to rule their territories and collect local taxes. Their lands were exempt from central government taxes. Moreover, the daimyo would also play a significant role in national governance. A subset of the daimyo were always senior advisors to the shogun. Most others participated in regular meetings with the shogun at which policies could be fine-tuned (Mason and Caiger 1997, 197–8; Roberts 1998, 17–21).

Although no written constitution existed during the shogunate period, it is clear that standing rules for governance and civil law existed, which for the most part were based on earlier forms. At the national level, there were informal rules dividing national policy-making authority between the shogun and emperor. Other more formal rules divided the policy-making authority of the central government and the daimyo. The standing procedures for making public policy included advisory councils and a standing bureaucracy, and those procedures were largely taken for granted by high and low government officials.

> [After the first three shoguns] their successors … came to office when the system was already in being. They had to rule as part of the established bureaucracy, abiding by existing laws and conventions and depending on the advice of serving ministers. (Mason and Caiger 1997, 217)

Japan's central government differed from the European template, however, in that it included two parallel governments based on the king-and-council template: a de facto government ruled by the shogun and his senior council of advisors that resided in Edo, and a de jure government ruled by the emperor and his council of advisors that resided in Kyoto. Regional rulers (daimyo) also had their own advisory and executive councils. Towns were often ruled jointly by an appointed head man and council of elders (Mason and Caiger 1997, 210–11).

As in medieval Europe, a broad range of positions in medieval Japan were formally hereditary, including those of the emperor, shogun, and the regional daimyo. Many other positions were limited to persons of particular social rank. For example, only children of samurai were eligible for military service. Ordinarily, the oldest son inherited his father's authority and wealth, although in Japan, as opposed to Europe, both illegitimate and adopted children could inherit the family title and lands. In cases in which no clear heir existed, a childless man would simply adopt a child (or grown man) or the relevant council would appoint someone to be the heir (Mason and Caiger 1997, 198–9).

As in medieval Europe, much of life was governed by standing rules that did not attempt to provide equality before the law. The bounds of one's acceptable behavior were largely determined by one's family and status. For example, strict rules governed relations between persons of different rank and regulated occupation and attire within each stratum.[2]

> Lords and Vassals, superiors and inferiors **must observe what is proper within their positions in life**. Without authorization, no retainer may indiscriminately wear fine white damask, white wadded silk garments, purple silk kimono … Persons without rank are not to ride palanquins … Marriage must not be contracted in private, without approval. (Laws of Military Households 1615 [*Buke Shohaato*], Lu 1997, 207–8)[3]

Educational opportunities were essentially limited to the top strata of society. In the positions in which exams, rather than family, determined positions, there was thus an implicit barrier, rather than a formal class-based one.

During some parts of the Tokugawa period, some positions in the civil service and medical profession were based on examinations analogous to those used in China and Korea at this time. This, in principle, created a path

[2] Many of these restrictions had parallels in medieval Europe, including class-based dress (sumptuary) codes (Jones 2003, 97).

[3] See Lu (1997, chapter 8) for examples from the civil code that specify different punishment for criminal activities, and status-based restrictions on sale of land, inheritance, clothing, and against taking private revenge.

for social mobility. However, access to tutors, books, and the examinations largely reflected the wealth and status of one's family until the era of public education emerged in the nineteenth century. To the extent that there was social mobility in medieval Japan, it was largely through adoption and appointment rather than examination (Levy 1996, 117–20).

Standing civil laws created institutions for dispute resolution, economic regulation, taxation, and limiting social mobility. There were laws governing inheritance and secession. And, as in Europe, land could not be easily sold. Most positions at the top of Japanese society were implicitly or explicitly hereditary.

Constitutional Exchange in the Shogunate Era

The center of government for much of Japanese history had been in or near Kyoto. The shogun was formally the emperor's agent, his supreme military commander.

During the civil war the shogun and his council had exercised essentially complete executive authority, while the emperor remained aloof from the mundane matters of day-to-day military strategy and governance in the territories won. This division of authority largely remained in place after the civil war was over. It was largely an informal arrangement that benefited both the emperor and shogun, but it should be noted that the shogun and his (hereditary) samurai army exercised considerable control over the comings and goings of the emperors and their courts through the Nijo-jo fortress, which was located near the emperor's palace in Kyoto.

As a consequence, for the next two and a half centuries, the emperor and his court lived comfortable, regal lives in Kyoto, but they had little control over the course of Japan's public policy. Constitutional bargaining took place, but for the most part it was between the daimyo and the shogun and between them and their respective councils, rather than between the shogun and the emperor.

The fiscal constitution of the shogunate period allowed the daimyo to offer tax revenue in exchange for increased authority over regional public policies, and the shogun and the central government often sought new revenues. Consequently, there were a number of peaceful shifts of authority between the central and regional authorities. Regional governments often obtained increased autonomy in exchange for higher tax payments to the central government. The shogun also gradually transferred (delegated) authority to his council and the Tokyo bureaucracy for day-to-day rule (Mason and Caiger 1997, 215–16).

In the course of two centuries of bargaining, a complex, decentralized, largely unwritten constitution emerged. More or less hereditary councils in the central and regional governments and their respective bureaucracies controlled most day-to-day policy decisions, while the shogun and the major daimyo lived comfortable lives of high politics and leisure in Edo. The regions maintained their separate identities and important ties among them were often familial, customary, and tacit, as in medieval Europe, rather than through formal alliances or national institutions (Mason and Caiger 1997, 201).

Japanese Economic Development and Mercantilism

The end of armed conflict in the seventeenth century and the stable system of property rights and law of the Shogunate helped promote economic development throughout Japan.

The income produced by commerce and manufacturing grew relative to that of agriculture. At the same time, agricultural production increased as new methods of farming were employed and more land was brought under cultivation. Increased commerce and specialization gradually produced a new middle class of merchants, manufacturers, and professionals, often from samurai families, whose services as soldiers were less often needed during times of peace. Many samurai became courtiers and businessmen, rather than full-time soldiers, and many daimyo diversified into manufacturing and commerce (Lu 1997, 228–35, 273–7).

The Closing of Japan

Prior to the shogunate period, Japanese markets had been open to traders and missionaries from China and Europe, but this ended in the first half of the seventeenth century. A series of laws adopted between 1620 and 1640 severely reduced Japanese contacts with other nations. The Spanish were expelled in 1624. A 1635 edict transferred control of international trade to the central government in Edo and reduced access to Chinese imports. The same edict eliminated opportunities for the Japanese to travel to other countries. A death penalty was to be imposed on Japanese who returned to Japan after foreign travel. A series of laws also ended the Christian religion in Japan (which had been promoted by Portuguese and Spanish missionaries in the previous century). A 1639 edict required that Portuguese ships were to be destroyed and their crews and passengers beheaded. Only the Dutch were permitted to retain commercial ties with

Japan, and these were as limited as those of the Chinese merchants (Lu 1997, 220–7).

Nonetheless, the advantages of peace and lawful governance were greater than losses from international commerce. The regional capitals became centers of commerce and culture in the seventeenth century, with populations that were significantly larger than those of comparable European capitals at the time. The population of Tokyo (Edo) was estimated to be about a million persons in 1700, at the same time that the population of London and Paris were about half a million each. Kyoto and Osaka had populations of about three hundred thousand each, while Amsterdam had a population of about two hundred thousand and Berlin and Stockholm had populations of about sixty thousand each.

Decentralized policy making in the two hundred fifty duchies and autonomous regions (*han*) of Japan allowed local variations in public policies, and yardstick competition among the daimyo encouraged best practices to gradually disseminate throughout Japan.

Decentralization within medieval Japan, however, also allowed local rulers to create monopolies and to regulate their borders. Sales of monopoly privilege and tariffs were significant revenue sources for the local rulers, as was also common in medieval Europe. Merchants might also be given monopoly privileges in exchange for providing public services, as, for example, the merchants of Akaoka, Taruya, and Saga were granted a monopoly on lumber in Kochi as a reward for building a canal for the city. Economic associations (guilds) were common among merchants in most trading centers (Roberts 1998, 29, 42–3; Lu 1997: 234–5).

The national policy of international isolation after 1635, local barriers to trade, cartels, relatively high taxes, and the illiquidity of land impeded the development of national markets, although local mercantilist policies were undermined to some extent by Japan's extensive sea coast.

> The system of **feudal government exercised a crippling influence, for each feudal chief endeavored to check the exit of any kind of property from his fief**, and free interchange of commodities was thus prevented so effectually that cases are recorded of one feudatory's subjects dying of starvation, while those of an adjoining fief enjoyed abundance. International commerce, on the other hand, lay under the veto of the central government, which **punished with death** anyone attempting to hold intercourse with foreigners. (Britannica 1911, "History of Japan," 33)

Economic historians report that commerce nonetheless grew steadily through the eighteenth century, but declined somewhat in the early nineteenth century (Lu 1997, 273–80).

CONSTITUTIONAL BARGAINING AND REFORM AFTER COMMODORE PERRY'S VISIT IN 1853

Although economic development continued in Japan without open markets, in the mid-nineteenth century it became clear that Japan was not developing as rapidly as Europe or North America. A new "yardstick" was introduced in 1853.

In 1853 Commodore Perry arrived with four steam-powered ships of war in Edo (Tokyo) bay. Perry's ships, his guns, and his gifts for the emperor and shogun revealed that Japan had fallen behind Europe in the past two centuries. Perry's return in 1854 produced negotiations and treaties of access (1854) and trade (1858) for the United States.[4] Subsequent treaties reestablishing trade with European states were also negotiated, in large part because it was clear that Japanese technology had fallen behind that of the West.

This conclusion was not a superficial one that focused on equipment alone. Many senior government officials in Japan clearly understood that Western technology reflected organizational as well as technological advantages. To catch up, many believed that a broad range of Western innovations in economic, political, and military organization had to be analyzed and adapted to Japanese circumstances. There were new unrealized potential gains from trade and travel.

The shogun convened a special council of the major daimyo to determine the proper response to the new yardstick and the West's insistence on more open international markets. A variety of long-standing quasi-constitutional domestic policies were reversed, and the Japanese people were henceforth encouraged to master Western technologies. Prohibitions on foreign travel and on the construction and purchase of seagoing ships ended. The translation of European scientific, legal, and political texts was broadened and accelerated as interest intensified and moveable type was introduced. New fortresses were built, cannons cast, and samurai troops trained in their use. The government ordered a battleship from the Dutch, who were also enlisted to "procure from Europe all the best works on modern military science." The emperor directed that "at the seven principal shrines, special prayers should be offered for the safety of the land and the destruction of aliens" (*Britannica* 1911, 239).

[4] Commodore Perry's negotiations with the Japanese in 1853 and 1854 involved presents and formal discussions, rather than gunshots or military intimidation. The proceedings are discussed in Forster (1903, 150–65).

The renewal of foreign trade after two centuries of closure clearly affected many Japanese family firms that now had to compete with distant foreign producers. It also clearly affected those in southern Japan, who previously had exclusive access to Dutch and Chinese merchants. A small liberal movement began to emerge that pressed for open foreign relations and more representative political institutions. The first newspapers were printed, and many were critical of existing government policies and results. These liberalizing pressures were countered by conservatives who pressed for a return to closure. Trade increased the presence of foreign persons who did not always follow the well-established etiquette of the shogunate era, which increased opposition to the intrusions of the uncouth foreigners.

The shogun was in the forefront of treaty negotiations and, by the standards of the time, could be regarded as a liberal in the sense that he and his advisors acknowledged the need for institutional reform and modernization. Southern daimyo were among the strongest opponents to foreign trade at the imperial court. Constitutional conservatism implies that it takes more authority to change the status quo than to maintain it, and much of the central government's authority had been traded away during the past century or so.

Neither the shogunate nor the imperial court was sufficiently powerful or influential to accomplish major reforms on its own. Negotiations between the imperial court and shogunate took place regarding foreign treaties, domestic policies, and institutional reforms, but without obvious results, because the shogun's and emperor's councils reached nearly opposite conclusions about the proper response. The shogunate argued for the expansion of trade, while many in the emperor's court argued for renewed closure. Naturally, both sides argued that the national interest would be advanced by their recommendations.

Disagreement between the Tokyo and Kyoto courts, in this case, implied that a constitutional crisis was at hand. With the failure of the shogunate to protect the homeland and enforce its own policy of closure, and with evidence of slow growth for many decades, support for the old "two-government" system diminished, even among those who had previously benefited from it. Consultations continued among representatives of the shogun, imperial court, and daimyo.

THE MEIJI RESTORATION OF 1867 AS CONSTITUTIONAL EXCHANGE

A shogun died and was succeeded by Yoshinobu Tokugawa in 1866, whose council continued to press for modest reforms. An emperor died and was replaced by one of his sons in 1867, who is now known as Emperor Meiji.[5] Both new leaders were relatively young and inexperienced, which shifted the balance of policy-making authority in favor of their councils. The following year, a major reform of Japanese governance emerged out of a long series of negotiations, reinforced by military efforts on behalf of the emperor by the southern daimyo.

The Meiji restoration is considered by some scholars to be a unilateral act of generosity on the part of the shogun to strengthen national governance and avoid civil war. By others, it is considered an act of surrender accepted out of necessity in the face of a superior military force. There is, however, much that suggests that the shift in authority to the emperor's court was part of an agreement worked out behind closed doors. Such an agreement would have been made easier by changes in the persons who formally headed the two branches of government. The Tokugawa regime evidently accepted a shift of day-to-day policy-making authority from the relatively new and weak (thirty-year-old) shogun to the relatively new and weak (fifteen-year-old) emperor Meiji. The emperor's regime, in return, accepted the need for a broad modernization of Japanese society.

In late 1867, the new shogun called a council of daimyo and high officials in Kyoto to announce his resignation, which was tendered the following day to the emperor.

> Now that **foreign intercourse becomes daily more extensive**, unless government is directed from one central authority, the foundations of the state will fall to pieces.... **If national deliberations be conducted on an extensive scale** and the Imperial decision be secured, **and if the empire be supported by the whole people**, then the empire will be able to maintain its rank and dignity among the nations on earth – it is, I believe, **my highest duty to realize this ideal by giving entirely my rule over this land**. (Tokugawa Yoshinobu, reprinted from Mason and Caiger 1997, 259)

A few months later in early 1868, a new "Imperial Oath" was required of all daimyo. It included five major commitments.

> **(i) We shall determine all matters of state by public discussion, after assemblies have been convoked far and wide** ... (ii) We shall unite the minds of **people high**

[5] The new emperor was selected to be the crown prince in 1860 from among the previous emperor's (Komei) male children. He was given the name Mutsuhito at that time and was known as Emperor Mutsuhito during his lifetime.

Japanese emperors and their periods of rule are renamed after their death. The name Meiji was given to the emperor after his death in 1912, which means "enlightened rule." I refer to this ruler as Emperor Meiji throughout this chapter, as is customary among historians writing in English and in Japanese after Mutsuhito's death. The term "king" Meiji would be equally appropriate for the purposes of this book, insofar as the daimyo can be regarded as dukes or barons, rather than kings.

and low … **(iii) We are duty bound to ensure that all people** … **may fulfill their aspirations** and not give into despair. (iv) We shall base our actions on the principles of international law. … (v) **We shall seek knowledge throughout the world and thus reinvigorate the foundation of this imperial nation**.

After the oath was read, four hundred eleven major and minor daimyo (including the thirty members of the emperor's advisory council) formally renewed their oath of fealty to the emperor by signing an official document (Breen 1996).

Bargaining and compromise is evident in that the imperial court had originally opposed shogunate efforts to negotiate treaties with the West and to modernize, but now fully embraced them, as implicitly did the four hundred eleven signatories. Bargaining is also evident in that the shift of governmental authority from the Tokugawa to the Meiji court was initially accomplished without substantial change in the central government bureaucracy or regional governments, although significant constitutional reforms soon followed. Moreover, the surrender of the Tokugawa lands (*tenryo*) to the new central government (Mason and Caiger 1997, 259–60) was followed by a similar surrender of lands by the four daimyo from the south that had provided military support for the Meiji restoration (Lu 1997, 305–15, *Britannica* 1911, 311).[6]

The emperor and his retinue moved from Kyoto to Edo and assumed control of the existing institutions of governance. The ruling council members were now selected by the emperor, rather than the shogun, and the city of Edo was renamed Tokyo (eastern capital), but the long-standing procedures for adopting and implementing public policies remained largely in place. Constitutional conservatism is evident in that policy-making authority remained largely in the hands of advisory councils at the central and regional government levels, and remained so to a considerable extent, even after the Meiji constitution was adopted twenty years later.[7]

Nonetheless, much was new. The imperial government had far more control over public policy than it had had for many centuries, and the new Imperial Oath included a commitment to use more open and representative procedures of governance than had been used in the past. The latter

[6] The oath was clearly negotiated and written by senior advisors, rather than the young emperor. The oath went through a number of drafts within the emperor's advisory council before being finalized (Pittau 1967, 11–15).

[7] Emperor Meiji was formally the source of the shogun's authority, and the emperor continued to be the formal source of authority under the Meiji constitution. (It was not until after World War II that the basis for constitutional government shifted from royal delegation of authority to popular sovereignty.)

played an important role in constitutional negotiations for the next several decades, because it was not clear whether the emperor's commitment to "determine all matters of state by public discussion, after assemblies have been convoked far and wide" was a commitment to create a parliament or simply a promise to call the daimyo occasionally to Kyoto. The ambiguity evidently reflected a lack of consensus among the emperor's council of advisors about the proper form the reformed government should take.[8] The details were slowly worked out through more than two decades of negotiation and institutional experimentation.

On other matters, the new Imperial Oath was quite clear. The emperor's commitment to "seek knowledge throughout the world and thus reinvigorate the foundation of this imperial nation" implied that all Japanese had a duty to study foreign theories, reforms, and outcomes. As a consequence, many high government officials and scholars traveled to Europe and the United States and returned home with new theories as well as practical ideas for the application of new industrial technologies and public-policy reform in Japan.

The experience of the European monarchies was naturally of particular interest for those advocating constitutional reforms, because liberalism had both theoretical and practical relevance for Japan.

THE LIBERAL TIDE AND EUROPEAN INFLUENCE IN THE EARLY MEIJI ERA

Before Perry's arrival, Japan's contact with Europe in the previous two centuries was mainly through a small Dutch trading post on the small man-made island of Deshima in the bay of Nagasaki. Schools of Dutch study were founded near the Dutch trading post, and nonreligious books and newspapers from the Netherlands were translated by Japanese scholars, albeit slowly and for limited distribution, because printing was done via wooden block, rather than with movable type. In this manner, some Western scientific ideas and philosophical ideas were available to interested scholars and students, particularly in the south. Indeed, the Dutch provided the shogun with advance notice that the United States would send ships to Japan a few years before Perry's arrived (*Britannica* 1911, 239). Contacts between the Satsuma and the Chinese continued via Okinawa. Additional international commerce also took place illicitly along the coast and with the Russians to the north (Mason and Caiger 1997, 205).

[8] It is interesting to note that proposed drafts of the oath were more explicit about the form of government to be adopted. Some called for representative assemblies and others for a federal council of daimyo. See Lu (1997, 307–8) for alternative drafts of the oath.

Changes in the laws governing travel and trade after Perry's arrival, together with encouragement from the shogun and emperor, caused a major increase in Japanese knowledge of Europe and America. After the new imperial oath, foreign travel and new translations brought Europe's political and economic theories to the attention of a broad cross-section of literate Japanese, including high government officials. For example, Nakae Chomin translated Rousseau's *Social Contract*. Nakamura Masanao translated J. S. Mill's *On Liberty* and Samuel Smile's *Self-Help*. The latter was a collection of rags-to-riches success stories that argued against the practice of using social status or class to determine a man's worth.[9]

Many of these European texts provided insights that were useful to persons interested in public policy, including senior officials in the Japanese government. For example, liberal economic theories provided an explanation for Japan's failure to keep pace with economic developments of the West. Japan's failure to keep up was not due to the cultural inferiority, but to policy mistakes. The closed nature of the Japanese mercantilist system (both internally and externally) would have reduced economic growth by reducing gains from specialization, economies of scale, and technological innovation. Liberal political theories, in turn, explained why needed economic reforms had not been adopted in Japan. Representation had been too narrow and grounded on the wrong principles to support the reforms necessary for economic development to take place. Elite forms of government often protect their interests by "protecting" the status quo from "unnecessary" innovations and by providing themselves with monopoly privileges. Liberal theories thus provided coherent explanations for Japan's relative weakness and, conversely, also suggested reforms that could allow it to catch up with the West.

Japanese Liberals

Literate Japanese did not become "Western" or "Westernized" any more than the English became Dutch or the French became English when they used

[9] Smile's *Self-Help* includes such challenges to the class system as: "Great men of science, literature, and art – apostles of great thoughts and lords of the great heart – have belonged to no exclusive class nor rank in life. They have come alike from colleges, workshops, and farmhouses – from the huts of poor men and the mansions of the rich. Some of God's greatest apostles have come from 'the ranks.' The poorest have sometimes taken the highest places; nor have difficulties apparently the most insuperable proved obstacles in their way. Those very difficulties, in many instances, would ever seem to have been their best helpers, by evoking their powers of labor and endurance, and stimulating into life faculties which might otherwise have lain dormant" (Available from the Gutenberg E-book Project).

innovations developed elsewhere. Rather, European ideas and experiences that helped identify constitutional, social, and economic problems and how those problems might be solved were taken into consideration when public policy and constitutional issues were being debated and reforms were being devised. For example, European experience provided evidence about how constitutional reforms had been introduced in other polities, and what their effects tended to be.

The "new" European texts also stimulated new policy and constitutional debates throughout Japan by inducing further analysis and refinement of older Japanese ideas. Shogunate-era scholarship, for example, included defenses for profits based on gains from trade and the promotion of persons based on their talents, rather than their class or status. Japanese theories also included norms for governance that implied that good rulers should rule with their subject's interest at heart, and that it was proper to allow free speech.[10] As in Europe, these early liberal ideas were by no means the dominant ones in eighteenth or early nineteenth-century. It is interesting to note, however, the regions of Japan where the most liberal views of economic activities were present were also regions from which a disproportionate number of Japanese entrepreneurs emerged.

During the second half of the nineteenth century, Japanese liberals and other proponents of reform used arguments that were in many ways similar to those used by European liberals and reformers, and such arguments were made both inside and outside government. As true in Europe at the time, however, Japanese liberals did not simply quote form Smith, Bastiat, Locke, Kant, Mill, and Rousseau. Rather, they produced arguments that reflected their own sense of culture, progress, and political opportunities in the Japanese context, given their new knowledge of European ideas. Japanese academics similarly produced syntheses of Western philosophers and older Japanese scholarship.

For example, various combinations of natural-rights, contractarian, and utilitarian ideas were used by Japanese political liberals at the time of the Meiji restoration.

Heaven bestows life and along with it the ability and strength needed to preserve it. But though man might attempt to use his natural powers, **if he lacked freedom his abilities and strength would be of no use. Therefore**, throughout the world, in all countries and among all peoples self-determined **free action is a law of nature**. In other words, each individual is independent and society is for the good of all …

[10] See Lu (1997, 228–55) for eighteenth-century excerpts from the works of Naito Kanji, Ishida Baigan, and Kumazawa Banzan.

The right to freedom and independence, which he receives from heaven cannot be bought and sold. (Fukuzawa 1867, quoted in Craig 1968, 107)[11]

The **people who have the duty to pay taxes to the government concurrently possess the right to be informed of the affairs of the government and to approve or reject such governmental matters.** This is the principle **universally** accepted in the world, which requires no further elaboration on our part. We humbly request that the officials not resist this great truth. [Opponents of reform] assert "Our people lack knowledge and intelligence and have not yet reached the plateau of enlightenment. It is too early to have a popularly-elected representative assembly." … We have **presented our case for the immediate establishment of a popularly elected representative assembly** and have argued also that the **degree of progress among the people of our country is sufficient** for the establishment of such an assembly. (Okubo 1874, quoted in Lu 1997, 327–9)[12]

As in Europe, Japanese liberals of this period did not completely accept notions of civil equality and rarely favored universal suffrage, rather they supported greater civil equality and more representative government. Liberal interpretations of the emperor's oath were commonplace.

Many of the first generation of newspapers published in the 1870s could be regarded as liberal insofar as they advocated a "wider opening of the door to official preferment" (*Britannica* 1911, 47). As in Europe, advancing relatively narrow economic and political interests often required expanded political and economic participation. Politically active writers in the 1870s also promoted liberal ideas and institutional reform in a variety of Japanese newspapers, periodicals, pamphlets, and books (Hane 1969).

More liberal newspapers were founded in the 1880s. For example, in 1882 Fukuzawa launched the newspaper *Jiji Shimpo*, which advocated liberal themes such as independence and self-respect (*History of Constitutionalism in Japan* [henceforth, *HiCoJ*] 1987, 55). Weekly periodicals promoting liberal reforms were begun, including the initially liberal *Kokumin no Tomo* in 1887 by Tokutomi Soho. Several books advocating constitutions

[11] Fukuzawa Yukichi is widely regarded to be one of the most influential of the liberal scholars in Japan. Yukichi Fukuzawa (1835–1901) attended university in Osaka, where he became familiar with European political thought through Dutch sources. In 1868, Fukuzawa founded a school in Tokyo named Keio Gijuku, as an institute of Western learning, which subsequently became one of the most prestigious universities in Japan. He had also traveled widely in Europe and the United States as a member of three missions sponsored by the shogun. Fukuzawa's picture appears on the present-day ten-thousand-yen note.

[12] Okubo Toshimichi (1830–78) was one of the most important members of the imperial council in the decade after the Meiji restoration. Okubo was, for example, the finance minister in 1871, and a strong proponent of economic and political modernization and an opponent of war in Korea. Okubo, a samurai himself, was assassinated in 1878 because of his successful suppression of the Satsuma Rebellion of 1877. He is often referred to as one of the three great nobles (Ishin-no-Sanketsu) of the restoration.

and representative democracy, among other reforms, were also written in the 1880s.

Hundreds of groups were organized to explore philosophical issues of constitutional governance, as with the Gakugeikodankai in Itsukaichi (Devine 1979). Politically active groups were organized to press for liberalization of political and economic life. The Movement for the Liberty and Rights of the People lobbied for a written constitution and national assemblies (Mason and Caiger 1997, 284; Devine 1979; Kaufman-Osborn 1992).

Ideas about hereditary privileges began to shift as notions of "equality before the law" began to replace older theories of family privilege among educated people, including many future members of parliament. Indeed, there were sufficient numbers of liberal groups and proponents of modernization that a confederation of liberal groups was organized (the Aikokushi or Patriotic League) to lobby for tax, regulatory, and political reform. Such groups attracted support from the growing rural and urban middle classes as well as liberal intellectuals and academics. Meetings were held by proponents of constitutional reform in 1877, and petitions favoring constitutional reform (with eighty thousand signatures) were submitted to the grand council in 1880 (*HiCoJ* 1987, 15, 19). In 1890, a nationwide temperance movement was launched.

The first political party was organized by liberals in 1881 (the Jiyuto), well before the first national elections were held, to lobby more effectively for reform. Two other liberal coalitions were organized shortly after Jiyuto, the Rikken Seito (Constitutional Party) in 1881 and the Kyushu Kaishinto (Kyushu Progressive Party) in 1882. The emperor's oath, which mentioned broadly representative assemblies, was often used by such groups to insist on a written constitution with an elected national assembly. In response, Okuma Shigenobu and other moderate conservatives organized the Rikken Teiseito (Constitutional Imperial Rule Party), which lobbied in favor of imperial government, although it also favored a written constitution and gradual reform.

Right-of-center liberals were affected by the new conservative arguments. For example, Tokutomi Soho was initially a moderate liberal, who favored constitutional representative government, equality before the law, and limited governance, although he rejected the natural rights and social contract theories of the state. Tokutomi gradually shifted his position in the 1890s in a more conservative direction, as he began to appreciate that military strength was an important determinant of evolutionary success (Pierson 1974). In much the same vein, Kato applies ideas from social Darwinism and Hobbes when he argues that:

> The world seems to be in the battleground of a struggle for existence, in which those who are superior, mentally and physically, through biological reason of heredity, are bound to win in life's race and control over the inferior for the same phenomena can be observed even more distinctly in the life of the lower animals and plants … hence there is no such thing as the natural rights of man. … Thus … unless there had been an absolute ruler, our State would never have been organized, nor the rights of our people come into existence. (Jinken Shinsetsu, 1882, quoted in Uyehara 1910, 115).

Many left-of-center liberals were similarly influenced by European arguments favoring labor law reform, expansion of social insurance, and redistribution.

German Influences on Japanese Moderates and Conservatives

Many senior Japanese officials found the German experience to be of special interest, because Germany was also in the process of creating a new central government and had only very recently reformed its medieval economic and political institutions. They, like Japan, did so in a setting in which regional nobles had long had significant political authority and in which liberal arguments were increasingly accepted. The particular attraction of Prussia's 1850 constitution within the imperial council reflected its success at preserving preexisting political authority, while incorporating many liberal ideas.[13]

Conservatives and moderates studied and were heavily influenced by German constitutional theorists. Among the German scholars mentioned by proponents of a strong monarchy were Stein, Gneist, and Roesler, who favored equality before the law with a strong royal government. Indeed, Roesler was invited to comment on proposed drafts of the Meiji constitution (Pittau 1967, chapter 5). Although accepting liberal arguments for civil equality and constitutional governance, moderate conservatives rejected arguments in support of strong parliamentary systems, arguing that a strong monarch can govern more justly because monarchs are less prone to capture by factions and class interests than are parliaments. Prussian influences are also evident in some of the early Meiji military reforms.

[13] It is interesting to note that Heinrich Rudolf Hermann Friedrich von Gneist was also very influential within Germany. Gneist was a moderate liberal by Prussian standards of the time, who served as a member of the Prussian parliament for twenty-five years. Besides writing books and providing advice to Japanese reformers while serving in the Prussian parliament, he also was employed by Friedrich III to teach his son, the future Wilhelm II, constitutional law.

By restoring its links to the world after the Meiji period began, and by looking for insights elsewhere, Japanese intellectuals of all political perspectives became far more connected to Western intellectual developments. And, as political theories and public debates among liberals and conservatives in Europe evolved during the late nineteenth century, similar shifts took place in Japanese theories and policy debates.

LIBERAL POLICY REFORMS OF THE EARLY MEIJI PERIOD

The impact of liberal ideas was evident in policy debates within the highest levels of government and in the policy reforms adopted throughout the second half of the nineteenth century. As in many European countries, liberal policies were supported by idealists because they advanced general national interests and human rights. As also true in Europe, such policies were also often supported by pragmatists in pursuit of narrower economic and political interests. Such liberal-pragmatic support produced educational reform and a reorganization of the military that reduced class privileges.

The educational reforms of 1871 include a preamble that summarizes the liberal perspective on education.

> The **only way in which an individual can raise himself**, manage his property and prosperity in his business and so accomplish his career **is by cultivating his morals, improving his intellect, and becoming proficient in the arts**. The cultivation of morals, the improvement of the intellect, and proficiency in the arts cannot be attained except through learning. **This is the reason why schools are established** ... **It is intended** that henceforth universally (**without any distinction of class or sex**) in a village **there shall be no house without learning and in a house no individual without learning**. (quoted in Pittau 1967, 24)

The preamble focuses on individual welfare, encourages nongovernmental applications of education, and clearly intends education to be class and status neutral for the first time. Before the reform, education had been more or less limited to the samurai and nobles who were thought likely to obtain senior posts in national and regional governments. The preamble breaks with this narrow view of the purpose of education.

A variety of other liberal economic reforms and policies were adopted during the same period. Restrictions on planting particular crops were eliminated in 1871. Internal barriers to trade were reduced and class-based rules that limited landownership, sales of land, and occupational choice were eliminated, as were restrictions on peasant ownership and careers. The first railroad was opened in 1872 as a demonstration project of less than twenty miles, but gradually railroad construction caught on and by

1900, three thousand miles of railroad tracks had been constructed. (As in the Netherlands, the early railroads were not superior to water-based shipping.) The ban on Christian churches was lifted in 1878. An income tax was introduced in 1887 that gradually replaced land taxes as the main source of government revenues (Mason and Caiger 1997, 272–7; Pittau 1967, 27–8; Minami 1994, 257–60; Lu 1997, 307–23).

Centralization and Civic Equality

Many of the quasi-constitutional reforms of government adopted in the first decades of the Meiji era advanced pragmatic interests in centralization. The duchy (*han*) system of the Tokugawa regime was formally ended in 1871, and regional nobles were encouraged to take up full-time residence in Tokyo, rather than continue their biannual migration. The smaller duchies (*han*) were merged into new prefectures. A series of land-tax reforms were introduced in 1873 that centralized taxing authority (although government expenditures continued to outpace revenues and produced significant deficits). The "Peerage Ordinance" of 1884 established five ranks of nobility. The "new" nobles were largely from the historically powerful regional families, although many supporters of the Meiji regime were elevated at the same time (HiCoJ 1987, 22–3).

In 1885, following several years of inflation, a new national Japanese currency was introduced that was convertible into silver (and subsequently gold), and regional currencies were eliminated. Such reforms further reduced opportunities for regional dynasties to organize opposition to the new central government.

Civic equality was indirectly increased by many of the early reforms, although inequality before the law was not eliminated. Opportunities were made more equal by reducing internal trade barriers and extending public education. The legal privileges of birth were revised, reduced, and simplified. Service in the military and national bureaucracy were opened to commoners. The centralization reforms also increased civil equality somewhat by reducing the authority of the daimyo and their families in their regions.

Military Reforms and the Conservative Satsuma Rebellion of 1877

Of course, not all Japanese accepted the need for greater openness in commerce and governance, and not all those favoring such reforms were liberals.

The most serious conservative challenge to the early Meiji reforms occurred shortly after the military reforms of 1872 and 1876 were adopted. The military reforms of 1872 created a new universal military service that was in many ways similar to that of Prussia at that time, with three years of active duty, followed by four more years in the reserves. This reform eliminated the samurai's exclusive hereditary right to serve in the Japanese military, which was very controversial among the samurai. About four hundred thousand samurai had rights to a lifetime pension as compensation for their military service, which was a substantial drain on central government revenues. Many of the pensions were hereditary (Britannica 1911, 313). Cash "buy outs" of lifetime privileges and pensions were offered to the samurai with some success.

The army was further reorganized in 1876 along more European lines. The remaining samurai pensions were reduced, and the exclusive samurai privilege of wearing two swords (daisho) in public was eliminated. The samurai also lost their right execute commoners who had shown them disrespect (kiri sute gomen).

A subset of the samurai refused to abide by the new laws, which had greatly reduced samurai privileges and income. The samurai opposition to the military reforms was partly pragmatic, as the reforms reduced their status and income. It was also partly ideological, as many samurai had a deep commitment to preserving Japan's medieval way of life and were skeptical about the effectiveness of the new Japanese army. As soldiers who shared the same concerns and were used to functioning within disciplined organizations, the samurai were able to organize an armed rebellion relatively easily, and did so in 1876–7.

The new nonhereditary Japanese army fairly quickly crushed the conservative Satsuma Rebellion in 1877. By doing so, the Satsuma Rebellion provided additional evidence that new organizations, new equipment, and new methods could be superior to the old ways. The new could be better than the old.

CONSTITUTIONAL BARGAINING AND REFORM AFTER THE MEIJI RESTORATION

Bargaining and compromise among liberals, pragmatists, and conservatives are evident throughout the Meiji period. Governance was subject to almost continual reorganization during the first two decades of the Meiji era, which reflected the usual difficulty of adopting major reforms in large organizations such as governments. Indeed, a policy of gradual reform was announced in 1875 (Mason and Caiger 1997, 286).

In 1868, shortly after the imperial oath was made and accepted, the central government was reorganized into three agencies: Sosai (office of the emperor), Gijo (office of administration) and Sanyo (office of councilors). These were staffed by members of the imperial family, its court, and its daimyo supporters. This provisional government would be the first of many formal and informal reforms of governance.

The daimyo responsible for the "assemblies" language in the emperor's oath continued to press for national representative assemblies with legislative authority, while the conservatives and pragmatists opposed sharing royal authority with such assemblies. As arguments and evidence shifted and as popular support for liberal reforms grew, laws were adopted to create national and regional assemblies, and these laws were revised several times. Four months later, a formal law (the Seitaisho) created a template from which the new national government gradually emerged.

It specified that policy-making authority would be delegated to a grand council of state (Dajokan). The new council of state consisted of twenty-six councilors, chosen mainly from the four regions (*han*) that had supported the emperor against the shogun. This royal council and its successors would function as the Japanese cabinet. The Seitaisho also provided for a delegation of authority among three subsidiary departments: one for legislation, one for administration, and one for judicial matters. The legislative department (Giseikan) was to consist of two chambers and may be regarded as the precursor to a Japanese parliament. The upper chamber was a noble chamber that represented the ruling families of Japan. The lower chamber was more or less a federal chamber with representatives from the regional (*han*) governments (Mason and Caiger 1997, 284; *HiCoJ* 1987, 11). Both legislative chambers were initially delegated legislative authority, but in the following year the lower chamber was changed into a consultative body without legislative authority (Pittau 1967, 16; *HiCoJ* 1987, 10–12, Lu 1997, 308–9). The Seitaisho also encouraged cities and provinces (han) to create representative assemblies (*HiCoJ* 1987, 10–12).

In 1871, significant reforms of the provinces and their governments were negotiated. The ancient feudal territories became prefectures to be governed, rather than family domains to be ruled. The regional daimyo continued to rule as governors of their old territories and retained their territorial treasuries.

National and regional tax bases were reformed at the same time. Taxes were to be based on land values, rather than agricultural output, which allowed tax rates to be reduced, but increased revenues because of the expanded tax base. Regional governments were assured of 10 percent of the new tax revenues, rather than 40 percent of that previously raised from agriculture alone (*Britannica* 1911, 312; Minami 1994, 259; Totman 2000, 292).

Lobbying and Negotiations for a Written Constitution

Proposals for a new elected lower chamber were also made in 1871, but no action was taken until four of the emperor's former state councilors – Itagaki, Goto, Eto, and Soejima – made a similar proposal in January 1874. A subsequent reorganization of governance created a new advisory "council of elders" (Genroin). The members of the Genroin were not elected, but rather chosen from the senior members of the council of state. The Genroin would deliberate on laws and accept petitions on various matters.

The Genroin was subsequently given responsibility to draw up a formal constitution for post-restoration Japan (Hackett 1968). Their 1878 proposal was surprisingly liberal. It called for a bicameral parliament with significant legislative authority and required the emperor to take an oath to "adhere to the constitution before a meeting of both houses" (Pittau 1967, 74). It was, however, too liberal to be adopted by the council of state as a whole (*HiCoJ* 1987, 14).

In 1878, a new law required that the provincial assembles be selected via elections, which changed the basis for holding seats in the provincial assembles and for drafting local election laws. The new local assemblies were also given the authority to veto new provincial taxes. These changes demonstrated that Japan's liberals were not simply making proposals, but were affecting constitutional decisions by the central government. However, as conservatives doubtless anticipated, the new local election laws were designed to minimize the effect that elections would have on the persons holding office. Those eligible to sit in the new representative assembly had to meet relatively high property qualification. Property qualification also determined who voted in the elections. Voting was by open, signed ballot. The assemblies normally met for just one month each year. (*Britannica* 1911, 150, 319–20; Wada 1996, 6).

As a consequence, the persons selected for regional assemblies and members of the second chamber appointed by them did not change very much after the reform was implemented. Most officeholders still came from the relatively wealthy families who had routinely served in advisory and administrative posts in the past. The effect of signed ballots helped to diminish the effect of voting because it allowed the most powerful families in a community or prefecture to make sure that "their" former vassals cast their votes for the "right" candidates. Without such assurances, it is clear that opposition from influential families at court would have been far greater and the new liberal architecture for local government far less likely to have been adopted.

Overall, the net effect of the education, tax, and military reforms of the 1870s was to reduce aristocratic privilege and centralize policy-making authority while increasing literacy, economic growth, and military strength. As in the United Kingdom, local government was liberalized somewhat before the national government, which tended to increase support for similar reforms of national governance.

Liberal economic reforms continued to be adopted during the 1890s, although these were often coupled with conservative political reforms that restricted the freedom of association, the press, and political parties. Censorship rules were toughened in 1882, 1883, and 1887 in response to public demonstrations of support for constitutional reform and remained in place until 1898 (Uyehara 1910, 182–3).

Nonetheless, constitutional debate and negotiations among conservatives and liberals inside and outside government continued throughout the 1870s and 1880s.

THE MEIJI CONSTITUTION IS ADOPTED

The emperor evidently remained interested in constitutional reform and solicited proposals from royal council members in 1878 and 1879. The proposals revealed both points of consensus and a broad range of opinion within the highest levels of Japanese government. Most of the proposals included a written constitution and representative assembly. There were, however, significant disagreements about the best division of policy-making authority between the emperor (and his royal council) and parliament. Proposed constitutions ranged from constitutional monarchies with a dominant parliament, similar to that of late-nineteenth-century England, to ones analogous to the Prussian system in which the authority of the king was maximized (Pittau 1967, chapter 3; Lu 1997, chapter 11).

The consensus in favor of a national assembly led to an 1881 imperial proclamation that a new national assembly would be convened in 1891. Efforts to determine how such an assembly would be assembled continued in earnest. After eight more years of negotiations among insiders, a compromise was reached, and Japan formally became a constitutional monarchy. A written constitution was adopted at an imperial ceremony in 1889.[14]

The Meiji Constitution of 1889

The Meiji constitution is grounded on Japan's version of the divine right of kings, rather than popular sovereignty, and thus it is formally a declaration by the sovereign.[15] The royal declaration states that the constitution is intended to bind future emperors as well as the current one:

> We, the Successor to the prosperous Throne of Our Predecessors, do humbly and solemnly swear to the Imperial Founder of Our House and to Our other Imperial Ancestors that, in pursuance of a great policy co-extensive with the Heavens and with the Earth, **We shall maintain and secure from decline the ancient form of government.**
>
> In consideration of the **progressive tendency of the course of human affairs** and in parallel with the **advance of civilization**, We **deem it expedient**, in order to give clearness and distinctness to the instructions bequeathed by the Imperial Founder of Our House and by Our other Imperial Ancestors, **to establish fundamental laws** formulated into express provisions of law, so that, on the one hand, Our Imperial posterity may possess an **express guide for the course they are to follow**, and that, on the other, **Our subjects shall thereby be enabled to enjoy a wider range of action** in giving Us their support.
>
> **We hereby promulgate**, in pursuance of Our Imperial Rescript of the 12th day of the 10th month of the 14th year of Meiji, **a fundamental law of the State, to exhibit the principles, by which We are guided in Our conduct, and to point out to what Our descendants and Our subjects and their descendants are forever to conform.**

Compromises between liberals, conservative, and pragmatists are evident throughout the new Japanese constitution (law of the state).

The principle of rule of law was accepted. The constitution created a new parliament and described the division of authority between the parliament, the executive cabinet (royal council), and the emperor. The Meiji parliament had veto power over new taxes, budgets, and new legislation. Meetings of parliament would take place annually, and its meetings would be open to the

[14] Hirobumi Ito (1841–1909) is usually given credit for the Meiji constitution, but the constitution was clearly a joint product of several of the emperor's closest advisors. Hermann Roesler, a German constitutional scholar, also played a significant role in this process, both suggesting a draft and commenting on revisions (Siemes 1962). Ito later served as prime minister several times and, perhaps surprisingly, is often said to have formed the first party government in 1900. He was assassinated in 1909.

[15] An English translation of the Meiji constitution is included in Dodd (1909).

public. All royal policy decisions would be cosigned by a cabinet minister. Elections would play a significant role for the first time. Following the English design, the new parliament was bicameral with a hereditary chamber of nobles and a directly elected second chamber.[16] The two chambers had essentially equal authority. The basic architecture and procedures thus satisfied liberal constitutional norms for the mid-nineteenth century.

The Meiji constitution, however, was crafted in a Prussian-like manner that preserved most of the emperor's and his council's autonomy.

Eligibility for seats in the elected chamber and for voting was based on tax payments. Suffrage for the elected chamber required payment of national taxes greater than fifteen yen, which at the time gave about 3 percent of adult men the right to vote in parliamentary elections, about 450,000 persons. The new electorate reached into the old samurai class and new upper-middle class, but no further. The election law also specified four-year terms of office and single-member districts (with minor exceptions), although the districts were based on population rather than number of voters. This, in combination with the existing distribution of tax payments, produced considerable variation in the number of votes that candidates would have to receive to win office. As few as twenty-three votes could determine a member of the new lower chamber (Uyehara 1910, 169–73, *HiCoJ* 1987, 20–2).

The Meiji constitution includes a bill of rights. However, all the rights listed could be revised by ordinary legislation, as could election laws. Free speech for members of the parliament was protected, but only inside parliament. Outside, it would be subject to the prevailing censorship laws (article 52). Other restrictions on the press and on political organizations remained in force (Uyehara 1910, 182–3, 219). Constitutional amendments required a two-thirds vote in each chamber and consent of the emperor. Proposals for amendments had to originate as executive (imperial) proposals, which made the constitution very difficult to amend in practice. On other matters, the emperor and chambers of parliament shared agenda and veto control.

Overall, the constitution was clearly a compromise, a constitutional bargain, rather than a "fraudulent" document imposed by conservatives on the emperor's council.

Parliament's veto power on new laws and would please Japanese liberals and others who felt their interests had not been well represented within

[16] The supplemental imperial ordinance concerning nobles, states that the noble chamber also includes persons appointed by the emperor and representatives of city governments. All higher nobles were eligible for seats, but only a fifth of the lesser nobles, who would elected by their fellow nobles (Dodd 1909, 33–4).

the Meiji council of state. The new noble chamber and by the restrictive wealth-based suffrage would please the regional governments outside the imperial court, which were largely controlled by noble families. The foundation of the constitution and the emperor's ability to appoint the council of state would please conservatives by preserving the ancient metaphysical foundation of the Japanese state (Siemes 1962).

Preserving royal autonomy also made the constitution acceptable to the emperor. Roesler's commentaries on the Meiji constitution make it clear that many of its provisions were written with preserving the historic (indeed mythic) authority of the emperor in mind. The emperor retained the power to declare war and peace, sign treaties, appoint and dismiss officials, elevate nobles, and determine the salaries of government officials (articles 1–16). In the absence of agreement for a new budget, the old budget would remain in effect (article 71). Parliament was also forbidden to reduce "fixed expenditures" adopted by the emperor before the constitution (articles 66, 67, and 76).

The two new royal councils that formally replaced the council of state and the Genroin are mentioned only briefly: the ministry or cabinet in article 55 and the advisory privy council in article 56. The practice of selecting a prime minister (cabinet president or chancellor) had become routine in the period prior to the constitution's adoption, but this important office is mentioned only in passing in the constitution, as a person who could break ties in the parliament (article 47). The ministers were all appointed by and responsible to the emperor, rather than parliament. The emperor and his councils retained formal control of day-to-day governance, as had long been common practice in Japan.

The emperor and his council were clearly important veto players in the negotiations that led to the final constitution's language. Beckmann (1957) argues that in practice the new constitution assured that the emperor's senior ministers and advisors would continue to exercise nearly complete control of many areas of public policy in Japan, assuring policy, procedural, and hierarchical continuity.

Although not a radical document in terms of the persons holding seats in government, the Meiji constitution created new institutionally induced interests and new formal procedures for adopting public policies. A national parliament with veto power over taxes and other legislation existed for the first time. Elections were used for the first time to select members of a standing chamber of the national government. These created incentives and political property rights through which subsequent constitutional negotiations and exchange could take place. The elected chamber of the

Meiji parliament initially represented major landowners for the most part. As a consequence, majorities in the elected chamber favored tax reform that would shift more of the tax burden to excise taxes; they also favored income-tax reform. (Land taxes were still the main source of government revenues.) Majorities in the second chamber also supported constitutional reforms that would increase parliament's authority, such as making cabinets responsible to parliament.

LIBERALISM, PARTY GOVERNANCE, AND SUFFRAGE REFORM, 1890–1930

Japanese constitutional history was very different from that of Europe before 1890, but after 1890, Japanese governance followed a similar path of constitutional reform through 1925.

In anticipation of parliament's veto power over new taxes, several tax reforms were passed in the 1880s, including a new income tax. As standing taxes, they were free from parliament's veto after the constitution took effect (articles 62), and as predicted, they increased the revenue of the central government. Unfortunately for the emperor and his advisors, Japanese military and economic efforts to expand Japan's empire on the Asian mainland (in Korea and subsequently China) proved to be very expensive, as were government subsidies to promote industrialization. Deficits continued to grow during much of this period and both government loans and revisions to the tax code were subject to parliament's approval (article 62). As a consequence, the government (emperor's council) was constantly negotiating with parliament for loans and changes in the tax system.

Negotiations in parliament took place on a number of dimensions, and support for higher tax revenues in the parliament was obtained partly by using the emperor's power of appointment. Even before disciplined political parties emerged, leaders of liberal and conservative coalitions in parliament used budget negotiations with the emperor's council advance their policy and constitutional interests. For example, Itagaki, the leader of a large coalition in the elected chamber, was invited into the cabinet in 1896. Supporters of coalition leaders in parliament also obtained senior positions in the bureaucracy and within regional governments.

Thus, shortly after the constitution was implemented, important posts in government were beginning to be filled by parliamentary leaders and their supporters. New taxes were also occasionally linked to proposals for suffrage extension in this period, although none passed in the 1890s (Akita 1967, 119).

The Gradual Emergence of Party Governance

Although suffrage was not very broad, the advantages of being a member of influential coalitions in parliament and of party organization in campaigns for office gradually induced more disciplined political parties to form. In many cases, the new parties simply reorganized and merged older conservative and liberal coalitions. For example, in 1898 the two leading liberal coalitions, the Jyuto and Shimpoto, merged to form the Constitutional Party (Kenseito). This merger created a liberal majority in the elected chamber and led to the first party cabinet in Japanese history, although a short-lived one.

The existence of the liberal coalition led to the resignation of Prime Minister Ito Hirobumi and the invitation of Itagaki and Okuma, the leaders of Kenseito, to form the first party government in June 1898.

> There is now hardly any doubt that [your party, the Kenseito] easily controls a majority in the Diet and that the Diet, if it so wishes, is in a position to hinder the accomplishment of state affairs. It is consequently unquestionable that if you are given the responsibility of forming the next cabinet the conduct of state affairs will not be hindered by the diet …
>
> … I do not have the help of the lowliest member of a political party. And realizing that this makes it impossible to control a majority in the House, I handed in my resignation yesterday. (Remarks of Ito at a meeting with Okuma and Itagaki on June 25, 1898, quoted in Akita 1967, 135)

Unfortunately, Itagaki and Okuma could not agree on how to share the fruits of office, and a few months later, before the next meeting of the parliament, Japan's first party government resigned and was replaced with another cabinet organized by one of the emperor's senior military advisors, Yamagata Aritomo.[17]

Prime Minister Yamagata held office for two years, passing significant reforms, some of which were intended to reduce the influence of future parliamentary majorities. For example, civil service reform was adopted in 1899, which reduced the politicization of the rapidly expanding bureaucracy (below the senior ranks appointed by the emperor) by requiring examinations and creating explicit qualifications for bureaucratic office. He also passed ordinances in 1900 that required ministers for the army to be

[17] Yamagata was one of Japan's most influential constitutional conservatives in this period. Yamagata Aritomo served as commander of the general staff in the 1870s and 1880s. Even earlier, he had been a staff officer in the military campaigns against the Tokugawa regime. After his term as prime minister, he held a variety of senior posts, including president of the emperor's privy council from 1909–22. (Yamagata died in 1922.)

selected from generals and lieutenant generals, and navy ministers from admirals and vice admirals, thus insulating the military from parliamentary control.

During Yamagata's term of office, former Prime Minister Ito attempted to form his own political party with its own electoral base of support. He believed that support in the directly elected chamber would be critical to legislative success and constitutional governance. He began forming a new party, the Rikken Seiyukai (Constitutional Political Friends Association), and managed to attract many former Kenseito members, after the Okuma and Itagaki cabinet failed. Ito was known to be a well-placed, effective, relatively liberal leader. He had been the prime minister three times in the past and had long been an influential member of the emperor's inner circle of advisors. The Kenseito party dissolved, and most of its members joined Ito's new party.

Ito's party won a majority in the elected chamber in 1900 (one hundred fifty-six seats of three hundred), Yamagata resigned in October, and Ito was invited to organize a new cabinet. Ito's cabinet is often regarded as the first party government.[18] (The Itagaki-Okuma cabinet had disintegrated before the parliament returned to session in 1898.) Ito's party-based government, however, was also short lived. It lasted only seven months. His new, moderate liberal party, however, played a major role in Japanese politics for the next four decades (Uyehara 1910, 243–6; Akita 1967, 138–58; *HiCoJ* 1987, 29–30; Scalapino 1968, 283–4).

Ito's acceptance of the necessity of party government was not shared by many others in the emperor's inner circle, and cabinet appointments alternated between party-based and nonparty cabinets for the next twenty-five years. The prime ministers of both party and nonparty-based governments were chosen from nobles who had served on the emperor's ministerial and advisory councils.

This pattern was broken in 1918 when Hara Takashi, a commoner who had become the leader of Ito's party, was asked to form a government. Unlike previous prime ministers, he had never been part of the inner circle of the emperor's ministers and advisors. Prime Minister Hara's entire cabinet, except for the military posts, was staffed by party members. (Hara's term of office was ended by his assassination in 1921.)

[18] Ito was among the most influential constitutional liberals of the Meiji period. Ito served in senior posts in later governments until he was assassinated in 1909 by a Korean nationalist who objected to Japanese efforts to rule Korea. Ito's 1900–1 term was his fourth term as prime minister, but it was the only one in which he formed a party cabinet (Akita 1967, 130–4, 152–4; *HiCoJ* 1987, 29). (See also: *HoCiJ* 1987, 30; Scalapino 1968, 264–71).

Another significant development occurred in 1924, when Kato Takaaki was appointed prime minister. Kato's term was followed by a series of party-based governments that alternated between the two major parties, the Seiyukai and Minseito, which routinely assembled majority coalitions in parliament during this period. During this period, party government can be said to have existed in Japan.

As in much of Europe, the necessity of parliamentary majorities to pass tax bills, as well as various palace intrigues, had gradually produced party governance without a formal constitutional reform (Uyehara 1910, 215–37, 244–6; Akita 1967, chapter 6; Scalapino 1968, 264–71; *HoCiJ* 1987, 32–6).

Gradual Emergence of Universal Male Suffrage

Members of the liberal and moderate parties often pressed for suffrage reform at the same time that they pressed for positions in the cabinet, bureaucracy, and regional governments. Proposals for suffrage reform were passed by majorities in the elected chambers of 1895 and 1899 that would have approximately quadrupled the electorate by lowering the tax threshold to five yen. However, both bills were vetoed by the noble chamber, in part because they were opposed by the Emperor's council (Uyehara 1910, 174–8; Akita 1967, 144–50).[19]

Support for suffrage reform was sufficiently broad that organized prosuffrage groups were formed inside and outside of government. Pressure from proreform groups outside government tended to rise as press and association laws were relaxed and fall as they were tightened. For example, after censorship was reduced in 1898 with the repeal of the Peace Preservation Law, a new suffrage reform organization was founded by urban business leaders in 1899 (the Shugiin Senkyoho Kaisei Kisei Domeikai). Several new political parties formed at about the same time, and many of them supported suffrage reform.[20]

In early 1900, parliamentary bargaining produced a complex constitutional exchange that involved suffrage expansion, a change in electoral procedures, and changes in the tax system. Suffrage was approximately

[19] Suffrage reform was mentioned in the very first meeting of the parliament in 1890. This does not necessarily imply that liberals elected to parliament lacked institutionally induced interests in the status quo, but it does suggest that their base of support was more liberal than that of the nobles in the emperor's inner circle.

[20] Most suffrage-reform groups were liberal ones in the sense used in this book, although other more radical groups also supported suffrage extension. As in Europe, most leaders of the labor and social-democratic movements can be regarded as left liberals, rather than Marxists or communists.

doubled by reducing the tax threshold from fifteen to ten yen. A secret ballot was introduced. As a compromise with conservatives, single-member districts were replaced with multiple-member districts (generally with three to five members) elected under a single nontransferable vote. Tax reforms also increased the relative importance of income and excise taxes, especially beer and sake, although land taxes remained the largest source of state revenues. The royal council supported multiple-member electoral districts to increase the number of parties, which would tend to make coalitions more fragile and increase their ability to engineer majorities in the second chamber (Uyehara 1910, 219–29; Mitani 1988, 71; Minami 1994, 258; Wada 1996, 6).

The new election laws caused older political parties to be reorganized, such as Ito's moderate party (Seiyukai), and new parties to be organized. A new Social Democratic Party was founded in 1901, and new conservative parties in 1906 and 1913. Although the socialist parties were subsequently banned, the social democrats re-formed as the Commoner's Party in 1906, which consistently advocated universal suffrage.

In 1919, during Prime Minister Hara's period of office, the electorate was doubled again by reducing the tax-vote threshold from ten to five yen, as had been proposed in the 1890s, but previously blocked in the noble chamber (Uyehara 1910, 174–8; Mitani 1988). Hara's suffrage reforms were heavily criticized by proponents of universal suffrage, but bills introduced by others to obtain universal male suffrage had failed to obtain majority support.

During the next few years, petitions were submitted to the emperor's advisory committee, and thousands of newspaper articles were written in support of universal suffrage (Quigley 1932, 250–55). Finally, during the Kato administration in 1925, the tax-based threshold for suffrage was eliminated, which created essentially universal male suffrage. All Japanese male citizens of age twenty-five or older were entitled to vote, provided that they were not on poverty relief or bankrupt and had not been convicted of a major crime (Lu 1997, 395; *Britannica* 1911, 144; Duun 1976, 170; Wada 1996, 7; Mason and Caiger 1997, 320, 331).[21]

At this point, parliamentary democracy can be said to have emerged in Japan. Elections for the second chamber were based on universal male suffrage, and party cabinets were routinely appointed during the next several election cycles.

[21] As noted in the previous chapters, such restrictions were also common in other universal suffrage laws of that period. A proposal was entertained to include suffrage for women who were heads of households but was not accepted. Women's suffrage movements were subsequently organized in the late 1920s, and bills extending suffrage to women passed

The Tide of Japanese Liberalism Retreats

The course of liberalization in late-nineteenth- and early-twentieth-century Japan was sufficiently well known that liberals from more conservative states in Eastern Asia, such as China and Korea, often sought refuge in Japan during repressive periods at home. Moreover, when East Asian countries became interested in Western theories and education, they normally sent their children to Japanese schools, rather than to Europe, where entirely new character sets would have to be mastered. For example, that China sent thousands of students abroad for education in the 1920s and most went to Japan.

Nonetheless, in contrast to most European transitions, the relatively liberal Japanese system of governance failed to sustain sufficient political support for competitive national elections and party governments.

In contrast to the German case, however, the de-liberalization of Japanese politics was a consequence of electoral competition, rather than constitutional coup, as conservatives won the policy debates inside and outside government. Emperor Meiji died in 1912 and was succeeded by Emperor Taisho who reigned until 1926, although he was in poor health for much of this time. Emperor Taisho was succeeded by Emperor Showa (Hirohito), who presided over Japan's militaristic period through World War II.[22]

Although liberal reforms did not end with Emperor Taisho's death, the liberal tide began to weaken at that point, as royal authority passed to a more ambitious and healthier men. The conservative resurgence was also associated with new ideological trends and a good deal of domestic violence. Social Darwinism, nationalism, and military success on the continent had caused ancient military values and conservative theories of governance to return to prominence. The two major parties, which had begun as moderate-liberal alliances gradually became more conservative. By the 1930s, both were led by senior military men.

Conservatives in parliament supported the divine right of kings (the divinity of the emperor), closure to the West, and the ancient warrior

in the elective chamber in 1930 and 1931, but they were vetoed by the noble chamber (Quigley 1932, 250–55). Suffrage was finally extended to women after World War II.

[22] Emperors in Japan have two names, a personal one under which they live and rule, and another honorary name created at the time of their death. The honorary name is used in the text, as customary, and is also normally used to describe the period of the emperor's term of office. Meiji's predeath name was Mutsuhito, and Taisho's predeath name was Yoshihito. Taisho's successor, Hirohito, is an exception for modern historians because of his long life and his regime's influence on world history during that period. Hirohito took office in 1926 and died in 1989, at which point he formally became Emperor Showa and his period of rule became the Showa era.

values – although few pushed for the end of industrialization. Censorship increased and tolerance for political debate diminished. Both liberal and socialist ideas were censored in parliament and increasingly restricted by law. Consider, for example, the censor of Tatsukichi Minobe, a member of the noble chamber who was a constitutional scholar at the Imperial University of Tokyo and a leading advocate of somewhat liberal interpretations of the Meiji constitution. His interpretations were severely criticized by conservatives.

A non-Japanese, **Blasphemous, European-worshipping ideology** which ignores our three thousand year old tradition and ideals is rife. **This liberalism which threatens to turn us into Western barbarians** is basic to Minobe's beliefs. (Attributed to one of the military reservist associations, Totman 2000, 368)

Professor Minobe's work was censored after 1935 and his courses at three universities suspended, in part for stating that Japanese soldiers fought and died for *their country*, rather than *for their emperor*. This was regarded within conservative circles as very disrespectful of the emperor.

The electoral reforms of 1925 were not undone, nor was parliament entirely ignored, but the mainstream of Japanese politics abandoned liberal economic and political ideas, and political authority shifted back to the emperor's cabinet and his military leaders. Conservative ideological trends were reinforced by the electorate's reaction to civil disorders and assassinations, including those of Prime Ministers Hara, Hamaguchi, and Inukai in 1921, 1931, and 1932. Broad popular support for Japan's military campaigns energized even more extreme military groups, who were responsible for many assassinations and assassination attempts, and who repeatedly sought to overthrow the Meiji constitution.

The conservative tide and the assassinations of prominent moderates affected the leadership and electoral campaigns of the two leading political parties (Totman 2000, 362–73; Power 1942).[23] After 1932, all the prime ministers were active military men. The last competitive national election was held in 1937. A few years later, in 1940, the two major parties and several minor parties merged to form a single progovernment party, the Imperial Rule Assistance Association.

[23] The number of major liberal and moderate leaders who were assassinated over the years is striking: for example, Okubo in 1878, Hoshi in 1901, Ito in 1909, Hara in 1921, Hamaguchi in 1931, and Inukai in 1932. There were also attempted assassinations of Itagaki in 1882 and Okuma in 1889. Itagaki is reported to have said "Itagaki may die, but liberty forever!" as he fell after his attack, words that made him famous among liberals for years to come (*HiCoJ* 1987, 56–69; Uyehara 1910, 95).

In this manner, electoral pressures, domestic violence, and political bargaining gradually ended parliamentary democracy in Japan. Although still formally grounded in the Meiji constitution, the government had become an illiberal one-party regime devoted to military values, activities, and objectives (Mason and Caiger 1997, 330–2; Scalapino 1968, 280–2; *HiCoJ* 1987, 35–8).

After World War II, it is sometimes said that the American General MacArthur imposed a new democratic constitution on Japan. It would be more accurate to say that MacArthur supported Japanese liberals in their efforts to reform the Meiji constitution. The preface was rewritten to ground the postwar constitution on popular sovereignty, rather than the divine right of kings. A new article 7 made the cabinet responsible to the parliament and eliminated the emperor's discretion to undertake a broad range of policies on his own account, as had been allowed by articles 7–16 of the Meiji constitution. Civil liberties were strengthened, women's suffrage was introduced, equality before the law was guaranteed, war was renounced, and academic freedom guaranteed. New elections were held, and the reforms were ratified by the new parliament of 1946, using the amendment procedures of the Meiji constitution (Lu 1997, chapter 15, Dean 2002, 193–4).[24]

CONCLUSIONS: IDEAS, INTERESTS, AND REFORMS

Over the course of seventy years, Japan's medieval order was gradually replaced by a new constitutional framework with more open markets, more parliamentary authority, broader suffrage and electoral competition, and greater equality before the law. The details of specific reforms, as in the European cases, reflected liberal theories of the state as well as the unique bargaining skills and tactics of those directly involved in negotiations and their supporters.

Japanese constitutional history is largely consistent with the models developed in Part I of the book. Constitutional reforms in both the shogunate and Meiji periods were normally multidimensional. Although there were two major series of reforms, most reforms were relatively moderate in scope. External shocks such as new technologies and ideas created new opportunities for constitutional reforms. Older institutions were rarely shed, but rather were gradually transformed into newer ones. In the late nineteenth century and early twentieth century, there were liberal trends

[24] Only six former members of parliament were reelected under the new constitution (Lu 1997, 481).

in the constitutional reforms adopted, which reflected the penetration of liberal ideas and support for industrialization. Parliament's power of the purse played a central role in the constitutional bargains worked out. As predicted, the liberal reforms were multidimensional and fine-grained and reflected mutual advantage and institutional conservatism.

As the ideological and economic interests represented in parliament and the royal council shifted away from liberal ones (partly as a consequence of assassinations), reforms shifted in illiberal directions, as also predicted by the theory. The bargaining equilibria shifted toward rule by the emperor's council in large part because it was supported by electoral outcomes, rather than imposed by a quasi-constitutional coup d'état. The Meiji constitution remained in force and elections continued to be held during the period in which policy-making authority shifted back to the emperor and his military leaders.

Revolutionary-threat theories of constitutional reform, such as those elaborated by Acemoglu and Robinson (2000), can account for relatively little of the emergence of parliamentary democracy or industrialization in Japan. Indeed revolutionary-threat theories seem to predict the opposite of what happened. In the 1870s and 1930s, the most credible threats of revolution were organized by arch-conservatives who wished to preserve or return to the old samurai ways, rather than by democrats. The conservative revolt of the 1870s (the Satsuma Rebellion) did not cause the trajectory of reform to shift in a conservative direction. Instead, the defeat of the samurai encouraged further liberalization. Although assassinations by conservative groups in the 1920s and 1930s helped push the center of gravity in Japanese politics to the right, they did not end popular suffrage or cause major changes in constitutional procedures, although civil liberties were curtailed.

Relevance of Ideas in Constitutional Debates

The manner in which European political theories affected Japan's policy debates and constitutional history sheds light on how ideological shifts occur and why such shifts tend to affect the course of constitutional development.

Although many politically active persons and scholars were influenced by texts and constitutional documents written by European authors, the Japanese did not simply copy European arguments and institutions. Rather, various Japanese persons used a subset of European ideas and technologies to advance their own purposes. Many of the objectives were similar to those of Europeans in the late nineteenth century: many in Japan wanted greater access to political and economic opportunities, many favored equality before the law, many were concerned about Japan's national security, and most sought more materially comfortable lives.

Ideas are portable, but new ideas tend to be used by persons who are already sympathetic to the conclusions reached or who are looking for explanations of events and solutions to problems that older ideas cannot provide. Liberal theories from Europe took hold in Japan for much the same reason that they took hold in Europe: They shed new light on problems of interest to Japanese businessmen, voters, and policy makers. It bears noting that other theories from the West did not make large inroads into Japanese culture during the nineteenth century. For example, there were no wholesale conversions to Christianity.[25]

Liberal theories, in turn, lost ground to new conservative theories and older nationalistic ones that were better aligned with military objectives on the Asian mainland, and with the steps that appeared necessary to preserve peace at home in the 1930s. Liberalism could not explain or solve the great macroeconomic problems of that period and it also failed to explain or cope with the domestic violence associated with the new antiliberal theories of the far left and right. Moreover, liberalism's emphasis on rationality, civic equality, open markets, and universal rights did not provide much intellectual or moral support for empire, military campaigns, and national superiority – ideas that captured the imagination of a broad cross-section of the Japanese in the first half of the twentieth century. Social Darwinism, military mysticism, stoicism, and a subset of traditional values provided better support for such perspectives and policies.

After World War II was over, the conservative theories lost favor and liberal ideas regained support. This reflected losses during the war and broad interest in rebuilding and catching up with the West (again).

Moreover, it was not very difficult to reverse the conservative policies of the past decade or two, because the liberalization of Japan's economy and constitution during the late nineteenth and early twentieth centuries provided useful points of departure. Indeed, it could be said that parliamentary

[25] It is interesting to note that Christianity had made significant inroads in several of the southern duchies during the sixteenth century. Many thousands of Japanese, including a few of the daimyos on the losing side of Japan's civil war, had converted to Catholicism. Christian churches were demolished in the early shogunate period, although thousands continued to secretly practice their Kirishitan faith until the reforms of the late nineteenth century allowed open forms of Christian worship (Lu 1997, 173–4, 197–201; Higashibaba 2001, chapter 6).

democracy was restored and improved after the war, rather than established. The present constitution has Meiji roots and is similar to the most liberal of the constitutional proposals made by senior government officials in the 1880s. The postwar constitution includes the same chapter titles and many articles from the original Meiji text. The contemporary Japanese state remains a constitutional monarchy with a bicameral parliament, although with a senate (House of Councillors), rather than a noble chamber.[26]

[26] See Dean (2002, chapter 4) for an overview of contemporary constitutional law and constitutionalism in Japan.

EIGHTEEN

The United States, an Exception or Further Illustration?

INTRODUCTION: AMERICAN EXCEPTIONS AND SIMILARITIES

The last case to be analyzed is the American transition to constitutional democracy. As in the case of Japan, this case also involves another continent's culture. It also involves a somewhat different catalyst for constitutional exchange, the absence of an obvious king, a war of independence, and differences in the timing and details of individual reforms. The emergence of liberal democracy in the United States of America is nonetheless consistent with the models of constitutional reform developed in Part I.

The transition to parliamentary democracy in the territories that became the United States began very early, but took an unusually long time to be completed. The first more or less democratic constitution in North America was the third charter for the Virginia colony, which was drafted in London and implemented in Virginia between 1619 and 1622. It called for a bicameral legislature, with one appointed chamber (the chamber of state) and another directly elected chamber (the chamber of burgesses). Initially, the first chamber was composed largely of English nobles who had made the trip to Virginia to look after their investments in the Virginia Company. Members of the second chamber were elected by the freemen (property owners) of the colony. The second chamber is of particular interest for the purposes of this book and for constitutional history, because elections for that chamber were based on unusually broad suffrage by the standards of world history. European suffrage would not reach similar levels for two more centuries. The transition to adult suffrage, however, took two or three times longer in the United States than in the other case studies. The colonies that became the United States all had relatively broad male suffrage by 1700, but the United States did not adopt women's suffrage until 1920, about the same time as this was done in Europe's parliamentary democracies.

The early start and long transition suggest that the path to democracy in the United States may have been quite different than in Europe, but this is less true than might have been expected. As in Europe, the power of the purse played an important role in the emergence of parliamentary authority. As in Europe, changes in the normative theories and economic interests of political elites (those with the authority to adopt constitutional changes) were also important determinants of constitutional developments. The path of reform in the United States was also largely peaceful, gradual, and lawful. A series of constitutional negotiations and reforms gradually produced relatively liberal forms of state and national governance over the course of a century and a half and adult suffrage another century and a half later. The War of Independence and Civil War had a smaller effect on the institutions of governance than often told to grammar school students, although both affected constitutional developments, as discussed later in the chapter.

It seems clear that exit options and best practices had important effects on town, county, colonial, and state governance. And, it can be argued that the exit options of other governments allowed the United States to emerge as a nation-state.

LABOR SCARCITY, CONSTITUTIONAL INNOVATION, AND COMPETITION IN THE COLONIAL PERIOD

Colonization of North America began nearly a century later than in South America, in large part because land, rather than gold, was the main source of profits for investors in the North American colonies. Land, unlike gold, is not portable. Land does not automatically produce income or wealth. It is not valuable, unless it is improved in some way. Farming requires clearing and tilling. Mining requires exploration, digging, and smelting. Forest products require lumberjacks, saws, and sawmills. To profit from land holdings requires labor and capital in addition to land. Consequently, those who received large land grants or purchased large tracts of land in North America had strong demands for labor and capital. Without those additional inputs, their large land holdings were essentially without economic value.

Formally, the English land grants were provided through charters of one kind or another from the English kings and queens, who had their own reasons for sponsoring development in the colonies. They were always interested in new tax revenues beyond the control of parliament and also interested in geopolitical power games. Wertenbaker (1914, 32), for example, suggests that colonial enterprises were undertaken largely to escape from fiscal constraints.

> The King [James I], who was always restive under the restraint placed upon him by the English Parliament had **no desire to see the liberal institutions** of the mother country transplanted ... **He wished, beyond doubt, to build a colonial empire which should be dependent upon himself for its government and which should add to the royal revenues.** In this way he would augment the power of the Sovereign and render **it less subject to the restraint of parliament**.

Investors in crown companies were also largely motivated by economic interests, although a few also had ideological or religious reasons to invest in the new international enterprises.

Credible Commitments and Other Contracting Problems

There were two unusual organizational problems faced by formeteurs in the North American colonies. First, there were a series of dictators dilemmas, because the persons and organizations that owned the colonies were in effect the rulers of those colonies. Colonial rulers were in principle constrained by English law, but local rulers also controlled the local dispute resolution (legal) proceedings. It was a long way back to England, so exit options were poor, which gave the local companies a great bargaining advantage over their employees. This weakened incentives to work hard in and emigrate to the colonies, because payments could be minimal and contract commitments arbitrarily revoked after arrival.

Second, and partly caused by the first, land was extraordinarily plentiful and labor was extraordinarily scarce in the colonies. In Europe, land was normally the constraining resource constraint, which is part of the reason that territorial wars in Europe were commonplace. Once new territory was possessed, the labor necessary for maintenance and improvement of that land would arrive almost automatically. In the colonies, labor was the constraining factor and had to be attracted from elsewhere.

Solutions to these problems were largely institutional. For example, property in the early commercial colonies such as Virginia was much like that within modern corporations. A firm's property is owned by its investors, and its employees normally have various use rights over that property. Office workers do not usually own "their" offices, but have stable use rights over them, including the right to exclude other employees from their office. In the colonial setting, employee surplus could be taxed away by the owners in various ways, so there was little incentive to work hard, save, or to emigrate to the colonies.

Selling control of a subset of the company's resources could address some of these incentive problems in much the same manner that the fiscal constitution analyzed in Chapter Six addressed the dictator's fiscal problem. Farm owners have more secure claims to their surplus production than farm renters and employees, insofar as terms can be renegotiated by landlords when the crops are harvested. Ownership of land, itself, was also valuable for many potential emigrants, who could only dream of owning their own piece of land in Europe. As it became clear that selling land was more profitable than managing or leasing it, land sales and land ownership became commonplace in the colonies.

This possibility of purchasing land encouraged middle class investors to participate in colonial enterprises and, once purchased, encouraged owners to work hard to improve their property; however, not all potential emigrants could afford to buy their own piece of the new world.

The most common method of attracting skilled and unskilled labor to the colony was with loans made to workers to pay for their journey and land in the colonies. Shipping agents and other entrepreneurs provided transportation to the colonies in exchange for promises of several years of labor, and those promises (contracts) were sold by shipping companies to landowners needing labor. These indentured-servant contracts also normally promised workers a substantial piece of farmland after their transport loan had been worked off. This gave the servants an interest in adhering to the contract and allowed them to become freemen after five to ten years of hard work for their colonial masters. About half of the European emigrants to the colonies in the seventeenth and eighteenth centuries had their trips financed through such indentured-servant contracts (Galenson 1986).

In some cases, however, promises were made and then new obligations required after the servants arrived in America, especially in the early days. In other cases, new laws were adopted that implicitly changed the terms of the contracts by adding new obligations or constraints. Such problems can be thought of as dictatorship or commitment problems, although not all of them involved governments or contracts per se. The rule makers in the colonies had significant autonomy in the early days and could rewrite rules and contracts and enact new regulations at their pleasure, as owners of firms are often able to do within their own organizations when exit costs are high.

> The Divine, Moral and Martial Laws, as they were called, undoubtedly brought about good order in the colony, and aided in the establishment of prosperity, but they were ill suited for the government of free-born Englishmen. **They were in open violation of the rights guaranteed to the settlers in their charters, and caused bitter discontent and resentment**. ("Regarding Governance in Virginia in 1610," Wertenbaker 1914, 23)

Once in America, indentured servants could not afford to purchase a ticket back to Europe to sue for damages if their master overstepped the bounds of the contract, reneged on his promise of fertile land at the end of the contract period, or added new conditions to the terms of contract. Exit costs to other colonies were falling through time, but not trivial in the early days, and in most places natural exit costs were reinforced by local laws. Moreover, as transportation networks among the colonies emerged and exit costs fell, masters would have difficulty with runaways, whether they overstepped the bounds of the contract or not.

Even without commitment problems, indentured labor "contracts" were risky both for the indentured servant and the contract holder. In the early days, many servants and other immigrants died from various diseases before paying off their debts. For example, in the first two decades of the Virginia colony, there were many years in which new immigrants simply replaced previous arrivals that had died from disease and conflicts with "Indians." Between 1619 and 1624, some five thousand persons immigrated to Virginia, but the net gain in populations was only two hundred (Wertenbaker 1914, 12–16, 46–7).

Similar problems faced communities and plantations that attempted to attract tradesmen who brought skills or capital to the new colonies in exchange for promises of land or other support.

People would be more willing to emigrate if contract terms were reasonable and enforced, and if subsequent promises and accumulated wealth were not broken or expropriated. And, of course, more people would provide labor-backed loans if they were likely to be repaid. To attract labor and capital to their colonies, landowners needed to assure labor, small businessmen, and other investors that they would be better off in their particular colony than at home.

In early-seventeenth-century America, this required establishing a reliable, credible method of enforcing land titles and contracts and for assuring that new laws would not be adopted that would undermine those titles and contracts. In principle, such contracting and governance problems can be solved through self-enforcing contracts, a well-functioning court system, or a combination of the two. However, in the early days, court systems did not always exist, and those that did exist tended to be biased in favor of major shareholders and/or associates of the proprietors receiving major land grants. Designing self-enforcing contracts in circumstances in which time is an important element and courts are nonexistent or unreliable is clearly problematic. Indeed, the worst indentured contracts were such that they probably would not have been enforced in England, and the worst indentured contract owners (masters) might well have been punished for violating criminal law in English courts.

Large landholders had a significant economic interest in developing methods for securing property rights and enforcing contracts in the colonies. If economic and political risks could be reduced for skilled and unskilled labor and for large and small capital investors, their land would become much more valuable. As in the case of the medieval tax constitution, a system of governance that protected the landed gentry, capital owners, and labor from arbitrary treatment would advance the long-run interests of all.

Virginia's Constitutional Solution: Representative Political Institutions as a Means of Protecting Property Rights and Increasing Cooperation

The Virginia colony's first governing body was characterized by the first charter of Virginia that was granted by James I in 1606. The first charter provided a land grant in North America to the Virginia Company in exchange for promised future payments to the king. Access to that land was to be determined by a council consisting of major investors in the Virginia Company, many of whom were nobles who naturally remained in England.

> And do therefore, for Us [James I], our Heirs, and Successors, GRANT and agree, that the said **Sir Thomas Gates, Sir George Somers, Richard Hackluit, and Edward-Maria Wingfield**, Adventurers of and for our City of London, and all such others, as are, or shall be, joined unto them of that Colony, shall be called **the first Colony**; And they shall and may begin their said first Plantation and Habitation, at any Place upon the said-Coast of Virginia or America, where they shall think fit and convenient, … And that **no other of our Subjects shall be permitted, or suffered, to plant or inhabit behind, or on the Backside of them, towards the main Land, without the Express License or Consent of the Council of that Colony**, thereunto in Writing; first had and obtained.

A second charter of the Virginia Company was granted in 1609, two years after the colony was founded. The second charter granted very extensive legislative authority to the company by the king for a period of twenty years, in exchange for promised payments to the sovereign. The company's ruling council, in turn, delegated much of its authority to an appointed governor who arrived in Virginia in 1610.

A third charter was obtained in 1611, which gave the company additional legislative ability:

> [The company] shall likewise have **full Power and Authority, to ordain and make such Laws and Ordinances, for the Good and Welfare of the said Plantation**

[colony], as to them from Time to Time, shall be thought requisite and meet: So always, as the same be not contrary to the Laws and Statutes of this our Realm of England; And shall, in like Manner, **have Power and Authority, to expel, disfranchise, and put out of and from their said Company and Society for ever**, all and every such Person and Persons.

Because the efforts of the company's appointed governor were not entirely successful, the company decided to revise its method of governing the colonies.[1]

King James had granted the Virginia Company the authority to create institutions of governance in their colony in the company's second and third charters, partly in exchange for a promise of additional revenues from the colony, although he evidently disapproved of the form finally chosen in 1619. In the years 1619–21, the Virginia Company replaced its system of governance in the colonies with a more representative one by adopting a system of governance based loosely on the English procedures. The new system of governance included a governor, an appointed chamber, and an elected chamber (the General Assembly).[2]

THE one of which Councils, to be called THE COUNCIL OF STATE (and whose Office shall chiefly be assisting, with their Care, Advice, and Circumspection, to the said Governor) shall be chosen, nominated, placed and displaced, from time to time, by Us.

[The other shall consist] of **two Burgesses out of every Town, Hundred, or other particular Plantation, to be respectively chosen by the Inhabitants**: Which Council shall be called THE GENERAL ASSEMBLY, wherein (as also in the said Council of State) **all Matters shall be decided, determined, and ordered, by the greater Part of the Voices then present**; reserving to the Governor always a Negative Voice. And this General Assembly shall have free Power to treat, consult, and conclude, as well of all emergent Occasions concerning **the Public Weal** of the said Colony and every Part thereof, as also to make, ordain, and **enact such general Laws and Orders, for the Behoof of the said Colony, and the good Government** thereof. (*Ordinances for Virginia*, July 24, 1621)

This template for governance solved many of the existing contracting and governance problems.

The Virginia model provided the sovereign company with considerable control over the office of governor and the membership of the first chamber, which consequently represented the interest of well-connected major landholders and merchants. The second chamber was elected by town

[1] See Salmon and Campbell (1994, chapter 1) and Wertenbaker (1914, chapter 2) for an overview of Virginia's first authoritarian and king-and-council-based governments.

[2] Copies of Virginia's three charters and the company's 1621 Ordinances for Virginia are available from Yale's Avalon Project (http://avalon.law.yale.edu/subject_menus/statech.asp).

and country property holders and therefore represented the interests of the middle class. Together, the veto power of the two chambers protected the middle class and economic elites from each other and provided similar protections for the proprietors. Changes in basic contract law, property rights, and other civil liberties could be adopted only if they advanced the interests (of majorities) of all three groups. The council and subsequently the assembly also served as Virginia's highest court of appeal (Wertenbaker 1914, 2, 8–10, 34–7, 40, 54–5).

The Virginia model thus provided fiscal and regulatory stability that was somewhat stronger than that noted by North and Weingast (1989) regarding England's parliament seventy years later (1689).[3] And, it is interesting to note that Virginia's 1621 constitution was written well before Hobbes, Locke, or Montesquieu put their pens to paper, and nearly two decades before the Levellers' contract.[4]

It was the success of this institutional template together with the mobility of labor and the interests of large landowners that induced the emergence of relatively liberal forms of representative government in the North American colonies during the next century and a half.

Gradual Liberalization of Colonial Governments

Although the Virginia template gradually became the standard one for governance in the colonies, the other colonies also began with nondemocratic forms of government: often a governor and unelected council of advisors. Initial variation in colonial governance was partly caused by cultural, economic, and religious differences. For example, Plymouth was a religious colony founded by Puritans, New York was a commercial trading post founded by Dutch merchants, and Maryland was a proprietorship (a colony initially purchased by a single person) that encouraged Catholic immigration. The Plymouth (1620), New Amsterdam (1624), and Maryland (1632)

3 The ordinances for Virginia adopted in 1921 describe the new bicameral representative government for the colony itself. See Wertenbaker (1914, chapters 2–4) for a detailed overview of how lawful governance gradually emerged under that new colonial constitution.

4 The Virginia template for governance is often attributed to Sir Edwin Sandys, who had served as a member of England's House of Commons for many years and as the treasurer of the Virginia Company of London shortly before Virginia's ordinances for the new government were issued. Sandys had previously been involved in contesting royal grants of monopoly (mentioned in Chapter Twelve) and debates on religious tolerance. He also had relations with the Leiden Puritans, many of whom migrated to Plymouth from the Netherlands in 1620 via the Mayflower. See Rabb (1998) for a biography of Sir Edwin and his roles in parliament and the Virginia Company.

colonies all began with unelected governments. This was also the case in West New Jersey, which was founded in 1664, and in North and South Carolina (initially a single colony) founded in 1664. Charter reforms were normally formally ratified in England in legal procedures initiated by colonial governors.[5]

Within a few decades of their colonies' foundings, the various colonial formeteurs and their successors found it useful to add elected chambers with veto power over taxes and laws in response to labor mobility and yardstick competition among the colonies. For example, in 1636 the Plymouth colony adopted a cabinet form of government with a governor and seven-person council of assistants elected by freemen. This was modified by adding provisions for equal protection of the law in 1641 and a bicameral legislature in 1644 (Massachusetts). Maryland adopted an elected assembly in 1638, equality before the law in 1638, and religious tolerance for all Christians in 1649. West New Jersey adopted a democratic bicameral government in 1681. Its elected chamber was called the General Free Assembly. New Amsterdam was taken from the Dutch by England and renamed New York, but its religious liberties were continued and a new, relatively weak representative assembly was adopted in 1683. (Similar assemblies had been proposed during the Dutch period, but not adopted.) Connecticut secured a charter that provided for an elected governor and bicameral legislature in 1698. By 1700, a good deal of the architecture for democratic governance had already been worked out and broadly adopted in the colonies.

The influence of early liberal political theories is evident in most of the charters. Consider, for example, these excerpts from the West New Jersey Charter of 1681, adopted a decade before Locke finished his influential treatise on government and several years before England's Glorious Revolution. The excerpts are from Lutz (1998):

> **We the Governor and Proprietors, freeholders and inhabitants of West New Jersey, by mutual consent and agreement**, for the prevention of invasion and oppression, either upon us or our posterity, and for the preservation of the peace and tranquility of the same; and that all may be encourage to go on cheerfully in their several places: We do make and constitute these our agreements to be as fundamentals to us and our posterity, to be held inviolable, and that no person or persons whatsoever, shall or may make void or disanul the same upon any presence whatsoever.

5 See Lutz (1998) for a collection of early colonial charters and codes. Many other colonial charters and ordinances are also available at Yale Law School's Avalon Project: www.yale.edu/lawweb/avalon/avalon.htm.

(i) There **shall be a free assembly of the people** for the Province aforesaid, **yearly** and every year at a day certain chosen by the said free people of said province, whereupon **all of the representatives of the free people of the said Province shall be summoned to appear** … to make and ordain such acts as shall be requisite for good government and prosperity of the free people of said province.
(ii) The Governor of said province **shall not suspend or delay** the signing, sealing and confirming of such laws as the General Assembly shall make.
(iii) That **it shall not be lawful for the Governor to make or enact any law or laws for said Province without the consent, act, and concurrence of the General Free Assembly**.
(iv) That it shall **not be lawful for the Governor and council, or any of them, to levy taxes without the consent, act, and concurrence of the General Free Assembly**.
(v) That **no General Free Assembly shall give to the Governor, his heirs, or successors any tax or custom for any time longer than one whole year**.

The West New Jersey charter of 1676 had previously provided for freedom of religion (chapter 16), for due process and jury trials (chapters 17–20), and public trials (chapter 23).

Although the North American colonies were often founded for profit and often run by chartered companies, they turned out to be great experimental laboratories of governance. Indeed, the freedom to conduct constitutional experiments could be counted as one of the great unexpected consequences of the discovery of the New World, perhaps the greatest in the long run.

Independence of the English Colonies

That the North American colonies remained independently organized and governed, rather than centrally administered under the tight control of England's kings was partly a matter of luck. Seventeenth-century England was a place of political turmoil, involving a major civil war, Cromwell's dictatorship, a restoration, and a Glorious Revolution, as discussed in Chapter Twelve. It was not until shortly before the Glorious Revolution that an English monarch, James II, began to centralize governance in the colonies.

James II initiated a series of lawsuits to revoke colonial charters for violations of English law. His success in court allowed him to create the Dominion of New England in 1685, which eventually placed all of New England, New York, and New Jersey under a single central, essentially authoritarian administration. James II appointed Governor Andros to rule the Dominion. Andros, as evidently ordered, restricted local assemblies and reduced judicial independence by appointing new judges and suspending the Massachusetts General Court. New taxes were imposed, and existing land claims were challenged. Enforcement of the Navigation Acts was stepped up. Writs against the charters of Maryland, the Carolinas, Pennsylvania, and the Bahamas were pending in English courts. If successful, those suits together with the Dominion would have greatly reduced political autonomy throughout the English colonies in North America (Taylor 2001, 276–7; Haffenden 1958; Osgood 1902).

This policy of centralization ended for several decades in 1689 when William III and the Dutch army induced James II to flee to France. William III reinstated the colonial charters (in some cases with minor revisions) and thereby restored decentralized governance in the colonies. It was not until George III that another English monarch made a serious attempt to centralize control over the colonies, which more or less directly led to the American War of Independence.

THE POWER OF THE PURSE, LABOR MOBILITY, AND CONSTITUTIONAL LIBERALIZATION IN THE COLONIAL PERIOD

Colonial governors and their governments were not as powerful in the North American colonies as in medieval Europe or as centralized as in the South American colonies. This was partly because the North American colonies were less profitable than colonies elsewhere and so were less directly supported by well-organized European armies, courts, and police. With little or no standing tax revenues and with little support from English taxpayers or sovereign companies, the royal colonial governors depended on taxes and fees approved by their legislatures for revenues and often for their salaries. Governors also needed reliable majorities in the colonial parliaments to secure the resources for governing, which made the governors dependent on their colonial legislatures (and also provided them with good reason to look for additional revenue from the British parliament). This made the colonial parliaments among the most powerful representative assemblies in the world at that time in terms of their control of legislation and taxation.[6]

[6] The governor of the Connecticut and Rhode Island colonies were (indirectly) elected by the colonists. Other governors held office through royal appointment, appointment by colonial companies, or proprietors.

The power of colonial government was also constrained by the desire to attract new residents (the demand for labor) and the exit options of those already in the colony. Migration to and among the colonies was constantly encouraged by the efforts of landowners and other formeteurs in Europe and in the colonies. In the North, religious leaders organized groups to found new settlements to promote narrow religious practices. Differences in the political and religious theories within colonies and towns, in turn, often induced subsets of the colonists to exit and form new communities. Connecticut and Rhode Island, for example, were founded by unhappy colonists from Massachusetts in the 1630s. Similar emigration and immigration occurred within and among other colonies, as new towns were founded and persons left old towns for new ones.

The motivation for exit was often poor and/or intolerant government policies and economic opportunities, rather than ideology. Insofar as more liberal governments tended to be more tolerant and less likely to impose unpopular taxes and policies, they tended to attract labor and capital, and so tended to produce more prosperous communities. This aligned the interests of landowners and land speculators with liberal political institutions in a manner that was not common in other places. Without relatively liberal political institutions, a colony's landed gentry might have a bit more political power and "their" people might exhibit greater cultural uniformity, but they would have been less wealthy because there would be fewer persons to farm, timber, mine, manage, purchase, and protect their land holdings.

Exit from poor or overly repressive colonies and communities also became increasingly easy in the seventeenth century. Colonial transport networks developed along rivers and bays, new towns were formed along those waterways, and the natives were gradually pushed out of the territory near the Atlantic seacoast. Many of the colonies were physically close together, because they were relatively small – as in the North with Massachusetts, Rhode Island, and Connecticut – and/or were linked together by common waterways – as with Maryland, Virginia, and Pennsylvania or New Jersey, Connecticut, and New York. Ships ran up and down the coast of North America, and the same rivers that allowed commerce to develop inland also allowed pioneers to move from town to town.

This is not to say that colonial governance was always routine, lawful, or liberal, but it is to say that competition for residents tended to make it so. Governments were often grounded on written documents, included representative assemblies, and relied upon relatively broad suffrage to select members of those assemblies.

Colonial suffrage was very broad by world standards in the late seventeenth century, although various restrictions on suffrage existed in most colonies during the seventeenth and eighteenth centuries (McKinley 1905; Brown 1955; Steinfeld 1989).[7] In the southern colonies, which depended relatively more on slaves, wealth requirements for suffrage and office, remained somewhat higher than in the north.

The success of the relatively liberal polities was evident in the emigration rates, land sales, use of new labor contracts, and economic growth. The south, although less liberal than the north, also had political and legal institutions that were liberal by historical standards. Population and economic development increased rapidly during the seventeenth century, and by century's end, the larger colonies were comparable in size to the smaller European states and duchies in 1700. Major commercial centers emerged along the eastern seaboard at Boston, New York, Philadelphia, and Charleston.[8]

These colonial governments demonstrated that representative governance based on broad suffrage was a feasible arrangement for territorial governance. The policies chosen under their institutions did not yield wholesale redistribution from rich to poor or to the middle class. Instead, it produced rule of law and relatively open trade, which contemporary research shows tend to increase economic growth. Wage rates in the colonies remained higher than those in Europe.[9]

7 The possibility of exit must also have moderated the behavior of other colonial governments around the world with respect to their immigrants as well. But many were more profitable than the North American colonies, and thus they were better policed and exit costs could be driven higher by local governments. European diseases had also greatly reduced the native "Indian" population, which simultaneously increased the demand for colonists and provided many more opportunities for resettlement (more open land) than in many other parts of the world.

8 There are several cases in which individual European monarchs encouraged immigration of relatively highly skilled groups that could produce services unavailable locally. Immigration was often encouraged with subsidies and by granting special civil and political liberties within specific communities or "free towns." In general, however, competition for unskilled labor was less intense in Europe, because the supply of labor was relatively large and its marginal productivity was relatively low. European political institutions also evolved to increase the value of land, but in a situation in which labor was not often scarce, because of Malthusian labor supplies.

9 Smith (1776, I.8.22) noted that "The wages of labor, however, are much higher in North America than in any part of England. In the province of New York, common laborers earn 23 shillings and sixpence currency, equal to two shillings sterling, a day; ship carpenters, ten shillings and sixpence currency, with a pint of rum worth sixpence sterling, equal in all to six shillings and sixpence sterling; house carpenters and bricklayers, eight shillings currency, equal to four shillings and sixpence sterling; journeymen tailors, five shillings currency, equal to about two shillings and ten pence sterling. These prices are all above the London price; and wages are said to be as high in the other colonies as in New York."

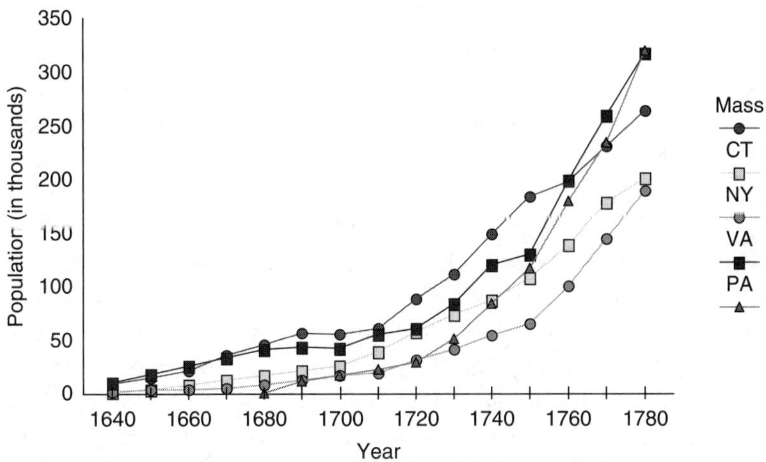

Figure 18.1. European-derived population of five largest colonies (1640–1780).

Mid-Eighteenth-Century Colonial Governments

The association between democratic bicameral forms of the king-and-council template and prosperity led essentially all of the North American colonies to adopt them during the late seventeenth and early eighteenth centuries. By the time of the Revolutionary War, only Pennsylvania had a unicameral legislature, although it too had briefly experimented with the Virginia model.

Eighteenth-century colonial governments typically included bicameral legislatures with one elected and one appointed chamber, each with veto power over new taxes and new laws. The upper chamber was often an elite chamber composed of senior government officials and major landholders, which was analogous to the noble chambers of European parliaments in that era, although membership was not entirely based on family bloodlines. Members of the second chamber were normally elected on the basis of much broader suffrage than in European parliaments.

The number of voters eligible to participate in elections for the lower chamber tended to increase as the number of freemen increased through time, although suffrage laws were occasionally tightened. (Racial, religious, and residency restrictions were often added during the eighteenth century.) Rather than 5 or 10 percent male suffrage, as was common in Europe until the nineteenth century, colonial suffrage was often greater than 50 percent and occasionally close to 100 percent of adult males, because so many families owned land and met minimum property requirements (Brown 1955; Brown and Brown 1964). Electoral politics, consequently, became mass marketing affairs in the North Atlantic colonies well before it did in Europe (as evidenced by local and regional newspapers and pamphlets).

The combination of parliamentary authority and broad suffrage implies that colonial governments were well on their way to becoming parliamentary democracies well before independence was declared in 1776.

This is not to say that the colonies were modern liberal states. Although more or less equal civil liberties were broadly in place, religious freedom in the northern colonies, for example, was often as limited as in Europe. In Massachusetts, Catholic priests were subject to lifetime imprisonment. In the southern colonies, slavery was commonplace, and in many places it was becoming more rather than less difficult for slaves to earn their freedom. (In the northern colonies, there were already politically active groups lobbying for the abolition of slavery.) Even in relatively tolerant states, suffrage and the right to hold elective office were often limited by religion and race in addition to wealth (Fiske 1888, 76).

By the standards of world history, however, the power of the purse had allowed colonial parliaments to become relatively powerful, while liberal political ideology, labor mobility, and plentiful land had made suffrage broadly based. As evidence of the breadth of suffrage, consider this analysis of the effects of typical wealth rules for suffrage in Pennsylvania by Thomas Paine:

> By a former law of Pennsylvania, prior to forming the Constitution, it was enjoined, that a **man is required**, should swear or affirm himself **worth fifty pounds currency** before he should be entitled to vote. The only end this answered was, that of tempting men to forswear themselves. **Every man** with a chest of tools, a few implements of husbandry, a few spare clothes, a bed and a few household utensils, a few articles for sale in a window, or almost any thing else he could call or even think his own, **supposed himself within the pale of an oath**, and made no hesitation of taking it; and to serve the particular purposes of an **election day**. (Quoted in Brown 1963, 269)

1776 AND THE "NEW" CONSTITUTIONS OF THE FORMER COLONIES

King George III's efforts to centralize policy-making authority in the English colonies, the Declaration of Independence, and war to secede from the British Empire all provided new opportunities for constitutional bargaining, experimentation, and exchange in the 1770s and 1780s. There were new constitutional problems to address, and after independence was declared, important veto players disappeared from those negotiations. The resulting constitutional bargains created the first sizable polities in human history grounded entirely on broad suffrage.

The new state constitutions, however, were not invented whole cloth, as the story is sometimes told. They reflected a century and a half of experimentation, bargaining, and competition with the Virginia political template. Two colonies, Connecticut (1662) and Rhode Island (1663), already had charters that provided for elected governors; their constitutions required only minor reforms to be serviceable. Connecticut continued to be governed under its colonial charter until 1818. Rhode Island continued to use its colonial charter as its state constitution until 1843. The others required reform after independence was declared in 1776.

The same history of constitutional experimentation also informed efforts to develop a new constitution for national governance.

Independence and the Adoption of "New" State Constitutions

Negotiations with King George III and the British parliament regarding that government's effort to centralize policy-making authority in the colonies proved fruitless, and so in July of 1776, the colonial governments jointly declared their independence.

The Declaration of Independence had immediate and direct effects on the organization of the executive branch at the colony-state level. The royal and proprietary governors who had run the executive branch of government lost their offices. At this point, the colonial parliaments could have dispensed with the executive office, but organizational conservatism and the advantages of executive administration prevailed, and governors were replaced, rather than eliminated. Two alternative procedures for selecting governors attracted attention, and both were adopted by subsets of the new sovereign state governments. The choice was between what would later be termed "prime ministerial" and "presidential" systems. Governors could be selected by elected state legislatures, or governors could be directly elected by state electorates.

Parliamentary appointment is consistent with an institutionally induced interest theory of constitutional reform, because this procedure maximizes the parliament's control over the executive, and thereby, public policy. However, institutional interests were not the only ones pursued by members of the colonial parliaments. The direct election of governors could also advance partisan interests and ideological interests. Colonial leaders who expected to win elections for governor had reason to favor directly elected governors, because it would provide them with a more powerful office than that of prime minister. Direct election of governors was also consistent with liberal theories of governance that were widely accepted within the colonies, because it would reduce problems associated with unified governance, what Thomas Paine termed the "vices of government." In the next few years, finely grained constitutional bargains were negotiated and accepted by the formerly colonial, now state, legislatures.

Most of the new states initially chose to create a prime ministerial system of governance.[10] In only three cases did a majority of the legislature initially favor direct election of governors.

This is not to say that ideological considerations affected only a few of the new state constitutions. Most state constitutions, for example, were explicitly grounded on popular sovereignty. Most of the new state constitutions also included lists of rights. Most also included provisions for broad male suffrage, subject to wealth or tax constraints, although in some cases, suffrage was also limited by race and religion. Only two states explicitly forbade voting by free blacks (Georgia and South Carolina). No new state constitution mentioned a state-supported church. Delaware's constitution explicitly ruled out the establishment of a state church. A few constitutions protected open worship by only Protestants (North and South Carolina) and others by all Christians (Maryland). A few state constitutions also explicitly forbade clergy from holding state offices. Complete freedom of religious conscience was assured by the state constitutions of Georgia, Massachusetts, New Jersey, New York, Pennsylvania, Virginia, and Vermont (Table 18.1).

National Governance and State Sovereignty

Before independence, a loose alliance of the colony-states was formed to coordinate and share the cost of lobbying the British sovereign and parliament. When these negotiations failed to yield the hoped-for results, independence was declared and new constitutional gains to exchange emerged at the national level. There were public-service areas in which economies of scale could be realized through national governance, especially national defense, and other policy areas in which a central authority could reduce unproductive conflict among the states.[11]

[10] In subsequent rounds of constitutional reform, several state constitutions were modified to include independently elected governors. New Hampshire did so in 1783, Pennsylvania in 1790, and Delaware in 1792 (Fiske 1888, 67–8).

[11] See Congleton (2004b) and Congleton, Kyriacou, and Bacaria (2003) for rational-choice-based theories of centralization produced through voluntary associations of regional (state) and national governments and also within treaty organizations.

Table 18.1. Characteristics of State Constitutions Adopted Immediately after the Declaration of Independence

	Date	Election of governor	Legislative form	Suffrage qualifications[10]	List of rights	Supreme court	State church
Delaware	1776	Legislature	Bicameral	Retained	yes	yes	no
Georgia	1777	Legislature	Unicameral[3]	10 pounds[4]	yes	yes	no
Maryland	1776	Legislature	Bicameral	50 acres	yes	yes	no[1]
Massachusetts	1780	Freemen	Bicameral	60 pounds	yes	no	no
New Hampshire	1776	Legislature	Unicameral[3]	Retained	no	no	no
New Jersey	1776	Legislature	Bicameral	50 pounds[2]	yes	yes	no
New York	1777	Freemen	Bicameral	100 pounds[8]	yes	yes	no
North Carolina	1776	Legislature	Bicameral	50 acres[5]	yes	yes	no
Pennsylvania	1776	Legislature	Unicameral[3]	Paid taxes	yes	yes	no
South Carolina	1778	Legislature	Bicameral	50 acres[6]	yes	no	no[9]

(continued)

Table 18.1. *(continued)*

	Date	Election of governor	Legislative form	Suffrage qualifications[10]	List of rights	Supreme court	State church
Vermont[7]	1777	Freemen	Bicameral	All men	yes	yes	no
Virginia	1776	Legislature	Bicameral	Retained	yes	yes	no

[1] Article 33 allows the possibility of supporting Christian churches using tax revenue.

[2] Article 4 says that "**all inhabitants** of this Colony, of full age, who are worth fifty pounds proclamation money" may vote. This gave independent **women** the right to vote until the wording was changed two decades later (Keyssar 2000, 54).

[3] An unelected second chamber (an executive council or cabinet) is chosen by the first (the assembly).

[4] Article 9 states that "All **male, white inhabitants** … of the age of twenty-one years and possessed in his own right of ten pounds value … shall have a right to vote at all elections."

[5] Articles 7 and 8 characterize different rules for House and Senate electors; one can vote for the House if one has paid public taxes.

[6] In addition, the right to vote is limited by race and religion: "free white man, and … who acknowledges the being of a God, and believes in a future state of rewards and punishments."

[7] Vermont was created as a new state from land originally part of New York in 1786, a few years after its constitution was written. It was, however, not admitted to the Union until 1791.

[8] Rules differ for the Senate and Assembly. Article 7 allows freeholders with more than twenty pounds of assets and renters to vote for members of the Assembly if they have "rented a tenement therein of the yearly value of forty shillings." Article 10 restricts votes for Senate to freeholders with wealth greater than one hundred pounds.

[9] Article 38 of the South Carolina constitution includes a characterization of acceptable Protestant religious beliefs.

[10] When different suffrage rules apply to the chambers of government, rules for the most stringent are listed.

Source: *State Constitutional Documents*, Thorpe (1909). Also available on the Web from Yale University's Avalon Project.

The new national government had to be acceptable to all member states, and consequently the result was a relatively weak central government. The resulting Articles of Confederation were analogous to those of the old Dutch Republic or the contemporary European Union. The states delegated significant policy-making authority to the central government and allowed a variety of decisions to be made with less-than-unanimous agreement, but the new national government had no authority to impose taxes or other laws on its members. The states retained all police authority. Article I adopts the name "United States of America" for the new confederation.

Articles 2 and 3 suggest that the new confederation preserved state sovereignty, while pursuing common ends:

(II) **Each state retains its sovereignty**, freedom, and independence, **and every power, jurisdiction, and right, which is not by this Confederation expressly delegated** to the United States, in Congress assembled.

(III) The said States hereby severally enter into a **firm league of friendship with each other, for their common defense, the security of their liberties, and their mutual and general welfare**, binding themselves to assist each other, against all force offered to, or attacks made on them, or any of them, on account of religion, sovereignty, trade, or any other pretense whatever.

Article 13, however, suggests that at least some at the bargaining table intended to create a national organization that was more powerful and durable than the usual treaty organization:

(XIII) **Every State shall abide by the determination of the United States in Congress assembled**, on all questions which by this confederation are submitted to them. And the Articles of this Confederation shall be inviolably observed by every State, and **the Union shall be perpetual; nor shall any alteration at any time hereafter be made in any of them; unless such alteration be agreed to in a Congress of the United States, and be afterwards confirmed by the legislatures of every State**.

The remainder of the articles define policy areas in which the national government would have jurisdiction and procedures for adopting public policy and settling interstate disputes.

Overall, the Articles of Confederation provided the architecture for a state-based, council-dominated form of the king-and-council template. Article 5 specifies that each state delegation would consist of two or more delegates and that "each state shall have one vote." It specifies three-year term limits for the delegates to the national congress and assures freedom of speech in the congress and immunity of delegates from arrest during sessions of congress. Article 6 delegates all international relations to the confederal government. Article 8 specifies that state-tax obligations for the "common defense" and "general welfare" are determined by the relative value of land holdings in the various states and are to be levied by the state legislatures. Article 9 creates a cabinet with a president (prime minister) to be chosen by the Congress. The president could hold office for only one year out of every three. It also provides for a national army and gives the central government exclusive power over war and peace. The central government also has the authority to regulate the minting of coins, regulate international trade, and serve as the highest court of appeal in disputes among states.

Supermajorities (9 of 13 votes) are required for most policy decisions. Article 9 also provides for establishing national courts to hear disputes among states and for establishing a standing committee with a president (limited to one-year terms) to govern while Congress is not in session. The Congress was to meet at least once every six months. Article 4 establishes free mobility among the states and assures persons migrating of the same rights as other citizens of the states in which they entered. It also provides for the extradition of criminals fleeing from state to state.

This design for a national government, completed in 1778, was used for the next two decades, although it was not ratified by all the member states until 1781. The tension between articles 2 and 13 would play a role in many of the constitutional controversies that took place in the next two centuries.

Governance under the Articles of Confederation proved adequate for a time of war, and the national Congress was able to pass significant legislation, such as the Northwest Ordinance governing the admission of new states. However, it was widely regarded to be too weak to advance national interests during the time of peace after the war was won in 1783. States ignored requests for contributions to the central government, trade barriers were being erected among the states, conflicts about the location of state boundaries were left unresolved, and national defense was poorly financed and orchestrated. Secession from the confederation was being discussed in several states.

A prominent group of state and national politicians believed that a stronger central government would be necessary if the United States was to survive in the long run (Fiske 1888, chapter 4). Negotiations for a stronger central government took place in assemblies of appointed state representatives in Annapolis and Philadelphia, many of whom had participated in drafting their state constitutions a decade earlier.

The architecture for a new central government was negotiated in Philadelphia, accepted by the assembled representatives, and submitted to the national congress for consideration.[12] The national congress accepted the proposed reforms of the Articles of Confederation without comment, and the proposal was sent to state legislatures for ratification or rejection in 1787, as required under article 13. After much public debate and some further negotiation regarding the addition of a Bill of Rights, the proposed Constitution was approved by all of the member states in 1790.[13] In this manner, the national government of the United States was peacefully and formally transformed into a more centralized one through negotiation and compromise.

In most respects, the new architecture for national governance was very similar to that already used by the member states. Those drafting the constitution sought a practical structure for governance and naturally looked to the governments with which they were familiar. The new constitution, however, substantially modified the architecture of the existing confederal parliament of the states by adding a directly elected chamber. It also strengthened the office of president and the Supreme Court.

The new congress was bicameral. One chamber, the Senate, essentially preserved the original Congress of state representatives, which helped obtain the approval of the smaller states. Each member-state government was entitled to appoint to representatives to the Senate. To this council of state governments, a new directly elected chamber was added, the House of Representatives. Its members were directly elected by voters in single-member districts (based on state population). The directly elected chamber had essentially the same policy authority as the Senate. It could veto and propose taxes and legislation.

[12] At the close of the Philadelphia assembly on September 17, 1787, it was agreed that everyone would destroy their notes or turn them over to the president of the assembly (George Washington). Fortunately for historians, a few of the delegates violated this rule. Madison's notes are by far the most complete and reveal both sophisticated bargaining and analysis of constitutional consequences throughout the meetings of the assembly.

[13] Several of the state assemblies and state constitutional conventions approved the Constitution, subject to the addition of a bill of rights that more clearly characterized the bounds of central government authority, as already found in most state constitutions. Twelve amendments were subsequently adopted in rapid succession by the Congress to satisfy this part of the constitutional bargain. Ten amendments (the Bill of Rights) were approved by Congress, the president, and the requisite number of state legislatures on December 15, 1791. (Two of the original twelve amendments passed by Congress did not receive sufficient state support to be adopted.) The first ten amendments thus are essentially part of the original Constitution.

The rotating presidency of the old Congress (essentially a prime minister) was replaced by a new, more powerful, indirectly elected president. The president would stand for elections every four years and could veto legislation from the Congress (although Congress could override that veto). He would be responsible for executing the laws approved by both assemblies and serve as commander in chief in times of war.

Majority rule was used for most decisions, including those that previously required supermajorities. Direct taxes were to be based on population, rather than land holdings (slaves were counted as two-thirds of a person). Senators and representatives were guaranteed free speech in Congress. Bills for raising revenues were to originate in the House of Representatives. Senators, representatives, and the president would receive a salary. Congress was to meet once a year, and the three-year term limits were eliminated. National elections for members of the House of Representatives would be held every two years. Section 9 forbids the granting of noble titles.

Bargaining and constitutional conservatism were evident at every step in the drafting and ratification process. For example, the list of areas of central government authority included in article 1, sections 8–10, of the new Constitution consists largely of the same ones listed in the Articles of Confederation. The general architecture of the revised national Constitution also followed closely the pattern of state constitutions, particularly those with elected governors, which in turn closely followed the architecture of the colonial governments that had evolved in the century before independence was declared.

Relevance for Constitutional Developments Elsewhere

Liberal political theory was significantly advanced by the debates and negotiations that produced the new U.S. Constitution.

Although liberal ideas had previously affected governance in the Dutch Republic, the colonies, and Great Britain, they were less clearly stated and less evident in written constitutional documents than in the United States. Significant intellectual progress is also evident when one compares Montesquieu's chapters on federalism and divided powers in his *Spirit of the Laws* with the far more sophisticated discussions included in Madison, Hamilton, and Jay's *Federalist Papers*.[14]

Those drafting the national Constitution sought an encompassing legitimizing authority, but as had been done at the state level, drew that authority

[14] Part of this difference, of course, may be the result of French censorship and treason laws at the time that Montesquieu wrote.

from the "self-evident" rights of man and contractarian justifications for the state, rather than biblical citations, as might have been expected from the representatives of a deeply religious society.[15] The Constitution of the United States begins with the words "We the people in order to form a more perfect Union."

That such a conception of the state preceded the French Revolution by a few years is unsurprising; Franklin, Adams, Jefferson, and Madison had all spent time in France before the new Constitution was drafted, and they were all familiar with contractarian theories of the state that had been worked out in Europe during the past century. That similar language had already been in use in colonial charters for more than century is, however, often overlooked by modern constitutional scholars and in contemporary tales about the founding of the United States.

Although it was not a radical experiment, the new national Constitution was a significant event in the history of Western democracy. It created the first government of a large territory that was completely grounded in elections with broad suffrage. Although not all senior officials were elected directly, those that were not were ultimately appointed (or elected) by directly elected officials. The new constitution included a Bill of Rights that would be supported by an independent Supreme Court. Its federal structure was scalable and was subsequently extended to govern a far larger territory simply by creating and adding new states.

During its first decades, the broadly elected governments of the United States demonstrated that rule of law could be implemented by popular government and that more or less moderate policies could be adopted by governments based on relatively broad suffrage. Wealth was not taken from the rich, huge deficits were not run, and law and order was not completely undermined by officials directly or indirectly selected by common persons.

The success of this relatively democratic national government supported nineteenth-century arguments in Europe about the feasibility of popular government. Such governments had previously been intangible speculations of political philosophers or rare forms of city government studied by political historians. If the liberal political institutions of the United States functioned reasonably well, perhaps the political ideas of the English Levellers, Locke, Montesquieu, and Rousseau were not impossible pipe dreams of idealists and scholars. Perhaps, such ideas could provide the intellectual foundations for practical alternatives to existing arrangements in Europe.

[15] See Miller (1991) for a discussion of the shift from traditionalist and religious theories of democracy and community to liberal ones in eighteenth-century America.

CONSTITUTIONAL REFORMS BEFORE AND AFTER THE CIVIL WAR, 1792–1870

Constitutional bargaining in the United States did not end in 1789, nor was it confined to national reforms. The reforms of the nineteenth and early twentieth centuries gradually transformed a relatively liberal representative system into a more completely democratic one. The national Constitution was formally amended nine times in the next eight decades and informally amended many more times. State constitutional and quasi-constitutional reforms were more commonplace and just as important in a highly decentralized federal system.[16] Consistent with the models of constitutional reform previously developed, the bargains struck reflected changing economic interests, ideological refinements, and preexisting institutions.

At the national level, the veto authority of the Supreme Court was extended to include constitutional review of national legislation and executive actions early in the nineteenth century, albeit largely through its own decisions (Rehnquist 2001, chapter 1). The balance of policy-making authority within the central government and between the central government and the states was also continually debated and adjusted at the margin. New territories were acquired, organized, and admitted as states to the Union.

Other significant constitutional and quasi-constitutional reforms were adopted by state governments. For example, governors became independently elected offices with broader powers in the late eighteenth and early nineteenth centuries (Benjamin 1985; Fiske 1888). Suffrage remained a state matter after the new national government was reformed, and was gradually expanded in the early nineteenth century as the definition of "freeholder" was liberalized and wealth requirements were reduced one state at a time. This was partly a result of interstate competition for labor, as the new states generally had more liberal rules than the original colonies. It was also partly a consequence of changing norms, expanding public education, and political competition, as in late-nineteenth-century Europe.

In some cases, however, new restrictions were adopted at more or less the same time as wealth or tax thresholds were reduced; for example, black suffrage was reduced, rather than expanded, in many states in the early

[16] It is easy to exaggerate how centralized the new national government really was. For the next century and a half, the main source of government services remained local (town and counties) rather than federal. It was not until about 1935, after the progressive amendments that federal expenditures exceeded state and local expenditures. See *Historical Statistics of the United States* Volume 5, 2006: Table Ea-A, 5–6.

nineteenth century.[17] Even with slavery and other new restrictions taken into account, suffrage remained substantially broader than in Europe, and many northern and new states approached universal male suffrage. The paper ballot was gradually introduced and reformed.[18]

Slavery, State Sovereignty, and the Perpetual Union

Unfortunately, in addition to the political effects of early liberalism, industrialization, and interstate competition for labor and capital, a problem postponed during the constitutional deliberations of 1787 led to a constitutional crisis and another war of secession in the middle of the nineteenth century. In this case, those attempting to secede lost the war, although at great cost to both sides.

Under the Constitution, slavery was a state regulatory issue. Support and opposition to this ancient institution varied by region, because of variation in ideological and economic interests. In the Northern states, where slavery was economically unimportant, abolitionists pressed for its elimination, and slavery was gradually abolished, beginning with Delaware in 1776, Vermont in 1777, Pennsylvania in 1780, and Massachusetts in 1780. In the South, where slavery was economically important for tobacco, rice, indigo, and subsequently cotton production, slavery was retained despite the efforts of Southern abolitionists.

Abolition of slavery throughout the United States became an increasingly important ideological issue in Northern elections, as support for civic equality increased during the first half of the nineteenth century. At the national level, this was most obvious within the House of Representatives, where representation was determined by state population. After the elections of 1860, the Southern slave states feared that the national government would adopt new, more liberal laws on slavery and other laws (chiefly tariffs) that would substantially reduce their wealth. Neither was very likely in the short run, given the balance in the Senate.

[17] Black suffrage was reduced or eliminated in several states as in Delaware (1792), Maryland (1809), Connecticut (1818), New Jersey (1820), and Pennsylvania (1838) (Grimes 1987, 32).

[18] Ballot design, perhaps surprisingly, continues to be controversial in the United States today. After the 2000 election for president, many significant changes in ballot design and counting were suggested, and a few were implemented. See, for example, Agresti and Presnell (2002) for a careful analysis of the effects on ballot design on the distribution of votes in Palm Beach County Florida. The Help America Vote Act was passed by Congress and accepted by the president in 2002.

Nonetheless, the Southern states attempted to secede from the Union to avoid these economic calamities in the long run and to preserve their political autonomy.[19]

The constitutionality of secession had been much debated in the period leading up to the war (Farber 2003, chapters 4–5). Articles 2 and 3 of the Articles of Confederation explicitly guarantees state sovereignty on all matters not transferred to the Congress, although article 13 commits signatory states to a "perpetual union." The legal and philosophical tension between perpetual union and state sovereignty, however, could no longer be peacefully resolved through constitutional bargaining and compromise. Rather, the perpetual union agreed to under article 13 was preserved by force of arms in a bloody Civil War (1861–65). According to President Lincoln's interpretation of the Constitution, sovereign states did not have the right to secede from a perpetual union.[20]

The Civil War took place from 1861 to 1865, and it ended with a victory for the North. It was by far the deadliest war in U.S. history.

Suffrage and Citizenship after the Civil War

Amendments of the U.S. Constitution require two-thirds majorities in both chambers of the legislature and approval by the legislatures of two-thirds of the states.

The secession of the Southern states changed the balance of interests represented in Congress and, thus, provided new opportunities for constitutional bargaining by reducing the number of states whose approval was required for amendments with respect to slavery and race. As a consequence, three liberal reforms of the Constitution were adopted by the Northern Republicans after the war was won. The Thirteenth Amendment (1865) made slavery illegal; the Fourteenth Amendment (1868) defined citizenship in inclusive terms (all persons born or naturalized in the United States) and guaranteed equal

[19] The seceding states listed their reasons in secession documents adopted by the state governments. For example, South Carolina's states that: "On the 4th day of March next, this party [President Lincoln and Northern abolitionists] will take possession of the Government. It has announced that ... a war must be waged against slavery until it shall cease throughout the United States. The guaranties of the Constitution will then no longer exist; the equal rights of the States will be lost. The slave-holding States will no longer have the power of self-government, or self-protection, and the Federal Government will have become their enemy." It bears noting that the "war" against slavery refers to the long political campaign undertaken by the Northern liberals against slavery, rather than a military effort.

[20] The army of the North was (and is) therefore called the Union Army. The army of the South was (and is) known as the Confederate Army, in honor of the new confederal constitution devised by the seceding states in 1861.

protection of the law to all citizens; and the Fifteenth Amendment (1870) forbade state laws that used race or color as a condition of suffrage, which changed suffrage laws in the North and West, as well as in the South.

These civil liberty reforms were largely motivated by liberal ideological interests (the civic equality of all citizens), although they also advanced the short-term political interests of the Republican Party, for whom the newly enfranchised were expected to vote. (The postwar governments in the South were often Republican governments.)

After the war was won, the Southern states were administered by the U.S. government and the Northern army for a few years. Provisional state governors were initially appointed for each of the Southern states. Elections for state constitutional conventions were held in 1866 to revise Southern state constitutions. These and other state elections initially used existing state suffrage rules, although senior members of the Southern army and government and wealthy plantation owners were not permitted to vote. The new state governments extended many civil liberties to former slaves (and blacks who had not been slaves), but in no case were blacks given the right to vote in elections, to serve as witnesses in criminal cases, or to serve on juries. Violence against freedmen (former slaves in this case) increased, state parliaments refused to cooperate with their provisional governors, and new discriminatory "black codes" were promulgated.

In 1867, the U.S. Congress replaced the provisional civilian governments with military governments, and new elections were held for another round of constitutional conventions, in which blacks and previously unenfranchised whites were allowed to vote. This time the result was eleven more liberal state constitutions, with broad suffrage and substantial equality before the law. In some cases, remaining wealth qualifications for high state office were totally eliminated. New state elections were held, which elected a number of blacks to high state offices.

To regain complete self-governance, each Southern state had to ratify the Civil War amendments to the U.S. Constitution. This was easily accomplished by the governments elected under the new suffrage laws. Georgia was the last of the "reconstructed" governments to ratify the Civil War amendments (in July 15, 1870). In this somewhat irregular manner, slavery was ended in the South and freed slaves became eligible to vote in federal elections (Morison 1965, 711–17).[21]

[21] Several Southern states were among the ratifiers of the Thirteenth Amendment in 1865, including South Carolina, Alabama, North Carolina, and Georgia. The politics of the Thirteenth Amendment are discussed in Grimes (1987, 31–9).

After control of public policy was returned to Southern state governments, however, suffrage laws gradually became more restrictive, as various literacy tests and fees (poll taxes) for voters were introduced to exclude former slaves and many other poor persons from voting (Keyssar 2000). Race per se could no longer be used as a criterion for suffrage, but many other criteria were allowed that had similar effects, and many of these criteria (informally) were unequally applied among the races. There was clearly no slippery slope to universal male suffrage in the southeastern United States.[22]

A DIGRESSION ON PARALLELS AND CONTRASTS WITH EUROPE IN THE NINETEENTH CENTURY

There was no equivalent to the Civil War in Europe, but economic and political developments in the United States nonetheless parallel developments in Europe in many respects. For example, slavery had been eliminated in most of Europe several decades earlier, albeit peacefully, as it had been in the Northern U.S. states. As in Europe, many of the political trends of nineteenth-century America were consequences of improved farming, industrialization, urbanization, and shifts in political ideology. Support for the expansion of public education, modest economic regulation, and social insurance increased during the century, as did support for women's suffrage.

Ideological changes were somewhat less obvious in the United States than in Europe, because there were very few true conservatives in the European sense. Although there were many who favored preserving past American traditions, there were few supporters of hereditary monarchs, privileged families, and a national church. The center of gravity of American political theories had been liberal (in the sense used here) since the middle of

[22] Poll taxes were used in eight states. Literacy tests were also used to reduce the electorate among both black and working class communities, in some cases with much tougher questions for blacks than whites. The Ku Klux Klan's illegal (but tolerated) campaign of terrorism against politically active blacks and Southern liberals clearly reduced open support among Southern liberals for the elimination of such policies.

(As a consequence of the interests represented in government and war damage, the South industrialized far more slowly than the North and had slower income and population growth. After suffrage was expanded in the late 1960s, per capita income in the Southern states began catching up with the rest of the country. Southern slave owners were not compensated for their capital losses as they were in many European countries, nor were losses reduced by phasing out slavery as it had been done in some of the Northern states. Slaves accounted for about half of Southern wealth in 1860.)

the seventeenth century, well before the term was first applied to politics.[23] Consequently, most policy and constitutional debates took place between left- and right-of-center liberals, who accepted the principles of constitutional governance, broad suffrage, open markets, and civic equality, although they did not always uniformly apply those principles to all races or to women. With respect to the latter, it seems clear that support for civic equality gradually increased during the nineteenth century, as developed later in the chapter.[24]

Economic Development: Industrialization and Urbanization

As in Europe, day-to-day life in North America was undergoing a major transformation. Specialization in economic production increased, and with it, life and livelihood changed for a majority of families.

The relatively open internal and external markets of the United States allowed new technologies with economies of scale in production to be applied. Steam engines, for example, were rapidly applied to manufacturing, mining, and transport. New, larger commercial enterprises were founded to organize the necessary teams and resources to create the new machines and networks. Other smaller organizations were created to provide new inputs and services to those industrial enterprises. Technological change, with support from state and national governments, also produced rapid improvements in transportation and communication networks, which increased the effective size of the domestic market by reducing transactions costs and allowing inputs and outputs to reach farms and factories further inland. Additional specialization and opportunities were induced by late-nineteenth-century innovations in electricity and chemistry and also liability and corporate law (Taylor 1951; Nye 1990; Gordon 1999; Wallis 2000).[25]

Population growth continued throughout the nineteenth century, reflecting increases in arable land and improved farming technologies and the

[23] See Miller (1991) for a discussion of the gradual spread of liberal political theory in eighteenth- and nineteenth-century America. Miller argues that liberalism gradually replaced earlier traditional (communitarian) and Puritan (Calvinist) political theories. The American version of liberalism, however, was influenced by these early theories and local traditions of direct democracy, as was true in some parts of Europe (Lutz 1983).

[24] Keyssar (2000, 168–9), argues that support for universal suffrage had waned somewhat toward the end of the century, although it seems clear that support for women's suffrage increased.

[25] Some economic historians debate the extent to which improved transport networks contributed to economic growth (Fogel 1962; Fremdling 1977). However, it seems clear that reduced transport costs, improved information, and increased specialization tend to increase economic output (Gordon 1999; Buchanan and Yoon 1994).

success of the new political institutions. Family sizes continued to be large, and there was substantial (net) immigration from Europe and Asia. For the most part, these were economic emigrants, who sought the opportunities that relatively open markets and abundant undeveloped land produced, although broader civil liberties also played a role at the margin during much of the nineteenth century. Immigrant neighborhoods emerged in larger cities, and entire regions of states were often dominated by particular immigrant groups. Newspapers were published in dozens of languages. New cities and towns emerged in the west, and older ones expanded in the east. Immigration was completely open during this period, and new immigrants could often vote before they were citizens, because the former was a matter of local regulations, and the latter, national regulations (passports did not yet exist).

The territory of the United States also increased during the nineteenth century through the purchase of Louisiana (1803) and Alaska (1867).[26] Other territories in the southwest were won from Mexico during 1846–8.

As in Europe, the rural landscape was transformed through a combination of legal reform and subsequent economic development. Most of the undeveloped land was initially held by the central government. To promote development, methods for transferring ownership of large blocks of government land to individual families were devised and implemented, as with various "homestead" acts. The homestead acts had effects that were similar to those involved in the European enclosure acts, as new deeds were devised, roads and fences were built, and lands converted from commons to private pasture and cropland.[27]

Agricultural technologies improved substantially during the nineteenth century with the introduction of better seeds and plows, mechanization of planting and harvesting, and chemical fertilizers. These techniques, together with rising demand from nonfarmers, allowed larger, less fertile areas to be profitably cultivated; farmland increased throughout the century.

[26] Several of the original thirteen states had previously privatized land that had been in the control of the royal governors and proprietors after independence was declared (Fiske 1888, 71).

[27] The various homestead acts, with their very favorable terms for land sales demonstrate that urbanization was voluntary in the United States, rather than the result of a shortage of farmland. In Europe, urbanization in the early nineteenth century is sometimes argued to be a consequence of privatization that evicted the landless, which induced them to move to cities as a last resort. (Involuntary urbanization can occur as medieval rights to commons disappear.) However, as noted earlier, research suggests that European enclosures often increased demand for rural labor to create new pasture from wastelands, drain swamps, and build new roads and fences.

Nonetheless, as in Europe, an increasing fraction of economic output (value added) was nonagricultural. Urban populations thus expanded more rapidly than did rural populations. People would not, of course, choose towns over farms unless real incomes and/or other conditions were preferable to those in the countryside. Urban life was systematically improving, as new technologies were applied and wages rose. Urban sanitation and transportation improved. Central heating was introduced, followed by electricity and telephones. Farm employment in the United States fell from 74.4 percent of total employment in 1800 to 55.8 percent of total employment in 1860, and to about 30.7 percent of total employment in 1910.[28]

The urbanization associated with the expansion of commerce and manufacturing also generated new demands for public services and regulation. Demand for public services in cities increased as median income increased, because government services tend to be normal goods. Demand also increased as some services became relatively more valuable or less expensive (public water and sanitation) and as new services became available (steel rails and mass transit). Public education expanded as economic returns to literacy and political support for equal opportunity increased. A broad range of local public-school and state-university systems were created and enlarged during the nineteenth century.

Infrastructure and education were subsidized by all three levels of government, although state and local governments were more important sources of services in the nineteenth century. At the national level, the Morrill Acts of 1862 and 1890 transferred lands from the central government to the states as a method of funding new public universities for the advancement of science, engineering, agriculture, and military science. National and state government grants of rights of way, together with other subsidies helped private turnpike, canal, and railroad companies create a more complete, rapid, and efficient transport network.

Increases in specialization, capital accumulation, and technological advance caused per capita (average) income to rise throughout the late nineteenth and early twentieth centuries. From 1870 through 1920, real per capita income more than doubled as population tripled.[29] Expenditures on local public services per capita increased sevenfold (Wallis 2000).

[28] See *Historical Statistics of the United States* (2006: vol. 2, tables Ba-A, 2–18). During the same period, clerical and manufacturing employment rose from negligible levels to about 34.9 percent of employment.

[29] It bears noting that estimates of the rate of increase in per capita income tend to be noisy and biased upward in this period. First, income has to be estimated, as the GDP surveys were not undertaken until the 1930s, which implies that the historical data series are less

Contrasts with Europe in the Nineteenth Century

Although much was similar in Europe and the United States, there were significant differences in the constitutional issues addressed during the nineteenth century. Male suffrage in the United States was already essentially universal (except for retrenchment in the South). International trade was less important for the United States because of its larger domestic markets and because free trade across state boundaries was guaranteed by the Constitution.[30] Political speech was constitutionally protected. This contrasts with much of Europe, where increased male suffrage and equality before the law remained prominent constitutional issues for most of the nineteenth century. With smaller domestic markets, tariff reduction also remained a central policy issue for economic liberals and many industrialists. Relatively liberal political and economic constitutions that had already been adopted in the United States gave its national politics a different cast than that in Europe, as emphasized by de Tocqueville (1835).

In Europe, the liberal constitutional reform agenda often induced left-of-center, moderates, and right-of-center liberals to cooperate in their persuasive campaigns and electoral strategies. This sort of cooperation was less common in the United States than in Europe, because liberals already dominated the major political parties. Day-to-day policy disagreements among liberals, rather than agreements, tended to dominate American political campaigns, rather than constitutional issues. These policy differences were sufficiently systematic that political parties representing right-of-center, moderate, and left-of-center liberals emerged in the United States. For much of the nineteenth century, the Republican Party represented left-of-center liberals and the Democratic Party right-of-center liberals, although this changed in the early twentieth century. Moderates floated between the two major parties as issues, interests, party personalities, and scandals varied at the margins of local, state, and national politics.

accurate than contemporary ones. Second, the substitution of trade for household production implies that both tax and flow of goods estimates tend to exaggerate national income, because these approaches neglect reductions in home production. The decision to use store-bought cloth and clothing implies that a net improvement in living standards occurred, but not that homespun cloth and homemade clothing was without value.

30 As in Europe, tariffs fell during the first half of the century in the United States in spite of the fact that it was a major source of the national government's revenues. Tariffs rose in the second half of the nineteenth century, in part to pay off bonds issued to finance the Civil War, but also because free-trade groups around the world were losing ground in this period.

As in Europe, it could be argued that liberalism in the United States tended to become more radical during the nineteenth century. For example, in the late nineteenth and early twentieth centuries, a *progressive* movement emerged in the United States. The short-lived political party with that name can be thought of as the American equivalent of the Social Democratic Party in Europe. American progressives were not generally opposed to private property or markets, but were interested in improving market outcomes for middle-class and blue-collar workers through institutional and regulatory reforms. For the most part, they sought reforms that would give those groups greater bargaining power within governments and firms. In the terminology used in this book, most progressives were left-of-center or radical liberals, rather than socialists, as was also true of moderate social democrats in Europe.[31]

It is interesting to note that the left-of-center liberals (the progressives) retained the name liberal in the United States in the twentieth century, whereas in Europe the right-of-center liberals kept that political label.

Toward the end of the nineteenth century, the economic and political reform agendas began to converge as European parliamentary authority increased and the members of those parliaments were elected on the basis of relatively broad male suffrage. Economic regulation, women's suffrage, and fine-tuning the institutions of parliament became constitutional issues for liberals on both sides of the Atlantic.[32]

Politically Active Interest Groups of the Nineteenth Century

A wide variety of politically active interest groups in the United States were organized in the late nineteenth century. Most groups had fairly narrow

[31] Prasch (1999) notes that "What distinguished the economists associated with the Progressive movement from their forebears in the liberal tradition was not their concern for rules per se, rather it was their belief that a free market could be the locus of systematic economic power. They thought that the proximate cause of this power was unequal bargaining power between employers and individual laborers. It was their observation that labor was typically constrained by a lack of wealth. This simple fact, operating in conjunction with the need to feed oneself and one's family, placed a distinct limit on the length of time that labor could 'hold out' for a better wage bargain." Nonetheless, progressives did include persons favoring broad public ownership of major industries, such as the railroads.

[32] The term liberal was not widely used in the United States during the nineteenth century to describe political positions, although it was occasionally used. The terms civil liberty, political liberty, and economic liberty were more widely used. Ross (1919) provides an account of American politicians who explicitly regarded themselves to be liberals, most of whom were Republicans.

policy agendas, although many such groups had overlapping memberships. Economic interest groups included regional and national business associations, trusts, labor unions, and farmer cooperatives that pressed for reforms that would improve the economic well-being of their members (profits, wage rates, and working conditions). Other interest groups had explicitly ideological and political agendas, such as the temperance and women's suffrage movements. Still other groups had both economic and ideological agendas, as with many free-trade and labor organizations. Technological advance and urbanization had reduced organizational costs at the same time that policy problems began to span state borders and personal income and free time increased.

Labor and progressive groups often joined forces in the United States, as did industrialists and laissez-faire liberals. In late-nineteenth-century Europe, such coalitions often led to the formation of new political parties. The former often formed new labor–social democratic political parties and the latter new liberal and/or conservative parties. However, this did not happen in the United States, because of its already competitive political system. In a polity with competitive elections based on broad suffrage in single-member districts, interest-group activities tend to affect the platforms of existing major political parties, rather than induce the formation of new parties. The Progressive Party did poorly in national elections, but it did induce the two major parties (Democrats and Republicans) to adopt more progressive positions on many issues.[33]

CHANGES IN THE ECONOMIC AND POLITICAL CONSTITUTIONS OF THE UNITED STATES 1870–1910

Although the Civil War, like the Revolutionary War, attracts considerable attention among historians and plays an important role in American political mythology, it was by no means the only significant period of

[33] A national Progressive Party was founded in 1912 by former Republican President Theodore Roosevelt, partly because he had failed to secure the Republican Party's nomination as their candidate for president (on a more or less progressive platform).

Many of its proposed policies were similar to those of the early Social Democratic Parties in Scandinavia, and the party did best in states where Scandinavian emigrants were large constituencies. In Minnesota, for example, the party received more votes than either of the mainstream parties. It ran second to the Democrats in the nation as a whole on a platform calling for a six-day work week, and eight-hour day in manufacturing, prohibition of child labor at ages below sixteen years, and women's suffrage. See Youngman (1913) for the 1912 Roosevelt platform and Davis (1964) for an analysis of the Progressive Party's base of support.

A People's Independent Party had previously been founded in 1892, which represented somewhat similar groups and interests and also drew much of its support from radical

constitutional reform in the nineteenth and early twentieth centuries. Indeed, the war itself and its three associated amendments can be said to have had a smaller effect on peacetime national governance and public policy than quasi-constitutional reforms adopted between 1870 and 1910 and also the constitutional amendments adopted between 1910 and 1920, in what is often called the progressive era. The Civil War amendments were civil-equality amendments, rather than procedural ones.

For example, during the late nineteenth century, there were several changes in what might be called the economic constitution of the United States, many of which paralleled those of the industrializing countries of Europe. The increase in population densities and the size of firms, together with persuasive campaigns led by progressives, helped increase electoral support for increased regulation of economic organizations. As a consequence, many states and cities adopted new laws to regulate firms and labor contracts, including antitrust laws and child-labor laws. By 1900, most Northern states had rules governing work days and work weeks for children and women, and similar laws were being adopted in the South in the period immediately after 1900 (Hindman 2002, 58–64). A variety of adjustments were also made to the rules that determined what is owned and how what is owned may be used without legal (or political) interference. Many of these adjustments were made shortly after independence was declared (Fiske 1888, 71), but many more were made in the second half of the nineteenth century. For example, tort law and corporate law were revised. Property rights concerning physical goods and services became individualized and alienable, at the same time that use rights were narrowed to take account of externalities and monopoly power.[34]

Centralization of Economic Regulation

However, not all problems of interest to progressives could be addressed by state and local governments, because they were regional or national in scope. Partly because of such interstate problems, there was a significant

Republicans. See, for example, Webb (1993) for a discussion of relationships among populists, progressives, and progressive Republicans. The progressive movement's base of support consisted largely of progressive Republicans and independents.

[34] Changes in property law were more obvious in Europe and Japan, where medieval family-based privileges for particular occupations, products, and services finally disappeared as matters of law during the nineteenth century. Debts often became individual, rather than family based, and land became freely bought and sold. However, it is clear that property and tort law changed in the United States as well. See, for example, Posner (2007).

increase in interest-group and electoral support for shifting some regulatory responsibilities from states to the national government.

The persuasive campaigns undertaken by progressives, together with support from economically aligned interest groups, gradually produced a series of new national laws that attempted to regulate large firms and transactions.[35] Examples include the Interstate Commerce Act, which regulated railroads (1887); the Sherman Antitrust laws, which regulated monopolies and other conspiracies to restrict open markets (1890); the Pure Food and Drug Act (1906), which created the Food and Drug Administration and provided for federal inspections of meat products and forbade poisonous patent medicines; the Federal Trade Commission Act (1914), which regulated "unfair methods of competition in or affecting commerce, and unfair or deceptive acts or practices ..."; and the Clayton Antitrust Act (1914), which strengthened the Sherman Act and exempted nonprofit institutions and organized labor from antitrust proceedings.

Arguments about the proper extent of governmental regulation of market activities and the constitutionality of such "ideal" regulations among right- and left-of-center liberals were evident in newspapers, political campaigns, scholarly books, and in the courts. Such debates occurred at every level of society. The main lines of arguments are nicely summarized in the Supreme Court's *Lochner v. New York* decision and dissent of 1905. The majority opinion includes the "right-of-center" liberal argument favoring complete freedom of contract, although this was not directly at issue in the case:

> The general right to make a contract in relation to his business is part of the liberty protected by the Fourteenth Amendment, and this includes the right to purchase and sell labor, except as controlled by the State in the legitimate exercise of its police power.
>
> Liberty of contract relating to labor includes both parties to it; the one has as much right to purchase as the other to sell labor. There is no reasonable ground, on the score of health, for interfering with the liberty of the person or the right of free contract, by determining the hours of labor, in the occupation of a baker. Nor can a law limiting such hours be justified as a health law to safeguard the public health, or the health of the individuals following that occupation.
>
> It is also urged, pursuing the same line of argument, that it is to the interest of the state that its population should be strong and robust, and therefore any legislation

[35] Many voters were skeptical of the ethics and tactics of the new industrialists. A significant subset of the new industrialists was referred to as "robber barons," although the new millionaires rarely resorted to obviously illegal behavior. (Many of the new industrial millionaires – Carnegie, Rockefeller, Morgan, Edison, and Ford – established large charitable foundations with large endowments partly to undermine such labels. See, for example, Johnson 1997, 536–60.)

which may be said to tend to make people healthy must be valid as health laws, enacted under the police power. If this be a valid argument and a justification for this kind of legislation, it follows that the protection of the Federal Constitution from undue interference with liberty of person and freedom of contract is visionary, wherever the law is sought to be justified as a valid exercise of the police power. Scarcely any law but might find shelter under such assumptions, and conduct, properly so called, as well as contract, would come under the restrictive sway of the legislature.

The minority dissent by Oliver Wendall Holmes includes the progressive argument, which supported government regulation of some contracts and gradually became the dominant opinion on the Supreme Court.[36]

This case is decided upon an economic theory which a large part of the country does not entertain. If it were a question whether I agreed with that theory, I should desire to study it further and long before making up my mind. But I do not conceive that to be my duty, because I strongly believe that my agreement or disagreement has nothing to do with the right of a majority to embody their opinions in law. It is settled by various decisions of this court that state constitutions and state laws may regulate life in many ways which we as legislators might think as injudicious, or if you like as tyrannical, as this, and which, equally with this, interfere with the liberty to contract.

Sunday laws and usury laws are ancient examples. A more modern one is the prohibition of lotteries. The liberty of the citizen to do as he likes so long as he does not interfere with the liberty of others to do the same, which has been a shibboleth for some well-known writers, is interfered with by school laws, by the post office, by every state or municipal institution which takes his money for purposes thought desirable, whether he likes it or not. The 14th Amendment does not enact Mr. Herbert Spencer's Social Statics.

Although the final *Lochner* decision was far narrower than the arguments applied, the opinions clearly demonstrate that the split between right- and left-of-center liberals occurred in the highest policy circles, as well as among politically active interest groups, political theorists, and editorial writers.[37]

Debates between liberals and progressives became significant factors in American policy and constitutional debates at about the same time that similar debates between moderate liberals and social democrats emerged in Europe, although the debate on adult male suffrage in the United State was essentially over (outside the South) by this point.

[36] See, for example, Rehnquist (2001, 107), who argues that *Lochner* was wrongly decided. The point of the quotes, however, is to demonstrate that liberal ideas and arguments were present at the highest levels of government, rather than to analyze the *Lochner* decision per se.

[37] Rehnquist (2001, 113–14) provides a short summary and critique of "anti-progressive" Supreme Court decisions.

Electoral and Bureaucratic Reforms Parallel Those in Europe

At the same time that progressives lobbied for changes in the economic constitution, they also successfully lobbied for reforms of political constitutions at the state and national levels. As a consequence, a number of significant procedural changes occurred during the progressive period, many of which also parallel those of Europe during this time.

For example, various forms of the secret ballot were adopted by individual states, beginning with Massachusetts in 1888. Ballots were placed in official envelopes before being placed in ballot boxes, which allowed votes to be cast without fear of rebuke by neighbors, landlords, and employers.[38] Nineteen states also added (or included) direct referenda and recall provisions to their constitutions, which allowed voters to decide specific issues, avoiding agency problems associated with representative systems of government.[39]

Bureaucracy was reformed to reduce political influence over the bureaucracy (although in the United States this was done to reduce incumbent advantage and corruption, rather than to reduce royal influence). The Pendleton Act (1883) established the U.S. Civil Service Commission, which placed most federal employees on a merit system, greatly reducing the extent to which political parties could determine jobs within the bureaucracy. After the Pendleton Act, only holders of the senior-most jobs in the U.S. bureaucracy were appointed by the president.

Such civil-service reforms improve efficiency by increasing continuity and institutional memory. To the extent that job-related skills are not highly correlated with partisan loyalty, merit-based hiring also tends to increase competence and productivity of the persons employed at the same time that the incumbent's ability to use the bureaucracy in political campaigns for reelection is reduced. The latter tends to increase political competition (by reducing incumbent advantage) and reduce corruption.

[38] Secret ballots were also known as the "Australian ballot," because the rules and ballots were heavily influenced by Australian electoral reforms of the previous decade. The new ballots included a list of all candidates, rather than favored candidates. Standard ballots were printed by government and distributed at voting places, although several exceptions existed (Ludington 1909). Heckelman (1995) notes that voter turnout fell as the secret ballot was adopted, which suggests that vote buying was diminished by the new voting rules.

Paper ballots had previously been used in several states. New York and Vermont had used paper ballots since independence.

[39] Provisions for referenda were mostly adopted by new states in the West that received statehood after the Civil War, but several other states amended their state constitutions to allow such referenda. Direct democracy continued to be used in some New England towns throughout this period, although it had not previously played a significant role in state governance.

The Suffrage and Temperance Movements

Prior to the Civil War there were broad American suffrage movements that attempted to expand suffrage for men and women. As in Europe, the American suffrage debates focused on qualifications for casting independent, meaningful votes. The suffrage movement initially attempted to reduce remaining property and residency qualifications for suffrage; it subsequently sought to eliminate religion, race, and sex as qualifications for suffrage. The early male-suffrage movements were quite successful, and property qualifications for men's suffrage were largely eliminated in the early nineteenth century, although other qualifications were sometimes added. These early successes did not entirely end men's suffrage campaigns, although they clearly became smaller and less effective as they began to focus on suffrage expansion for smaller groups, such as Southern blacks and native Americans.

A women's suffrage movement emerged in the early nineteenth century at about the same time that property restrictions for men's suffrage disappeared in most of the United States. Their influence is evident in the Fourteenth Amendment (which guaranteed "due process of law" and "equal protection of the laws" to *all* citizens). Supporters of women's suffrage had almost been able to add the word "sex" to the Fifteenth Amendment, which ruled out legal discrimination on the basis of race (see Keyssar 2000, 178–9). The Fourteenth Amendment was subsequently used in legal challenges of state suffrage laws that discriminated against women. These challenges were unsuccessful, however, in part because the legislative history of the Fifteenth Amendment was well known, and in part because the Fourteenth Amendment itself included provisions based on the sex of voters.[40]

After the Civil War, organized support of women's suffrage and women's equality before the law was by far the most active and best known of the American suffrage movements.[41] The women's suffrage movement gained support in the late nineteenth century, and it began to have significant effects on public policy in the twentieth century. For example, several states

[40] The Fourteenth Amendment distinguishes between equality before the law in general and political equality. Seats in the House of Representatives after 1868 were allocated among states in proportion to the number of men qualified to vote, rather than state population. This provided states with a strong incentive to eliminate their remaining restrictions on male suffrage. The Fifteenth Amendment prevents the use of race as a qualification for suffrage.

[41] Evidence of this can be easily obtained. For example, typing in the words "suffrage movement" into the search engine Google returns only women's suffrage movement links.

adopted women's suffrage laws in the early twentieth century (Keyssar 2000, 203–12).[42]

Roughly during the same period, another long-standing movement gained in strength and began to influence public policy and induce constitutional reforms at the state and local level. Various temperance movements were organized to oppose alcohol abuse and lobbied for new laws restricting alcohol access, production, and consumption. For example, the American Temperance Society was organized in 1826. Temperance societies were founded in Ireland in 1829, in Sweden in 1837, in Denmark in 1840, and in Norway in 1845. Energetic temperance movements also emerged in Germany and England. Some of these organizations were international in scope, as with the Independent Order of Good Templars; others simply paid attention to the efforts of other similar groups in other places, copying their best practices.[43]

Temperance appealed to the Puritan strand of American thought, which had long opposed "demon rum." Support for temperance laws in the United States and in Europe increased toward the end of the twentieth century, partly as a consequence of the new urban lifestyles based on wages, where many men were reputed to "drink up" a significant fraction of their week's wages on the way home to their families on pay days. As a consequence of lobbying campaigns by a broad cross-section of antialcohol groups, many towns, counties, and a few states tightened their regulations for alcohol production, sale, and consumption. Pressures to do so at the national level intensified in the early twentieth century.[44]

The long-run constitutional success of the women's suffrage and temperance movements are consistent with the suffrage-reform model of Chapters Seven and Eight. A majority of male voters had gradually been persuaded that women were qualified to cast their own independent votes and that alcohol was undermining the quality of life and the productivity of a broad cross-section of the American labor force. In no case was the women's or temperance movement a serious revolutionary threat.

[42] Qualified women had been granted suffrage in some colonies and in the state of New Jersey from 1776 through 1807. Idaho adopted women's suffrage in 1896, Washington in 1910, California in 1911, and Kansas in 1912 (Keyssar 2000). A useful timeline of the U.S. women's suffrage movement and women's suffrage is available at http://dpsinfo.com/women/history/timeline.html.

[43] The temperance and women's suffrage movements in Europe are less studied, because they operated in the political shadow of various men's suffrage movements. See Johnson (1997) and the *Catholic Encyclopedia* for overviews of European temperance movements.

[44] For a contemporaneous overview of the pro- and antiprohibition campaigns in the United States, see the *New York Times*, July 16, 1911, "Prohibition the Issue of 1911." (Some states and counties had long been "dry" states, as, for example, Maine had been since the mid-nineteenth century.)

PROGRESSIVE REFORMS OF THE NATIONAL CONSTITUTION 1910–20

A number of progressive amendments were proposed at the national level in the late nineteenth and early twentieth centuries. Only four eventually generated sufficient support to pass with the required supermajorities in the Congress and to be ratified by three-quarters of the states. (In the United States, the executive branch does not have veto power over amendments, so negotiations take place within and among the chambers of the national and state legislatures.) Two of the progressive amendments were similar in spirit to those adopted in Europe at about the same time, insofar as they further democratized American governance. One of the amendments addressed tax-reform issues that were normally addressed with ordinary legislation in Europe. The last addressed a public-health and morality issue using constitutional amendment procedures, whereas in Europe such reforms were normally adopted through ordinary legislation.

Changing the U.S. Tax Constitution: The Income Tax and Prohibition

The federal government had relied entirely on excise taxes and tariffs for its revenues before 1913 (with a short exception during the Civil War), because the Constitution forbade direct federal taxes – taxes borne directly by individuals. In this, the federal government had a standing tax constitution that proscribed a tax base analogous to that of the medieval kings of Europe during times of peace. The use of tariffs and excise taxes limited the range of services that could be centrally provided, which helped assure that governance in the United States would remain a decentralized federal system.[45]

As demands for central government services increased and confidence in the central government's ability to provide those services increased, it became clear that old tax rates would have to be increased or new taxes introduced. Those most affected by existing tariffs and excise taxes, of course, generally preferred that a new tax be introduced that would shift the

[45] Neither the colonial governments nor the state governments were similarly restricted. Colonies had used taxes similar to income taxes as early as the seventeenth century. States had used income taxes throughout the nineteenth century, beginning with Virginia in 1843 (Comstock 1921). The federal government's occasional use of an income tax had been ruled unconstitutional by the Supreme Court in 1895.

burden of taxation to others. There were also ideological arguments in support of income taxation. For example, proponents such as Edwin Seligman argued that the income tax was a fairer tax because the burden of excise taxes and tariffs tended to be disproportionately borne by middle-class and poor persons.[46] The Democratic Party proposed a national income tax in their 1896 platform, and a series of income-tax proposals were introduced in Congress, but voted down during the next decade.

However, economic growth, electoral pressures, free-trade lobbies, and expenditure pressures, including those associated with national security, increasingly favored income taxation in the early twentieth century (Brownlee 2004, chapter 1). Congress passed the Sixteenth Amendment allowing income taxes on July 2, 1909, which was ratified by the required number of state legislatures on February 3, 1913.

The first income tax was incorporated into a tariff reduction bill in 1913. Tariffs were reduced as the income tax was implemented, which suggests that fiscal exchange had played a role in the amendment process.[47] The income tax was subsequently expanded during World War I, because the war caused tariff revenues to fall at the same time that American participation in the war caused federal expenditures to increase. The importance of income taxes as sources of revenue was further increased when the Eighteenth Amendment (prohibition of alcohol sales) was adopted in 1919.

The temperance movement, as noted earlier, had long lobbied for laws that limited alcohol consumption. There were state and national campaigns to reduce and/or eliminate alcohol consumption in most states throughout the nineteenth century. As a consequence, many cities, counties, and states adopted rules prohibiting alcohol consumption, especially in the early twentieth century.

By 1913, a majority of persons in the United States lived in places in which alcohol consumption was prohibited, and the temperance movement turned its attention to a national program. Representatives from these congressional districts and states pressed for similar rules for the nation as a whole (Cherrington 1920, 323–30). However, a constitutional amendment was necessary, because at that time, regulations of alcohol was an area of

[46] Seligman was an economist at Columbia University who had written widely on the effects of an income tax. He testified before Congress on May 20, 1911 in support of the amendment (*New York Times*, May 21, 1911).

[47] Although tariff rates were reduced, tariff revenues initially increased as a consequence of the Underwood Simmons Tariff Act of 1913. The new national income tax was somewhat progressive. It included a 1 percent tax on personal and corporate incomes above $3,000 and a 6 percent rate on incomes above $20,000. About 98 percent of U.S. taxpayers paid no income tax (Brownlee 2004, 56–7).

state, rather than national, policy. An antialcohol amendment was passed by Congress on December 18, 1917 and ratified by the required number of state legislatures on January 16, 1919. (The Eighteenth Amendment was subsequently repealed by the Twenty-First Amendment in 1933.)

This amendment was motivated by ideological and public-health interests, although concerns about the latter were partly ideological in nature. Prohibition, in contrast to the income-tax amendment, reduced national, state, and local tax revenues from excise taxes on alcohol products.[48]

Reforming the Selection Process for Members of Congress

The two other progressive amendments were similar in spirit to those adopted in Europe in the early twentieth century. The Seventeenth Amendment placed the American first chamber – the Senate – on an electoral basis. The Nineteenth Amendment expanded suffrage by eliminating sex as a criterion for suffrage. As in Europe, support for these reforms reflected a mixture of pragmatic, partisan, and ideological interests.

The Senate was initially designed to represent the interests of state governments, so its members were appointed by state legislatures. This gave its members somewhat different institutionally induced interests than members of the House of Representatives. Support for reform of the Senate was based partly on a number of scandals in the late nineteenth century, including procedural ones in which state legislatures were unable to select a senator for months at a time, leaving their state unrepresented. There were stories about senators who received their seats through campaign contributions to state parties. Critics began to refer to the Senate as a "millionaire's club."

Progressives and left liberals in the United States, as elsewhere, favored direct elections over indirect ones and pressed for reforms, largely because they thought that representative assemblies produced better public policies than appointed ones. A consensus for reform of the Senate became evident in 1893, when two-thirds of the House of Representatives voted to place the Senate on a directly elected basis. The Senate, however, vetoed the proposed amendment and similar proposals for the next eighteen years.

As a method of getting around the constitutional provision that senators be appointed by state legislatures without amending the constitution,

[48] Equally effective temperance movements were also active in Scandinavia during this same time period, and the result was also often prohibition. For example: Norway, Finland, Iceland, and Russia experienced periods of prohibition at about the same time as the United States. The Swedes transferred all sales to state stores and regulated consumption through a coupon system.

reformers encouraged states to conduct nonbinding elections for senators and encouraged state legislators to promise to vote according to those electoral outcomes. This and other shifts in state politics gradually changed the institutional interest of the senators in the Senate.

Ten senators who voted against reform of the Senate lost their reelection campaigns in 1910 and were replaced with progressives favoring reform. Thirty-one state legislatures formally announced their support for the direct election of senators (Zelizer 2004, 356–62). Negotiations between the Senate and House of Representatives finally produced a compromise amendment early in 1912. The Seventeenth Amendment, providing for the direct election of senators, was passed by Congress on May 13, 1912 and ratified by the required number of state legislatures (many of which already used this procedure) on April 8, 1913.

Women's suffrage also reflected the effects of long, persuasive campaigns on the men who were entitled to adopt the reforms, as suggested by the models of Chapter Eight. American's left liberals (reform Republicans) and progressives supported suffrage extension, while moderates and conservatives initially opposed it. The Progressive Party supported a constitutional amendment for women's suffrage in 1912, and the Republicans did so in 1916 (Zelizer 2004, 370–7).

Democrats opposed a constitutional amendment and argued that women's suffrage should be adopted one state at a time. A compromise on amendment language was worked out between the House and Senate in 1919 and accepted by the required supermajorities in the two chambers on June 4, 1919. It was ratified by three-quarters of the states on August 18, 1920. The Nineteenth Amendment, as was true of women's suffrage laws in Europe, extended the logic of "qualified voters" to women. What is unusual about the U.S. case is the long gap between the last major male suffrage reforms (1869) and women's suffrage (1920). Support for further suffrage expansion among male voters clearly increased very gradually in the United States.

Voting patterns within the Congress for all four of the progressive amendments reflected ideological and economic interests of the states and voters represented. Berman's (1987) empirical work based on voting patterns in western states and McDonagh and Price's (1985) analysis of voting patterns in Midwestern states and California support the hypothesis that ideological considerations played a significant role in male support for women's enfranchisement (support for the amendments rose with votes for the Progressive Party and fell with votes for Democrats). Support for women's suffrage among male voters was also linked to other policy agendas – in particular prohibition – which is consistent with the ideological model of suffrage reform developed in Chapter Eight. Holcombe and Lacombe (1998) provide statistical evidence that relatively low-income states favored the income tax , and states that had already adopted direct election of senators favored the new method of selecting senators.

Consequences of the Progressive Amendments

The individual progressive amendments were modest relative to the constitutional reforms adopted in Europe at this time, but they also significantly altered the procedures and resources of the national government.

By changing the electoral basis of the Senate, the government became a less federal system of government. No longer were state-government interests in preserving state authority directly represented in the national government. The possibility of an income tax implied that national revenues were no longer limited to excise taxes and tariffs. These were significant reforms. Indeed, some legal scholars argue that the progressive reforms were the first truly fundamental reforms of American political procedures and constraints since the ratification of the Bill of Rights amendments in 1791 (Epstein 2006).

Together, the Sixteenth, Seventeenth, and Nineteenth amendments removed earlier constitutional constraints on the size of the central government and increased the demand for and supply of central government services.[49] State and local governments had been the main sources of public services in the years before the progressive amendments, but after 1913, state expenditures grew more slowly than federal ones. Various income taxes rapidly became the most important revenue sources for the federal government, and subsequently allowed federal programs for international security and social insurance to expand steadily for several decades after the Great Depression and World War II.

CONCLUSION: THE GOVERNMENT OF THE UNITED STATES EMERGED FROM A LONG SERIES OF CONSTITUTIONAL NEGOTIATIONS AND COMPROMISE

With the adoption of women's suffrage, the United States can be said to have completed a three-hundred-year-long transition to constitutional democracy. The foundations of national governance had been electoral since 1776,

[49] There is evidence that women's suffrage produced a new median voter with a higher demand for social insurance than the previous one (see Lott and Kenny 1999).

but the members of America's parliament were more directly elected in 1920 than they had been in the past.[50] Equal protection of the law was guaranteed by the Fourteenth Amendment. Race and sex were no longer allowed to be used as qualifications for suffrage under the Fifteenth and Nineteenth Amendments. Suffrage was essentially universal among adults, except in the southeast, where other qualifications for suffrage were still in place.[51]

Two of the most important periods of reform reflected changes in the number of parties directly participating in constitutional negotiations. This demonstrates that the standing procedures for amendment were significant constraints on the possibilities for constitutional reform throughout U.S. history. Reforms were not simply imposed by successful revolutionary leaders. The historical record includes a good deal of direct evidence of negotiations and compromises that were necessary to obtain the necessary support under the amendment procedures. Commercial interests, mobility, and ideology played central roles in the colonial deliberations of the seventeenth and eighteenth centuries. Similar interests, augmented by politically active interest groups and industrialization, helped induce additional reforms in the nineteenth and twentieth centuries.

As predicted by the models of Part I, the rise of parliament and the broadening of suffrage were largely independent of one another. The rise of parliament occurred for the most part in the colonial period, well before independence and well before universal adult suffrage was adopted. There were advantages associated with sharing policy-making authority in the colonial context that were analogous to those analyzed in Chapters Five and Six. Labor and capital were mobile, and formeteurs and their successors

[50] Elections for the president are still indirect. Votes are tabulated at the level of states, and state electors cast their votes for the president. The number of electors in each state is equal to the sum of their senators and their representatives. With very minor exceptions, however, the electors have always voted in the manner recommended by the majority of their state's voters.

It bears noting that the chief executive in prime ministerial systems is also indirectly elected, which suggests that the electoral system adopted in 1787 was a compromise between those favoring selection of presidents by both chambers of Congress and those favoring direct elections. (Madison's notes for August 6 and September 4, 1787, regarding section 1 of article ten of the draft constitution are not clear on this point, although suggestive.)

[51] Suffrage was not extended to poor whites or most blacks in the South until the late 1960s, although both groups had briefly been free to vote in national and state elections after the Civil War.

Suffrage among adults in most European countries in most cases excluded minorities in 1925, as noted earlier. Citizenship for native-born "foreign workers" was often difficult to obtain until after World War II. Persons on welfare were also generally ineligible to vote even after "universal" adult suffrage was achieved, as, for example, in Denmark, Japan, Sweden, and the United Kingdom.

wanted to attract them to their territories. The balance of authority that emerged between colonial governors and parliaments reflected colonial institutions and circumstances that generally favored the colonial parliaments. Suffrage in the United States began at relatively high levels during its colonial period, because it helped assure free labor that their interests would be represented in government.

In spite of this early relatively broad suffrage, the transition to universal suffrage took nearly three hundred years (three hundred fifty, if suffrage restraints in the southeastern United States are taken into account). Male suffrage was gradually extended as property, religious, educational, and racial qualifications were eliminated, although there were periods in the eighteenth and nineteenth centuries in which suffrage contracted. In the nineteenth and twentieth centuries, constitutional amendments extended suffrage to former slaves, Native Americans, and women.

The United States was affected by liberal and technological tides in the nineteenth century that were broadly similar to Europe. For example, ballot and bureaucratic reforms and women's suffrage were adopted in Europe and the United States at about the same time. With respect to women's suffrage, it seems clear that suffrage norms had changed on both sides of the Atlantic during the late nineteenth century in a manner consistent with the models of Chapter Eight. Women's suffrage was clearly not the product of strikes or revolutionary threats. Although industrial strikes did occur in the United States during this period, it was largely men who were already eligible to vote that conducted the strikes.

The nonrevolutionary basis of the contemporary Constitution of the United States of America is clearly suggested by its architecture for governance. The Virginia template of 1619 remains evident, although significant reforms were adopted during the course of three centuries of constitutional negotiation, conflict, and compromise. A revolution (war of secession) did lead to the drafting of new state and national constitutions in 1776, but the "new" state and national constitutions adopted at that time reflected a century and a half of constitutional negotiations and experimentation by colonial governments.

PART III

ANALYTICAL HISTORY AS SOCIAL SCIENCE

NINETEEN

Quantitative Evidence of Gradual Reform

Anyone who has attempted to keep a diary knows that faithfully recording history is nearly impossible, even in very small number settings. There is much that must be left out because of space and time constraints. Both deductive and inductive approaches to history face similar problems. Just as every historical narrative can potentially be more complete, so can every model. Indeed, many, perhaps most, debates among historians, political scientists, and economists arise from disagreements about whether variable *x* or event *y* has been inappropriately neglected or focused on by others. In this, the preceding chapters are no different from other models and alternative historical narratives and so are naturally open to such criticism. The historical narratives of Part II suggests that the models of Part I can shed useful light on the emergence of Western democracy, but no proof is possible.

For many readers, the predictions of the models will seem so evident in the historical narratives that further empirical analysis seems unnecessary. On the other hand, the historical narratives were written with the models in mind, and it is possible that the factors focused on were given greater prominence than they deserved. It is also possible that the pattern of reform was less regular and predictable than the narratives make them appear, because so much has been left out. It is possible that constitutional bargaining played a smaller role in constitutional developments than the narratives suggest.

More evidence is always useful. With this in mind, Chapter Nineteen develops quantitative evidence and statistical tests to assess the explanatory power of the model of constitutional reform developed in Part I. Statistical inference rarely ends debates over the relevance of models or variables, but it does allow hypothesized relationships to be examined systematically and often sheds light on the extent to which particular relationships and variables can account for the events of interest.

The estimates and tests conducted in Chapter Nineteen broadly support the main hypotheses about the emergence of Western democracy: (a) that democratic governance arose gradually through a series of parliamentary and electoral reforms and (b) that constitutional and economic liberalization were interdependent phenomena during the nineteenth century.

THE TEMPORAL STRUCTURE OF POLITICAL AND ECONOMIC DEVELOPMENT

Subjecting the models to statistical tests requires a somewhat more quantitative and coarse formulation of both the models and historical experience than used in the narratives.

Recall that the models of Part I imply that the bargaining equilibrium determines the nature of a government's constitution (C_t) in period t. These reflect preexisting distributions of ideological (I_{t-1}) and economic (W_{t-1}) interests; the preexisting constitutional architecture (C_{t-1}), and political (v_{t-1}) and other random "shocks" in the previous period. All these factors affect the bargains reached by the parliament and the king. Some of these shocks may be sufficiently large to be considered crises, but crises are not necessary for constitutional reforms to be adopted.

The extent of economic liberalization (L_t) in period t reflects past political decisions and so the extent of economic liberalization is determined by the same political and economic variables as those that determine the current constitution. The distribution of human capital (E_t) reflects past education policies and the distribution of wealth (W_t); so it is largely determined by the same past political and economic variables as constitutional and economic liberalization. The distribution of economic interests (W_t) is largely determined by economic regulations (L_t), the past distribution of available resources (including human capital), the state of production technology (T_t), and economic shocks (u_t). Economic inertia exists because the distribution of natural resources and capital (physical, human, and organizational capital) and past regulations tend to change relatively slowly because of institutional conservatism with respect to economic regulations and within the economic enterprises themselves. Consequently, W_{t-1} is an important determinant of present economic opportunities.

The general temporal logic of the models can be summarized with a series of intertemporal equations:

$$C_t = C_{t-1} + c\left(I_{t-1},\ W_{t-1},\ v_t\right) \tag{19.1}$$

$$L_t = l\left(I_{t-1}, W_{t-1}, C_{t-1}, v_{t-1}, u_{t-1}\right) \tag{19.2}$$

$$E_t = e\left(I_{t-1}, W_{t-1}, C_{t-1}, v_{t-1}, u_{t-1}\right) \tag{19.3}$$

$$W_t = W_{t-1} + x\left(L_t, T_t, E_t, u_t\right) \tag{19.4}$$

To simplify for the purposes of statistical analysis, C_t can be thought of as an index of liberal democracy, W_t as average real wealth, and I_t as an index of the liberalness of the ideology of the median member of parliament. Natural resources are assumed to be determined by national boundaries, geographic location, and geological factors, which are taken as given for the period of interest. Technology and ideology are exogenous variables in this model, and reflect past innovations and experience in science and philosophy.

Note that even with these simplifications, time dependency in a constitutional bargaining model is not an unexplained property of the "error term," but rather is predicted by the internal logic of the model. The implicit function theorem allows the constitutional and economic systems to be characterized as functions of the predetermined and exogenous variables.

$$C_t = C\left(u_t, v_t, C_{t-1}, W_{t-1}, I_{t-1}, T_{t-1}, v_{t-1}, u_{t-1}, I_{t-2}, T_{t-2}, v_{t-2}, u_{t-2}, \ldots\right) \tag{19.5}$$

$$W_t = X\left(u_t, v_t, C_{t-1}, W_{t-1}, I_{t-1}, T_{t-1}, v_{t-1}, u_{t-1}, I_{t-2}, T_{t-2}, v_{t-2}, u_{t-2}, \ldots\right) \tag{19.6}$$

These reduced forms demonstrate that constitutional and economic systems are interdependent and substantially determined by similar past chance events and innovations. That is to say, constitutional liberalization and economic development are predicted to be highly correlated, because they are determined by the same variables, although through somewhat different processes, as reflected by the two functions.

Unfortunately, there are no good quantitative measures of the magnitude of past ideological and technological changes. Indeed, the importance of particular innovations are normally assessed by looking at their economic and political impacts, rather than through independent measures of the innovations themselves (Burke 1978, Mokyr 2002).

These data problems can be bypassed to some extent if technological and ideological innovation can be characterized as stochastic processes. For example, it can be argued that innovations are substantially unpredictable insofar as they are produced by men and women with random collections of talents and knowledge whose new ideas are catalyzed by chance events.[1] This makes the ideology and technology sequences analogous to those of v and u, and they can be treated in a similar manner for purposes of statistical tests.

This additional assumption allows equations 19.5 and 19.6 to be approximated as:

$$C_t = \gamma\left(C_{t-1}, W_{t-1}, u_t, v_t, z_{t-1}, z_{t-2}, \ldots\right) \tag{19.7}$$

$$W_t = \chi\left(C_{t-1}, W_{t-1}, u_t, v_t, z_{t-1t}, z_{t-1}, \ldots\right) \tag{19.8}$$

with

$$z_{t-1} = v_{t-1} + u_{t-1} + T_{t-1} + I_{t-1} \tag{19.9}$$

Equations 19.7 and 19.8 are similar to those used in most contemporary empirical work on the political economy of institutions, although the models predict that the stochastic parts of the reduced-form models are likely to be serially correlated and mixed, rather than pure, distributions. The models also differ from others used (often implicitly) in this area of research in that they do not imply unidirectional causality or particular trigger points at which democratic politics or market economies become feasible.[2] The assumed continua of government and market types allows peaceful and gradual transitions to parliamentary democracy and to market-based economies when there are what might be called "liberal trends" in the random shocks, but stability when there are no trends.

History and the Intertemporal Equations

The historical narratives suggest that both kinds of periods have existed in Europe. Medieval forms of king-and-council governance were stable for centuries at time, although there were reforms and counter-reforms. Trends in

1 If ideological and technological shocks are not completely exogenous, one could represent such innovations with functions such as $T_t = s(T_{t-1}, E_{t-1}, L^E_t, W_{t-1}, z_t, u_t)$ and $I_t = i(I_{t-1}, E_{t-1}, C_{t-1}, W_{t-1}, v_t, z_t, u_t)$. These relationships can be substituted into equations 19.5 and 19.6, and would yield reduced forms similar to those of equations 19.7 and 19.8, but without explicit technological and ideological variables. Nonetheless, if genius and/or luck are required for innovation, the "genius factor" z_t remains an important variable both in the T and I models and in the reduced forms. In such cases, "genius" and "luck" drive both economic and constitutional development in the long run, which provides a role for exceptional men and women in the model.

2 For an extensive overview of the contemporary literature on the interdependence between economic and political development, see Paldam and Gundlach (2008). Congleton and Swedenborg (2006) provide an overview of the contemporary rational-choice-based empirical research on the policy effects of alternative democratic constitutions.

economic and political reforms are evident in the nineteenth century. The historical narratives suggest that the trends reflect increased rates of technological innovation, new economies of scale, and the "radicalization" of liberalism.

There is also historical evidence of the predicted boot-strapping effects. The early market and educational reforms contributed to increased rates of innovation, which tended to increase support for further liberalization of economic rules insofar as new economies of scale became possible. Broader markets, in turn, allowed new industrial organization to be profitable, which increased specialization and helped expand the middle and upper-middle classes, who generally favored greater openness in politics and markets. Upward mobility required eliminating medieval privileges in economics and politics.

Economic liberalization often advanced political liberalization, and political liberalization often supported economic liberalization. There was no conflict between democracy and economic development in the nineteenth century. Although each transition includes unique features, the Western transitions were qualitatively similar and occurred during roughly the same time period, largely between 1825 and 1925.

The remainder of this chapter suggests that Western transitions were also quantitatively similar.

DESCRIPTIVE STATISTICS FOR THE NINETEENTH CENTURY

Economic historians and political scientists have constructed macroeconomic and macro-political data sets for the nineteenth century. These data are less precise than their contemporary counterparts, but they are sufficient to demonstrate that the historical narratives developed in Part II are consistent with recent efforts to quantify institutional developments. Estimates of reduced forms of the models based on that data demonstrate that the models provide useful causal theories of western constitutional developments in the nineteenth century.

It should be acknowledged that the quantitative data are imperfect in many respects. For example, per capita gross domestic production data is, for example, often used as a measure of average personal income or welfare. There are conceptual problems with doing so, because not all sources of income or economic welfare are measured (or estimated) by contemporary formulations of GDP. There are additional problems with using nineteenth-century data to approximate average income, because GDP is less precisely measured and to some extent measures the wrong thing.

Nineteenth-century GDP data are not based on extensive market survey data, but are estimated from economic models that link GDP to other available quantitative data, such as tax and trade flows. Moreover, gross domestic product measures market activity and neglects domestic sources of goods and services. Household production was a much larger fraction of personal income during the first part of the nineteenth century than at the century's end, because more of economic life took place in the home in 1800 than in 1900. The gradual reduction in household production during the nineteenth century implies that GDP per capita provides an estimate of average income that is biased downward in the early part of the century relative to the last part of the century. This tends to bias growth rates of personal income upward and exaggerate the effect of business cycles on personal income in the first half relative to the second half of the century.[3]

Quantitative political indicators are also problematic for much of the nineteenth century. With the exception of vote counts and seats in parliament, evidence about the nature of constitutions is inherently less numerical than data about economic income. Even election data tend to be sparse in the early part of the nineteenth century, because voting was often by voice and division, rather than ballot, and because elections for seats in parliament were often not contested. Data on party affiliation are also unreliable during the first half of the nineteenth century, because disciplined political parties emerged in most of Europe only in the late nineteenth century, although various more or less stable factions have long existed. The absence of party platforms and good voting records implies that the standard measurements of party and voter ideology are unavailable.

One can say with some confidence that average wealth, suffrage, or turnout are twice as large in country A than in country B, but one cannot so easily conclude that the parliament in country A is twice as powerful or its government is twice as democratic as that of country B. The breadth of suffrage and the division of authority between the king or president and the parliament are quire different things and the historical narrative suggests that they are not always highly correlated.

Quantitative Indices of the Relative Authority of King and Council

Nonetheless, several attempts have been made to construct indices of democracy for the nineteenth century. For example, the Polity IV database extends back to 1800 for many countries. That data series is based on expert appraisals of a number of common characteristics of governance for the

[3] This bias may be offset to some extent by reductions in environmental amenities, but tends to be increased by reduced access to communal resources.

countries in the data set. These characteristics are used to create numerical "subindices," which are then aggregated into widely used indices of democracy (essentially added together). The subindices of Polity's 0–10 index of democracy assess both formal constitutional procedures and de facto political procedures, as judged by various country experts.

The widely used Polity index is a similar −10 to +10 index that subtracts an index of autocracy from the democracy index. Democracies (10) have broadly competitive systems for choosing their chief executives, institutional constraints on governance, and guarantees for civil liberties. Autocracies (−10) have executives that are chosen by a narrow elite who can govern without significant institutional constraints.

Unfortunately for the purposes of this book, the Polity indices focus for the most part on the procedures through which a country's "chief executive" comes to office, rather than on the distribution of policy-making authority between the executive and parliament, or the election laws for parliament, which are the main focus of this book. In nineteenth-century parliamentary systems, determining who the chief executive is and whether he or she is elected or not requires determining whether the prime minister or king is actually the chief executive in a given year, and who ultimately chooses the prime minister.

As developed in Part II, the precise manner in which prime ministers are chosen and their policy-making authority relative to the king is not entirely determined by constitutional documents. Consequently, the Polity indices implicitly require assessing the relative importance of policies controlled by the king and cabinet and the extent to which the king or parliament determines the membership of the cabinet. Because of this, one of the democracy subindices, XrComp, indirectly sheds light on one of the key shifts in authority required for the emergence of parliamentary democracy in the nineteenth century. The other subindices for the democracy index provide equally coarse assessments of the extent to which chief executives are politically and constitutionally constrained.[4]

The subindex XrComp characterizes the competitiveness of executive recruitment. It focuses the selection process for the executive (hereditary, designated, or elected). In nineteenth-century Europe, a value of 1 implies royal dominance, 2, sharing between a king and an (indirectly) elected prime minister, and 3, dominance by an (indirectly) elected prime minister (Marshall and Jaggers 2005, 24). Clearly, three categories can only roughly measure the continuum of policy-making authority.

[4] The democracy index focuses on three characteristics: (a) the existence of institutions through which citizens "express effective preferences about alternative policies and leaders," (b) the extent to which there are "institutionalized constraints on the exercise of

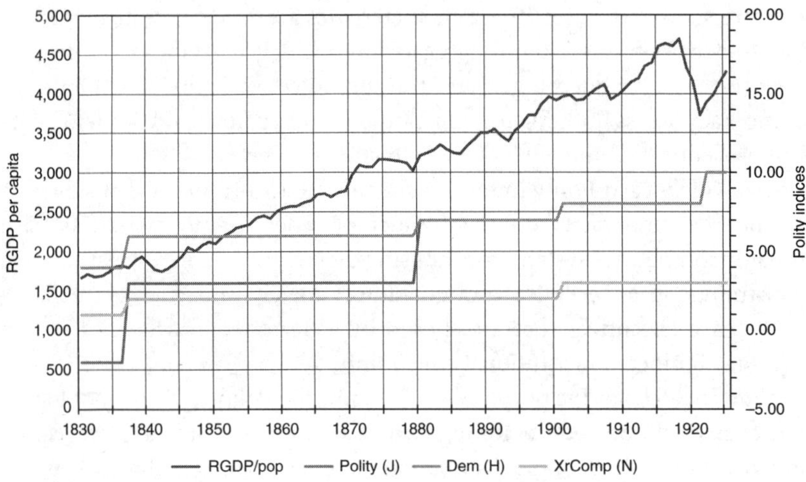

Figure 19.1. The British transition 1830–1925.

Some Suggestive Data Plots

Figures 19.1, 19.2, and 19.3 plot economic and political indicators for the United Kingdom, Sweden, and the Netherlands. The figures include per capita gross domestic product in constant dollar terms (RGDPpp) and three Polity indices. The RGDPpp data are from Officer (2006) for the United Kingdom, from Smits, Horlings and Van Zanden (2000) for the Netherlands, and from Edvinsson (2005) for Sweden. The political liberalization indices include (a) Polity's executive competition subindex, XrComp, which takes integer values from 1 to 3, (b) Polity's democracy index, which takes values from 1 to 10, and (c) the Polity index, which takes values from −10 to +10. Because there are different experts for different countries, cross-country comparisons are less than completely reliable, although the country indices are internally self-consistent.[5]

The data plots reveal that average income increased more or less continuously during the nineteenth century in Great Britain, the Netherlands, and Sweden, although there were several business cycles. Business cycles

power by the executive," and (c) aspects of civil liberties and the rule of law. Overall, the index attempts to measure "the competitiveness of political participation, the openness of executive recruitment, and constraints on the chief executive." Many of the subindices are simple 0–1 variables. (Marshall and Jaggers 2005, 17–18).

5 See Jacobs and Smits (2001). Van den Berg et al. (2006) note that business cycles in the nineteenth century had significant effects on quality of life and mortality.

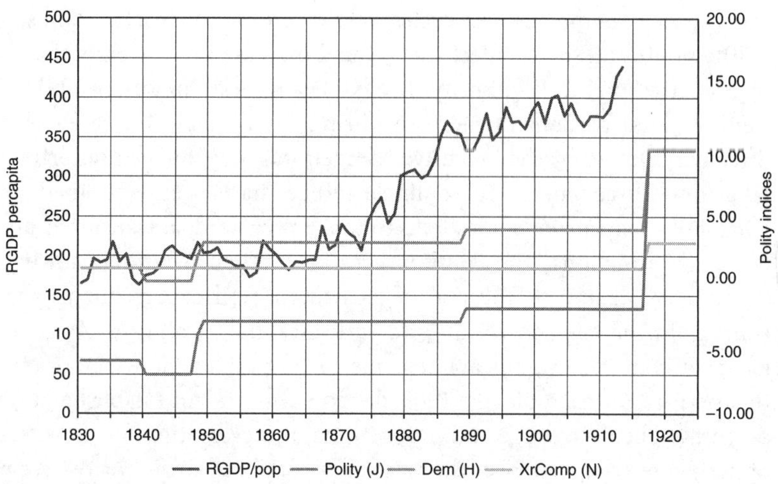

Figure 19.2. The Netherlands transition 1830–1925.

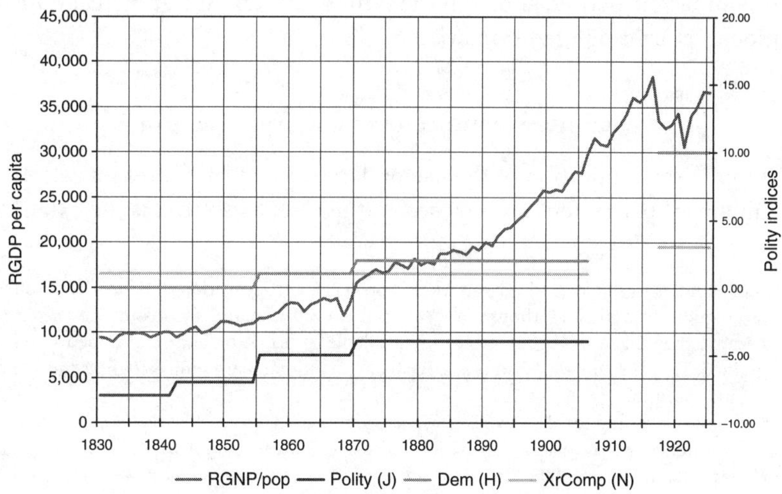

Figure 19.3. The Swedish transition 1830–1925.

are evident in spite of the fact that the estimated RGDPpp data have been smoothed somewhat by researchers to reduce various measurement errors. Indeed, many of the business cycles were severe and international in scope.[6]

The political indices reflect the gradual increase in the democratic basis of executive political authority. Kings became less important and prime ministers and parliament more so during the century. The latter is most directly indicated by the executive competition index, which unfortunately takes only three values. The political indices have been smoothed somewhat, but their integer values tend to make very gradual transitions appear to be step functions. The Polity indices for Sweden rise more slowly than seems consistent with the rise of parliament and expansion of Swedish suffrage in the late nineteenth and early twentieth centuries. As noted in Chapter Fourteen, significant reforms of its parliament were adopted in that period. For example, the 1907 election-law reforms established universal (unweighted) suffrage and proportional representation for the selection of parliament. Control over the cabinet (as opposed to authority over budgets), however, was not completely resolved until the period of World War I. Unfortunately, the effects of parliamentary reforms are only indirectly measured by the Polity indices.[7]

Overall, real per capita GDP and liberal democracy increased gradually throughout the period, although the timing of economic growth and institutional reforms differed somewhat.

Quantitative Indicators of Suffrage Reform

A more direct indication of the use of democratic procedures for selecting members of parliament, as opposed to the chief executive, is the extent to

[6] Most studies of this period rely on Maddison's (2003) compilation of data. The country-level studies of Smits, Horlings, and Van Zanden, Officer, and Edvinsson are used here because they make use of more recently available information and tend to be more fine grained. Trends in the Maddison RGDP per capita estimates are similar to these individual country studies.

[7] Some of the coding for the Swedish case is coded as "88" from 1907 to 1916, which indicates a period of "transition" in which the usual indices cannot be definitively judged (Marshall and Jaggers 2005, 18). This coding indicates that there was greater ambiguity in this period than usual over who could appoint the cabinet and prime minister.

Chapter Fourteen suggests, however, that intermediate values of XrComp (2) would have been appropriate for this period. Although there were several large public demonstrations in favor of economic and political reform, elections continued to be held as constitutional reforms were introduced, debated, and adopted. Some of the reforms adopted in this period had delayed effects; for example, turnover in the upper chamber took place over nine years (Congleton 2003c, chapter 3; Verney 1957, chapters 8–9).

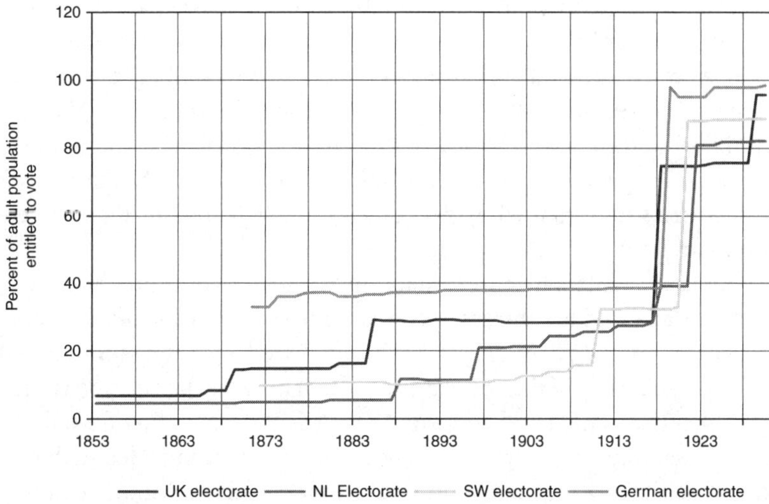

Figure 19.4. Electorates in four European countries.

which persons were eligible to vote and actually cast votes in national elections for seats in parliament. Records exist for suffrage law reforms, population, and the number of votes cast in late-nineteenth-century elections. This information has been used by Flora et al. (1983) to estimate the eligibility to vote within several Europe countries, although the estimates do not cover the entire nineteenth century. Time series of eligibility for the United Kingdom, the Netherlands, Sweden, and Germany are plotted below in Figure 19.4. (Toke Aidt kindly provided the interpolated values of the Flora estimates.) The Flora calculations clearly indicate a gradual expansion of suffrage – more or less as step functions for the countries depicted. (The individual "steps," however, should tilt upward somewhat, reflecting the suffrage effects of increasing personal wealth and tax payments under the suffrage laws of that period.)

Suffrage reform was not an all-or-nothing revolutionary event; rather, significant reforms were adopted occasionally throughout the nineteenth century. Several significant revisions are evident in each of the four countries.

Voter turnout in the early nineteenth century is more difficult to assess than eligibility to vote, because early elections were often by voice vote, and many candidates for parliament ran unopposed before the emergence of well-organized national political parties. These factors, together with parliaments' limited authority, tended to make casting votes less important in

the early nineteenth century. Vote tabulations, however, are available for the second half of the nineteenth century, as more elections for seats in parliament were contested and as paper ballots and secret ballots were introduced. Table 19.1 lists votes cast, population, and fraction of the population voting using data from Cook and Paxton (1978, 1998) for the number of voters and population. The Cook and Paxton data for the Netherlands and Sweden are supplemented by data taken directly from Dutch and Swedish election records.

Population figures from national census data do not align perfectly with election dates and are interpolated from the nearest available data points. Turnout rates are rough approximations, based on the assumption that adults make up half of the population and that the adult population is equally divided between men and women. As long as the true ratios are stable, the relative magnitudes of turnout will be similar to those included in the table. Note that electoral participation gradually expands both numerically and proportionately throughout the century. It also bears noting that the largest single suffrage reforms occur just before or after World War I, when most adult women became eligible to vote.

In combination with the Polity indices, the election data support the contention that substantially new procedures for selecting public policy gradually emerged in the nineteenth century. Parliaments gradually obtained broad authority over public policy (through their prime ministers) and the members of parliament were elected by increasingly broad electorates.

Overall, the data plots and table support the hypothesis that the political and economic "revolutions" of the nineteenth century were the consequence of a long series of reforms, rather than a single great innovation or change in institutions.[8] Similar diagrams and tables could be constructed for Belgium, Denmark, Italy, and Japan, and also for the republics of the United States, Switzerland, and France. Although each of these countries had a somewhat different path of electoral and parliamentary reform, their beginning and end points were remarkably similar. Liberal parliamentary democracy did not emerge in a single great step, even in France, where major reforms were experimented with.

[8] It seems clear, for example, that women's suffrage was based on ideological considerations, rather than a response to revolutionary threats or economic development. The women's movement never organized armed militias, nor did economic income expand at unprecedented rates in the decade before suffrage was granted to women. A majority of men (who were directly represented in parliament) had become persuaded that women were sufficiently competent and independent to cast a thoughtful vote.

Table 19.1. *Votes Cast in National Elections and Population*

Nineteenth-Century Netherlands, Sweden, and the United Kingdom (in thousands, from Cook and Paxton, European Political Facts 1848–1918*)*

	Netherlands			Sweden			United Kingdom		
Election Years (NL and UK)	Voters	Pop (interpolated)	Turnout (est)	Voters (nearest yr)	Pop (interpolated)	Turnout (est)	Voters	Pop (interpolated)	Turnout (est)
1831							435.4	26081.571	0.033
1833							652.8	26211.457	0.05
1866							1056.7	30206.1	0.07
1869							1995.1	30973.32	0.129
1883							2618.5	35454.42	0.148
1886							4380.5	36308.85	0.241
1888	292.6	4471.267	0.131	274.7	4719.196	0.116			
1891	293.8	4629.92	0.127	288.1	4784.98	0.12		37732.9	
1894	299.1	4807.7	0.124	339.9	5101.258	0.133			
1897	576.6	4985.48	0.231						
1901	609.6	5254.84	0.232				6730.9	41458.7	0.325
1905	752.7	5556.52	0.271						
1909	843.5	5858.2	0.288	503.1	5445.2	0.185	7710	44976.44	0.343
1913	960.6	6243.4	0.308	1066.2	5558.837	0.384			
1918	1081.5	6690.1	0.323	1124	5777.462	0.389	21392.3	43833.754	0.976
1922	1844.8	7079.36	0.521				21127.6	42957.442	0.984

STATISTICALLY SIGNIFICANT CORRELATIONS

The same data sets allow statistical tests of some of the boot-strapping hypotheses of the bargaining model of constitutional reform. For example, equations 19.7 and 19.8 imply that there will be significant correlation between per capita RGDP and the democracy indices during the nineteenth century. Such correlation is evident in the figures described earlier, insofar as RGDP per capita and the various Polity indices of democracy generally increase throughout the century.

To determine whether or not these visual regularities are statistically significant, regressions were run on real per capita gross national product (GNP) and the democracy index for the period from 1830 to 1929 for the United Kingdom, the Netherlands, and Sweden. These are the countries that best fit the model, which are also the ones for which the democracy index provides the best measure of the degree of political liberalization. Linear estimates of equations 19.7 and 19.8 are reported in Table 19.2.

The hypothesized positive correlations between economic and political developments are present at statistically significant levels. Similar correlations between income and political developments are often found in studies of late-twentieth-century governance in cross-sectional and panel studies. See, for example, Lipset (1959), Grier and Tullock (1989), Knack and Keefer (1995), Przeworski et al. (2000), Mosquita et al. (2003), and Paldam and Gundlach (2008).

The model also has predictions about the stochastic components (residuals) of the estimates. The models imply that both systematic and stochastic components should be evident in the residuals. Note that the linear estimates support both predictions. The error terms account for a significant fraction of the variation in the economic and democratic developments in the United Kingdom, the Netherlands, and Sweden. The predicted time dependency is evident in the Durban-Watson statistics, which indicate the presence of statistically significant autocorrelation.

Overall, the regression estimates suggest that choice-framing variables focused on in the models are relevant ones that help to describe the course of constitutional history, notwithstanding the various measurement problems.

JOINT CAUSALITY TESTS FOR ECONOMIC AND POLITICAL LIBERALIZATION

The regressions reported in Table 19.2 support the contention that economic and political liberalization were associated with one another in

Table 19.2. *Ordinary Least Squares Estimates of the Relationship between Real Domestic Product Per Capita and Polity's Democracy Index*

	United Kingdom, Netherlands, and Sweden 1830–1929			
	UK RGDP per capita (LS)	UK RGDP per capita (Arch)	NL RGDP per capita (LS)	SE RGDP per capita (LS)
Constant	−588.435 (−2.47)**	−1017.974 (−8.32)***	140.654 (8.86)***	12584.35 (23.97)***
Democracy Index	545.860 (34.16)***	630.203 (38.78)***	46.751 (8.94)***	2515.341 (19.31)***
R-square	0.72	0.68	0.49	0.81
F-statistic	255.33***	39.83***	79.93***	373.21***
DW	0.16	1.7	0.15	0.06
N Observations	100	100	84	90
	UK Democracy (LS)	UK Democracy (Arch)	NL Democracy (LS)	SE Democracy (LS)
Constant	2.667 (9.89)***	3.863 (13.72)***	−0.0864 (−.25)	−3.584 (−10.37)***
Real GDP per capita	0.001 (15.97)***	0.001 (15.25)***	0.011 (8.94)***	0.000322 (19.32)***
R-square	0.72	0.94	0.49	0.81
F-statistic	255.33***	252.98***	79.93***	373.21***
DW	0.19	1.42	0.15	0.05
N Observations	100	99	86	90

* Denotes statistical significance at the 10 percent level. ** Denotes statistical significance at the 5 percent level. *** Denotes statistical significance at the 1 percent level.

the nineteenth century, but they do not shed much light on the nature of that dependence. The estimates suggest that somewhat more than half of Western economic and constitutional developments in the nineteenth century were jointly determined. Similar results can be found for other countries of interest for the purposes of this study, including Belgium, Germany, and the United States, although the Polity indices less faithfully reflect the path of parliamentary reform in these other countries.

The theory developed in Part I suggests that constitutional and economic liberalization are jointly determined, rather than causally related. This is consistent with the hypothesis that both are induced by trends in technological and ideological developments that produce new constitutional gains from exchange and compromise.

Direct tests of the boot-strapping and joint-causality hypotheses can be undertaken with the statistical causality tests developed by Granger (1969). The Granger approach uses past values (lags) of the two variables as estimators for each other. If past values of variable *X* contribute to the explanation of current values of variable *Y*, then *X* is said to "Granger cause" *Y* in the sense that past values of *X* help predict current values of *Y*. Joint causality is said to exist if past values of *Y* also help to predict present values of *X*.

The existence of statistically significant joint causality between average income and democracy indices would provide evidence that economic and political liberalization are outcomes of other similar (or correlated) variables. Granger causality tests are possible for five of the six case-study countries using data similar to that used above. Table 19.3 summarizes the results.

The results reveal somewhat stronger causality from economic to political developments, although joint causality for economic and political developments is found in three of the five cases. Joint causality of economic and political liberalization in the United Kingdom, the United States, and the Netherlands – cannot be rejected at plausible levels of statistical significance. Swedish causality is stronger from economic to political liberalization. German causality is stronger from political to economic reform.

Given the coarseness of the Polity indices and the fact that the democracy indices focus on the executive, rather than parliament or parliament-executive relations, the statistical results are stronger than might have been expected. In general, they are consistent with the predictions of the models of Part I and the narratives of Part II. The joint-causality result for the United States is the most surprising because so much of its economic and political liberalization took place before 1830.

EMPIRICAL SUPPORT FOR THE CONSTITUTIONAL BARGAINING AND REFORM MODEL

The visual and statistical tests of this chapter demonstrate that the predictions of the models of Part I and the conclusions of the historical analysis are supported by statistical analysis of the data available for the nineteenth century. The regression estimates account for between 50 and 80 percent of the aggregate economic and political developments in the West, which suggests that the choice settings modeled in Part I were commonplace and

Table 19.3. *Granger Causality Tests for Economic and Political Change*

United Kingdom (U.K.), the Netherlands (NL), Sweden (SE), Germany (DE), and the United States (U.S.) Mid-Nineteenth Century to Early Twentieth Century (two lags)	
U.K. Rgdp per capita does not Granger cause U.K. democracy	7.96***
U.K. democracy does not Granger cause Rgdp per capita	2.12*
NL Rgdp per capita does not Granger Cause NL democracy	242.62***
NL democracy does not Granger cause NL Rgdp per capita	25.77***
SE Rgdp per capita does not Granger Cause SE democracy (logs)	3.48**
SE democracy does not Granger cause SE Rgdp per capita (logs)	0.49
DE Rgdp per capita does not Granger Cause DE democracy	1.59
DE democracy does not Granger cause DE Rgdp per capita	3.81**
U.S. Rgdp per capita does not Granger Cause U.S. democracy	7.00**
U.S. democracy does not Granger cause U.S. Rgdp per capita	26.87***

* denotes significance at the 10 percent level.
** denotes significance at the 5 percent level.
*** denotes significance at the 1 percent level.
(The period of interest is 1830–1929, although the data sets were somewhat incomplete for the Netherlands and Germany. Some periods in Germany and Sweden are coded as not available.)

important in Europe during the nineteenth century.[9] Evidently, relatively similar constitutional gains to trade emerged at more or less the same time throughout the West. Causality between economic and political development tends to be bidirectional in most cases, as predicted.

The unexplained residuals suggest, as historians often argue, that men and women of genius and luck clearly mattered in each case, and that the negotiations reflected chance events and states of mind. On the other hand, the rise of Western democracy was not entirely the result of chance and heroic efforts. The statistical analysis of this chapter and the historical narratives of Part II suggest that there was much that was systematic. Together with the historical narratives, the statistical analysis suggests that constitutional and quasi-constitutional bargaining produced a long series of liberal

[9] It bears noting, however, that the variance of the true error term is likely to be somewhat larger than the results suggest, because both the RGDP and Polity data series have been smoothed by the social scientists who assembled them to reduce measurement errors, which tends to increase intertemporal correlation within and across data series.

reforms during the nineteenth century. The political subset of those reforms produced what we refer to today as Western democracy.

That liberal reforms can increase civil liberties, civic equality, and promote economic development remains evident in the 20th century. Most contemporary indices of *institutional quality* are simply indices of the *liberalness* of a polity's political and economic institutions. Such indices may be said to measure how far a given polity has moved from its medieval (authoritarian) political and (mercantilist) economic systems toward a liberal one. A correlation between the quality of institutions and economic income and growth have been found in many contemporary studies. (Holcombe, Lawson, and Gwartney 2006; Keefer and Knack 1995; Congleton 2007b).

TWENTY

Ideas, Interests, and Constitutional Reform

The theory of constitutional design and reform developed in this volume explains the essential architecture of parliamentary democracy and the path of reform that produced it. It explains why policy-making authority tends to be divided, why the distribution of policy-making authority changes through time, and why this normally is done without radically changing the standing procedures for governance. It demonstrates that significant shifts of the distribution of policy-making authority within divided governments can occur peacefully and lawfully through a process analogous to exchange in markets. The analysis suggests that a series of such constitutional reforms can gradually transform a more or less authoritarian system into a parliamentary democracy.

The historical narratives of Part II suggest that liberal democracy emerged in this manner. Trends in economic and ideological interests allowed a series of liberal reforms to be negotiated and adopted by kings and parliaments during the nineteenth and early twentieth centuries. These constitutional and quasi-constitutional reforms gradually produced the rules of economic and political life that we largely take for granted in the West. Indeed, those new rules can be said to have created the West.

This concluding chapter reviews the book's main arguments and conclusions, and contrasts them with other macro-political theories and histories. It also argues that the analysis of this book can also be used to understand and predict contemporary constitutional developments. Other methodological issues are taken up in the appendix.

THE LOGIC OF CONSTITUTIONAL GOVERNANCE AND REFORM

The theory of constitutional governance and reform developed in this volume is based on a theory of organizational governance. All organizations, including political ones, have to overcome internal incentive and governance problems to be viable in the short run and long run. Solving incentive problems requires artificial incentive systems that attract team members and align the interests of the team with the organization's (formeteur's) long-term interests. Solving governance problems requires establishing standing procedures for gathering information and selecting policies (standing internal rules) that advance organizational interests and for revising those policies through time as circumstances inside and outside the organization change.

An organization's standing procedures for choosing policies can be regarded as its constitution. An organization's constitution normally specifies the persons (officeholders) that participate in policy decisions, the scope of their authority, and how particular policies are made. In small organizations, there may be only a single person with the authority to choose policies. In larger organizations, a policy-making team is likely to choose the organization-wide policies. Such policy-making teams (governments) may be subdivided in various ways, as with the king-and-council architecture, and authority for making policies may be divided in various ways among the team members and component institutions. All durable organizations have constitutions in this sense, although not all such constitutions are written down.

Specific implementations create political property rights over policy areas. Political property rights, in this sense, characterize the procedures (and constraints) through which public policies are to be adopted. These assignments of authority tend to be fairly stable through time, because the existing rules tend to advance the interests of the persons with the ability to change them. At points in time when that is not true, there will often be constitutional gains to trade that can be realized by reforming the "rules of the game," and reforms will be bargained over and (occasionally) adopted.

Such constitutional reforms are commonplace in both the private and public sector, although they tend to be modest and do not usually exhibit strong trends.

Choosing among Constitutions

All formal organizations have a beginning, at which point their formeteurs normally choose from tried and true templates for governance, such as the king-and-council template. In doing so, they acknowledge the difficulty of constitutional design. The use of familiar templates reduces the extent to which formeteurs have to engage in institutional analysis, which frees time and attention for other purposes. The use of a familiar template also reduces risks. If a template has worked well in other organizations they are familiar with, it is likely to work for their new organization as well.

The king-and-council template is widely used for organizational governance because it solves a variety of informational and agency succession problems and reduces unproductive intraorganizational conflict. It is scalable in the sense that it can be used to make policy decisions in small and large organizations, within the subdivisions of a large organization, and by confederations of independent organizations. It is flexible in that it can be adjusted along various margins to take account of the talents, interests, and circumstances of formeteurs and their successors.

The knowledge and time constraints and risk aversion that induce formeteurs to rely on preexisting templates for governance also imply that constitutional reforms tend to be modest and infrequent. There are costs – risks and uncertainties – associated with all reforms, and there are benefits associated with stable routines. Stable routines reduce the cost of creating and maintaining stable and profitable relationships with persons and groups inside and outside an organization.

Both amendment procedures and the institutionally induced interests of those holding high offices thus tend to favor continuity over revolution in constitutional design. Moderate reforms allow organizations to adjust to changing circumstances, while preserving most of the benefits of standing procedures and policies. Such conservative propensities are not entirely accidental or consequences of risk aversion; rather, they are products of past experiments, experience, and selection.

The rationality of formeteurs (and their successors) and the importance of survivorship imply that the procedures of organizational governance tend to improve through time. Improved governance helps organizations to survive and flourish by making more effective use of information, personnel, and resources.

STABILITY AND TRENDS IN ECONOMIC AND POLITICAL REFORM

This somewhat terse summary of the theory of the design and evolution of organizations developed in Chapters Two to Five has surprisingly direct implications for territorial governance and its evolution.

It provides an explanation for periods in which governments are more or less stable and for periods in which trends in reform exist. It also predicts that reforms are likely to occur when the economic and ideological interests represented in government change, but only if potential gains to constitutional exchange emerge under the preexisting distribution of political property rights.

Because most constitutional reforms are small and many are informal, such reforms will be most evident when there are trends in the reforms. Trends eventually produce cumulative reforms that are sufficiently large to be noticeable to outsiders.

Violence, per se, does not play a central role in the analysis, although threats of violence may be used to increase a regional government's organizational stability and efficiency by reducing the cost of aligning the interests of team members and citizens with their governments. Threats of violence and other major crises may also induce reform, although such threats are neither necessary nor sufficient to do so.

A Point of Historical Departure: The Medieval Constitution

In the late-medieval period, most governments in Europe were based on relatively standard forms of the king-and-council template. Most regional and national governments had strong kings and weak parliaments.

Although parliaments were commonplace throughout medieval Europe, their members were for the most part members of elite families who served in government as a birthright. Even those elected to office were often from aristocratic families. The locus of policy-making authority was centered in a single royal man or woman and his or her appointed councilors. Prior to 1700, there were no national governments whose policy makers were selected on the basis of broad suffrage. Only citizens, narrowly defined, could vote in Athens; only the wealthiest 5 to 10 percent of men voted in medieval cities such as Siena and Florence during their "republican" periods; only a small fraction of citizens could vote for the English House of Commons until well into the nineteenth century. The parliaments (or tax councils) normally had veto power over new taxes.

Most kings delegated part of their executive authority to a council or cabinet of ministers that managed the day-to-day operations of the government. The latter suggests that there were three institutional centers of policy-making authority, but the executive council was normally controlled by the king and so could be regarded as a royal instrument, rather than an independent policy-making authority. In the nineteenth and early twentieth centuries, control over appointments to the executive council became an indicator of the balance of authority between kings and parliament.

The division of authority between kings and their parliaments and between kings and their executive councils were not entirely static during the medieval period, but they did not exhibit obvious long-run trends. The parliaments (or tax councils) normally had veto power over new taxes. Parliaments occasionally traded taxes or support on issues of particular interest to kings in exchange for royal approval of policies of interest to parliament or for a bit of additional policy-making authority. Similar fiscal bargains also occasionally shifted authority to kings, especially during times of national crisis. Most such reforms tended to be small and many were undone after a decade or two. Somewhat larger reforms occurred at times when important veto players changed, as at times of succession, although these also tended to be reversed in subsequent decades.

Some kings and some parliaments were stronger than others. Some kings also delegated more policy-making authority to their executive councils than others. Nonetheless, the medieval balance of authority was quite stable, because the constitutional reforms of the medieval period had conservative self-correcting tendencies. Kings were nearly always the dominant policy maker.

The stability of the medieval constitution diminished in the seventeenth and eighteenth centuries, but did not disappear. For example, English policy making in 1630 was characterized by a relatively strong king and weak parliament. From 1640 until 1653, English policy making was dominated by parliament. It returned to executive dominance with Cromwell's protectorate (1653–8) and to royal dominance in the years following the restoration (1660–88). The Glorious Revolution of 1688 shifted significant policy-making authority back to the parliament, although the king retained the dominant authority (Morgan 2001, 310, 326, 334).

Sweden began the eighteenth century with a dominant, nearly authoritarian king, followed by a period with a dominant parliament, the so-called Age of Freedom in 1719–72. Sweden ended the eighteenth century with a king-dominated government and the restoration of royal prerogatives after 1789 by Gustav III (Weibull 1993, 53, 61, 74). The century-long moving average remained, nonetheless, at approximately the medieval norm.

The stability of medieval constitutions did not imply that all persons or all members of parliament preferred the medieval order – with its hierarchical society, numerous trade barriers, monopoly church, royal rituals, and magnificent buildings – to other political and economic systems that they could imagine. There were nearly always persons and groups that lobbied for political, economic, and religious reforms during the medieval and early-modern periods. For example, upper-middle-class farmers and town merchants generally regarded themselves to be underrepresented in parliament and believed that their interests were often neglected or harmed by national policies. Many supported reforms of parliamentary procedures that would later be called liberal reforms. However, support for such reforms among those who could adopt them was not sufficiently strong or sustained for durable reforms to be adopted.

King-dominant systems of divided governance with mercantilist internal and external economic regulations were stable and robust for many centuries.

Technological and Ideological Trends Induce Constitutional Reform

Clear trends in the reforms of European governance emerged in the nineteenth century when new technological and ideological trends emerged. These created new alignments of economic and ideological interests that pressed for more open economic and political systems. There were new economies of scale in production and new theories of governance and economics. Liberalism motivated a number of politically active idealists and provided useful arguments for economic pragmatists favoring such reforms.

The new support for economic and political liberalization altered the balance of support and produced a long series of liberal economic and political reforms in much of Europe, North America, and Japan. The result is often called Western democracy.

CONTRAST WITH BIG-BANG THEORIES OF REFORM

The importance of the political and economic reforms adopted have induced many scholars to propose explanations of the rise of the West. Their theories can be divided roughly into two categories: "big-bang" or revolutionary theories and "evolutionary" or reform theories.

The big-bang theories of Western democracy are quantum leap theories in which new institutions for governance emerge suddenly, normally because of revolutions, constitutional conventions, or combinations of the two. Revolutions provide a possible mechanism through which outsiders can influence the policies of a government. Constitutional conventions provide a mechanism through which new institutions for governance can be drafted whole cloth. These two explanations for new constitutional regimes can be combined. A constitutional convention might be called after a civil war or war of secession is won.

Analysis of constitutional conventions assumes that agreement about new institutions can be discovered at such assemblies, and often attempt to explain why a community might adopt a constitution that incorporates particular institutional features (usually ones that the scholars are already familiar with). Hobbes (1959), writing in authoritarian France, for example, suggests that there will be a single sovereign body, as a means of escaping anarchy. Buchanan and Tullock (1962), writing in the United States, suggest that the particular voting procedures and federal institutions may advance general interests. Revolutionary theories often accept such "general-will" contractarian theories of constitutional design, but insist that violence or threats of violence are key to the creation and reform of government. In such models, government officeholders never have interests in reform, only in continuity, unless there is a military threat from within.

Both peaceful and violent big-bang theories of constitutions tend to imply that (a) constitutions are developed whole cloth at times of crisis (b) followed by a period in which the new constitution remains entirely stable, until (c) another major crisis and/or revolution occurs.

With respect to the emergence of democracy, most big-bang theories focus entirely on the extreme forms of governance, dictatorships and parliamentary democracy. Given that focus, transitions cannot be gradual because there are no intermediate forms of government. Such a focus also tends to imply that constitutional transitions require revolutions of one kind or another, because constitutional exchange is essentially impossible if the choice is only between liberal democracy and autocracy.

Simplistic big-bang explanations suggest that "the people" organize a revolution to overthrow an authoritarian regime, and, if successful, adopt a radically new democratic government by holding a national constitutional convention. (Grammar-school treatments of the French and American Revolutions often adopt such narratives.[1]) More sophisticated theories acknowledge that there are several ways that an authoritarian regime can be overthrown and a new constitution implemented. Within a violent revolution model, the first step requires the organization of sufficient military power to overthrow the existing regime, which is often acknowledged to be a difficult process. Within a peaceful revolution model, the persons in power must be persuaded to voluntarily surrender their authority to large peaceful demonstrations, rather than use the army and police to disperse the demonstrations.

[1] A useful book-length critique of such explanations for the American War of Independence and the Constitution of the United States is provided by Raphael (2004).

Once the overthrow of an authoritarian regime is accomplished, the desired constitutional reforms can be adopted in several ways. The formeteurs of revolutionary movements (revolutionary leaders) may simply impose a new (hopefully democratic) constitution on the country, or they may organize a constitutional convention that does so. The members of the constitutional convention may be appointed or elected. Why revolutionary leaders call a constitutional convention is not explained. Evidently, revolutionary leaders are postulated to be contractarians.

Big-bang theories of historic change are numerous and a complete survey of them is beyond the scope of the present volume. Such chasm-jumping theories of democracy include historical ones by Marx and Engel (1959) and Palmer (1959), contemporary sociological and economic ones by Goldstone (1993), and Acemoglu and Robinson (2000). The critical assessments of revolutionary theories developed in this book parallel those of Goldstone (1993, 2001), who argues that most revolutionary theories lack causal micro-foundations.

As an explanation for the emergence of Western democracy, big-bang models suffer from several defects. There is an implicit assumption that an overthrow is undertaken with the aim of liberal reform, rather than simply to take over the top offices of the existing government. There is also an implicit assumption that the governments of the revolutionary military organizations that conduct the wars or liberation tend to adopt democratic institutions after the war is won, rather than simply adopting the slogans and vocabulary of democrats. Democratic institutions are, of course, not easy to design or implement, nor is it ordinarily in the interests of revolutionary leaders to adopt them. Constitutional conservatism supports the continuation of military governance. After all, their "transitional" governance must have been reasonably effective to have won the war, and it would be risky to experiment with major institutional reforms.

This is not to argue that no liberalizing civil wars or constitutional conventions took place in the nineteenth century. Belgium successfully seceded from the Netherlands and established a relatively liberal form of constitutional monarchy based on the British-Dutch template. There were also large, peaceful demonstrations during the mid-century that helped promote liberalization, but usually as one of many factors that induced modest reforms to be adopted, rather than a major force that induced major reforms. For example, the Netherlands, Denmark, and Prussia adopted significant reforms in the period just after the popular demonstrations of 1848, but their constitutional negotiations and reforms were already under way at the time. Dutch and Danish reforms began a decade or two before those demonstrations. Prussia's new constitution included liberal provisions, but it did not shift very much authority from the king and his council to the new representative chamber of the new parliament. Subsequent liberal reforms were adopted in each case without further "revolutions."

It also bears noting that popular demonstrations, uprisings, and civil wars do not always produce liberalization or democracy. Peasant revolts were fairly common before the nineteenth century, but they never produced parliamentary democracies. Instead, they usually elicited more repressive laws and enforcement (Tilly 2004). Censorship increased and other civil liberties were curtailed both during and after the period of the French Revolution. Germany's grand constitutional convention of 1848–9 did not cause a new German constitution to be adopted. The violent revolutions of the early twentieth century (in Russia and China) produced authoritarian regimes, rather than parliamentary democracy. This can also be said of the French revolutions of the late eighteenth and mid-nineteenth centuries.[2]

Peaceful and violent big-bang theories also have problems explaining the timing and institutions of Western democracy. Authoritarian regimes (king-dominated governments) had long held power. Was repression worse in 1900 than in 1800 or 1200? Moreover, in many Western democracies kings still have a place in government and live a royal lifestyle. If the old authoritarian governments were overthrown, why do kings and queens remain in office? There is also the matter of elections and suffrage. There were normally elections for a significant number of the members of parliament before 1900. Was this democracy or not? Why are there so many ways to elect members of parliament used today?

Such details would naturally be of little interest if the only choice is between dictatorship and democracy. If there are only two possible forms of government, then one or the other form of government is always in place before and after a revolution is won. Quantum-leap accounts also neglect the fact that even when relatively large reforms are adopted, as in Belgium in 1830, the reforms adopted are large only relative to the ordinary course of reform. Most of the constitutional and legal framework that existed before such "revolutions" remains in place.

The constitutional-bargaining model developed in this volume provides a better explanation of the observed path of reform, the conservative

[2] A contributing factor for the failures of some wars of liberation is that the leaders of the revolutions have ideological reasons for rejecting the forms of governance that history has demonstrated to be viable. By rejecting templates that work, rather than simply modifying them, the probability of failure increases. As noted in Chapters Two and Three, there are good reasons for institutional conservatism.

nature of reforms adopted, and the general architecture, procedures, and continuity of Western governance. It is the intermediate forms that make modest reforms and institutional continuity possible. It is also the intermediate forms that allow reforms to be voluntarily adopted by those already holding office at times when new constitutional gains to trade emerge.

By ignoring the intermediate forms of governance, the big-bang theories implicitly assume away the continuum that allows gradual transitions to take place.

CONTRAST WITH OTHER EVOLUTIONARY THEORIES OF REFORM

In addition to the revolutionary theories of constitutional reform, there are also many evolutionary theories of society in general and governance in particular. For example, most historians that focus on national histories suggest that both national cultures and nation-states emerge gradually over the course of many centuries. Many economists and political scientists take such historical research seriously; and, as social scientists, rather than historians, they attempt to develop theories that can account for such evolutionary tendencies. Well-known twentieth-century examples include Hayek's (1948, 1973) analysis of spontaneous orders (culture and market networks) and North's (1981, 1990) analysis of the role of institutional change in economic development. Their evolutionary historical theories led to two Nobel prizes in economics. The approach of this book is largely compatible with their research, but focuses on formal rather than spontaneous organizations and on political rather than economic institutions.[3]

Other evolutionary theories tend to be sociological rather than economic in nature and include political developments as simply one of many areas in which customs and institutions change through time. When done well, social historians weave together a variety of historical threads to produce a series of rich tapestries that together provide a more or less coherent moving picture of the society of interest. Some, such as Tilly (2004), include roles for politically active groups who may occasionally induce

[3] The recent book by North, Wallis, and Weingast (2009), for example, includes much that is very compatible with this volume, although it focuses more attention on economic developments than on political ones and does not really analyze the politics of institutional reform or governance except in very general (bargaining among elites) terms.

institutional reform by staging minor uprisings. Unfortunately, by analyzing the whole of society, such general histories can only include a few snippets about each development, and by stressing general tendencies they neglect the individual decisions and circumstances that produced the patterns and changes of interest. The broad brush often hides nearly as much as it reveals.

Although evolutionary theories account for continuity and general trends in a manner that revolutionary theories cannot, the narratives often fail to explain why particular institutions exist, the factors that promote their stability and continuity, or the process through which those institutions are modified through time. With respect to government, for example, they may describe the general architecture of a government that exists, but not why the architecture tends to be more stable than the assignment of authority within it, nor how the division of authority changes through time. Apart from Finer's (1997) three-volume history, there are very few contemporary efforts to track the emergence and evolution of the rule-making bodies that we call governments.

This may be because constitutional historians have lacked a general framework for thinking about changes in the distribution of policy-making authority. Historical narratives that do not begin with the king-and-council template and that do not focus on constitutional bargaining cannot easily analyze shifts in governance during the medieval period or the gradual transition to parliamentary democracy that occurred in Europe and Japan during the nineteenth century; nor can they explain why so many democratic governments still have hereditary kings and unelected members of parliament. They lack the conceptual framework for doing so. Similarly, rational-choice models that assume officeholders have only institutionally induced interests cannot account for all the bargaining that takes place within parliaments and between kings, cabinets, and parliaments, nor why the bargaining equilibrium changes through time.

Without taking account of the non-institutional interests of formeteurs and their successors, it is difficult to explain why independently governed polities often use similar constitutional architectures. Without accounting for non-institutionally induced interests, such as may emerge from economic and ideological changes, it is also difficult to explain why no countries industrialized without democratizing and why no countries democratized without industrializing during the nineteenth century. Without taking account of possibilities for constitutional exchange, it is difficult to explain why so many democracies still have kings.

Industrialization: Cause or Effect?

Economic and political historians almost routinely argue that industrialization plays a central role in the constitutional reforms that produced liberal democracy both in the nineteenth and twentieth centuries (Przeworski and Limongi 1993). Such theories, however, have a difficult time accounting for differences in the timing and rate of industrialization among countries, because both technology and public policy rules are completely portable.

Whether economic development induces constitutional reform or constitutional reform induces industrialization is not obvious. Political decisions often determine what can and cannot be traded by determining how contractual obligations will be enforced and the subset of user-rights that can be bought and sold. Economics suggests that such political decisions can have large effects on a nation's path of economic development by affecting transaction costs, market size, and rates of technological innovation. Indeed, it is far easier to argue that national governments determine market activity than the converse, even in fairly complete models of political economy.

To the best of my knowledge, no other volume provides peaceful political mechanisms through which industrialization – itself largely an economic activity – may induce or contribute to constitutional reforms.

That industrialization often precedes political reform is likely to reflect the politics of policy reform, rather than economics per se. Officeholders and the persons whose interest they represent often benefit more directly from economic liberalization than from changes in parliamentary authority or expansions of suffrage. As a consequence, it may appear that economic developments encourage political developments, although it is politics that allows economic reforms to be adopted.

The present analysis suggests that this is true not only for minor regulations and tax laws, but also for major economic policies and constitutional reforms. The politics of economic and political liberalization cannot be ignored.

The technological innovations of the eighteenth and nineteenth centuries produced new political alignments, decreased the costs of political interest groups, and increased preexisting support for liberal reforms. Individually, pragmatists and liberals could produce very few reforms, but acting as a coalition they were in many cases able to advance a broad liberal reform agenda. Liberal reforms were not adopted simply to advance liberal ideals, but also in pursuit of profits and policy-making influence.

When such coalitions were not sufficient to produce reforms, the status quo remained in place as, for example, in Turkey, China, and Korea. In such places, very few liberals or economic entrepreneurs (if any) held influential offices in government.

Importance of Liberal Ideas

The present analysis differs from most economic explanations of historical developments in that the models and historical narratives take account of ideological as well as economic interests. Although economic interests helped push many reforms through in nineteenth-century Europe, the overall pattern of reform was not a new web of rent-creating regulations and barriers to entry, but rather more open and competitive economic and political systems. The reform agenda tended to be liberal, rather than economic in the sense of the rent-seeking literature.

The liberal economic and political theories of the late eighteenth and early nineteenth century were well suited to such ends. Adam Smith's *Wealth of Nations*, for example, included a variety of arguments against regulations that created local monopolies and in favor of expanding national transport networks. Smith did not argue that "bigger was better," but that "more open" was better than "more closed." His analysis included warnings about cartels and corporations as well as government regulators. Contractarian and utilitarian theories of the state similarly supported systems of government in which representation was broad and more or less proportional to population. They argued that everyone's interest should be accounted for, which required everyone's interest to be at the table. If representation was to be fair, then representation should be distributed according to citizen-voters. Such arguments challenged law-based preferences in economic and political life and favored civic equality.

Both contractarian and utilitarian theories were increasingly used as normative theories by educated persons in the West during the late eighteenth and nineteenth centuries, often in combination with other older norms, because the theories were taught in public and private schools and were promoted by a variety of economic and ideological interest groups. (Religion-based normative arguments faded somewhat as state church monopolies were eliminated.) As a consequence, liberal theories influenced insiders as well as outsiders and were often used in the policy and constitutional debates within national parliaments and bureaucracies. Indeed, liberal economic and political theories were probably more widely used by officeholders, bureaucrats, and other well-educated and well-traveled persons than by the general public.

This is not to say that all educated persons were liberal idealists. In many cases, the use of liberal arguments was simply a means to an end, a rationalization for higher profits or greater political influence. However, such arguments are useful only if liberal norms have been internalized by a sufficient number of those listening to the arguments to be effective. In such cases, the use of liberal arguments can help produce decisive coalitions, because coalitions are easier to assemble when there are broad interests that can be advanced, rather than only narrow interests.

Liberal arguments also indirectly undermined support for the medieval balance of authority within parliaments and between the king and parliament. Indeed, even simply shifting debates in parliament to systematic, rational analysis of policy and institutional alternatives tends to favor reform by reducing the range of arguments that can be used to support the status quo. "Mere" appeals to custom and national traditions become less persuasive. The shift from divine right of kings to contractarian explanations of governmental institutions also implies that institutional improvements are conceptually possible. God may make no errors in his designs, but man-made institutions may be imperfect and/or unjust, and such "imperfections" might be "perfected."

By undermining traditions of royal deference, the popular-sovereignty rationale for government authority also increased the cost of producing what Wintrobe (1998) terms "loyalty." It reduced the effectiveness of royal efforts to maintain control and reduced the moral authority of unelected chambers. Conversely, when kings and nobles come to accept popular-sovereignty justifications for their offices and authority, a bit more royal deference to elected chambers of parliament and to large-scale public demonstrations in support of particular reforms naturally occur.

Together, political, economic, and philosophical liberalism provided a rough direction for policy and constitutional reform and a series of persuasive arguments and convenient metrics for analyzing the relative merits of alternative policies.

Role of Liberal Interest Groups in the Emergence of Western Democracy

In evolutionary theories, interest groups are often mentioned in passing as evidence that general interests have already changed, rather than as agents for change. Consequently, only broad social movements are given much attention by most historians. For example, both sociological and revolutionary theories suggest that labor organizations are important phenomena.

In some revolutionary accounts, they are the main source of democratization. In contrast, the analysis of this book suggests that a broad range of interest groups, often organized around narrow issues such as education, trade, and suffrage reform helped produce the long series of reforms that produced liberal democracies and relatively open economic systems.

The peaceful, patient, persuasive activities of such groups are argued to be of greater interest and import than their occasional violent efforts. Peaceful activities are easier to organize than violent ones, because they are (often) legal. Such activities are normally more effective than militant efforts, because they do not attract repressive sanctions from the state, yet allow outsiders to influence the ideas and reform agendas of insiders.

Interest groups can disseminate facts and theories to persuade those represented in government to reassess their policy goals and/or normative theories. They can organize public demonstrations in support of reform and so provide cover for advocates of reform in government and undermine public-interest arguments of their opponents. If there are elections, they can also organize and increase political support for particular candidates, policies, and parties in parliament. They can also organize boycotts and strikes in support of (or opposition to) policy reforms, but these tend to be costly for participants and so they occur relatively infrequently and normally are employed only after long periods of peaceful persuasion. That such nonviolent efforts can be successful is clearly indicated by the reforms of the nineteenth century.

In many cases, the adoption of reforms catalyzed the formation of new politically active groups and/or shifts by existing groups to other reform issues in a manner that helped produce trends in reform. For example, successful efforts to reduce censorship and restrictions on voluntary association reduced the cost of forming politically active groups. New groups formed in support of other reforms, often liberal ones in the nineteenth century. As suffrage expanded, election campaigns by parties and interest group support for campaigns naturally became more important determinants of public policy.

Political competition in the late nineteenth century also affected the relative influence of organized interest groups and political parties. Many formerly conservative groups began to support modest liberal reforms as a method of attracting new members and retaining current members. Traditional nongovernmental organizations, such as churches and guilds, did not disappear, but they faced greater competition for voter attention and access to policy makers, which reduced their political influence relative to what it had been in years past.

In countries in which the conservative-pragmatist defenders of the status quo won most early policy debates, rather than the liberal-pragmatist coalitions, the formation of interest groups was suppressed and the status-quo ante was largely continued.

A TWENTY-FIRST CENTURY WHIGGISH HISTORY?

Several colleagues have suggested that the theory and historical narratives developed in this volume are similar to the optimistic "Whiggish histories" written in the nineteenth and early twentieth centuries by liberal historians. Although the term Whiggish is normally used to denigrate rather than compliment a line of historical research, this book agrees with many Whiggish conclusions. For example, liberal historians of the nineteenth and early twentieth centuries often argued that institutions and reforms of institutions have important effects on economic and political developments. They also argued that reform tends to be gradual and that there were systematic improvements of Western political and economic systems in the eighteenth and nineteenth centuries.

The historical narratives of Part II reach similar conclusions insofar as they suggest that there was economic and political progress in the West during the nineteenth and early twentieth centuries and that most of it was the result of peaceful reforms of preexisting economic and political institutions, rather than great revolutions in constitutional design motivated by internal military threats or adopted at grand constitutional conventions. A bit of direct Whiggish influence is also evident in that early-twentieth-century historians are cited fairly often in the text because they devoted greater attention to institutional details than the generations of comparative historians that followed them.

It bears noting, however, that the optimism of the theory proposed and tested in the present volume is a long-run optimism that hinges on the emergence of substantial liberal-reform interests. When other interests increase in importance, the course of constitutional reform can become authoritarian, rather than liberal, and so less attractive by contemporary Western sensibilities. This, for example, occurred in Japan in the 1930s, when conservatives (antiliberals) reversed a three-decade-long tide of liberal political reform. Similar reversals also occurred in some periods and places within the United States when states reduced or eliminated suffrage for women (in New Jersey) and subsequently for persons of non-European descent.

A bit of pessimism is also introduced by the implication that popular revolutions are unlikely to be successfully organized, and when organized, are unlikely to induce constitutional liberalization. Effective governments, essentially by definition, suppress revolutionary organizations, and so a credible threat of revolution tends to produce additional repression, rather than liberalization, within all reasonably well-run polities.

Moreover, the analysis and historical studies undertaken in this book do not imply that particular events had to occur in the nineteenth century. Instead, they suggest that, given certain conditions, some constitutional and policy reforms were more likely than others. In particular, increasing acceptance of liberal economic and political theories in Europe, together with technological innovations that increased the efficient scale of production, made liberal regulatory and constitutional reforms more likely to be adopted. Whether they are adopted or not depends on the nature of preexisting political institutions and the interests of officeholders with the ability to adopt reforms.

Moderately, But Clearly Liberal

Overall, the analysis of this book makes it clear that the Western transitions to parliamentary democracy were broadly similar, although they were not identical. In nineteenth-century Europe, liberal and commercial interests were well represented in government and constitutional reforms were adopted through tough opportunistic bargaining within parliaments and between parliaments and their kings and queens.

The reforms were not entirely dependent on industrialization or entirely culture specific. Northern European societies were culturally linked in various ways through trade, history, and religion. Many of their political and economic institutions had Germanic and Latin origins in the distant past. Scandinavia and Germany, however, had never been ruled by the Romans. The British had never been part of the Hanseatic League, and the influence of the Protestant Reformation varied widely across northern Europe. There were few Lutherans in Great Britain. Similar political and economic transitions took place in Belgium during the nineteenth century, which was not Protestant, and also in Japan, a country where trade, culture, and religion were only very weakly linked to northern Europe. The transition to democracy in Europe suggests that industrialization can be a catalyst for liberal reform, but the transition of the United States suggests that it is not the only possible catalyst.

Liberalism, however, played a central role in each of the transitions. The direction of reform was provided by liberal political and economic theories. Liberal politicians and constitutional scholars such as Madison, Grey,

De Geer, Thorbecke, and Ito provided much of the logic and language of the legislative and constitutional reforms adopted. Indeed, parliament's veto power over royal revenues (now largely in the form of household allowances) continues to support the contemporary balance of authority between European parliaments and their kings or queens (most of which remained sovereign well into the twentieth century, and many of which remain formally sovereign in the twenty-first century).

The polities produced by nineteenth-century reforms were not the laissez-faire minimal states advocated by "doctrinaire" liberals of the mid-nineteenth century, because they were determined by moderate liberals, whose preferred policies shifted during the nineteenth century. Economic competition was limited by rules against fraudulent practices and monopoly power. Slavery and several other forms of labor "contract" were forbidden. International tariffs were low, but not as low as they had been earlier in the century. There continued to be significant government support for transport, energy, and communication infrastructures, as well as for court systems that enforced civil and criminal law. Government services included public education and modest social insurance.

Nor were the new Western political systems completely democratic in the sense that majorities could adopt whatever policies they wished. The new governments were constrained by their constitutions through divisions of authority, constitutional review, and civil liberties of various kinds. Most of these policies and institutions were broadly supported by mainstream liberals in 1925, and most had long been advocated by liberal interest groups.

Liberalism and the Twentieth and Twenty-First Centuries

At the time that liberal reforms were first being implemented in North America and Europe, their long-term effects were open to question. After all, the medieval systems of governance with their associated economic regulations, monopoly religions, and hereditary-based politics had produced law and order, reasonable prosperity, and significant progress. Europe had gradually passed China, Japan, and Turkey during the seventeenth and eighteenth centuries, and had done better than most of the rest of the world for an even longer period.

The economic and political consequences of the nineteenth-century political and economic reforms must have surprised late-medieval conservatives by demonstrating that (a) prosperity could be increased and extended throughout the income distribution by freer internal and external markets, (b) such wealth-increasing reforms could be sustained by the new, broadly representative governments, and (c) democratic public policies tended to be more predictable and law bound than those of the aristocratic systems they replaced and somewhat less susceptible to political fads and deficit finance than their kings had been.

There was essentially no tradeoff between long-term growth and political liberalization in the nineteenth century. Markets and politics were simultaneously improved as institutions for promoting broadly shared interests in prosperity, equality before the law, and the provision of public services. The success of the new liberal political-economic systems relative to medieval systems accounted for much of their appeal in the late nineteenth and twentieth centuries, particularly among relatively pragmatic voters and government officeholders.

The success of these new political-economic systems was not unnoticed and did not disappear in 1925. At or near the top of most contemporary lists of "political openness" are the countries analyzed in the case studies of Part II. The same countries also top lists that measure "economic openness" and per capita national income.

Contemporary indices of governmental quality imply that (a) the more open and democratic a nation's political institutions are, (b) the more uniform and enforced its civil liberties are, (c) the more independent its judiciary is, and (d) the more literate its citizens are, the better governed are the countries of interest. Similarly, mainstream indices of the quality of economic institutions imply that: (a) the more open and competitive are the internal and external trade networks, (b) the less arbitrary (and discretionary) is its economic regulation, and (c) the more effectively a nation's civil law is enforced, the better are its economic institutions. Among such indices are the Worldwide Governance Indicators of the World Bank, the civil and political liberty indices of Freedom House, and the Economic Freedom index of the Heritage Foundation.

That liberal political and economic arrangements tend to increase the quality of life and have done so for more than a century has induced other countries to adopt liberal reforms and also induced a good deal of migration from "undeveloped" (illiberal) to "developed" (liberal) countries during the past century.

Whether the connection between liberal political and economic theories remains sufficient to produce future transitions, however, is subject to challenge. For example, Hardin (1999) suggests that there is no necessary connection between political and economic liberalism. There is, however, evidence of similar internal liberalizing pressures in many rapidly developing countries, as in South Korea and Taiwan and more recently in China and

India. Liberal economic and political ideas have influenced policy debates and decisions in the highest councils of state in those countries.

If the analysis of this book is as general as the author believes, gradual liberalization is likely to continue for the next several decades in these and other countries in which liberal ideas become widely accepted and political institutions are sufficiently flexible to allow constitutional gains to trade to be realized. In such cases, the course of reform is likely to be peaceful and lawful, although not noncontentious.

Appendix: Methodological Approach, Limits, and Extensions

Perfecting Parliament surveys a good deal of history and reflects many years spent reading constitutional documents, political treatises, and hundreds of books and papers written by careful historians. However, *Perfecting Parliament* is not intended to be mainly a historical work, but rather a contribution to social science. The book attempts to develop and test a particular theory of constitutional design and reform, rather than to induce patterns from past experience. This is not because induction is logically impossible or without interest. Indeed, my recognition of the importance of the king-and-council template was a consequence of research on Swedish constitutional history (Congleton 2001b, 2003c). Rather, it is because the main goal of this book is to advance constitutional theory.

The book develops a general theory of rule-based governance and reform. It uses that model to explain the emergence and properties of king-and-council-based systems of governance and peaceful transitions from authoritarian regimes to constitutional democracies. The case studies, historical overviews, and statistical analysis are undertaken to assess the explanatory power of that analytical approach to history. The evidence developed in Part II and in Chapter Nineteen suggest that relatively simple rational-choice models can shed significant light on important episodes of Western constitutional history.

Although the models cannot predict every detail of the constitutional bargains adopted, the choice settings characterized by the models and prose are evidently sufficiently realistic and universal that their implications are evident in American, European, and Japanese constitutional histories. The specific transitions focused on in the case studies are important ones, and the narratives suggest that a theory of constitutional reform that focuses on bargaining between parliaments and kings can shed useful light on the emergence of liberal democracy in the countries examined.

In addition to the evidence developed in this book, a good deal of other case-specific quantitative evidence also supports the contention that economic and ideological interests have influenced important policy and constitutional debates within parliaments. For example, Schönhardt-Bailey (2003, 2006) provides statistical evidence that such ideas influenced the repeal of the Corn Laws (reduction in agricultural tariffs) in the United Kingdom. Aidt and Jensen (2009) provide evidence that franchise extension and the size of government were correlated for a broad cross-section of European countries and in a manner that is consistent with the model of constitutional exchange developed in this volume.

BLUNTING ANTICIPATED CRITICISMS: ON THE SCOPE OF HISTORICAL NARRATIVES

The historical narratives do, however, make minor contributions to historical research by providing unusually tight and focused constitutional histories for six countries and general overviews of liberal policy debates and reforms. The historical narratives developed are not simply summaries of existing research. Very few historical narratives devote as much attention to institutional history and institutional detail as the case studies of Part II do, and those that do tend to focus on single institutions within rather short periods. No other comparative study examines as many constitutional documents as those used in the present study or clearly links constitutional developments to liberal and technological innovations.

That six countries are covered, rather than one or two, makes it clear that constitutional negotiations were not isolated events of individual countries. Much was taking place inside parliaments and between parliaments and their kings that was essentially universal in nature. The level of detail focused on made the historical part of this project manageable and allowed a good deal of constitutional history to be discussed within a single volume. That six countries were covered, rather than a dozen, allows more of the details of the reforms adopted and the contributions of particular individuals to be developed in a manner that allows readers to judge for themselves what is general and what is idiosyncratic in the constitutional reforms adopted.

Nonetheless, several criticisms can be made regarding the scope of the historical analysis. For example, some critics might argue that the book neglects work by particular historians that might be relevant for a complete analysis of the emergence of Western democracy. A basis for this criticism clearly exists, because only a few hundred of the many thousands of references that could have been brought to bear on the subject are cited. Moreover, as true of most broad historical accounts, nearly every sentence in the historical chapters of this book could be expanded into a chapter, and nearly every section into a book in its own right. (Indeed many subsections are short summaries of such books.)

A partial defense is that the references listed in the bibliography do not include all the references consulted, and that hundreds of other references are indirectly accounted for in the secondary texts written by the historians that are cited. The latter are assumed to give accurate summaries of additional historical resources for the periods and areas analyzed. The use of both narrow and broad case studies and general histories implies that the book's historical narratives are based upon a more thorough analysis of historical details than actually undertaken by the author.

An analogous criticism could be directed at those who study institutional reform, or history in general, without taking proper account of all contemporary research in economics, statistics, and political science. There is a sense in which all historical research requires an interdisciplinary approach because people are influenced by a variety of social, political, economic, and legal factors. Every historical analysis could be improved by taking greater account of research in other fields. This conclusion also demonstrates that the usefulness of such criticism is quite limited, because it applies to every possible research project that could be undertaken by individual scholars or small teams of scholars. Complete historical or social science research in this sense is impossible!

However, useful research is not impossible, although it should be acknowledged that both historical and social science research are always at least partly statistical in nature. Given the breadth and depth of the available historical resources and social science research, a reasonably thorough sampling of primary and secondary sources should provide a reasonably complete understanding of the material, research, and conclusions available elsewhere. To the extent that there are general patterns in history and in preexisting research, it should also be possible to discern those patterns with a finite sample of the relevant literatures and data. Prospects for useful research in the social sciences are further enhanced to the extent that social systems can be divided into sufficiently independent and uncomplicated subsystems for a human mind to understand them, a few parts at a time.

With respect to the latter, the proper degree of abstraction and detail can help. Just as an impressionist painting is clearest when one is a bit too distant to see the individual brush strokes, and the notion of impressionism itself is clearest when one studies several such paintings, so too are constitutional developments easiest to see when one focuses on the core procedures of governance and studies several countries in which similar changes in core constitutional procedures are evident. And just as impressionism as a genre might be missed by roaming through a great museum in a single day or focusing exclusively on a single painting, similarities in Western transitions may easily be missed by work that focuses on the great sweep of history or that focuses entirely on the idiosyncrasies and genius of the unique men and women whose pen strokes and compromises determined the exact expression of particular constitutional documents and reforms.

BLUNTING ANTICIPATED CRITICISM: LIMITS OF RATIONAL-CHOICE-BASED ANALYSIS

If a theory of constitutional political economy is possible, common factors must exist that influence both constitutional design and constitutional reform.

Part I of the book uses rational-choice models to identify general factors that are likely to influence constitutional design and reform. The models do so in part by focusing on specific choice settings and by subjecting the models to a variety of methodological norms. A model should be logically consistent, which eliminates many intuitively plausible representations of relationships among people, markets, and political factors. To obtain clear results, a model should employ Ockham's razor to minimize the factors used in one's explanation. Models should focus on *important* or *essential* factors in particular choice settings. A rational-choice model should thus rely as much as possible on narrow self-interests as explanatory factors, not because such interests always dominate, but because they are essentially universal and likely to influence the decisions of most persons in most settings – at least at the margin. Rational-choice models should also be consistent with earlier models and existing historical and statistical research on the topics of interest.

Such methodological norms have produced simple but sophisticated models that provide considerable insight into the operation of economic markets and political systems in the short and medium run. This book suggests that similar models can be used to help understand the factors and relationships that lead more or less self-interested men and women to adopt and reform constitutions in the long run.

It should be acknowledged, however, that the implications of rational-choice models are never as precise as their associated mathematics seems to imply. For example, predicting the behavior of specific persons who are completely rational and well informed is difficult if individuals pursue a large number of goals in a large number of circumstances. The more complex are the goals and circumstances of individuals, the more difficult it is for social scientists to catalog them all and to take account of their associated choice-relevant tradeoffs. Even if mistakes were never made and persons behaved exactly as modeled, it would be impossible to predict individual choices perfectly without complete information about the particular aims and tradeoffs of particular individuals.[1]

One very sensible method of dealing with the multiplicity of goals and circumstances that characterize many decision settings is simply to ignore them and, instead, to focus on the subset of goals and circumstances that can be plausibly assumed to be more or less universal and relevant for most of the decisions being analyzed. This allows a theorist to conduct other-things-being-equal analyses that yield useful explanations and predictions of typical behavior. The neglected factors are often assumed to have little effect at the margin, and/or are assumed to be sufficiently unsystematic that their average effect on decisions is approximately zero and so can be neglected without significant loss of explanatory power. These are stronger assumptions than necessary, but they are often reasonable first approximations of the effects of simplification.

Such considerations often induce economists to assume that the persons modeled are concerned only with maximizing their own personal wealth. An interest in personal wealth is nearly universal because most other goals require resources (wealth) to advance them. Efforts to increase wealth are consequently very likely to play a role in a wide variety of individual decisions, even if maximizing wealth is not the direct aim of many persons in the real world. Additional resources also advance biological and group purposes as well as idiosyncratic individual ends, and so a preference for greater wealth tends to be genetically and culturally reinforced.

Economists and game theorists often assume that persons have such "narrow" self-interests partly to make their models tractable and in some cases because some theorists evidently believe that all the other goals are indirectly determined by such interests. It is the universality of such interests, however, rather than their narrowness, that accounts for their usefulness (Pareto 1897, Stigler and Becker 1977).

[1] Rationality does not imply that outcomes are always what one might have hoped for. It means that alternatives are considered and (reasonably) consistent choices are made. Even a fair game will have losers along with winners. Mistakes can, however, occur. In the case of lottery tickets, a series of purchases may be mistaken in that it reflects a poor understanding of probability theory, although the purchases may have been entirely rational given what is known at the time the decisions were made.

Nonetheless, the importance of personal idiosyncrasies, chance events, ideas, and errors has to be acknowledged, and such effects are evident in the historical narratives. The more idiosyncratic the choice-relevant aims of individuals and the more important information problems and theories are, the less likely a rational-choice model will explain or predict the specific decisions made or bargains struck, because the individual idiosyncrasies and mistakes will be relatively more important determinants of the choices made than the general factors analyzed.

For example, each of the narratives mentions exceptional persons (by name) who played pivotal roles in the course of their nation's reforms: Willem I, William III, Washington, Madison, Thorbecke, De Geer, Bismarck, and Taisuke. The historical narratives also imply that slightly better or worse luck might have altered history on many occasions. The Spanish Habsburgs might have subdued the Dutch revolt in the sixteenth century. King James II might have correctly anticipated the landing point of Willem III in 1688, defeated the Dutch intervention, and continued his centralization of political authority in England and in the North American colonies. Wilhelm II might have agreed to surrender a bit more authority to the German parliaments of the 1890s, which might have allowed an orderly transition to parliamentary democracy in the next two or three decades, rather than a somewhat chaotic one at the end of a very costly war. The assassination of influential liberals and moderates in Japan during the early twentieth century might have failed or been prevented by minor changes in personal schedules and security.

The conclusions derived from models are necessarily somewhat imprecise and incomplete because models always ignore idiosyncratic factors that are often significant determinants of specific decisions by individual consumers, firms, voters, and politicians. The importance of idiosyncratic factors should, of course, be acknowledged at the same time that systematic factors are focused on in one's analysis and historical research.

More than good or bad luck was involved in the emergence of Western democracy, although idiosyncratic and chance factors cannot be ignored.

PREDICTABILITY AND CONTROVERSY IN SOCIAL SCIENCE AND HISTORICAL ANALYSIS

The usefulness of models is not a result of their precision; rather, it is their ability to identify key variables and to improve our understanding of key relationships among those variables. In this respect, the scientific aim of a humble model builder differs from that of the most ambitious historians. For many historians, completeness is very important, and identifying what is unique is at least as important as identifying what is general. Consequently, historians devote enormous time and attention to studying particular people and events, especially unusual ones. Such unique people and events, however, are nearly without interest for a model builder, because their main purpose is identification of a few relatively universal determinants of the phenomena of interest.

For example, social scientists and statisticians can provide explanations of particular histories of governmental dice rolling in more or less similar circumstances, and can make predictions about as yet unrealized "histories" that would emerge in the future. A government official will roll a seven about one-sixth of the time using unweighted dice in ordinary circumstances. A series of rolls may test and refute various possible hypotheses about dice rolling – for example, that "dice can be hot" if they are fair.

We can predict with absolute certainty that the numbers on ordinary dice can add up to no less than two and no more than twelve, but we cannot predict the result of any single roll of the dice, even though the number of factors that need to taken into account is far less than the number that need to be taken account of in most political and economic settings. Nonetheless, statistics implies that although little can be said about a single roll of the dice, a variety of predictions can be made about the outcomes of a series of dice rolls. Perhaps surprisingly, a series of cases in which government officials roll the dice repeatedly is more predictable than any single case.

For historians, the purposes of research are different and in many ways more interesting than those addressed by social scientists and statisticians. Having observed a particular roll of the dice, the historian wants to explain exactly how the values observed arose. Here, there are clearly proximate causes – more or less the same ones used by a physicist – and also indirect causes: the government official rolling the dice was upset, was under pressure, had been exposed to different theories of rolling dice, was affected by beliefs about divine causality, was left-handed, near-sighted, weak from age, lived north of the equator, and so forth. All these factors might affect the manner in which the dice were thrown and, therefore, would largely determine the flight of the dice actually observed. It is entirely possible that this partial list of factors might have determined the exact trajectory of the dice imposed by the official who controlled the dice and the numbers that appeared on top.

Such completely accurate histories may thus explain exactly what happened, without shedding any light on what will happen on the next roll of the dice. Although "history will repeat itself" about one-thirty-sixth of the time in this case, little of the detail that applies to a particular instance of dice rolling will be relevant for explaining the next similar event (roll of the dice), because either the underlying chain of causality is too complex to be fully understood or truly stochastic phenomena occur.

This is not to say that social science is only about prediction or that history is only about explanation, because the persons who engage in these enterprises are often themselves interested in both questions to varying degrees, and properly so. Social science provides a lens through which particular events can be made sense of, and historical research can stimulate the formation of new hypotheses to be tested, as well as provide facts that can be used to test existing hypotheses. Such "convex combinations" of research interests produce a more useful and compact body of knowledge for fellow travelers, scholars, and practitioners than would have been produced by methodological "purists."

Moreover, in cases in which there are few determining factors, the explanations of historians and theories of social scientists tend to be very similar. The light went on because a person flipped the wall switch. The building survived a direct lightening strike unharmed because it was protected by Ben Franklin's invention (the lightning rod). The battle was lost because one side was greatly outnumbered, outgunned, and caught by surprise. Prices rose in seventeenth-century Spain because of the influx of gold from South America.

In cases in which causal relationships are simple, even a single instance may generalize perfectly to a wide variety of settings. In other cases in which causality is more complex, there are often many plausible claims and counter-claims. Here, disagreements are commonplace across disciplines and within disciplines. This book, it is hoped, may induce a few historians to think a bit differently about special persons and events in the past, just as their work has induced this author to think more carefully about constitutional theory and practice.

Unexplained Residuals and Beliefs about Determinism

Controversy and fresh insights are not caused only by differences in methodology or research aims, as might be said about differences between social scientists and historians. Controversies within social science also occur because disagreements exist about the extent to which human behavior is predictable in general or in particular circumstances, and therefore about the extent to which a single theory can possibly explain particular events.

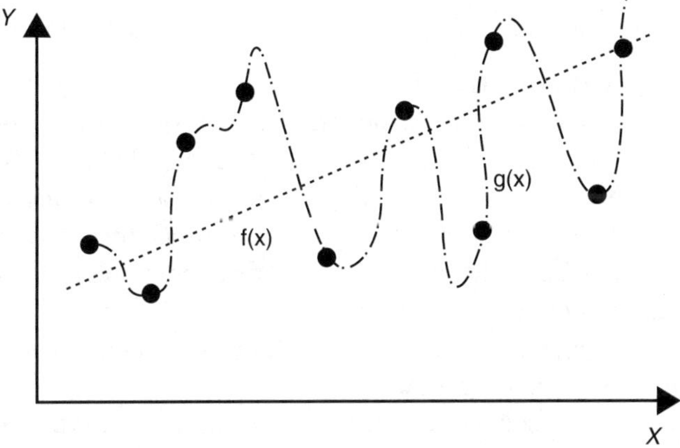

Figure A.1. How predictable?

To appreciate this point, consider the time series of data points depicted in Figure A.1. For those who believe that the world is completely determined, the "finely nuanced" dashed fitted line, g(x), will be the sort of theory to which they aspire. For those who believe that the world is not so readily explained, whether because of complexity or the existence of truly random factors, the "essentialist" dotted linear line, f(x), is all that they believe can be accounted for. Disagreements of this sort may cause social scientists from the same field of research to disagree for reasons that seem similar to those discussed earlier, but which are subtly different. Some social scientists would insist that we can or will be able to predict each successive dice roll; others would regard such precision to be impossible. For the former group, a very small error term does not imply that other explanations or factors do not exist. For the latter group, an error term can be too small as well as too large; and, moreover, a very large error term does not necessarily imply that a faulty analysis has been undertaken or that a theory can be improved upon.

It seems clear that we know a good deal about social phenomena that can be generalized and a good deal that cannot be generalized. Yet there is little systematic evidence on the "meta-questions" that might allow us to assess the degree to which present theories will explain new cases, or the extent to which new explanations and new theories will be required to understand cases not yet analyzed. Indeed, each side of the debate can point to scientific episodes in which they have been proven correct.

Limits of Systematic Theories of Constitutional History

With respect to the focus of this book, it is not immediately obvious how much of the rise of Western democracy can be explained by general features of the political and historical setting. Nor is it obvious how much is peculiar to the men and women that advocated particular constitutional designs or reforms and to the circumstances in which their arguments and decisions were made. Chapter 19 suggests that about half of the constitutional path can be explained by interdependencies between economic and political developments. Much remains unexplained, but may be impossible to explain with a general theory.

For example, three major episodes of constitutional reform occurred in Sweden during the nineteenth and early twentieth centuries, although proposals for major and minor constitutional reforms were nearly continuously proposed during the entire period. Why significant new constitutional gains to trade emerged in three particular decades is not obvious. It also seems clear that the details of reform were affected by the specific persons holding high offices and unique Swedish circumstances. Nowhere else in Europe was an explicit wealth-weighted-voting system adopted. However, broadly similar patterns of reform were adopted in several other European kingdoms during approximately the same period. For example, the United Kingdom, the Netherlands, Belgium, Denmark, and Norway also adopted reforms in the nineteenth century that gradually shifted power from their kings to their parliaments and increased the importance and breadth of suffrage in elections for parliament.

How much of this pattern of reform is explainable by general economic, social, and political forces might be debated by serious and well-informed scholars for a variety of reasons. They may be interested in somewhat different aspects of history or view it from different methodological perspectives, as noted earlier. This book takes an intermediate position on these issues and also about the extent to which a single model can account for long-term social phenomena.

PARALLELS BETWEEN SCIENTIFIC AND CONSTITUTIONAL DEVELOPMENT

Political constitutions are the durable rules through which ordinary day-to-day, year-to-year, and decade-to-decade public-policy decisions are made. In this, durable constitutions can be said to be the "natural laws" of the political game in a particular place at a particular time. The same can be said about scientific theories that have withstood the tests of time within a particular society. Yet in both cases, "natural laws" may be changed as new information or new circumstances come to attention.

Although some flexibility is desirable (and unavoidable) in each case, there are also advantages to stability. A constitution must be taken as given for purposes of ordinary legislation if it is to determine the process through which policies are adopted. Without standing procedures, conflict over decision-making procedures would dominate and governments would consist of disorganized groups engaged in intense fighting over their organization's (potential) surplus. Similarly, a standing paradigm allows a variety of research questions to be asked without simultaneously analyzing (or debating) the core principles of the paradigm. Without standing procedures for making policies and standing paradigms to frame research questions, a good deal of the productivity of their respective enterprises would be lost.[2] It is therefore completely reasonable to assume that stable decision-making rules and theories are in place when analyzing the kinds of policies that a government is likely to adopt in a given year or decade.

However, neither assumption is appropriate for long-run analysis. Constitutions, unlike star systems but like astronomical theories, can be revised and copied, which implies that understanding contemporary constitutional designs requires a theory of constitutional reform as well as a static theory of constitutions, just as a long-run theory of science requires a theory of scientific refinement and innovation.

Most constitutions include formal and informal procedures for changing the rules of the game because most constitutional designers believe that some flexibility is necessary for their constitutions to be robust, and thus include durable rules for making rules. By including procedures of amendment, constitutional designers acknowledge the limits of their own ability to foresee future conditions and the fact that even very good constitutions are somewhat context specific. The norms of modern scientific work are similarly modest, in that no answer or theory is to be exempt from challenge and revision.

The procedures specified for constitutional amendments are normally designed to be more demanding than those required for ordinary legislation and tend to require more repeated reviews of proposals and/or greater supermajorities. This suggests that most constitutional designers believe that stability is of greater importance than flexibility at the margin. The

[2] See Congleton, Hillman, and Konrad (2008) for an extensive overview of the rent-seeking literature. See Hillman and Katz (1987) for a model of intra-organizational rent-seeking.

rules of the game have to be stable enough to determine day-to-day politics. Similarly, the demands for shifting a paradigm are far more demanding than for changing theories or conclusions for minor sub-areas of a broad research program in part because of advantages associated with stable frames of reference.

The institutions of science and scholarship reflect similar tradeoffs between stability and flexibility. Education requires stability in the facts and explanations of relationships among facts if knowledge is to be transmitted to students and other scholars (indeed, in order to claim that knowledge exists). On the other hand, orthodox theories are subject to nearly constant challenges, particularly at their various frontiers, and are gradually revised as a consequence of those challenges. As in governance, a series of minor experiments can have important effects on mainstream historical and scientific theories.

The more closely one examines any nation's constitutional or field of scientific research, the more evident are the nearly continuous efforts to advance and oppose reforms of standing procedures, theories, and constraints, although relatively few reform proposals gain sufficient support to be broadly adopted (Rasch and Congleton 2006). As a consequence, both constitutional liberalization and paradigm shifts are often gradual and are most evident many years after they have occurred, as proponents of older institutions and theories gradually accept new evidence, and as older ideas and persons in senior positions at major institutions are gradually replaced by new generations of men and women with "new" ideas.

LIBERALISM, REFORM, AND SCIENTIFIC ADVANCE

It is interesting to note that much of the methodology and domain of modern science emerged at roughly the same time as Western political and economic systems. This was not a coincidence, but another area in which bootstrapping occurred. Liberalism and economic development played significant roles in determining the broad outlines of science as it emerged from the nineteenth century. Conversely, scientific attitudes also affected the development and penetration of liberal ideas in the countries analyzed in this book.

Although many liberals acknowledged limits in a person's or society's ability to determine what the best policies are, they generally agreed that a scientific approach is better than an unthinking adherence to traditional ways of doing things. Liberal political and economic theories thus produced a number of hypotheses about how public policies could be improved. Economic liberals argued that monopolies and many other barriers to trade reduced economic income and national wealth. Political liberals argued that more representative, but rule-bound governments provided better public policies, more tolerance, and broader opportunities for most people. Insofar as liberal policies produced the hypothesized results, the theories were affirmed and became more widely accepted.

Support for the deduction-experimental approach was itself partly empirical and partly ideological (or methodological). Technological progress tended to support the contention that improvements were possible, insofar as the new modes of transportation, communication, and farming were widely considered superior to horseback, letters, and old wooden plows. Good things followed from the better understanding of animals, plants, minerals, and energy produced through scientific methodology. The countries that allowed these new technologies to be employed grew more rapidly than the countries that maintained their medieval institutions, and the nation-states that allowed and/or supported industrialization tended to become militarily more powerful, as well as more prosperous.

Many of the reforms that promoted political and economic liberalization also promoted scientific advance. Reductions in censorship and greater openness in markets both allowed and indirectly encouraged people to experiment with new technologies and new theories. As technological advance and specialization inside firms and among firms increased, new, higher-paying jobs for middle managers, accountants, engineers, and researchers emerged. These higher wage rates and the advantages of innovation induced new investments in secular forms of human capital and in research and development.

Commercialization and industrialization also affected the national government's interest in expert knowledge and in technological advances. Taking advantage of the new technologies for finance, infrastructure, and military operations often required specialists who understood the new methods and who could provide policy makers with answers to technical or scientific questions. This increased the informational advantages of representative parliaments, the bureaucracy, and organized economic interest groups and indirectly increased their influence over domestic and trade policies relative to the king or queen. It also increased the demand for experts who could provide advice about public finance and the organization of government and who could make use of the new technologies of transportation, communication, and warfare. Better-trained bureaucrats were needed.

New polytechnic universities were founded, and scientists and other scholars hired during the second half of the nineteenth century. At the new universities, both science and science students were produced at "knowledge factories," where middle-class students could obtain advanced technical and scientific training in relatively large, standardized classes at a reduced (and subsidized) price. There were, in effect, new economies of scale in technical education and innovation.

Moreover, technological, economic, and political developments (what we call "progress") created a variety of new phenomena to be interpreted and understood by practitioners and academic scholars. Efforts to provide answers gradually produced new, more specialized scientific fields of research, including new social sciences, new fields of engineering, and new physical sciences. Much of present-day science emerged as distinct fields of research in the nineteenth and early twentieth centuries.

In this manner, liberalism opened and widened the doors of science in much the same manner that it opened politics and economics: by reducing entry barriers, exploiting economies of scale, and increasing specialization. The list of significant innovations in agriculture, mining, materials, machines, electronics, and organizational theory is nearly endless. Constitutional theories and technologies also advanced during this period, as for example alternative voting systems and architectures for parliament were analyzed by academics and proponents of constitutional reform.

PERFECTING PARLIAMENT CONTINUES

Of course, to say that progress has been made is not to say that either Western institutions or Western science are perfect. Efforts to further improve governance, as in the sciences, continued unabated during the twentieth century, although gains from constitutional exchange were less commonplace than scientific innovations during most of that century. Even in more or less democratic polities, constitutional reforms can have significant effects on public policy and the quality of life (Congleton and Swedenborg 2006).

The broad consensus about the constitutional foundations of a "good society" that emerged throughout the West in the late nineteenth century did not produce completely stable institutions or public policies, as might have been predicted (Fukuyama 1992). But they helped sustain the routines and institutions that had produced a new form of economic and political life, a form of life that most of us take for granted today.

Although the liberal constitutional consensus crumbled somewhat in the half century following World War I, it reemerged in the second half of the twentieth century. Contemporary Western conservatives, moderates, liberals, and social democrats are thus nearly all liberals in the sense used in this book. They continue to accept and support representative governance, broad suffrage, civil equality, and the rule of law, albeit with a good deal more social insurance and economic regulation than accepted by most liberals (or social democrats) in 1925.

The aristocratic, religious, and historical arguments used against nineteenth-century liberals have all but disappeared in the West, along with a good deal of mysticism, traditionalism, intolerance, and cultural variation. There are relatively few advocates for government-assured national-church monopolies or privileged families today, except perhaps in the Middle East. The radical departures on the left and right that produced great mid-twentieth-century wars have also largely disappeared in the West and other parts of the world as well.

In these respects, it can be argued that liberals won the late-twentieth-century constitutional debates as well as those of the eighteenth and nineteenth centuries. Moreover, in both cases it can be argued that it was the left liberals who won those debates (much to the lament of the right-of-center liberals of those two centuries). For example, although modern social-insurance programs were started by liberal and conservative parties in the late nineteenth and early twentieth centuries, they did not really become major programs until after World War II (Congleton and Bose 2009). However, that and other twentieth-century developments are subjects for another book.

References

Acemoglu, D. and J. A. Robinson (2000) "Why Did the West Extend the Franchise? Democracy, Inequality, and Growth in Historical Perspective," *Quarterly Journal of Economics* 115: 1167–99.

(2005) *Economic Origins of Dictatorship and Democracy*. Cambridge: Cambridge University Press.

Ackerman, B. (1991) *We the People, Volume I*. Cambridge, MA: Harvard University Press.

Adams, C. (1998) *Those Dirty Rotten Taxes: The Tax Revolts that Built America*. New York: Free Press.

Adeweg, R. B. and G. A. Irwin (2002) *Governance and Politics of the Netherlands*. New York: Palgrave-MacMillan.

Agresti, A. and B. Presnell (2002) "Misvotes, Undervotes, and Overvotes: The 2000 Presidential Election in Florida," *Statistical Science* 17: 436–40.

Aidt, T. S., J. Dutta, and E. Loukoianova (2006) "Democracy Comes to Europe: Franchise Extension and Fiscal Outcomes 1830–1938," *European Economic Review* 50: 249–83.

Aidt, T. S. and P. S. Jensen (2009) "Tax Structure, Size of Government, and the Extension of the Voting Franchise in Western Europe, 1860–1938," *International Tax and Public Finance* 16: 362–94.

Akita, G. (1967) *Foundations of Constitutional Governance in Modern Japan 1868–1900*. Cambridge, MA: Harvard University Press.

Alchian, A. A. and H. Demsetz (1972) "Production, Information Costs and Economic Organization," *American Economic Review* 62: 777–95.

Aldrich, J. H. (1995) *Why Parties? The Origin and Transformation of Political Parties in America*. Chicago: University of Chicago Press.

Alesina, A. and H. Rosenthal (1996) "A Theory of Divided Government," *Econometrica* 64: 1311–41.

Allen, R. C. (1982) "The Efficiency and Distributional Consequences of Eighteenth Century Enclosures," *Economic Journal* 92: 937–53.

Anderson, G. M. and A. Gifford Jr. (1996) "Between the Constitution and the Deep Blue Sea: Contractual Controls on Opportunism Aboard Pirate Vessels," *Constitutional Political Economy* 7: 49–61.

Aristotle (330 BCE/1962) *The Politics*. (Translated by T. A. Sinclair) New York: Penguin.

Arrow, K. J. (1963) *Social Choice and Individual Values* 2nd Ed. New Haven: Yale University Press.

Aspinall, A., A. Smith, and D. C. Douglas (Eds.) (1996) *English Historical Documents 1783–1832*. London: Routledge.

Axelrod, R. (1984) *The Evolution of Cooperation*. New York: Basic Books.

(1986) "An Evolutionary Approach to Norms," *American Political Science Review* 80: 1095–1111.

Bailkey, N. (1967) "Early Mesopotamian Constitutional Development," *American Historical Review* 72: 1211–36.

Balla, S. J. and J. R. Wright (2001) "Interest Groups, Advisory Committees, and Congressional Control of the Bureaucracy," *American Journal of Political Science* 45: 799–812.

Banks, J. S. and B. R. Weingast (1992) "The Political Control of Bureaucracies under Asymmetric Information," *American Journal of Political Science* 36: 509–24.

Barker, J. E. (1906) *The Rise and Decline of the Netherlands, A Political and Economic History and Study in Practical Statesmanship*. London: Smith, Elder & Co.

Barnard, H. (1854) *National Education in Europe*. Hartford, CT: Case Tiffany and Co.

Barnea, M. F. and S. H. Schwartz (1998) "Values and Voting," *Political Psychology* 19: 17–40.

Baron, D. P. (1998) "Comparative Dynamics of Parliamentary Governments," *American Political Science Review* 92: 593–609.

Baron, D. P. and J. A. Ferejohn (1989) "Bargaining in Legislatures," *American Political Science Review* 83: 1181–206.

Beckmann, G. M. (1957) *The Making of the Meiji Constitution: The Oligarchs and the Constitutional Development of Japan, 1868–1891*. Lawrence, KS: University of Kansas Press.

Beer, S. H. (1956) "Pressure Groups and Parties in Britain," *American Political Science Review* 50: 1–23.

(1957) "The Representation of Interests in British Government: Historical Background," *American Political Science Review* 51: 613–50.

Bellquist, E. C. (1935) "Foreign Governments and Politics: The Five Hundreth Anniversary of the Swedish Reksdag," *American Political Science Review* 29: 857–65.

Bély, L. (2001) *The History of France*. (Translated by A. Moyon) Paris: Jean-Paul Giserot.

Benjamin, G. (1985) "The Diffusion of Executive Power in American State Constitutions: Tenure and Tenure Limitations," *Publius* 15: 71–84.

Benneh, G. (1973) "Small-Scale Farming Systems in Ghana," *Africa* 43: 134–46.

Berman, D. R. (1987) "Male Support for Woman Suffrage: An Analysis of Voting Patterns in the Mountain West," *Social Science History* 11: 281–94.

Berman, H. J. (2003) *Law and Revolution (Vol. II), The Impact of the Protestant Reformation on the Western Legal Tradition*. Cambridge, MA: Belknap.

Bernard, H. (1874) *History and Progress of Education from the Earliest Times to the Present*. Chicago, IL: A. S. Barnes & Co.

Besley, T. (2006) *Principled Agents? The Political Economy of Good Government*. Oxford: Oxford University Press.

Besley, T. and S. Coate (1997) "An Economic Model of Representative Democracy," *Quarterly Journal of Economics* 112: 85–114.

Bienen, H. and N. Van de Walle (1989) "Time and Power in Africa," *American Political Science Review* 83: 19–34.

Black, D. (1948) "The Decisions of a Committee Using Special Majority," *Econometrica* 16: 245–61.

(1987) *The Theory of Committees and Elections*. Dordrecht: Kluwer Academic Publishers.

Blackbourn, D. and G. Eley (1984) *The Peculiarities of Geman History, Bourgeois Society and Politics in Nineteenth-Century Germany*. Oxford: Oxford University Press.

Blackbourn, D. (1998) *The Long Nineteenth Century: A History of Germany 1780–1918*. Oxford: Oxford University Press.

Blackstone, W. (1765) *Commentaries on the Laws of England*. Oxford: Oxford University Press.

Blankart, C. B. (1998) "Was Knut Wicksell a Conservative or a Radical?" *Public Choice* 94: 355–65.

Blockmans, W. P. (1978) "A Typology of Representative Institutions in Late Medieval Europe," *Journal of Medieval History* 4: 189–215.

Blok, P. J. (1912) *History of the People of the Netherlands*. (Translated by O. A. Bierstadt) New York: Putnam.

Blom, H. W., W. P. Blokmans, and H. de Schepper (1992) *Bicameralisme. Tweekamerstelsel vroeger en nu*. The Hague.

Blum, J. (1981) "English Parliamentary Enclosure," *Journal of Modern History* 53:477–504.

Boyd, R. and P. J. Richerson (1985) *Culture and the Evolutionary Process*. Chicago: University of Chicago Press.

(1992) "Punishment Allows the Evolution of Cooperation (or Anything Else) in Sizable Groups," *Ethology and Sociobiology* 13: 171–95.

Boylan, R. T. and R. D. McKelvey (1995) "Voting over Economic Plans," *American Economic Review* 85: 860–71.

Breen, J. (1996) "The Imperial Oath of April 1868," *Monumenta Nipponica* 51: 407–29.

Brennan, G. and J. M. Buchanan (1977) "Towards a Tax Constitution for Leviathan," *Journal of Public Economics* 8: 255–73.

(1980) *The Power to Tax*. New York: Cambridge University Press.

(1985) *The Reason of Rules*. Cambridge: Cambridge University Press.

Brennan, G. and F. G. Castles (2002) *Australia Reshaped: 200 Years of Institutional Transformation*. Cambridge: Cambridge University Press.

Brennan, G. and A. Hamlin (2000) *Democratic Devices and Desires*. Cambridge: Cambridge University Press.

Brentano, L. (1894) *Hours and Wages in Relation to Production*. (Translated by W. Arnold) New York: Scribners and Sons.

Breton, A. and R. Wintrobe (1975) "The Equilibrium Size of a Budget-Maximizing Bureau: A Note on Niskanen's Theory of Bureaucracy," *Journal of Political Economy* 83: 195–207.

Brook, C. N. L., J. R. L. Highfield, W. Swaan (1988) *Oxford and Cambridge*. Cambridge: Cambridge University Press.

Brown, R. E. (1963) "Rebuttal," *William and Mary Quarterly* 1963: 265–76.

(1955) *Middle Class Democracy and the Revolution in Massachusetts*. Ithaca: Cornell University Press.

Brown, R. E. and B. K. T. Brown (1964) *Democracy or Aristocracy?* East Lansing: Michigan State University Press.

Brownlee, W. E. (2004) *Federal Taxation in America: A Short History*. Cambridge: Cambridge University Press.

Buchanan, J. M. (1954) "Social Choice, Democracy, and Free Markets," *Journal of Political Economy* 62: 114–23.

(1975) *The Limits of Liberty: Between Anarchy and Leviathan*. Chicago: University of Chicago Press.

(1983) "Rent Seeking, Noncompensated Transfers, and Laws of Succession," *Journal of Law and Economics* 26: 71–85.

(1987) "The Constitution of Economic Policy," *American Economic Review* 77: 243–50.

Buchanan, J. M. and G. Tullock (1962) *The Calculus of Consent, Logical Foundations of Constitutional Democracy*. Ann Arbor: University of Michigan Press.

Buchanan, J. M. and R. D. Congleton (1998) *Politics by Principle, Not Interest*. New York: Cambridge University Press.

Buchanan, J. M. and Y. Yoon (Eds.) (1994) *The Return to Increasing Return*. Ann Arbor: University of Michigan Press.

(2000) "Symmetric Tragedies: Commons and Anticommons," *Journal of Law and Economics* 43: 1–14.

Buchanan, J. M., Tollison, R. D. and Tullock, G. (1980) *Toward a Theory of the Rent-Seeking Society*. College Station: Texas A & M University Press.

Bueno de Mesquita, B. (1990) "The Origins of German Hegemony," *World Politics* 43: 28–52.

Bueno de Mesquita, B., A. Smith, R. M. Siverson, and J. D. Morrow (2004) *The Logic of Political Survival*. Cambridge, MA: MIT Press.

Burke, E. (1790) *Further Reflections on the French Revolution*. (Edited by D. F. Ritchie 1992) Indianapolis: Liberty Fund.

Burke, J. (1978) *Connections*. Boston: Little, Brown.

Bush, W. (1972) "Individual Welfare in Anarchy," in G. Tullock, *Explorations in the Theory of Anarchy*. Blacksburg, VA: Center for Study of Public Choice.

Caldwell, P. C. (1997) *Popular Sovereignty and the Crisis of German Constitutional Law*. Durham, NC: Duke University Press.

Carson, C. S. (1975) "The History of the United States National Income and Product Accounts," *Review of Income and Wealth* 21: 153–81.

Carter, J. R. and D. Schap (1987) "Executive Veto, Legislative Override and Structure-Induced Equilibrium," *Public Choice* 52: 227–44.

Castels, F. G. (1978) *Social Democratic Image of Society*. New York: Routledge.

Chadwick, M. E. J. (1976) "The Role of Redistribution in the Making of the Third Reform Act," *Historical Journal* 19: 665–83.

Chase, M. (1991) "Out of Radicalism: The Mid-Victorian Freehold Land Movement," *English Historical Review* 106: 319–45.

Cherrington, E. H. (1920) *The Evolution of Prohibition in the United States of America*. Westerville, Ohio: American Issue Press.

Clark, G. (1998) "Commons Sense: Common Property Rights, Efficiency, and Institutional Change," *Journal of Economic History* 58: 73–102.

Clarkson, T. (1786) *An Essay on the Slavery and Commerce of the Human Species*. London: Cadell and Phillips.

Claydon, T. (2002) *William III*. London: Pearson Education.

Cohn, S. K. (2004) *Popular Protest in Late Medieval Europe*. Manchester: Manchester University Press.

Comstock, A. P. (1921) *State Taxation of Personal Incomes*. New York: Columbia University.

Conacher, J. B. (Ed.) (1971) *The Emergence of British Parliamentary Democracy in the Nineteenth Century*. New York: John Wiley and Sons.

Congleton, R. D. (1980) "Competitive Process, Competitive Waste, and Institutions," in J. M. Buchanan, R. D. Tollison, and G. Tullock, (Eds.) *Towards a Theory of the Rent-Seeking Society*. Texas A & M Press: 153–79. Reprinted in Congleton R. D, A. L. Hillman, and K. A. Konrad (Eds.) *40 Years of Research on Rent Seeking*. Heidelberg: Springer-Verlag (2008): 69–96.

(1982) "A Model of Asymmetric Bureaucratic Inertia," *Public Choice* 39: 421–5.

(1984) "Committees and Rent-Seeking Effort," *Journal of Public Economics* 25: 197–209.

(1989) "Efficient Status Seeking, Externalities and the Evolution of Status Games," *Journal of Economic Behavior and Organization* 11: 175–90.

(1991a) "Ideological Conviction and Persuasion in the Rent-Seeking Society," *Journal of Public Economics* 44: 65–86.

(1991b) "The Economic Role of a Work Ethic," *Journal of Economic Behavior and Organization* 15: 365–85.

(1997) "Political Efficiency and Equal Protection of the Law," *Kyklos* 50: 485–505.

(2001a) "Rational Ignorance and Rationally Biased Expectations: The Discrete Informational Foundations of Fiscal Illusion," *Public Choice* 107: 35–64.

(2001b) "On the Durability of King and Council: The Continuum Between Dictatorship and Democracy," *Constitutional Political Economy* 12: 193–215.

(2003a) "Economic and Cultural Prerequisites for Democracy," in A. Breton, G. Galeotti, P. Salmon, and R. Wintrobe (Eds.) *Rational Foundations of Democratic Politics*. New York: Cambridge University Press.

(2003b) "On the Merits of Bicameral Legislatures: Policy Predictability within Partisan Polities," M. J. Holler, H. Kliemt, D. Schmidtchen, and M. E. Streit. (Eds.) *Year Book of New Political Economy*. Tübingen, Germany: Mohr Siebeck. Vol. 22: 29–54.

(2003c) *Improving Democracy through Constitutional Reform: Some Swedish Lessons*. Dordrecht: Kluwer Academic Press.

(2004a) "Economic Development and Democracy, Does Industrialization Lead to Universal Suffrage?" *Homo Economicus* 21: 283–311.

(2004b) "Mutual Advantages of Coercion and Exit within Private Clubs and Treaty Organizations: Toward a Logic of Voluntary Association," *Revista de Political Economy* 4: 49–78.

(2006) "Constitutional Exchange in Japan: from Shogunate to Parliamentary Democracy," *Public Choice Studies* 47: 5–29.

(2007a) "From Royal to Parliamentary Rule without Revolution, the Economics of Constitutional Exchange within Divided Governments," *European Journal of Political Economy* 23: 261–84.

(2007b) "Informational Limits to Democratic Public Policy: The Jury Theorem, Yardstick Competition, and Ignorance," *Public Choice* 132: 333–52.

(2007c) "The Moral Voter Hypothesis: Economic and Normative Aspects of Public Policy and Law within Democracies," *Journal of Public Finance and Public Choice* 25: 3–30.

(2008) "America's Neglected Debt to the Dutch," *Constitutional Political Economy* 19: 35–60.

Congleton, R. D. and F. Bose (2010) "The Rise of the Modern Welfare State: Ideology, Institutions, and Income Security: Analysis and Evidence," *Public Choice* 144: 535–55.

Congleton, R. D., A. L. Hillman, and K. A. Konrad (Eds.) (2008) *40 Years of Research on Rent Seeking*. Heildelberg: Springer.

Congleton, R. D., A. Kyriacou, and J. Bacaria (2003) "A Theory of Menu Federalism: Decentralization by Political Agreement," *Constitutional Political Economy* 14: 167–90.

Congleton, R. D. and R. D. Tollison (1999) "The Stability Inducing Properties of Unstable Coalitions," *European Journal of Political Economy* 15: 193–205.

Congleton, R. D. and S. Lee (2009) "Efficient Mercantilism? Revenue-Maximizing Monopolization Policies as Ramsay Taxation," *European Journal of Political Economy* 25: 102–14.

Congleton, R. D. and B. Swedenborg (Eds.) (2006) *Democratic Constitutional Design and Public Policy: Analysis and Evidence*. Cambridge, MA: MIT Press.

Congleton, R. D. and V. Vanberg (1992) "Rationality, Morality, and Exit," *American Political Science Review* 86: 418–31.

(2001) "Help, Harm or Avoid: On the Personal Advantage of Dispositions to Cooperate and Punish in Multilateral PD Games with Exit," *Journal of Economic Behavior and Organization* 44: 145–67.

Cook, C. and J. Paxton (1978) *European Political Facts 1848–1918*. New York: Facts on File.

Cooter, R. (2002) *The Strategic Constitution*. Princeton: Princeton University Press.

Cowling, M. (1967) *1867 Disraeli, Gladstone and Revolution: The Passing of the Second Reform Bill*. Cambridge: Cambridge University Press.

Craig, A. M. (1968) "Fukuzawa Yukichi: The Philosophical Foundation of Meiji Nationalism," in R. E. Ward (Ed.) *Political Development in Modern Japan*. Princeton: Princeton University Press, 99–148.

Craig, F. W. S. (1977) *British Electoral Facts 1832–1885*. New York: Macmillan.

Cross, A. L. (1914) *A History of England and Greater Britain*. New York: Macmillan.

Cruickshanks, E., S. Handley, and D. Hayton (2002) *The History of Parliament: The House of Commons 1690–1715*. Cambridge: Cambridge University Press.

Daalder H. and G. A. Irwin, (1989) *Politics in the Netherlands: How Much Change?* London: Frank Cass and Co.

Danstrup, J. (1947) *A History of Denmark*, 2nd Ed. Copenhagen: Wivels Forlag.

Davis, A. F. (1964) "The Social Workers and the Progressive Party 1912–1916," *American Historical Review* 69: 671–88.

Dean, M. D. (2002) *Japanese Legal System*. London: Cavendish Publishing.

Demsetz, H. (1967) "Toward a Theory of Property Rights," *American Economic Review* 57: 347–59.

Devine, R. (1979) "The Way of the King. An Early Meiji Essay on Government," *Monumenta Nipponica* 43: 49–72.

Diamond, J. (1999) *Guns, Germs and Steel: The Fates of Human Societies*. New York: Norton and Co.

Dicey, A. V. (1887) *The Privy Council*. London: Macmillan and Co.
Diermeier, D., H. Eraslan, and A. Merlo (2006) "The Effects of Constitutions on Coalition Governments in Parliamentary Democracies," in R. D. Congleton and B. Swedenborg (Eds.) *Democratic Constitutional Design and Public Policy: Analysis and Evidence*. Cambridge, Mass.: MIT Press.
Dixit, A., G. M. Grossman, and G. Faruk (2000). "The Dynamics of Political Compromise." *Journal of Political Economy* 108: 531–68.
Dodd, W. F. (1908) *Modern Constitutions: A Collection of the Fundamental Laws of Twenty-Two of the Most Important Countries of the World, with Historical and Bibliographical Notes* (Volume 1). Chicago: University of Chicago Press.
(1909) *Modern Constitutions: A Collection of the Fundamental Laws of Twenty-Two of the Most Important Countries of the World, with Historical and Bibliographical Notes* (Volume 2). Chicago: University of Chicago Press.
Drescher, S. (1990) "People and Parliament: The Rhetoric of the British Slave Trade," *Journal of Interdisciplinary History* 20: 561–80.
Dudley, L. (2000) "The Rationality of Revolution," *Economics of Governance* 1: 77–103.
(1991) *The Word and the Sword: How Techniques of Information and Violence Have Shaped Our World*. Oxford: Blackwell.
Dumke, R. H. (1978) "The Political Economy of Economic Integration: The Case of the German Zollverein of 1834," *Journal Economic History* 38: 277–78.
Duun, P. (1976) *The Rise of Modern Japan*. Boston: Houghton Mifflin.
Edvinsson, R. (2005) *Growth, Accumulation, Crisis: with New Macroeconomic Data for Sweden 1800–2000*. Stockholm: Almqvist and Wiksell International.
Encyclopedia Britannica 11th Edition (1911). Available online at http://www.1911encyclopedia.org/Main_Page
Engerman, S. L. (1986) "Slavery and Emancipation in Comparative Perspective: A Look at Some Recent Debates," *Journal of Economic History* 46: 317–39.
Epstein, R. A. (2006) *How Progressives Rewrote the Constitution*. Washington DC: Cato Institute.
Ertman, T. (1997) *Birth of the Leviathan: Building States and Regimes in Medieval and Early Modern Europe*. Cambridge: Cambridge University Press.
Farber, D. A. (2003) *Lincoln's Constitution*. Chicago: University of Chicago Press.
Feld, L. P. and M. R. Savioz (1997) "Direct Democracy Matters for Economic Performance: An Empirical Investigation," *Kyklos* 50: 507–38.
Feld, L. P. and S. Voigt (2006) "Judicial Independence and Economic Development," in R. D. Congleton and B. Swedenborg (Eds.) *Democratic Constitutional Design and Public Policy*. Cambridge, MA: MIT Press.
Ferrero, M. (2002) "The Political Life Cycle of Extremist Organizations," in A. Breton., G. Galeotti, P. Salmon, and R. Wintrobe (Eds.) *Political Extremism and Rationality*. Cambridge: Cambridge University Press.
Fregert, K. (2009) "Fiscal Institutions and Fiscal Outcomes in Sweden 1720–1809: The Role of Constitutional Checks, Transparency and Delegation," Working Paper, Lund University.
Ferguson, N. (2002) *The Cash Nexus: Money and Power in the Modern World, 1700–2000*. New York: Basic Books.
Fetscher, E. B. (1980) "Censorship and the Editorial: Baden's New Press Law of 1840 and the 'Seeblatter' at Konstanz," *German Studies Review* 3: 377–94.
Feuchtwanger, E. J. (2002) *Bismarck*. London: Routledge.

Field, J. (2002) *The Story of Parliament in the Palace of Westminster*. London: Politico's Publishing.

Finer, S. E. (1997) *The History of Government II, The Intermediate Ages*. Oxford: Oxford University Press.

Finkelstein, J. J. (1968–69) "The Laws of Ur-Nammu," *Journal of Cuneiform Studies* 22: 66–82.

Firth, C. H. (1902) *Cromwell's Army*. London: Metheun & Co.

Fiske, J. (1888) *The Critical Period of American History 1783–1789*. New York: Houghton, Mifflin & Co.

Flora, P. (1983) *State, Economy, and Society in Western Europe 1815–1975: A Data Handbook*. Frankfurt: Campus Verlag.

Floud, R. (1997) *The People and the British Economy, 1830–1914*. Oxford: Oxford University Press.

Fogel, R. W. (1962) "A Quantitative Approach to the Study of Railroads in American Economic Growth: A Report of Some Preliminary Findings," *Journal of Economic History* 22: 163–97.

Foster, J. W. (1903) *American Diplomacy in the Orient*. New York: Houghton, Mifflin and Co.

Frank, R. H. (1985) *Choosing The Right Pond, Human Behavior and the Quest for Status*. Oxford: Oxford University Press.

Fremdling, R. (1977) "Railroads and German Economic Growth: A Leading Sector Analysis with a Comparison to the United States and Great Britain," *Journal of Economic History* 37: 583–604.

Frey, B. S. and R. Jegen (2001) "Motivational Crowding Theory," *Journal of Economic Surveys* 15: 589–611.

Fukuyama, F. (1992) *The End of History and the Last Man*. New York: Free Press.

Fulbrook, M. (1990) *A Concise History of Germany*. Cambridge: Cambridge University Press.

Galenson, D. W. (1984) "The Rise and Fall of Indentured Servitude in the Americas: An Economic Analysis," *Journal of Economic History* 44: 1–26.

(1986) *Traders, Planters, and Slaves: Market Behavior in Early English America*. Cambridge: Cambridge University Press.

Gardiner, S. R. (Ed.) (1906) *The Constitutional Documents of the Puritan Revolution 1625–1660*, 3rd Edition. Oxford: Oxford University Press. (Also available on the World Wide Web at: www.constitution.org/eng/conpur_.htm)

Garfinkel, M. R. and S. Skaperdas (1996) *The Political Economy of Conflict and Appropriation*. Cambridge: Cambridge University Press.

Garrard, J. (2002) *Democratization in Britain, Elites, Civil Society, and Reform since 1800*. New York: Palgrave.

Gibbons, R. and K. J. Murphy (1990) "Relative Performance Evaluation for Chief Executive Officers," *Industrial and Labor Relations Review* 43: 30–51(S).

Gilligan, T. W. and K. Krehbiel (1989) "Asymmetric Information and Legislative Rules with a Heterogeneous Committee," *American Journal of Political Science* 33: 459–90.

Gladdish, K. (1991) *Governing from the Centre: Politics and Policymaking in the Netherlands*. London: Hurst & Co.

Goldstone, J. A. (1993) *Revolution and Rebellion in the Early Modern World*. Berkeley: University of California Press.

(2001) "Toward a Fourth Generation of Revolutionary Theory," *Annual Review of Political Science* 4: 139–87.

Gordon, R. J. (1999) "U.S. Economic Growth since 1870: One Big Wave?" *American Economic Review* 89: 123–28.

Gordon, S. (1999) *Controlling the State: Constitutionalism from Ancient Times to Today.* Cambridge, MA: Harvard University Press.

Gould, A. C. (1999) *Origins of Liberal Dominance: State, Church and Party in Nineteenth-Century Europe.* Ann Arbor: University of Michigan Press.

Granger, C. W. J. (1969) "Investigating Causal Relations by Econometric Models and Cross-Spectral Methods," *Econometrica* 37: 424–38.

Grantham, G. W. (1980) "The Persistence of Open-Field Farming in Nineteenth-Century France," *Journal of Economic History* 40: 515–31.

Grey, H. E. (Ed.) (1867) *The Reform Act of 1832: The Correspondence of the Late Earl Grey with His Majesty King William IV and with Sir Herbert Taylor, from November 1830–June 1832.* London: Murray.

Grier, K. B. and G. Tullock (1989) " Empirical Analysis of Cross-National Economic Growth, 1951–80," *Journal of Monetary Economics* 24: 259–76.

Grimberg, C. (1935) *A History of Sweden.* Reprinted in 2007 by Alcester, UK: Read Books.

Grimes, A. P. (1987) *Democracy and the Amendments to the Constitution.* Lanham, MD: University Press of America.

Groenveld, S. and M. Wintle (Eds.) (1992) *State and Trade: Government and the Economy in Britain and the Netherlands since the Middle Ages.* Den Haag: Cip-Gegevens Koninklijke Bibliotheek.

Grofman, B. and A. Lijphart (Eds.) (2002) *The Evolution of Electoral and Party Systems in the Nordic Countries.* New York: Algora Publishing.

Grossman, H. I. (1991) "A General Equilibrium Model of Insurrections," *American Economic Review* 81: 912–21.

Grossman, G. M. and E. Helpman (1996) "Electoral Competition and Special Interest Politics," *Review of Economic Studies* 63: 265–86.

Grotius, H. 1625/1901 *The Rights of War and Peace, Including the Law of Nature and of Nations.* (Translated by A. C. Campbell) Washington, DC: M. Walter Dunne.

Grubb, F. (1992) "Fatherless and Friendless: Factors Influencing the Flow of English Emigrant Servants," *Journal of Economic History* 52: 85–108.

Guizot, F. (1861/2002) *The History of the Origins of Representative Government in Europe.* (Translated by Andrew R. Scoble) Introduction and notes by Aurelian Craiutu. Indianapolis: Liberty Fund.

Hackett, R. P. (1968) "Political Modernization and the Meiji Genro," in R. E. Ward (Ed.) *Political Development in Modern Japan.* Princeton: Princeton University Press.

Hadenius, S. (1999) *Swedish Politics during the 20th Century: Conflict and Consensus.* Stockholm: The Swedish Institute.

Haffenden, P. S. (1958) "The Sovereign and the Colonial Charters, 1675–1688: Part II," *William and Mary Quarterly* 15: 452–66.

Hall, P. A. and R. C. R. Taylor (1996) "Political Science and the Three New Institutionalisms," *Political Studies* 46: 936–57.

Halévy, É. (1987) *The Liberal Awakening (1815–1830).* London: Routledge.

Hamer, D. A. (1977) *The Politics of Electoral Pressure: A Study of Victorian Reform Agitation.* New Jersey: Humanitarian Press.

Hammon, T. H. and G. J. Miller (1987) "The Core and the Constitution," *American Political Science Review* 81: 1155–74.

Hane, M. (1969) "Early Meiji Liberalism, An Assessment," *Monumenta Nipponica* 24: 353–71.

Hardin, R. (1999) *Liberalism, Constitutionalism, and Democracy.* Oxford: Oxford University Press.

Harris, J. F. (1987) "The Authorship of Political Tracts in Post 1848 Germany," *German Studies Review* 10: 411–41.

Hart, O. and J. Moore (1990) "Property Rights and the Nature of the Firm," *Journal of Political Economy* 98: 1119–58.

Hayek, F. A. (1948) *Individualism and Economic Order.* Chicago: University of Chicago Press.

(1954) *Capitalism and the Historians.* Chicago: University of Chicago Press.

(1973) *Law, Legislation, and Liberty: Rules and Order.* Chicago: University of Chicago Press.

(1979) *Law, Legislation, and Liberty: The Political Order of a Free People.* Chicago: University of Chicago Press.

Heckelman, J. C. (1995) "The Effect of the Secret Ballot on Voter Turnout Rates," *Public Choice* 82: 107–24.

Heckscher, E. F. (1954) *An Economic History of Sweden.* Cambridge, MA: Harvard University Press.

Heclo, H. and H. Madsen (1987) *Policy and Politics in Sweden: Principled Pragmatism.* Philadelphia: Temple University Press.

Heffernan, W. (1973) "The Slave Trade and Abolition in Travel Literature," *Journal of the History of Ideas* 34: 185–208.

Heiner, R. A. (1983) "The Origin of Predictable Behavior," *American Economic Review* 73: 560–95.

(1986) "Imperfect Decisions and the Law: On the Evolution of Legal Precedent and Rules," *Journal of Legal Studies* 15: 227–61.

Hehenkamp, B., W. Leininger, and A. Possajennikov (2004) "Evolutionary Equilibrium in Tullock Contests: Spite and Overdissipation," *European Journal of Political Economy* 20: 1045–57.

Helle, K., E. I. Kouri, and T. Jansson (2003) *The Cambridge History of Scandinavia.* Cambridge: Cambridge University Press.

Helmfrid, S. (1961) "The Storskifte, Enskifte and the Laga Skifte in Sweden: General Features," *Geografiska Annaler* 43: 112–29.

Henderson, W. O. (1950) "Prince Smith and Free Trade in Germany," *Economic History Review* 2: 295–302.

Herlitz, N. (1939) *Sweden: A Modern Democracy on Ancient Foundations.* Minneapolis: University of Minnesota Press.

Higashibaba, I. (2001) *Christianity in Early Modern Japan.* Leiden: Brill.

Hill, B. (1996) *The Early Parties and Politics in Britain, 1688–1832.* New York: Macmillan Press.

Hillman, A. L. and E. Katz (1987) "Structure and the Social Costs of Bribes and Transfers," *Journal of Public Economics* 34: 129–42.

Hillman, A. L. and H. W. Ursprung (1988) "Politics, Foreign Interests, and International Trade Policy," *American Economic Review* 78: 719–45.

Hinch, M. J. and M. C. Munger (1996) *Ideology and the Theory of Public Choice*. Ann Arbor: University of Michigan Press.

Hindman, H. D. (2002) *Child Labor: An American History*. New York: M. E. Sharpe.

Hirsch, F. (1976/1995) *Social Limits to Growth*. London: Routledge.

Hirschman, A. O. (1994) "The On-and-Off Connection between Political and Economic Progress," *American Economic Review* 84: 343–48.

Hirshleifer, J. (2001) *The Dark Side of the Force: Economic Foundations of Conflict Theory*. New York: Cambridge University Press.

History of Constitutionalism in Japan (1987) Tokyo: House of Representatives.

Hobbes, T. (1651/1959) *Leviathan*. New York: E. P. Dutton.

Holcombe, A. N. (1916) *State Governments of the United States*. New York: Macmillan.

Holcombe, R. G. and D. J. Lacombe (1998) "Interests versus Ideology in the Ratification of the 16th and 17th Amendments," *Economics and Politics* 10: 143–60.

Holcombe, R. G., R. A. Lawson, and J. D. Gwartney (2006) "Constitutions and Prosperity: the Impact of Legal and Economic Institutions on the Wealth of Nations," in R. D. Congleton and B. Swedenborg (Eds.) *Democratic Constitutional Design and Public Policy, Analysis and Evidence*. Cambridge MA: MIT Press.

Holmberg, E. and N. Stjernquist (1995) "Introduction," in *Constitutional Documents of Sweden*. Stockholm: The Swedish Riksdag.

(1996) *The Constitution of Sweden: Constitutional Documents of Sweden*. (Translated by U. K. Nordenson, F. O. Finney, and K. Bradfield) Stockholm: The Swedish Riksdag.

Holmberg, T. (2002) "Great Britain: The Treasonable and Seditious Practices and Seditious Meetings Acts of 1795," Web site: *the Napoleonic Series*. www.napoleon-series.org/research/government/british/c_gagging.html

Holborn, H. (1959) *A History of Modern Germany: The Reformation*. Princeton: Princeton University Press.

(1964) *A History of Modern Germany: 1648–1840*. Princeton: Princeton University Press.

(1969) *A History of Modern Germany: 1840–1945*. Princeton: Princeton University Press.

Holmstrom, B. and P. Milgrom (1994) "The Firm as an Incentive System," *American Economic Review* 84: 972–91.

Hudson, R. (1891) "The Formation of the North German Confederation," *Political Science Quarterly* 6: 424–38.

(1891) "The Formation of the North German Confederation," *Political Science Quarterly* 6: 424–38.

Hurst, J. W. (2004) *The Legitimacy of the Business Corporation in the Law of the United States, 1780–1970*. Charlottesville: University Press of Virginia.

Iannaccone, L. R. (1992) "Sacrifice and Stigma: Reducing Free-Riding in Cults, Communes and Other Collectives," *Journal of Political Economy* 100: 271–91.

(1998) "Introduction to the Economics of Religion," *Journal of Economic Literature* 36: 1465–96.

Immergut, E. M. (2002) "The Swedish Constitution and Social Democratic Power: Measuring the Mechanical Effect of a Political Institution," *Scandinavian Political Studies* 25: 231–57.

Israel, J. I. (1998) *The Dutch Republic: Its Rise, Greatness, and Fall 1477–1806*. Oxford: Clarendon Press.

(2002) *Radical Enlightenment*. Oxford: Oxford University Press.

Jacobs, J. and J. P. Smits (2001) "Business Cycles in the Netherlands 1815–1913," Working Paper, University of Groningen.

Jacobson, D. (2000) "Mill on Liberty Speech and the Free Society," *Philosophy and Public Affairs* 29: 276–309.

James, J. A. (1981) "The Optimal Tariff in the Antebellum United States," *American Economic Review* 71: 726–34.

Jennings, I. (1961) *The British Constitution*. 4th Ed. Cambridge: Cambridge University Press.

Johnson, P. (1997) *A History of the American People*. New York: HarperCollins.

Jones, E. (2003) *The European Miracle: Environments, Economics and Geopolitics in the History of Europe and Asia*. 3rd Ed. Cambridge: Cambridge University Press.

Judson, H. P. (1894) *Europe in the Nineteenth Century*. New York: Flood and Vincent.

Kahan, A. (1973) "Notes on Serfdom in Western and Eastern Europe," *Journal of Economic History* 33: 86–99.

Kan, F. J. W. van (1995) "Elite and Government in Medieval Leiden," *Journal of Medieval History* 21: 51–75.

Kaufman-Osborne, T. V. (1992) "Rousseau in Kimono: Nakae Chomin and the Japanese Enlightenment," *Political Theory* 20: 53–85.

Keefer, P. and S. Knack (1995) "Institutions and Economic Performance: Cross-Country Tests Using Alternative Institutional Measures," *Economics and Politics* 7: 207–27.

(1997) "Why Don't Poor Countries Catch Up?" *Economic Inquiry* 35: 590–602.

Keyssar, A. (2000) *The Right to Vote, the Contested History of Democracy in the United States*. New York: Basic Books.

Kindleberger, C. P. (1975) "The Rise of Free Trade in Western Europe, 1820–1875," *Journal of Economic History* 35: 20–55.

Kirzner, I. M. (1978) *Competition and Entrepreneurship*. Chicago: University of Chicago Press.

Knight, F. H (1921) *Risk, Uncertainty, and Profit*. New York: Houghton, Mifflin & Co.

Koch, H. W. (1984) *A Constitutional History of Germany*. New York: Longman.

Kolb, E. (2004) *The Weimar Republic*. London: Routledge.

Konrad, K. A. and S. Skaperdas (2005) "The Market for Protection and the Origin of the State," CESifo Working Paper 1578.

Konstam, A. (1998) *Pirates 1660–1730*. New York: Osprey.

Koselleck, R. (1998) *Critique and Crisis: Enlightenment and the Pathogenesis of Modern Society*. Cambridge, MA: MIT Press.

Kossman, E. H. (1978) *The Low Countries, 1780–1940*. Oxford: Clarendon Press.

Krehbiel, K. (1991) *Information and Legislative Organization*. Ann Arbor: University of Michigan Press.

Kuran, T. (1989) "Sparks and Prairie Fires: A Theory of Unanticipated Political Revolution," *Public Choice* 61: 41–74.

La Court, P. de (1662) *The True Interest and Political Maxims of the Republic of Holland*. (The English title and quoted text is from John Campbell's 1746 translation of La Court's book.) Originally published as *Interest van Holland ofte gronden van Hollands welvaren*, Amsterdam, 1662.

Laffont, J. J. and J. Tirole (1993) *A Theory of Incentives in Procurement and Regulation*. Cambridge, MA: MIT Press.

Landes, D. S. (1999) *The Wealth and Poverty of Nations: Why Some Are So Rich and Some So Poor*. New York: Norton.

Lang, S. (1999) *Parliamentary Reform 1785–1928*. London: Routledge.

Laursen, J. C. and C. J. Nederman (Eds.) (1997) *Beyond the Persecuting Society: Religious Toleration before the Enlightenment*. Philadelphia: University of Pennsylvania Press.

LeMay, G. H. L. (1979) *The Victorian Constitution: Conventions Usages and Contingencies*. London: Duckworth.

Lee, S. J. (1994) *Aspects of British Political History, 1815–1914*. London: Routledge.

Leeson, P. T. (2007) "An-arrrgh-chy: The Law and Economics of Pirate Organizations," *Journal of Political Economy* 115: 1049–94.

Levy, D. M. (2001) *How the Dismal Science Got Its Name*. Ann Arbor: University of Michigan Press.

Levy, D. M. and S. J. Peart (2005) *The Vanity of the Philosopher: From Equality to Hierarchy in Post-Classical Economics*. Ann Arbor: University of Michigan Press.

Levy, M. J. (1996) *Modernization and the Structure of Societies*. Piscataway, NJ: Transaction Publishers.

Lewin, L. (1988) *Ideology and Strategy, A Century of Swedish Politics*. Cambridge: Cambridge University Press.

Lijphart, A. (1968) *The Politics of Accommodation: Pluralism and Democracy in the Netherlands*. Berkeley: University of California Press.

Lindert, P. H. (1986) "Inequal English Wealth Since 1670," *Journal of Political Economy* 94: 1127–62.

Lipset, S. M. (1959) "Social Requisites of Democracy: Economic Development and Political Legitimacy," *American Political Science Review* 53: 69–105.

LoPatin, N. D. (1999) *Political Unions, Popular Politics, and the Great Reform Act of 1832*. London: Macmillan.

Locke, J. (1689/1988) *Two Treatises of Government*. Cambridge: Cambridge University Press.

Lott Jr., J. R. (1990) "Predation by Public Enterprises," *Journal of Public Economics* 43: 237–51.

Lott Jr., J. R. and L. W. Kenny (1999) "Did Women's Suffrage Change the Size and Scope of Government?" *Journal of Political Economy* 107: 1163–98.

Lovejoy, P. E. (1982) "The Volume of the Atlantic Slave Trade: A Synthesis," *Journal of African History* 23: 473–501.

Lu, D. J. (1997) *Japan, A Documentary History*. New York: M. E. Sharpe.

Ludington, A. (1909) "Present Status of Ballot Laws in the United States," *American Political Science Review* 3: 252–61.

Luebbert, G. M. (1991) *Liberalism, Fascism, or Social Democracy*. Oxford: Oxford University Press.

Lutz, D. S. (1994) "Toward a Theory of Constitutional Amendment," *American Political Science Review* 88: 335–70

(1983) *American Political Writing During the Founding Era, 1760–1805*. Indianapolis: Liberty Press.

(1998) *Colonial Origins of the American Constitution: A Documentary History*. Indianapolis: Liberty Press.

Lyon, B. D. (1980/1960) *A Constitutional and Legal History of Medieval England.* 2nd Ed. New York: Norton.

Machin, I. (2001) *The Rise of Democracy in Britain, 1830–1918.* London: Macmillan.

Macfarlane, A. (1978) *The Origins of English Individualism.* Oxford: Basil Blackwell.

Maddison, A. (2003) *The World Economy: A Millenial Perspective.* New Delhi: Overseas Press.

Magnusson, L. (2000) *An Economic History of Sweden.* London: Routledge.

Margolis, H. (2002) *It Started with Copernicus: How Turning the World Inside Out Led to the Scientific Revolution.* New York: McGraw Hill.

Marshall, M. G. and K. Jaggers (2005) "Polity IV Project, Political Regime Characteristics and Transitions, 1800–2004, Dataset Users' Manual," Fairfax, VA: George Mason University School of Public Policy.

Marx, K. and F. Engels (1908) *Manifesto of the Communist Party.* New York: New York Labor News Co. (Also available from Project Gutenberg: www.gutenberg.org/etext/31193)

Mason, R. H. P. and J. G. Caiger (1997) *A History of Japan.* Rutland, VT: Tuttle.

Mathias, P. (2001) *The First Industrial Nation: the Economic History of Britain 1700–1914.* London: Routledge.

McDonagh, E. L. and H. D. Price (1985) "Woman Suffrage in the Progressive Era: Patterns of Opposition and Support in Referenda Voting," *American Political Science Review* 79: 415–35.

McKelvy, R. D. (1976) "Intransitivities in Multidimensional Voting Models and Some Implications for Agenda Control," *Journal of Economic Theory* 12: 472–82.

McKinley, A. E. (1905) *The Suffrage Franchise in the Thirteen English Colonies in America.* New York: Burt Franklin.

McLean, I. A. (2001) *Rational Choice and British Politics, An Analysis of Rhetoric and Manipulation from Peel to Blair.* Oxford: Oxford University Press.

McLean, I., A. Spirling, and M. Russell (2003) "None of the Above: The UK House of Commons Votes on Reforming the House of Lords, February 2003," *Political Quarterly* 74: 298–310.

McLean, I. A. (2004) "Thomas Jefferson, John Adams, and the Déclaration des Droits de l' et du Citoyen," Working Paper, Oxford University.

McLennan, A. (1998) "Consequences of the Condorcet Jury Theorem for Beneficial Information Aggregation by Rational Agents," *American Political Science Review* 92: 413–18.

Mesquita, B. B., A. Smith, R. M. Siverson, and R. D. Morrow (2003) *The Logic of Political Survival.* Cambridge, MA: MIT Press.

Metcalf, M. F. (1987) *The Riksdag: A History of the Swedish Parliament.* New York: St. Martins.

Miller, J. (1991) *The Rise and Fall of Democracy in Early America, 1630–1798.* University Park: Pennsylvania State University Press.

Minami, R. (1994) *The Economic Development of Japan.* 2nd Ed. New York: St. Martins.

Mitani, T. (1988) "The Establishment of Party Cabinets, 1898–1932," in J. Duun (Ed.) *Cambridge History of Japan,* Volume 6, Cambridge: Cambridge University Press.

Möckel, K. (Ed.) (1979) "Der Moderne Bayerische Staat – Eine Verfassungsgeschichte vom aufgeklärten Absolutismus bis zum Ende der Reformepoche," in (K. Bosl, (ed.) *Dokumente zur Geschichte von Staat und Gesellschaft in Bayern* – Abteilung

III Bayern im 19. und 20. Jahrhundert Band 1; München: C. H. Beck'sche Verlagsbuchhandlung.
Mokyr, J. (2002) *The Gifts of Athena, Historical Origins of the Knowledge Economy.* Princeton: Princeton University Press.
Mommsen, W. J. (1995) *Imperial Germany 1867–1918.* (Translation of *Der Autoritäre Nationalstaat,* by R. Deveson) New York: Oxford University Press.
Montesquieu, C. (1748/1914) *The Spirit of the Laws.* London: G. Bell and Sons.
Moraw, P. (1989) "Cities and Citizenry as Factors of State Formation in the Roman-German Empire of the Late Middle Ages," in (C. Tilly and W. P. Blockmans (Eds.) *Cities and the Rise of States in Europe.* Oxford: Westview.
Morgan, K. O. (Ed.) (1997) *The Oxford Illustrated History of Britain.* New York: Oxford University Press.
Morgan, K. O. (Ed.) (2001) *The Oxford History of Britain.* Oxford: Oxford University Press.
Morison, S. E. (1965) *The Oxford History of the American People.* Oxford: Oxford University Press.
Mork, G. R. (1971) "Bismarck and the 'Capitulation' of German Liberalism," *Journal of Modern History* 43: 59–75.
Morris, H. L. (1921) *Parliamentary Franchise Reform in England from 1885 to 1918.* New York: Columbia University Press.
Morris, J. (1978) *The Oxford Book of Oxford.* Oxford: Oxford University Press.
Mueller, D. C. (1996) *Constitutional Democracy.* New York: Oxford University Press.
(2003) *Public Choice III.* New York: Cambridge University Press.
(2009) *Reason, Religion, and Democracy.* New York: Cambridge University Press.
Newton, G. (1978) *The Netherlands: An Historical and Cultural Survey 1795–1977.* Boulder: Westview Press.
Nicolson, H. (1946) *The Congress of Vienna, A Study in Allied Unity: 1812–1822.* New York: Grove Press.
Niskanen, W. A. (1968) "Nonmarket Decision-Making: The Peculiar Economics of Bureaucracy," *American Economic Review Papers and Proceedings* 59: 293–305
Nitzan, S. and J. Paroush (1985) *Collective Decision Making,* Cambridge: Cambridge University Press.
Nordstrom, G. J. (2000) *Scandinavia Since 1500.* Minneapolis: University of Minnesota Press.
North, D. C. (1981) *Structure and Change in Economic History.* New York: Norton.
(1987) "Institutions, Transactions Costs and Economic Growth," *Economic Inquiry* 25, 419–28.
(1990) *Institutions, Institutional Change and Economic Performance.* Cambridge: Cambridge University Press.
North, D. C. and R. P. Thomas (1971) "The Rise and Fall of the Manorial System: A Theoretical Model," *Journal of Economic History* 31: 777–803.
(1973) *The Rise of the Western World.* Cambridge: Cambridge University Press.
North, D. C. and B. R. Weingast (1989) "Constitutions and Commitment: the Evolution of Institutions Governing Public Choice in Seventeenth Century England," *Journal of Economic History* 49: 803–32.
North, D. C., J. J. Wallis, and B. R. Weingast (2009) *Violence and Social Orders: A Conceptual Framework for Interpreting Recorded Human History.* Cambridge: Cambridge University Press.

Nozick, R. (1974) *Anarchy, State, and Utopia*. Englewood Cliffs, NJ: Prentice-Hall.
Nye, D. E. (1990) *Electrifying America: Social Meanings of a New Technology*. Cambridge, MA: MIT Press.
Nye, J. V. C. (1991) "The Myth of Free Trade Britain and Fortress France: Tariffs and Trade in the Nineteenth Century," *Journal of Economic History* 51: 23–46.
Officer, L. J. (2006) "The Annual Real and Nominal GDP for the United Kingdom, 1086–2005," *Economic History Services*, (September). www.eh.net/hmit/ukgdp/.
O'Gorman, F. (1989) *Voters, Patrons and Parties: The Unreformed Electoral System of Hanoverian England: 1734–1832*. Oxford: Clarendon Press.
Ogg, F. A. (1918) *The Governments of Europe*. New York: Macmillan.
Olson, M. (1965) *The Logic of Collective Action*. Cambridge: Harvard University Press.
(1982) "Environmental Indivisibilities and Information Costs: Fanaticism, Agnosticism, and Intellectual Progress," *American Economic Review* 72: 262–66.
(1993) "Dictatorship, Democracy, and Development," *American Political Science Review* 87: 567–76.
(1996) "Big Bills Left on the Sidewalk: Why Some Nations Are Rich, and Others Poor," *Journal of Economic Perspectives* 10: 3–24.
(2000) *Power and Prosperity*. New York: Basic Books.
Olson, M. and M. C. McGuire (1996) "The Economics of Autocracy and Majority Rule: The Invisible Hand and the Use of Force," *Journal of Economic Literature* 34: 72–96.
Orlow, D. (2008) *A History of Modern Germany: 1871 to Present*. 6th Ed. Upper Saddle River, NJ: Pearson Education.
Osgood, H. L. (1902) "England and the American Colonies in the Seventeenth Century," *Political Science Quarterly* 17: 206–22.
Ostrom, E. (1991) *Governing the Commons: the Evolution of Institutions for Collective Action*. Cambridge: Cambridge University Press.
(2005) *Understanding Institutional Diversity*. Princeton: Princeton University Press.
Ostrom, E., J. Walker, and R. Gardner (1992) "Covenants with and without a Sword: Self-Governance Is Possible," *American Political Science Review* 86: 404–17.
Ostrom, V. (1999) "Polycentricity (Parts 1 and 2)," in M. McGinnis (Ed.) *Polycentricity and Local Public Economies: Readings from the Workshop in Political Theory and Policy Analysis*. Ann Arbor: University of Michigan Press.
Oye, K. A. (1986) *Cooperation under Anarchy*. Princeton: Princeton University Press.
Paldam, M. and E. Gundlach (2008) "Two Views on Institutions and Development: the Grand Transition vs. the Primacy of Institutions," *Kyklos* 61: 65–100.
Palmer, R. R. (1959) *The Age of Democratic Revolution: A Political History of Europe and America, 1760–1800*. Princeton: Princeton University Press.
Palmer, R. R. and J. Colton (1994) *A History of the Modern World*. New York: Alfred Knopf.
Pareto, V. (1897) "The New Theories of Economics," *Journal of Political Economy* 5: 485–502.
Park, J. H. (1931) "England's Controversy over the Secret Ballot," *Political Science Quarterly* 46: 51–86.
Persson, T., G. Roland, and G. Tabellini (1997) "Separation of Powers and Political Accountability," *Quarterly Journal of Economics* 112: 1163–202.
Persson, T. and G. Tabellini (2003) *The Economic Effects of Constitutions*. Cambridge, MA: MIT Press.

Petersson, O. (1994) *The Government and Politics of Nordic Countries*. (Translated by F. G. Perry) Stockholm: CE Fritzes AB (Kluwer).

Phillips, J. A. (1992) *The Great Reform Bill in the Boroughs: English Electoral Behavior, 1818–1841*. Oxford: Clarendon Press.

Philpott, H. J. (1881) *Free Trade vs. Protection; or A Tariff for Revenue Only vs. A Tariff for Spoils Only*. Des Moines, Iowa: State Leader Co.

Pickering, P. A. (2001) "'And Your Petitioners & C': Chartist Petitioning in Popular Politics 1838–48," *English Historical Review* 116: 368–88.

Pierson, J. D. (1974) "The Early Liberal Thought of Tokutomi Soho: Some Problems of Western Social Theory in Meiji Japan," *Monumenta Nipponica* 29: 199–224.

Pirenne, H. (1925/1980) *Medieval Cities: Their Origin and the Revival of Trade*. Princeton: Princeton University Press.

Pittau, J. S. J. (1967) *Political Thought in Early Meiji Japan*. Cambridge, MA: Harvard University Press.

Plott, C. R. (1967) "A Notion of Equilibrium and Its Possibility under Majority Rule," *American Economic Review* 57: 787–806.

Pomeranz, K. (2000) *The Great Divergence: China, Europe, and the Making of the Modern World Economy*. Princeton: Princeton University Press.

Poole, K. T. and H. Rosenthal (1991) "Patterns of Congressional Voting," *American Journal of Political Science* 35: 228–78.

Posner, R. A. (2007) *Economic Analysis of Law*. 5th Ed. Amsterdam: Wolters Kluwer.

Power, J. E. (1942) "The Japanese Constitution and the Militarists," *Pacific Affairs* 15: 188–94.

Prasch, R. E. (1999) "American Economists in the Progressive Era on the Minimum Wage," *Journal of Economic Perspectives* 13: 221–30.

Price, W. H. (1913) *The English Patents of Monopoly*. Cambridge, MA: Harvard University Press.

Przeworski, A. and F. Limongi (1993) "Political Regimes and Economic Growth," *Journal of Economic Perspectives* 7: 51–69.

Przeworski, A., M. E. Alvarez, J. A. Chibub, and F. Limongi (2000) *Democracy and Development*. Cambridge: Cambridge University Press.

Pugh, M. (1999) *Britain Since 1789, a Concise History*. New York: Palgrave.

Qian, Y. and B. R. Weingast (1997) "Federalism as a Commitment to Preserving Market Incentives," *Journal of Economic Perspectives* 11: 83–92.

Quigley, H. S. (1932) *Japanese Government and Politics*. New York: Century Co.

Rabb, T. K. (1998) *Jacobean Gentleman: Sir Edwin Sandys, 1561–1629*. Princeton: Princeton University Press.

Raico, R. (1990) "Eugen Richter and the Late German Manchester Liberalism: A Reevaluation," *Review of Austrian Economics* 4: 3–25.

Ramlinger, G. V. (1968) "Social Change and Social Security in Germany," *Journal of Human Resources* 3: 409–21.

Rallings, C. and M. Thrasher (2000) *British Electoral Facts 1832–1999*. Aldershot: Ashgate.

Ransome, C. (1883) *Rise of Constitutional Government in England*. London: Rivingtons.

Raphael, R. (2004) *Founding Myths: Stories that Hide Our Patriotic Past*. New York: New Press.

Rasch, B. E. and R. D. Congleton (2006) "Amendment Procedures and Constitutional Stability," in R. D. Congleton and B. Swedenborg (Eds.) *Democratic Constitutional Design and Public Policy: Analysis and Evidence*. Cambridge, MA: MIT Press.

Rawls, J. (1971) *A Theory of Justice*. Cambridge, MA: Harvard University Press.
Rawski, T. G. (Ed.) (1996) *Economics and the Historian*. Berkeley: University of California Press.
Ray, J. L. (1989) "The Abolition of Slavery and the End of International War," *International Organization* 43: 405–39.
Rediker, M. (1989) *Between the Devil and the Deep Blue Sea: Merchant Seamen, Pirates, and the Anglo-American Maritime World, 1700–1750*. New York: Cambridge University Press.
Rehnquist, W. H. (2001) *The Supreme Court*. New York: Alfred A. Knopf.
Reitan, E. A. (1970) "From Revenue to Civil List, 1689–1702: The Revolution Settlement and the 'Mixed and Balanced' Constitution," *Historical Journal* 13: 571–88.
Renzsch, W. (1989) "German Federalism in Historical Perspective: Federalism as a Substitute for a Nation State," *Publius* 19: 17–33.
Rich, N. (1977) *Age of Nationalism and Reform, 1850–1890*. New York: Norton.
Richardson, G. (2005) "The Prudent Village: Risk Pooling Institutions in Medieval English Agriculture," *Journal of Economic History* 65: 356–413.
Richardson, H. G. (1928) "The Origins of Parliament," *Transactions of the Royal Historical Society*. (Fourth Series) 11: 137–83.
Rietbergen, P. J. A. N. (2002) *A Short History of the Netherlands: From Prehistory to the Present Day*. Amersfoort: Bekking Publishers.
Riker, W. H. (1957) "Dutch and American Federalism," *Journal of the History of Ideas* 18: 495–521.
(1962) *The Theory of Political Coalitions*. New Haven: Yale University Press.
Roberts, L. S. (1998) *Mercantilism in a Japanese Domain*. Cambridge: Cambridge University Press.
Roberts, M. (1986) *The Age of Liberty, Sweden 1719–1772*. Cambridge: Cambridge University Press.
Rogozinski, J. (1996) *Pirates!: Brigands, Buccaneers, and Privateers in Fact, Fiction, and Legend*. New York: Da Capo.
Rorty, A. O. (1998) "Philosophers on Education," *New Historical Perspectives*. London: Routledge.
Ross, E. D. (1919) *The Liberal Republican Movement*. New York: Holt and Co.
Rubin, P. H. (2002) *Darwinian Politics: the Evolutionary Origin of Freedom*. Piscataway, NJ: Rutgers University Press.
Ruin, O. (1990) *Tage Erlander: Serving the Welfare State, 1946–1969*. Pittsburgh, PA: University of Pittsburgh Press.
Runkle, D. E. (1998) "Revisionist History: How Data Revisions Distort Economic Policy Research," *Federal Reserve Bank of Minneapolis Quarterly Review* 22: 3–12.
Sack, J. J. (1980) "The House of Lords and Parliamentary Patronage in Great Britain, 1802, 1832," *Historical Journal* 23: 913–37.
Salmon, E. J. and E. D. C. Campbell (1994) *The Hornbook of Virginia History*. 4th Ed. Richmond: Library of Virginia.
Sap, J. W. (2000) *The Netherlands Constitution 1848–1998, Historical Reflections*. Utrecht: Uitgeverij Lemma BV.
Särlvik, B. (2002) "Party and Electoral Systems in Sweden," in (B. Grofman, and A. Lijphart (Eds.) *The Evolution of Electoral and Party Systems in the Nordic Countries*. New York: Algora Publishing.

Sawyer, B. and P. H. Sawyer (1993) *Medieval Scandinavia*. Minneapolis: University of Minnesota Press.

Scalapino, R. A. (1968) "Elections and Political Modernization in Prewar Japan," in R. E. Ward (Ed.) *Political Development in Modern Japan*. Princeton: Princeton University Press, 249–91.

Schap, D. (1986) "Executive Veto and Informational Strategy: A Structure Induced Equilibrium Analysis," *American Journal of Political Science* 30: 755–70.

Schonhardt-Bailey, C. (1991) "Lessons in Lobbying for Free Trade in Nineteenth-Century Britain: To Concentrate or Not," *American Political Science Review* 85: 37–58.

(1998) "Parties and Interests in the 'Marriage of Iron and Rye,'" *British Journal of Political Science* 28: 291–332.

(2003) "Ideology, Party, and Interests in the British Parliament of 1841–47," *British Journal of Political Science* 33: 581–605.

(2006) *From the Corn Laws to Free Trade: Interests Ideas and Institutions in Historical Perspective*. Cambridge, MA: MIT Press.

Schumpeter, J. A. (1934) *The Theory of Economic Development: An Inquiry into Profits, Capital, Credit, Interest, and the Business Cycle*. Harvard: Harvard University Press.

Scott, F. D. (1950) "An 1813 Proposal for a Zollverein," *Journal of Modern History* 22: 359–61.

Seligman, E. R. A. (1914) *The Income Tax: A Study of the History, Theory and Practice of Income Taxation at Home and Abroad*. 2nd Ed. New York: Macmillan.

Seymour, C. and D. P. Frary (1918) *How the World Votes: The Story of Democratic Development in Elections*. New York: Little and Ives.

Shapley, L. and B. Grofman (1984) "Optimizing Group Judgmental Accuracy in the Presence of Interdependencies," *Public Choice* 43: 329–43.

Sharp, A. (Ed.) (1998) *The English Levellers*. Cambridge: Cambridge University Press.

Shepsle, K. A. (1979) "Institutional Arrangements and Equilibrium in Multidimensional Voting Models," *American Journal of Political Science* 23: 27–59.

Shepsle, K. A. and B. R. Weingast (1981) "Structure Induced Equilibrium and Legislative Choice," *Public Choice* 37: 503–19.

Siemes, J. (1962) "Hermann Roesler's Commentaries on the Meiji Constitution," *Monumenta Nipponica* 17: 1–66.

Simon, H. A. (1978) "Rationality as Process and as Product of Thought," *American Economic Review* 68: 1–16.

Simon, H. A. and J. G. March (1958) *Organizations*. New York: Wiley.

Skogh, G. and C. Stuart (1982) "A Contractarian Theory of Property Rights and Crime," *Scandinavian Journal of Economics* 84: 27–40.

Smith, A. (1776) *An Inquiry into the Nature and Causes of the Wealth of Nations*. Dublin: Whitestone.

Smith, F. B. (1966) *The Making of the Second Reform Bill*. Cambridge: Cambridge University Press.

Smits, J. P., E. Horlings, and J. L. van Zanden (2000) *Dutch GNP and its Components, 1800–1913*. Groningen Netherlands: University of Groningen.

Spulber, D. F. (2008) *Market Microstructure: Intermediaries and the Theory of the Firm*. Cambridge: Cambridge University Press.

Spruyt, H. (1994) *The Sovereign State and its Competitors*. Princeton: Princeton University Press.

Stasavage, D. (2003) *Public Debt and the Birth of the Democratic State: France and Great Britain 1688–1789*. Cambridge: Cambridge University Press.

Steinfeld, R. J. (1989) "Property and Suffrage in the Early American Republic," *Stanford Law Review* 41: 335–76.

Steinmo, S. (1993) *Taxation and Democracy*. New Haven: Yale University Press.

Stephens, H. W. and D. W. Brady (1976) "The Parliamentary Parties and the Electoral Reforms of 1884–85 in Britain," *Legislative Studies Quarterly* 1: 491–510.

Stephenson, C. and F. G. Marcham (1938) *Sources of Constitutional History*. London: Harrop.

Stern, F. R. (1977) *Gold and Iron*. New York: Knopf

Sterzel, F. (1994) "Public Administration," in H. Tiberg, F. Sterzel, and P. Cronhult (Eds.) *Swedish Law: A Survey*. (translated by J. Hurst) Stockholm: Juristförlaget.

Stevens, D., B. G. Bishin, and R. R. Barr (2006) "Authoritarian Attitudes, Democracy, and Policy Preferences among Latin American Elites," *American Journal of Political Science* 50: 606–20.

Stigler, G. J. and G. S. Becker (1977) "De Gustibus Non Est Disputandum," *American Economic Review* 67: 76–90.

Strayer, J. R. and H. W. Gatzke (1979) *The Mainstream of Civilization*. 3rd Ed. New York: Harcourt Brace, Jovanovich.

Stringham, E. (Ed.) (2006) *Anarchy, State, and Public Choice*. Cheltenham: Edward Elgar.

Strode, H. (1949) *Sweden, Model for a World*. New York: Harcourt Brace and Co.

Stuurman, S. (1989) "Samuel Van Houten and Dutch Liberalism, 1860–90," *Journal of the History of Ideas* 50: 135–52.

Sutch, R. and S. B. Carter (2006) *Historical Statistics of the United States*, Volumes 1–5. Cambridge: Cambridge University Press.

Suval, S. (1985) *Electoral Politics in Wilhelmine Germany*. Chapel Hill: University of North Carolina Press.

Svanstrom, R. (1934/2008) *A Short History of Sweden*. Stubbe Press.

Hart, M. C. (1993) *The Making of a Bourgeois State: War Politics and Finance During the Dutch Revolt*. Manchester: Manchester University Press.

Taylor, A. (2001) *American Colonies, the Settling of North America*. New York: Penguin Books.

Taylor, G. R. (1951) *The Transportation Revolution, 1815–1860*. New York: Rinehart.

Thatcher, O. J. (1901) *The Library of Original Sources, Volume V (9th to 16th Century)*. Chicago: University Research Extension (Reprinted by the University of the Pacific Press, 2004).

Thompson, E. A. (1974) "Taxation and National Defense." *Journal of Political Economy* 82: 755–82.

Thorpe, F. N. Ed. (1909) *The Federal and State Constitutions Colonial Charters, and Other Organic Laws of the States, Territories, and Colonies Now or Heretofore Forming the United States of America*, Washington, DC: Government Printing Office (compiled and edited under an Act of Congress adopted on June 30, 1906.)

Tideman, T. N. (2006) *Collective Decisions and Voting: The Potential for Public Choice*. Aldershot: Ashgate.

Tilly, C. (2004) *Contention and Democracy in Europe, 1650–2000*. Cambridge: Cambridge University Press.

Tilly C. and W. P. Blockmans (Eds.) (1989) *Cities and the Rise of States in Europe, A. D. 1000–1800*. Oxford: Westview.

Tocqueville, A. de (1835/2010) *Democracy in America: Historical-Critical Edition*. Translated by J. T. Schleifer) Indianapolis: Liberty Fund .

Totman, C. (2000) *A History of Japan*. Oxford: Blackwell.

Toyne, S. M. (1948) *The Scandinavians in History*. London: Arnold.

Tridimas, G. (2005) "Judges and Taxes: Judicial Review, Judicial Independence and the Size of Government," *Constitutional Political Economy* 16: 5–30.

Tridimas, G. and S. L. Winer (2005) "The Political Economy of Government Size," *European Journal of Political Economy* 21: 643–66.

Tsebelis, G. and J. Money (1997) *Bicameralism*. Cambridge: Cambridge University Press.

Tsebelis, G. (2002) *Veto Players: How Political Institutions Work*. Princeton: Princeton University Press.

Tullock, G. (1965) *The Politics of Bureaucracy*. Washington DC: Public Affairs Press.

(1967) "The Welfare Costs of Monopolies, Tariffs and Theft," *Western Economic Journal* 5: 224–32.

(Ed.) (1972) *Explorations in the Theory of Anarchy*. Blacksburg, VA: Center for Study of Public Choice.

(1974) *The Social Dilemma*. Blacksburg, VA: Center for Study of Public Choice.

(1987) *Autocracy*. Dordrecht: Marinus Nijhoff.

(1980) "Efficient Rent Seeking," in J. M. Buchanan, R. D. Tollison, and G. Tullock. *Toward a Theory of the Rent-Seeking Society*. College Station: Texas A&M University Press, 97–112.

(2002) "Undemocratic Governments," *Kyklos* 55: 247–64.

(1929) "The Anti-Slavery Movement Prior to the Abolition of the African Slave Trade (1641–1808)," *Journal of Negro History* 14: 373–402.

Upton, A. F. (1998) *Charles XI and Swedish Absolutism*. Cambridge: Cambridge University Press.

Usher, D. (1989) "The Dynastic Cycle and the Stationary State," *American Economic Review* 79: 1030–44.

Uyehara, G. E. (1910) *The Political Development of Japan 1867–1909*. London: Constable and Co.

Van Raalte, E. (1959) *The Parliament of the Kingdom of the Netherlands*. London: Hansad Society for Parliamentary Government. Printed in Den Haag.

Vanberg, V. (1994) *Rules and Choice in Economics*. London: Routledge.

Vanberg, V. and W. Kerber (1994) "Institutional Competition among Jurisdictions: An Evolutionary Approach," *Constitutional Political Economy* 5: 193–219.

Van Bunge, W. (Ed.) (2003) *The Early Enlightenment in the Dutch Republic, 1650–1750*. Leiden: Brill.

Van den Berg, G. J. M. Lindeboom, and F. Portrait (2006) "Economic Conditions Early in Life and Individual Mortality," *American Economic Review* 96: 290–32.

Van Gelderen, M. (1993) *The Dutch Revolt*. Cambridge: Cambridge University Press.

Verney, D. V. (1957) *Parliamentary Reform in Sweden 1866–1921*. London: Oxford at the Clarendon Press.

Vickers, J. (1985) "Delegation and the Theory of the Firm," *Economic Journal* 95: 138–47.

Voigt, S. (1999a) "Breaking with the Notion of Social Contract: Constitutions as Based on Spontaneously Arisen Institutions," *Constitutional Political Economy* 10: 283–300.

(1999b) *Explaining Constitutional Change: A Positive Economic Approach (New Thinking in Political Economy)*. Cheltenham: Edward Elgar.

Volckart, O. (2000) "State Building by Bargaining for Monopoly Rents," *Kyklos* 53: 265–91.

Von Der Dunk, H. (1978) "Conservatism in the Netherlands," *Journal of Contemporary History* 13: 741–63.

Wada, J. (1996) *The Japanese Election System: Three Analytical Perspectives*. London: Routledge.

Wagner, R. E. (1988) "The Calculus of Consent: A Wicksellian Retrospective," *Public Choice* 56: 153–66.

Walker, A. and E. Wood (2000) "The Parliamentary Oath," *House of Commons Research Paper* (00/17): 1–50.

Wallis, J. J. (2000) "American Government Finance in the Long Run: 1790 to 1990," *Journal of Economic Perspectives* 14: 61–82.

Ward, A. W., G. W. Prothero, and S. Leathes (Eds.) (1909) *The Cambridge Modern History, Volume VI, the Eighteenth Century*. New York: Macmillan.

Webb, S. L. (1993) "From Independents to Populists to Progressive Republicans: The Case of Chilton County Alabama, 1880–1920," *Journal of Southern History* 59: 707–36.

Weber, M. (1930) *The Protestant Ethic and the Spirit of Capitalism*. (Translated by T. Parsons) New York: Dover Publications.

(2003) *The History of Commercial Partnerships in the Middle Ages*. (Translated by L. Kaelber) Oxford: Rowman and Littlefield.

Weibull, J. (1993) *Swedish History in Outline*. (Translated by P. B. Austin) Stockholm: The Swedish Institute.

Weingast, B. R. (2006) "Designing Constitutional Stability," in R. D. Congleton, and B. Swedenborg (Eds.) *Democratic Constitutional Design and Public Policy: Analysis and Evidence*. Cambridge, MA: MIT Press.

Weingast, B. R. and W. J. Marshall (1988) "The Industrial Organization of Congress; or, Why Legislatures, Like Firms, Are Not Organized as Markets," *Journal of Political Economy* 96: 132–63.

Welby, G. C. B., R. Rea, and J. A. Murray-MacDonald (1908) *Report of the Proceedings of the International Free Trade Congress*. London: Unwin Brothers.

Wertenbaker, T. J. (1914) *Virginia Under the Stuarts*. Princeton: Princeton University Press.

Whyte, W. H. (1956/2002) *The Organization Man*. Philadelphia: University of Pennsylvania Press.

Wicksell, K. (1894). *Våra Skatter. Hvilka Betala Dem, och Hvilka Borde Betala? Synpunkter och förslag [Our taxes. Who Pays Them and Who Should Pay Them? Views and Proposals]*. Stockholm: Albert Bonniers Forlag.

(1896). *Finanztheoretische Untersuchungen*. Jena: Gustav Fischer. In English "A New Principle of Just Taxation," in A. Musgrave and A. T. Peacock (Eds.), 1958, *Classics in The Theory of Public Finance*. London: Macmillan.

Wigmore, J. H. (Ed.) (1912) *A General Survey of Events, Sources, Persons and Movements in Continental Legal History*. Boston: Little, Brown and Co.

Williamson, O. (1967) "Hierarchical Control and Optimal Firm Size," *Journal of Political Economy* 75: 123–38.

(1996) *The Mechanisms of Governance*. Oxford: Oxford University Press.

(2002) "The Theory of the Firm as Governance Structure: From Choice to Contract," *Journal of Economic Perspectives* 16: 171–95.

Willink, B. (1991) "Origins of the Second Golden Age of Dutch Science after 1860: Intended and Unintended Consequences of Education Reform," *Social Studies of Science* 21: 503–26.

Wilson, N. G. (1992) *From Byzantium to Italy: Greek Studies in the Italian Renaissance*. Baltimore: Johns Hopkins University Press.

Wintrobe, R. (1998) *The Political Economy of Dictatorship*. Cambridge: Cambridge University Press.

(2006) *Rational Extremism, the Political Economy of Radicalism*. Cambridge: Cambridge University Press.

Wit, J. (1998) "Rational Choice and the Condorcet Jury Theorem," *Games and Economic Behavior* 22: 364–76.

Wordie, J. R. (1983) "The Chronology of English Enclosure, 1500–1914," *Economic History Review* 36: 483–505.

Yasutake, R. (2006) "Men, Women, and Temperance in Meiji Japan: Engendering WCTU Activism from a Transnational Perspective," *Japanese Journal of American Studies* 17: 91–111.

Youngman, E. H. (Ed.) (1913) *Progressive Principles*. New York: Progressive National Service.

Zelizer, J. E. (2004) *The American Congress: The Building of Democracy*. New York: Houghton Mifflin Harcourt.

Index